KT-142-964

C016248825

The Countess

The Scandalous Life of Frances Villiers, Countess of Jersey 1753–1821

TIM CLARKE

AMBERLEY

This work is dedicated to Henrietta, Matthew and Veronica

First published 2016

Amberley Publishing
The Hill, Stroud
Gloucestershire, GL5 4EP

www.amberley-books.com

British Library Cataloguing in Publication Data.
A catalogue record for this book is available from the British Library.

ISBN 978 1 4456 5626 7 (print)
ISBN 978 1 4456 5627 4 (ebook)

Map and table design by Thomas Bohm, User design.
Typesetting and Origination by Amberley Publishing.
Printed in the UK.

Contents

Acknowledgements

The writing, over a period of very nearly ten years, of the biography of Frances Villiers, Countess of Jersey, has been both enormous fun and an enormous adventure. It has been a fascinating voyage of discovery of the Countess and of her life, ending in the first biography ever written of an extraordinary lady and an extraordinary life, and the telling of a story which has not been known for many years. It has taken me, too, to some wonderful places including the bowels of Chatsworth, the private side at Castle Howard, the Round Tower at Windsor Castle and Duke Humfrey's Library in the Bodleian.

In the course of this journey, I have incurred many debts which it is my pleasure to acknowledge. First I am grateful for the permission of Her Majesty Queen Elizabeth II for access to and use of material from the Royal Archives, including some previously unpublished material in relation to George, Prince of Wales and Lady Jersey. I am grateful, too, to the Chatsworth House Trust for allowing me access to the archives at Chatsworth; to the Howard family for granting me access to the archives at Castle Howard, and their kind permission to reproduce their manuscripts; to the Earl of Home for allowing me to read his private papers, in particular the journal of Lady Mary Coke; and to the Earl Spencer for allowing me to quote his family papers. Finally I thank the Earl of Jersey for his courtesy and kindness.

I am grateful, too, to the staff of various institutions who have helped me on my way. These include the staff of the Bodleian Library; the Borthwick Institute for Archives at the University of York; the British Library, Department of Manuscripts; the Huntington Library, San Marino, California; the London Metropolitan Archives (where I discovered what the authorities say no longer existed – a letter from the Countess to the Prince dated to the time of their affair); the National Archives at Kew; the National Records of Scotland, Edinburgh, General Register House, Historical Research Room; and, by no means least, the staff of the London Library.

I am very greatful, as well, to the unknown (to me) owners of Thomas Beach's portrait of the Countess of Jersey for kindly permitting me to use a photograph of their painting. I recognise, too, and am grateful for the invaluable assistance in very different ways of Dr Nicholas Draper of University College London (and St Peter's Square, London), Peter Jenkins CMG who, appropriately for a former ambassador, was diplomatic in reading an early draft of this work, and Alice Munro-Faure for the information she kindly gave me in relation to Charles Nathaniel Bayly.

Finally I must thank Amanda Foreman. She does not know it but it was in the pages of her biography of Georgiana, Duchess of Devonshire that I first encountered the Countess and it was that which caused me to embark on a wonderful journey.

Tim Clarke
St Peter's Square, London
January 2016

Twysden Family

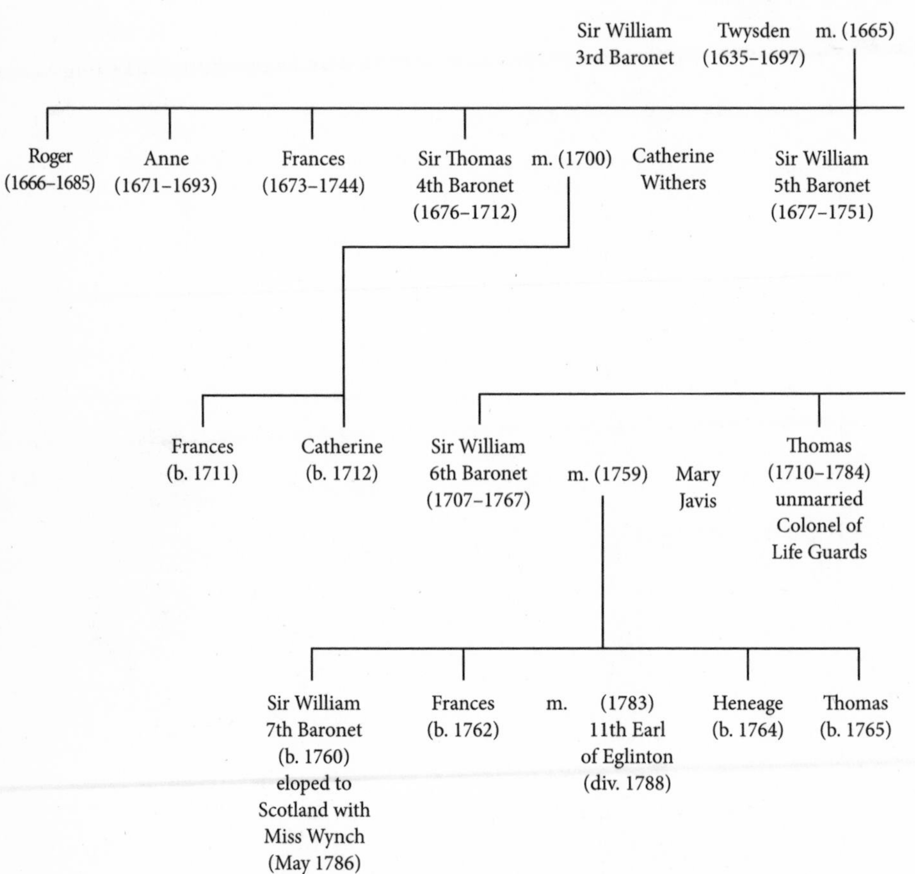

Twysden Family (continued, left to right)

Frances Crosse

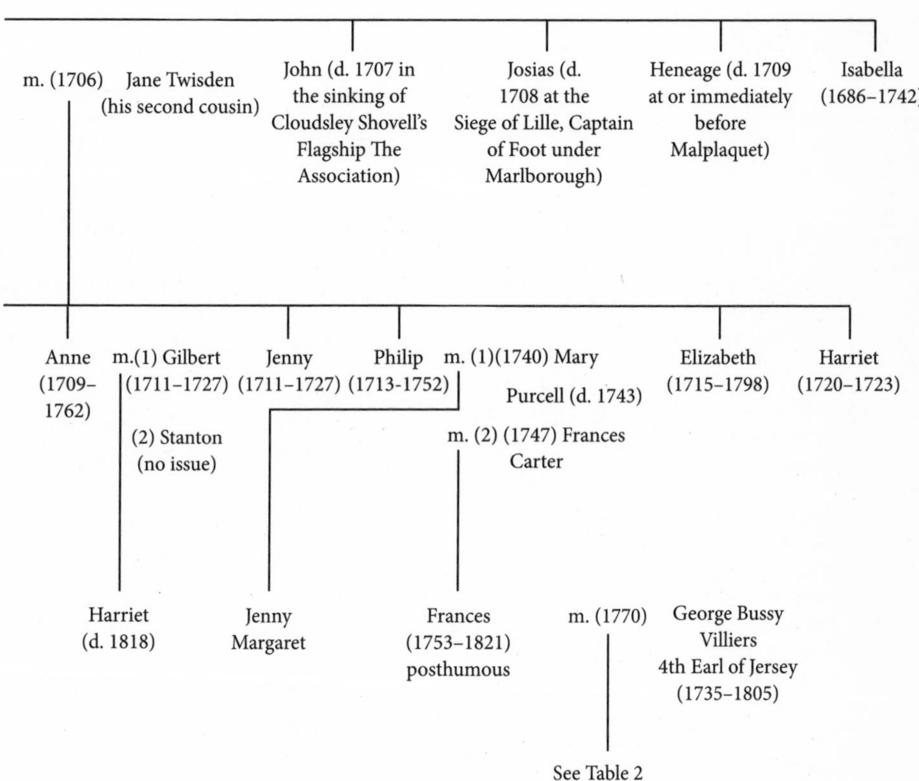

Villiers family – Earls of Jersey

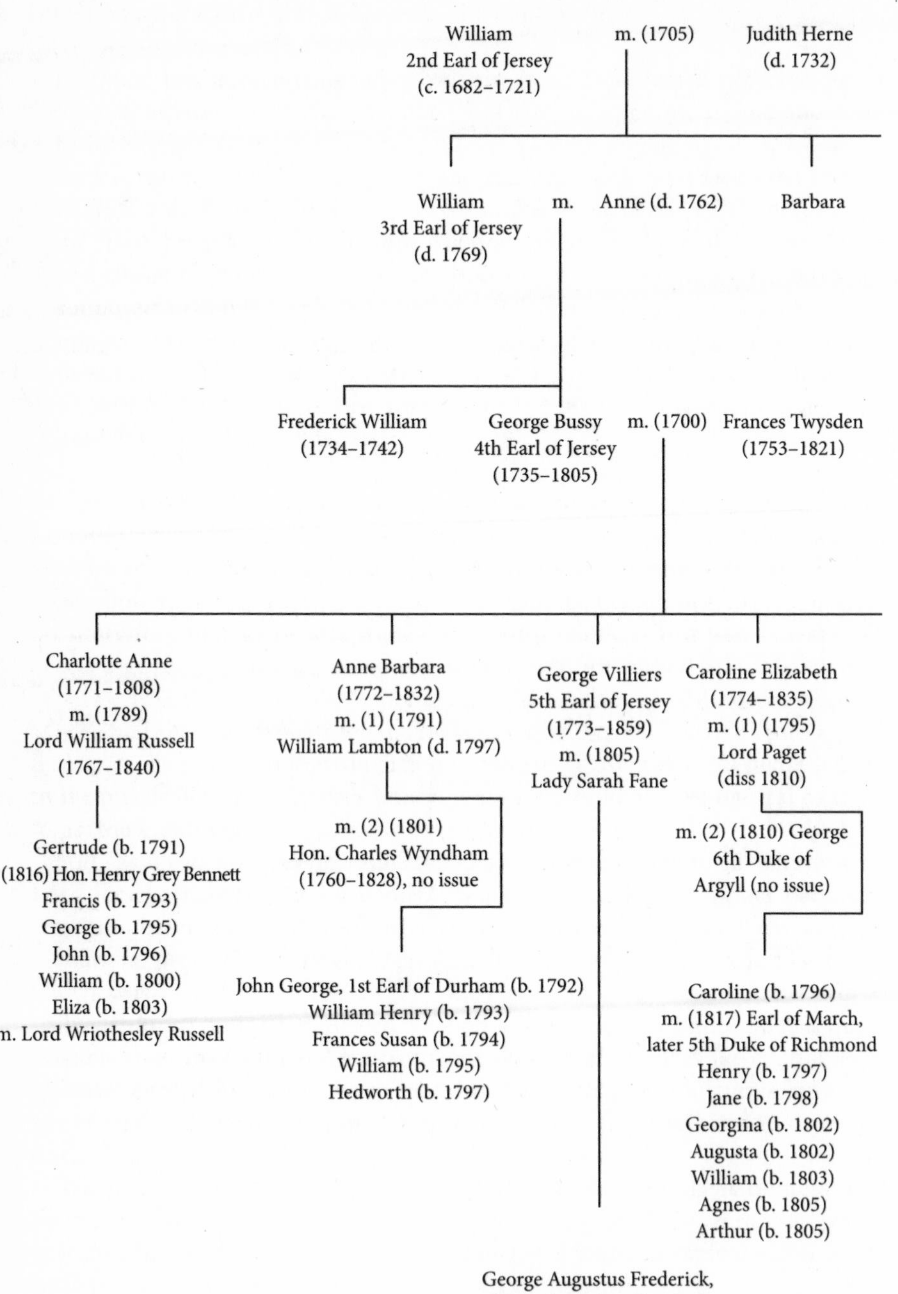

George Augustus Frederick,
6th Earl of Jersey (b. 1808)
Augustus John (b. 1810)
Frederick William (b. 1815)
Francis John Robert (b. 1819)
Sarah Caroline Frederica (b. 1822)
Clementine Augusta Wellington (b. 1824)
Adela Corisanda Maria (b. 1828)

Villiers family – Earls of Jersey (continued, left to right)

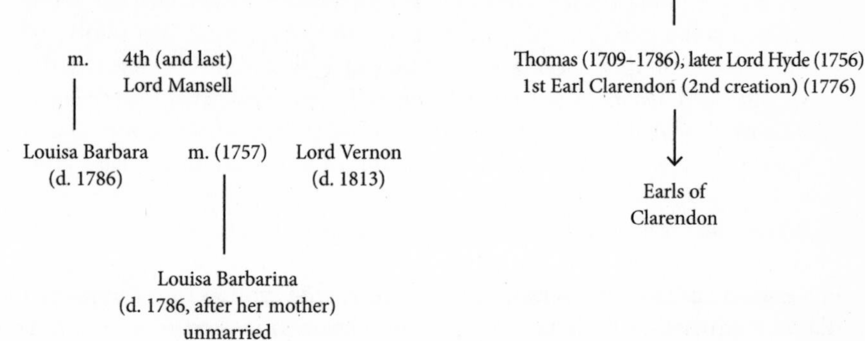

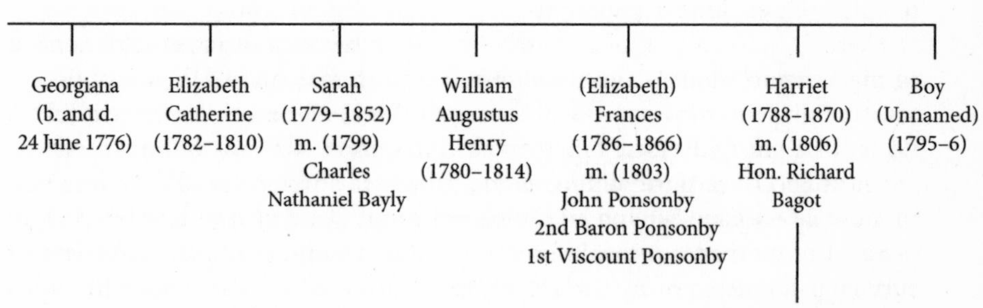

(Two other daughters)
Emily Mary (d. 1853)
May Isabel (d. 1900)
Edward Richard (1808–1874)
William (1809–?1810)
Henry (1810–1877)
Charles Walter (1812–1844)
Lewis Francis (1813–1870)
George (1818–1867)
Richard (1821–1840)
Frederic (1822–1892)

Foreword

In a golden age of letter writing, the late eighteenth century, it is not surprising that there are many references to Frances, Countess of Jersey, in the letters of her contemporaries. She was not only a leader of Society but also for some years one of the most vilified women in the Kingdom. However, compared with many of those contemporaries, including her husband, very few letters to or from the Countess survive.

There is a handful of her letters in the Jersey family papers on deposit at the London Metropolitan Archives and a dozen in the Hickleton Papers at the Borthwick Institute, University of York. Similarly, there are just a dozen or so of Lady Jersey's letters at Chatsworth, the seat of her friend the Duchess of Devonshire, only one at Castle Howard, home of the 5th Earl of Carlisle (one of her long term lovers), and none at all in the papers of William Fawkener, another of her lovers, at Mannington Hall. The largest surviving collection of her letters are the forty-two letters to one of her most loyal friends, Edward Jerningham, which are now in the Huntington Library in San Marino, California.

Apart from these there is evidently very little, which is supported by the 10th Earl of Jersey having kindly confirmed to the author in May 2012 that he did not retain any other letters to or from the Countess.

This absence of surviving letters is also implied in Margaret, Countess of Jersey's history of the Jersey family, *Records of the Family of Villiers, Earls of Jersey,* published in 1924, which, despite its title and its author presumably having access to all the family papers, is predominantly based on printed sources with very few original documents referred to. Further support is provided by the *8th Report of The Historical Manuscripts Commission*, published in 1881, which in listing the manuscripts of the Earls of Jersey at Osterley Park, their house west of London, mentions nothing of relevance to Frances Jersey.[1]

As regards the National Register of Archives at the National Archives in Kew, London, Lady Jersey is almost non-existent.

We do know that, following the Countess's death in 1821, Lord Clarendon (ironically a kinsman of hers) is reported to have destroyed her correspondence with the Prince of Wales, the most famous of her lovers.[2] We also know that, in 1964, the 9th Earl of Jersey confirmed to Professor Arthur Aspinall, the editor of the Prince of Wales' published correspondence, that none of the correspondence between Lady Jersey and the Prince survived at that time.[3]

In the eight volumes of Professor Aspinall's edition of the published correspondence of the Prince of Wales in the years 1770 to 1812 there appears only one letter to Lady Jersey (from Thomas Tyrwhitt), two letters from her (one to Col McMahon and one to the Prince of Wales), three letters from Lord Jersey (one to each of King George III, the Prince of Wales and Col McMahon) and one to Lord Jersey (from Col McMahon). Aspinall in his preface says however that 'nothing of substantial historical importance, however objectionable from a personal point of view, has been omitted [from the eight volumes]. The main omissions are a few letters or passages of slight interest whose text is obviously unsuitable for publication, and letters containing birthday greetings' in addition to some doubtless duplicated official documents.

Aspinall also comments: 'That the King [as the Prince became] had a very vulnerable past is common knowledge, and many letters which would have thrown a somewhat lurid light on his more dubious connections were naturally destroyed by his executors or by others.'[4]

Similarly, in his Introduction to Aspinall's edition of the correspondence of King George IV in the years from 1812, Professor C. K. Webster writes: 'The mistresses of George IV's youth do not appear much in these papers since their letters were for the most part destroyed.'[5]

In fact, it seems that one letter from the Countess to the Prince of Wales dated to the period of their affair has survived.

It also seems likely that outside the Royal correspondence, given the nature of some of her relationships, parts of the Countess's correspondence would not have been kept. It is possible too that, given her place in history, some may have been inclined to destroy her correspondence after the event. An equal factor, though, is likely to be that Lady Jersey was simply not a letter writer. Hers was a different nature. There are virtually no letters to her in the Jersey family papers – though she may not have been one for keeping letters either – and such letters written by her as survive tend to be short and hasty affairs.

Whilst the contemporary politician and commentator Thomas Creevey may have bemoaned the destruction by Lord Clarendon of the Countess's correspondence with the Prince as 'damned provoking to think that such capital material for the instruction and improvement of men and womenkind should be eternally lost', it may well be that there was not much more which has been lost.[6]

Whatever the reason, the picture of Lady Jersey which follows is, perforce, based largely not on what she wrote but on the writings of those who knew her – or thought they knew her.

1

The Beautiful Miss Twysden

Fanny Twysden, the future Countess of Jersey, was one of the great beauties of her time. Clever and witty, she had enormous charm. She was a leader of Society, in its grandest sense, and a woman of 'irresistible seduction and fascination'. She was also unprincipled and malevolent and was destined to become the most hated woman in the country, burned in effigy and her carriage pelted by the mob.

Marrying high above her station, she was to be responsible for arranging the disastrous marriage of her lover, the future King George IV, and to play a major part in blackening the name of a king who was, in the words of *The Times* on his death, unregretted by his subjects.[1]

She in her turn was to die with a reputation so infamous that two centuries later it is still unchallenged, with no attempt being made in the intervening years to redeem it.

Her life began, too, in unusual circumstances.

Fanny's father, Philip Twysden, was a bishop. He was also a highwayman. He was killed before she was born.

Even in the eighteenth century a certain romance attached to highwaymen; stories of their gallantry to lady passengers abounded, and they really did say 'stand and deliver'. It was, nevertheless, a dangerous occupation. Not only was it the habit of travellers and their servants to carry guns in self-defence but also, on capture, hanging was almost inevitable. Despite this, in addition to the Philip Twysden, there seem to have been several instances of young men of respectable backgrounds 'taking to the road to counter ill-fortune and rebuild their finances'. James Maclean, known as 'the Gentleman Highwayman', who had held up Horace Walpole in 1749, was one; he was the son of a Scottish Presbyterian minister and had squandered a small fortune in London before taking his chances on the highway. As we shall see, Philip Twysden had similar grounds for taking to Hounslow Heath.[2]

Philip was the youngest son of Sir William Twysden, 5th Baronet of Roydon Hall in East Peckham, Kent, a long-established Kentish family.[3]

The three Twysden brothers followed the practice of the time. The eldest, another William, as a matter of course inherited both the title and the estate; the second, Thomas, became a soldier; Philip went into the Church.[4]

Philip Twysden was talented and personable enough to attract the attention of Lord Chesterfield who, when he went to Ireland as Lord Lieutenant, took Philip with him as his private chaplain. It was there that Philip was appointed to the Irish Bishopric of Raphoe.[5]

It was probably also in Ireland that Philip met his second wife, Frances Carter, whom he married in 1747 and who was to become Fanny's mother.[6] Frances was the daughter of Thomas Carter, a member of the Irish Privy Council and Master of the Rolls in Ireland. Prominent in Irish politics, Carter was also a man of substance. He had bought the Mastership of the Rolls for more than £11,000 and built a magnificent house in Henrietta Street, supposedly with the finest staircase hall in Dublin. He was also very able: Lord Chesterfield described him as the leading man in the Dublin Parliament.[7]

Philip Twysden clearly married very well in his second marriage, and the daughter from this union was to become one of the most famous ladies of her time.

Before then, though, dramatic events intervened. On 14 October 1752, the bluestocking Mrs Delaney wrote to her friend Mrs Dewes:

> The Bishop of Raphoe is dead.[8]

That the death was unexpected is clear. Not much else is; it is both mysterious and murky.

There are differing accounts of Philip's death. Margaret, Countess of Jersey, in her *Records of the Family of Villiers, the Earls of Jersey,* says there is 'a mysterious story to the effect that his death resulted from some encounter with his dogs'; the Bishop, being a keen huntsman, apparently keeping a pack of hounds. But she goes on to say that 'his enterprises earned him the nickname of "slip gibbet"' and this accords more with the Twysden family version of events.[9]

In this, having originally claimed that the Bishop had been killed by a highwayman on Hounslow Heath, the Twysdens later admitted the truth – the Bishop was a highwayman who was killed whilst carrying out a robbery.[10] In doing so they accepted the claim of one of Fanny's enemies that

> the archives of the British Museum tell us that the 'Lord Bishop Twysden of Raphoe', a member of the old Kentish family of that name, was found suspiciously out at night on Hounslow Heath, and was 'most unquestionably shot through the body', and adding sarcastically that for a dignitary of the established church this was 'collecting tithes in a rather promiscuous way'.[11]

This version is supported by one Amos Logan of Aylesford in Kent. He relates being told by Mr Merryweather, vicar of East Peckham, a variation of it. According to this, a doctor who was staying at Roydon Hall when Philip was also there was warned by a servant that his pistols had been tampered with and so checked them. Finding they had been unloaded, he reloaded them. Later, on Wrotham Heath, his coach was stopped by two masked men, one of whom, pointing his pistol, approached the doctor fearlessly – but the doctor fired and killed the man, who proved to be Philip Twysden.[12]

Whatever the truth – and the claim of Philip being a highwayman is persistent – the bishop died. What is more, despite his rich wife, he died a bankrupt, which may account for his second career, and which certainly left his pregnant widow in an unhappy position.

As the Countess of Westmorland wrote: 'He left a wife in the most afflicting circumstances, in a strange country, big with child, and not a penny of money. Lady Sandwich ... very kindly took her into the country with her, where she is at present, but intends going immediately to her father in Ireland.'[13]

If Frances Twysden did go to Ireland, she was to return quite soon, for *The London Evening Post* reported on Sunday 25 February 1753 that 'the Lady of the late Dr Twysden, Bishop of Raphoe, was safely delivered of a Daughter at her house in St James's Street', in London. The daughter was Fanny Twysden.[14]

It is said that Fanny Twysden's mother was a stern and stately lady who brought her daughter up strictly.[15] It is likely that she and her daughter spent a considerable time in Ireland. But it seems they also maintained a friendship with Fanny's cousins at Roydon Hall. This probably developed further, to the benefit of neither's reputation, when her mother was remarried to another Englishman, Colonel Johnston, and came back to England permanently.

Fanny Twysden grew to be a young lady of great charm and accomplishment. She was spirited and vivacious with considerable social skills. She was an accomplished musician and, though small, was 'exceedingly pretty and fascinating' – as well as inheriting her father's love of hunting.[16] In future years, she was described by Queen Charlotte as Lord Jersey's 'bewitching little wife' and it is said that, 'In her youth, Frances Twysden had been famous throughout all Ireland for her beauty.'[17]

By the time she was seventeen, the bewitching and beautiful Fanny Twysden had married into one of the great families of England. This was the first step in a new life in which her pursuits were her pleasure and her lovers: a life which was bitterly to divide society, set the Prince of Wales against his wife, the Queen against her daughter-in-law and the public against both the Prince and the Countess of Jersey in a display of exceptional vitriol – even in a century when, surrounded by beauty and elegance, cruelty and crudeness were the language of the day.

2

The Prince of Macaronies

Nobody knows how the paths of Fanny Twysden, the granddaughter of a Kentish baronet, and George Bussy Villiers, 4th Earl of Jersey, crossed. Over more than forty years the Earl wrote many hundreds of letters to his friend and confidante Georgiana, Countess Spencer, but not even these give any real clue as to how the two met – though they do show vividly the agonies of indecision the Earl went through before he finally decided to marry Fanny Twysden.

The Earl's bloodline has been described as 'the real blood-royal of England'. The Villiers were, in the small society of the eighteenth century, one of the great families of England, related to many noble families including the Dukes of Devonshire, Grafton and Marlborough as well as the Pitts, the Herveys and Charles James Fox, and to the mistresses of three monarchs.[1]

George Villiers was physically very small even as an adult. Horace Walpole remarked (almost incredibly) that George's eldest daughter, Lady Charlotte Villiers, was already taller than him when she was only four years old.[2] This did not make him a freak in his time; for example, Lady Mary Coventry was described by Creevey as 'decidedly under three feet in height' and was known by her mother-in-law, Lady Holland, as her 'little doll'.[3] Further, George was good looking and had the most exquisite manners. When he was only fifteen, Jane Hamilton, Lady Cathcart, described an entertainment where 'I had Lord Villiers for my partner the first part of the evening. He is indeed the handsomest and genteelest Boy I ever saw and dances in the greatest perfection.'[4]

As the heir to a great name, George led a gilded youth.

In 1754, with Lord Nuneham, the eldest son of Earl Harcourt, George set off, as was the fashion of the aristocratic youth of the day, on a Grand Tour across Europe to complete his education. He did not return for two years. On the tour, the two young aristocrats were accompanied by George's tutor, the future Poet Laureate William Whitehead, as their leader and mentor.[5]

The Jerseys, though, were not rich in comparison to their peers, even though a Grand Tour of three years could cost up to £5,000.[6] Horace Walpole, admittedly a man of high standards, describing a visit to Oxfordshire in 1753 wrote:

> I did look over Lord Jersey's [house, Middleton Park at Middleton Stoney], which was built for a hunting box and is still little better.[7]

This lack of wealth accounts for the scale of a new house built soon after, when a fire at Middleton destroyed the entire house apart from some domestic offices.[8] The fire had begun 'in a Garret that had been shut up for some time past, but that by the help of Sir James Dashwood's servants, whose seat is near Lord Jersey's, and the country people, most of the Fine Furniture was saved'.[9]

The new house was not large. It was built with two wings, in the Palladian fashion, 'with a particularly large pillared porch, satisfactorily filling the eye at the end of a mile long avenue' through the Park.[10] The diarist Mrs Philip Lybbe Powys said of it

> tho' on a small plan, I hardly ever saw so clever [a house] for its size, as every room is good, tho' only four in the whole. You enter a hall, the staircase behind; on one side an eating room 36 by 22, on the other side a drawing-room the same dimensions, with a most excellent library out of the first, behind the hall, 70 feet long. In this room, besides a good collection of books, there is every other kind of amusement, as billiard and other tables, and a few good pictures.[11]

The small scale of the house clearly troubled the Earl, even if its hospitality was splendid. Years later, Lord Jersey commented to Lady Spencer that he had not the wealth that enabled some of his friends to build and run great houses like the Fitzwilliams at Wentworth Woodhouse and the Devonshires at Chatsworth – or even, though this he did not say, the Spencers at Althorp or his neighbours, and both their relatives, the Marlboroughs at Blenheim. Indeed, in the early 1800s Lord Jersey flirted with bankruptcy and after his death his widow needed the financial support of her son, who by then had married enormous wealth in the form of the banker Robert Child's heiress.

Villiers was an earnest and serious young man. The nineteen-year-old Edward Gibbon, who met him in Lausanne on his Grand Tour, described him as a 'good, sensible, modest young man'.[12] His portrait by Edward Dance shows an elegant and contemplative man. He was not one to enjoy the frivolities of Society or many of its habits and was by nature cautious or even pessimistic ('green spectacled' as he was once described) in outlook. His very spirited future wife, of whom he was in some awe, once nicknamed him 'Hem! Hem!' Indeed, this sensitive and serious man was to be dominated, and made miserable, over many years by his adored, magnetic but very strong and forceful wife.

On his return from the Grand Tour, Villiers embarked, in the normal way for a peer's son, upon a career in politics and as a courtier. In 1756 he had been elected an MP and was to remain one until he succeeded to the Earldom.[13] In his political career he was active in following the interests of his great friend and future Prime Minister the Duke of Grafton; his standing was such that, as Horace Walpole records in his *Memoirs of the Reign of George the Third*, in 1765 he was one of those at a meeting of the chiefs of the opposition which took place at Claremont, near Esher in Surrey.[14]

In later life his serious side revealed itself as he fussed about the hours his wife kept, but that he was more than just sensible and trustworthy is shown by the work he did for some of his oldest friends, the Spencers. John Spencer, the 1st Earl Spencer, was the great-grandson of the great Duke of Marlborough. His father had inherited the bulk of the Duke's estate, other than Blenheim Palace, under the will of the Duke's widow (his elder brother, having offended Duchess Sarah, had to rest content with the Dukedom and Blenheim Palace). As a result Lord Spencer was a man of considerable wealth. When he was building Spencer House in St James's, London at enormous expense, he and Lady Spencer spent a considerable time travelling on the continent and had to enlist the support of Villiers, who took on the role of project manager at a time when their architect James Stuart was losing control of the project with progress slow and estimates soaring.[15] His work appears to have been diligent and effective and we find no complaints of it.

There was, too, a less sober side to Villiers and that was as a 'macaroni', those fashionable, or perhaps foppish, young men in Society who acquired their nickname as a result of admiring everything foreign, including food. Starting from the mid-1760s and reaching a crescendo in the early 1770s, their attention was focused on ever more lavish and fantastic clothes and extremes in manners and sensibilities.

Thus *Town and Country Magazine* wrote of macaronis:

> They make a most ridiculous figure with hats an inch in the brim that do not cover but lie upon the head, with about two pounds of fictitious hair formed into what is called a 'club' hanging down their shoulders. The end of the skirt of their coat reaches the first button of their breeches which are either brown-striped or white; their coat sleeves are so tight that they can with difficulty get their arms through their cuffs ... Their legs are covered with all the colours of the rainbow. The shoes are scarce slippers and their buckles are within an inch of the toe. Such a figure, essenced and perfumed, with a bunch of lace sticking out of under *its* chin, puzzles the common passenger to determine the thing's sex.[16]

Well known for his courtly manners, Villiers was to Mrs Montagu, the author and literary hostess, 'the Prince of Macaronies'.[17] When he appeared at court in 'a pale purple velvet coat, turned up with lemon colour, and embroidered all over with "SS"'s of pearls as big as peas, and in all the spaces little medallions of beaten gold, real solid, in various figures of Cupids the world gasped with wonder, but Mrs Delaney, hating ostentation ... pronounced that it was "only a fool's coat".'[18]

Mrs Delaney was not alone in such views. The macaronis were much derided in the press.

He might have been 'The Prince of Macaronis', but Villiers was also devoted to country sports. He hunted and shot with a passion, and was dauntless in the saddle. William Whitehead frequently wrote in his letters of Villiers' sporting activities, as when he wrote to Lord Nuneham in 1763 that Villiers was at Middleton and spending six or eight hours every day shooting so that 'he quite stocks Lord Jersey's table with game ... The hounds too, I think they say, are to be out tomorrow.'[19]

By that time, Villiers was eighteen and minds were turning to his marriage or at least romance. Whitehead had written to Lord Nuneham the previous month, as if rumours were about, saying 'I most heartily wish Lord Villiers was really going to be married, but I literally know nothing of the matter'.[20] Who the subject of that rumour was is unclear, but in October 1763 the not long married daughter of the Duke of Richmond, Lady Sarah Bunbury, wrote of Villiers:

> That little toad pretends to be seriously in love with me; he is a very good actor, for his likeness never make better love, or rather looked it better (for I insisted on his not speaking whether in joke or earnest), than he does. He is so like him when he makes *les yeux doux* & sighs, etc., etc. it's quite ridiculous, you would be in love with his looks I quite assure you.[21]

This may have more to do with Lady Sarah Bunbury than with Villiers. In May 1767, Lady Mary Coke, the often waspish daughter of the 2nd Duke of Argyll, who had been visiting Holland House, wrote:

> I found only the Family but as Ly Sarah Banbury [*sic*] was one you may guess Lord Carlisle came in soon after. I am not of a censorious disposition, & yet cannot help saying I think Lady Sarah's conduct highly imprudent, to say nothing worse, & her good Grace of Richmond is almost as particular with Mr Sackville as Lady Sarah is with Lord Carlisle.[22]

In any event, there is no further mention of Villiers' romantic ventures for some years to come.

Outside politics, Villiers instead concentrated on his friendships and his sport. First amongst these was his friendship with the Spencers, to whom he was very close. The depth of Villiers' obviously Platonic (his wife, clearly piqued at the time, was later to suggest the contrary) relationship with Lady Spencer, in particular, is shown by the many hundreds of beautifully written, chatty, informative, wistful and sometimes complaining letters in an elegant hand which he wrote to her in the forty or so years from 1759.

All of this was to change, and not just his relationship with Lady Spencer. In August 1769 George's father died in Bath and Villiers succeeded to the Earldom as the 4th Earl. This and the need for an heir was the catalyst for change and for the marriage which was to transform his life, and his friendships, at whose centre lay Fanny Twysden.

3

Courtship and Marriage

At the time of his father's death, Villiers was inching slowly towards that marriage.

English Society in the mid-eighteenth century was small. In 1770 there were 196 English peers, of whom twenty-three were dukes, one a marquess, eighty-one earls (including Lord Jersey), thirteen viscounts, and sixty-seven barons – in addition to which there were 129 Irish peers and eighty-one Scottish ones.[1] Not only did they all know personally many of the other peers but also many of their families were related either by blood or by marriage.

The social standing of the peerage was such that it was seen to be threatened by marriage outside the group. Accordingly, in the eighteenth century peers married predominately within the peerage. Between 1730 and 1780, some 60 per cent of the first wives of peers were themselves from families of peers, foreign nobility or royalty. Compared to the 162 marriages in this period within this wide definition of the peerage, the clergy (where the fathers were bishops or deans) provided only nine wives, and just ten wives were the daughters of baronets.[2]

That the new Earl of Jersey was not conforming to the natural order of things in his choice of wife coupled with the fact that, at thirty-four, he was nearly twice her age, may explain some of the diffidence displayed by him during his courtship of Fanny Twysden. There may, too, have been some concern about her and her cousins' reputations.

The circumstances and progress of the courtship are mysterious. Lord Jersey's references to it in his letters are oblique, and even Margaret Jersey throws no light on how the couple met in her *Records of the Family of Villiers, Earls of Jersey.*

From the very start there appears to have been some tension over the topic with Lady Spencer. In an undated letter written from Berkhemstead, possibly in September 1769, Lord Jersey said:

> I must own the apprehension that dislike or anything untoward in the, I mean any Person, whom it is necessary almost I should chuse to share my

fortunes with me, should produce a distance or coolness between us three [that is Jersey and the Earl and Countess Spencer] (forgive if I put her a little out of the question in that sincere attachment to you) retards very much any resolution I might wish to take upon that Plan.[3]

It almost seems that Jersey's relationship with Lady Spencer and her husband was more important to him than any marriage.

Initially there was more than one candidate to become Countess of Jersey. The Earl, desperate for advice, wrote to Lady Spencer, who was about to go abroad, on 10 October 1769 from Délapré Abbey in Northamptonshire, the seat of the Bouverie family:

> What conversation passed between us lately upon a certain subject … you would help one to the right track … let me have good advice by letter … I will own the younger person has somehow or other got the upper hand, though it is easy to be checked yet, & hurry I know is the Devil.[4]

So Fanny was, for the moment at least, the favoured candidate in what appears to be a decision by the Earl that it was time to get married. Still, he remained undecided, and who the other candidate was is unknown.

Fanny at this time was also in Northamptonshire and, in November, Lord Jersey was back there, too, but having second thoughts. On 26 November he again wrote to Lady Spencer from Délapré Abbey:

> You see I am in this county, but I have not made a single visit or seen any of the neighbouring ladies since I writ last; do not imagine it runs in my thoughts, indeed it does not, that is very little if at all; I shall go away in a short time and shall not return.[5]

But things rapidly took a turn in Fanny's favour. On 4 December, Lord Jersey told Lady Spencer that whilst out hunting with Bouverie:

> Who should meet us in the field, but the little Lady herself, so much for fortune. Why not are you here to advise one to continue to think, as I do, upon the subject, what steps to take … I see I cannot live alone, & why should she not share that place, as well as another, I mean with as good a prospect of mutual content … if it should so happen that during this week we should meet again, I am terrified with the fears of what lengths I may not go.[6]

Doubtless, on this occasion the beautiful Miss Twysden was her bewitching self and her passion for hunting a common interest.

Back in London in December, the Earl was becoming even more desperate; he seemed more decided on marriage but more worried about its consequences. Lady Spencer was still abroad so unable to advise him and, after bemoaning that two of his letters to her at Nice in France had not arrived, Lord Jersey wrote on 18 December that those letters

> contained much on the old Northtonshire [*sic*] subject, which I cannot repeat, but I think the subject gains ground very fast upon my discretion & prudence, and could I have but one long reasoned discourse with you, I believe I should decide at once, one way or the other.[7]

By the end of January 1770, things were crystallising. On 29 January, Lord Jersey wrote in mysterious terms to Lady Spencer:

> The whole is now fixed, & tomorrow I believe the Cat is to be let quite out; our friend is no longer in the situation he was ... What the Consequences will be are ... not yet even to guess ...[8]

Who the friend and what the change in situation was is unknown, but on 1 February Lord Jersey wrote to Lady Spencer once more from Délapré Abbey:

> The tremendous resolution is at last taken; & not only taken, but really executed; that is yesterday morning the proposal was accepted in this neighbourhood; so it is all over & I must never look back, the prospect is clear but the climate is uncertain – I knew it would come to this ... I do not think you could have prevented it [even if Lady Spencer had not been abroad], and I hope you do not disapprove...'

He added that if he perceived any change in Lady Spencer's friendship and confidence as a consequence 'I shall wish it all undone again'.[9]

Lord Jersey's concern about the effect of his marriage on his friendship with Lady Spencer was a recurrent theme in their correspondence at the time, as was his desire for her approval of his choice. It seems he already understood the threat his new wife represented but expressed the hope that 'The person in question will I think if, I am not mistaken in my judgement of her, at least not thwart it & then it will be alright'. On the other hand, he certainly knew that Lady Spencer did indeed disapprove of the match, as an undated letter to Lady Spencer acknowledges a great argument between them on the subject of him marrying 'so young a person.'[10]

Lord Jersey's impending marriage certainly provoked comment in society too. On 9 February Lord Jersey wrote that it 'is no longer secret, it has been known & talked of as such from one friend or another in London for some days, but now the Cat is quite out, she is a pretty large Cat it is true, yet I have made up my mind to it now and am Benedict at once' and consoled himself by saying that, despite all his ambivalences, 'to all appearances I have made a choice the most promising for my own happiness'.[11]

Lord Jersey did not enjoy, either, all the bustle that went with weddings. He said, 'I am now getting more confusion & in more hurry than well [*sic*] be imagined, impatient to have it over as soon as possible makes one so busy that I scarcely have time to do anything ... my house is all about my ears but

I hope before you come [back from the Continent] we shall be in the family way.' He wrote again on 13 February, 'I hope of getting the Business over very soon. I am now in the utmost hurry and confusion ... Yet I learned this morning that, do what I will, it cannot be completed for sometime, which is a shocking piece of news.'[12] Lord Jersey was clearly not enjoying himself and his nerves were suffering accordingly.

By the end of February the date of the wedding had still not been decided. On 22 February he wrote, ever more frantically, to Lady Spencer, who was now at Dover on her way home:

> Tho' I have every day more and more reason to approve of my choice, I cannot help feeling myself in a most anxious and alarming situation. You will ask me immediately when it is to be; I know not, nor have the least guess ... The present is a horrid time; one is the joke of everybody.

Though he did not say whether that was because friends enjoyed the discomfiture of a seasoned bachelor getting married or, more unkindly, because of the disparity in the bride and groom's ages or their social standing.[13]

The latest delays may have been caused by discussions on the marriage settlement. Finally 'Articles of Agreement' were signed on 26 March 1770 between Lord Jersey and 'Frances Johnston wife of Col. Johnston widow of Ld Bishop of Raphoe for infant daughter Frances Twysden (over 17) ... re the settlement of Mrs. Johnston's fortune'. The same day, Lord Jersey and Fanny Twysden were married at Col Johnston's house in St Martin's-in-the-Fields in London.[14]

The wedding was duly reported in the next day's newspapers with the additional information that the ceremony was 'performed by the Rev Mr Alt, his Lordship's chaplain'.[15]

The newly married couple went on honeymoon to Wimbledon Park, the Spencers' country house south-west of London. From there Lord Jersey wrote the next day to Lady Spencer with characteristic lack of enthusiasm that 'the [marriage] ceremony ... passed off as these things usually do, I suppose, a horrid performance indeed'. He did not seem to have enjoyed much of either his engagement or the marriage ceremony. He was, however, a lot happier with Wimbledon Park, and perhaps was now more relaxed, for in thanking Lady Spencer for its loan he went on to say, 'We have now only to thank you for our situation here which is comfortable to a degree & there is everything in the world provided and offered to us that we can possibly want, & more indeed than we can have thought ... pray come early [tomorrow morning] ... before the others arrive, Johnstons &c.'[16]

Society's commentary on Lord Jersey's choice of wife did not cease on his marriage. Viscountess Irwin may have been joking when on 2 April she wrote to Lady Gower: 'I perceive it is the fashion to have two wives at a time Lord Jersey being married to Miss Johnston & Miss Twysden, but which is he really possessed of?'[17] Lady Mary Coke was clearly not joking when writing to Lady Greenwich from Paris the following day:

> I think Lord Carlisle has made a very proper choice. I approve of that marriage [in March that year Lord Carlisle had married Lady Caroline Leveson Gower, daughter of the 2nd Earl Gower, afterwards 1st Marquess of Stafford] much more then [*sic*] of Ld Jersey's: not that I have anything to say against the lady, but I don't think her Birth suitable to his.[18]

Whatever Lady Mary Coke thought on this score, Fanny Twysden, having married high above her station in an aristocratic century, was now the Countess of Jersey. By right and by nature she was now to occupy a leading position in Society and at court, where her husband had now become Master of the Horse to Queen Charlotte.

4
Respectability

Frances, Countess of Jersey was ranked alongside the Duchess of Rutland and Georgiana, Duchess of Devonshire as one of the reigning beauties of the day. She had great personal charm. Slim and elegant, she was small but also a woman of great spirit, style, wit and, at bottom, steel. Margaret Jersey describes her as 'small and exceedingly pretty and fascinating'.[1] Sir Nathaniel Wraxall, a contemporary writer and memoirist, described her as having 'irresistible seduction and fascination'.[2] Another, the Margravine of Ansbach, more prosaically 'allows for her beauty but says she has thick legs'.[3]

Years later, Lord Melbourne, who had known all these beauties in his youth, related to Queen Victoria that George IV always used to say that the women were much handsomer in his time but, said Melbourne:

> One couldn't judge unless one saw them all together. The Duchess of Rutland ... was reckoned so excessively beautiful; &c. Lady Hertford &c.; Lady Jersey ... she was a handsomer but a wickeder woman ... little with large black eyes ... very handsome.[4]

As a leading member of Whig Society by virtue of her marriage, the Countess was to become a member of the Devonshire House Circle, the hundred or so habitués of Devonshire House who, sharing Whig loyalties, were centred on Countess Spencer's daughter Georgiana upon her becoming Duchess of Devonshire. Where Frances Jersey differed from Georgiana, and many of her contemporaries, was that she took little interest in politics and did not indulge in the passion of the age, gambling. When Edmund Burke said to the writer Fanny Burney in 1782 that the eighteenth century was 'an age distinguished by producing extraordinary women', Frances Jersey might well have been one of those he had in mind.[5] She certainly was, with Lady Melbourne, the basis for the nasty Lady Sneerwell in Sheridan's *The School for Scandal*, first performed in May 1777.[6] What is not true, as has been alleged, is that she was also the inspiration for Diana Villiers in Patrick O'Brian's Aubrey-Maturin naval novels of the Napoleonic wars. Rather, that character was inspired by the same not totally respectable Margravine of Ansbach in her younger days when she was still (the Beautiful) Lady Craven.[7]

The Countess was a talented musician. She played the harp well, practising a good deal, and aspired, on his visiting, to make 'fine harmony' with her closest friend Edward Jerningham – and fretted when much needed harp strings did not arrive at Middleton. Typically, she greatly enjoyed there being much music at Blenheim when staying with the Marlboroughs in 1770, and in a letter from Lord Jersey to Lady Spencer in October that same year he wrote:

> I shall be very glad if you will think of making out a little music for Ly J at the Christmas Party at Althorp [the Spencers' seat in Northamptonshire], she plays everything at sight & seems to accompany upon the thorough Bass readily enough.[8]

In the 1790s, when she spent much time with the Royal Family along with the Prince of Wales, she often employed her talents on the harp in entertaining Queen Charlotte.

Frances Jersey was an intelligent woman but one of impulse and enthusiasm – not always guided – who was dedicated to the pursuit of pleasure in all the forms it took amongst fashionable Society. She was witty and supremely sophisticated, style personified. She loved Society's balls, assemblies, masquerades, concerts and operas, and threw herself into everything with breathless energy – so much so, and with so little restraint, that her health frequently suffered as a result, to the regular disapproval of her husband. Her enthusiasm in the hunting field, at least in the eyes of her husband, verged on the reckless and also commonly provoked his reproof.

She was devoted to fashion in an age of high fashion and loved rich and beautiful clothes like so many of the cream of Society, the '*ton*', of both sexes. We shall see this later with her becoming a leader of a fashionable set, but an early example can be found in the *Lady's Magazine* of 1784, telling of 'the Jersey Turban, a large band of tiffany pinned on the hair with a heron's feather and one diamond pin on the left side'. Frances Jersey was not to be outdone by the Duchess of Devonshire having a hat, the eponymous Devonshire hat, named after her.[9]

She was capable of real kindness and loyalty and was a caring and affectionate as well as ambitious mother; her kindness to children, too, was not limited to her own. At the same time, she inspired real affection in those looking beyond her faults, as shown by the attentions of those close to her including Whitehead, Jerningham and Georgiana Spencer and, even more tellingly, the much more critical Countess Spencer.

However, this deeply attractive and complex woman, once described by a contemporary as 'clever, unprincipled, but beautiful and fascinating', coupled kindness and loyalty with a sharpness which increasingly over the years merged into scorn and selfishness.[10] Conscious of her charms, she could also be haughty, manipulative, malicious and cruel. Her tongue could be biting. Friends came and went accordingly; some treated her with caution from the first. Nevertheless, from the beginning, her marriage opened wide the doors of Society to her.

Whatever the origins of their marriage, Lord Jersey clearly adored his wife and would continue to do so over many years, despite consummate provocation, with a *naivité* which sometimes defies belief. He was also not a little in awe, if not in fear, of her. For her part, she clearly had affection for him although this did not prevent her treating him very badly over many years.

In the first years of her marriage, though, Frances Jersey led a life of respectability, made up of domesticity, child bearing, and visiting, punctuated by regular bouts of illness, until the birth of a son and heir to the earldom gave her independent spirit release. In short, in the early years she led a pastoral, conventional and respectable life which was, for one of her kind, rather dull – relieved only by such excitements in the hunting field or elsewhere that she could find.

Although shortly after their marriage Lord Jersey, along with the Duke of Grafton, visited Lord Sandwich at Hinchinbroke (where 'Miss Ray', Sandwich's mistress, later to be murdered by a would-be paramour, 'does the honours'), the newly marrieds spent the first few months of their marriage in London where the excitement-seeking Lady Jersey was either rash or accident prone. Whitehead wrote to Lord Nuneham from Mount Street on 25 June 1770:

> Your friend Lady Jersey has wanted a great deal of scolding since you left town; she must needs be a driver as well as a rider. The horses ran away with her in one of the little chaises at Wimbledon, & she was obliged to throw herself out of it to avoid being drowned. This fright has, I hope, cured her; I wish she would learn the prudence of Lady Nuneham.[11]

It seems she failed to do so. In an undated contemporaneous letter to Lady Spencer from Grosvenor Square, the Jerseys' house in London, Lord Jersey wrote:

> In the first place Lady Jersey is not at all hurt by the most shocking fall which she had had from her horse just now, I send this to you lest you should hear a contrary account from others; also to ask you whether I should send for anybody or do anything. She does not seem the least affected by it.[12]

Frances Jersey would demonstrate over the years that she did not lack strength of character.

Leaving London for Middleton for the summer, the Jerseys led a quieter life in the country. Whitehead related to Lord Nuneham at the end of June that he had received a letter from Lord Jersey there:

> He has forgot something, and she has forgot something, and I am to send this, and to bring that: Lord bless them, they are both very young, but they are absolute turtles at present.[13]

In July, Lord Jersey told Lady Spencer:

> We are now entirely settled here ... Our first arrival here has been a little uncomfortable by my little Lady's being ill. She was very much so for several days, but has been relieved by a strong rash, which probably will go through the family [i.e. the household] ... In the end though I suppose it will do her good; bad as that method is of being well – she stands by me and says give my love to her – the Nunehams and Brudenels are our company.[14]

This is the first mention of Lady Jersey being ill. Over the next few years she was to be ill nearly as regularly as she was to be pregnant.

Later that month, they had her mother Mrs Johnston to stay for a few days whilst Lady Jersey was already involving herself in the coming London Season and her new place in society – Lord Jersey relaying a message from her to Lady Spencer that she wished Lord Spencer 'would call himself a subscriber to her Box at the Opera; he has a silver ticket, she says and can do it easily'.[15]

The Jerseys then embarked on a series of visits to introduce the new Countess to the Earl's closest friends, the Duke of Grafton, Lord and Lady Nuneham, and the Spencers, as well as their nearest neighbours, the Duke and Duchess of Marlborough.

First they went to Wakefield Lodge in Northamptonshire, one of the Duke of Grafton's estates, for the Races, where 'the house begins to fill with the Set, such as it is', and for the hunting. Lord Jersey reported that as yet 'she has had no falls &c &c' resulting from her enthusiastic approach in the field,[16] although when he wrote to Lady Spencer on 30 July that 'Ly J is tolerably good about hunting, but when she does go she rides as she did at Farming Woods' (where Lords Spencer and Jersey stayed when hunting with the Pytchley Hunt near Althorp) he clearly thought that her lack of falls was due more to luck than to prudence.[17]

Then in early August they were at Nuneham, Earl Harcourt's seat about six miles from Oxford, to stay with the Nunehams. Actually, as Lord Jersey said to Lady Spencer:

> We are in fact performing [that is, as the local aristocracy, acting as patrons at Oxford races] ... [and] stole the middle day of three to pass at this Place, & delightful indeed it is.[18]

Nuneham was certainly a lovely place. 'It is a place possessing great natural beauties, which have been much improved by Browne, Whitehead and Mason ... Mason laid out the flower garden in excellent taste. It is one of the most perfect I have ever yet seen' wrote the Bishop of London to Hannah More some years later.[19]

Back again at Middleton at the end of the month, Lord Jersey wrote that 'Ly Jersey has not been able to ride once she has been here, her horse has never been sound, which is unlucky enough, but we have a little chaise that is made a good deal of use. As to company to stay [with] us we have not had much: we expect some however soon.'[20]

Perhaps it was fortunate that her horse was unfit and the company limited since Lady Jersey was now pregnant. This, however, did nothing at first to restrain her youthful high spirits – or bad manners. Whitehead describes a visit with the Jerseys to Ditchley Park, near Chipping Norton, in August where the maid who showed them around the house had 'the tone and manner of the man who shows the tombs', and 'Lady Jersey, fie upon her, began giggling as soon as the poor girl spoke, & put her quite out of her narration'; later when they came to a ceiling 'which the young woman assured us was paper misshé [*sic*], I was obliged to leave the room, because I would not be a witness of so much ill-behaviour; in short her Ladyship must never go to Dr Bacon. At Lord Shrewsbury's she behaved better.'[21]

For the rest of the summer, the Jerseys continued with a quiet life at Middleton, from where, in advance of their visit to the Spencers at Althorp, Lady Jersey was diligently polite to the older and more sedate Lady Spencer. Lady Jersey expressed her impatience to see the Spencers, as the epitome of courtesy, Lord Jersey, accounted in a letter: '[it] is natural for her when you [Lady Spencer] have shown so much kindness & attention to her. She is tolerably well.'[22]

Then in October they completed their round of visits. First they spent two nights at Blenheim Palace with the Marlboroughs where Frances Jersey's love of music was indulged; 'I was very glad we executed it, for Ly J got a great deal of Music, which is what she likes' said her husband.[23] Then the Earl went to Farming Woods and on to Wellingborough to hunt, with Lady Jersey meeting the party there, although, presumably given her pregnancy, she was not hunting on this occasion.[24] From Wellingborough, the Jerseys at last made their way to Althorp.[25]

Lady Jersey commonly became depressed during the later stages of her pregnancies, perhaps regretting the loss of excitements open to her or even, vain as she was, the loss of her figure. There is however no further news of the Countess on this score or otherwise until, on 2 May 1771, she gave birth to the Jerseys' first child, Lady Charlotte Anne Villiers, prompting Lord Jersey to write to Lady Spencer:

> I can safely say [Lady Jersey] is hitherto most amazingly well, as if nothing had happened, indeed she was so expeditious, that her sufferings were much less than I believe even she herself apprehended.

The Earl did however confess that 'a son would have been most welcome to us both' and that he felt some disappointment on that score, although he never admitted that to his wife and she 'does not appear to suffer at all from whatever may be her feelings' on the child not being a boy.[26]

At Lady Charlotte's christening 'Lady Jersey [seemed] quite well, and not at all fatigued' by it.[27] Afterwards, though, she suffered another of her now periodic bouts of illness, in which she suffered from one or both of a persistent cough and hoarseness and a pain in her side. On this occasion, a Tuesday, as Lord Jersey wrote to Lady Spencer, she 'coughed a great deal all night, & was very low & weak this morning, but the Doctors thought her fever abated and on the whole that she was better, her pulse being much mended – she has been blooded again today, and her breath seems relieved'. She was not so ill, though, as to take to her bed but, as Lord Jersey went on to say, 'she is to go to bed soon after 7 o'clock, and if Lady Spencer [stays] at home LJ will call upon her Ladyship.'[28]

The report on her health the next day was that 'Lady J has had a good night, & is certainly much better today, & the Doctor says the strictest adherence to rigid rules is all that is wanted. – She coughs however a good deal.'[29] During the course of the day Lady Spencer called on Lord Jersey to enquire after the invalid, and in a note to Lady Spencer the same night Lord Jersey told her that 'Lady J has continued without fever all day and seems to promise to have a good night; but her cough is still also frequent and troublesome that the least imprudence or accidental check would destroy the present amendment'.[30]

Quiet, something foreign to the Countess, was not for the last time the prescription.

Fortunately, Friday's report was that 'Lady J continues to mend, as she should do, and is to go out on Sunday, if the weather is but tolerable'.[31]

The improvement continued and by the end of June the Countess was well enough to go to Euston Hall in Suffolk to stay with the Duke of Grafton. Little Lady Charlotte was left behind at Middleton. Of Charlotte, Lord Jersey commented that we 'fancy that she is grown to be nearly half as big as other children of the same age'. With both the Earl and his wife being physically small, the Jersey children when young were generally noticeably small, too. In the same letter he also jokingly complained to Lady Spencer that:

> I do not know how many more bad habits Ly J is to learn from you for she has already caught the fancy of angling, and desires me to tell you what excellent sport she has had today ... She rides about a great deal, and is grown rather plumper.[32]

The quiet life, with or without fishing, resumed on their return to Middleton in mid-July, with Lady Jersey once more pregnant, less than three months after Lady Charlotte's birth.[33] This time she exercised some caution; having fallen from her horse once, and though she 'rode him many times afterwards without the least danger, and [Lord Jersey thought him] the best going horse ... anywhere', by July she preferred riding the Earl's old chestnut, 'Bobbings', to her own. This discretion, prompted one assumes by her pregnancy, was not to last.[34]

The Nunehams stayed with the Jerseys in August, but that apart Middleton was 'the quietest place in the world'[35] – so quiet, said Lord Jersey to Lady Spencer, that 'Ly J says she has nothing to communicate' to you.[36]

The Jersey's second child, another daughter, Lady Anne Barbara Frances Villiers, was born on 22 March 1772, a mere ten months after her elder sister.

It seems that this birth, or at least its aftermath, was considerably worse than the first.

Possibly unwisely, the Countess having a habit of over exerting herself in her enthusiasms, the Jerseys soon embarked on a busy social life. In May, with the Nunehams, the Duke and Duchess of Queensberry, Lord and Lady Temple and others, they visited Horace Walpole at Strawberry Hill, Walpole's Gothic Revival masterpiece of a house at Twickenham, where they 'had a very agreeable day, though the weather was not good enough to allow of walking'.[37] When back at Middleton in June they were so busy entertaining or being entertained that Whitehead wrote to Lord Nuneham:

> So kind have the natives been that this is the first day I dined with Lord and Lady Jersey alone. They are both perfectly well, and very much employed making a dog kennel, & digging earths to invite foxes to making Middleton their abode. Some disturbances will probably attend their labours in the long run, & I may have a new Chevy Chase to write in beginning of winter*. Lady Jersey is an arrant little tigress upon the subject, & even trimmings and contreband caps are little thought of for the time being by the fashion loving Countess as she concentrated on the hunt.[38]

No longer pregnant, she also abandoned her short-lived discretion in riding mild-mannered horses. By July she was riding frequently and, said Lord Jersey, 'her old horse has failed her; & she has boldly ventured on one of my hunters, a horse of infinite spirit, but hitherto he has carried her well. Spencer calls him the Dresden China horse.' He also told Lady Spencer that the 'little creatures are well and much grown. The oldest begins to be amusing enough to be a great deal with us.'[40] Lord Jersey's often mocking tones when talking about his children belie the fact that he clearly doted on them.

July also found the Jerseys at Lord Temple's seat at Stowe, a Neoclassical palace in sublimely landscaped gardens, having supper in the illuminated grotto with Lord and Lady Coventry and Prince Poniatowski.[41] But by the middle of the month Lady Jersey had another attack of her illness, this time a bad one – she was to remain ill for some months to come. She had, said her husband, 'almost a constant hoarseness upon her every evening & a more troublesome pain in her side – she frequently looks very ill.'[42]

In mid-August she was no better, rather

> much the same, sometimes tolerably well, sometimes the reverse. She has almost a constant hoarseness, rather a thickness of voice with a very frequent pain in her side … and [said her husband] if we had not had so remarkably fine a summer I am confident she would not have been so well as she is even now; and the Autumn & damp weather will undoubtedly lay

* These sporting activities lie rather oddly, at the height of the Macaroni craze that year, with the 'Macaroni Magazine' printing portraits and memoirs of some of the more celebrated members of the set and featuring the Earl under the title of the 'Nosegay Maccaroni'.[39]

> her up in my opinion, unless she will require some degree of prudence ... However at her own request I write by this post to Dr Warren for his advice which I fear she will not follow when it comes ...[43]

Dr Warren was the highly regarded, and ubiquitous, doctor to Society. Whether it was his advice (which Lady Jersey unexpectedly both requested and followed), a new-found prudence on the part of a normally impatient Countess, or merely nature at work, by the end of the month the Earl was able to report:

> We are just returned from a three days absence to Oxford Races ... [Lady Jersey] begins drinking some [steel?] waters of the neighbourhood tomorrow; in which she will persevere about two days, but she is certainly much mended and if the autumn does not produce cold, she will get fat by degrees.[44]

Improvement in her health was nevertheless slow. In September, Lord Jersey went to London to do his 'waiting' at court, leaving the Countess behind at Middleton. In his absence, the doubtless bored Countess visited Blenheim and Nuneham, finding scarcely anybody at the former and a full house at the latter. On his return to Middleton, Lord Jersey found her 'not at all well' and, to make things worse, that young Lady Charlotte was also ill, having had 'a fit & is not as she should be, though they are both better now, and on the whole Lady J is stronger'.[45]

By October, the Countess had convinced herself that she was well enough to go on what the Earl described as

> a foolish hurrying journey to Bath to see her Mother & that unfortunate child, which continues still in the same deplorable state. She comes back [wrote Lord Jersey to Lady Spencer] tomorrow ... [Thereafter] Lady J if she can manage it may take some hunting with you at your return. She now rides with hounds that go much faster, indeed she has been out with us two or three times, & by setting [a servant] Shipwith before her she has been more prudent than her inclinations would have led her. She has got good horses, which is the great article, for Prudence in Ladies I never expect to see.

So, too, the skill of her horses tempered her impetuosity.[46]

There is no clue to who the 'unfortunate child' was or its relationship to Mrs Johnston. There is, though, a clear recognition of the need to curb Frances Jersey's impetuosity when out with the hounds.

The Earl's concerns about his wife's journey to Bath proved well-founded. On his way to Euston Hall for a fortnight's hunting and shooting in early November, he wrote:

> Lady J is at Mid. not long returned from her Bath Journey ... not the most prudent in the world and so it has proved in an essential circumstance, but she is reasonably well ... She wants something to reinstate her effectually,

> for she has strong symptoms of the most delicate frame, which will not bear what she thinks it can, and those symptoms ought to be removed.[47]

And so her illness rumbled on. It had now lasted for nearly six months. The Jerseys went *en famille* to Euston for Christmas, with the hope of much hunting.[48] Lord Jersey did manage some before badly bruising his leg in a fall in the field. Lady Jersey, though, continued to be 'indifferent, not well enough to have hunted more than once, the pain in her side hangs constantly upon her'.[49]

The Earl's injury, too, was quite serious. Whilst some days later he was 'a great deal better, tho' still confined', it was unclear when he would be able to walk. Nevertheless,'he certainly is better than we could have expected' said his wife to Lady Spencer.[50]

Despite all of this, they were both fit enough to return to London in early January 1773.

Once there, Frances Jersey subscribed for a box in the theatre, one of the new vantages which had been 'added to the Theatre ... upon the Stage, & a tolerably good one'. In the eighteenth century the theatre was, in the words of a leading historian of London, London's greatest pleasure, in which all but the poorest could share. What is more, 'on several nights throughout the season, they might find themselves sharing it with the King. From journeyman to monarch, all sorts and conditions of Londoners were found in the theatre and all had their place.'[51]

Professor White quotes a publication of 1747, *The Tricks of the Town Laid Open,* which describes the workings of the theatres at the time:

> In our play houses at London, besides an Upper-Gallery for Footmen, Coachmen, Mendicants, &c. we have three other different and distinct classes; the first is called the *Boxes*, where there is one peculiar to the King and Royal Family, and the rest for Persons of Quality, and for the Ladies and Gentlemen of the highest Rank ... the second is call'd the *Pit* where sit the Judges, Wits and Censurers ... that damn or sink the Play at a venture ... in common with these sit the Squires, Sharpers, Beaus Bullies and Whores and here and there an extravagant Male and Female Cit. The third is distinguished by the Title of the *Middle Gallery*, where the Citizens' Wives and Daughters, together with the Abigail's, Serving men, Journey-men and Apprentices commonly take their Places.[52]

In these performances, the audience itself was 'just as fascinating as much of the action on stage, the theatres "glittering and gaudy because our spectators love to be an exhibition themselves". The house lights were undimmed throughout the performance for ease of observation. Fashionable people in the boxes were most regarded and had most regard for each other: "Gentleman and ladies ogled each other through spectacles; for my companion observed, blindness was of late become fashionable." '[53]

The Countess's health now continued, said the Earl, 'tolerably well; how long London will leave her so is not a matter of doubt ...' He was right in this. She would, doubtless over-taxing herself as ever, continue to struggle with illness for months more to come, both in London and at Middleton.

Meanwhile their daughters, having been left behind at Middleton, now joined the Jerseys in town, 'the youngest complaining of her teeth, but crying out as the Beauty, though I [said the Earl] retain my partiality to the jolly riot of the eldest, who is an excellent companion, walks and runs.'[54]

Lady Anne may have been regarded as a beauty even as an infant, but all the Jersey daughters grew up to be great beauties, including Lady Charlotte.

When Lord Jersey went back to Middleton in March 1773, 'Lady J staid in town, for reasons you know, & I hear she is better of her cough, which was bad enough when I came away', he wrote;[55] whether her reasons for staying in town were for her health or other purposes, what is clear is that she was pregnant again.

Perhaps learning from past mistakes, a quiet and pastoral existence resumed. May was spent at Middleton and, although Lord Jersey came up to London for the King's Birthday, Lady Jersey remained in Oxfordshire where her mother was staying with them for a few days.[56] It was quite a domestic scene; as Lord Jersey said, 'I am grown a regular family man, & have a wife of my own to look after; Business enough for any one man ... Her Grace [the Duchess of Marlborough] and Lady J being in the same way neither of them can travel much.'[57] Her inability to travel at least gave Lady Jersey the opportunity, through her husband, to invite Lord Spencer to 'belong to her box at the Opera', and Lord Jersey went on, in a comment foreshadowing his future treatment at the hands of his wife, 'you must not be as long answering the request as I have been proposing it, for I shall pay for it at home.'[58]

For her part, the Countess told Lady Spencer: 'I propose to take great care of myself in order to be very robust at Farmers Wood [*sic*] in October', where they hoped they would be joining the Spencers after Lady Jersey's next child had arrived.[59] Despite that, by mid-June Lord Jersey was writing from London that his wife had been ill again: 'I have left Lady J better, but she has been much out of order in the country,' where he had left her.[60] Indeed, on 18 June Lord Jersey felt the need to write to Lady Spencer, saying that although she may have heard that his wife was dangerously ill it was not true – 'she has been out of order and narrowly escaped fever; [but] is tolerably well now and has been entertained in my absence by a visit', paid by the French Ambassador and Monsieur de Lauzun.[61]

And then she appeared recovered. There was a flurry of visits in the final months of Lady Jersey's pregnancy. The Earl and Countess of Essex, who in these years were good friends of the Jerseys, visited Middleton which, said Lord Jersey, 'will assist in keeping up Lady J's spirits which always sink as she advances near her time. She is amazingly increased [in size] as of late, she means to lie in here and to be attended by Kerr. Most probably before you arrive in this country [he wrote to Countess Spencer who was once more abroad] she will be up & riding about Fields again after hounds.'[62]

Then the family was at Blenheim and afterwards, in early July, they spent a few days at Nuneham during 'the magnificent doings at Oxford for Lord North's installation' as Chancellor of the University.[63]

At the end of July, though, Lord Jersey wrote to Lady Spencer from Middleton: 'We are now, for the first time almost this summer, left alone, which is an extraordinary thing to us ... Lady J considering how soon she expects is amazingly stout and active.'[64]

By 9 August he reported:

> Lady J is now in daily expectation; Mr Kerr has taken up his Residence at Middleton so that we can be in no hurry or difficulty and she is perfectly well. The weather is hot & close as ever, but our rooms are ... large and airy, & she is out a great deal in her little chaise so that she finds as little inconvenience from the heat as possible. I have fixed the event to happen with a very few days, she thinks it will be much longer.[65]

The Countess was right. It was ten days before the child was born but, eventually, on 19 August 1773, Lord Jersey could write to Lady Spencer who was now at Spa:

> I have waited two posts to give you the news I am now able to do, that is *d'un Figlio maschio*. Ly J was a very few hours ago brought to bed, after a short suffering & is in great spirits and perfectly well.[66]

The Earl now had his son and heir. Viscount Villiers had been born a little before 3 o'clock that morning and, wrote Whitehead to Lord Nuneham, 'Her Ladyship and Lord Villiers are according to the phrase as well as can be expected.' He went on to say that 'Lady Charlotte Villiers (whose nose poor thing, did not want to be put out of joint) hopes Lady Nuneham will retain some degree of affection for her'.[67]

Lady Jersey recovered well. The Earl wrote again to Lady Spencer on 23 August:

> By the last post you will have received an [account] of Lady J being brought to bed of a son ... she seems perfectly well, has hitherto had no complaint whatever; & it seems to depend entirely of herself to proceed in a course of gaining strength; without any unfortunate drawback ...

In that same letter, he further asked if Lady Claremont was also at Spa with Lady Spencer, adding, 'if she is no doubt you have mentioned Ly Jy's situation to her; for I was desired to write to her.'[68]

A week later he added:

> Lady J continues quite well, with much increase of strength and no complaint whatever. She is got out of her bedchamber & seems fit for anything, but I hope the being so well will not tempt her to be imprudent,

> having suffered so much by it last time. She has seen nobody & I believe the quietness may have contributed much to her well-being; she is all impatience to see you ...[69]

The arrangements for the christening were soon in hand. It will, said Lord Jersey, 'probably be on a Saturday; when I hope we shall have your [Lady Spencer's] company. His [Majesty] I mean to ask, the others are [Lord Jersey's cousin] Lady Hyde and the Duke of Marlborough [i.e. to be godparents].'

He went on to thank Lady Spencer's daughter Georgiana for her compliments on the birth of Villiers: 'We know the eagerness of her affection for Lady J ... many thanks to her we beg ... Lady J continues quite well and is grown absolutely fat; it is now almost three weeks, & I flatter myself she is quite safe.'[70] Indeed, such was Georgiana's delight at the new arrival that she 'acquainted everybody she met at Spa [where she was with her Mother] that Lord Jersey had brought forth a son'.[71] Georgiana Spencer was, as the Duchess of Devonshire, to loom large in years to come both in Society and in the life of Frances Jersey.

So far as the Countess was concerned, she now had done her duty. At the age of only twenty the spirited, beautiful and fascinating Frances Jersey had delivered a son and heir to the Earl. A chapter had been closed. She could now put behind her the pastoral, conventional and respectable, not to mention dull, life she had led until now. Henceforth her life would take a less respectable and, for her, a more exciting direction. Over the years she would as a result acquire an increasingly unenviable reputation as one of the faster set of society.

5

Les Liaisons Dangereuses

In the eighteenth century, perhaps in reaction to the puritanism of the seventeenth, the aristocracy of England rejected the concept of matrimonial chastity. In 1724, Lady Mary Wortley Montagu alleged that not only husbands but also wives amongst the higher aristocracy were freely committing adultery. In 1739 an anonymous author wrote that female adultery in high circles was now 'rather esteemed as a fashionable vice rather than a crime'.[1] Forty years later nothing had changed, as a pamphleteer wrote in 1785: 'It is a melancholy reflection that infidelities are much more frequent amongst people of elevated rank, than those of less exalted stations ...' They were certainly much better publicised.[2]

In the case of a wife, this behaviour was subject to the critical precondition that she must first have produced the incontrovertibly legitimate heir, as Frances Jersey had now done.

After that the wife could regard herself as fancy-free and, in a very real sense, faithful couples were greeted with some incredulity.[3] So in 1780 the Earl of Pembroke wrote, '*nos dames, douces commes des agneaux, se laissent monter par tout le monde*'.[4] Such was the acceptance of this state of affairs that the children of such dalliances, known as 'children of the mist', were brought up alongside their legitimate siblings. Thus the Duke of Devonshire's children by Lady Elizabeth Foster were raised with his children by Georgiana, and it is generally accepted that all but one of Lady Melbourne's six surviving children were the offspring of several men other than his Lordship, including in the case of her son George – so it was widely believed – the Prince of Wales.[5]

Whilst a certain amount of discretion was called for, prominent well-known affairs beyond Lady Melbourne's included those of Georgiana, Duchess of Devonshire with Lord Grey; Lady Elizabeth Foster's affair with the Duke of Devonshire in a *ménage à trois;* and that of Georgiana's sister, the Countess of Bessborough, with Lord Granville Leveson Gower, who subsequently married the Countess's niece, Georgiana's daughter Harriet.

Charles Piggott in his *The Female Jockey Club or a Sketch of the Manners of the Age*, published in 1794, wrote mockingly of this way of life:

> Perhaps in expatiating the wide field of humanity we should discover amongst the *privileged orders* more *excressences* of this kind [that is cuckolded husbands], than in any other walk of life. It has never been held the virtue of nobility to cultivate domestic happiness; their minds are devoted to far more sublime pursuits. The sober drudgery of matrimonial employments must be intolerable to a man or woman of fashion, educated in the genuine principles of aristocracy. To confine sensibility to one *thing*, and that thing a husband, would very ill become a woman of spirit, sprung from an *ennobled* and most *loyal* family.[6]

It is entertaining against this background, as well as that of her life, to read Georgiana, Duchess of Devonshire's views on Pierre Choderlos de Laclos' novel *Les Liaisons Dangereuses*, published in France at the time. In it, two decadent French aristocrats plot in their correspondence the seduction of an innocent. In October 1782, Georgiana was to answer her mother's question:

> If by *Les Liaisons du Coeur* you mean *Les Liaisons Dangereuses*, a book lately come out and much in fashion, I am afraid I have read it, as I was lent it when it was very rare. It is very indecent, but the description it gives of the too like manners of the world (and indeed they say it is founded on truth) is far from being uninstructive ...[7]

In the case of Lady Jersey there was already a real-life correspondence strikingly similar to that of de Laclos' novel. This was between William Augustus Henry Fawkener, Esq. (the significance of his full name will become apparent later) and his friend the Hon. Richard Fitzpatrick, in which they recount their lives, loves and conquests in sometimes graphic detail and which seems to touch closely on Frances Jersey – to such an extent that it seems quite possible that from 1773 there was some form of liaison between Fawkener and the Countess.

William Fawkener was certainly to play a significant part in Frances Jersey's life. He was the elder son of Sir Everard Fawkener, former Ambassador to the Porte and Secretary to the Duke of Cumberland, after whom William appears to have been named. Sir Everard's greatest claim to fame was that he was a friend of Voltaire and played host to him when Voltaire visited England.[8] William's mother was the natural daughter of General Charles Churchill, brother of the great Duke of Marlborough.[9] His sisters were Mrs Crewe, 'the fashionable beauty, whose mind kept the promise ... made by her face ... the woman who [Fox] said he preferred to any living ...' and the celebrated Mrs Bouverie, herself a great beauty.[10]

Fawkener lived and moved in the highest circles, although he was 'of little fortune' and had to work for a living, his father having died insolvent. Probably his greatest friend was the 5th Earl of Carlisle, to whom he wrote in 1781: 'You know I have not many friends, but the few whom I really love make my happiness by their partiality to me, and I believe I need not tell you that you stand very high in the list.'[11]

Perhaps one should not be surprised that Lord Carlisle was also to feature large in Frances Jersey's life.

Whilst at Eton, William Fawkener was 'famed for a turn of gallantry with the Windsor milliners.'[12] He was elegant and refined; the actress and courtesan Sophia Baddeley, whose portrait was painted by Zoffany, and who admittedly had an affair with him, said of Fawkener that he 'wanted not the ornament of dress to set him off. Nature had been bountiful to him, both in features and person and he was a man whom the ladies much admired.'[13]

In December 1773, Fawkener had set off to the Continent for several months, judging from his correspondence not entirely of his own volition. Certainly it was a curious thing to do for a man who needed to earn a living. The focus of his tour was to travel around Italy, although on his way he visited Paris (where he charmed Walpole's friend and correspondent the celebrated Marquise du Deffand) and then Geneva in order to see his father's friend Voltaire.[14] During his travels Fawkener maintained a sometimes racy correspondence with Fitzpatrick. Fitzpatrick was the second son of the Earl of Upper Ossory and an intimate of Charles James Fox, with whom he shared a 'love of reckless gambling, fast living, and witty conversation' as well as being a talented writer of satiric verse.[15] In a letter to Fitzpatrick, written from Calais within half an hour of his arriving in France at the start of his tour, Fawkener said 'remember me to Charles [presumably Fox] and lay me at the Countess's feet'.[16] As yet there is no clue as to who this Countess was, but when Fawkener wrote again from Paris on 15 December he divulged:

> I am exceptionally disappointed and hurt at not receiving an answer to my last letter. I did not think her capable of so much ... I enclose a few lines, which I beg you would contrive to get delivered to her as soon as possible. They shall, I am determined, be the last unanswered ones ... [My thoughts] dwell on what I have left in England. But if she persists in this resolution [illegible] will extinguish the last sparks of my love.

Fawkener went on to ask Fitzpatrick if he knew 'what has passed on the subject. I know it is the fate of the absent to be forgotten.'[17].

Not much more can be drawn from this save that, whoever she was, it seems that the mystery lady was at the very least having a flirtation with Fawkener and that he was sending surreptitious love letters to her. Unfortunately a second unknown enters the mystery, as revealed when Fawkener wrote to

Fitzpatrick from Florence on 22 February 1774, referring both to *'la petite'* as well as to 'the Countess'. In this letter, after thanking Fitzpatrick for three letters which awaited him at Florence, he continued:

> Distance has a surprising effect on my love. I confess I expected an answer of some sort from *la petite*, but she [disappointed?] me and is as little cruel as any I ever felt ... If the Countess enquires how I bear my misfortunes tell her whatever you think proper: my reputation and character as a lover will I am sure be safe in your hands. [Deliver?] her my [best?] thanks for the honour she does me in thinking of me and say everything that one of her greater [most ?] respectful admirers can be supposed to think ... Fortune has granted you what she denied me, an opportunity of recovering your reputation, and of effacing by a series of successes, the shame and weakness of a [manner] I am condemned to pass in the opinion of one woman for the man of all others the most unworthy of a Lady's favours.[18]

By this juncture messages were evidently being relayed both to and from 'the Countess'. Given that within a very few years Fawkener and Frances Jersey were lovers, it is easy to speculate that the Countess he refers to was Frances Jersey and that the affair between them had its beginnings in 1773. It is possible, too, that there was some connection between this and Fawkener's absence abroad which he obviously found a chore rather than a pleasure. What is clear, though, is that *'la petite'* and the Countess are different women, as we shall see later from a letter Fawkener wrote to Fitzpatrick from Rome in August that year, so that there is no merit in arguing that *'la petite'* refers to the physically small Frances Jersey, whom it would also be natural to refer to as 'the Countess'.

Still, as Lord Glenbervie said later, Fawkener cuckolded, in addition to Lord Jersey, 'many other husbands.'[19] Further, even whilst Sophia Baddeley was still being kept by Lord Melbourne, Fawkener 'boasted [to her] of favours he pretended to have received from a married lady of the first rank, which was notoriously false ... The lady was, in every sense of the word, truly virtuous'; he further alleged she had a dissipated husband. So it is quite possible that 'the Countess' was someone other than Frances Jersey, not least because, even if his claims were true, his description of a virtuous lady and her dissipated husband do not ring true in relation either to Frances or to the Earl.[20]

Whether or not there was any such liaison between the Countess and Fawkener, following Lord Villiers' birth in August 1773, Frances Jersey launched herself into London Society's whirlpool with her typical enthusiasm. In January 1774 Whitehead wrote to Lord Nuneham:

> The Jersey family is now settled in Town, the little boy christened for the second time, and her Ladyship looking very handsome, & beginning her gambols. I dined with them yesterday at Lord Edgecombe's.

He went on to describe the glory of her Ladyship's dress and, as an aside, her sense of humour:

> Lady Jersey desires me to tell Lady Nuneham that she meant to have written yesterday, but a birthday is so perplexing a thing, when one's trimming is not quite ready, that it was impossible to attend to anything else. She is to-day all over ducks' feathers, green and gold, faintly shining upon red silk. I told her she seemed to me to be in second mourning, but it is called vastly elegant & indeed the stomacher, robings, &c., with diamonds upon them, looked extremely well. The flounces on the petticoat had only the appearance of dyed ermine. Her head however, was extremely well drest, & I was treated with contempt for my occasional censures upon other parts.[21]

London in the late eighteenth century had its own rules and practices. Parliament generally sat from November to April with breaks at Christmas and Easter, filling London with visitors and requiring the political classes and the nobility to be present to attend the Houses.[22] Then there was the 'London season', which had its origins in seventeenth century and was consolidated in the first half of the eighteenth. From the 1740s, the social season shrank from January to July and further from March to July by the end of the century. These were the 'frantic months in the London luxury trades' as the rich and fashionable thronged to town.[23]

London in 1770 had around 700,000 inhabitants – about one in eight of all Englishmen.[24] It had been transformed during the course of the century by the introduction of street names, paving and street lighting so that by 'the early 1770s it could be said with some confidence that "London is the best paved and best lighted city in Europe".' Its paving remained a wonder to foreigners till the century's end.'[25] William Hutton, returning to London from Birmingham in 1784 after a gap of some years, marvelled at this 'collection of magnificence', its houses 'on the average about one storey higher then I have ever seen'. At night 'not a corner of this prodigious city is unlighted'.[26] A German visitor in the 1780s, Sophie von la Roche, marvelled at Oxford Street, noting 'watchmakers, silk shops, fan stores, china shops, glass shops, "spirit booths" or gin shops ...' She found the array on offer dazzling, with its 'lights behind shelves of crystal flasks, confectioners, fruiterers; lamp shops providing "a dazzling spectacle" and all "so beautifully lit ... Up to 11 o'clock at night there are as many people along this street as at Frankfurt during the fair, not to mention the eternal stream of coaches."'[27]

Lord Jersey though, as was his wont, was enjoying London society rather less than his young wife. That same January he wrote to Nuneham:

> This town is, as usual, dull *à l'extrême*; we are at present in a little round of dinners with the Edgcumbe's &c, according to custom at the beginning of winter, but I think one of my chief amusements is my little girl; she grew so conversable that she makes a much greater fool of me than ever.[28]

Frances Jersey on the other hand did not find it dull. She had her portrait painted by Daniel Gardner, who had worked as an assistant to Sir Joshua Reynolds, become a friend of Constable, and never let his sitters see his portraits before they were finished. Such was her repute and her personal charms that her portrait was of more than just personal interest. In February, Thomas Watson published his mezzotint of the portrait, copies of which were for sale by W. Shropshire and T. Watson in New Bond Street.[29]

The social whirl continued. At the end of February 1774, Whitehead wrote to Nuneham, somewhat drolly:

> Lady Jersey is going tonight to a ball at Lord Gordmanstown's, but it is etiquette not to be over drest any more than a proper regard to one's person requires. All of the *bon ton* go to it, but it is, nevertheless, to be treated with a kind of nonchalance: this, amongst inferior beings, would be translated impertinence; but I bow with reverence to the resolutions of the supreme authority ... [30]

By the end of March, the whirl was taking its toll. Lady Jersey, said Whitehead, 'has raked herself into being very thin & not at all well, but still goes on. The doctor & the dance succeed each other, for everybody dances now, at every assembly, & every night. A royal christening, the opera, & Almacks [the smartest private assembly] afterwards, in one night, nothing but female delicacy could possibly undergo.'[31]

At the same time the inevitable occurred, no doubt due to the carelessness, impetuosity and cussedness of Frances Jersey, who cared little for the opinions of others even though, if needed, she was prepared to submit to chastisement. There was a falling out between her and Lady Spencer. On 24 February, Lord Jersey wrote to the very proper and very different Countess Spencer:

> I must beg to trouble you with [one matter] ... It is some time that Ly J has conceived an opinion that you have, either from disapprobation of her conduct or whatever other motive, taken a particular dislike to her. The unhappiness which this occasions to me who have been so many years devotedly attached you, you may easily conceive ...

He went on to ask whether Lady Jersey was right and begged Lady Spencer not to mention the issue to anyone.[32]

This is probably not the same occasion as when Lord Jersey wrote in similar terms, in an undated letter, to Lady Spencer but it is worth quoting that letter, too, to show the continuing fragility of the relationship between Frances Jersey and her husband's greatest friend. In this letter the Earl wrote that he could not

> be any longer silent upon a subject which has for some time given to me so much real uneasiness. It is your total neglect of Lady Jersey – I will confess one great argument with me for marrying so young person, was the confidence that you would take her under your protection, & give her

> that countenance in the world which must establish her credit, & fix the line of life, in which she was to walk. This I hoped and trusted in from the friendship you have always shown to me … I can easily see that her Society can be no amusement to you, but you have not a common acquaintance who comes into your house of fashion you have taken so little notice and I trust her behaviour has not given room for such disregard.

Writing with tears in his eyes, Lord Jersey reminded Lady Spencer that his wife did not know he was writing to her.[33]

We do not know what caused the falling out but it is clear that the two Countesses were very different characters and that it would be easy for the young, impulsive, strong-willed and selfish Frances Jersey to offend the older, staider and religious Lady Spencer – even if she did not go so far as to commence an affair with Fawkener. It is also easy to see the *naiveté* of Lord Jersey in hoping that Lady Spencer would be the guide and mentor to his wife, who was unlikely to be grateful to anyone for taking that role.

Lady Spencer's reply confirmed that Frances Jersey was right in her suspicions and prompted the Earl to write back:

> It was with no less sensible grief that I read … your letter, from which I find that Ly J's conjectures are so near being well grounded … [I] am miserable with every thought … And whatever may be her failings which have produced this time may … show her more deserving … I firmly believe she wishes to be thought worthy of your friendship & and society … God bless you.[34]

Whatever the cause, and whatever Frances Jersey's reasons for her submission, this exchange obviously cleared the air, temporarily at least. It was not the last time Frances Jersey submitted herself to her elder patron, for on 7 March Lord Jersey wrote to Lady Spencer from Délapré Abbey:

> If you could know the very great happiness you have given Lady J by your kind behaviour to her lately, you would be a little convinced how much she really loves you & yours, & overlook…whatever the failings are in her which produced your shyness to her.[35]

This may be doubted, at least so far as the Countess herself was concerned, but the charade, to use a word which was soon to be invented in the court of Georgiana, was to continue as the Duchess of Devonshire, as Georgiana was to become on 7 June 1774, wrote to her mother later that year: 'I hope you will be able to find time for your Middleton visit as I know Ly J wishes to have you there.'[36]

Frances Jersey's love for the Countess's family (or at least the younger members of it), or perhaps just her enthusiastic approach to life, had on the other hand been recently illustrated. Whitehead, in his letter to Lord Nuneham of 26 March 1774, referred to Lady Georgiana Spencer's recent engagement to the Duke of Devonshire which 'everybody seemed delighted with' and went on to say 'Lady Jersey and Lady Clermont are quite in their element; they are the projectors, buyers, & supervisors of all wedding cloaths & trinkets.'[37]

In fact, after four years of marriage in the highest society, Frances Jersey was beginning to emerge as one of its central figures. Always immensely attractive, strong-minded and spirited, she had acquired the confidence to show her real nature. No longer constrained, she was sure of her charms and determined to do what she wanted to do and the way she wanted do it – and if this was thoughtless, selfish or merely self-indulgent, so be it. Part of this was formed by her ability and desire to bend other people to her will to achieve what she wanted, a manipulative streak which became increasingly apparent as the years passed. Whilst still prepared to play a role if necessary, she wanted to exploit and enjoy the freedom that her position and charms gave her even if, on occasion, this caused offence.

These were the beginning steps of a journey which was to lead her to the summit of Society – and to be the object of near universal hatred.

Meanwhile there were more domestic concerns. In early April Lord Jersey was hunting in Northamptonshire, staying at Farming Woods with Lord Spencer and his heir Lord Althorp.[38] As we shall see, it is possible that Lady Jersey took advantage of his absence. However, on 9 April he wrote to Lady Spencer that 'Ly J's difficulties about this Business have determined me to come to town to relieve her mind'.[39] This 'Business' was probably the decision whether to inoculate her daughters against smallpox at a time when this was no risk-free matter. Frances Jersey was deeply fond of her children and doubtless found the decision whether to proceed with inoculation a very difficult one. William Whitehead had written to Lord Nuneham on 26 March that the Jerseys 'are on the brink of a resolution to inoculate their two girls' against smallpox.[40]

Smallpox was more prevalent in London than elsewhere and was furthermore most prevalent in the middle two quarters of the eighteenth century, when it claimed over 2,000 Londoners a year. It was said that almost all children caught smallpox, and the disease was a prominent killer in the early years of life.[41]

When Whitehead wrote again on 23 April, the decision had been taken. He said:

> The young ladies in Grosvenor Square were this morning inoculated; I have not seen them, nor shall, I presume, till they are well. You are certainly right, I am a monstrous fidget, but I conceal it admirably, and only teize myself at home. It will be a lying-in to me till it is over, for I am fond of them both; yet even that fondness I never dare show, because I am said to spoil them.[42]

Lord Villiers, who was too young to be inoculated, was sent to Lady Spencer's house at Wimbledon Park to keep him away from his infectious sisters.[43]

Once the children became infectious, Lady Jersey would, as convention required, also be confined to the house and not be able to go out into society.

Before then she sought to enjoy herself. Accordingly, the night before the inoculation the Jerseys went to the pleasure gardens at Ranelagh. Ranelagh Gardens was one of the two principal pleasure gardens of eighteenth-century London. Situated on the River Thames next to the Royal Hospital in Chelsea, and with its Rotunda and private boxes, its masquerades and concerts, it was also the most fashionable one, frequented by the elite of society, often seething with its paying guests and a place to see and be seen – though not to the exclusion of more disresputable ladies using it as an opportunity for advancing their careers. Edward Gibbon described it as 'the best market we have in England' for marriages. The other main London pleasure garden was Vauxhall, which, on the other hand, was by far the most famous of the London pleasure gardens, described by a German visitor in the 1760s as 'an entertainment which has no equal, that I have heard, in Europe.'[44]

Unfortunately, that night at Ranelagh things took an unpleasant turn. As Lord Jersey related, the crowd in attendance was excessive, and one of his servants was attacked by the mob who 'used him in the most cruel manner' whilst Lord and Lady Jersey remained 'encompassed by those outrageous wretches' in their coach nearby. This resulted in Lady Jersey having 'a fit', although by the following day she had recovered from the fright which 'shook her much'; the servant, who had earlier seemed likely to lose an eye, fortunately made a full recovery.[45]

Even so, when on 25 April Lord Jersey wrote to Lady Spencer, he reported that 'today we are going to Langley ... I think the country air will do Ly J no harm after her late sitting and this fright' at Ranelagh.[46] Langley was presumably Langley Park, one of the Marlboroughs' houses in Buckinghamshire.

The two girls did well following their inoculation. On 29 April, Lord Jersey told Lady Spencer, 'our little animals scarcely deserve your attention & Goodness. The Small Pox is now upon the turn & Anne was very complaining yesterday & Charlotte a little less so, but the Baron [their Doctor] says the whole is over.' As early as 1 May, Lord Jersey was writing, 'Ly J has not yet gone out, but the Baron says she might have done so, with the greatest safety in the world, two days ago. Whenever she does go she will be abused, yet I'm sure now she errs on the right side.' Whilst there were some relapses in the girls' health, by the second week of May it seemed that not only had the inoculations been successful but also that the girls had returned to their former selves.[47]

This also meant that Lord Jersey was able to join Lord Spencer at Harrow to hear Lord Althorp speak at a school dissertation – Lord Jersey was ever diligent in his attentions to the heir of his greatest friends.[48] The Jerseys were also able to go to Wimbledon on 12 May, presumably to bring Villiers back home now that girls were no longer infectious.[49]

For Frances Jersey, there followed over the coming months the familiar themes of illness and pregnancy. After a fête champêtre given by Lord Stanley, heir to the Earl of Derby, at his house at Epsom, 'The Oaks', early in June, the Jerseys were back at Middleton by the end of the month.[50] Lady Jersey was once more pregnant, and the despondency which typically accompanied her pregnancies was probably not helped by some very dismal weather, described by her husband in a letter to Lady Spencer:

> These Rains too have almost entirely prevented Ly J going out ever since she has been here, which in a gentle way might possibly have done her some good. She now however remains in the same state as when she left town, is frequently extreamly low & has been two or three times on the brink of fainting away. The Opinions here are the same as in London, & must wait the Event, whenever it may chuse to happen.
>
> What her strength will be for the Summer Expeditions I know not, but I am impatient to hear from you relating to Chatsworth.

In the same letter Lord Jersey proposed a visit to Chatsworth House in Derbyshire where the Countess's Devonshire daughter was now the mistress.[51]

In fact, Lady Jersey's health was beginning to cause real concern. On 29 June Lord Jersey wrote:

> [Our future motions] are in a most uncertain state owing principally to Lady J's health, for she continues still in the same way, nothing decided, but certain they say to be worse; & therefore till all that is over we can say or know nothing. The air however & the singular quiet of this place have given her rather better looks, though not much to brag of ... We have been quite alone & the report of Ly J's not being well has kept off almost all our neighbours so as to enforce a quiet life on her.[52]

Whitehead was a little more phlegmatic (though perhaps just as critical of Lady Jersey's pursuit of pleasure) as the often rather gloomy, 'green spectacled' Lord Jersey, in writing to Lord Nuneham on 1 July:

> As to the Jerseys, I dare say you will inform me how their health goes on; I am very uneasy till she gets better. From your Lordship I shall have less flattering accounts than from herself, & less desponding ones than from Lord Jersey; she is an absolute martyr to *bon ton* [i.e. from throwing herself into the doings of Society][53]

Things did not improve. A week later, Lord Jersey was telling Lady Spencer that he was

> driving Lady Jersey out in the Chaise in the intermediate times [between farming] ... We have engaged to go to [stay with the Marquess of Bath at] Longleat; that is if Ly J is well enough, and how that will be I can not tell, she seems to day much lower and worse than she has been since she left London. I do not wonder at from the state of Doubt in which she is. The journey will have an effect ... to decide the Matter one way or another.

> She is anxious to see her Mother at Bath; and therefore I fancy will not be easily put by the Visit [to Longleat as it was on the way to Bath].[54]

Indeed, whilst many of the Countess's other relationships became strained – and more – over the years, she had a strong and lasting relationship with her mother.

The visit to Longleat and Bath duly took place. Nevertheless, whilst 'Lady Jersey was part of the time not stout, she recovered herself at last, & bore the travelling tolerably well, but is today [20 July] complaining again. In short, she remains in the same uncertain state, & the longer it continues the worse it will be.'[55] Indeed, Lady Jersey's illness continued well into the summer.

Whilst Frances Jersey continued to ail, Fawkener remained in Italy and was clearly not enjoying it. In July he was in Rome and bored. He wrote to Fitzpatrick that his younger brother 'Everard desires his best compliments to you. It is a dreadful boar [*sic*] for him, but he bears it with great fortitude.'[56] Indeed, Fawkener too was heartily sick of Rome and, although enjoying a liaison with a Mme Lempri, complained that the weather was so hot that exercise was impractical 'and fucking itself a *corvée*', or painfully hard work. He went on to ask whether 'the Countess & *la petite* absolutely broke with that little foolish bitch Lady Barrymore, or do they still see her and abuse her only with their particular friends', a question which raises two thoughts. First, that such behaviour would be typical of Lady Jersey, so adding a degree of credibility to the suggestion that she was indeed Fawkener's 'Countess'; and second, that it makes it clear that 'the Countess' and *'la petite'* were indeed different people whilst leaving open the possibility that there already was a *liaison dangereuse* between Frances Jersey and William Fawkener (which was to resurface very publicly a few years later).[57]

6

The Social Whirl

Over the next few years, the Jerseys led the life of fashionable society, the *ton*. In these years, too, the first cracks appeared in Lady Jersey's reputation. There are grounds for believing that as early as 1774 Lady Jersey's infidelities resulted for the first time in a child fathered by someone other than the Earl – though several more were to follow.

The poet Thomas Moore tells a story about the Jerseys' lifestyle: the Earl's porter 'complained he could not stay with the Jerseys, because my Lady was the very latest woman in London – "Well, but what then? All women of fashion are late [&] you can sleep afterwards"–"Ah, no, Sir that's not at all – for my Lord is the earliest gentleman in London and, between the two, I get no sleep at all."'[1]

This tells us firstly of Lady Jersey's committed pursuit of pleasure and secondly that this pursuit was commonly without her husband, who frowned on much of the frivolities of Society.

But first there was her continuing illness. The proposed visit to the Devonshires at Chatsworth was postponed to late August 1774 when they would go only 'if Ly J is well, because she continues just the same, or rather in my own opinion not so well, especially yesterday; But it is still all a mystery. I hope you will have no such mysteries,' wrote Lord Jersey to Lady Spencer from Middleton in July of that year.[2] Why there was a mystery is unclear, for Lady Jersey was now well advanced in pregnancy, when she always struggled, and would give birth to another daughter in December. Such mystery as there is seems to be as to who was the father of the unborn child.

Whitehead had another, and now familiar, explanation for the Countess's illness: the over-enthusiastic pursuit of pleasure. On 31 July he wrote to Lord Nuneham, with whom the Jerseys were staying:

> Lady Jersey is now, I presume, under your care & directions, and you must, as her host 'against the murderer shut the door, nor hold the knife yourself:' that is in plain English, you must force her to be quiet, grow well whether she will not, & not lead her into rakeries & vagaries. She may study botany with Walter Clarke in the flower garden but not scamper to balls and races.

He went on:

> I hanker after my Oxfordshire friends [the Jerseys] and heartily wish some of them [particularly Frances Jersey] capable of tasting the quiet pleasures I at present possess [at Middleton].[3]

For a while at least, Lady Jersey was actually doing just that, for upon the very moment of his writing Whitehead received a letter from her in which she told him 'she is making a herbal; dissecting flowers, gumming them on paper, drying plants entire, & doing everything that is mild & rural'.

She might have been enjoying quiet pleasures but, even so, there was a touch of spice, for Whitehead went on to say that if 'she had not mixed a little scandal upon the neighbours in her innocent epistle, I should tremble for what the *bon ton* would think and say of her. That last happy foible secures her …' from such a fate.[4]

Whitehead's affection for the charming Frances is clear.

Her impatience to go to Chatsworth and see her friend Georgiana was also clear. At the beginning of August her husband wrote, that 'no roads let them be ever so rough or bad will stop Lady J taking the journey unless she is absolutely in her bed, she has that love for Georgiana as well as yourself [Lady Spencer], that all advice that tends to delay the meeting is very ill received indeed; at the same time I know & see that every little travelling and additional exercise makes her ill, but she is too intent upon this object to suffer to allow it & it is only left for me to wait the event with just apprehension.'[5]

Before that though they were to go to a ball at Blenheim Palace to which 'the whole county of Oxford [was] invited'. This prompted a letter from Lord Jersey which suggested that Lady Jersey's pregnancy was by another man. He wrote on 14 August 1774, 'How Lady J is to do this, & to perform the journey immediately I do not know, nor can guess at all what her situation is; she says she is sure the accident happened before she left town; however she is well enough now and I hope will continue so.'[6]

Although he gives no clue as to what the 'accident' was, it is credible that it was the fact of her being pregnant. The uncertainty as to the 'accident's' timing, or the timing of conception, is consistent with the next Jersey child being born in December that year, a full month earlier than everyone – other than perhaps the Countess – expected it (as we shall see). It is also more than possible that this uncertainty was engineered by Lady Jersey to conceal a conception which happened when her husband was away, as he was, hunting at Délapré in March, nine months before the birth, rather than when he was back in London. The use of the word 'accident' could well have been used to suggest a failed attempt at contraception at a time when the two of them were together in London. Finally, the baby when born was indeed small but, as we have seen, the Jersey babies generally were. Unfortunately, though, there is no hint as to who the father of the child might be so as to prove or disprove the theory, although it could not have been Fawkener who was still abroad at the time.

As the Earl foresaw, Frances Jersey was sufficiently fatigued by the ball at Blenheim for the journey to Chatsworth to be deferred a few more days.[7] She made the trip eventually, though, leaving the children behind at Middleton. For once, Lady Jersey was sensible and, despite wanting to visit the Derby races whilst at Chatsworth, 'she perceived it would create difficulties & therefore acquiesced in giving up the Idea'. From Chatsworth, the Jerseys went on to visit the Duke of Grafton at Wakefield Lodge. Lady Jersey's health was perhaps now on the mend for this event as, wrote her husband, she was 'without difficulties and seems the better for it'.[8]

Returning to Middleton in September, they found the children well, but not without some drama:

> An event has … occurred which is very inconvenient in relation to … their health in our absence & also to Lady J [said Lord Jersey]. The doctor, or apothecary in whom we had much confidence & who used to be continually here, hanged himself two days ago.

In her recurrent illnesses the Countess had doubtless commonly called upon the Doctor's services and was bound to feel the loss of a trusted source of help.

More mundanely, shortly after their return Lord Jersey's uncle, Lord Hyde (later the 1st Earl of Clarendon) and his family came to stay for a few days, along with Lady Clermont. Entertaining the Hydes was something of a chore since they were always rather dull guests.[9] Fortunately, other more entertaining visits to Blenheim, Nuneham and Althorp followed and, as an additional blessing, the Countess had it seems recovered her health. As Countess Spencer wrote:

> Lady Jersey was likely vastly happy with little raid she would answer it today as of her Morrow, she is vastly well as Mr Kerr assur'd me who came to her yesterday to bleed her if it had been necessary before her journey [back to London], but he thought there was no occasion for it.[10]

What the 'raid' was, possibly a brief trip to Chatsworth, is unclear. In any event, at the end of the month the Jerseys returned to London, where on 16 December 1774 the Countess gave birth to her third daughter, Lady Caroline Elizabeth Villiers.[11] Whilst there, Lady Jersey enjoyed the Opera, leaving her less gregarious husband to complain to Lady Spencer, tongue-in-cheek, 'tell Ld S that I fancy my children and family will not have much reason to thank him for endeavouring to ruin my moral constitution by putting me up [i.e. proposing him for membership] at Almacks', the club at the summit of society of which his future daughter-in-law was to become 'the Queen'.

Perhaps the Countess's pregnancy explains why, even when back in town, the ever fashionable Lady Jersey was not yet following the latest mode of extravagantly tall hairstyles surmounted with feathers. Her husband wrote in November, 'I have not yet seen the high heads & feathers which grow universal, but Ld Edge [that is Lord Edgecumbe] says my Lady has not begun them yet.'[12] It did not, though, prevent her participation in other extravaganzas. During the winter of 1774 London was 'in its usual state as to amusements, gaming, and extravagances ... There was an intention of a play being acted when all the fine ladies and gentlemen were to perform. There was to have been a grand ballet in which the Duchess of D., Lady B. Stanley, Lady Jersey, Lady Melbourne, Lady Cranbourne, Mrs. Hubert, etc., were to have showed off, but friends and husbands interposed.' Nevertheless, a few months later, Lady Elliott continued:

> The same people, with the two Royal Dukes, are to have a grand fête on the river the 5th of June. It is to be a race of boats; twelve small boats, just large enough to keep above water and to contain two men, are to sail from Westminster Bridge, and row against one another, and it is thought they will go sixteen miles an hour. All the city barges are now painting and decorating for it, and the different trades are to have barges with pageants. The whole is to end in a masquerade at Ranelagh. It will cost an immense sum, but nobody knows how it will be paid; in short, never were people so foolish as in the great world just now; but, thank God! It does not seem to have spread below a certain set, who are laughed at by the rest of the world.[13]

The 'certain set' were of course the *ton,* the so-called leaders of fashion, which included Frances Jersey. On this occasion the extravaganza on the river eventually took place in the summer of 1775.

That year illustrates vividly the motions of the beau monde at the time and Frances Jersey's part in them.

In the spring of 1775 the Jerseys were at Newmarket where they 'lead the normal life, out upon the Course all day, and the Evening ... the Ladies play at Whist'.[14] Then there was an invitation from Horace Walpole to dinner at Strawberry Hill.[15] In June Whitehead was writing mockingly:

> I shall go on Saturday to The Grove [Lord Hyde's seat near Watford], to meet Lord & Lady Jersey; a day or two's country air will do her Ladyship no harm, at least she would be safe from the midnight air of Vauxhall and Ranelagh. I have not seen her or Lord Jersey since yesterday. They are at Wimbledon [the Spencers' house] today, and tomorrow is a compleat something of breakfast & dinner at Petersham, & will probably conclude with a moonlight frolic upon the water for fear they should not be quite tired to death.[16]

So the social round continued, although in early July they were again at Nuneham for several days for more serious matters. They were there 'to endeavour to be of some assistance' to Lady Nuneham, who was extremely ill.[17] Horace Walpole also visited Nuneham at around this time when he 'found

Lady Jersey ... with a pretty little girl [Lady Charlotte], who will be the picture of her father as soon she cuts her nose, and is bigger already'.[18]

Thereafter they returned to Middleton, dining with the Marlboroughs at nearby Blenheim and then entertaining a party of country neighbours who 'were so obliging as to dine here'.[19] In August it was Chatsworth again, this time with a visit to Chesterfield races 'where the Ladies perform only one day's Ceremony, the Course, Ball & Supper & come home at night'.[20]

Back in Middleton in September, Whitehead paints a picture of such visits:

> I arrived safe [at] Middleton, & dined exactly at four o'clock. The Lady and the children I find perfectly well; the Lord is not quite so well as he should be, but has condescended to take a slight medicine, which I hope will remove his complaint. We dine today at Sr [*sic*] Charles Cotterel's, & they will probably have finished all their visits before you come to Middleton; Lady Caroline Stuart is to be here tomorrow.[21]

Adding to this, Lord Jersey recounted that, whilst at Middleton, Lady Caroline sang and played 'exceedingly well and [painted] also; and at night we have the most determined party at whist you ever knew: I take to it very much ... Lady J plays ... much better than me'. One can easily picture Lady Jersey's determination at the card table.[22]

Then, to complete the picture, they were joined a few days later by the Nunehams, who complained to Lady Spencer that in waiting for her letters 'one might as well think of waiting dinner for Ly Jersey', such was the Countess's modish preference for fashionably late dinners.[23]

Another short visit to Blenheim followed, of which Lord Jersey expressed, for some undisclosed reason, a degree of concern – 'the visit perhaps will be a little awkward, that is you know one can never tell how all are together' – before the Jerseys returned to London for the Winter where the social whirl continued, albeit in a different form.[24] This was despite the fact that, as Lord Jersey wrote to Lady Spencer, 'you will find us all sad invalids; the whole town is seized with a general Cold & Cough ... Lady J was quite ill yesterday & nobody escapes.'[25]

The Countess recovered soon enough and shortly was to be found at Mrs Vesey's drawing-room, whose reputation for elegance and learning rivalled Mrs Montagu's. As a fellow bluestocking, Mrs Boscawen said: 'I went to Mrs Vesey, where there were fine ladies indeed! Duchess of Devonshire, Lady Jersey, Lady Claremont, Mrs Crewe, Mrs Walsingham, Lord Edgcumb, Mrs Dashwood.'[26]

And so it went on. And on. And, despite Lady Clermont writing in January 1776 that 'I never hear anything of Lady Jersey', the Countess remained very much in the public eye.[27] Indeed, as one of the Devonshire House Circle, consisting both of respectable aristocrats and of less respectable ones along with a congeries of artists, actors, scroungers, libertines and wits, the Countess could hardly be anything else. With Georgiana Devonshire the almost unchallenged leader of society the press were fascinated with the Circle and its doings.[28]

Mrs Delaney summed up the Lady Jersey of these years:

> I have seen Lady Jersey two evenings this week to meet her mother, who is gone out of town today with her general [as Colonel Johnston had become], in order to go to Ireland for two years ... She *is* very fine, *superbly à la mode*, and has lost much of her prettiness, and will soon, I fear, lose her life if she continues her present absurd and ruinous course of life. It is a pity, for she wants neither parts nor sensibility; but every good quality is lost in vanity and love of what is *falsely* called *'pleasure'*.[29]

Such was the essence of Frances Jersey, even though Mrs Delaney does not use any of the harsher epithets which would in the future soon attach to her. Mrs Delaney was right, too, to be concerned about the effects on Lady Jersey's health, for in the summer of 1776 she was once more ill. This bout did not initially seem serious, her husband writing to Lady Spencer that 'Ly J is better but has more fever today.'[30]

Once again, however, there may have been more to this illness than just the result of an exhausting social whirl. A contemporary edition of Debrett, although no other source is available to corroborate it, records that on 24 June 1776 Lady Jersey gave birth to a daughter, Lady Georgiana Villiers, who died the same day.[31] This is to an extent consistent with Countess Spencer having noted around Christmas 1775 that 'Ly J looks very well but is monstrously big and fat'.[32]

Be that as it may, Lady Jersey's illness proved to be both severe and persistent. In July Lord Jersey wrote, 'Lady Jersey has been growing better in looks & some degree of strength, till yesterday, when she seem [*sic*] to fall back again entirely & is under the greatest apprehension of a relapse of her complaint.' Later, at Nuneham in August he wrote to Lady Spencer: 'Lady J is better, grown fatter, but cannot walk; she was very near fainting away in Oxford Streets [i.e. in the streets of nearby Oxford] yesterday; but I cannot think this to be a weakness entirely; it certainly must be the complaint being fixed in her legs.'[33]

Frances Jersey described her maladies to Georgiana Devonshire: 'I am not well, my legs swell & I am nervous, some times we talk of going to Brighthelmstone but I believe it won't be necessary ... my children are delightful.'[34]

Brighthelmstone, as Brighton on the Sussex coast was then known, was a popular resort for sea bathing, thought at the time to be restorative for one's health. It was a favoured locale of the Prince of Wales, who was to build his Pavilion there, and his set. The King and the rest of the royal family, together with the more conservative elements of the court, on the other hand favoured Weymouth, in Dorset in the south-west, as the resort for sea-bathing.

The Jerseys did in fact go to Brighton for the Countess's health in early August 1776, from where Frances Jersey wrote again to the Duchess, this time with some astringency:

> I already find myself better, I am even good-humour'd before breakfast. I have got the best house here at the corner of ye Steine … I am growing strong hourly & I believe I shall never like lying abed again. I was at a Vile Ball last night all the publick things are detestable. I don't intend to prostitute myself any more to the mob …[35]

Nevertheless, because of Lady Jersey's continuing illness she was soon to return there. In September Lord Jersey was writing: 'We set out tomorrow for Brighthelmstone, Lady Jersey was so fatigued when she returned [from a visit to Althorp] that she has a mind to try sea bathing to recover her strength. I wish it may succeed.'

A week later the Earl was positively optimistic, albeit in his rather grudging way:

> You may have some curiosity to know how the bathing agrees with Lady Jersey: it seems to do exceedingly well, she is much pleased with it & in great spirits when she comes out. She is no doubt infinitely better & stronger than when she was at Althorp, but I cannot quite attribute that to two dippings in salt water. Good hours & that together I daresay will be of service to her and if nothing calls us away sooner we shall stay here all this month.

Despite the good effect of bathing and rest on his wife's health, Lord Jersey loathed Brighton, saying 'the place in itself I think abominable …' He expanded on this when he wrote on 19 September that, despite there being some company, including the Pelhams and Lady Pembroke, 'the whole is dreadfully tiresome & if it was not for some music, singing particularly by Miss Shrine the sejour would be scarcely tolerable … on the 29th we mean to go, but Lady Jersey has unluckily caught a very bad cold, which will prevent her bathing for some days. The water has been of use to her I believe & the early hours of as much,'[36]

One wonders what the pleasure-loving Lady Jersey thought. She did not enjoy Brighton on her previous visit. Perhaps she was too unwell to care or perhaps her desire to be able to resume the pursuit of pleasure made her ready to pay the price of a few weeks of boredom. In any event, the treatment seems to have worked since even after the first visit Lady Spencer was writing from Middleton in late August that 'we have found Ly Jersey much improved in looks & strength and the children all in high beauty'.[37]

Back in Grosvenor Square at the end of September the Earl wrote with relief:

> We are at last got back from Brighton … Lady J is come back much the better for the Sea, & I hope she will now be induced to keep good hours. We go tomorrow to Nuneham and home the next day …

From where, two days later, he added, 'we staid only one night in town on our passage home, and saw little more than ladies ready to fall to pieces' as they emulated his wife's social habits, to his obvious disapproval.[38]

Meanwhile the Countess, writing from Middleton to Georgiana Devonshire a little later, expressed her relief at her recovered health: 'I am here all alone, mon Mari is [away] & I am wonderfully comfortable ... I had been so long a miserable rag that I really enjoy a little health.'[39]

Apart from the constant social round there was also a more domestic aspect. After their falling out in the early years of her marriage, relations between Frances Jersey and Lady Spencer remained friendly if not cordial, with Lady Jersey perhaps playing a role of attentiveness and even fawning to Countess Spencer. In these years, too, relations between Lady Jersey and Georgiana Devonshire were not only close but also sometimes intense.

In November 1774 the Jerseys were staying with Lady Spencer at Althorp when the men went off to hunt at Pytchley. Lady Spencer described the domestic scene to Georgiana Devonshire:

> Lady Jersey, your sister [Harriet] & I shall be left alone ... our chief employments will be reading & playing at chefs ... tuning the harp & the Viol da Gamba together ... Lady Jersey & I had a very good drive ... Lady J & Harriet plaid at chess.[40]

The following month Lady Jersey was carrying out commissions for Lady Spencer 'as fast as she can' and writing somewhat winsomely of their domestic affairs:

> I have the whole petticoat ... the price is 40 [guineas?] ... the whole thing is long and large enough ... your purses did not arrive till Monday, I have sent a white one ... I hope they are fine enough ... I do not know what you have done with my Husband and, I assume you've done everything that I [would?] with yours.[41]

Later, Lady Jersey was scribbling Lady Spencer a note:

> Will you lend one the delightful Bed Gown for an hour or two, that I may have one made; for I find it impossible to *live* without one. If you have seen the Dss [of Devonshire] pray write a word to say how she is.[42]

Nevertheless there continued to be friction between the two very different ladies. On one occasion, described by Lady Spencer, after the actor David Garrick made an incantation at supper at Althorp:

> Lady Jersey made one which I told her I would not on any acct send [to anyone] because I think the making of it was improper & the producing of it still more ill judged, but it is clever & therefore I will send it for yourself only –

'Mon premier est un Tyran
Mon second est un Monstre
Et les deux ensembles sont le Diable'.[43]

That is Frances Jersey in three words: improper, ill-judged and clever.

Whilst relations between Lady Spencer and Frances Jersey were fragile, those between Lady Jersey and the Duchess of Devonshire were intimate, with Georgiana demanding regular news from Lady Jersey,[44] and Frances Jersey mocking her husband, the Earl, in front of her, saying to Georgiana: 'Hem! Hem! has been more hemish than ever, but mightily fond of me.'[45] In fact, Georgiana's intensity in their relationship could be disturbing, and on one occasion a letter full of endearments from her to Lady Jersey provoked the response: 'some part of your letter frightened me.'[46] Still, the two were friends, on one occasion going together to the House of Commons to listen not only to some very bad speaking 'but *en revange* we had some very fine speeches ... Charles Fox outdid himself' – foreshadowing the Westminster election some years later in which Georgiana was to play such a prominent role.[47]

Even so, in the summer of 1776 the two Countesses were cooperating in getting 'a poor child ... into the lace manufactury' as a means of earning a living, and Lady Jersey was recommending a new servant to Lady Spencer, closing with the words: 'I suppose Ld Jersey has settled about our going to [visit the Spencers at] Wimbledon. I mean to crawl there on Saturday if you like it.' In June 1777 Lady Spencer went to considerable trouble to enquire after a possible new Governess for the Jersey children – which, unfortunately, Lord Jersey had to acknowledge on his careless wife's behalf. Still, that same month, Lord Jersey wrote to her: 'Lady J proposes to wait upon you on Wednesday next either at dinner or in the evening ... We are going to Tunbridge for Lady Jersey's health.'[48]

The mid-1770s were, for Lady Jersey, continuing years of ill-health, pregnancy and childbirth. The birth, seemingly after a full term, and death the same day of Lady Georgiana Villiers in June 1776 has already been mentioned. Eighteen months earlier, in December 1774, there had been as we also know a happier event. Whitehead wrote to Lord Nuneham on 16 December 1774 that Lady Jersey had sent for him the previous evening to sit with and read to her for the greater part of that evening. At 5 a.m. the next day Lady Jersey gave birth to her third daughter, Lady Caroline Elizabeth Villiers. The girl, Whitehead told Lord Nuneham, 'is a very little one'. An express was sent to give Lord Jersey the news since, doubtless in the belief that the baby was not due for another month, he had just left for some hunting at Althorp.[49]

He rushed back home and promptly reported to Lady Spencer: 'I find Lady Jersey this morning perfectly well, & a little creature of a girl, about half as big as any of the others, but to all appearances well.'[50]

Two days later he wrote again:

> Lady Jersey continues perfectly well, as does the diminuitive creature, which I am told is remarkably plump tho' it is so small you cannot dress it ... Lady J desires you will beg [Georgiana] to write immediately ... for she can read letters tho' she must not answer them; and I am to tell you something that your stomacher & C is ready, tho' I might miscall it & it may be your trimmings.[51]

If, as seems likely, Lady Caroline was not the Earl's daughter, he probably did not know that. She was not, though, the last of the Countess's 'children of the mist', and these others the Earl certainly did know about.

Despite Lady Jersey's apparently rapid recovery, Lord Jersey was forced to postpone his return to Althorp. He commented, either in disappointment on his part or in suggesting hypochondria on his wife's, 'Lady J is become exceedingly low & alarmed at her situation, that I cannot leave, tho' I believe she goes on as well as possible.' Even this mildest of criticism of his wife was rare indeed from a habitually pessimistic man who was devoted to his spouse.[52]

Lady Spencer's anxious response resulted in the reply, on Christmas Eve, that he had 'many thanks to return to you from Lady J as well as myself for your anxiety upon her account ... in regard to her health ... if she continues as she is I mean to be with you on Monday', though he had been equally determined the previous Wednesday. He continued, 'she is at present up & I think as free from Complaints as I have known her in this situation.'[53] Whether he ever got back to Althorp is unclear, though it seems unlikely since on 3 January 1775 he wrote that there were few people in town and there was no Opera, but Lady Jersey and the child were quite well.[54] – well enough indeed to enable him, after the initial alarm, to be with the Graftons at Euston for the hunting by 7 January.[55]

Lord Jersey hunted regularly with the Duke of Grafton. He was also a stalwart of two nearby hunts run by Earl Spencer in Northamptonshire, the Althorp Hunt and the neighbouring Pytchley Hunt. The latter had a club based at Pytchley Hall,[56] whose earliest list of members in 1766 shows both Lord Spencer and Lord Villiers (as he was then) as members.[57] Until 1777 Lord Spencer, presumably by choice, had no regular rooms at the club but, along with Lord Jersey, stayed at nearby Farming Woods when the hounds were at Pytchley, which he rented especially for the purpose from the Earl of Upper Ossory.[58]

Whilst Lady Spencer did not hunt, other ladies did. There is a painting by Wooton of the 3rd Duke of Marlborough, who died in 1758, and his Duchess hunting in Althorp Park.[59] Although ladies were not often, as Lord Jersey once lamented, part of the party there, Lady Jersey was at Farming Woods in April 1775 and, as we have seen, hunted with great gusto if not outward rashness, as you would expect.[60] *The Althorp Chace Book,* which maintained a contemporary record of the doings of the hunt, records that on 27 November 1773 the chase, faced with an impassable brook, 'were obliged to come round to the Stag hunting bridge near Merry Tom ford which the huntsman and Lord and Lady Jersey had luckily seen before'. Lady Jersey was also included in a list, dated to about 1780, of the twelve 'ladies who wear the uniform' of the Althorp Hunt.[61]

These years also saw the withering of Lord Jersey's political career. In October 1775, along with his friend the Duke of Grafton, he had voted against the government's policy in relation to the rebellious North American colonies.[62] As a consequence, as George Selwyn told Lord Carlisle, 'neither Lord Jersey or [*sic*] his Grace [the Duke of Grafton] were spoken to at the [King's] dressing last Friday but [their removal from office] are not yet'; as it happened, their removal did not come to pass until 1777 when it had become more expedient for the King.[63]

In these years, too, whilst Lady Jersey continued to glitter in Society her reputation began to suffer; no longer was she the young innocent; now she was a beautiful, mature and charming woman of the world. Writing from Venice in September 1774 to Richard Fitzpatrick, William Fawkener had said that he hoped to be back in England in less than two months and asked Fitzpatrick to 'lay me at the Countess's feet'.[64] Perhaps this along with Frances Jersey's character was part of the problem, for by the time the grand fête on the river finally took place on 23 June 1775 its patronesses included 'many who [the Duchess of Hamilton and Argyll] would not have chosen as the companions [for her daughter Lady Betty Hastings]. For the Ladies Tyrconnel and Jersey ... had earned already, or were fast acquiring, an unenviable reputation.'[65]

The regatta, when it happened, was immense – and much more than just a regatta. With a procession on the river and a boat race, the Thames was also crammed with pleasure craft. There were fairs on both banks of the Thames and stalls selling food and drink of every description as well as, inevitably for the time, numerous ladies of easy virtue selling other things. It culminated with a ball that night at Ranelagh Gardens whose beautifully engraved tickets depicted the River Thames as a naked man standing at the front of a conch on the river, with Abundance and a putto behind him and Ranelagh's Rotunda in the background. The supper for the 2,000 descending quality was organized by Mrs Cornelys, an 'entrepreneur of whimsical genius ... [who] held leading strings of London's pleasures in the 1760s and 1770s, when luxury and show heeded no bounds' – and whose daughter Sophie had Casanova for a father. The music at Ranelagh was provided by Giardini with an orchestra and chorus of 240.[66]

The following year *The Morning Post* gave a summary commentary on Frances Jersey's reputation. It published under the heading 'Scale of Bon Ton', an analysis of the charms of the reigning toasts of London including Georgiana Devonshire, Lady Jersey, Lady Barrymore, Lady Melbourne, Mrs Crewe and Mrs Bouverie. It gave each of the thirteen ladies scores under the separate headings of beauty, figure, elegance, wit, sense, grace, expression, sensibility and principles. Lady Jersey was unique in being given zero for sense. She was also unique in being given zero for principles.[67]

In one respect, though, she did have sense, or at least more sense than Georgiana Devonshire. Unlike many of her friends and contemporaries,

Frances Jersey did not indulge in the scourge of the age: gambling. By the late eighteenth century, gambling had become a way of life amongst the rich and fortunes were lost and gained at the tables in short order. The original purposes of clubs such as White's, Boodle's and Brooks's was chiefly gambling, and wagers could be placed on every aspect of life, on lives and deaths, on politics and on other bets – the only limitation was the imagination. The enormous gambling losses of Georgiana Devonshire and others such as the Earl of Carlisle are well known, but what was so extraordinary was the recklessness of society as a whole at the gambling tables. Losses in a single night's play of hazard, a game of dice, could amount to £5,000; in 1772, Charles James Fox lost £11,000 in just one night's gambling session, albeit one staggered over twenty-two continuous hours.[68] The Countess did not play but many who could no more afford to lose than her did so to ruinous extremes.

Then in May 1777 the premiere of Sheridan's new play *The School for Scandal*, a satire on the Devonshire House Circle, took place at Drury Lane. In it 'the evil Lady Sneerwell [modelled on a combination of Lady Jersey and the political hostess Lady Melbourne] connives with the Journalist Snake and Joseph Surface to bring about Lady Teazle's ruin'. Whilst members of the Devonshire House Circle 'thought it was a tremendous joke to see themselves caricatured on stage … [and arrived] *en masse* to watch the first night', the caricature contained an essential grain of truth and doubtless was recognised as such, though probably not by the Countess herself.[69]

Lady Jersey was certainly a difficult woman, one of contrasts and contradictions. Chameleon like, she could switch on her enormous charm at will, but never far beneath was something else which left an air of unease amongst those she consorted with, even those who liked her. So Lord John Cavendish wrote of her:

> I have seen more of her lately than I ever did before, & think her exceedingly agreeable; but am not yet cured of an opinion I have formed that she would not quite do for a Ly John; but I like her well enough to wish she would take rather more care than she does for the sake of her own happiness; my Lord is 18 years older than her, not of a very patient temper, & I doubt she takes the liberty of [teasing?] him a little too much: I have no scruples in acknowledging that my Lady is much more to my taste than my Lord … I am afraid if any mischief does come that her Ladyship shall have the worst of the bargain; not only in the talk of the world (which is no truth to a Woman) but in real comfort of the remainder of her life.[70]

How prescient Lord John was.

Writing at a time when she was no longer close to the Countess, Georgiana Devonshire put some flesh on these bones:

> I think when Lady Jersey pleases there is a real fascination about her, at least I have often & often gone to her resolving to arm myself against her flattery … & have found myself quite forgetting why I resolv'd and

> believing her as sincere as myself. Yet she is not a person one should trust. It would be the height of folly to suppose she was not as [false] to oneself as she is to all the world. However she is often I believe accus'd of what she does not deserve – when I saw more of her I had been often warned that she repeated things I [raised] to her – now if she did she must have invented them for I never said anything to her I could care about whilst she on the contrary always [presumed?] to [reveal?] herself even with impudence in her opinion &c to me & it was then I lik'd her best all because it seems to contradict the opinion of her being ... false.[71]

There was at that time, too, another public recognition of the Countess's failings. Sir Herbert Croft's *Abbey of Kilkhampton,* a collection of satirical epitaphs written for some of his more famous contemporaries, published in 1780, contained one for Frances Jersey. After acknowledging, doubtless tongue-in-cheek, her 'Beauty, Good–sense and Sweetness of Disposition', it went on:

> Had she possessed more Prudence, with less Vivacity; more
> Affection, with less Inconstancy; more Sincerity, with less Insinuation;
> She would have lived a Pattern to the Wives and Daughters of Great Britain.[72]

So beneath the beauty and the charm people saw inconstancy, insincerity, untrustworthiness and manipulation, which they did not like and which cost her friendships and loyalty in the small world of high society; that and her lifestyle certainly provoked disapproval amongst the more conservative set. Possibly it was this which once prompted Georgiana Devonshire to write to her sister 'I had a note from Ly Jersey today in a very good humour', as if to say the reverse was equally possible.[73] Maybe it was this too that caused a dispute between Frances Jersey and Lady Westmorland a few years later to become very public knowledge. An account of the row, based on a letter Lady Jersey had written to Lady Westmorland's daughter, apparently had been circulated throughout society, or, in Lord Jersey's words as he sought to get a copy to see what was being said about his wife, had 'been shown throughout London'. Worse, apparently the account had been leaked, for whatever reason – though it seems unlikely that the reasons were other than malicious – by none other than Georgiana's sister Harriet, now Lady Duncannon, to whose husband Lord Jersey wrote: 'I must declare that I do not think Ly J's greatest enemy could have acted more unfairly by her than Lady Duncannon has alone.'[74]

The Countess certainly provoked strong feelings.

Even so, whilst she might disturb and even anger people, until now the shadows cast on Lady Jersey's reputation were largely the result of her relentless and uninhibited pursuit of pleasure and a certain fastness not always combined with discretion or good judgement. Perhaps this was compounded by the fact of an affair and having another man's child. Now, though, events in Tunbridge Wells in the summer of 1777 were to do her reputation much greater damage. When Lord Jersey wrote to Lady Spencer in June that they were going to the spa town to drink the waters for his wife's health, he did not know that this was to be the beginning of the next chapter of his wife's life and of his marriage. The coming months would also put Lady Jersey's relationship with both Lady Spencer and her daughter Georgiana Devonshire under great strain.

The initial catalyst was William Fawkener who, back from abroad, had dined with the Countess in April and, as we know, saw her again in June.[75]

7

Tunbridge Wells and Coxheath Camp

July 1777 found the Jerseys in Tunbridge Wells, a place which Lord Jersey hated as much as he did Brighton. 'We go on as usual here,' he bemoaned, 'Only the weather is excellent ... We are going to day to dine on a family visit with Lady Twysden [Frances Jersey's widowed aunt] at Peckham near Merryworth ... The company here is but little increased or changed, Whist is our constant Evening Resource.'[1]

The company at Tunbridge included William Fawkener – and a dalliance, if not a full-blown affair, was soon taking place between him and the Countess. At the end of the month Fawkener wrote to Richard Fitzpatrick that he was embarked upon a

> fool's errand & have suffered myself to be ensnared like an idiot as I am with hopes and promises that never will be realised. It is not of her I complain nor could I without the greatest injustice, the difficulties are insurmountable & if I had been wise I should long ago [have formed?] a resolution which I shall at last be obliged to take & which becomes every day more difficult & disagreeable.[2]

So the initiative apparently had been taken by Frances Jersey. She was the seductress of a handsome though not too unwilling partner, setting a pattern for future affairs in future years; in short, Lady Jersey with her beauty and irresistible fascination was, when she decided upon it, rather the seducer than the seduced. Further, her attractions were so powerful that she was able to bend her lovers to meet her desires even when opposed to their own. This ability was to earn her the nickname in the press of 'the Enchantress'. And so it was in the case of William Fawkener, who was clearly getting ever more deeply involved with Frances Jersey against his better judgement.

The newspapers soon picked up the story. The number of papers published had grown substantially over the century but all were very reliant for their news on word of mouth which, when combined with a degree of deliberate fabrication, compounded their inaccuracies. There was also a marked trend towards scandal-mongering, often in very abusive terms. To Georgiana Devonshire, who was clearly in a position to judge, *The Morning Post* was 'that *Hydra* of scandal'.[3]

On 21 July it was the same widely read *The Morning Post* which, for these reasons, published the following 'announcement':

> In a few days will be published …
> The *Jealous Husband*, by the E__l of J____y …
> *An Ode to Melancholy*, by W___m F_____r, Esq.

On 6 August *The Morning Post* followed that up with an article in the guise of a letter from Tunbridge Wells dated 2 August:

> Our chief beaux [here in Tunbridge] are Capt F__k__ r and Mr W___n (your old acquaintance) these two gentlemen seem to engross the attention of *almost* all the female circle … — E______r [*sic*] lays close siege to a certain beautiful Countess, who I think will join for a *discretionary surrender*; for the sake of her husband, the writer of this, ardently wishes her Ladyship should be cautious of her conduct, and consider, before too late, that her indiscretion will be attended with infamy and dishonour and to inforce the matter further, her ruin will be involved with a tender husband, and four lovely children.

The Captain referred to is obviously Fawkener, who until 1775 had been in the 1st Regiment of Foot Guards and was known to some, such as Sophia Baddeley, as 'Captain Fawkener'; the reference to 'E_____r' is a clear typographical error for 'F_____r'.[4] Equally, there is no doubt that the Countess referred to is Frances Jersey.

It is also clear that the writer saw it as more than a mere dalliance.

More followed. On 11 August, *The Morning Post* published another 'letter from Tunbridge Wells':

> Mr Editor
>
> My last letter has caused the devil to pay for here. In one general voice, death and destruction are announced against you and your correspondent. We are called the *common disturbers* of society and execrated as pests to every social enjoyment … The hint about F_____ and the *pretty Countess* cannot possibly be attended with bad consequences, but, on the contrary, if rightly reflected upon, will *nip in the bud* a growing evil, which, to a certainty, if not timely administered to must involve a family in misery and dishonour. —It serves to convince the indiscrete parties that they are observed; that the public eye is upon them, and that detection, most assuredly, will follow their indiscretion.

At this stage, Lady Jersey seems to have taken fright and become more discreet in her behaviour because when a third 'letter', dated 13 August, was published it read:

> Mr Editor
>
> Your Mount Sion correspondent ... in direct terms declares Mr F_____ and Lady_____, to be the only persons of fashion at the Wells! In good faith 'tis a pleasant fellow, and *altogether* comprehensive.
>
> I am sorry to be obliged to make an appear [*sic*] to the observation of every individual at Tunbridge, whether or not the conduct of Lady _____ was not highly censurable, till within these very few days;—in other words, till my public animadversion on her conduct; the change in her carriage proves to me that I have acted *right*, and *gratefully* repays me for the trouble I have taken to save her from *destruction*.

The reaction of Lord Jersey to these reports was forbearing if not naive. Georgiana wrote to her mother:

> Have you seen *The Morning Post* about Ly Jersey – Ld Jersey saw them for the first time in town – & has behav'd very handsomely about them – for he told Ly J he should think it right to be the more indulgent to her, to shew the world he did not believe them.[5]

As we will see, this forbearance was not to last, but in the meantime salt was to be rubbed into the wound.

If Lord Jersey did not believe the reports, everyone else did. In mid-September the Jerseys were due to join a house party at Chatsworth. Somewhat awkwardly, Fawkener preceded them there, arriving three days before they did. Georgiana Devonshire commented to her mother, 'Mr Fawkener arrived here this evening. I am glad since he did come that it was some days before we expected [the Jerseys].' When she went to meet the Jerseys on their arrival she noted that 'Ly Jersey looks extremely well & Ld Jersey in pretty good humour. Fawkener had the prudence to stay out at shooting all morning.'[6] *

---

* Amanda Foreman in her biography of Georgiana Devonshire puts the Jerseys' stay at Chatsworth in late August 1777 (p. 66). It was, though, impossible for the Jerseys to have been at Chatsworth then, notwithstanding the dating of some letters suggesting the contrary. Apart from the fact that Georgiana Devonshire commonly misdated her letters, the Jerseys had been in Tunbridge since mid-July and were still there on 14 August, when they were due to leave on 16 August. On 20 August they were at Middleton having, according to a letter dated 27 August, got back there on 17/18 August and having not left Middleton since. On 26 August they were expected, with the Clermonts, at Chatsworth at some later date. On 27 August they were still at Middleton. On 28 August they left for Wakefield Lodge, getting back to Middleton from there on 3 September. On 15 September they set out for a fortnight at Chatsworth getting back home to Middleton on 28 September.[10]

Once at Chatsworth, it was impossible for Fawkener and the Jerseys not to be thrown together. On one day they rode together with the Duchess, Lady Clermont, and others to Castleton cave; on another the Jerseys went to watch the Duke of Devonshire and Fawkener shoot.[7] On another occasion, 'The D of Devonshire & Ld Jersey [went together] to their dear Harry Turner the horse dealer,' but on this occasion Lady Jersey went with the Duchess and Fawkener for a ride in the open carriage on the Buxton Road.[8]

All of this may have contributed to Lord Jersey, despite his earlier forbearance, not being in the best of humours. After a week at Chatsworth, Georgiana Devonshire reported to her mother that he had 'been two or three times out of humour & has threatened the old story of parting but she [Lady Jersey] has put him in good humour & he is in great spirits now', her display of charm doubtless being with a view to enabling her to stay close to her lover.[9]

One imagines the sceptical Lady Spencer had no trouble believing *The Morning Post* story despite pleadings to the contrary in a letter from Lord Jersey on 27 August (the reference to 'some friends' of hers means him and his wife):

> Lady J received much benefit from the Waters, & seems now to be quite well – I came away with the idea that, contrary to custom, there had been no ill-nature, but I have since heard & seen indeed that such an idea was not well grounded, for some friends of yours were amongst others the objects of their malice. As you take in I believe the [*Morning Post*] I trust you will not suffer those friends to be run down. If you have read the papers you will know what I mean. It is scarcely possible to escape censure at such a place, & with cheerfulness & spirit, it becomes more difficult ... Ly J always desires her love.[11]

So, explained Lord Jersey, malicious minds fabricated the story on the basis of facts which, with his normal naivety, he saw only as his wife's high spirits. In quoting this letter (and she seems unaware of *The Morning Post* articles), Margaret Jersey in her *Records of the Family of Villiers, Earls of Jersey* says that it shows that rumours were afloat, even then, about a relationship between Lady Jersey and the Prince of Wales. Given the terms of *The Morning Post* articles quoted earlier that is clearly incorrect, even ignoring the fact that the Prince was then only fifteen.[12]

A letter, apparently from Earl Harcourt (as Lord Nuneham had now become on his father's death), described the Jerseys to Lady Spencer on their return to Middleton from Tunbridge Wells:

> Both of them [are] looking in better spirits than I have seen them for some years – he is something nearer being fat, than ever he was in his life – she is in perfect good humour, and has behaved so amiably to him, & with such propriety to every other person during her 7 weeks residence at Tunbridge, that there is every appearance of friendship, affection and mutual confidence between them.

He went on, knowing the Spencers' affection for Lord Jersey, 'I am sure you & Ld Spencer will be rejoiced at this intelligence.'[13]

In saying this Harcourt may have been guilty of wishful thinking or merely believing what Lord Jersey told him. More plausible is that Lady Jersey was now behaving herself and playing a proper role after the stories in the papers. Her admirer Whitehead, though, was lyrical when he wrote from Middleton the same month, 'The garden is very neat, but not so full of flowers as it ought to be; the greatest improvement I have observed in it was Lady Jersey walking there this morning before breakfast, "herself a fairer flower."'[14]

Ten days at Middleton were followed by further visits, first to Wakefield Lodge, where since 'Ly J is come back so stout from the Wells ...' she intended to join the hunting field, followed by a fortnight at Chatsworth with a house party which included Fawkener.[15]

Back from Chatsworth, the Jerseys had the less exciting company of Lord Clarendon (as Lord Hyde had now become) and his family once more: 'We are going to make not a very cheerful exchange of Company, the Clarendon family come tomorrow: & that is rather of a different style from what have we left' wrote Lord Jersey.[16] Indeed, when Lady Jersey invited the Rev. William Mason to join them at Middleton, Mason jokingly asked his friend Lord Harcourt to recommend a route to Nuneham which avoided Middleton.[17]

In December the King finally dismissed Lord Jersey from his post as a Lord of the Bedchamber. Commentators were scathing about the reasons for it, Horace Walpole retorting that the dismissal was more to convey an appearance of firmness to the rebellious American colonies than anything else. He went on, 'there did not seem any particular reason for marking two friends [Mr Hopkins also being dismissed] of the Duke of Grafton ... there were a few other opponents [of Government policy] in place.'[18]

More happy was Christmas at Althorp with the Spencers and, amongst others in the large party, the Devonshires, the Marlboroughs, Rachel Loyd (the housekeeper at Kensington Palace and a society favourite) and the actor David Garrick.[19] Since one of Garrick's jobs over the festivities was to read a new play by Hannah More, the dramatist, writer and philanthropist, to Lady Spencer, Lord Jersey was commissioned to bring it from London when he joined the party.[20] Before she came, Rachel Lloyd reported on the latest London fashions which, of course, both Georgiana and Frances Jersey would be espousing. She wrote to Lady Spencer saying that she had heard that, in London, the Duchess of Devonshire was looking very 'handsome, her gown was white satin trimmed with flowers and Blond', and 'Lady Jersey's the same, white satin is the fashion this year'.[21]

1778 commenced in the normal way, with the Jerseys in London but with snow preventing a return to Middleton. Relations with Georgiana Devonshire remained cordial and she dined with them in the middle of January.[22] When they did get back to Middleton

> Lord Villiers (the prince of maccaronies) gave ... a play in a Barn. He acted Lord Townley; Miss Hodges, Lady Townley. I suppose [wrote Mrs Elizabeth

> Montagu drily] the merit of this entertainment was, that people were to go many miles, in frost and snow, to see in a barn what would have been every way better at the theatre in Drury Lane or Covent Garden. There was a ball also prepared after the play, but the barn had so benumbed the vivacity of the company, and the beaux' feet were so cold, and the noses of the belles were so blue, many retired to a warm bed at the inn at Henley, instead of partaking of the dance.[23]

Amateur theatricals were commonly put on in Society but, sadly, there are no other reports to show whether Mrs Montagu was as alone in her scepticism of Lord Jersey's theatricals as she was in ignoring his long since succession to the Earldom.

There followed a further mystery concerning Frances Jersey. Early in March 1778, writing to congratulate Lady Spencer on some happy event, she wrote: 'I did not come last night for I was so low, I shd have done you more harm than good.' A few days later she wrote again, saying 'you are very good to think of me, I am quite well today but I had another agreeable cry, before Dinner and felt so fatigued all the eveng that I fancied I was going to be ill but staying 12 hours in bed has set me up again, and I can bear joy very well'.[24]

No clues are given as to what lay behind this, but there are some grounds for speculation. Apparently about this time and certainly some time in 1778, Lord Harcourt wrote to Lord Jersey about Harcourt's plans for his garden, and went on 'whenever your pregnancy, or Lady Jersey's, which is almost the same thing, allows you to quit London, we shall be glad to see you'. There is, though, no record of Lady Jersey having any child between 16 December 1774, when Lady Caroline Villiers was born, and the birth of Lady Sarah Villiers on 17 November 1779, other than Lady Georgiana Villiers who was born and died on 24 June 1776. It is therefore possible that the depression which Lady Jersey was suffering in March 1778 was due to the loss of another baby.[25]

There is however some contrary indication. Three days after Lady Jersey's second letter to Lady Spencer, Georgiana Devonshire wrote to her brother: 'My Father and Lord Jersey make bitter lamentations at being kept by this inconvenient business from [hunting at] Pytchley and Lord Jersey especially for he is obliged to stay for the divorce of a Mr Hammond a friend of his.' This might suggest there were other reasons for Lady Jersey's depression since neither the loss of a baby nor Lady Jersey's depression itself could or would in any way be described as an 'inconvenient business' and neither were likely to cause Lord Spencer to stay in town, even if they did Lord Jersey – although the possibilities are not mutually exclusive.[26]

Whatever the cause, her depression did not last and Lady Jersey was, in the summer of 1778, able to play what had now become her familiar role, this time in the extraordinary pageant that was Coxheath Camp.

Coxheath was a 'wild heath' two or three miles south of Maidstone in Kent. Britain in 1778 was under threat of invasion; the war in America was going badly, and the previous year France had allied herself with Britain's rebellious American colonies, and joint French and Spanish fleets controlled the English Channel. In response, the Army set up a camp for training recruits as well as serving as a reserve against any French invasion in the south-east of the country at Coxheath which, over the course of time, became the Army's largest training camp.[27]

A Prussian visitor, Johann von Archenholz, wrote that the King's review of the troops at Coxheath in June was

> one of the most singular spectacles that I ever beheld during the course of my travels. The camp consisted of eighteen thousand soldiers, all of whom, but two or three battalions, were militia. For many years there had not been such a great army in the neighbourhood of the capital. Prodigious crowds were, therefore, attracted by the novelty of circumstance; the sovereign himself, to whom it was also new, having never before seen but a few regiments in Hyde Park, was so transported by the scene that he cried out to the commander-in-chief "O ... what a fine sight this is!"'[28]

The camp became a major social event. All of Society flooded there. 'The Duchess of Devonshire, Lady Clermont, Lady Melbourne, Lady Jersey and Mrs Crewe were only a handful of the glamorous women who could be seen striding across the parade grounds ... With its round of social calls and parties, life continued much as it would have in London or Bath.'[29]

Many brought their own militia with them. In June the Duke of Devonshire's militia joined the camp, along with the Duke and his wife who lived in a 'tent' made up of several marquees.[30] One contemporary source described the Duke of Devonshire 'who commands the Derbyshire militia [as] more distinguished for the exercise of social virtues than for his activity in either military or political concerns'.[31] The Jerseys, at this stage at least, were there without any militia, although in July Whitehead told Lord Harcourt, 'Lord Jersey, like a true patriot, has attended a Justice meeting, & sworn in fifty ragamuffins, substitutes, & others. I am sorry to find that many of the substitutes were weavers from Coventry, who would get no employment.'[32]

Originally, General Keppel, the commander of Coxheath Camp, had ordered that 'all women, exc. Soldiers' wives on strength and officers' wives during the day, were to be excluded from the camp. No married lady was to be admitted after the evening gun.' The ruling was, however, soon waived.[33]

With large numbers of the *ton* at Coxheath, the camp soon won a reputation for fast living and moral laxity 'which both outraged and titillated the public'. Before long, caricatures, typically ribald depictions of the time, were for sale in London, such as J. Mortimer's *A Trip to Cock's Heath* which featured phallic cannons, one ejaculating smoke, being admired by enthusiastic ladies.[34] A contemporary novel, clearly based on actual events, *Coxheath Camp: a novel. In a series of Letters by a Lady*, after recording the scene of Queen Charlotte's arrival at Coxheath and praising her conjugal felicity, went on to say that 'Conjugal felicity had begun to be deemed, by our Wits, conjugal folly'.[35]

Nor was this unmerited. Between 'June and early November ... Lady Melbourne became pregnant with the Earl of Egremont's child ... Lady Claremont aborted a baby she had conceived through a liaison with a local apothecary', and 'the Duke of Devonshire had taken Lady Jersey as his mistress'.[36]

As to the last, Georgiana Devonshire discovered one day that, whilst she had been busy organising a 'female auxiliary corps' of her aristocratic friends, 'the Duke and Lady Jersey had been taking advantage of her parades through the camp to visit each other's tents ... the Duke made no effort to keep the affair secret. Lady Jersey went further and flaunted her conquest in front of Georgiana, who was too frightened and inexperienced to assert herself.'[37]

This was typical of Frances Jersey's delight in taunting and humiliating people, both her friends and others – it was said of her that she was never happier than when tormenting a rival. Here she was even crueller. According to Lady Clermont, 'she [Frances Jersey] asked the Duchess if she could give her bed [at Coxheath]. She said she was afraid not, the other said, "then I will have a bed in your room" [that is close to the Duke's room] so that in the house she is to be.'[38]

The Countess's affair with the Duke continued until October with remarkable insouciance on the part of the principal players, or perhaps just brazenness on the part of Frances Jersey and *naiveté* on the part of her husband.

So when in late June the Jerseys were at Middleton, although they saw a 'great deal of the Children, indeed they will never let us be without them',[39] including the occasion of young Lord Villiers being put, for the first time, on the back of a real horse and thereafter despising his wooden one,[40] they found time to invite Georgiana Devonshire to stay. When she did not come Lord Jersey wrote to Lady Spencer with extraordinary innocence, that 'we were much disappointed at the Duchess not coming hither as we had fully expected it, but I understand she is gone to Tunbridge or still at Coxheath'.[41]

How anybody, except perhaps Frances Jersey, could expect the Duchess to stay in the house of her rival and tormentor defies belief.

In August they returned to Tunbridge, enabling Lady Jersey to display her sharp tongue and to give a flavour not only of nearby Coxheath but also of society of the time, in a letter to her friend Lady Ponsonby:

> I have been here nearly a fortnight. We came to see the Duchess who was desired to drink waters which she has done about three times in three weeks ... I remain here mon mari is gone to town ... the camp at Coxheath I went to see the other day, & liked it very well ... this place is full of people which makes it rather disagreeable ... one Lady here who has actually five lovers, past & present, at her House the other night & carried it off with a sangfroid that would amaze anybody who did not know what an idiot she is.[42]

More sangfroid (or self-deception) followed in September when Frances Jersey wrote to Lady Henrietta Spencer (also known as Harriet), Georgiana's as yet unmarried younger sister, asking her to arrange for some books like the ones Lady Spencer had to be sent to her as she meant to teach her children to write. After apologising for not seeing Lady Harriet when in town because 'I had a thousand things to do', she went on:

> I am here [at Middleton] almost alone. Don't expect your sister tho' she has promised to come, & I dare say intended it. I wish you would come with her, but I suppose, you are not to be trusted [by Lady Spencer to come] here, tho' you went to Nuneham. Ly Sp. will see at the day of judgement that I am as good as other people, tho' I don't cant, pray give my love to her & tell her so – adieu you see I am as stupid as an old post.[43]

Such a blunt message was unlikely to be well received by Countess Spencer.

What it tells us, too, is that Frances Jersey knew well what some of the staider elements of Society thought of her, that she was not *comme il faut*, and, just as important, that not only did she not care what their opinions were but also thought them wrong and was prepared to say so.

In September Lord Jersey visited Lord Spencer and, afterwards, asked both him and Lady Spencer to come to stay it Middleton. As ever, Lady Spencer was – despite their long friendship but probably due to her dislike of Frances Jersey – the more reluctant to come but eventually, it seems, they both did go to Middleton in October.[44]

It may be this was the occasion when Lady Spencer decided to take the initiative and ordered an end to Lady Jersey's affair with the Duke. Angered by Georgiana's unwillingness to interfere, Countess Spencer outlined to Lady Jersey the consequences if it were to continue. Lady Spencer also let the Duke of Devonshire know that the Spencers were disgusted with him.[45]

The result was recounted by Lord Althorp in a letter to his mother on 29 October where he described one from his sister Georgiana

> in which she gave me some satisfaction by telling me of a considerable change that has happened in a certain marriage [i.e. that of the Devonshires] … [and that] the lady [i.e. Frances Jersey] has written to her & expressed in very strong terms the great obligations she has to you for advice on the subject. I think that looks very well & most heartily hope for my sister's sake as much as anyone else's that the shame [of Frances Jersey] maybe sincerely lasting.[46]

That indeed was the end of the affair although quite why the strong minded Frances Jersey was, once more, so submissive is curious. Perhaps she did not care, as it was only a matter of days before she had acquired herself another lover. This time the affair was to continue much longer. Her new lover was, perhaps, not so new. It was William Fawkener.[47]

There was a postscript to the Duke's affair with Frances Jersey. Some years later, Georgiana recorded that her sister Harriet was staying with some Cavendish cousins in Dorset in October 1783, when 'Lady George

[Cavendish] teased her cruelly about ... Canis [Georgiana's nickname for the Duke of Devonshire] and the Infernal [as Lady Jersey was called], and so blended with some truth that she was quite hurt ... but what Canis thinks most ill-natured is that she said his intrigue with the Infernal was upon his feeling angry with me about Eyebrow [that is Charles James Fox]', with whom there had been rumours that Georgiana was having an affair.[48]

The story of Frances Jersey's affair with the Duke, though, was not quite over. In November 1778 what proved to be a thinly disguised autobiographical novel, *The Sylph*, written by 'a young lady', was published. The book caused a considerable stir and, before long, Georgiana Devonshire was identified as its author.[49]

The novel is the story of an innocent country girl, Julia Stanley, married to a cruel and dissipated roué, Sir William Stanley. One friend of Julia's, Lady Besford, is modelled on Lady Melbourne, but it is another character, Lady Anne Parker, who is of greater interest here. Of her Julia wrote, 'if I dislike Lady Besford, I think I have more reason to be displeased with Lady Anne Parker. —She has more artifice, and is consequently a more dangerous companion' who enjoys making trouble.[50] In another place, Julia writes that 'Lady Anne Parker is even more infamous than Lady Besford' and reveals that Lady Anne is having an affair with Julia's husband.[51] Lady Anne Parker is clearly the image of Lady Jersey.

There is a further entertaining caricature in *The Sylph* in the character of 'Lord L_____'. The same adulterous Lady Anne Parker regales the company at a supper party with the story of Lord L_____and his wife:

> Did you not take notice of Lady L_____, how she ogled Captain F_____ when her booby Lord turned his head aside? What a ridiculous fop is that! The most glaring proofs will not convince him of his wife's infidelity 'Captain F_____' said he to me yesterday at court; 'Captain F_____ I assure you, Lady Anne, is a great favourite with me.' 'It is a family partiality,' said I; 'Lady L_____ seems to have no aversion to him.' 'Ah, there you mistake, fair Lady. I want my Lady to have the same affection for him as I have. He has done all he can to please her, and yet she does not seem satisfied with him.' 'Unconscionable!' Cried I, 'why then she is never to be satisfied.' 'Why so I say; but it proceeds from the violence of her attachment to me. Oh! Lady Anne, she is the most virtuous and discreetest Lady. I should be the happiest man in the world, if she would but shew a little more consideration to my friend.' I think it a pity he does not know his happiness, as I have not the least doubt of F_____ and her Ladyship having a pretty good understanding together.[52]

One wonders what both Lord and Lady Jersey made of this; it is likely they read and certainly knew about it. The references to Captain Fawkener in 'Captain F_____', and the *naivité* of the Earl in relation to the events at Tunbridge and thereafter are unmissable. Georgiana's barb at Lady Jersey's malevolence and Lord Jersey's foppishness and gullibility cannot be avoided nor the reality denied. It was very public mockery of them both.

By this time, too, Frances Jersey's already doubtful reputation was becoming ever more so, even without the aid of *The Sylph*.

In December 1778 the Countess of Derby had fled from her husband and taken refuge with her lover, the Duke of Dorset. Society, which was prepared to tolerate private indiscretions but not public immorality, was scandalized, and public censure and ostracism of Lady Derby followed. Two camps formed: those who would and those who would not visit Lady Derby. Lady Jersey was one of the younger, and faster, generation who did.[53]

This was despite her husband, in a unique exercise of authority over his wife, initially prohibiting her from doing so (Lord Spencer also prohibited Georgiana Devonshire from visiting Lady Derby), prompting a self-serving letter from Frances to Lady Ponsonby: 'You may guess what we felt at being obliged to abandon a person ... whom we loved so much ... I believe the Dss & myself are the only people who have not been to see her.'[54]

The last was of course as she knew nonsense, though whether she visited Lady Derby in defiance of her husband or whether – and this seems more likely – she bullied her husband into submission is unclear. In contrast, when Georgiana Devonshire asked her mother's permission to visit the disgraced Lady Derby, Lady Spencer responded caustically:

> If you sacrifice so much for a person who never was on a footing of Friendship, what are you to do if Lady J[ersey] or Lady M[elbourne] should proceed (and they are already on their way) to the same lengths.[55]

Lady Spencer was not alone in her views of Frances Jersey. In a letter of the same month the acerbic Lady Mary Coke wrote to her sister, Lady Stafford:

> Lady Jersey is much talk'd of & not to her advantage. tis [*sic*] thought she will be the next lady parted or divorced ... I shou'd not mention a report of this nature before it was confirmed of any Lady who bore a good Character but so much has already been said of [her] that I don't think these reports will do [her] much injury.[56]

Parting, let alone divorce, was an almost irredeemable sin in those times, and yet such was her reputation.

And then there was a much more public recognition of Frances Jersey's growing ill-repute, along with the fact of her affair with Fawkener, in an anonymous satire published the following year, entitled *Sketches from Nature, in High Preservation, by the most Honourable Masters; containing upwards of eighty Portraits, or Characters of the Principal Personages in the Kingdom*. This purported to be a catalogue of portraits of eminent people and described one portrait by 'Lord J_____' of 'Eve tempted by the Serpent' as follows:

> By the blooming elegance of our general mother's person [that is Eve], we should judge the painter to have copied the figure from some British beauty of the age. Different enquirers will fix on different ladies as the most natural originals in such a case. For our part we meddle not with _____ affairs. The scene is well described and embellished in masterly taste. Eve has in all her all that we think lovely, but speaks, in the language of the eyes, her subjection to female frailty. One thing will plead in her behalf – The artist has given her a very personable serpent.[57]

Lord J_____ was obviously Lord Jersey, Eve was of course his beautiful wife and, for the present, the serpent was (the very personable) William Fawkener.

8

The Fawkener Years

Frances Jersey's affair with Fawkener was to last until his marriage nearly five years later. Of course, whilst it lasted, and despite it being public knowledge, in the manner of the day the Countess continued to play the role of a loyal wife as Society expected, and the Earl somehow accepted his wife's behaviour without much complaint but with considerable unhappiness.

It seems that, for whatever reason, Lady Jersey admitted her affair with Fawkener, which had indeed commenced in Tunbridge Wells in August 1777, to her husband in the early months of 1778. As Georgiana Devonshire wrote to her mother in April:

> Ly Jersey has at last confessed but you must not own you know it even to Ld J, as it is to be kept secret ... I have seen Ly Jersey, I spoke to her of yr knowing of his been here, I think it will be of use for the future.[1]

A second letter written only six days after this shows Lady Spencer, writing from Farming Woods, asking her daughter:

> Was it not very imprudent of Lady [here the name is very thoroughly scratched out] to go to the [Races?] so soon after the illness she has had & to meet such people, surely she is infatuated. I have said nothing of all that here you may be sure.[2]

It seems clear that this too is a reference to Lady Jersey and that it was her name which has been so vigorously deleted. The facts bear out that conclusion. First, Lady Jersey had been ill the previous month. Second, her husband was an habitué of Farming Woods, and if he was there then that would be a reason for Lady Spencer to keep silent on the topic. Finally, a man of Fawkener's reputation would naturally fall within Lady Spencer's dismissive categorization of 'such people'. The clear implication is that Lady Jersey's affair with Fawkener, yet to be interrupted by her brief dalliance with the Duke of Devonshire, was visibly taking wing and had been challenged by Lord Jersey, so resulting in his wife's confession.

This also explains Lady Spencer's letter to her daughter in July 1778 asking whether Lord Jersey had yet arrived in Tunbridge, which is near Coxheath, and continuing, 'I am afraid the Company he will find [there] will occasion a few [Clowds?] – pray take care to avoid as much as you possibly can the having anything to do in that horrid business.[3]

The 'infatuation' accounts too for the unhappiness which palpably prevailed in the Jersey household at the time. After visiting Lord Jersey at Middleton in October that year, when Fawkener had clearly succeeded the Duke of Devonshire in the Countess's affections, Lady Spencer described to her daughter the unhappy state she found there:

> The want of harmony in that house is but too visible & prevents a possibility of enjoying oneself, they both received me very kindly, their children are charming & I could only grieve that with so many ingredients to make them happy they had so little prospect of being so. After dinner Ly J & I had some conversation, I had determin'd to say nothing, but I could not help it – I can not see her without loving her & and one can not feel interested for her without feeling that she is hoarding up a weight of misery that must in time burst & overwhelm her. She received all I said in such a manner that I cannot help pitying her & thinking she has better heart than she appears to have ... she has no religion [to guide her] which is her misfortune ... In short I went to Middleton with a heavy heart & came away with it rather heavier for I can foresee nothing but misery for them.[4]

The first striking thing about this letter is how even Lady Spencer could still be charmed by Frances Jersey. The second is Lady Jersey's reaction to this 'conversation', as reported by Georgiana to her mother:

> I have had another [letter] from Ly Jersey – I must copy out one part of it because it delights me – after saying that you have been there she says, 'I am too sleepy to enter into particulars but I must tell you that I have had a great conversation with Ly Spencer, I am all gratitude and [attendrement?] and if anything could make me what I ought to be it would be her she is the most enchanting woman in the world.'[5]

It is difficult to reconcile these descriptions with some of the Countess's earlier reactions. Was she being respectful to an older woman; was she playing a part, even fawning, to avoid an argument; or was she merely biddable? The last seems unlikely: at twenty-five she was a grown woman who knew her own mind. Clearly there remained a degree of affection and goodwill in both directions, and equally clearly Lady Jersey took the advice in good spirit. Nevertheless – and perhaps this is the answer to the conundrum – her conduct did not change despite Lady Spencer's advice and the pretence of harmony with her husband had to continue. In December 1778, when they were staying at Althorp, Lord Jersey had a very serious accident whilst hunting, 'a horrid & distressful scene' resulting 'from the absurdity of wishing to emulate the glory of a whipper in'. But Lady Spencer's 'account of Ly J delights me, [wrote Lord Harcourt] and her conduct makes her husband happy even in his current situation'.[6]

The answer seems, therefore, that the bewitching Frances Jersey was merely playing a part – but playing it very well at least as far as Lady Spencer was concerned. However, by no means was everybody fooled, and the parlous state of the Jerseys' marriage was well known. Lady Mary Coke when reporting Lord Jersey's accident to her sister, after acknowledging that Frances Jersey had set out immediately from London to visit her dangerously ill husband, put the knife in with the following:

> But to everybodys surprise she is already return'd [to London] & the message from the door that Ld Jersey is mended, but why she left him so soon nobody can tell. That they are on bad terms is well known & yet upon such an occasion as a dangerous illness it does not seem decent to leave him.[7]

Frances Jersey's affair with Fawkener did not always run smoothly. Despite the affair Fawkener seemed determined to marry but was a poor judge both of his own interests and of his own mind. In the spring of 1799 William Hamilton MP was giving 'suppers to all the fine ladies and of course, as he feasted some, he affronted others. Amongst the latter is Lady Jersey who [was already] in the dumps because F_____ will most probably marry Lady Laura [Waldegrave]', another of the beauties of the time. As it happened, that marriage did not take place, in part because Lady Laura's mother, the Duchess of Gloucester, not surprisingly did not approve of the match.[8]

Still, in spite of Lady Spencer's advice and Fawkener's vacillations, in June 1779 Lady Jersey was once more pregnant, this time with Fawkener's child which had been conceived in February. As a result the Countess could not travel and the Jerseys stayed in London. Whitehead saw

> no likelihood of the Middleton family leaving London; Lord Jersey is come back again from Euston. Her Ladyship can drive herself out for many hours every day, can go to Ranelagh, &c, &c, but can not yet venture on a journey. The fresh air about London does her an infinite deal of good, & it is not so raw as the country air; the dust softens it exceedingly.[9]

Lady Jersey's view on things, as she told Lady Ponsonby, was less benign:

> I have had a thousand chagrins of different natures beside the old constant torment I waited till my heart was at ease and my mind too.... I am with child & suffer amazing from sickness & c.[10]

By the end of July, however, it was thought safe enough for the Jerseys to travel, so they set out for Middleton where all the children had been for more than a month.[11]

Lady Jersey stayed at Middleton when, in September, her husband went to hunt with the Bouveries at Délapré Abbey. Apart from the usual company, wrote the Earl to Lady Spencer, staying at Délapré were also 'Mr Evd Fawkener & Mrs Fawkener with whom I had the honour to dance, & I will say no more on that subject', he commented in a tone of total dismissal. Everard Fawkener was not only Mrs Bouverie's brother but also William Fawkener's, so just possibly this was Lord Jersey acknowledging his wife's conduct, perhaps provoked by knowledge of the parentage of her imminent child.[12]

There is, though, a more likely explanation. In the words of the worldly Lady Mary Coke:

> Mrs Bouverie has her youngest brother & his wife now in the House with her & she carried her to the Races at Northampton where Lord Jersey danced with her – is it right that a lady of so infamous a character should meet such support & protection.[13]

Quite what Mrs Everard Fawkener had done to deserve so infamous a 'character' is sadly not known.

As Lady Jersey's pregnancy progressed the Jerseys planned their return to London for her lying in. They were due to leave Middleton at the end of September but 'the fever and sore throat which has been all summer in our neighbourhood, & had just before got into our Village ... broke out in the Family [a word which encompasses the whole household]. I have been and am at a great loss what to do about the children [wrote Lord Jersey], but the illness appears slight upon the Servants & nobody else being taken ill, I am in hopes it will go no further.' He hoped they could return to London early in October.[14]

Whitehead recorded his views in a letter to Lord Harcourt on 30 September:

> By her size it seems high time that Lady Jersey should be in town, unless she would do a better thing for her health, which is, lie in in the country ... Pray heaven it may be a boy and a stout one; the present boy still keeps your Lordship's letter in his pocket and always laughs at the same places.[15]

Presumably, Whitehead's anxiety for another boy was to provide insurance for the succession.

Once in London, Lady Jersey was 'at home' every evening. Loving company, society and gossip, she was 'the rendezvous for the stray people in town' out of season.[16] One of those stray people was Georgiana Devonshire, who wrote to her mother in October:

> I am to dine with Lady Jersey ... to tell you the truth tho' I love her tenderly, I have learnt to feel a kind of uneasiness in being with her, that makes our

> society very general – I am discontented in being with her and can't tell her so, *et ma bonhomie en souffre.*

It is remarkable after all that had passed, as well as a tribute to the Countess's charms, that Georgiana could still love Frances let alone love her tenderly. Less remarkable was that there was now some tension in the air, as both behaved as if nothing had happened between them and Georgiana's comment marked the first hint of a parting of the ways between the two of them.[17]

When the Jerseys came to London they had left their children at Middleton. The children's health, despite the earlier optimism, caused real concern. On 22 October Lord Jersey wrote to Lady Spencer:

> This last week I had been in great alarm about the children at Middleton, they were attended by the Physician from Oxford, and being recovered from the attack they had of this epidemic fever, which continuing or rather increasing with great violence in our Village, they are now got to town & seem perfectly well.[18]

As a result, he was able spend a few days hunting with the Spencers before his wife gave birth, which she did on 17 November 1779. Despite Whitehead's prayer, the infant was another girl, Lady Sarah Villiers. Lady Jersey commented on this, after excusing herself for not writing to Lady Ponsonby before on the grounds that 'I was too uncomfortable [from being an enormous size] to answer your last letter ... I suppose you know *la signora mit au monde une fille*, to the great grief of everybody I am less miserable at it than other people, for I like my Children so much as soon as I have seen them.'[19]

It is clear this time that Lord Jersey was not the father of the new-born baby – and this time we do know who the father was.[20]

In the late eighteenth century, the daughters of the nobility were presented at court when they were about sixteen. On 20 October 1796, some sixteen years after Lady Sarah's birth, Lady Jersey presented one of her daughters to Queen Charlotte at the Queen's Drawing Room. Only Sarah of her daughters was, at that time, of the right age to be presented and accordingly it is clear that the daughter she presented was Sarah – even though the following day's *Lloyd's Evening Post* referred to her as Lady Susan Villiers (none of the Jersey daughters was called Susan).[21]

The politician and diarist Lord Glenbervie was also at that Drawing Room and wrote in his diary 'Fawkener stood near when the daughter was presented to the Queen. I thought him anxious and agitated. Several ladies were whispering to one another to observe the likeness.'[22]

The proposition that Lady Sarah was William Fawkener's daughter is compelling. We know the affair was continuing; we know Frances Jersey's propensities; and we have contemporary evidence as to likeness as well as signs of guilt (or at least embarrassment) on the part of Fawkener, if not on the part of the supremely self-confident Countess. Margaret, Countess of Jersey acknowledges that the Earl was not Lady Sarah's father in her

Records of the Family of Villiers but her statement that Sarah was 'commonly accepted as the Prince's daughter' is unsupported by any evidence (as well as being based on a misinterpretation of Lord Jersey's letter to Lady Spencer of 27 August 1777 about the reports in *The Morning Post*), and her assertion that Lady Sarah bore a striking resemblance to the royal family appears to be wishful thinking – or, given Lady Sarah's acknowledged beauty, precisely the converse. Only her argument, that contemporary catalogues described Lady Sarah as 'sister to the 5th Earl of Jersey' rather than, as the other Jersey daughters were described, 'daughter of the 4th Earl', remains, and that is equally consistent with Fawkener being her father – but even so at least one further Jersey girl was publicly recognised as being another man's child, as we shall see.[23]

The last argument also raises the interesting suggestion that the illegitimacy of Lady Sarah was not only known but also acknowledged by Society as well as by Lord Jersey himself. The birth of the next Jersey child, to be conceived in February 1780, would reinforce the message.

The Countess made a good recovery from the birth and her husband was soon frequenting the hunting field when not complaining about the lack of entertainment in town. One of his hunting companions was Lord Althorp. In 1780 the Jerseys took him even further under their wing than usual. On 24 March Althorp wrote to his mother that, after dining at the Star & Garter Tavern:

> I went afterwards by invitation to Lady Jersey's, who had a very private party & a supper. My sister, Ly Melbourne, Ld Frederick, Tom Grenville, Mr Fawkener and I composed it ... this morning ... dressed so as to dine early with the same party and at the same place as yesterday for the purposes of going in time to the [belle?] assembly.[24]

It seems that Lord Jersey was not one of the party. Lord Althorp dined with Lord Jersey on 8 April, having told his mother beforehand that he had not seen Lord Jersey yet. On that occasion Sir W. Boothby 'was the whole company there'.[25]

He was back dining with Lord Jersey a few days later and followed this in turn by going to 'a most charming concert at the opera house. [Since it was crowded] & as I came after it began I could only get a little corner in Lady Jersey's box to stand up in.'[26]

Apart from the concert, the Jerseys enjoyed a ball at Lady Clarges and 'a comical sort of party' at Lady Lucan's, together with a French play at Lady Aylesbury's. As to 'other little public matters the only novelty I see [wrote Lord Jersey to Lady Spencer] is that the young ladies [Ly Hume amongst them] have adopted Lady J['s] manner of dressing her hair *En Taureau* & they are all now like so many female bulls'.[27]

Lord Jersey went back to Middleton at the end of April with a view to visiting Lady Spencer in Bath. Once more, though, Lady Jersey who, for reasons which are now obvious, had developed a habit of remaining in

London after her husband had left for the country, was 'far from well; she has been ailing for this past week very unpleasantly, her spirits are excessively bad & the more so because they do not know what is her complaint, & of course try different medicines with equal ill success'. In fact, once again she was pregnant. As a result, Lord Jersey returned to London and postponed his visit to Bath. At his wife's request he asked Lady Spencer 'not to say anything of Ly J Illness because she wishes [her mother] Mrs Johnston not to know it'.[28]

Eventually, even though Lady Jersey continued to ail, her husband did go to Bath to meet the Spencers in mid-May; [29] Lady Jersey still remained in London and was fit enough to entertain friends. One of these, Lady Clermont, told Lady Spencer that she had called on Georgiana Devonshire at Devonshire House. When she said she 'was going to see Ly Jersey who was confined, she [Georgiana] desired I would not say anything of her … I think she seems quite tired of the set' – perhaps another indication that the uncomfortable relationship with Frances Jersey was now proving too much for Georgiana.[30]

When Lord Jersey returned from Bath to London the first story he heard was that he had died in Bath and 'several persons had sent last night to enquire of the Porter if it was true'. This, though, he said 'was rather different from the other rumor that I had taken a Lady to Bath with me. My death is certainly not true, as to the other I shall beg to be silent …'[31] This is intriguing, since when writing to Lady Spencer to say that he would be joining her in Bath he added 'whether I shall bring any Companion or I cannot say, I rather think the contrary'. There are no more clues and no evidence that the Earl at any time reciprocated his wife's infidelities.[32]

In his absence Lady Jersey's health had not improved. Indeed, 'Lady J does not appear to have made the least progress; she is daily seized with hysterical low [fits?] & as well for that as other reasons I cannot fix upon any day for going to Midd.; tho' I mean it should be about Friday or Saturday.'[33]

Lady Jersey's health however soon benefited from an unlikely source.

In June 1780 London was rocked by severe riots lasting for over a week, the Gordon Riots. Large anti-Catholic mobs, swayed by the oratory of Lord George Gordon, indulged in an orgy violence and destruction.[34] London in the eighteenth century was a violent place, with many brutal and lawless elements, and what had started as a (relatively) peaceful protest against the relaxation of restrictions on Catholics rapidly snowballed into a major riot. Protestors roamed around large parts of the town wreaking destruction on Catholic chapels and shops, as well as houses, dressing it up as a protest against 'Popery', although in reality seeking a wider vengeance. Lord Mansfield, believed to support the relaxations, had his house set alight, his valuable library destroyed and his possessions looted. Nor was he alone in being attacked. The rioting escalated still further on Wednesday 7 June, when its violence and destruction reached its peak.

Langdale's brewery in Holborn was torched with spectacular effect. But it was the symbols of authority which were the principal targets of the mob's anger. In addition to Newgate prison being sacked, the

> King's Bench Prison [being] set on fire and burned out; the ancient Borough Clink was burned to the ground and never rebuilt; the Southwark New Prison was emptied of prisoners; the Marshalsea was attacked but saved by the military [and] the round-houses in Borough High Street and Kent Street pulled down and fired.[35]

Initially, the authorities' response to the riots and the widespread destruction was one of confusion and inactivity. But, with the escalating violence, more determined heads prevailed. The regular army was brought in to support the militias and, by Thursday 8 June, it had arrived. Prompted by the extremes of destruction on Wednesday, violence was met with violence. The army and the militia was now ruthless in its response, and with 'some 210 rioters shot dead in the streets; another seventy-five or so dying in hospitals; unknown others dead from drinking neat liquor at Langdale's or elsewhere or dying at home from their wounds', and soldiers now everywhere on the streets. By Friday the disturbance had been crushed and the rioters and the force of the riots were now spent.[36]

After describing the effects of the riots, as seen from the relatively unscathed West End of town, as 'all riot, confusion, & hourly expectation of more', with London 'so full of troops that it is impossible the mob can make any very great impression', Lord Jersey wrote in early June that 'I meant to have gone out of town today, whether I shall tomorrow God knows; what is a man with a Wife in one place and a family in another to do' – the children still being at Middleton. The next day he wrote: 'We shall remove to Mid. tomorrow – you cannot conceive how families had been leaving this hitherto, if not still, hazardous spot: & Goods removing from all houses.'[37]

It must have been very frightening, though Whitehead, in writing to Lord Harcourt at the time, said with remarkable coolness: 'The newspapers tell you all our calamities, sometimes a little exaggerated.'[38]

By 9 June, the troops had done what was required to restore order, so enabling Lord Jersey to write: 'Quiet seems now to be the Idea of everybody and that this mob is crushed ... In this interval of rest we are setting off for Middleton, if possible to enjoy some little peace with my Children & at my home, endeavouring to fancy that this whole country is not on the brink of ruin.' Lord Jersey ever was the pessimist.[39]

When they arrived in Middleton in mid–June, 'the difference of the scene from what I have left [he said] is not to be described ... It begins to appear like a dream; as the Children's Arabian Nights are laying about the room, I shall very soon fancy that such horrid scenes of desolation, cruelty & and rapine must have been Baghdad, & not in London.'[40]

It was not all bad, however. Referring to the riots he wrote: 'Lady Jer seem[s] to have received benefit from it; the spirit & animation of the business certainly rouzed her nerves for a time ...' Perhaps her illness was in the mind; perhaps she no longer suffered from morning sickness. Whatever its cause, or cure, there was no more mention of it.[41]

The family were quite alone at Middleton until Frances Jersey's mother joined them for a few days 'on a sudden' later in the month.[42] When Whitehead arrived a few days after that, he found – perhaps prompted by the Countess's recent illness – that

> the reform in the family [as to their time of dining] is prodigious. Be it known to all persons that we now dine at three o'clock, by the Middleton clock too, which is a quarter before that at Nuneham, & a full half hour before those in Oxford & London ... I found Lord and Lady Jersey going out upon a neighbourly visit, to junket with their friends, but the two eldest young ladies did me the honour of accompanying me in my repast.[43]

In early August Lady Jersey, never afraid of staining her reputation by association when fun was to be had, stayed in Richmond upon Thames in Surrey with the not entirely respectable Lady Di Beauclerk, the artist daughter of the 3rd Duke of Marlborough who had left her husband Viscount Bolingbroke and had an affair with Topham Beauclerk (the great-grandson of Charles II and his mistress Nell Gwynn) before her divorce enabled her to marry him. Whilst the Countess was in Richmond she also 'drank tea' with Horace Walpole at nearby Strawberry Hill.[44]

The family were still at Middleton at the end of August after the Clarendons had come and gone. Villiers was back home from Harrow for the holidays, and the Jerseys socialised with their neighbours: 'We were [wrote Lord Jersey] at Blenheim this morning ... We have in our neighbourhood the new & handsome Ly Dashwood, and the neither new, nor handsome Lady Newhaven. They dined with us yesterday, & I was so much afraid of the little figures [that is his children] producing remarks that I would not let one of my children see her.'[45]

As autumn approached, they started to plan a return to London due to Lady Jersey's pregnancy. On 6 October Lord Jersey wrote, 'Lady Jersey begins to take fright every day more & more & therefore it is now fixed that we leave [Middleton] on Thursday. She will stay one night at Nuneham, I shall perhaps remain there a day or two more.'[46]

That is indeed what happened, so Lord Jersey was back in town long before Lady Jersey gave birth to her second son and sixth child on 15 November. It is barely credible but the son was named William Augustus Henry Villiers. There is no proof but the likelihood must be that he, too, was not the Earl's child and was named after his real father or, at the very least, his mother's lover. Either way, the brazenness of Lady Jersey was extraordinary and the humiliation which her husband must have felt in the face of all Society can only have been profound.

The following year, 1781, brings the first mention in the Countess's life of another man who was to have a large role in it, Frederick Howard, 5th Earl of Carlisle – Byron's guardian, one of Fawkener's closest friends and ultimately his successor as Lady Jersey's lover. *The Gentleman's Magazine* described Lord Carlisle as 'possessing a small but elegant figure, in which symmetry blended with agility and strength, he shone as one of the meteors of fashion. Elegant in his dress and manners with his green riband [of the Order of the Thistle, the second highest order of chivalry] across his vest, and a brilliant star sparkling at his side, he was considered one of the chief ornaments of the Court.'[47]

If one word were to summarise the Earl it would be 'elegance'. Like Fawkener, he was also a man of pleasure; one of his previous and publicly known affairs had been with Lady Sarah Bunbury, as Lady Mary Coke had noted in 1767.[48]

Horace Walpole, though, was less than flattering when he wrote of Carlisle in 1778, when the Earl had been appointed one of the Commissioners to the troubled American colonies:

> Lord Carlisle was a young man of pleasure and fashion, fond of dress and gaming, by which he had greatly hurt his fortune, was totally unacquainted with business, and though not void of ambition, had but moderate parts, and less application.[49]

Notwithstanding Walpole's assessment of him, by 1781 Lord Carlisle was in Dublin acting as Viceroy of Ireland, where Fawkener visited him and Lady Jersey wrote to him.[50]

In England the Countess continued to glitter. August 1781 saw the publication of a collection of twenty-four sonnets entitled *The Bevy of Beauties,* which was much admired.[51] The collection was dedicated to the Duchess of Devonshire and each sonnet took as its subject a particular beauty of the day, including the Duchesses of Devonshire and Rutland and Lady Laura Waldegrave. Sonnet number XVI was on the Countess of Jersey, 'Scene, A Retirement; Time, the close of the day', and this time there were no barbs, only 'characters nicely discriminated, and the praise ... appropriate without flattery'.[52]

The Countess's elder children were now growing up and she and the Earl enjoyed spending time with them. Whatever her treatment of her friends, Lady Jersey was genuinely fond of children, as is shown by the attention she paid to Georgiana Devonshire's when Georgiana was banished abroad for her adultery by the Duke some years later. Her own children were obviously no exception even though, as was the norm for the times and her position, she spent much time away from them. In July, she bought young Lord Villiers 'a new horse from Bath ... called Millikin',[53] and whilst at Middleton in August Lord Jersey said that 'the children do take a good deal of the time, besides we have had an alarm amongst them. Sarah was taken exceedingly ill a few days ago, but by the application of a Blister she is pretty well again.'[54]

As to her friends, Frances Jersey continued to be on friendly enough terms with the Spencers who, after postponing a visit to Middleton as a result of a bad cold which Lady Spencer did not want to give to the children, arrived there early in October along with Lady Clermont and, eventually, the Ponsonbys.[55] Whilst Countess Spencer was at Middleton she wrote to Georgiana Devonshire to tell her that 'Lady J is quite uncomfortable with your not writing', so close did Frances Jersey continue to feel to the Duchess.[56] Another example of that apparently continuing closeness occurred a year later when Georgina Devonshire was beset with some serious difficulties. Whether this was her latest pregnancy or the burgeoning affair between her husband and Lady Elizabeth Foster is not clear but it prompted her mother, in the latter's words, to tell Georgiana that

> the only persons I mean to mention your situation to are Ly Jersey, Ly Clermont, Mrs Howe, Miss Lloyd & your sister – to all whom I have lied to intolerably that I must make it up by telling them the truth ...[57]

Meaning that Lady Jersey was, despite all, even now still part of some inner circle of Georgiana's.

In October at Middleton a less welcome guest, at least for Lord Jersey, was apparently William Fawkener – although he did not seem to be enjoying himself much either, writing drolly, and somewhat ungratefully, to the Earl of Carlisle from there on 14 October:

> I hunt three days a week, the others and all the evenings I pass in reading, or now or then playing cards with any unfortunate people whose bad luck has brought them to this place. Nothing could be more insipid than this life, yet I rather enjoy such a state of vegetation, and I think with horror at the fat women and macao, the stupid men and long suppers.[58]

Whether in between times he was able to enjoy the presence of his mistress is unsaid. Even so, one wonders at the very fact of his presence and whose initiative it was.

The countryside, however, then began to pall. By 4 November Lord Jersey was writing: 'We go on here as usual, beagling and complaining of the weather, but tomorrow we are to be enlivened by a Ball at Blenheim, of what magnitude I do not know, but I should suspect nothing very great.' He was right:

> It was composed of neighbouring misses and Oxford scholars ... The daughters of the house dance delightfully & are the most accomplished young women I know ... We returned home after supper but not quite

> successfully for we run [*sic*] against the Gateway at Blenheim and broke our Carriage completely, it might as well have been a very bad accident.[59]

It was time to go back to town, although there is the slightest suggestion that the Jerseys went further and went on to France. The diarist Laetitia Hawkins, writing years later, reported, as we will see, that in February 1782 the Jerseys were 'newly returned from France', though there is no other evidence of their having gone there and she is probably wrong; they were in France later the following year so that it is possible she simply got the dates wrong.[60]

There were other events in 1782 which kept Lady Jersey in the public eye amongst which was a very vivid description by Lady Augusta Murray:

> All the fine ladies, and the *bon ton* then were last night Assembled, I assure you I never saw such a number of handsome women and all well drest. Miss Wooodley looked very beautiful, Ly Jersey *se surpassait* and Lady Melbourne exceeded the [illegible] of any reasonable being that ever was seen.[61]

And then in February there was the publication of Sherwin's engraving *The Finding of Moses,* of which George Selwyn wrote to Lord Carlisle:

> There is a picture engraving at the man's house in St James's Street where your picture is to be engraved. The design is ingenious; it is the story of Pharaoh's daughter finding Moses in the bullrushes. The Princess Royal is introduced as Pharaoh's daughter, and all the other ladies, celebrated for their beauty – the Duchess of Devonshire, Lady Jersey, &c. &c.; on *briquera les places*. The portraits will be originals, and the whole, if well executed, will be a very pretty print.[62]

Laetitia Hawkins added some retrospective colour:

> To see the picture in its progress, to see themselves and one another, the women of fashion were in Sherwin's drawing-room from two to four daily; and the *cortege of beaux* may be conjectured. Horses and grooms were cooling at the door, carriages stopped the passage of the street; and the narrow staircase ill sufficed the number that waited the cautious descent or the laborious ascent of others.

She went on to describe the ladies in the picture:

> The then young Duchess of R_____, queen of beauty! but of manners the most chastised; her graceful grace of 'Deva'; Lady Jersey, newly returned from Paris, where her lord and herself had obtained the distinguished title of 'the English couple!' the Waldegraves daughters of a mother still retaining

> traces of almost unrivalled beauty ... and many others, were there, who claimed places, or were solicited to accept them.[63]

Portrait painting at that time made up by far the largest part of the art market in London, built on the growing number and wealth of the middling sort, and demand far exceeded supply.[64] In the 1750s, Joshua Reynolds was charging 12 guineas for a head and 48 for a full-length portrait. By the late 1770s, the respective prices were 50 and 200 guineas and, in 1787, Thomas Gainsborough was charging the comparable price of 160 guineas for a full-length portrait.[65]

Indeed a passion for pictures was a marked feature of London life in the eighteenth century, as we can see from the crowds Laetitia Hawkins describes. It gave employment to some thousands of artists, printmakers and related tradesmen: 'Pictures also provided some of the great public spectacles of London life in the annual exhibition of the Royal Academy and the Incorporated Society of Artists. Amongst the throngs of spectators of the quality and many ranks below were those, never few in number, who come more to be seen that to see.'[66]

However the event which cast the most limelight on Frances Jersey at the time was her name being linked with the nineteen-year-old Prince of Wales, on which topic, at almost exactly the same time, James Hare was writing to the Earl of Carlisle:

> The Prince of Wales has been to the Duchess of Cumberland's public nights, and sups there every Saturday with about about twenty people. He shows a great fancy for Lady Melbourne and Lady Jersey, but is supposed to like the first best. He wishes to be invited to private suppers, and without any form, but as Mrs Broadhead and Mrs Thornhill are the only ladies who have hitherto received that honour, the others do not like the precedent.[67]

The press soon picked up the relationship.[68] So did the satirical part of it which recorded the Prince of Wales' 'great fancy' to Lady Jersey and Lady Melbourne and cruelly went on to describe Lord Jersey as 'the pretty-pacing, sweetly simpering, beauty-blended, odoriferous ... all-bewitching, all-indulging, all-deluding swain'.[69] Sadly there is more than an element of truth in this. Lord Jersey, however, was not alone in his mistreatment, as George Selwyn related in March to Lord Carlisle:

> The P of W supped the night before last at Lord Derby's; there were as I am told no less than six courses; the women were Lady Payne, Lady Jersey, perhaps the Lady Meilbourne [*sic*]; I have not as yet been informed of particulars. He stayed there till six ... Lord Meilbourne [*sic*] stayed away at his instigation.[70]

There is no suggestion, though, that in the 1780s Lady Jersey sought to ensnare the Prince. More likely is that the young Prince succumbed to the attractions of two very handsome and charming women of the world. Indeed, Lady Jersey's reaction when told that the Prince was in love with her was forthright, if not totally honest, and certainly not without typical astringency or hypocrisy:

> They have been so good as to put something ill natured in the papers about me & the P of Wales if he is in love with me I cannot help it, it is impossible for anyone to give another less encouragement than I have, I hope you can take my word for it but I can bring witnesses whom you will believe ... I have not seen the P above six times all the winter, he has met the Dss just as often ... judge then my Dr Louisa if he could prefer me to her ... he has not said anything particular to me, I hope this scandal will drop with as little reason as it was raised. Ly Lucan is the most diligent in spreading it, as long as Ld J takes my [part] & does me justice I do not care much.[71]

For the time being that was end of any particular relationship between the Prince and Lady Jersey for more than a decade. It was enough, though, to enable the Prince in 1795 to describe – rather disingenuously – Lady Jersey, then his mistress, to his wife Princess Caroline as being 'one of my oldest friends'.

One of the few surviving letters from Lady Jersey dates from this time and exhibits her style of letter writing, which reflecting her personality is rushed, often peremptory and breathless. It also shows that relations with the Spencers continued to be friendly. The undated letter, apparently sent on 1 June, invited Lord and Lady Spencer 'to a very stupid party at cribbage this Evg ... my children are all ill, & I am going it is now in my head as you may perceive'.[72]

Perhaps she had an excuse in that once more she was expecting. When inviting Lady Clermont to Middleton in August, a vain Frances Jersey bemoaned that she was 'cross ... at being gross but that [Lady Clermont would] find her agreeable as she has learnt a new secret to keep her ennui to herself'.[73]

At the same time, the Jerseys' way of life was affected, not always as they would wish, by a new appointment which Lord Jersey had received at court. Following the dismissal by George III of Lord North's administration in the Spring and the appointment of a new one under Lord Rockingham (with the consequent 'universal removal of all those attached to the late Ministry'), Lord Jersey had been appointed Master of the King's Stag Hounds.[74] Whilst this doubtless provided welcome income, it involved more than a purely ceremonial role and required the Earl to travel to and fro to join the King when hunting.

So as Whitehead said to Lord Harcourt in September:

> His Majesty begins hunting next week, which will oblige Lord Jersey to be backwards & forwards; & her Ladyship will have her excursions likewise. [On this occasion that suited Lady Jersey for her current view was

that] Anything is preferable to being long at home, & she is thoroughly convinced that all pretensions to love, or even bear with, the country, are affectation, especially in women ...'[75]

As normal, Lady Jersey did not enjoy her pregnancy. Originally the plan was that she would return to London for her confinement on 10 November;[76] this plan soon changed, as Rachel Lloyd wrote on 17 October:

> Lord Jersey overtook me on Tuesday just on the other side of Oxford, he had been hunting with the King, and was riding from the chase to Middleton he told me he and Lady Jersey ment [*sic*] to settle in London the end of next week and she was not very well.[77]

Countess Spencer echoed this, writing to Georgiana Devonshire at the end of October: 'Lady Jersey is I hear not quite well & is coming to town sooner than she intended.'[78]

On 14 November, Lord Jersey wrote to Lady Spencer from London, that 'I find Lady J quite low in spirits and therefore I shall not take the chance of collecting more news by going out; particularly as it is most likely, unless this frost will kind enough to last, that I shall be obliged to go tomorrow to Wickham for the Saturdays [*sic*] Stag-hunt.'[79]

Despite this the Countess continued to go out 'moderately, [and had] a party most nights which is some relief to her but her apprehensions increase & her spirits fail every hour', as they always did when she was pregnant, wrote her husband some days later;[80] some at least of these parties were, in an empty London, small cribbage parties attended by Rachel Lloyd, Mrs Howe, Lord Frederick (presumably Cavendish) and Lady Clermont.[81] By late November, though, her husband thought her 'worse than ever I knew her in the same situation', continuing 'in hourly expectation & not the better'.[82] Loving her children as she did, she could no longer bear her continued separation from them, left behind at Middleton for her lying in, so the children were then brought to town.[83] On 28 November her husband wrote: 'Lady J is not yet released, tho' I expect it every hour, nothing can be more uncomfortable than she is.'[84]

Even with all this discomfort and expectation, another month was to pass before on 30 December 1782 Lord Jersey could write:

> Lady Jersey being brought to bed of a Daughter this morning ... So Lady J is at last released from her burthen ... she seems hither to be quite well ... a Girl, which sex is certainly very partial to me in my decline of life.[85]

The new daughter was Lady Elizabeth Catherine Villiers; on this occasion there is no suggestion as to who her father was. It could have been Lord Jersey but, given the parenthood of the last two children as well as at least one of those who followed, one wonders to what extent conjugal felicity continued between the Jerseys. It is quite possible that on this occasion too Fawkener was the father.

Following the birth, Lord Jersey planned to visit the Spencers at Althorp in the New Year of 1783. This was postponed a few days, only in part owing to Lady Jersey's situation. The postponement brought forth an embarrassing confession from him as he wrote to Countess Spencer on 13 January 1783:

> Ly J not being able yet to write herself has desired me a topic, not very agreeable, to trouble you upon. We cannot recollect whether Lord Spencer has been so kind to stand Godfather to one of our Girls; if he has not we must ask the favor now; if he has, I fear we must apply to your Ladyship.[86]

In the spring there was another change of ministry, with the king asking the Duke of Portland to lead a new one. As a result there were, once more, changes to positions at court, and Lord Jersey lost his position as Master of the King's Stag Hounds, with it going to Lord Hinchinbrook, the heir to the Earl of Sandwich. Lord Jersey had clearly performed his duties well during his brief tenure since a draft letter from George III to the Duke of Portland at the time ran: 'I hope Ld Hinchinbrook will exactly follow the steps of Lord Jersey in the management of the Hounds, as he has done them great justice.'[87]

Again Lord Jersey appears a man of much greater effectiveness than is commonly credited. His consolation for the loss of the Stag Hounds position was his appointment as Captain of the Band of Gentlemen Pensioners.[88]

London in 1783 was awash with eminent visitors from France, not all endearing themselves. 'The D de Chartres & his companions [reported Lord Althorp to his mother in May] are sad blackguards ... there are some very strange stories concerning them; he will soon get out of repute in the fine world for the other night at Mr Fox's he went to sleep sitting between Mrs Crewe & Ly Jersey.'[89] One wonders how Lady Jersey reacted to this.

A week later, Althorp wrote his to his mother again:

> There is an amazing tribe of French both men and women coming over the next week amongst whom I hear are the Duc de Coigny ... Monsr de Polignac ... the beau Dillon again who is very much enamoured with Ly Jersey as the *chronique scandaleuse* will have it. I can't help [a] concatenation of ideas but I must tell you here that the match between Fawkener and Ly Jemima Asburnham is declared.

He went on to say that Lady Jemima so adored William Fawkener that her father could hold out against the marriage no longer and that Fawkener, lest his motives be doubted (obviously his reputation was doubtful to say the least), insisted that, despite his own lack of fortune, the marriage settlement should be for her children only, with him taking no interest under it.[90]

Lady Mary Coke, as ever, had a more colourful take on events:

> Lady Gemima Ashburn [*sic*] report now says is to marry Mr Fawkener sh'll get more beauty and less money than if she had married Mr Watson – inclination must be the motivation on both sides for Ly Gemima has not fortune enough to make it a match of interest for Mr Fawkener.[91]

So here appeared once more cracks in Frances Jersey's affair with Fawkener. However, it seems that she was already positioning herself for a new affair, this time with Fawkener's friend the Earl of Carlisle, although some put the final ending of her affair with Fawkener some months later. Certainly Lady Mary Coke's report in June 1783 is clear that Frances Jersey was getting close to Lord Carlisle even if it was to be some while before their affair really blossomed:

> There is another thing said with a good deal of confidence that Lady Jersey is all powerful at Lord Carlisle's & that the last ball at his House was wholly directed by her & that Lady Carlisle's cousins Lady Caroline Waldegrave & the pretty Miss Vernon were neither of them asked because her Ladyship had friends of her own she liked better.[92]

Whatever the truth, Lord Ashburnham's scruples about his daughter's match with Fawkener proved correct. Once again Fawkener did not know his own mind and jilted Lady Jemima with the result that a mere fourteen days after Althorp's letter, on 31 May, Horace Walpole was writing to his friend Mason:

> There is no discouragement to infamous proceedings. Mr Falkener [*sic*] has just abandoned a daughter of Lord Ashburnham with worse circumstances if possible than Lord Egremont did my niece. You will not wonder when you reflect who was his patron.[93]

The reference to Lady Jemima and Fawkener's patron presumably is William Augustus, Duke of Cumberland, who has been described as one who 'loved gaming, women and his own favourites and yet had no sociable virtue'.[94]

Whether or not her affair with Fawkener survived this episode so as to continue in parallel with her getting close to Lord Carlisle, Lady Jersey threw herself into entertaining the French visitors.

After reporting the arrival of 'the French Ladies &c viz Madames de Coigny, Chalons, & Dandeleau Messrs Duc de Coigny, another Coigny, Polignac, Dandeleau, & Esterhazy …' Lord Jersey went on to tell Lady Spencer that the Duchess [of Devonshire being pregnant and accordingly] not being in a situation to take much labor upon her, Lady J undertakes a good share of the foreign ladies ... We are now setting off with them, last night they were at Marl. House – tonight at Mrs. Meynell's & the Duchess's, tomorrow at Ranelagh with Ly J – Thursday Masque: Lady J. Friday somewhere but I forget where, Saturday opera & supper at Ly Salis. & so we must keep them going whilst they stay here; which is to be only a fortnight. – Adieu I am in a great hurry.[95]

In addition to everything else, on the day of the visit to Ranelagh 'Esterhazi [*sic*] dined at Ld Jersey's'. For once, though, the pregnant Georgiana Devonshire showed some restraint; on hearing that her sister-in-law had just given birth to a stillborn daughter, 'the news had the effect on her to make her take a sudden fit of prudence & go quietly home to bed instead of supping at Ly Jersey's with the foreigners'.[96]

Lord Jersey summed up the ceaseless round:

The French visitors engross the whole Conversation & object of the town at present ... we have endeavoured to amuse them by not leaving them a moment to themselves ... I should imagine they will be quite happy to find themselves on the other side of the Water ... bye the bye they are coming in a morning to breakfast here in their way to see Kew & Richmond Gardens ... They press us exceedingly to go to Paris this autumn for a month or five weeks.[97]

And so it went on. The *London Chronicle* of 27 May reported: 'On Sunday morning, the Duke and Duchess of Devonshire gave a most elegant breakfast to a select number of the nobility at Burlinghton [*sic*] House', at which the guests included the Duc de Chartres, the Prince of Wales and Lord Jersey. Since the Earl was there as well as Lady Melbourne and Lady Duncannon, as Georgiana's sister Harriet had now become, it is more than probable that Lady Jersey, though not mentioned in the *London Chronicle*, was also at the breakfast.[98]

She certainly played her part to the full. Lady Mary Coke wrote two days later:

Lady Clermont & the Dutchess of Devonshire have made an absolute monopoly of the French Ladies they are not allowed to go anywhere but by their direction, they came in an equipage of her Graces to Lord Stormont conducted by Lady Jersey.[99]

And then at the end of the month: 'The Duke [of Queensberry] ... gave a breakfast to the French ladies but invited only two English – Lady Derby & Lady Jersey.'[100] So perhaps it is no coincidence that the same month Horace Walpole, when writing to his friend Sir Horace Mann in Florence, described two of the leading lights in this whirlwind, the Duchess of Devonshire and the Countess of Jersey, very much to the latter's advantage:

> The Duchess of Devonshire, the Empress of fashion, is no beauty at all. She was a very fine woman, with all the freshness of youth and health, but verges fast to coarseness. A more perfect model than any of them [Walpole had also been describing his three beautiful Waldegrave nieces], but in miniature, Lady Jersey, is going to Paris – and will be very angry if they do not admire her as much as she intends they should.[101]

And, indeed, that seemed to be the case. Althorp had also heard that the Jerseys had decided to go to Paris after the king's birthday.[102] His mother's response to this followed: 'Lord Jersey does not seem by his letter to be determined upon going to Paris – it will be a perilous expedition for her and not a pleasant one for him.'[103] Quite why it would be perilous for her is unclear, unless she shared Walpole's thoughts – or perhaps Lady Jersey was again pregnant, although there is no evidence of it. Presumably the unpleasantness for him would be the result of inevitable flirtations (at the least) from her.

Lady Spencer was wrong, however, for when Lord Jersey wrote to her on 3 June he said, first, that a new wave of French visitors was currently expected, and that 'suppers for the French are taking place at a variety of houses' but that he 'had a good dose of the last [wave of French] & shall escape from these the beginning of next week for Brighthelmstone'; and, second, that 'an expedition for Paris is fixed for the 15th of Sep'.[104]

Before that expedition the Jerseys spent two months at Brighton. Despite Lord Jersey's dislike of the place, writing to Lady Spencer he said:

> We are settled here for some time, & as bathing is the object of the journey ... the cheerfulness of the Place matters not much, but indeed there is not one person I speak to ... In this situation our children are at present our only society, & I will own to you I do not dislike them very much; the two eldest are big enough to be companions – Sarah I understand, has been left with the Duchess to be spoilt by her; if they do not make her sick, I am sure she will entertain her Grace as a plaything, for I can feel the loss of her in that character.[105]

Lord Althorp, at Brighton some time thereafter, was more trenchant:

> This place [he said] is [except for sea bathing and the sea air which are delightful] stupid as possible. Ld & Ly Jersey have gone to Petworth [the Earl of Egremont's nearby seat in Sussex] & there is no one remaining that I know ...[106]

By the beginning of August the company had improved so that Daniel Pulteney, an impecunious but well connected man about town, was writing to the Duke of Rutland:

> This place contains, besides Pitt, a great number of very distinguished names, and amongst them your favourite Lady Jersey, who has shown no

> great reserve to some of her friends, though at present she is waiting for a successor to Lord Carlisle.[107]

So not only was Lady Jersey behaving badly but also her affair with the Earl of Carlisle, which was to last a decade and more, does seem to have begun somewhat tentatively despite Lady Mary Coke's report of Lord Carlisle's ball; and despite Lady Jersey, too, at a ball given by Lord Carlisle, presumably the same one and as part of her plan to seduce him, in Althorp's words having taken 'a freak, & danced for the first time for some years'.[108]

By coincidence that month another Frances Twysden also caused news. This was Lady Jersey's twenty-year-old cousin (not niece as some have said), the daughter of the 6th Baronet, who was getting married. Like her elder cousin, she married a man much older than her and married much higher in society than was to be expected. She married as his second wife the fourty-six-year-old Earl of Eglinton. Also like her cousin, she was to cause scandal before many years had passed.[109]

Back at Middleton in mid-August, both Lord and Lady Jersey went up to Wakefield Lodge to hunt. Left alone, Whitehead described the visit somewhat mockingly:

> The Lord & Lady are taking the delightful diversion, this warm weather, in hunting in the forest; I could almost say, with Shakespear's clown, 'the more fools they'. This is the third day since their departure, & they are to return when the destinies decree, which I fancy will be tomorrow; & they may possibly bring some dear friends with them and, if they have any there whom they cannot avoid asking, or chuse to invite.[110]

Lord Jersey's description of the expedition to Wakefield Lodge was more prosaic. The hunting 'went on well, but unfortunately for me, on Tuesday last, I was seized in the field ... with [a] Rheumatic spasm ... As I took laudanum as soon as I could be got home the pain was more expeditiously relieved [than when some years previously he had a similar attack when staying with the Spencers].' He was, nonetheless, 'a good deal shaken by the attack' and was unable to ride for some days.[111]

Fortunately this did not impede the planned journey to France. They duly left in mid-September, and discovering by chance that Lady Clermont was going at the same time arranged to meet her at Dover. When they arrived there their departure was postponed, much to the chagrin of an ever impatient Lady Jersey. Her husband described what happened:

> Beside a very high contrary wind & compleat stormy weather, a band of sand is driven up the mouth of the harbor, which prevents any ship going out; the Packet has not been able to sail, nor is likely; and she [that is Lady Jersey] your Ladysp knows must go the first moment she can, in weather which perhaps [does] not please our Ladies, however impatient part of the

> company may be. Lady Clermont is at a different Inn from ourselves ... but she is patient & we must study under her.[112]

The crossing to Calais, when it did take place, was 'quiet [*sic*] tedious'.[113]

The life the Jerseys led in Paris was not:

> We attend the theatres constantly [wrote the Earl] ... There are many English here ... but we receive so many civilities from the French of our acquaintance that we have not time to live in any other society than the French ... We shall go to Fontainebleau on Sunday ... We are going today to dine at la Muette [Louis XVI's Chateau in the Bois de Boulogne, outside Paris] with the D and Dss de Polignac who remain there with le Dauphin. The Queen goes by water from Choissy to Fontainebleau.[114]

James Hare was also in Paris. The son of an apothecary, Hare had become a friend of Fox, the Duke of Devonshire, and Lord Carlisle at Eton and Cambridge and was a social celebrity much in demand for his wit and social polish.[115] He told Lord Carlisle that 'Lady Jersey has been amazingly good natured to me, and carried me to dine at the Duc de Coigny's ... The English here are very numerous, but not such as I like to live with ... Lord Jersey is, I believe, much admired, at which I am not surprised.'[116]

When the Jerseys got to Fontainebleau in October, they found that apparently all of France went there at that time of year:

> We meet with an excess of attentions & politenesses from every body ... there are at present but few English; last week we had Mister Pitt and some others: he excited the greatest curiosity and of course was much fêtéd ... the abominable fogs which we have had these last three or four days .... we hunt the Stags & Wild Boars in the same great & magnificent style that I believe you remember [Lord Jersey wrote to Lady Spencer] ... our poor beagles will appear wonderfully quiet after this.[117]

There is also a letter from Lady Jersey sent whilst she was at Fontainebleau in the Chatsworth archives, this one addressed to Georgiana Devonshire. It has been retrospectively dated to the following year, 1784, but taking its content with that of the letter from Lord Jersey just quoted (both refer to the Jerseys arriving in Fontainebleau on 13 October), it is clear that its correct date is 1783 so as to refer to the same visit. It is interesting to read in this letter what Lady Jersey thought worthy of mention:

> The Com D'Artois is to lend me horses to hunt ... I am very well lodged in Msr de Chalons apartment, it adjoins the castle & opens into the gardens ... They will spoil me here ... This place grows more & more delightful, but the hurry is not to be conceived ... it is impossible to conceive anything so pleasant as the Queen's mannner, she improves upon acquaintance astonishingly ...[118]

Despite all of this, it seems Walpole was right. Writing after the Jerseys had returned to England, Miss Lloyd told Countess Spencer: 'Lord Trentham ... hears Lady Jersey was not admired at Paris, they only said she was very tolerable considering she had had so many children.'[119]

This may have been only malice but, if it was true, a proud Frances Jersey would not have enjoyed it and, even if it was not, not the telling of it either.

Whilst the Jerseys had set off to France, Lord Carlisle had retired to Castle Howard for the summer. On this occasion, an inveterate gambler like so many of his contemporaries, the Earl doubtless did so in a happy frame of mind as, in Lady Mary Coke's words, he was 'five and twenty thousand pounds the richer from play within these few months'.[120]

That enormous sum, though, was not sufficient to detain him long in Yorkshire and his early return to London in October, coincidentally or not at about the same time the Jerseys arrived back from France, provoked comment from Lady Mary Coke: 'Lord and Lady Carlisle are come to Town. I don't think they can be fatigued with the Country for I believe they have not been there above two months.'[121]

Given her earlier comments, Lady Mary Coke clearly did not think the timing of the Earl's return to London was a coincidence. In that supposition she was probably right – and too in supposing that the Countess's campaign was now proving to be a success.

Whether or not that is right, the Jerseys' return to England from France was certainly a time of great change, and for Lord Jersey great sadness. On 31 October 1783, Lord Spencer, who had long struggled with ill-health, died in Bath. Lord Jersey felt this a very heavy blow, so heavy as to need the doctor to be summoned, as Lady Jersey said, writing to Mrs Howe and asking her to tell Lady Spencer, that her husband would 'be happy to go to her any morng she will appoint, for both their sakes I hope it will be soon – he is better Warren came, & is not prescribed'.[122]

Lord Jersey was still struggling from his friend's death at the end of November, when the new Lord Spencer asked the Earl to introduce him into the House of Lords. The now Dowager Countess Spencer wrote to her son: 'you cannot imagine how pleased he [Lord Jersey] is with your intention in thinking of him, & he has beg'd me to say it as strongly as possible & how glad he should be to do it if he was able – but that his spirits were not equal to it, & indeed I do not believe he could go through it.[123]

The second change concerned William Fawkener. As Georgiana Devonshire wrote to her mother early in January 1784: 'I will not mention anything about Fawkener's whim, I might say to him what the King of France did to the D. of Chartres: *Tout ce que vous faites, mon cousin, est extraordinaire*.'[124]

The 'whim' was that on 29 January 1784 Fawkener married Georgiana Devonshire's cousin, Georgiana Ann Poyntz, known as Jockey. The marriage was to prove a disaster. Not only did it raise eyebrows at the time but also after the event it was reported to be 'much against [the bride's] inclination, both because he was considerably older, and on account of a scandalous report which is said to have reached her ears that he (who was one of the most fashionable men of the day) had been engaged in an intrigue with her mother about the year of her birth'.[125]

In little more than two years the great cuckolder was himself cuckolded. The new Mrs Fawkener eloped with Lord John Townshend, Fawkener and Townshend fought a duel in Hyde Park, and Fawkener was awarded £5,000 damages against Townshend for 'criminal conversation' or adultery. By 1787 the Fawkeners were divorced.[126] Whilst Georgiana Devonshire was godmother to Jockey's first child, Jockey's second marriage was not a success either.[127]

Whilst much of that lay in the future, Fawkener's marriage enabled Lord Glenbervie to write that 'Lord Carlisle ... replaced William F——r, when he discarded [Lady Jersey] to marry Miss Poyntz and to be afterwards treated by her as he treated Lord J and many other husbands'.[128]

Although this drollery was not entirely true, Lord Carlisle did now possess the field and so became the *amant en titre* of Frances Jersey.

9

The Westminster Election and a New Lover

Once more it was Frances Jersey, ever confident of her attractions, who had taken the initiative to start her affair with the Earl of Carlisle. Early in 1784 she continued her campaign against a now clearly not unwilling Earl. There is a charming, and flirtatious, letter from her to the Earl in the Castle Howard archives which may mark the final establishment of the affair after some months of hesitation, possibly prompted by the fact of Fawkener's marriage. Dated only 'February the 19th', intriguingly it is the only letter from Frances Jersey which survives in the whole of those archives despite an affair lasting nearly a decade. It goes:

> I should have wrote to you long ago, but I took a panick at the thoughts of anybody seeing my letter, for I can'd write nonsense with great comfort to you which I should not like to have read by others, & if you will promise me upon your honor never to show my letters, you shall hear from me often enough ... pray write to me soon & tell me a great deal about yourself.
>
> Ever Yrs Sincerely F. J.[1]

Presumably the Earl did write back soon; of his own admission he was not one to resist temptation. At a time when sexual activity was positively prescribed on medical grounds, and the retention of semen believed to be harmful, he once confessed fear of an attack of gout on the grounds of living too chaste a life, adding 'it is not a common fault with me'.[2] Certainly an affair did indeed now commence between the Earl and the captivating Countess, which was to last many years and to produce at least one child.

Nathaniel Wraxall, traveller and memoirist (or perhaps simply gossip), wrote in 1784 of the comparative virtues of the great beauties of the time, describing the Countess of Jersey as having 'irresistible seduction and fascination'.[3] An astute and intelligent lady, she could play different parts to suit different occasions and audiences artfully, although – and we shall see more of this – not without a degree of self-deception or serious misjudgements.

Thus Lord Harcourt wrote in January that year:

> Ly Jersey dined with us & brought Ld Villiers, whom I conveyed to the Opera, she was very pleasant, & not so terribly political as she generally has been of late; why she has taken up this new character I cannot guess, unless it be in imitation of her *chaste* friend Mme de Polignac, who in more senses of the word than one, is a very intriguing and very absurd woman; nor can I see without wonder that a woman of Ly J's understanding should persuade herself that she is in the secrets of a party, when it is really impossible that she should be entrusted with them, and when, on the contrary, I am apt to suspect that somebody, seeing her weakness, is [deceiving?] her, to make her look ridiculous.[4]

Similarly, he wrote later in the month: 'Today I was at the Drawing Room, and Ly J & Mr Cholmondley dined with us; she met him at her request, that she might talk about France, & talk of it she did increasingly, so that Ly H and myself could bear no part in the conversation.'[5]

Again he wrote in April: 'Lady Jersey and Mr Whitehead dined with us; she chose to be captivating, and of course was so.'[6]

Frances Jersey was certainly captivating and charming, as well as clever, but she was also increasingly self-centred and domineering whilst lacking in both judgment and discretion. She enjoyed provoking a reaction to an extent which went beyond the mischievous. All of these weaknesses grew ever more apparent with the passing of the years.

At this time the Harcourts were still intimates of the Jerseys, although in the course of time, like many of Frances Jersey's relationships, this would change – in this case dramatically. Harcourt, having previously been a republican, was in 1784 becoming a courtier and, as an amused Horace Walpole recorded, 'it made me smile indeed that Lord Harcourt on his change had given away his ring of Brutus [the republican assassin of Julius Caesar] to the Jersey's little boy,' the same Lord Villiers.[7]

By February Lord Jersey wrote: 'Great assemblies are beginning; Ly Amhersts tomorrow, D'adhemar's [the French Ambassador] on Thursday, the Prince of Wales's on Friday and his Levee on Saturday Morng.' The Prince of Wales's assembly was, he later wrote, 'magnificent, and not formal, for the sort of thing'.[8]

The Jerseys made their contribution to the round of parties. Lord Harcourt wrote sardonically to Lady Spencer later that month describing the Countess and her performance in Society:

> I am going to dine at Ld Jersey's, where the company is not appointed to meet till 6 o'clock, as she cannot endure to dine earlier. What a strange place this London is, where to rise to the rank of good company a woman must keep late hours, be very impertinent and ill bred, and make everybody wait for her, and if she wants to get a step higher & to be at the head of anything, must have the parade of a gallant, if not the reality of one.

He went on, now tongue-in-cheek, to advise Georgiana Devonshire's mother that if Georgiana wanted to keep her leading place in Society she should copy Lady Jersey and commit adultery, 'or [be] suspected of it, for to cover the *sin* of so many virtues she must have the merit of some fashionable glaring vice, or her reign will soon expire'.[9]

At the time, Georgiana – whose own adultery was not long in coming – was actually at Chatsworth, lonely and miserable following money problems from her gambling, her father's death and the death of a baby.[10] She confessed to her mother: 'I feel a dread of going to London, tho' Lady Melbourne, whom I love, and Ly Jersey whose society is so remarkably amusing, wd certainly do their best to entertain and dissipate me.'[11]

Lady Melbourne was of a kind with Frances Jersey, 'beautiful, clever and ruthless'. She was reputed to have been party to an arrangement under which her lover, George Hanger, later Lord Coleraine, 'sold' her to Lord Egremont for £13,000 with, so it is said, her getting some of the proceeds.[12]

In due course, Lord Harcourt described the Jerseys' dinner to Lady Spencer and in so doing also further illuminated his hostess's character:

> The dinner on Friday, as a dinner was very handsome [he wrote], and in other respects neither formal nor disagreeable, but the Lady of the House and myself had not much conversation & since I gave her a contemptuous rap in return for a flippant scratch, she has or I think she has looked shy on me, for I am one of the few either sex who neither court nor fear her.[13]

So a few more words of observation encapsulate the Countess: amusing, mischievous and dissipated, impertinent and ill-bred in a refined society, but despite all that both courted and feared.

Georgiana Devonshire did eventually come to town in mid-March. Before arriving she told her sister Harriet Duncannon that she would be staying at home on the day of her arrival, 'all the evening and see only you & Peste and [some others] ... Peste has ordered an Eveg gown for me but I have nothing but my smock for the morning ...', 'Peste', or Plague, alongside 'the Infernal', being one of her nicknames for Lady Jersey.[14] When she did arrive, she told her mother that she 'saw Ly Jersey who looked beautiful, she had been at Ly Betty Dobrées & was going to a Ball at Dadhemars', the spelling of whose name varies considerably even by the standards of those times.[15]

Despite the nicknames and some unease, Georgiana clearly continued on amiable enough terms with Frances Jersey, not only because the evening gown had been ordered for her by Lady Jersey but also because the day after Georgiana's arrival, as she told her mother, 'I went to the opera with Lady Jersey and my sister, [to see] the *Reine de Golconde*, it was very pretty.'[16] Nevertheless the dominant, if not domineering, role of Lady Jersey in that relationship is illustrated in an undated letter from the Duchess to Lady Melbourne:

> I expect with patience to hear from you, but don't put anything about Davé [?] in yr letters in case by any accident Ly Jersey might insist on seeing

> them – however I shan't let her if I can help it, so pray tell me all you know about Lubin, Bess and the adorable schoolboy.[17]

Very soon, though, politics were going to take a dramatic turn so that electioneering, rather than evening gowns, opera and assemblies, would be the focus of Society. Before then much of the Jersey family were to be struck down by illness of a familiar kind.

At the end of March, Lord Jersey reported: 'Lady J has been confined ever since Wednesday with a sore throat, & more even than a little fever; that has abated, but she is extremely low, & out of spirits.' The next day Villiers was back home from school at Harrow 'very sick, & is now in bed with a violent fever and sore throat: Lady J has not been out yet'. The day after that, the report was: 'George has been very ill these last days of a fever & ulcerated sore throat; it seems now to have taken the turn & he will probably mend fast: that the others may not catch it is to be hoped, but they have been all together.' The hope was not to be fulfilled. Within a week, Lord Jersey noted: 'At present I am in a fidget (unreasonably) abt one of my girls who has caught George's throat & we are endeavoring if possible to prevent its going so bad as his was …' Still, these events were not unqualified bad news. Another wave of French visitors was pouring into London and the various illnesses, which anyway were soon on the mend, gave the Earl the welcome opportunity 'to get out of their reach'.[18]

Political drama then ensued. On 25 March 1784, George III dissolved Parliament. This was the culmination of a political struggle between power and favour. The Whigs in the form of Charles James Fox represented power in that he controlled a majority in Parliament. The king, however, detested Fox and the Whigs. Pitt and the Tories represented the favour which the king bestowed upon them even in opposition. The king, by dissolving Parliament, sought to destroy Fox's power. A general election followed and, in the contest for the two seats for the Westminster constituency, Fox stood for the Whig interest against Hood and Wray. Society polarised into two camps behind the candidates, and over the two months the election lasted they actively and vividly did all they could to get their own men elected. During this period the Westminster election dominated both the newspapers and Society. The Devonshire House Circle being ardently Whiggish at its core threw itself behind Fox – and this included the ladies.[19]

There was a strong tradition of electoral canvassing by ladies in eighteenth-century Britain. For example, in 1767 Lady Susan Bunbury canvassed most effectively for her husband in Morpeth. In the following year, Lady Glyn, canvassing for her husband in Coventry, 'courageously visited every voter personally on his behalf', and in 1774 Lady Craven was canvassing, also in Coventry, during the election there.[20] In fact, 'women of rank were expected to participate in the political life of the nation … [and] to use the power at their disposal.'[21] This is exactly what happened in the Westminster election of 1784.

The ladies set to work with great energy. In the words of Nathaniel Wraxall, 'Neither entreaties nor promises were spared. In some instances even personal carreses [*sic*] were said to have been permitted, in order to prevail upon the surly or inflexible.' Famously, Georgiana Devonshire was said to have promised a butcher a kiss in exchange for his vote.[22]

The election was a bearpit. Of it, the soldier, beau and eccentric (and former lover of Lady Melbourne) George Hanger wrote:

> No one, in my humble opinion, has seen *real-life* or can know of it, unless he has taken an active part in the contested election for Westminster. In no school can a man be taught a better lesson of human life than at a contested Westminster election: there he can view human nature in her basest attire; riot, murder, and drunkenness are the order of the day and bribery and perjury walk hand in hand.[23]

A more modern description tells of Westminster being littered in a deluge of handbills, encounters on the hustings being so fractious that the hustings themselves on occasion gave way, the crowds on the streets being frequently violent and hundreds of constables being brought into Westminster from all over London in a vain attempt to keep order.[24]

Mrs Papendiek, a keeper of the wardrobe to the Queen, also wrote eloquently of the election, describing the procession before polling: 'entertained indeed we were, if it may be so called. Fighting, drumming, screaming, singing, marrowboning, hooting, hurrahing, &c were going on the whole time. Elegant carriages passed, Fox in that of the Prince Wales, with dress liveries, fox-tails, ribbons, flowers &c.'[25]

The leader of the female cohort in the election for the Whigs was Georgiana Devonshire. She was, though, not alone and she was joined by many other women on both sides of the political aisle – even if she attracted more attention and more criticism than any other.[26] Thus Mary Hamilton tells of severe strictures being passed on the Duchess's behaviour and describes meeting her 'in her coach with a mob around her canvassing in the Strand for Mr Fox; what a pity that any of our sex should ever forget what is due to female delicacy. The Scenes the Dss has been in lately, were they noted down, would not gain credit by those who were not in London at the time of the Election.'[27]

Those who joined Georgiana Devonshire in the campaign included her sister Lady Duncannon, the Duchess of Portland, Lady Carlisle, Mrs Bouverie, the three Ladies Waldegrave and others, including, it is commonly said, Lady Jersey.[28] Indeed it would be very untypical if Frances Jersey had not participated in the election to some extent at least, being a member of Georgiana's set and a friend of hers and given her excitement-seeking character. It is more than likely, too, that she was one of those who appeared at the opera 'decorated with Fox's tails' as a show of support.[29] The evidence is, though, that Frances Jersey's participation in the Westminster election was marginal – decorative rather than substantive, probably disdaining the vulgarity which featured so largely in the process.

This is firstly because there is no mention of her participation in the 400 or so pages of the contemporaneous *History of the Westminster*

Election containing every material occurrence from its commecement [*sic*] *on the first of April to the final close of the poll*, published in 1784. Indeed the first mention of Lady Jersey in that work appears on page 377 in the context of the Prince of Wales' celebratory fête after the poll had closed. On the other hand, in the preceding pages many other ladies are mentioned by name or clearly identified as being actively involved. These include not only Georgiana Devonshire and Lady Duncannon, but also the Ladies Waldegrave, Mrs Bouverie, the Duchess of Portland and Dowager Duchess of Portland, the Dowager Duchess of Bedford, Lady Grosvenor, Lady Dornhoff, Lady Cr[aven], Lady Worsley, Lady A——r, Mrs S——n, Lady Sal–sb–y, Lady Beauchamp, the Countess of Carlisle, the Duchess of Rutland, Lady Willoughby, the Duchess of Ancaster, Lady Margaret F——e, Lady Southhampton and Mrs Hobart. Whilst there are periodic references such as to the 'Rt Hon Beauty', the 'canvassing Countesses', and 'Countess ——', it is inconceivable, given Lady Jersey's public profile, that had she been actively involved she would not also be mentioned by name or otherwise identified.

The second reason is that there are no contemporary references elsewhere to Lady Jersey having actively participated in the campaign and, specifically, none at all in the correspondence – admittedly much reduced from its norm during the election – of Georgiana Devonshire or that of Frances Jersey's husband over the period of the election. The Earl in particular confines himself to comments such as the 'gay part of the world have been reduced this week to small Cribbage parties',[30] commenting disparagingly on the French Ambassador's Ball,[31] and writing on 15 May that 'the Westminster election is thank God nearly over ... London goes on as usual, Assemblies and suppers ... and so forth'.[32]

When Fox ultimately triumphed on 17 May the celebrations were manifold. After Fox's triumphal procession that day of some thirty coaches whose destination was Devonshire House, a breakfast at Brooks's was planned 'for the ladies', and on 18 May the Prince of Wales entertained 650 people to a morning fête at his home, Carlton House, to celebrate Fox's victory.[33] There were nine marquees and four Bands at the fête, with the company dancing 'country dances and cotillions'. The Prince of Wales opened the dancing with the Duchess of Devonshire and, as a sign for the future, amongst others dancing were Lady Jersey with the Earl of Carlisle.

Many of those at the fête, including the Prince and Lord and Lady Jersey, went on to a celebratory ball at Mrs Crewe's that evening, many of the guests sporting Fox's colours of buff and blue – Fox had made his name as champion of the rebellious American colonies and had taken to wearing the buff and blue of the American forces, a blue jacket and a buff waistcoat.[34] After the toasts, Lady Jersey, the Duchess of Portland and Lord North who were in an upper room called upon Captain Morris to join them to sing 'The Baby and Nurse' and then all returned to the main room where he sang some more with a 'spirit that made every fair eye in the room dance with delight. In short never was an evening spent so much true pleasure and comfort.'[35]

After the excitements of the election, life returned to normal, although the Prince of Wales seemed to have acquired a taste for entertaining. In the last week of May, Lord Jersey told Lady Spencer he had a 'magnificent breakfast at Carlton House, & it was extended to a dinner Ball & supper', and only a few days later the Jerseys were both at a Ball at Carlton House.[36]

Thereafter there was a temporary respite at Middleton (where it was so cold that on Midsummer's day they still had fires burning) before 'an expected invasion of foreigners' was due.[37] As it happened, the invasion of French did not materialise, although the Duke du Lauzun did come to stay, along with the Earl of Carlisle, before Frances Jersey left Middleton in mid-July to meet Mme de Coigny in Brighton.[38]

This visit to Middleton by Lord Carlisle is significant. It was the first time he is recorded as a guest of the Jerseys. One imagines that it was at the initiative of the Countess; the Carlisles had not previously featured in the Jerseys' circle. It was soon to be followed by the first recorded visit by the Jerseys to Lord Carlisle's seat in Yorkshire, Castle Howard.

Before that visit, Lady Charlotte Villiers was very ill with 'a most violent fever' in August.[39] In September, Frances Jersey was 'confined for some days with a rheumatic pain in her face & fever, and she is now [wrote Lord Jersey at the time] at this moment complaining heavily of a most acute relapse'.[40] And then there was a stay at Chatsworth, where Lord Jersey was to make something of a fool of himself.

From there in September, Lord Jersey wrote to Lady Spencer: 'We arrived late in the evening yesterday ... in our way we accidentally, by meeting Lady Aylesford on the road lay one night at Packington [Hall, the Earl of Aylesford's seat in Warwickshire] ... the house is an excellent one and he lives excellently.' Lord Jersey went on to bemoan the inconvenience caused on the journey as a result of 'the Perch of Lady Jersey's Chaise breaking short in two in Matlock town, & besides the inconvenience of leaving it there, the moving all the bundles, parcels, hat boxes & c & c in such a gaping place before so many spectators late in the evening is always a disagreeable ceremony enough'.[41]

To add to their discomfiture Frances Jersey was still not well. As Georgiana Devonshire commented on the Jerseys' arrival at Chatsworth, 'she is far from looking or being well & I think has many dropsical symptoms.'[42]

Amongst the company at Chatsworth was the beautiful twenty-six-year-old Lady Elizabeth Foster, friend and confidante of both the Devonshires. Several of the company of 'Lord Jersey, Sir William Jones [an elderly orientalist], Colonel Crawford, witty Mr Hare and the Duke himself ... swarmed around the alluring honeypot' that was Bess Foster.[43] Bess Foster was the daughter of the Earl of Bristol, who went on to be the mistress of the Duke of Devonshire, forming part of a famous *ménage à trois* at Chatsworth before marrying the Duke after Georgiana's death.

Writing to her mother on 13 September, Georgiana Devonshire said of this:

> Poor Lord Jersey got very drunk, but we agreed not to tease him about it as he went to bed. You know he cannot bear a joke, so don't ever tell him, but he really is quite fallen in love with Ly Eliz.

A week later, she told her mother that 'Sr Wm has succeeded Ld Jersey in being lover of Ly Eliz, he is quite desparate, I tell her she is like Susannah tempted by the Elders', because of the difference in age between Elizabeth Foster and her admirers.[44]

After a week at Chatsworth, the Jerseys left for a short stay with Lord Fitzwilliam at Wentworth Woodhouse, his spectacular house in Yorkshire which boasts the longest front of any house in the country; from 'thence [wrote Lord Jersey] we shall go on to Castle Howard. Lady J never having seen these places it will be no fatigue to her but I own seems to me an unconquerable journey.' 'Lady J' had more reasons than common interest, though, to enjoy the journey to visit Lord Carlisle.[45] Even the Earl would probably not find the journey unconquerable because since the 1750s such journeys were much easier as a result of the trunk roads connecting London with major cities such as York having been turnpiked. As a result, for example, the journey to Bath which had taken 50 hours in 1750 took a mere 16 in 1800.[46]

Clearly the normally astute Lady Spencer had not yet made any connection between Lord Carlisle and Frances Jersey, for her dismissive comment on the Jerseys' departure from Chatsworth was 'Lord Jersey (how can he be so silly) gives a very moderate account of Miss Lloyd ... I should think from what he says he is in a decline – what are he & Lady Jersey rambling about & why do they go so far North?'[47]

Three days after their arrival at Castle Howard, Lord Jersey was writing to Lady Spencer: 'Our landlord has a fit of the Gout ... There is no company but ourselves & that will make it awkward if his gout should continue.' Clearly, therefore, so far as the Lady Jersey and Lord Carlisle were concerned there was only one object to the visit. It is easy to speculate, too, that an 'attack of the gout' enabled Lord Carlisle to disappear to his rooms whenever it suited him and Lady Jersey to follow him. As to the *naiveté* of Lord Jersey, one struggles for words.

In the meantime, Lord Jersey mused about the houses he was staying at, Wentworth Woodhouse and Castle Howard. Little needs to be said about the latter, but the former, a lesser-known eighteenth-century masterpiece, was the largest non-royal residence in Europe. '[A]ll these seats [wrote Lord Jersey] have had & demand great fortunes to contribute to the greatness & enjoyment of them, & the idea of the contrary raises rather a melancholy reflexion in one's mind.' He went on, in a more down-to-earth manner, to say that 'they tell me Lady J's chaise will not reach home, it has already broken down once; and at this distance what is to be done? I seriously fear it will happen again'.[48]

At the end of September, Lord Jersey was again writing to Lady Spencer from Castle Howard: 'I shall leave this place in a few days, but I am rather stopped by Lady Jersey's Chaise being broken to Pieces, the length of this journey & it's [*sic*] age have not agreed at all, & I must wait till it is mended.'[49]

Whether it was in fact the broken chaise, Lady Jersey's use of that as an excuse to prolong their stay, or Lord Carlisle's recovery from gout which delayed their departure will remain unclear since they seem to have got home without the chaise.[50] By 8 October they were back at Middleton where the ever gloomy Lord Jersey was still bemoaning the chaise's absence – 'for it is broken entirely to pieces, so as I believe scarcely to make its appearance again' – and continued to complain of the unforeseen inconvenience it had caused, although later that month he was able to write that 'I have contrived to set it up on its legs again' so that it might be able to get back to London.[51]

When returned to Middleton for the winter, the children were much involved. In October, Lord Jersey wrote that

> we have been diverting ourselves & the Children with letting [off some balloons], one to be sure took fire, to our great disgrace, & the disappointment of the Village, but another mounted yesterday to admiration ... for the heighth [*sic*] it rose was beyond our Eyes, & tho' we had our horses ready & pursued it as hard as we could over open country, it beat us entirely & we are still at a loss to know where it has fallen. It was [fuelled?] by a spunge dipped in spirits of wine.[52]

The following month, when the Harcourts along with Lord Charles Spencer and Lady Clermont were staying with them, the children were putting on 'a puppet show: it is now finished, & we have had last night a regular representation to a full house. They play the puppets themselves & I assure you succeed very well. The dance of *Le Deserteur* is one of the pieces, & Charlotte speaks a Prologue', said his proud Lordship.[53]

These family entertainments were interrupted by balls given by their neighbours, the Fermors at Tusmore and the Marlboroughs at Blenheim. Lord Jersey described the Marlboroughs' second ball, at Christmas, as 'magnificent'.[54]

Frances Jersey was clearly enjoying herself too once back in London in January, prompting Lady Mary Coke to comment acidly: 'The Duchess of Devonshire is not yet come to Town but her friend Lady Jersey is, & going on as usual.'[55]

But then it was the turn of Lord Villiers and, probably, Lady Elizabeth to be inoculated against smallpox, with the consequence, once more, that the Jerseys were largely confined to home for fear of infection.[56] This, at least in the eyes of Lord Jersey, was not without its advantages.

Early in the New Year of 1785, the Prince of Wales had got into the routine of prevailing upon people to hold balls to which, of course, he was to be invited. Lord Jersey, in his typical manner, fearful that he would become one of the chosen individuals, was hopeful that he would 'find some loophole to decline the honor; the children had been confined at a lucky time'. Their infectiousness provided just the excuse he needed.[57]

That did not, though, prevent the Prince of Wales attending on the Jerseys at home. Writing at the end of February Lord Jersey said, 'the Gay world seems worn out almost with the Balls & Suppers of last week & I say *tant mieux* – the Pce of W called upon Lady J for a moment last night and I do not think his looks shew much disposition to more dancing.'[58]

The Jerseys were now beginning to live increasingly separate lives. In January 1785, Lady Jersey went by herself to Bath, leaving her husband to 'move to town with all the children, &c' by himself after which he was proposing to go to Euston 'for an in-definite period'.[59] Soon too the Countess would routinely stay in London after he and the children had left for the summer, for reasons we can work out.

Meanwhile, there was once more trouble with the Spencers as Frances Jersey continued to push the boundaries of respectability. In March, the young Lord Spencer wrote to his mother:

> I have some how or other seen very little of [Lord Jersey] since I came to town & I am afraid he thinks so; I am really under a little difficulty about it, for if it was only himself there is nobody almost than I should like to see more of, & for whom on many accounts I have more sincere regards, but as there is a Lady in the case who is I think *entre nous* more uncultivatable (if you will accept the word) than ever, it makes it very difficult to me to know how to separate them.[60]

The problem was clearly Frances Jersey, whatever 'uncultivatable' meant in practice (perhaps irredeemable). The result was twofold. First, to avoid seeing her Lord Spencer also had to avoid seeing Lord Jersey, and the Earl could see that happening. Second, whether out of loyalty or otherwise, there was friction between the Earl and Lady Spencer. At the end of April, Lord Jersey writing to Lady Spencer was complaining of 'the unfortunate loss I have lately had. It is of a nature to be daily felt, nay hourly, from the long habit of intimacy, a habit of 40 years which has subsisted between us; but I do & will endeavour to have recourse to your good advice.'[61]

The friction did not appear to last long, at least in his wife's absence, since in May Lady Spencer was inviting Lord Jersey to join a fishing party 'at Farmer Floyd's'.[62]

In the middle of June the family, or most of it, returned to Middleton for the summer, Lord Jersey writing on 23 June that 'we have been here by ourselves & keeping what is called children's hours, but it has been very comfortable' and relating that they had enjoyed some good carp fishing in the ponds whilst there.[63] Lady Jersey, though, in accordance with what was now her practice, was still in town on 30 June.[64] She was still there a fortnight later when Lord Jersey had to rush up to London on account of her being ill. He said 'she was seized with a putrid sore throat on Thursday, but the Disorder has been of the easiest sort & she is now allowed to take the air, but the Doctor Warren says she is too infectious to be allowed to go to her Children'.[65]

It is clear Lady Jersey stayed in London to pursue her affair with Lord Carlisle. There is some interesting arithmetic to be done. The Jerseys' next daughter, Lady Fanny Villiers, was to be born on 15 April 1786, which implies a date of conception of July 1785. It seems that between mid-June 1785 and 7 July 1785, the date (apparently) when Lady Jersey was laid low by her illness, Lord and Lady Jersey were never in the same place at the same time, whilst it is reasonable to speculate that conception took place on or prior to 7 July. Add to this the fact of the known affair of Lady Jersey with Lord Carlisle, and the contents of a letter dated 4 October 1802 from the Countess of Bessborough to Lady Holland, and the conclusion is clear. In that letter, after referring to Lady Fanny Villiers' forthcoming marriage to John Ponsonby, Lady Bessborough continued: 'Ly Fanny Villiers ... is indecently like Ld Morpeth'.[66]

Since Lord Morpeth was the eldest son and heir of Lord Carlisle, Lady Fanny's parentage is clear, as are the opportunities afforded to Lady Jersey whilst staying in London without her husband. One wonders whether Lord Jersey also did the arithmetic but it is probable that he did not need to.

Whilst little was said in public, Lady Jersey's affair with Lord Carlisle was public knowledge. This doubtless included his wife who, in the manner of the times, ignored it to such an extent that in September Lady Jersey spent more than a week staying with Lady Carlisle at Downe Place, the Carlisles' house in the country.[67] In Dr Johnston's words, such was the acceptance of lack of chastity of husbands in those times that 'wise married women don't trouble themselves about infidelity in their husbands ... the man imposes no bastards upon his wife'.[68]

10

A Growing Family and Growing Ill-repute

The 1780s saw an increase both in the Jersey family and in the ill-repute of the Countess herself. They also witnessed the final disintegration of the long since brittle relationship between Frances Jersey and her husband's oldest friend, Countess Spencer.

Both Lord and Lady Jersey doted on and were proud of the children, whoever their father. As we have seen, they were not alone in bringing up children of different paternity without any distinction between them. Further, all the Jersey daughters were to become great beauties. Lord Melbourne, who was of age with them, described them to Queen Victoria many years later as 'all very handsome', picking out in particular Lady Sarah as being just that and Lady Fanny as being 'very pretty'.[1] With the benefit of hindsight he was much less complimentary about their characters. With the sole exception of Lady Harriet, whom he described as 'much the cleverest', the rest were condemned as 'very foolish'.[2]

Naturally, the Countess in particular was diligent in the pursuit of the best marriages for all of them. The Jerseys were anxious, too, that their friends should approve of the children. When writing to Lady Spencer in September 1785 to congratulate her on Georgiana Devonshire giving birth to a daughter, Frances Jersey invited Lady Spencer to Middleton, adding 'I am sure you will be pleased with all my children, & I will be quite proud of showing my two eldest Girls, to you, for I know you will think them perfectly sensible, good humor'd and unaffected creatures'.[3] In January 1786, Lady Spencer having just fulfilled Lord Jersey's long-held ambition for her to meet his growing son again, Lord Jersey wrote after giving her other news: 'I cannot finish this without adding how much satisfaction I received from your approbation of George's behaviour; it ought & I am sure will encourage him to grow up with the same manners' – he had displayed on an expedition with the Countess.[4]

A few days after Lord Jersey's letter, Countess Spencer had written to Georgiana Devonshire a letter which showed that there were much deeper and nastier undercurrents at play. It showed, too, Lady Jersey in a very different light to the role she had played over many years, and that any pretence of warmth between her and Countess Spencer was at an end. As Lady Spencer wrote:

> Ly Jersey came to me yesterday & sat a good whilst, she talked of her children who I commended as every Lady must but she went on saying so much of her care of them ... that I could not help saying it was a subject which always affected me & made me inclined to say things that were unpleasant & that I had better let alone ...

In short, that Lady Jersey's selfish and disreputable behaviour was tantamount to cruelty to her children, so difficult did it make their lives.

Lady Jersey's response was both immediate and angry, as Lady Spencer continued:

> Upon which she burst into such outrageous hysterical crying & said I must not such say any hard things to her now, that instead of assurancing me with pity & tenderness as she generally does I felt the hardness she reproached me with & great indignation at the idea, that all her fondness for her children could not prevent her injuring them in a thousand ways – by disobliging behaviour which has made enemies of every lady she knows & a conduct that will soon make her as despicable as she is infamous.[5]

So on both sides the charade was over and both presented their real opinions. No longer was Lady Jersey mollifying and submissive, rather she was hard and indignant to someone who was not of her kind. For her part, Lady Spencer thought Frances Jersey unpleasant, disreputable and, by indulging herself indiscriminately, cruel and embarrassing to her children, though this was to prove minor compared with what was to follow; her disapproval and dislike of Frances Jersey was patent. The message was reinforced two years later when, unexpectedly, Countess Spencer encountered Lord and Lady Jersey with their three eldest daughters at a house party. She described to Georgiana what happened:

> She [Lady Jersey] ran up to me & kissed me, & I am such a fool that I never can help feeling *attendré* when any thing I have long known comes in my way and seems glad to see me – I took an opportunity whilst she was alone at breakfast of just asking her how she did & saying I could not help feeling glad to see her. She said she had her doubts of that & seemed inclined to ride the high horse, upon which I said she was quite at liberty to think what she pleased, but she stopped me, insisted on shaking hands with me & so we parted.[6]

So that was the end of that. Frances Jersey no longer cared what Lady Spencer thought and was happy to make that clear. The long pretence was over. Whilst it was not yet also the end of Frances Jersey's relationship with

Georgiana Devonshire that too would follow before long, though for some time it was to be a qualified rupture. The Earl's relationship with Lady Spencer survived for the time being but from here it too would eventually succumb to Lady Spencer's now acknowledged disapproval, and dislike, of his wife.

Unaware of these angry undercurrents, the Earl had added some bad news in the postscript to his otherwise blithe and contented letter: 'Augustus has been extremely ill, & was yesterday in a dangerous state'. Lord Jersey was a pessimist by nature but this illness was to dog Augustus for some considerable period. Still, in February Augustus (was he called that rather than by his first name in order to avoid associations?) received some, in a sense, better news on the death of his kinswoman Lady Vernon.

Louisa Barbara, Lady Vernon, was the daughter of the 4th and last Lord Mansell and granddaughter of the 2nd Earl of Jersey and so was second cousin to Lord Jersey. In her will of 5 August 1783 she had left to young William Augustus Villiers, subject to life interests first for her husband and then for her uncle Lord Clarendon, an estate in the Vale of Glamorgan in South Wales known as Briton Ferry, which had descended to her through the Mansell family. Lady Vernon died on 1 January 1786 – the Earl of Clarendon was to die later that year – so that young William's inheritance was now certain.[7]

It has been estimated from the sale catalogues and tithe apportionments of the early nineteenth century that in 1774 the Briton Ferry estate amounted to 3,200 acres.[8] Lord Jersey certainly was able to write to Lady Spencer in February 1786:

> You have heard without doubt that Lady Vernon is dead, & I understand that by her will, the Estate of Briton-Ferry (a very considerable property) is left to my second son, after the death of Lord Vernon and Lord Clarendon.[9]

In writing to her son the same day, Lady Spencer put a figure on this, saying 'Ly Vernon wife to present Lord has left Ld Jerseys 2nd son an estate of £3,000 a year after Lord Vernon's death'.[10] The only price to be paid was that the will required Augustus to change his surname to Mansell.

The other Villiers children were also 'tolerably well'. Three-year-old Elizabeth had a muscular or nerve problem with her face which was being treated with some success, as Lord Jersey said to Lady Spencer:

> I am certain you will be glad to hear confirmed by me the sudden and good effects of the Electricity on Elizth; she is in a manner quite well, & a few times more I think will strengthen her eyelid intirely; that being the only part that now remains a little weak.[11]

As to George, having just collected him from Harrow, in April Lord Jersey commented that he 'is not only improved in growth … But he seems to think & conduct himself with more notions of right & wrong than I believe comes within the reflexion of boys of his age; in short I am quite pleased with him.'[12]

Meanwhile, Lady Jersey's time was approaching, not without some impatience on the part of her husband who seemed to think the baby overdue (perhaps he thought that the baby had been conceived before he left London and so was his rather than Lord Carlisle's) and wanted to get on with his own pursuits.[13] Eventually, on 15 April 1786 he was able to write: 'This morning Lady J added another female to the family, & she is herself as well as can be expected.'[14]

The new female was, of course, Lady Fanny Villiers.

One of the consequences of Frances Jersey's confinement was that Lord Jersey had to escort his elder, now growing up, daughters to various balls which otherwise, unchaperoned, they could not attend. On 9 May he was bemoaning that there were so many balls and assemblies that 'it will be scarcely be possible [to] *assist* at them all ... tonight I attend my Children first to their Ball at Ly Camelford's & afterwards I shall go to one at Lady Melbourne's'.[15]

In the summer, the family went in the normal way to Middleton.[16] Once more, though, Lady Jersey stayed on in London for some time after the rest of the family had gone, but on this occasion no baby was to result.[17] When at Middleton, Lord Jersey spent a day at Nuneham before going to The Grove and then on to Holywell to see Lady Spencer.[18] The previous September some of the royal family had stayed with the Harcourts at Nuneham – and there is a telling story told by one of them, Prince Ernest, the fourteen-year-old future King of Hanover, who slept in a room with a yellow damask bed, of which he said: 'Beautiful Lady Jersey has that Room when she is here. I suppose it is a great favour to let me have it; I fancy strangers in general are not allowed to sleep in it ...'[19]

That has the ring of truth to it; one can almost hear Lady Jersey's voice.

That summer there were two elopements which touched on the Jerseys. First, in May Frances Jersey's cousin, the forty-six year-old Sir William Twysden, ran off to Gretna Green 'with a Miss Wynch, a young lady of 15'.[20] The second was less successful. Georgiana Devonshire's sister, Harriet, Lady Duncannon, was secretly planning to leave her husband and elope with Charles Wyndham, the younger son of the Earl of Egremont and a more than somewhat dissolute friend of the Prince of Wales. In this case, though, her brother and mother discovering her plans nipped matters in the bud and prevented the elopement before Lord Duncannon even knew of it, and Harriet fairly rapidly agreed to give Wyndham up.[21] One of the many ironies of this story is that Harriet Duncannon, no saint as we will see, was to regard Frances Jersey as evil personified. Another was that in 1801 the Jerseys' second daughter, Lady Anne Villiers, was to marry the same Charles Wyndham as her second husband, which may well not have happened had the elopement succeeded. As it turned out, the marriage soon disintegrated and Lady Anne rapidly left her new husband.

More respectably, the autumn of 1786 brought a rite of passage for the two eldest Villiers girls as Lord Jersey wrote on 6 November:

> We had on Friday a famous Ball at Blenheim; *famous* I call it because my two eldest daughters were there; & it was the first of the male & female

> kind at which they had been; they were delighted as you may imagine & I think they did not disgrace themselves.[22]

Lady Charlotte and Lady Anne appeared again in Society in a different form in the spring of 1787. The era of portraiture was blossoming, and at the Royal Academy's exhibition in April there was a painting by Maria Cosway, entitled *Young Cybele with two nymphs*, of the two of them holding their little sister Fanny on a lion. There was also second picture by Mrs Cosway of Lady Jersey herself with two of her children, in which Frances Jersey was dressed in black as a witch and, seemingly, performing an incantation. This picture was entitled *The Enchantress*, a title which was to resonate and was in future years used by the press as a not very complimentary nickname for the Countess.[23]

The Earl of Ailesbury for one was not impressed and wrote in his diary: 'the exhibition in general thought a very indifferent one. Mrs Cosway's ideas for Lady Jersey and two children in one and three of her children in another, very odd.'[24] A happier response, reflecting Lady Jersey's renowned charms, was the following epigram, also entitled *The Enchantresss*, prompted by the Countess's portrait appearing in a contemporary newspaper:

> Jersey! Why wave thy wand around?
> Or trace the magic circle on the ground?
> More potent charms and strong enchantments lie
> Within the magic circle of thine eye
> Those are the fascinating spells, that prove
> Thy proud dominion o'er the realms of love.[25]

There was a second portrait of Lady Jersey in progress at this time. It was in Joshua Reynolds' studio and was, in his words, '*The Duchess of Devonshire and Lady Jersey in conversation*. This was begun some years since; it is resumed for Lady Jersey who is sitting for its being finished.' The mere thought of such a portrait is delicious but sadly, even if it was finished, it now seems lost.[26]

The first few months of 1787 also give a snapshot, as viewed from the outside, of other aspects of the life Lady Jersey led in Society, for it was Society which formed the central theme of her life whilst in London.

First there was the court whose formal occasions she regularly attended. She was present at the Queen's Birthday event on 18 January, when she was reported in the press as wearing:

> Black velvet body and robe, the petticoat white and blue and black intermixt, laid crossways on the coat; and between each a stripe bordered with a row of gold flowers, and a gold fringe, of an uncommon breadth.[27]

Then there was the opera. She, with Georgiana Devonshire and the Earl of Carlisle and, of course, many others, were at the Opera House in early May to see a performance of *Ridotto*. After the performance, 'at half past one the supper rooms opened and gave every rareity in season with every choice of French wines … the provision for supper was very abundant, and the wine was given unsparingly … About three, many of the female assemblage … had retired,' reported *The World & Fashionable Advertiser*. The times of day referred to were of course the early hours of the morning.[28]

The same newspaper reported a performance of *Peeping Tom* at the Haymarket Theatre in June:

> The House, driven by stress of weather, was abundant; and there were names of consequence: the Duchess of Richmond, Lady Jersey, Lady Mexborough, Lord Carlisle, and many others, graced the boxes.[29]

In between, in May, there was another influx of French visitors. The French ladies, Lord Jersey reported, 'have been entertained & feted as much as they could possibly wish & more I think that they can stand; and a large part of them go off to Bath tomorrow … Mons D'Adhemar gave them a great Ball last night, more ample and full than any one hitherto given'.[30]

In June, Lord Jersey and the children went to Brighton for some time, with the Earl returning to London after settling the children in. Whilst we know Lady Jersey spent some time in Brighton, it is not clear whether she remained behind in London for a time as she had in recent years.[31] The significance of this is that, almost exactly nine months later, on 19 March 1788, she gave birth to her seventh surviving daughter, Lady Harriet Villiers. Given her practice in recent years, it is tempting to assume that Harriet, too, was the daughter of the Earl of Carlisle.

Either way, the family then went on to Middleton for the Summer, Lord Jersey commenting from there in July on their time in Brighton: 'Sea Bathing has answered what I believe it was expected to do for the Children but in other respects there never was more triste business, scarcely anybody I have ever seen before, & what few were there not living in Society together.'[32]

Even back at Middleton, they were not isolated from the scandals of Society. At this time, the Duke of Devonshire was much taken by Lady Elizabeth Foster, to his mother-in-law's considerable disgust, and in September Lady Augusta Murray was telling the Marchioness of Stafford the latest news on this front:

> The Duke of Devonshire is now less smitten Lady Spencer *est très en colère*, Ly Jersey says she does not see why such a trifle can put her Dowagership [of Spencer] in such a passion when she herself had Lord Harcourt and Ld Jersey at one time. This is the latest scandal I have heard.[33]

Apart from the acerbity of Lady Jersey's comment, one wonders not only at her clear acceptance of such a life style but also about whether the comment about Lady Spencer was true and, indeed, whether she really believed what she said. The answer to both these last seems to be clearly not, even if Lady Augusta's failure to deny the allegation might imply its truth. There is no indication in the many hundreds of letters between Countess Spencer and Lord Jersey to suggest anything other than the deepest Platonic relationship. Of course, any letters indicating the contrary would be likely to have been destroyed. Nevertheless, the characters which emerge from that correspondence – not least in their loyalty to the late Lord Spencer, Countess Spencer's self-evident religious faith and probity, and the Earl's formal prose – argue strongly that the relationship between Lady Spencer and Lord Jersey was never anything else. It seems certain that Lady Jersey knew her words to be untrue, and one is left to remark only on the sharpness of her tongue. She was quick to be dismissive of those who did not share her views on life.

This obviously also raises the question whether Lord Jersey ever followed the example of his wife in taking a lover, which would be by no means unusual amongst his peers. There is little direct evidence either way but the answer seems that he did not. Apart from the fact that having a lover would seem quite out of character for the transparently faithful Earl, nothing survives to indicate any possible affair on his part. There is, of course, the rumoured female companion on his trip to Bath in 1780 and the, very brief, infatuation with Lady Bess Foster at Chatsworth in 1784 but both of these incidents appear completely innocent and isolated. Of course, there can be no certainty but the impression of the Earl's total loyalty to his disloyal wife rings true.

This time also saw the beginnings of the Countess's correspondence with Edward Jerningham, a genteel if not affected poet and playwright who was the youngest son of Sir George Jerningham Bt. Moving in fashionable as well as literary circles, he numbered amongst his friends not only the Jerseys but also the Harcourts and Lord Carlisle. Immersed in the world of theatre, he knew Sheridan well, and some say that the foppish poet Sir Benjamin Backbite in *The School for Scandal* is based on him.[34]

Jerningham became one of Frances Jersey's closest and most faithful friends and was frequently invited to Middleton. The previous year he had been invited in September, Lady Jersey writing to him:

> Lord Jersey desires me to say that we shall certainly be here the 29, and very glad of the pleasure of seeing. Pray don't forget to make my uniform. The darkest Courbeau you can find. A black cape. The buttons are made by Williams in St Martin's Lane. The summer waistcoat is sold by by Willis in Bond Street and the winter one by Bargman Taylor in Charles Street, Grosvenor Square. If you have any new French books, I hope you will bring them.[35]

Was this the black costume in which Maria Cosway painted *The Enchantress*, exhibited a few months later?

In 1787 Frances Jersey again invited Jerningham to Middleton, this time in October when she would be 'very happy to see' him. She did, though, complain to him about her health, saying, 'I have been unwell almost ever since I was at Brighthelmstone. My health and temper have mended, and I believe I am fit to live with human creatures again. Pray bring your harp. I have practised a great deal lately, and I think we shall make fine harmony.'[36].

The New Year of 1788 began with another scandal in the family. Frances Jersey's cousin, Frances, Countess of Eglinton, was something of a magnet for scandal. Having married a man considerably older than herself, her becoming pregnant in 1786 had been regarded by many in society as an 'extraordinary', if not suspicious, event – and in this she was not helped by her cousin's reputation. Lady Mary Coke recounted the views of the world on this pregnancy:

> The scandalous part of the world says she has behaved cruelly to Lord Eglington's [*sic*] heirs but the more candid allow he may be the Father of the Child. The circumstance the most against Lady Eglington is her intimacy with her cousin Lady Jersey – who no Lady of strict morals (I should think) cou'd live in friendship with.[37]

In fact it seems that the child was indeed Lord Eglinton's despite public suspicion to the contrary, for which, as we will see, there may have been some (physical) justification. The most telling aspect of the story is, though, the unenviable reputation that Frances Jersey had now clearly acquired, at least amongst the more prim sections of Society, and the guilt by association which it, through her friendships, inspired.

Now the scandalous part of the world was to be proved right in its judgement on the Countess of Eglinton. She had for some time been conducting an affair with the Duke of Hamilton and was once more pregnant, this time by the Duke. Eventually her husband became suspicious and, on being challenged by him, the Countess admitted to the affair. All this was reported, with an additional twist, in *The Morning Chronicle* in January 1788:

> His Grace of H is shortly coming up to London; but we do not hear that he brings with him his beautiful and amiable Duchess.
>
> It rarely happens that a female, whose husband sues for divorce, has the ingenuousness, like Lady Eglinton, to acknowledge her guilt, and thus preclude the necessity of a regular trial. Yet her Ladyship has not only done this, but confessed herself to be three months advanced in her pregnancy in consequence of her connexion with the Duke.
>
> There have been some circumstances to palliate the crime of the chaste Lady E——; for her husband is not only considerably advanced in years but it said to have long ago received like Corporal Trim – a wound – but when or where that is the question.[38]

The reference to Corporal Trim is presumably to that character in Laurence Sterne's novel *The Life and Opinions of Tristram Shandy* but should instead have been to Tristram Shandy himself, since it was he who, when young, was encouraged by a chambermaid, in the absence of a chamber pot, to urinate out of a window – when in the course of so doing the sash came crashing down so circumcising him. It is unknown whether the former soldier Lord Eglinton had really suffered 'a wound' but even if he had it had not prevented the couple from having the earlier child.

Lady Eglinton was mistaken if she thought that, by confessing her affair, the Duke of Hamilton would leave his wife for her. Instead the Duke and his Duchess were reconciled and the Earl of Eglinton rapidly divorced his Countess.[39]

As the star of Frances Eglinton waned, so that of the eldest Jersey daughter, Lady Charlotte Villiers, grew in the ascendant. Like all the Jersey daughters, whoever their father, the eldest girl, Charlotte, was very pretty and in 1788 was coming out into Society. Of the Jersey girls and their mother, the poet Samuel Rogers wrote:

> Did I tell you of my flirtation with a very celebrated Countess? ... How I dined alone with her, rode alone with her, spent an evening alone with her ... and how I was domesticated with her daughters? And such daughters – but *n'importe*. I shall only observe *en passant* that if you have any notion of what perfection a woman can attain to you are quite mistaken, and should be punished for your presumption.[40]

Following Lady Harriet Villiers' birth in March, Frances Jersey was far from well.[41] Accordingly it fell to her husband to play a large role in Charlotte's coming out. First she was presented at court;[42] next her proud father escorted her to a series of balls, the first occurring in early May:

> We had a most magnificent Ball yesterday at Devon're H. including all the town I think & I was in a manner under the necessity of staying it out as it was Charlotte's first public exhibition. I was kept there the whole night, that is till six o'clock this morn'g, but I cannot feel to regret or grudge it much because I had the satisfaction of flattering myself that her public deportment was so consonant with her real character; & a better one does not exist.[43]

A month later the Earl was writing: 'lately I have seen a good deal of the world from my attendance on Char'tte & the public is civil enough to be partial to her appearance at the Birthday ... at this moment there is multiplication of Balls &c which Charlotte will attend & consequently I shall be long in this neighbourhood.'[44]

By September, Lady Jersey's health had improved sufficiently for her to visit Cheltenham, ostensibly to try the waters, as Rachel Lloyd wrote: 'Ly Jersey has been here on a visit to Ly Carlisle for ten days, but her true reason for her coming, as she says, is to try if these waters will agree with her, for if they do so she will take a House next year.'[45]

Rachel Lloyd may have believed Lady Jersey's reasons for the visit but it is easy to surmise others. Indeed it seems that some did just that as when Lady Mary Coke commented that, unusually: 'The Carlisles don't go to Yorkshire till the Autumn.'[46]

This visit and delayed removal to Yorkshire may have been just as well because in November a planned family visit by the Jerseys to Castle Howard was repeatedly postponed 'to the great mortification of the young ones', owing to the onset of a period of madness in George III and the consequent need for Lord Jersey to be available to attend Parliament.[47] Ultimately, in mid-December he was writing to Countess Spencer that 'my northern expedition has no chance of taking place'.[48] Presumably it was not only the Jersey children who were mortified at this although one imagines that Lord Carlisle also spent much time in London.

In 1789 it was Lady Anne Villiers' turn to be presented at court, on this occasion with some drama. Like her sister, Lady Anne was a beauty. A table published three years later set out an 'estimate of the personal attractions of our ... reigning beauties. This arbitrary mode ... was the invention of Akenside, who first applied it to poets'. The 'reigning beauties' included the Duchesses of Devonshire and Rutland as well as both Lady Anne Villiers and her elder sister Charlotte. Under the heading 'Loveliness', Lady Anne scored 20, which represented perfection and was more than both the celebrated Duchesses scored.[49]

Lady Anne was presented to the Queen by Lady Jersey at the Drawing Room on 26 March; Lady Charlotte was also in attendance. Unfortunately, in her father's words, an 'excess of a finely dressed crowd or mob', that is the cream of English society, being unable to leave at the ends of the great Drawing Room and all having to go out the same doorway, 'the squeeze & pressure was intolerable to those who had not patience to wait to a late hour ... the consequences were natural, faintings away, screamings, loss of caps, bags, shoes, & I suppose almost every part of the dress that was not quite attached strongly to the wearer'.[50] Frances Jersey was taken ill afterwards with 'a slight fever increased by the fatigue' of these events and even on 31 March was still confined to the house in Grosvenor Square.[51]

The family followed suit. At the beginning of April, Lord Jersey was taken ill with a fever and swelling which Dr Warren put down to St Anthony's fire.[52] By the middle of the month he was much better although, said Lord Villiers, still very weak, and a week later was complaining,'I am left with the most troublesome complaint in the world; I'm totally deaf in Company so that I cannot mix in Society,' although this did not prevent him going to Euston by way of Newmarket early in May.[53]

The next to succumb was William, as Augustus was now called, Lord Jersey telling Lady Spencer on 23 May:

> The day I returned from your house I was obliged to fetch my second son from School & he has been extremely ill ever since of a scarlet fever ...

> the hourly alarms arising from an attack, so long & uncertain in it's [*sic*] progress, especially upon one so young & delicate a frame as his.[54]

Lord Althorp wrote to his mother two days later:

> I saw Lord Jersey this morning who is in great anxiety about his son William, who has been for a week in violent scarlet fever, & is not yet pronounced out of danger; he seems much affected by it, & is still so deaf that he cannot manage his own voice at all, or hear without difficulty what anybody else says, otherwise I think he looks reasonably well.[55]

It was only at the end of the month that Lord Jersey was able to write to Lady Spencer:'you are very kind to enquire about Will'm, he has been extremely ill, but his fever has now left him, & it only remains for him to recover his strength. He is reduced to a very great degree indeed.'[56]

Against this background, Lady Charlotte continued to step out. Betsy Sheridan writes of a masquerade at Mrs Sturt's house in Hammersmith early in June at which the Royal Princes, including the Prince of Wales, were present, as were 'Lady Jersey and her daughter (very pretty woman) as black veiled nuns' – a costume Lady Jersey, to the amusement of the press in later years, was fond of wearing at masquerades, fashionable entertainments at the time. The daughter was Lady Charlotte.[57] The big event, however, occurred in the middle of June, as her father related: 'I came to town this day from an excursion into the country & am saluted with Lord William Russell's proposal to Charlotte; she has given her consent, & we are now in the usual bustle, produced by an event of that sort.[58]

The man the eighteen-year-old Charlotte had agreed to marry was a younger brother of the 5th Duke of Bedford, recently elected an MP and in later years to become more than eccentric (and to die murdered by his valet slitting his throat in bed). His engagement to Charlotte was something of a triumph, on the appearance of things if nothing else, because there were at least two competitors (of sorts) for her hand. The first was Lord Titchfield, son of the Duke of Portland, who, as Lord Minto said to his wife, 'was violently in love with her, and is gone abroad, I believe, on her account. She is supposed to have preferred Lord William, and I believe the Duke was not desirous of Lord Tichfield's marrying so immediately. Lady Charlotte Villiers is extremely pretty, and will be like her mother.'[59] The second was the Marquess of Lorne, heir to the Duke of Argyll, once described as 'the highest bred man in England' and a man of acknowledged beauty.

It is said in fact that Lorne had scorned the opportunity to marry Lady Charlotte. It is certainly true that, from the very time of her marriage to Lord William Russell, Lady Charlotte had an affair with Lorne which was to continue until her death nearly twenty years later, an affair which was very public and which survived despite Lorne having, for some years in the early 1800s, a concurrent affair with the celebrated courtesan Harriette Wilson. Despite this competition from Harriette Wilson, Lorne refused to leave Lady

William Russell, as Charlotte had now become, and it was said that 'after sharing Lady Charlotte's box at the Opera, he would share his bed with Harriette back at Argyll House'.[60]

All of which casts a rather a different light on Lord Jersey's comments on Lady Charlotte's character and public deportment at the time of her stepping out into Society. One wonders, too, whether Lady Mary Coke knew something when, hearing of Lady Charlotte's engagement, she wrote: 'Lord William Russell's marriage with Lady Charlotte Villiers was this day declared, the Lady has her Mother's Beauty but I hope not her Character.'[61]

For the present, arrangements for the wedding proceeded at the normal rapid pace of the time with *The Oracle* reporting the engagement on Saturday 20 June:

> Hymen will soon tie the Gordian Knot between Lord William Russell and Lady Charlotte Villiers, daughter of Lord Jersey.
>
> The Duke [of Bedford] is said to behave on the occasion with princely liberality; a noble jointure is granted on the Bedford estates, leaving Lord William in clear possession of fully fifty thousand pounds, which he is entitled to under the late Duke's will.

On 22 June Lady Jersey gave a grand dinner at home in Grosvenor Square for 'the Duke of Bedford and all the Russell family',[62] whilst Lord Jersey, after saying the lawyers had been put to work on the marriage settlement, summed up for Lady Spencer his views on the marriage:

> Charlotte's situation, considering the man & every other collateral circumstance will be such as will entitle her to a prospect of real happiness. The fortune is enough for comfort certainly (for your ears only) ... the settlement is £300 pin money and £1,000 jointure with proper fortunes for younger children. This point is not absolutely essential for happiness, but ease at home contributes much to it. His character is excellent ... they know each other well, & what can one desire more than such a foundation to start with.[63]

One of Lord Jersey's weaknesses was, perhaps as a result of his naivety, that he was a poor judge of character. Lord William was to prove a weak, eccentric and financially incompetent, if tolerant, husband.

It was also reported in the papers that, on the marriage, the Duke of Bedford gave his brother £10,000 and an addition to his annual income of £1,500, making Lord William's 'rent-roll' £4,000 per annum, a considerable sum.[64]

The wedding was fixed for 11 July at the Jerseys' house and was planned to take place 'as privately as the connexions of the family will admit'.[65] Privacy may have been the intention but, as the press reported, 'about three hundred persons assembled about Lord Jersey's door, with fiddles and marrow bones and cleavers and played to the performance of the ceremony'.[66]

Following the wedding, the Jerseys retreated for the summer to Middleton but not before embarking on a series of 'family visits and dinners upon Charlotte's marriage' to celebrate the union, after which the Earl remarked on how everybody commented on the couple's 'happy countenance'. Lord Jersey adored his children, but in the circumstances one wonders about the degree of wishful thinking on his part.[67]

That autumn, unlike the last, the Jerseys were able to go and stay with the Carlisles at Castle Howard. Indeed they stayed rather longer than they originally intended. In early October, Lord Jersey wrote from there: 'Our stay here will probably [be] all this month ... Charlotte & Lord William came to us yesterday & I do not think we can yet accustom ourselves to live without her.'[68]

Instead, they were still there six weeks later in the middle of November and, even then, it was unclear how much longer they would have to stay, as Lord Jersey had fallen down some steps and had been confined for a fortnight 'unable to bear the motion of horse or carriage'.[69] In the meantime, Lady Carlisle had rushed off to Derby to look after her daughter, who had had a miscarriage whilst on her way to Wales.[70] This unfortunate combination of circumstances may have suited both Lord Carlisle and Lady Jersey particularly since it was not until the end of November that Lord Jersey felt fit enough to travel.[71]

There is a different version of this story, given to Georgiana Devonshire by James Hare in a letter dated 15 December:

> The Jerseys staid at Castle Howard two months: Lord Jersey fell down just before they were to have left it and a most [unusual?] fall it must have been for did not prevent his hunting or shooting but made travelling very inadvisable ... Lord Carlisle is now with Ly Carlisle at Middleton.[72]

The Jerseys had arrived home at Middleton on 1 December.[73] It only took until 15 December before it was reported that the Carlisles had joined them there. On 23 December, *The World* announced that 'Lord and Lady Carlisle stay with Lady Jersey until January – then they all come to London.' Lord Carlisle and Lady Jersey clearly knew what they were doing as the two families spent nearly three months living together. It is inconceivable that Lord Jersey and Lady Carlisle did not, too, but what they thought about it can only be imagined.

When the Jerseys did arrive in London it was some time before the Countess went out into Society. As she explained to Georgiana Devonshire, she was troubled with an old ailment:

> I came to town with the old pain in my side increased, and so many bilious symptoms that I expected soon to die of a disorder in my liver but [Warren?] has entirely cured me & assures me that I had only a slight obstruction of the gall duct however his remedys were violent Physick very often which confined me several days in each week.

Her letter went on to tell news of the family and then to acknowledge (to the Countess's regret) that, after years of being under pressure, the relationship between her and the Duchess now seemed to have broken down completely:

> Anne is so much improved that I think it will be odd if I do not marry her this year … Caroline is as tall as I am & now I will not mention my children again … I cannot talk to you without saying pray write to me, tho' I have not much hope that you will resume the thread of discourse so broken as ours, yet I will believe that there is in your head & heart a great deal of old affection for me & a perfect conviction of my unalterable attachment to you, I still cherish the hope that a time will come when we shall live together again, it is so delightful to me that I shall retain it whilst I live … God bless you my love.'[74]

But the thread of discourse was not yet completely over. Somehow the Countess wove her magic and her wish was fulfilled, at least for a few more years. Indeed, it only really irretrievably broke down when Lady Jersey became the Prince's mistress, so the best part of three years later the discourse was continuing as Frances Jersey, then in Dover, was commissioning errands from the Duchess. She wrote to her:

> Thank you my dear love for your [letter] … I have been here one week after having passed three at Cheltenham & find myself in better health than I have been for many years excepting the pain in my right side which I believe nothing will ever cure but if it don't kill me I will be content … I am now established with a house full of people … [including] Lord C & his son …

Who, she said, were shortly going north, presumably to Castle Howard, for two months, where they would be 'without any society but Madame who is more silly & tiresome than ever. I have escaped her for the whole summer.' She went on to ask Georgiana to send her two pairs of those 'worsted things to wear over my shoes. They use them at Geneva … I shall be satisfied with one pair, but I had rather have another for Caroline.'[75]

One can only be amazed at her acid tongue, the more so that she felt at liberty to use it openly in describing Lady Carlisle in such terms. This, and her hauteur, was a trait which would make her many enemies, as Lady Spencer had remarked upon in the past.

One wonders too what Lady Jersey made at that time of Lord Morpeth, the nineteen-year-old son of her lover Lord Carlisle. A few years later she was to make a great deal of him.

Meanwhile Lady William Russell was expecting. In a letter of 2 December 1789 to Lady Spencer, Lord Jersey said, 'I hope I may soon have a Grandchild too; Charlotte was ill, but has got to town safe, I believe, & I am told in little apprehension.'[76] In January 1790 she was, once more, presented at court by her mother as etiquette required following her marriage.[77] Then in June her father said of her, 'I do not know whether I shall defer my visit to Mid. till Charlotte's confinement, or rather recovery sets us at liberty. She is still going about perfectly well.'[78] However, in early July there is the first hint of trouble as Lord Jersey wrote to his friend: 'I am detained in town … till Charlotte is brought to bed: an event that seems to grow daily further off instead of approaching; but she is perfectly well.'[79] Thereafter there is no mention of Charlotte until the end of the month, when Lord Jersey wrote: 'Char is quite well, & it is not from any accident matters are postponed. From this state however, we shall now soon move into the country; the Broad wheeled wagon is ordered and every black symptom attending it.'[80] The implication of 'black symptoms' seems clear; either she had lost the baby or the child was born but died soon afterwards, causing her father to write on 15 September: 'Charlotte continuing still very well,' presumably in her recovery.[81] This is consistent with Lady William Russell's first recorded surviving child, Gertrude, not being born until the following year.

Early in October Frances Jersey went to Bath on her own, presumably to see her mother.[82] Her husband was detained at Grosvenor Square by Charlotte who still needed some looking after.[83] The Jerseys were reunited in time to see Lord Villiers off to Geneva for the next stage of his education in November.[84] Villiers was to remain in Geneva, causing his father to alternate between fretting over him and proudly receiving good reports of him, for more than a year.[85] At that time, wrote Lady Frances Shelley, Geneva was 'much frequented by the best society in England', which included her future husband who was there at the same time and became a lifelong friend of Villiers as a result, a friendship doubtless cemented by their joint love of the turf – Shelley later winning the Derby twice and Villiers, when the 5th Earl, three times.[86] On his return from Geneva Villiers' education was to be completed at Cambridge, where he was admitted as a Nobleman of St John's College in February 1792.[87]

In January 1791 Lady William Russell left London apparently feeling, for some reason, the need to declare she was 'not with child'.[88] Happily by August she was and staying with her parents at Middleton before going up to town for her confinement.[89] Lady William's attempts to have children were clearly the stuff of Society gossip, and there is a series of letters from Mrs Caroline Howe to Lady Stafford on the topic. On 25 September 1791 she wrote: 'Madme de Coigne is in England, & gone to her friend Lady Jersey, they must soon come to town to attend Ly Will: Russell who is this time really to be confined, and in a few weeks.'[90] Then on 14 November she wrote, 'Ly W Russell is just as she was & I find it is very much believed, contrary to the opinion of the wise & who ought to know best, that she will not produce anything more this year than the last.'[91] A week later she wrote, 'Lady William Russell is not [yet?] in bed but Ly Carlisle told me [t'other?] night, her family do not doubt that she will be so.'[92]

The doubters were proved wrong although the birth was very difficult. On 25 November Lord Jersey wrote to Lady Spencer that Charlotte

> was this morn' brought to bed of a daughter & is they say going on well. We are very happy and released from a great anxiety … [Lady Jersey] will

> scarcely perhaps be able to write by this post, the fatigue and anxiety of last night having nearly overset her.[93]

It seems Lord William did not suffer any such fatigue or anxiety. At the time of the birth he was at supper with the Duchess of Bedford, and it was only when intelligence was received of his wife's delivery that the party set out for Grosvenor Square.[94]

The news was greeted with relief elsewhere. Lord Spencer, writing to his mother a few days later, said, 'I have just written a letter to Ld Jersey to congratulate him on becoming a Grandfather by the birth of Ld W Russell's daughter. I am ... glad it has at last come to pass.'[95]

Some dramatic developments followed. On 27 December, *The Times* reported: 'Lady William Russell continues without hope of recovery.' She had indeed been taken very ill but it was not quite that bad. Lord Jersey described what happened:

> We have been in the utmost scene of distress; poor Charlotte, having had originally a cruel time, was taken ill after seven days, has suffered the most inexpressible pain, & has been in every respect in the most alarmg situation, & it is only now that we look forward to a slow & gradual recovery.

She had been attended by a team with Dr Warren at its head, without whom, Lord Jersey was sure, the results would have been fatal.[96] Even so, the illness was protracted, and it was not until beginning of February 1792 that 'her fever, & the cruel symptoms attending it' left so that there was then 'nothing to look forward to but a re-establishment of strength & spirits'.[97]

Fortunately, when Lady William next gave birth, to a son in March 1793, 'she was perfectly well from the beginning. Nothing similar [to the previous birth], or indeed anything untoward' occurred.[98]

Lady Anne Villiers was getting married also in 1791, as the Earl had forecast. The first public intimation of this came as a report in *The Times* on 18 May, stating that 'A treaty of Marriage is ... on the tapis between Mr Lambton, Member for Durham, and Lady Charlotte Villiers.' Apart from naming the wrong (already married) daughter – the reference should have been to Lady Anne – the story was true. On 23 May, *The Times* wrote: 'Lady Jersey is in high luck, – not at Faro – but in marrying her daughter to Mr Lambton who is heir to twenty thousand pounds a year, – and is in actual possession of as many virtues.'

This time the article was completely accurate. The Lambtons had been great landowners in County Durham for hundreds of years and, in the eighteenth century, had acquired enormous wealth as a result of good marriages and the coal which lay under their land. The result was that they were amongst the richest families in the country. William Lambton was the heir to the fortune and he was to marry Lady Anne.[99]

It was a splendid match, and Anne's parents were delighted. Lord Jersey wrote to Lady Spencer on 6 June: 'from all I hear I have every day more & more reason to rejoyce and confide in Anne's prospect of happiness – I do not exactly know when the Ceremony is to be, but I think it cannot exceed three weeks,'[100] whilst Lady Jersey's friend Edward Jerningham described the Countess as 'overjoy'd at this match – she has five more daughters to dispose of'.[101]

The wedding was eventually fixed for 20 June, and after the ceremony the new couple were to stay at a friend's house at Marlow for some time.[102] Back in London later in the year they bought the Duchess of Ancaster's house in Berkeley Square for £6,000.[103] It was there that, on 12 April 1792, their first child was born; this new arrival was John George Lambton, named after his two grandfathers, General John Lambton and George Villiers, who was later to become the 1st Earl of Durham.[104] Unlike her sister's experience a few months earlier, all seemed to go well for Lady Anne with the birth and, on 30 April, Lord Jersey was writing: 'she has now got over almost three weeks without a complaint & the Boy as well as herself are as we could wish them.'[105]

Alongside these family events, the formal workings of Society continued. On 26 February 1792 the third Jersey daughter, Lady Caroline Villiers, was presented at St James's. The same day, her mother and she were invited to supper at Cumberland House but when they went up there was no room at the Duchess of Cumberland's table, so they came away; apparently there were only two tables and, presumably, only the greatest were seated at them, rather than Lady Jersey taking umbrage at royal discourtesy.[106] The following week, Lord Jersey presented his son-in-law Mr Lambton to the King at a levée at St James's.[107]

At the end of May Lady Caroline was preparing for the Birthday, and Lord Jersey took the opportunity to give news of his family to Lady Spencer. Charlotte, he said, 'is I think as well as ever she was in her life, & her little girl delightful ... Caroline ... is taller than her sisters, & the world seems disposed to think her not ill-looking, some say the best of the three' – which was quite something. Villiers, he added, was 'at Cambridge gaining some advantage ... in a more improving way that he could otherwise in this or foreign countries'.[108]

During this time another portrait was commissioned. Lady Stormont describes a visit to Maria Cosway's studio

> where there is a little whole length of Lady Jersey's youngest girl [this is Lady Harriet] in her shift going to Hush and playing with her foot. I don't think a quite pretty attitude, it has very large dark eyes, black hair and seems a pretty little thing ...'[109]

Some parts of Society, though, were more controversial, and Lady Jersey in her usual way rose to the challenge where fun was to be had. In March that year the Margravine of Ansbach was sending out invitations to parties at her house 'to a great many people who have no intention to visit her'. The Margravine, a traveller, writer and society hostess daughter of the 4th Earl of Berkeley, had in earlier years had an indiscreet affair with the Duc de Guines which was followed by several other affairs; Walpole described her as 'pretty ... good-natured to the greatest degree' but '*infinitamente* indiscreet'.[110] She was much disapproved of and all those that knew her formerly had been, at a recent party at Mrs Sturt's, 'anxious to avoid her'. Many, such as the Duchess of Marlborough and Lady Salisbury, ignored her invitations or treated them as a mistake. However, as Rachel Lloyd told Lady Spencer, 'Lady Jersey was at her house and [took] her daughter Caroline with her, many people are surprised at her for doing so,' the implication clearly being that it was bad to go and worse to take her unmarried daughter with her.[111]

Lady Jersey did not take any notice of such disapproval, as Mrs Howe told Lady Stafford in July:

> There was a great, turtle dinner at the Margravine's at Brandenburgh House [her villa in Hammersmith west of London] last Tuesday, the Margravine acted 3 different *petites pièces* in different drapes in the evening, after which there was a cold supper & fireworks. M Texier had a great share in the performances about 40 people, the Duke of Clarence, the Jerseys, Bouveries, Ly Julie Howard &c &c and the whole was not over [until] 2 the next morning.[112]

All of this – weddings, marriage settlements, portraits and society doings – seems to have been taxing Lord Jersey's limited wealth because, in late November 1792, he was writing to the king. After expressing his loyalty to George III, who had 'granted him condescensions & favours from his earliest years', he went on:

> With these sentiments I venture to throw myself on your Majesty's goodness and presume to offer the warmest wish to be restored to your Majesty's service; particularly in any situation in which I might be honored with that friendship, if I dare use the expression, which has been the unfeigned boast of my life.[113]

The king had immense powers of patronage at court and through the Civil List, with over 1,000 paid appointments connected with The Royal Household.[114] Unfortunately for him, Lord Jersey had not held any position at court since he ceased to be Captain of the Gentlemen Pensioners in December 1790. Nor was he to do so until his wife was in a position of influence and favour.

The position of Lady Jersey was shortly going to change to just that. Before describing those events, which were to bring out some of the ugliest sides of the Countess's character, we should look at some of her lighter and more personable traits and her softer and kinder sides which are so often overlooked. The first can be found in her correspondence, peremptory, witty and even self-mocking, with Edward Jerningham; the second in her kindnesses to others, not least Georgiana Devonshire and, whilst the Duchess was in exile abroad, her children.

Very few letters from Lady Jersey survive. The largest surviving collection is the forty-two letters from her to Edward Jerningham (and one letter to a third party) which are now in the Huntington Library in California – perhaps it is no coincidence that Edward Jerningham was one of Lady Jersey's most loyal friends, standing by her in the worst of times even though on occasions his actions were not appreciated by her.

These letters, many of them undated, can largely be attributed to the 1790s.Thus in August 1791 she wrote to Jerningham about some harp strings she needed at Middleton:

> No news of my harp strings! I can only account for their not arriving by supposing the box was not sent to you. If so, pray go directly to Grosvenor Square and carry it away. When it is filled desire your maitresse d'hôtel to pay and seal it up, and order the maid in my house to send it by coach, not the wagon. I am in the utmost distress for those strings.

She went on to aim a barb at the Countess of Mount Edgecumbe, with whom Lady Jersey did not get on, asking, 'with which of her gentle and amiable qualities has the "Sea Cowcumber" endowed [her daughter] Miss Edgecumbe? Pray tell me all the news and gossip of the remains of London, and when the good Bishop [that is Jerningham] will come here.'[115]

Then again she wrote to him from Middleton:

> To tell you why I did not write to you from Brighton would be to describe a life of hurry, variety [?] and noise which, though very delightful at the time, would make you giddy to think of. Since I came here I have passed a month in the other extreme and have found Mr Whitehead's observations on this place true, that the extreme quiet is as disturbing as a paper-mill. However [her daughter] Caroline and I have passed through the month without being stopped by the ennui of the others, which has been very fatiguing. I intend that October should more agreeable, and having first finished Dr Beattie's 'Elements of Moral Science,' I choose to study modern wits, and command or entreat you (choose which you like best) that you should come here as soon as you can pack up your yellow waistcoat. I should have made this proposal sooner, but that I have lived in daily fear of going to Bath. My *beau-père* [that is General Johnston] has the gout, and detained my Mother. If his illness had continued I must have gone to her; but it is over and she comes here. You shall have a warm room, a great deal of hot bread for breakfast, and every nastiness to eat that you can think of. Your friend Elizabeth is well, and fat, and

> handsome ... I can and will not take any excuse: so pray let Wednesday's post tell me the day on which I may expect you.[116]

And there was an exchange in September 1792 starting with Lady Jersey once more writing from Middleton:

> This is to inform you that I am established at Middleton, and that if it finds you at Park Place, I order you to come here immediately. If you delay you will not find the director of this, whom I conclude you wish to meet. If this should follow you to [Jerningham's brother's house in] Norfolk I entreat that you will make your arrangements for visiting us at your return. I shall stay here until after Xmas, unless I go for a week to Nuneham; but that will suit you too. Adieu.[117]

Not receiving a reply to this, she wrote again on 23 October:

> I wrote to you the last week in August or in the beginning of September. You have not answered my letter, and I conclude you have not received it. It contained only an order to come to Middleton, which I hope you will obey now. I return [there] on Friday next. The sooner you arrive the better; but you will find me there until after Xmas. We have been acting, and I played 'Mrs. Oakley' [the leading female character in George Colman the Elder's comedy *The Jealous Wife* which had been premiered at Drury Lane in 1761] to perfection. We wanted you as a performer; and if we do continue to get up a play, I depend on you. Pray tell me when we may expect you.[118]

Jerningham eventually replied, prompting the following response:

> Thank you very much for your letter. It was a great whilst coming; but it was full of too many friendly and partial ideas to admit any reproaches. I intended informing you that I remain here till about the 15th of January, and shall probably act again during one week, from the 23rd to the 30th of December or from the 30th to the 6th of January, and entreating your company and performance. If you are in London before that time you can easily come and Lord C[arlisle ?] would be an agreeable companion in a post-chaise. The horrible accounts from Brussels [the French having invaded the Low Countries and won a victory at Jemappes on 7 November had now become masters of the southern parts of the Austrian Netherlands] make me conclude that Lady Jerningham will not remain there; and her arrival in London will probably bring you and Sir William southward sooner if the charms of Lady Mount [Edgecumbe], Lady Cic [Lady Cecilia Johnston] and Lady Mary Coke are not unusually powerful. I do not see why you should stay in that vile town of London at this season. We think of getting up *'the Rivals'*. We want an excellent actor for the part of Acres. What do [you]

> say to it. I am sure you would surpass Dodd, if you would undertake it. I find that our plays must be from the 6 January; but if you are amiable, you will come sooner. Pray answer this directly. Lord Car[lisle] bids me say you will find him in London in a few days.[119]

As to her kindnesses, we have already seen Frances Jersey working with Countess Spencer to get a poor child a job in a lace works some years earlier. Another example would arise in the spring of 1795, when the Countess was at the apogee of her power. Whilst the background is quite unknown, she was the means of relieving a Mrs Poole, an officer's widow, from starving. By November of that year it seems that Mrs Poole's situation had worsened as a result of 'enemies [with] cruel designs' and, fearing that she had been committed to Marshalsea prison as a result, Frances Jersey sent to the prison to get her released. Finding that Mrs Poole was not in fact in Marshalsea but still facing the threat of imprisonment for debt, the Countess, through the agency of Edward Jerningham, sought to help her further. As a result, Mrs Poole wrote in November to Jerningham saying: 'as at all points it is absolutely necessary that I should lose no time in thanking Lady Jersey for her repeated goodness to me, which can never be eradicated from my grateful heart.'[120]

In these years, too, we see the softer side of the Countess. When between October 1791 and September 1793 Georgiana Devonshire was banished abroad by the Duke as a result of her affair with Earl Grey, by whom she had a child, she left her and the Duke's children, aged 9, 7 and 2 in 1792, behind in England. Not surprisingly, the children were deeply upset by their mother's absence.

Frances Jersey was very fond of children and this was not limited to her own. She took a real interest in the welfare of the Devonshire children in their mother's absence and often brought her own children to play with them at Devonshire House.[121] So in May 1792 she was to write to Lady Spencer, then in Geneva, 'a full account of the good looks of the children of Devon're house'.[122] Nor was her interest in the children limited to visits to Devonshire House. It seems that the young Devonshire children had a practice of being invited regularly to visit the Jerseys in London from Chiswick, west of London, where the Devonshires had a country villa, the Palladian Chiswick House. So in February 1793 Lord Jersey wrote: 'The two young ladies from Chiswick have been here … Lady J['s] account of the little ones was perfectly good, and soon as I can I will see them myself' – Lord Jersey, having influenza, kept away from the children on this occasion.[123]

Again in June of that year he was writing: 'two days ago I had the satisfaction of seeing the young ladies from Chiswick in the most perfect health & exactly what ought to be.'[124]

Nor was it just the welfare of the Devonshire children that Lady Jersey was taking an interest in. At the same time that Georgiana Devonshire was in exile, her sister, Lady Duncannon, was spending much time abroad for her health. When in Hyères in the south of France in 1792 she wrote:

> Ly Mexborough, [writes] very often; Ly Jersey too ... I have been remarkably lucky not only in my friends but even my acquaintances, most of them I mean, the time of my illness & my long absence has shown those who really car'd for me & those that only affected it. But with regard writing, people really have been very good.[125]

Sadly in the next few years both these personable and gentler sides of Frances Jersey would be lost to view whilst the uglier ones would loom large. The result would both cost her friendships and, ever more so, her reputation in much more profound ways than until now.

11

Mrs Fitzherbert's Overturn

The contemporary politician and diarist Lord Glenbervie wrote that, at the time war broke out with revolutionary France in February 1793, the connection between Lord Carlisle and Lady Jersey had been at an end for some time. This was 'in consequence of her having formed a new *liaison dangereuse* (for such all such instances with her proved to be)'. This new liaison was with the Prince of Wales.[1] On 22 February 1793, *The Times* published a poem entitled 'On Mrs Fitzherbert and Miss Bell Pigott's overturn'; Maria Fitzherbert was, of course, the Prince of Wales' secret (and unlawful) wife and his acknowledged lover, and Bel (or Isabella) Pigot was her resident companion.*

Whilst Lord Glenbervie was right, *The Times* was premature. Lady Jersey was indeed finding her way into the affections of the Prince of Wales but it would take many months before either she was his recognised lover or Mrs Fitzherbert definitively overturned, and even then the Prince of Wales remained in two minds about Maria Fitzherbert.

It is unclear whether the affair between Lady Jersey and Lord Carlisle died a natural death or whether its end was precipitated by Frances Jersey preferring the opportunities from having a royal lover. As we shall see, Lady Palmerston thought at the time that it was the latter and the choice, once more, of Frances Jersey. Either way, Lord Carlisle, who remained on good terms with the Jerseys, was not slow in filling the vacancy. 'Some little time after Lady Sutherland ... returned from Paris where Lord

* With this role, one would imagine that Bel Pigot, daughter of Admiral Pigot, was very respectable. She does, however, figure in the scandalous publication *The Jockey Club, or, a Sketch of the Manners of the Age,* published in 1792 to 'hold the mirror up to nature'. In this, although the reference may be to someone else, it is said that Bel Pigot encouraged 'that liberal unshackled intercourse between the sexes which yields such an exquisite zest to the enjoyment of fashionable life'. She was 'transcendently happy in possession of universal esteem ... her chief delight is in conferring gratuitous favours on those who enjoy her friendship'. 'Descending into the vale of years, her constitution still retains its original predilection for the powerful attractions of youth, and the v-g-r-s Captain L-sc-lles, the gay Lothario of modern times, is reported to have inspired a romantic passion into her breast that disdains the shackles of restraint.'[2]

Gower her husband was Ambassador when the war broke out in 1793, a particular intimacy began to be observed between her and Lord Carlisle,' and 'Lady Sutherland ... had the reputation of having an intrigue with Lord Carlisle,' an intrigue which resulted in a son being born to the relationship in January 1800.[3]

Lady Jersey's acquisition of a new lover was much slower and more qualified. Nevertheless, her insinuation into the affections of the Prince was regarded by Mrs Fitzherbert as a much more serious threat than any of the previous lovers the Prince had had during his relationship with her. The Prince and the Jerseys lived in the same set. Lord Jersey had held various offices in the King's household and he and his wife were friendly with several ladies about the court. Further, Lady Jersey was on friendly terms with the Queen, who enjoyed her playing of the harp. With these advantages and with her extraordinary charms Lady Jersey could become a serious competitor to Mrs Fitzherbert, should the opportunity arise. In fact it is commonly suggested that Lady Jersey deliberately set out to create that opportunity and to ensnare the Prince. So, for example, it has been said that 'her allurements were exercised with the practised care of an ambitious, experienced, sensual though controlled and rather heartless woman'.[4] That is possible but seems an *ex post facto* assertion based on the virulence with which Lady Jersey was regarded in later years. There is no direct evidence either way – although she had indeed rejected some form of opportunity ten years earlier – but it seems likely that, as with her former lovers, over the months Frances Jersey took the initiative in acquiring a royal lover by seizing the opportunity that was presented by the often stormy relationship between a self-indulgent and fickle Prince of Wales, with a history of 'extra-marital' affairs, and Mrs Fitzherbert.

The fact that Lady Jersey was almost ten years older than the thirty-one-year-old Prince and already a grandmother may have caused Napoleon to comment on the Prince's propensity for older women – *'Il paraît que vous aimez les vieilles femmes en Angleterre'* – and give cartoonists ammunition for their work, but it was no hindrance to the growing intimacy between them. In this Frances Jersey was no exception; in particular Maria Fitzherbert herself was six years older than the Prince. In other respects the Countess was different from Mrs Fitzherbert in that she 'did not even possess the generous figure that [the Prince of Wales] usually demanded'. Indeed, when the competition for the Prince's favours became public, the *Bon Ton* magazine asked the question: 'which is the woman – the plump dame or the thin lady?'[5]

Whilst the Prince's affair with Lady Jersey unfolded, Society continued in its normal way. In April, a newspaper reported on the opening of a new theatre at the Margravine of Ansbach's Brandenburgh House, and a splendid dinner after the performance at which the Prince of Wales was present and was served on gold – his presence presumably doing something to redeem the Margravine's reputation; 'the company consisted of about 100 persons', including Lady Jersey. The company did not separate until five o'clock in the morning.[6]

A short visit to Brighton by the Jerseys in May ('all my children are this morning gone to Brighthelmstone & to stay some time, one of them, Eliz'th, not having recovered the effects of a violent fever, sea bathing we are told is absolutely necessary, nothing could be more inconvenient or disagreeable,' wrote Lord Jersey) was followed by a longer one in July.[7] That too was occasioned, in part at least, by the health of one of the Jersey daughters, as the Earl said:

> We are obliged to come for the bathing of one of our children (Anne) and I mean only to come & go till she has staid her time out, which ... must still be of some weeks longer duration ... The Pce of W leaves [on the occasion of the Brighton races] & returns some days hence.[8]

That may have been his intention but it was probably not his wife's. Brighton in August 1793 was busy, as *The Gazetteer* reported on 9 August:

> The weather being at last auspicious, the public breakfast at the Grove, so long announced and so impatiently expected took place [on 6 August]. All that is gay and fashionable in Brighton were collected in one spot. The Prince ... Lord and Lady Carlisle ... Lord and Lady Jersey &c all agreed in approving the elegance of the entertainment. Only one thing was wanting ... dance – this was proposed, but the Duchess of Marlborough objected that it was too [hot?] to which Mrs Fitzherbert, who was of the same party, seemed to look assent.

The World's report from Brighton of 14 August recounted:

> We have had an amazing influx of company within these few days ... There is to be a Public Breakfast tomorrow morning at the Promenade Grove, under the patronage of the Prince of Wales ... Lady Jersey and her charming daughter, and Mrs. Musters, take the lead here in point of beauty as well as fashion.[9]

At that 'very elegant and fashionable' second public breakfast not only was the Prince present but also 'Mrs Fitzherbert, Lady Jersey, Lady William Russell &c' although, reported *The Gazetteer*, 'Lord Carlisle has disappeared'.[10]

It seems that the mutual interest between the Prince and Lady Jersey was apparent. Whilst that may not have accounted for the 'disappearance' of Lord Carlisle, Frances Calvert, who was also in Brighton that August, subsequently wrote: 'Lady Jersey was there at that time, and I saw the beginning of that flirtation.'[11] At the time, however, others may have thought differently, as, in an undated letter which can be attributed to 1793, the Countess of Sutherland wrote to Lady Stafford: 'I saw the Pce of Wales last night ... he looks very well & does not seem to have suffered from the skirmishes at Brighthelmstone.'[12]

If that was a reference to Lady Jersey, she was to be proved wrong just as, on the other hand, the Duke of Gloucester was to be proved right; some years earlier he had been discussing with Mrs Harcourt the Prince's relationship with Mrs Fitzherbert and expressed the hope that the Prince would remain in Mrs Fitzherbert's hands, 'as she was no political intriguer & probably if they parted he would fall into worse hands'.[13]

For the time being that event lay in the future. In October, Frances Jersey was back in Middleton writing to Edward Jerningham in her normal style:

> Thank you for your letter and the print which I think excessively good. The idea and the execution are excellent, and I am impatient show it to my neighbor Mr Fermor who has sacrificed two daughters. It is very vexatious that you cannot come here now. The Aylesburys and Mrs. Damer are going to Meilleraie* next week why will you not accompany them? And then the journey would be nothing. You could never give me a greater proof of friendship than by doing this. Think of it, and at all events let me hear from you immediately. Enclose letters to Lord J.

She went on:

> I was in perfect health and spirits when I came here; but I have been entirely alone, and *l'Epée use le fourneau*. This is a confession entirely for yourself: I depend upon your secrecy. Your expectations of my stupidity cannot be disappointed, let them be raised to the highest pitch; but I hope to recover in the brilliant atmosphere of Grosvenor Square, whenever I am so happy as to enjoy its fogs. Tell us all the news you hear. I tremble at the next from France: trying the Queen is murdering her [Queen Marie-Antionette of France was tried and guillotined that month]. Send me the book you talked of; it will not hurt my spirits, for I have none to hurt. I have been expecting my mother every day this month, and am now uncertain when she arrives; but she will, I am sure, be delighted to see you.
>
> Adieu, Father Edward! Pray for the soul of Sister Frances.[14]

The Countess's clerical nickname for Jerningham is intriguing as is her reference to herself as a nun. Her custom of dressing as a nun at masquerades has already been noted. Add to this her future nickname for the Prince as 'the Primate' and one could speculate as to how Frances Jersey perceived both herself and her relationships in a spiritual, or possibly another and less respectable, light.

The word 'nun' acquired certain nuances in the eighteenth century – much like Shakesperian 'nunneries'. In common parlance the many brothels which

* The reference is presumably to Meillerie, a village in France on the shores of Lake Geneva and much painted in the eighteenth century. Its rocks were greatly admired at the time, with Samuel Rogers at page 63 of his *Recollections* describing them as 'very beautiful'.

existed in London at the time employed a 'stable of "nuns" maintained by the "Abbess" or "Mother"'. In the words of Professor White, 'the fact is that prostitution was found all over London, certainly everywhere that men with money in their pockets came together for enjoyment, from Hockley-in-the Hole to Mrs Cornelys's masquerades ...'. 'The *filles de joye* ... are generally deemed the life, and soul, of a Masquerade,' it was said in 1777, when it was a matter for public lament that 'Not an Abbess or a Nun was to be seen from King's-Place'.[15]

It is inconceivable that Frances Jersey was unaware of these connotations when describing herself, and dressing, as a nun. Whilst she was not alone in the latter, one is almost forced, even though her daughter was similarly dressed, to admit she was mockingly flaunting her sexuality and refined availability in these years of loose living amongst the aristocracy. That would certainly be in character.

This letter was followed by another at the beginning of November:

> I am angry with myself and ashamed of having been a great whilst without answering your letter. A multitude of little grievances have worn out my patience, and subdued my spirits, and made me for some time incapable of doing anything. They have at last produced a bilious attack, which, after having made me very ill for a few hours, has done me good. And I am able to tell you how sorry I am that you cannot come here – you must send me the play [Jerningham's tragedy *The Siege of Berwick* which was to be premiered at Covent Garden later that year].The secret is in the newspapers; but I will continue to deny your child, as much as if you was a maid of honour. – *Vous vous moquez de moi* when you talk of epilogues. I never had the courage to produce that which I invented from my theatre. As to Lord C. he must speak for himself. I wish I could attend the first performance; but I fear I have no chance of seeing London for a great while. Lord Jersey will be there on Wednesday, and you will probably see the Harcourts. Perhaps you may come with them when you are safely delivered, this when your month is up. Don't talk of my having been ill. I have not been confined, and I hate tormenting people about my liver like Mrs St John. Pray continue to send me as much news as you can collect or invent. I am convinced that surprise makes a greater ingredient in composition than people generally imagine. The murder of the Queen [Marie-Antoinette] has not had half the effect which that of the King had. – Adieu once more! Send us the play. You have not even told me the subject.[16]

As it happened, *The World* reported on 13 December that amongst the titled fashion at Covent Garden to watch a performance of a 'Tragic Drama' by Mr Jerningham was the Countess of Jersey. What she thought of the play we do not know. *The World* thought very little of it, giving it a very poor review and commenting that Mr Jerningham 'certainly mistook his talent'.

By now Lady Jersey was well entrenched in the affections of the Prince, even though for a long time he could not bear to cut all ties with

Mrs Fitzherbert. Indeed, even at the height of his affair with Frances Jersey it is clear that the Prince had greater affection for Mrs Fitzherbert than for the Countess. Nevertheless, it is said that as early as April Mrs Fitzherbert was so concerned by the threat of Lady Jersey as to having a retaliatory affair herself with a young French aristocrat, Charles de Noailles, who, at twenty-two, was said to be *'beau comme le jour'*. Whether or not this was true (and it seems unlikely), the Prince was reduced to fury by the mere report of it.[17] The affair was said to continue until Maria went to Brighton in the summer.[18] Even so, by the autumn the Prince's affair with Lady Jersey had caused Maria Fitzherbert's relationship with the Prince to deteriorate rapidly and her friend Lady Anne Lindsay was urging her 'if there is no final rupture have none for God's sake – if there is, remain where you are – no nothing – nothing is final to those whom have hearts & affections & who have loved totally & sincerely'.[19] However, in a number of ways Maria Fitzherbert did not help her own cause. Perhaps one of these was reported in the newspapers at the end of November when they announced that her 'chief residence will continue to be in the neighbourhood of the Pavillion, Brighthelmstone', whilst the Prince spent the final months of 1793 in London. Even so, as was his practice, an emissary was sent to Brighton in November find out how Mrs Fitzherbert was.[20]

Frances Jersey had been in Bath shortly before coming to London and attending Jerningham's play at Covent Garden.[21] There is an interesting letter in the Granville manuscripts from the Countess of Sutherland to Lady Stafford that has been attributed to the time – and is indeed difficult to attribute to a later period – which is suggestive of Frances Jersey exercising her charms on the Prince:

> Ly Jersey is unwell & is going to Bath ... except the few people who happen to have any curiosity about Ly Jersey there is never a word said about them. She is supposed to have a considerable degree of anxiety about settling the Regency for the Prince whilst she remains at Bath: probably Lady Harcourt may be sent to Town on the occasion.[22]

The nuance, and there is another reference supporting this, is that the 'Regency' is the Prince's assumption of a role which another man holds by right: his relations with his own wife.

If there was some manipulation going on, there was certainly more to follow. Frances Jersey sought to consolidate her position with the Prince by encouraging his breaking with Maria Fitzherbert. To this end, she employed a series of arguments that his association with Maria was unwise. The first was that Mrs Fitzherbert, as a Roman Catholic, was the cause of his considerable unpopularity. She went on to argue that without that association the Prince would have no difficulty in putting his disastrous financial affairs to right. Over and above this, she said that Maria Fitzherbert was not really fond of the Prince but (so claimed

Frances Jersey) had been heard to say that it was not so much his person as his rank that she loved.[23]

In this campaign Frances Jersey had an ally. The Prince's mother, Queen Charlotte, disliked his relationship with the Catholic Mrs Fitzherbert and, despite Lady Jersey's reputation, the 'bewitching little wife' of Lord Jersey was a friend of the Queen, who was happy that Lady Jersey should be the means of separating the Prince of Wales from Maria Fitzherbert.[24]

In the early months of 1794 the Jerseys were much at court. This was nothing out of the ordinary but doubtless was fuelled by the burgeoning relationship between the Countess and the Prince. So *The Morning Post* reported on 3 January 1794 of a 'Drawing Room' that day where the Prince of Wales, Lord and Lady Jersey and 'Lady C Villiers', presumably Lady Caroline, were present. Again the *London Chronicle* reported on 18 January on 'dancing in the Royal Ballroom where their Majesties were present and where in the minuets, led by the Prince of Wales, Lady Caroline Villiers featured. Then, as Lord Jersey wrote on 27 January: 'We are all now assembled in town as usual at this Season ... all my family, children & their children are perfectly well, & in a few days my son, by being presented at court, launches fairly into the world, a tall Gentle'mn almost six feet heighth [*sic*].'[25]

The presentation took place at the levée on 31 January.[26]

Lord Villiers was also at the King's Birthday on 4 June with his mother and his sister Lady Caroline, but not seemingly Lord Jersey. All were beautifully dressed. Lady Jersey wore 'a lilac crape train, edged with silver fringe, and fastened round the arms with two diamond beads; the petticoat richly embroidered with silver and lilac foil'. Lady Caroline wore 'a pink sarsnet train trimmed with silver; the petticoat covered with a drapery of pink crape richly embroidered in silver stripes intermixed with white beads'. Villiers was not to be outdone and was wearing a 'puce colour and light blue striped rich silk coat and breeches, and white silk waistcoat, the whole richly embroidered in coloured and white silk, spangles, and network, forming pleasing bouquets and wreaths of flowers, in a very curiously and masterly manner'.[27]

A rather different perspective of the reality of Lady Jersey's Society life was provided by an outsider, the twenty-three-year-old George Canning. After a brilliant career at Eton and Christ Church, Oxford, the future Prime Minister wrote in his diary earlier that year:

> I went to Mrs Villiers and supped there. There were the Dss of Devonshire – and Ld. and Ly. Jersey and their beautiful daughter and Lord Carlisle – and God knows what other fine people besides – so as to be on the whole a rather a dullish aristocratic meeting and had I not been relieved in some degree by sitting at supper next to Lady Sutherland and Mrs. Villiers I should have been most exceedingly bored.[28]

The beautiful Lady Caroline's presence at all these occasions was not a matter of chance. One of the Countess's motives was to find her a suitable husband.

Nevertheless it provoked a delightful – at least to Frances Jersey – report in *The Morning Post* of 23 June:

> Our *Belles*, of the *haut-ton*, are very shy of being seen with their *grown up daughters*. Amongst these may be mentioned the D——s of R——d, Mrs Mu——rs, Lady M—ln—r and several others. The lovely Lady Jersey, alone, is above such childish Vanity – for she has no rivalship to dread.

There were stories, too, that Lord Jersey himself was back in royal favour. *The Sun* reported on 28 February, perhaps more influenced by the visible royal preference his wife was receiving than by reality, that it understood the office of Rangership of the Parks was to be given to him.

On 21 June, *The Oracle* reported the arrival of the Countess of Jersey along with Lady Caroline Villiers in Brighton, and it was from there, a few days later, that the hammer blow fell on Mrs Fitzherbert's relationship with the Prince. On 24 June, she received a message from him: he was also in Brighton, arranging for them to meet at the Duke of Clarence's house at Bushey, west of London. The letter started with the words 'My dear love' and ended with 'Adieu my dear love excuse haste. Ever thine'. The same day, having arrived at the Duke of Clarence's, she received a further note from the Prince terminating their relationship. Receiving this at dinner, Maria straightaway returned to her house at Marble Hill where she endorsed the Prince's first letter: 'This letter I received the morng. of the day the Prince sent me word he would never enter my house (Lady Jersey's influence)'.[29]

Matters did not prove to be quite as clear-cut as this. Whilst the hammer blow had indeed been orchestrated by Lady Jersey, there was, once more, considerable wavering on the part of the Prince.

In early July he was writing to his friend Captain Payne, who he was using as an intermediary with Maria:

> My dear Jack, I cannot leave London without leaving you these few lines, just to say that I shd not feel comfortable did I not think I shd have a few lines from you this evening telling me how you left *dear Mrs Fitz.* Indeed my dear Jack, you know I love her too truly not to have felt more than words can almost express, at leaving her in the temper wh. I saw she was determin'd not to get the better of.

He went on to justify himself by adding:

> I really think myself too ill used. God knows what I've done to merit it ... If you think this note will be of service you may shew it [to Maria]. But pray don't let me have any highflown letters from her upon this subject for they really are too painful for me to be able to bear ym.[30]

On receipt of this self-justifying letter Jack Payne rushed to Mrs Fitzherbert seeking an interview between her and the Prince. This she refused, resulting in a further letter from the Prince, now at Windsor Castle, on 8 July making another attempt at a rapprochement, which Jack Payne was commanded to deliver to Maria Fitzherbert. In the self-serving covering letter to Payne the Prince said:

> To tell you what it has cost me to write it, & to rip up every and the most distressing feelings of my heart & which have so long lodg'd there is impossible to express. God bless you my friend, whichever way this unpleasant affair now ends I have nothing to reproach myself with. I owe nothing to her family, whatever was due was due to herself, but in either case this letter is a final answer to everyone. Your affectionate but unhappy friend.[31]

In all this the hypocritical and self-deluding Prince sought to justify his latest affair, going on to say that he was 'anxious to make [Frances Jersey] appear not only in his own eyes but in those of the World in general, as the most amiable of her sex, & consequently as the most deserving of the sentiments he was known to profess for her', and went on to urge Maria Fitzherbert not to listen to 'nonsensical' stories about Lady Jersey or to criticise his choice of allegedly 'improper' friends.[32]

For the time being this seemed to be the end for Maria Fitzherbert. On 15 July Lord Mornington was writing to Lord Grenville, the Foreign Secretary: 'I heard last night from no less an authority than Tom the Third [Thomas Coke] that a Treaty of separation and provision is on foot (if not already concluded) between His Royal Highness and the late Princess Fitz. I think you ought to marry His Royal Highness to a frow [*sic*] [ie frau] immediately.'[33] Even at this time, though, there were some who did not believe the separation was final. Three days later, Lady Stafford was writing to her son that the Prince and Mrs Fitzherbert remained friends 'and the mischief maker is left to find out another, or to go on with you know who', that is presumably Lord Carlisle.[34] In this she was wrong and it was left to *The Times* of 23 July to report, this time correctly, what had now become the reality – although it took a month more before the parties recognised the fact:

> We have hitherto foreborne to mention the report in circulation for many days past of the FINAL SEPARATION between a GENTLEMAN of the most DISTINGUISHED RANK, and a LADY who resides in *Pall Mall*, until we had the opportunity to ascertain the facts beyond all doubt.
>
> We are now able to state from the most undoubted authority, that a final separation between the parties in question has ACTUALLY TAKEN PLACE ... MRS FITZHERBERT has no intention of retiring to Switzerland, as has been reported. She is looking out for a house at or near Margate where she means to reside for six months.

Two days later, *The Sun* also reported the reality, with some irony: 'Lady Jersey, though a *Grandmother*, is many years *younger* than Mrs. Fitzherbert – and in personal attraction there can be no comparison made! Lady Jersey is now one of the loveliest Women in the Kingdom.'[35]

The Prince, though, remained deeply unhappy and continued to waver. Recognising this, the Duchess of Cumberland, his sister-in-law, offered to act as an intermediary between him and Maria.[36] At the same time her friend, Lady Anne Lindsay, sought to console Mrs Fitzherbert by saying of Frances Jersey that 'it is not in her power, a married woman as she is, with other dutys [*sic*] to fulfill, to supply your place to him';[37] Maria Fitzherbert resisted all approaches from various intermediaries on behalf of the Prince seeking reconciliation.[38] She continued to do so even though it appears that, at some stage, a meeting was arranged between her and Prince, which was to take place at Jack Payne's house.[39]

The reconciliation was not to be. Mrs Howe summed up matters in a letter to Lady Stafford on 20 August:

> I had a long conversation one morning ... with the Prince of Wales but not such a one as I can write, he certainly would have made up all before she [Mrs Fitzherbert] went to Margate that is if she had behaved so in return as to encourage it. But how long that inclination may continue in his breast I cannot say, nor can I guess, if she may wish it, when she returns again to Town.[40]

In short, Mrs Fitzherbert had refused all attempts at rapprochement.

The writer Hester Piozzi actually welcomed the Prince's melancholy which she saw as a sign of good sense: 'surely our Heir Apparent has more Wit than to be fretting after Mrs Fitzherbert; who I hear is very happy, and will I hope soon be married – to some Man of Delicacy, and a nice Sense of Honour.'[41]

She was right in part. Ultimately the Prince accepted that his relationship with Mrs Fitzherbert was over and on 21 August wrote to Jack Payne:

> I have at last taken my resolution and all I can say is that I shall ever be happy to contribute anything that lays in my power to render Mrs. Fitzherbert's situation as comfortable as possible and to testify every sort of attention and kindness to her in the manner that can be most pleasing to her feelings *mais tout est fini*.[42]

It was indeed the end and left the Countess of Jersey in possession of the field. It was also the beginning of another, unhappy, chapter in the Prince's life, although when the King wrote to Pitt on 24 July neither he nor the Prince had any idea of what was to follow:

> I have [wrote the King] this morning seen the Prince of Wales who has acquainted me with his having broken of all connection with Mrs Fitzherbert and his desire of entering into a more creditable line of life by marrying; expressing at the same time the wish that my niece, the Princess of Brunswick may be the person.[43]

Whilst engineering the Prince's break with Mrs Fitzherbert, Lady Jersey had not only been consolidating her position with the Prince but also encouraging, as we shall see, the Prince in the new idea of marriage, both by the use of her extraordinary charms and by appealing to his other ambitions.

The same day that the King was writing to Pitt, Prince Ernest wrote to his brother the Prince of Wales. His letter contains the first reference in the royal correspondence to Lady Jersey, so recognising the position she had now achieved. Prince Ernest reported that the King and Queen were to give a grand ball and, presumably influenced by the Prince of Wales, 'Lady J & daughter is to be invited; *je connais du monde qui ne sera pas mécontent de cela*.'[44]

By then Lady Jersey was in Brighton having 'taken a house near the Prince's on the Steine'. He too was there, and as *The Oracle* reported 'his principal amusement was manoeuvring his regiment; for at the Pavilion everything is dreary and disconsolate with him'.[45]

An undated letter from about this time from Lady C. Campbell describes how the Prince sought to assuage his melancholy:

> They say the Prince is still miserable for Mrs Fitz: who first broke of [*sic*] their *Arrangement*. He goes, However, every Night to Ly Jersey pour se consoler; she (Ly J) never goes out, & they sit & talk all Night till one or two o'clock. These New Loves & Misery's for ye old Love are strange Contradictions'. [Whilst their Mother was consoling the Prince, her daughters were enjoying themselves at the opera, where 'Lady Abercorn was dres'd in and looked devinely, so did Lady William Russell & her sisters, Caroline Villiers and Anne Lambton'].[46]

Meanwhile, the Prince was increasingly at the ascendant Lady Jersey's beck and call. *The Times* reported on 5 August that the previous day he had set off, once more, to Brighton, from where William Churchill wrote to Jack Payne on 22 August:

> He [the Prince] was in town for one week from the 9th which time I find was taken up with Ly J. I thought a trip to Margate would have taken place; fortunately for Mrs F it did not, and he return'd here the 17 as wise as he went. A letter from Lady J carried him back again Wednesday.[47]

There is a delightful, and almost certainly false, story about the Prince's visit to Brighton in Robert Huish's 1831 (almost fictional) memoir of George IV, which is worth repeating not only for its own sake but also as an illustration of the reputation that history was to give Frances Jersey: 'A female we deprecate whenever we mention her, and who may be considered in the human race as the type of the serpent – beautiful bright and gloss in its exterior – in its interior, poisonous and pestiferous: we allude to Lady Jersey.'

Huish goes on to relate that whilst the Prince was at Brighton that year he had an affair with one Lucy Howard, a woman 'sent on earth to show to man what angels are in heaven ... a masterpiece of God's creation'. Apparently, said Huish, the Prince visited Lucy Howard in the company of Lord Rawdon to avoid suspicion, leaving the Pavilion at twilight and riding over the downs. Lady Jersey being suspicious sent a stable boy to follow the Prince to find out what was happening; the boy tracked him to a particular house but could not establish the purpose of the visit. An increasingly suspicious Lady Jersey sent the boy back but he was discovered by the Prince who, demanding an explanation of his presence, 'inflicted summary chastisement' on him, crippling him for life and nearly killing him. Indeed some reported, said Huish, that he did kill him, but Huish says that this was not the case and that the Prince gave his parents £50 per annum for his support.[48]

The mythology of Lady Jersey was beginning to take form.

There was also increasing speculation about what lay behind the Prince's ending of his relationship with Mrs Fitzherbert. On 5 August *The Times* reported: 'It is said that the late separation was brought about at the earnest solicitation of her MAJESTY,' which in a substantive sense was true as the Queen never liked Maria Fitzherbert. What was also true, as Lady Margaret Fordyce, a friend of Mrs Fitzherbert's, wrote a little later, was that Lady Jersey's plan was for the Prince to leave Maria so that the King would pay his debts.[49] *The Bon Ton* magazine accurately summed things up and reflected Lady Jersey's new position of influence in the following way:

> The separation so anxiously and so long desired by certain august personages, was effected solely by the management and address of an active countess. Hence the influence she possesses in all the royal circles, and hence the envy which attaches on her, as a natural consequence of female pre-eminence.[50]

In short, the Queen was very grateful to her and the Countess was in favour.

There was a further natural consequence of Lady Jersey's new position in those days of scatological popular cartoons. On 26 August the newspapers published a Cruikshank print entitled *My Grandmother, alias the Jersey Jig, alias the Rival Widows* in which a crone-like Lady Jersey is sitting on the Prince's knee, taking snuff whilst being fondled by the Prince, with him saying:

> I've kissed & I've prattled with Fifty Grand Dames,
> And chang'd them as oft, do you see;
> But of all the Grand Mammy's that dance on the Steine,
> The Widow of Jersey give me.

In the background Mrs Fitzherbert, who the Press had reported was to receive £6,000 per annum from the Prince, was clasping her forehead and a bond for £6,000, crying: 'Was it for this paltry consideration I sacrificed my______ my______my______? For this only I submitted to______to______! Shame for ever on my ruined Greatness!!!'[51]

There were also some very salacious rumours to be heard. In the early months of 1795, Mrs Piozzi recorded stories in circulation that the Prince would not marry unless his debts were paid, and went on:

> Some of these Debts too are of a nature so disgraceful, that he dares not show the Articles ... others say he has paid 10 or 20 Thousand for quiet possession of Lady Jersey – a Woman who has no less than six Grand Children – What Times! what Manners are these? besides the immense expense of buying Mrs Fitzherbert's consent to his Marriage – another Old Grimalkin of fifty Years standing at least.[52]

Clearly Robert Huish heard the same story although with a gloss to it. Writing of the same time, he said that Princess Caroline later

> declared, that George III, had disclosed to her, that the ... Duke of Gloucester, in a conversation, positively stated that an arrangement was made with Lord Carlisle to give up Lady Jersey to the Prince; that this was agreed at Rochester when Lady Jersey first set out to meet the Princess of Wales, and that there was an understanding that she should always be the objectives of his [that is Carlisle's] affection.[53]

The truth of the story may be doubted, and Huish's chronology is clearly wrong. Nevertheless what cannot be doubted is that the story was in circulation and that, given Lady Jersey's reputation, credence was given to it.

Much more credible are the reports of the role that Lady Jersey played in arranging the Prince's disastrous marriage to Caroline of Brunswick, a marriage which was to cause an unpopular Prince to become a despised one and, indirectly, to result in the royal family itself feeling under threat.

Lady Jersey was now in a position of favour and influence within the royal family and her behaviour began to change dramatically. It was as if her new position had gone to her head, realising the opportunities open to her at the summit of Society. No longer was she simply a spirited, selfish and somewhat fast member of the *ton*. Now she quite rapidly became an authoritarian and increasingly arrogant and manipulative lightning rod who sought to manage both the Prince and Society in her own interests. So in her biography of Georgiana Devonshire, Amanda Foreman says of Lady Jersey that once she had become the Prince's mistress: 'She was insufferable, making it a point to be as vicious as possible to anyone who had once been connected with the Prince. She was vile to Mrs Fitzherbert and sneering towards Georgiana and Lady Melbourne.'[54]

We shall see, too, many of the loyal and disinterested intimates of the Prince being ousted from his circle by her in the near future as she sought to concentrate influence over the Prince in her own hands, an outcome the Duke of Gloucester had rightly feared might happen if Mrs Fitzherbert was replaced in the Prince's favours. The result was that a very foolish and self-centred Prince was bereft of wise and impartial advice, to be guided only by the Countess.

She had also

> at last accomplished her ardent desire to be admitted to the Queen's parties at Windsor. – It is understood to have been accomplished by the Prince of Wales. – The Princess Royal told Lady Beverley [wrote the artist Farington in his diary early in September] before the last entertainment given at Windsor, that the wish of Lady Jersey was known at Court, but that it would not [be] complied with. – When Lady B went there she was surprised to see Lady Jersey in conversation with the Prince of Wales.[55]

The favour shown to Lady Jersey extended to her husband. At the same time, Lord Jersey was writing to Countess Spencer that she would have heard from Lady Jersey that the Prince intended to marry, and added (in confidence) that the Prince, no doubt prompted by the Countess, had asked him to become his Master of the Horse in the following terms:

> My desire to appoint to that situation a person who from their manner and their knowledge & habits of a [Court] will do honour to the Office naturally makes me desirous of knowing whether such an appointment would be agreeable to your Lordship.[56]

It is widely accepted that the Prince's decision to marry was the work of Lady Jersey as part of her strategy to separate him permanently from Mrs Fitzherbert. She appealed to his self-interest by encouraging the belief that, on his getting married, Parliament would settle his debts, whilst the Prince's marriage suited Lady Jersey, as the Duke of Wellington said to Lady Salisbury, 'simply because she wished to put Mrs Fitzherbert on the same footing as herself, and deprive her of the claim to the title of lawful wife to the Prince', which, being already married, she could not achieve herself.[57]

Persuading the Prince to marry seems a simple task. More extraordinary was the influence that Lady Jersey exercised over the Prince in his choice of the lumpen and unsophisticated Caroline as his wife. Nevertheless, as Lord Holland wrote at the time:

> All well-informed persons agree that the preference of the Princess [Caroline] of Brunswick was the choice of Lady Jersey and Lady Harcourt; though some suppose that a reluctance to gratify his mother by raising a second

> Princess of Mecklenburgh [the first being Queen Charlotte] to the throne of England, was an ingredient in that determination.[58]

Lord Holland also explained the reasons for Lady Jersey's choice of Caroline, saying that Lady Jersey had no objections to, nor was her position threatened by, the Prince marrying a woman of 'indelicate manners, indifferent character and not very inviting appearance, from the hope that disgust for the wife would secure constancy to the mistress'.[59]

In short, Caroline would provide no competition to the beautiful, elegant and witty Countess of Jersey as the Prince's paramour. How she convinced the Prince that Caroline was the right choice can only be explained by Frances Jersey's charms and persuasiveness and her emphasising the acceptability of the choice to the King as a precondition to the settling of the Prince's debts. In a word, the marriage Lady Jersey orchestrated was designed to consolidate her position with the Prince of Wales and her indirect standing, power and patronage that went with that.

The interests of the Prince, let alone of the country, did not enter the Countess's calculations.

This was to prove the most fateful decision of her life. It would result in the destruction of both her and the Prince's reputations, and a display of vitriol directed against them rarely seen even in a century when, surrounded by beauty and elegance, cruelty and crudity were the language of the day.

In the meantime onlookers were fascinated with the unfolding events. The Countess of Mount Edgecumbe, no friend of Frances Jersey, was asking Edward Jerningham scathingly, 'Will your friend the Lucretia, by her virtue, gain any situation in the new establishment?' of the household of Prince and his future bride.[60] At the same time, Horace Walpole was writing to Mary Berry in response to news that Mrs Fitzherbert was in Margate driving away her sorrows: 'I suppose our Countesses (I don't mean *my* two [that is Ladies Ailesbury and Ossory; rather he had in mind the Countesses of Jersey and Harcourt], but especially the latest, are now thinking on, or ordering their robes, since Mrs F has waived her claim to *Ich Dien*.'[61]

The Queen was more ambivalent about her son's marriage, despite her desire to separate him from Maria Fitzherbert. She never liked Caroline or the Prince's choice of her as his bride (and was to become very unpopular as a result of her treatment of Caroline). As Prince Ernest wrote to his brother early in October:

> She said she had resolved never to talk, no never to open her lips about your marriage, so that no one should say she had any hand in any thing; though she never liked the Dutchess of Brunsvic [*sic*] yet she should treat the Princess very well. Her opinions she could not give, as she never intended to speak about it. She hoped you would be happy, & all this she

> said with tears in her eyes. God knows what is the matter with her, but she is sullen.[62]

The Queen's antipathy to Caroline was later to prove a prop to Frances Jersey in her hard-hearted relations with the Princess.

In the midst of all of this, unfavourable reports on Caroline were circulating in England. It was 'too late to recede. [This fact] had allayed all Lady Jersey's disposition to soften or contradict; and it [was] most probable that she encouraged such gossip and scandal' in order to cement her position with the Prince, wrote Lord Holland. So it was, he went on, that when eventually Caroline was to arrive in England she would be escorted by the Countess of Jersey, 'her bitterest enemy (a lady well practised in the arts of tormenting, insulting, and degrading a rival ...)'[63]

Lady Jersey also took control over the composition of the Princess's future establishment. Lord Glenbervie later wrote: 'the Prince, who named all the Princess's establishment at that time, and amongst the rest, Lady Jersey. More correctly speaking, I believe she named them all.'[64] So it was that Lord Jersey wrote to Lady Spencer on 30 October: 'In addition to what I told your Ladyship regarding myself, I have further to say that Lady Jersey is to be one of the Ladies of the Bedchamber, the List will all be known today of the whole establishment.'[65]

In other respects life continued in the normal way. Early in September, Frances Jersey wrote to Edward Jerningham to assure him that 'anything in my power you shall always command' – perhaps one of the factors behind his loyalty to her in coming years.[66] For some reason, though, their relationship needed to be shrouded in mystery. On 30 September, the Countess wrote to him from Middleton:

> I shall be in town tomorrow night, and glad to see you as early as you please on Wednesday morning. I wish now to remind you that our appointments are still a secret, and that you must express surprise as well as joy when you are informed of them. Adieu. Ever most sincerely yours. FJ.[67]

The Prince too was continuing a relationship. On 25 October Prince Ernest, presumably at his brother's behest, breakfasted with Mrs Fitzherbert, afterwards writing to the Prince of Wales to say that 'she received my brother & myself v civilly ... Mrs F seems to me to be very low spirited, never mentioned your name once, but, however, she was very low at anything mentioned that have any regard to you.'[68] Perhaps it was this that caused the Prince of Wales to request all his friends to 'show the same attention as before' to Mrs Fitzherbert, which prompted Georgiana Devonshire to comment 'what an odd situation'.[69] Despite that, Prince Ernest had closed his letter to his brother with the words: 'My best compliments to Lady Jersey. All I hope is that you may both be sincerely happy.'[70]

So Lady Jersey's position at court, in particular with the Queen, was now assured. Of this Lord Malmesbury, the diplomat who was to play a pivotal role in bringing Princess Caroline to England, wrote perceptively in his diary on 7 December 1794:

> Lady Elizabeth Eden, whom I carried home from Court, said Lady Jersey was very well with the Queen, that she frequently went to Windsor, and appeared as a sort of favourite ... This, if true, is most strange and bodes no good.[71]

Lord Malmesbury was to be proved right: it did not.

12
The Arrival of Princess Caroline

Even more than in earlier years, the absence of Frances Jersey's own correspondence makes it difficult to see into her mind during the turbulent years which were now beginning. Apart from a telling letter, probably written in 1796, we have few clues as to what she thought apart from that which outsiders surmised. What is more, the formerly voluminous correspondence between her husband and Countess Spencer was dwindling in these years, not least because of the growing distance between the families and the growing unpleasantness of the Countess and her reputation.

What is clear is that, with her position with the Prince now secure, an increasingly confident and self-important Lady Jersey sought to consolidate her influence. Not only did she seek to control the Prince and his future wife but also she sought to replace the Prince's inner circle with those she favoured and who favoured her. In all of this she became increasingly autocratic and assertive, and the faults in her character became increasingly apparent. By controlling the Prince she sought to buttress her own position and from that position she sought the status, the patronage, the domination and the influence she so much enjoyed, both for herself and for her family.

Of pressing interest was the imminent marriage of the Prince of Wales.

'Lady Jersey goes to meet the Princess of Brunswick, at least she is to be one of the Ladies that go,' wrote Mrs Howe to Lady Stafford on 11 November 1794, so marking the start of an episode which would plunge Frances Jersey's already doubtful reputation into one of disrepute.[1] One has to assume that her fetching of Princess Caroline was Lady Jersey's idea. It seems equally certain that when the Prince wrote to his mother on 19 November 1794 putting forward the names of four bridesmaids for the Princess it was Lady Jersey who suggested the names. The four proposed were Lady Charlotte Spencer, Lady Mary Osborne, Lady Charlotte Legge and the Jerseys' third daughter, Lady Caroline Villiers, all daughters of Dukes or Earls in accordance with precedent. The Queen replied to the Prince the next day that the King 'approves greatly of yr choice'.[2] All of which enabled Lord Jersey to write proudly to Lady Spencer at the end of the month:

> Lady J is to go over for her RH … and the whole Etiquette is settling fast. Our Caroline is to be one of the Bride maids: which she is not a little pleased with. I wish you knew her, not only by sight, but by her character; I will venture to refer you to Lord Spencer for her looks.[3]

On 11 December Lady Jersey and Mrs Aston, who was to join her in fetching the Princess, were presented to the Queen at the Drawing-Room following their appointment.[4] Even now, though, Lady Jersey's reputation was preceding her. Lord Malmesbury, who was in Brunswick arranging the details of the marriage, noted in his diary on 9 December a conversation with Princess Caroline in which she asked about Lady Jersey, appearing to suppose her an '*intriguante*' but not to know of any partiality or connection between Lady Jersey and the Prince of Wales.[5]

More stories were to emerge in Brunswick before very much longer but, in the meantime, preparations for the Princess's journey to England, at a time when England was still at war with France, were going ahead. On Friday 5 December *The Sun* reported:

> Yesterday the Squadron of Yachts which are to bring the Princess of Wales over, dropt down the River from Deptford, to take in provisions and ammunition; they are expected to sail in a few days … The Admiralty have engaged that the squadron which is to bring her to England shall be completely equipped by Monday next …[6]

And on 15 December Lord Jersey wrote to tell Lady Spencer that all the details of the trip to fetch Princess Caroline would shortly be fixed, and that 'Lady J is all in the hurry of preparation for her journey'.[7]

As part of these preparations, Lady Jersey was making her presence felt by asking constant and importunate questions. It was presumably to her that Captain Payne, who was in charge of carrying out the arrangements for Princess Caroline's sea crossing, was referring when he wrote to the Home Secretary, the Duke of Portland (apparently) on 11 December in the following terms:

> The whole artillery of female chicanery has been played off against me, without success, and your judicious interposition will render them totally abortive. The day is not far off when you [as the person in overall charge of the arrangements] will receive the thanks to which your Grace is entitled in guarding a *person* [that is the Prince] from his own indiscretion.[8]

The Countess was also bombarding the Queen with questions. Princess Elizabeth responded to the Prince of Wales that the Queen

> would most willingly answer all the questions Lady Jersey *most naturally* wishes to have *answer'd,* but she is *as unknowing as yourself*, though as

> anxious to have everything as comfortable and proper as you can wish. She has twice try'd to talk to the King on this subject, & *he* has so positively said that the Duke of Portland had received *his orders to settle everything* … About the ladies' dress, mama orders me to say that if they receive the Princess on board it had better be undress, but in case of their being *unwell & forced to go onshore* she advises them to take a Court dress, that if the Princess wishes to see *them there* they may appear in gala.[9]

The same day, the Prince received yet another letter from the Countess asking ever more questions which, in order to save time, on this occasion he passed on directly to the Queen for answers.[10]

But some of this was, nevertheless, done by the Countess with self-deprecating humour and grace. There are three undated letters amongst the Jersey family manuscripts which can be dated to this time. In them the Countess gives detailed instructions in relation to the transport of her and Mrs Aston's luggage. Written with charm, they are almost playful, recognising 'the tiresomeness' of her letters, acknowledging the kindnesses shown to her and offering the reward variously of some not terribly good verses and an invitation to dinner and an introduction to her children. One of the letters closes with:

> Ever your most obliged Humbl Servant & Eternal Ketchup Eater
> F. Jersey.[11]

The Countess, as she was to show many times in her life, could charm at will.

However, she was also becoming exercised about the safety of their journey in wartime Europe, as the Prince of Wales wrote on 23 December: 'such an alarm has been conceived by the ladies, & indeed by Lord Jersey, of the dangers of going in yachts … it would be impossible to prevail upon them, or even for him to ask them, to embark,' that is unless they were to go on a warship. Lady Jersey's qualms prevailed and, not without some difficulty, a warship was duly provided.[12]

Even at this stage during all the comings and goings, with his marriage imminent and Lady Jersey his established lover, the Prince was concerned for Mrs Fitzherbert – a state of affairs which continued through all the years of his affair with the Countess and which speaks volumes for Frances Jersey's charms and resources as well as the Prince's malleability. In the first of numerous incidents which illustrate that, despite the thrall which the 'Enchantress' that was Lady Jersey threw over him, the Prince's real and overriding love even during the years he was under the Countess's spell was for Maria Fitzherbert, the Prince was troubled. Having made provision for Mrs Fitzherbert of £3,000 a year, he was now worried about what would happen should he die. Accordingly, through Lord Loughborough, he raised with the King the issue of whether the King would continue its payment on his death. Lord Loughborough's response, dated 19 December, was that, having spoken to the King, the Prince should have no 'uneasiness on this account'.[13]

At the same time there was increasing uneasiness in Brunswick. Lord Malmesbury noted hearing 'hints about' Lady Jersey there in his diary on

28 December and later at dinner he described the Duchess of Brunswick and the Princess as 'alarmed, agitated and uneasy' as a result of receiving an anonymous letter from England, 'warning them in the most exaggerated terms against Lady ——, who is represented as the worst and most dangerous of women'. Malmesbury had no choice but to dismiss the letter, which he initially described as 'evidently written by some disappointed milliner or angry maid servant, and deserving no attention'. There was also some deeper speculation that the letter was designed by Lady Jersey to encourage the idea in Caroline that she would be led into 'an affair of gallantry'. This did indeed frighten the Duke and Duchess of Brunswick, but Malmesbury dismissed the idea saying, 'Lady—— would be more cautious than to risk such an audacious measure.'[14]

On two scores, therefore, the circumstances surrounding the preparations for Princess Caroline's journey to England were not propitious.

The naval expedition to collect her was also encountering difficulty. On 29 December the welcoming party were at Sheerness ready to leave for the Continent. 'Last night,' reported the next day's *The Morning Chronicle*, 'the Prince of Wales returned to town from Sheerness, where he had been to see Lady Jersey and her suite embark to bring over the Princess of Brunswick.'[15] However the squadron's departure was delayed by contrary winds.[16] Then, when it eventually sailed a week later, as Lord Jersey told Lady Spencer:

> I attended Lady Jy to Margate, the whole party being sent thither under the notion that they were to embark from thence; we were then called to Sheerness, & they sailed from thence, they got no further than about five Leagues beyond the Nore, when the changing of the wind forced them back again to Sheerness.[17]

For the time being the expedition was abandoned because of the weather, and the Prince of Wales went back to Sheerness to accompany Lady Jersey and Mrs Aston to London.[18] As *The Morning Chronicle* reported: 'Commander Payne, the Earl of Clermont, Lady Jersey, Mrs Aston and the whole of the Mission to bring over the Princess of Brunswick are returned to town from Sheerness, to wait for better times, or better weather.'[19] Once there, were one to believe the pro-Caroline polemic, Lady Anne Hamilton's *Secret History of the Court of England* – which, not being written by Lady Hamilton nor secret, and being largely fictitious, one should not – 'the Prince was still as dissolute as ever, and associated with the very dregs of society of both sexes', which clearly included the Countess in the mythology of Frances Jersey.[20]

All the while, Frances Jersey was continuing to seek to separate the Prince from his former inner circle, in particular those who remained loyal to Maria Fitzherbert, so as to maximise her own influence and patronage for her family especially – in addition to the Earl becoming the Prince's Master of the Horse and her daughter one of the Princess's bridesmaids, she herself was to become one of Caroline's Ladies of the Bedchamber and her eldest son too was soon to receive a royal appointment. One of that former inner circle who was to suffer was Lord Hugh Seymour, brother of the Marquess of Hertford, who in December was already feeling unmerited royal mistreatment, prompted without doubt by the Countess. On 21 December Seymour wrote to his friend Jack Payne:

> I do assure you my dear Jack, that your admonition on the subject of giving way to my feeling about the Prince's conduct to me was not necessary, as my own pride is sufficient to keep me quiet on that score, and except to yourself, Mrs Fitz and the person who has so much right to look into every circumstances which may at any time make me grieve, I feel that I could not be brought to express my contempt for the false and base part the P. has acted towards me in return to [*sic*] the sincere regard every act of mine has manifested towards him.[21]

A few days later Seymour was writing again to Jack Payne to tell him of a letter his wife, Lady Horatia Seymour, had received from Mrs Fitzherbert in which she regretted the influence Lady Jersey was exercising over the Prince, and saying that Maria's letter

> does her heart much honor, as the interest she still feels for the welfare of the Prince makes her dread his being without a friend to turn him from the mischief and numberless difficulties which his present connection exposes him to ... but alas ... he is doom'd to be led by some bad character, male or female.[22]

The power of the manipulative and self-serving Countess over a weak and self-indulgent Prince was manifest to all his friends.

The Countess's next target was Jack Payne himself, as Lord Hugh Seymour wrote to Payne on 14 January:

> How very sorry I feel that the P is so thoroughly under the influence of Ly J who will certainly not fail to complete his ruin. I understand that she is working hard to separate you from him, & if she succeeds it will be difficult for him to apply to any person to relieve him from his difficulties, which nothing could bring home to his feelings with advantage but being reminded of his own description of that very strange character.[23]

Nevertheless, it was Seymour who, for the time being, bore the brunt of Lady Jersey's intriguing. Two days later he was writing again to Jack Payne:

> I shall beg you to take an opportunity ... of learning from him [that is the Prince] whether he is really anxious to turn me out of his family or whether it is only the object of that bitch under whose influence he is at present to remove from him those that the world has approv'd of being about him.[24]

The reference to the Prince's 'family' was, in the parlance of the day, to his household, where Seymour held the post of Privy Purse and Master of the

Robes. Seymour's concerns that he was to lose this position seemed unjustified when, on 19 January, the Marquess of Hertford wrote to the Prince supporting his brother's application for a seat on the Board of Admiralty, to which the Prince replied the following day that this would not prevent him retaining the situation 'which he at presents holds'.[25] Within a fortnight, though, and despite the Marquess seeking to have the change delayed until Hugh Seymour returned from sea, Seymour had been appointed instead as an additional Lord of the Bedchamber. This was a change which the family, and the world at large, regarded both as a demotion and as a sign of the loss of the Prince's favour, despite his earlier assurances – the Prince responding abruptly to the Marquess that the matter was now out of his control.[26]

It did not really matter whether it was the Prince or 'the bitch' who lay behind this (it was certainly the Countess), the effect was the same and more enemies were made. It was not until about 1800, when Lady Jersey was no longer in favour, that the Prince sought a rapprochement with Lord Hugh, who before the ascendance of Lady Jersey had long been one of his closest friends.[27]

When Lord Darnley, the new Groom of the Stole, as one of his first official acts, wrote reluctantly on 7 February to tell Lord Hugh of his unwelcome demotion, he too deplored the Prince's behaviour, writing that the Prince stood very much in need of a sincere friend. He wrote: 'If those who answer that description could by any means prevent him from listening too much to evil counsellors and adding to the follies he has already committed, they would not only do essential service to him individually, but, what is much more important at this very serious and alarming moment, to this country and the world.' The evil counsellor was of course Frances Jersey.[28]

Darnley was not alone in this view. In her letter to Jack Payne of 12 February, Lady Horatia Seymour said: 'I am most grateful to the world for the indignation they have shewn at anything that appear'd like a slight shown towards a Man of Hugh's superior character. This alone has brought the Prince to his senses.'[29]

Sadly it had not. The Countess's malice towards Princess Caroline was to become a common topic of conversation, as did her greedy insistence that the Prince place all the patronage at his disposal in her hands. Lady Jersey's misjudgement of this was summed up by Georgiana Devonshire in a letter to Lady Melbourne at about this time: 'It is very odd that clever as she is she should not have guessed that the extent of patronage she took would be unpopular.'[30]

An example of this came in the form of an announcement from Carlton House on 6 March which not only informed the world of Lord Hugh Seymour's demotion to the Bedchamber but also rubbed salt in the wound by stating that young Lord Villiers had also been appointed a Gentleman of his Highness's Bedchamber.[31]

The real dynamics behind the Prince's marriage, however, were yet to become clear. On 24 January 1795, Gillray's s caricature *The Lover's Dream* was published, showing the public's unjustified expectations. In it the Prince sleeps in a four-poster bed as a cupid raises its curtains and his bride-to-be approaches. Meanwhile the King offers him a sack of gold and the Queen extends a book to him entitled *The Arts of Getting Pretty Children* as Lady Jersey and Maria Fitzherbert slink furtively out of the room.[32]

The reality of the situation was more accurately displayed elsewhere. On 5 February the Prince gave an entertainment at Carlton House where he was joined by the King and Queen, the Princesses and the Royal Dukes of York, Clarence and Gloucester. As *The Oracle* reported, following a concert and cards, 'supper was served up in the greatest order and most brilliant style,' adding portentously, 'Lady Jersey did the honours of the house.'[33]

By now the plan that Lady Jersey and others should go to fetch Princess Caroline had been abandoned. Instead, the Princess was to be greeted on her arrival in England. Until then, the Prince retreated (not alone) to his country house in Hampshire, Kempshot. As Lord Palmerston wrote to his wife in early March:

> The Princess is expected very soon. The Prince and Lady J are at Kempshott. The P is highly offended on two accounts because Lady J is not invited to the private parties at B[uckingham] House and because he is not promoted to the rank of Major-General in the Army![34]

Whilst Palmerston did not mention that Lord Jersey too was at Kempshot, the long-suffering Earl was indeed there, writing from Kempshot on 13 March: 'We remain here I believe one day longer & then I fancy the Pss may be expected very shortly indeed, when we shall all be put into function'[35]

By now Lady Jersey's behaviour, her arrogance, self-importance, domineering disposition and her flaunting of her royal favour, was beginning to provoke public criticism. *The Times* of 26 March reported that the previous Monday the Prince of Wales was so indisposed with a fever that he had 'an ounce and a half of blood taken from him'. Nevertheless, *The Times* went on, 'On Tuesday his Royal Highness was sufficiently recovered to go to Lady Jersey's where he spent the day.' The next day *The Times* thundered:

> If a certain Lady, very much connected at present with a Gentleman of high distinction, proceeds to conduct herself much longer in the manner she now does, there will not be found an honourable Lady who will not give in her resignation in a newly appointed household. Her conduct gives general disgust and unease.

Despite being clearly besotted with Lady Jersey, and with his marriage imminent, the self-indulgent Prince could still not let go of Maria Fitzherbert. She had withdrawn to her house at Marble Hill near Richmond, where early in April, as she was 'taking a dismal airing in my carriage, the first thing that presented itself to me close to my own house was the Prince riding furiously by my carriage so near I could have touched him I really thought I should have died'. They did not speak but later Maria learned that he had been opposite her house for some time.[36]

The inevitable continued to unfold. On 5 April, Lady Jersey was at Greenwich to greet Princess Caroline upon her arrival in England – and here mythology begins to take over. As Robert Huish has it:

> The Princess was received by Sir Hugh Palisser, the Governor [of Greenwich Hospital] who conducted her to his house; but Lady Jersey did not arrive there until an hour after the Princess had landed [the implication, probably correctly, is that this was a deliberate slight on the part of the Countess]. They both soon retired into an adjoining room, and the dress of the Princess was changed for one which was brought from town by Lady Jersey.[37]

The story goes that Lady Jersey made 'derogatory comments on Caroline's muslin gown and blue satin petticoat' and ordered Caroline to change into 'a less flattering white satin dress which she had brought with her'. Lady Jersey was also alleged to have insisted 'that dollops of rouge be applied to Caroline's cheeks'.[38] All of this, so it is said, was designed by Frances Jersey to put Caroline in the least attractive light, in particular in the eyes of the Prince.

As in all myth there is an element of truth. *The Sun* certainly reported that, 'On her landing [the Princess] wore a blue dress, and on her leaving Greenwich [for London she] was dressed in an elegant satin dress,' and it may well be that after her travels rouge was applied to her face; nevertheless, there is more to be said on both sides.[39]

It is clear that Princess Caroline was forced to wait for the King's carriages to meet her at Greenwich. Lord Malmesbury, who was in attendance, confided to his diary that this was 'owing, as I have since heard, to Lady —— not being ready'. Whilst this is hearsay after the event, if, as seems probable, it was true, it was an unforgiveable breach of etiquette – even though there could be any number of explanations for it, only one of which was that it was deliberate slight on the part of Lady Jersey.[40]

Lord Malmesbury in the same diary entry also confirms that 'Lady —— [was] much dissatisfied with Princess's mode of dress … and expressed herself in a way which induced me to speak rather sharply to her.' This too does not substantiate the charges against Lady Jersey of deliberately demeaning the Princess, though it does seem that, typically, she spoke sharply. More important is the account by Caroline's protagonist, Nightingale, in his *Memoirs of Princess Caroline*, published in 1820:

> The dress of the Princess was changed, from a muslin gown and blue satin petticoat, with a black beaver hat, and blue and black feathers, for a white satin gown, and a very elegant turban cap of satin, ornamented with white feathers: a plume, in imitation of the Prince of Wales' own crest, studded with brilliants, which, as it played backwards and forwards in the light produced a most beautiful effect. This cap and the rest of the Princess's

> dress, were a present ordered by his Royal Highness, and were carried from town by Lady Jersey to Greenwich for that purpose.[41]

So it appears the dress was the Prince's choice, though doubtless influenced by Frances Jersey, and the effect was not 'unflattering'. Add to that the advice from the Princess's own mother that she 'strongly recommends that her daughter's cloathes [*sic*] should be chiefly white, as that becomes her most', and the alleged malevolence of Lady Jersey's actions at Greenwich appears doubtful indeed.[42]

Even more doubtful is the story, typical of numerous canards which emerged in later years as a result of the vitriol that Frances Jersey was to attract, that she gave Princess Caroline onions to eat, on the grounds that the Prince liked nothing so much as the smell of onions.[43]

What on the other hand is clearly true is the account Lord Malmesbury wrote in his diary that day of the party travelling to London in the King's coaches. At first, he recorded, Lady Jersey, who was to travel in the Princess's coach, insisted that she could not travel facing backwards but must sit forward, as if to assert her position, even though 'it was strictly forbidden by the King' as contrary to etiquette. To this Malmesbury offered Lady Jersey that she could come in his coach, sitting forward, with Mrs Aston moving into the Princess's. This, Malmesbury tersely noted, 'of course settled the business'.[44]

The arrival of Princess Caroline in London the same day prompted Horace Walpole to draw a historical parallel. Writing to Mary Berry two days later he said: 'The Princess arrived at St James's on Sunday at three o'clock – Madame des Ursins was not arrested, and sent out the kingdom full dressed with all her *old* diamonds *new set*.'

In comparing Lady Jersey to Mme des Ursins Walpole was referring to the Princess des Ursins, who had formerly been all-powerful at the court of Philip V of Spain eighty years earlier but who had been dismissed from court and country by Philip's second wife, Elizabeth Farnese, whom the Princess had gone to meet as she entered Spain on her way to her marriage in Madrid.[45]

In Princess Caroline's case not only was there no dismissal of the reigning favourite but also the Princess was to be surrounded by those chosen by Frances Jersey. The Countess herself was a Lady of the Bedchamber to the Princess, which would mean her being intimately involved in the Princess's day-to-day life. Furthermore, as Lord Glenbervie said of the selection of her other servants, 'Lady Jersey … named them all'.[46]

Contemporary observers were scathing of the unfolding events.

Initially there was hope, as the publication of an anonymous 'letter' to the Prince said:

> Another beneficial consequence was anticipated [of the wedding] by the moral and decorous part of the community, that it would terminate, as

decency and propriety demanded it should, the open and undisguised intercourse you then had with the wife of an Earl, your neighbour.[47]

That hope was to remain unfulfilled, as Lady Charlotte Bury wrote in her journal:

> Who and what was the woman sent to escort her Royal Highness to England? Was there any attempt made on the part of the Prince to disguise of what nature his connection with Lady J——y? None. He took every opportunity of wounding the Princess, by showing her that Lady J——y was her rival. The ornaments with which he had decked his wife's arms he took from her and gave to his mistress, who wore them in her presence and suffered Lady J——y to do so in the most open and offensive manner.[48]

Another commentator, Mary Frampton wrote in her diary of these times:

> The Prince was then under the influence of Lady Jersey, a clever, unprincipled, but beautiful and fascinating woman, though with scarcely any retrieving really good quality. She had lived a good deal with the Harcourt society, being very clever ... Amongst other freaks she was a very fine lady'.

Mary Frampton also tells a story illustrating Lady Jersey's style, describing how this very fine lady insolently approached Mary's aunt at an assembly, saying, 'Oh, Miss Fauquier, you are just the person to have a pincushion about you,' to which the aunt responded, 'Yes, I always have a pincushion and plenty of pins, but I am just the person *not* to give you one of them.'[49]

More immediately, on the evening of her arrival in London Princess Caroline and the Prince of Wales had dinner together. They were joined, *The Sun* reported, by Lady Jersey, Mrs Aston, Mrs Harcourt [*sic*], Lord Malmesbury, Lord Clermont, Col Grenville and Major Heslop – Malmesbury apart a veritable troupe of the Prince's cronies.[50]

The dinner was a disaster. Perhaps this was the occasion which transformed the Countess's attitude to Princess Caroline. Instead of regarding her as she had until now as a puppet to be manipulated in the Countess's own interests, the Princess's behaviour caused Lady Jersey, ever the epitome of elegance and style and one to exploit the weaknesses of others, to despise, and in her own words 'abhor', her – and ultimately to mistreat her, in the style of a woman who, in the words of her critics, was never happier than when tormenting a (losing) rival.

As the Princess told Charlotte Bury some years later: 'the first moment I saw my *futur* and Lady J——y together I knew how it all was, and I said to myself, "Oh, very well!"'[51]

At the dinner a clearly nervous, unsettled and unsophisticated Princess Caroline did herself no favours. As Lord Malmesbury recorded, he was 'far from satisfied with the Princess's behaviour', describing her as 'flippant, rattling, affecting raillery and wit, and throwing out coarse vulgar hints about

Lady [Jersey], who was present, and though mute, *le diable n'en perdait rien*. The Prince was evidently disgusted.'[52]

This would only be compounded were it true, as Robert Huish has it that earlier in the day Princess Caroline had mentioned to Lady Jersey (who, so he said, passed it on to the Prince) that she, Caroline, had had a previous attachment and that she 'loved one little finger of the individual [concerned] far better than she should love the whole person of the Prince of Wales'.[53]

It is probably not true, but come what may the effect of all of this was to fix the Prince's, and indeed the Countess's, dislike of his future wife and in so doing to fulfil the Countess's original objectives. Nevertheless the Princess was not slow to challenge the Prince and his relationship with Lady Jersey. As the self-deluding, or perhaps bewitched, Prince reminded her a year later:

> The intimacy of my friendship with Lady Jersey, under all the false colour which slander has given to it, was perfectly known to you before you accepted my hand, for you yourself told me so immediately on your arrival here, reciting the particulars of the anonymous letters which transmitted the information to Brunswick, & giving yourself credit for having suppressed all mention of their purport but *to myself*. This Madam, was two days before we were married: I then took the opportunity of explaining to you that Lady Jersey was one of the oldest acquaintances I had in this country & that the confidence resulting from so long friendship had enabled her to offer advice which contributed not a little to decide me to marriage.[54]

Despite which it was really Maria Fitzherbert that the Prince yearned for. Even on 7 April, the evening before his marriage to Caroline, the Prince said to his brother, the Duke of Clarence, 'William tell Mrs Fitzherbert she is the only woman I shall ever love.'[55] The next day, as he was on his way to his wedding, the Prince said to Lord Moira: 'It is no use, Moira, I shall never love any woman but Fitzherbert.'[56]

For her part, Mrs Fitzherbert largely disappeared from public view, although the two parties to the illegal marriage of 1785 were both miserable.[57] Despite, or perhaps because of, this there is a story, attributed to Princess Caroline in 1820, that two days after his wedding the Prince actually called for his carriage with the intent of going to Mrs Fitzherbert and had to be physically prevented from doing so.[58]

The dynamics of the story of the royal wedding are extraordinary: manipulation by a mistress, greater love for a former mistress, and disdain for a future wife – and all in the context of the sorry tale of the Prince's imminent wedding, the culmination of a journey illustrated in one near-contemporary cartoon which showed Caroline being helped down into a boat to take her to England by an elderly crone wearing a crown, the stern of the boat bearing the name *The Hag of Jersey*.[59]

The wedding took place on 9 April. Princess Caroline's mantle 'of crimson velvet, trimmed with ermine, was supported by Ladies Mary Osborne, C. Spencer, C. Legge and C. Villiers who attend as Bride-Maids … Their dress consisted of a crape petticoat, richly embroidered with stripes of silver foil and spangles, with a white satin body and train … Their caps were an embroidered bandeau, with three large ostrich feathers,' reported the *Whitehall Evening Post,* which went on to note that amongst 'The Ladies whose dresses were much noticed for their superior elegance' was Lady Jersey herself.[60]

The 'Lady C. Villiers' was of course Lady Caroline Villiers, whom Lady Ailesbury particularly admired, describing her as 'a most beautiful girl'.[61]

During the ceremony the Duke of Leeds noted a remarkable 'coolness and indifference' on the part of the Prince towards Princess Caroline and was afterwards told that during the ceremony the Prince 'was perpetually looking at his favorite Lady Jersey'.[62] Lady Maria Stuart put it more strongly, saying that 'the Prince was so agitated … it was expected he would have burst out in tears', and afterwards that he 'looked like Death and full of confusion, as if he wished to hide himself from the looks of the whole world. I think he is much to be pitied … What a wedding.'[63] Another person there, Lady Anne Lindsay, recalled the Prince of Wales, on his way out of the Chapel Royal, giving her a look that she remembered as 'miserable'.[64]

At the reception that followed the Prince was drunk;[65] and, again in the words of the Duke of Leeds:

> A circumstance happened … which was thought to confirm the unfortunate suspicion of his ill-fated attachment to [Lady Jersey]. The Earl of Harcourt whose wife was also a Lady of the Bedchamber to Her Majesty, and the most intimate friend of Lady Jersey, was desired by the Prince to hold his hat during the ceremony which over when his Lordship sought to return the Hat HRH insisted on his keeping it. The hat was ornamented with a most beautiful and costly Button and Loop of Diamonds.[66]

If the wedding was miserable, the honeymoon, at least for Princess Caroline, was hardly less so. Even so, before its disintegration the Prince and his new wife had consummated their marriage, and the Princess was pregnant within days of the wedding.

Of course, Lady Jersey accompanied the newly married couple on their honeymoon and clearly caused the Princess discomfort at the least, even if some of the stories which abound are, as is most likely, untrue.

It will be enough to quote just one example of the widely circulated, and apparently believed, canards about Lady Jersey before moving on to the undisputed truth:

> All through the honeymoon Lady Jersey had spared no pains to make the life of the Princess miserable, by means of continual practical jokes and humiliations. Even on the wedding night Lady Jersey caused Epsom salts to

> be put into the pastry served to her for supper, arranged for her to be given the most unmanageable horses to ride at military parades and caused spirits to be added to the wine she drank' so as to get her drunk.[67]

The Princess provided a less contentious – but still scathing – description of the honeymoon to Lord Minto three years later, which he retold to his wife:

> It appears they lived together two or three weeks at first, but not at all afterwards as man and wife. They went to Windsor two days after the marriage, and after a few days' residence there they went to Kempshot, where there was no woman but Lady Jersey, and the men very blackguard companions of the Prince's, who were constantly drunk and filthy, sleeping and snoring in boots on sofas, and in other respects the scene, she says, was more like the Prince of Wales at Eastcheap in Shakespeare than like any notions she had acquired before of a Prince or a gentleman. The conversation was suited to the rest, and the whole resembled a bad brothel much more than a Palace.[68]

Another well known story of this time is recorded by Hare. In this, one evening after pipes and punch had been produced: 'When Lady Jersey drank, the Regent kissed the spot where her lips had rested: upon which the Princess took a pipe from Lord Coleraine's mouth, blew two or three whiffs [into the Prince's face] and handed it back to him. The Prince was quite furious …'[69]

The Prince may have been furious but the Princess was deeply unhappy. Lady Charlotte Bury records Caroline saying to her at the time: 'If anybody say to me at this moment – will you pass your life over again, or be killed? I would choose death; for you know a little sooner or later we must all die; but to live a life of wretchedness twice over – oh! Mine God no!'[70]

The Prince's behaviour to the Princess was now dividing the *ton* into two camps, and the Countess was regarded in the same light. His flagrant unfaithfulness, flaunting Lady Jersey as his consort in public, and his open bullying of Caroline, with Lady Jersey seizing every possibility to humiliate her, prompted Countess Spencer to write to Georgiana Devonshire in April: 'Lady J is in every thing & by everybody most thoroughly disapproved. What a prospect of wretchedness seems gathering round every individual in that sad group … I feel happy that you & your sister are unconnected with them all.'[71]

Whilst public support for the Princess, and not just within the *ton*, grew ever more sympathetic and enthusiastic (on her appearance at Covent Garden on 20 April, accompanied by the Prince and Lady Jersey, she was rapturously greeted with the 'warmest acclamation'), the behaviour of Lady Jersey was increasingly manipulative, grasping and peremptory and she was becoming ever more unpopular, with the Prince seemingly meekly acquiescing in her demands as putty in her hands.[72]

First there was the Prince's new carriage. This was a superb yellow chariot adorned with the Prince of Wales' arms and crest and ornamented with festoons and oak leaves heightened in gold, with the Royal Arms and, on the side panels, the Order of the Garter. This truly magnificent coach was presumably built by John Hatchett, the Royal coachmaker, of Long Acre, near St Martin's Lane where the most celebrated coachmakers were to be found. At the time Hatchett employed several hundred workmen on three floors, from smiths to gilders, although few coach makers made a complete coach, with bits of the enterprise being farmed out to specialist trades like draughtsmen, 'coach livery lace-makers', and wheel-wrights, each based nearby.[73] This splendid carriage was, however, appropriated to Lord Jersey, in theory in his capacity as Master of the Horse, on the grounds that, although it was first designed for the Princess of Wales, it was really only suitable for state occasions so had better be used on a more regular basis by Lord Jersey – and, to public indignation, his wife.[74]

Then there was the story related by Princess Caroline to Lady Charlotte Bury, also picked up by the press, that not long after her wedding 'the pearl bracelets, which had been given her by the Prince, were taken from her to decorate the arms of Lady J—y', who apparently wore them in the Princess's presence.[75]

Finally, the Countess was seen to arrogate to herself the standing of a royal mistress of Carlton House, as Lady Spencer described to her daughter on 20 April: 'Mrs Howe writes me word that she was sent to on Saturday to go to Carlton House, a card by order of the Princess (as those from the Queen) from Lady Jersey, to desire she would come at 9.'[76]

Some thought the reign of Lady Jersey would not last. Mrs Piozzi wrote in April that 'Lady Jersey's favour they say will wane away fast mean time, and all the Town will be happy to see her kicked out'.[77] Only the latter sentiment was to be proved true. Three weeks later, she was writing: 'the world though wicked is so enraged against Lady Jersey, that people expect her to be hissed in her carriage, or at the Theatre: and our new Princess's popularity daily increases I think ...'[78]

In May a new arrangement, imposed by the Prince, was in place. Known as 'the Carlton House system', under it Princess Caroline was effectively confined to Carlton House and her visitors limited to those approved by her now estranged husband, who was encouraged and probably led in this by his mistress. This provoked Lord Palmerston to write to his wife: 'Everybody I hear is in the highest indignation at the proceedings at C[arlton] H[ouse]. She is quite shut-up and not permitted to see any person but such as are approved of,' with visitors being refused admittance to the Princess at the door. A day later he wrote again to his wife: 'the public mind is highly irritated and all reserve seems to be laid aside. Lady J is hissed and insulted and I hear is afraid to go to C[arlton] H[ouse] in her own chair' – many noble families kept private sedan chairs, readily identifiable by their coats of arms on the sides or the liveried retainers carrying them.[79] Lady Jersey, though, pretended that none of this was her doing, as Palmerston continued: 'All the harsh things are put upon [Lord Malmesbury] to do [vis-à-vis Princess Caroline] and [Lady Jersey] affects great kindness with a degree of familiarity in public that has more than once disgusted all the spectators.'[80]

Lady Palmerston's response was even more telling, clearly seeing that the driving force behind all the unhappy events was Lady Jersey rather than the Prince of Wales:

> I quite lament over our poor captive Princess ... I cannot comprehend the motive which induces Lady Jersey to behave so injudiciously and what advantage she can derive by making the Prince behave not only like a fool but also as a complete brute. I thought Lady Jersey was as cunning as a serpent, though not quite as harmless as a dove, and that she would have done everything to conciliate not to disgust the wife and the world. Her worst enemy cannot wish her to pursue a line of conduct so destructive to the stability of her empire. She must feel like her cousin Robespierre (I am sure they must be related) and that ere long she may not be murdered but she will be driven from society. How silly not to be content with cajoling and dressing Lord Carlisle. She might have gone out to the end of their days in a quiet respectable attachment.[81]

Frances Jersey, as we shall see, not only pretended to disapprove of the Carlton House system but also, acute as she was, recognised the damage it was doing to the reputations of her and her lover. Nevertheless, in a manner of self-destruction they persisted in it, for reasons that can only be ascribed to malice on her part and dislike of the Princess on his. The Countess's pretences, though, were seen through, and Lady Palmerston was to be proved right. It would not be long before Lady Jersey was indeed to be driven from Society.

Before then, as Mrs Piozzi wrote on 12 May: 'They write *no Lady Jersey* on the Walls now.'[82]

Despite this, Frances Jersey remained in Queen Charlotte's favour, as *The Times* of 25 May commented in words clearly critical of the queen. After announcing to the world that 'Lady Jersey is reported to be pregnant' it went on to say 'and strange as it may seem, was particularly distinguished during the late superb fêtes at Frogmore'.

The report of Lady Jersey's pregnancy was true – but nobody thought that the Earl was the baby's father.

The Countess continued to strengthen her grip on the Prince and his circle. Jack Payne, as an ally of Maria Fitzherbert and, in Nathaniel Wraxall's words, 'one of the most honest and honourable men of his time [who] enjoyed during many years his Royal Highness's favour', was now banished from Carlton House – although as *The Times* reported on 13 June, 'Commodore P——, lately wrecked on the *rocks* of Jersey, was fortunately picked up by the Fitzherbert *jolly-boat* and safely carried in to harbour.'[83]

There were happier events amongst the Countess's own family. Also in June, Lord Paget, heir to the Earl of Uxbridge, and later to be a distinguished soldier who was to command the cavalry and lose a leg at Waterloo, proposed to the Jerseys' third daughter, Lady Caroline Villiers. Lord Jersey commented, 'I have not hesitated to accept [the proposal]: trusting with confidence that in every respect her happiness can be obtained.'[84] On 25 July the marriage of the twenty-one-year-old Caroline Villiers, 'a girl of simple, dreamlike beauty', duly took place. Over the next nine years, according to Caroline's own version of events, she was to live very happily with Paget, giving him three sons and five daughters before the marriage spectacularly imploded when Paget, provoking huge scandal, abandoned her and his family for another woman.[85]

Before returning to London for the wedding Lady Jersey had accompanied the Prince and Princess to Brighton, riding with them in the same carriage.[86] The presence in Brighton that summer of the Prince's two pregnant ladies – for Caroline was also pregnant from the first days of her marriage – prompted Horace Walpole to relate to Mary Berry: 'It seems it has been reported that of the two pregnancies at Brighton the greatest is a timpany, and the biggest a dropsy. "What,' said William Fawkener, "is the Prince still between wind and water?"'[87]

Lady Jersey's pregnancy also produced satirical, if premature, comment in the press, *The Morning Post* reporting:

> Lady Jersey's *accouchement* is hourly expected. The Prince stands Godfather, and the Princess honours the baptismal font with her presence. Ladies Jersey and Kingsborough are probably two of the most handsome and youthful looking *Grandmothers* that this or any other country can boast.[88]

At the same time Lord Hugh Seymour's fall from grace continued. His wife had not been appointed to the Princess of Wales's household and, in the summer, he received a letter of dismissal from the Prince's household from Lord Cholmondley. Admittedly he was not alone in this and the dismissal was justified on the grounds that 'the arrangement Parliament has thought proper to make relative to the Prince of Wales' affairs, not allowing his Royal Highness to continue the establishment of his family' also resulted in the dismissal of the bulk of the Prince's establishment,[89] with amongst the few to survive being Lady Jersey as a Lady of the Bedchamber and Lord Jersey as his Master of the Horse.[90]

The fact that the Jersey interests survived the cull of the Prince's household was mockingly recorded in the *True Briton* of 29 July:

> Lady Jersey, having seen her Daughter married, returns to *her own duty* in Brighton. Lord Jersey possesses a high character for *hospitality* at this moment; but considering the source from which the hospitality is derived, it might perhaps be more suitably adjourned to a more *convenient period*.

Frances Jersey's hauteur continued to annoy. Amongst the small retinue that accompanied the Prince to Brighton was one Miss Gertrude Vanneck. 'Lady

Jersey's high-handed ways enraged all the establishment at Brighton. Miss Vanneck is come away furious also ... on never being asked to play cards; nay, she was desired for her amusement to bring her spinning wheel into the [card] playroom.'[91]

Back in London there were arrangements to be made, before the Countess's accouchement, as to where the Jerseys were to live. The plan was that they were to move into the former house of the late Field Marshal Conway in Warwick Street and, presumably on that basis, they had proceeded to sell their house in Grosvenor Square.[92] However, on 22 August Mrs Howe wrote to Lady Stafford saying, 'I now understand Ly Jersey is not to be in the house in Warwick Street but that which Ld and Ly Russel inhabited in Palmal, tho' there is this moment a Bill on it.'[93]

According to Lady Louisa Macdonald, though, there was a reason for this, as she also told Lady Stafford: 'Lord & Lady Jersey are to have the House Lord William Russel [*sic*] lived in last winter until that which the Prince of Wales bought of Marshall Conway can be got ready for them, Mr Stuart Wortley has taken Lord Jersey's in Grosvenor Square.'[94]

The significance of this was that, not only was Field Marshal Conway's former house in Warwick Street now owned by the Prince and being made available by him to the Jerseys, but also that it was next to Carlton House. Clearly there was a gathering scandal here, which explains the nuances Horace Walpole added to the whole affair when writing to Mary Berry a few days later:

> The Jerseys do not go into the house in Warwick Street – some say on the remonstrance of the present [Lord Loughborough], others, of the last Chancellor [Lord Thurlow]. They are to have the house of their son-in-law Lord William Russel, which was his Grandmother Bedford's in Pall Mall – still harping after Carleton House.[95]

This, though, proved to be only a delay before the Jerseys did eventually move into the house in Warwick Street. Perhaps Lady Jersey had not yet summoned up the courage to endure another outcry against her.

In the same letter Walpole recorded (mockingly but prematurely, it seems) the downfall of another of the Prince's inner circle, Thomas Tyrwhitt, his private secretary, at the Countess's hand. In Walpole's words, Tyrwhitt 'is gathered to his numberless predecessors, for having roundly lectured Lady Jersey on her want of reverence for the *legal* Princess and the poor injured lady had no way to escape but by inventing a swoon, in the height of which came in the Prince who, learning the cause, dismissed him [Tyrwhitt]'.[96] This was rapidly followed by a rumour that the Countess's ever loyal friend Edward Jerningham was to be appointed as a Groom to the Bedchamber, causing Walpole to comment, in the hope of propriety and good order, 'I wish with all my heart he may! He will not offend by lecturing his old friend Madame de Maintenant' – as Walpole, with a pun, nicknamed Lady Jersey in imitation of Louis XIV's mistress Mme de Maintenon – as to a proper course of conduct.[97]

Lady Jersey's position now seemed both secure and recognised as is shown by a letter to the Prince from his brother Prince Ernest on 28 August that closed with the words: 'My best complts to Lady J.'[98] It was also acknowledged, with some trepidation, by more impartial observers, as witness the letter of 4 September comparing the situation with revolutionary France, from Lord Auckland to the future Earl Minto: 'The world talks very freely of the Prince of Wales and Lady Jersey, who has not taken warning by the histories of the French Court.' Auckland went on to add the not surprising but significant news that 'she has her bed in the Prince's dressing room', formalising, and acknowledging, her as the royal mistress she had now become.[99]

As Lady Jersey's pregnancy advanced, preparations continued for the imminent birth. *The True Briton* of 2 September reported that Lady Jersey had let her town mansion 'and was content to take her straw', more than brazenly but ultimately incorrectly, at the Brighton Pavilion. A fortnight later, reported *The Oracle*, 'Lady Jersey expects an increase in family, and that, shortly, at the Brighton Pavilion,' adding that her fourth daughter (the fifteen-year-old Lady Sarah Villiers who was with her in Brighton), 'is spoken of as rivalling in beauty even her sister graces.'[100] Accordingly, when the Prince gave a grand ball at the Pavilion in Brighton after a masquerade on 1 October, 'to which were invited nearly all the fashionable company in the place', not only did 'the Princess, who is very palpably a couple ... not dance, nor did Lady Jersey who is in a situation exactly similar'.[101]

Actually, Lady Jersey's pregnancy was more advanced than Princess Caroline's and on 16 October it was reported: 'Lady Jersey, at the house of Lord Jersey ... [in] Brighton [gave birth to] a son. Her Ladyship and the infant are in a fair way of doing well, and the greatest precaution has been taken prevent them being disturbed by noises in the street, to which end the road has been littered [with straw], and the drums silenced' – a treatment which it seems no ordinary Countess would be afforded.[102]

Lady Sarah reported the birth to Edward Jerningham that day: 'I am sure you will be glad to hear that Mamma was brought to bed this morning at seven o'clock of a very fine little boy, and they are both as well as possible.'

More drily, but accurately, Lewis Bettany (the editor of Jerningham's letters) notes that the boy, who was to die in infancy, was 'too important (or unimportant) to be included in Burke's [Peerages'] account of the Countess of Jersey's children'.[103]

The Oracle was more sarcastic about the baby's parentage, reporting: 'Lady Jersey's young son promises to do very well, and bears a strong family likeness. One of her Ladyship's *grandsons* is to stand *godfather.*'[104]

Society was scarcely less scathing. Mrs Howe, writing to Lady Stafford on 24 October after reporting 'I fear to say' the birth of the boy, went on to add 'she intends to suckle it herself, what is that for I wonder? I have been answered perhaps she intends to nurse the royal child' – that is, the Prince's imminent child that Princess Caroline was carrying, suggesting an ambition to control the child who would be second-in-line to the throne as much as its father.[105]

When this story became more publicly known it provoked a different reaction in *The Times*:

> An amiable great lady, though very accomplished in the English language, now and then makes some innocent mistake. She lately asked Lady Jersey if her child would not like *new* milk.[106]

At the same time, there were the beginnings of a fightback by the Princess against Lady Jersey's activities. Elizabeth Montagu's sister wrote to her on 13 September:

> I hear (I wish it may be true) that the P of W has plucked up spirit enough to tell her husband that tho' it may not be in her power to dismiss Ly J from her post yet it is in her power to forbear speaking to her, and that if she follows them to Brighton she is determined to take no notice of her. I wonder that his Father and Mother do not exert themselves to prevent such a glaring impropriety of conduct, as is his, it is cruel to suffer a young Woman so situated to be exposed to such treatment. I suppose the purchase of the house for Ly J is the first fruits of his economical reform of expences. What a pitiful fellow Ld J must be. I hope his H——ss leaves his slippers at her Chamber Door on proper occasions.[107]

Princess Caroline's mother was also getting concerned, writing to her brother the king from Brunswick a fortnight later:

> I fear some black design, Lady Jersey turns every word the poor Princess says, and her whole thrust is to hurt her in your opinion and the Queen's ... You know, dear brother, that the innocenter [that is more naïve] one is the easier one falls into scrapes, the Prince has told her ... that he will not constrain her in nothing, that she may live with whom she pleases ... she is frightened out of her senses ... the Prince made the point that she should treat [Lady Jersey] with distinction and indeed until now she has obeyed him blindly.[108]

The Princess summed it up in a letter to a friend in Germany: 'The Countess is still here. I hate her and I know she feels the same towards me. My husband is wholly given up to her, so you can easily imagine the rest.'[109]

13

Love in High Life

On 11 January 1796 *The Sun* reported:

> Carlton House, Jan 7
>
> This morning, between nine and ten o'clock the Princess of Wales was happily delivered of a Princess.

Amongst those present at the birth of the next heir to the throne, along with the Archbishop of Canterbury, the Lord Chancellor and various other peers, were Lord Jersey as Master of the Horse and the ladies of Her Royal Highness's Bedchamber, including, of course, the Countess of Jersey.

Frances Jersey's presence was doubtless barely noticed at the birth. More galling for the Princess was the christening which took place in the Gold Room in Buckingham Palace a month later, where not only was Lady Jersey present despite the ceremony being of a private kind where 'a few of the Nobility only, who are usually honoured with invitations to their Majesties' private parties were invited',[1] but also the infant Princess Charlotte, named after her Grandmother doubtless at the prompting of the ingratiating Countess, was 'presented by Lady Jersey to the King, Queen, and Princesses'.[2]

By now, the Countess had not only the Prince but also his mother in her thrall, and the Queen was to make herself very unpopular from her support of the Countess's treatment of Caroline. The King on the other hand never succumbed to her charms but, despite his obvious disapproval of her, he was never able to outmanoeuvre her against the wishes of both his wife and his son.

Lady Jersey was now living openly with the Prince and was 'insufferably insolent' to those around her – and not only in riding through the courts of Carlton House attended by servants in the Prince's livery.[3] Her hauteur and pride flourished in the reflected glow of royalty and she took advantage of it at every opportunity. So, later in the year, as the *General Evening Post* of 22 October reported, at a 'public day' at St James's attended by royal princesses, foreign envoys, cabinet ministers, senior soldiers and civic dignitaries: 'The Earl and Countess of Jersey, unexpectedly made their appearance; her Ladyship, with her daughter, Lady Charlotte Villiers [*sic*], retired from the Presence Chamber through Prince Ernest's [private] apartments.'

Lady Spencer summed it up in a letter to Georgiana Devonshire in January 1796:

> She has reigned with too much despotism to last long … I am unwilling to warn you and your sister about her, because I think most of the warnings I have given you both have generally failed completely. However, I would wish you both to remember that she has fairly dropt you, & that there is no necessity when others drop her, that you should take her up. In a good cause such a conduct is highly laudable but surely not in a bad one.[4]

But then came one of the most extraordinary events of the whole affair. On 10 January, three days after the birth of his daughter, the Prince of Wales made his will. A long and rambling affair of ten pages, it can be summarised by the following statement:

> By this my last Will & Testament, I now bequeathe, give & settle at my death all my worldly property of every distinction, denomination & sort, personal & other, as shall be hereafter described to my Maria Fitzherbert, my wife, the wife of my heart and soul … who is dearer to me, even millions of times dearer to me, than the life
> I am now going to resign.[5]

In all of this the Prince left just one shilling to his wife. Further, there is not a single mention of his current paramour who had overthrown Maria Fitzherbert and organised the humiliation of his wife. Despite her extraordinary hold over the Prince, the Countess of Jersey was totally ignored in his will.

It was to be some years before the Prince told Mrs Fitzherbert about the will. One would love to know if Frances Jersey ever knew about it and its terms, although the gift of just a shilling to his wife has the whiff of Lady Jersey's malice so perhaps she did.

By now the Carlton House system had become something of an open scandal. The Princess was, as she put it, 'shut up all long day' with the Countess when she was in waiting until after dinner, at which the Prince might or might not present. The Princess then retired, whilst the Prince and Lady Jersey attended 'parties of pleasure together'. In operating this system, under the management of Frances Jersey, the Prince ignored cries in the public prints that Caroline was a 'state prisoner'.[6]

Of this Glenbervie wrote in his diary for 18 January:

> If the twentieth part of [the reports and anecdotes in circulation] have any foundation, that is sufficient to fix the highest degree of blame on

> his [the Prince's] conduct, which has the less chance of a very favourable interpretation from the public, as his great female friend and adviser is Lady Jersey ... the only confidential man who remains about him is Tommy Tyrwhitt, the Prince's Secretary. Tyrwhitt, I believe, is neither suspected of being able to influence him in any respect, nor, were he able, of the inclination of doing so in any improper manner.[7]

The reports and anecdotes were indeed much more than one-twentieth part true, despite a clever and self-serving, or perhaps self-deluding, letter from Lady Jersey written probably to Colonel McMahon, the Prince's Private Secretary, around this time.

In this, after acknowledging that she was 'advising' the Prince as to his conduct, she went on to say that she had entreated the Prince to reject limiting the Princess's visitors unduly, and went on to say that the Prince wished the Princess to enjoy every amusement and comfort in *his* house that will not interfere with his own. She continued, perhaps out of self-interest since to impose isolation on the Princess would soon become public knowledge, to say that the

> perfect retirement [of Caroline] would have appeared cruel to the world, & in fact would have been exercising a degree of tyranny which could only be gratifying to a mean & narrow breast ... you know the reasons I have to abhor her & you must be convinced that I can have no motive for wishing the Prince to be gentle & indulgent to her, but that he may appear in a true light, & that we may still have the satisfaction of thinking that *we* have *always* acted generously by *her*. Though Lord Moira dreads any communication with me, I *am* ambitious of his good opinion & wish him through you to know what my sentiments are upon this occasion.[8]

What the reasons were for the Countess to abhor the Princess are nowhere articulated and probably did not exist beyond the elegant Countess's scorn of a gauche and unattractive girl – but Frances Jersey did have an extraordinary talent for persuading others to accept her view of the world, even when it was palpably wrong.

Despite her protestations, nothing changed. This was in spite of the sarcastic report of *The True Briton* on 27 January that 'amongst the gossipping [*sic*] reports in the upper circles, it has been stated that Lady Jersey is about resign; but we have no reason to believe in the report, as Lady Jersey is highly in favour with the Princess of Wales, to whom her attentions are of the most affectionate and endearing kind'.[9] On the contrary, she continued to play the central role so that when the Prince visited the Countess at home, according to the Margravine of Ansbach, she was 'accustomed to drop the linen blinds of the window' – though whether this was for privacy or advertisement is unknown.[10] Further, said *The Sun*, with a hint of sarcasm, her dearest friend Edward Jerningham was a frequent visitor 'at Carlton-House and it must be owned that the Prince of Wales can hardly select a man more recommended by taste, knowledge, literary talent, and suavity of manners'.[11]

Although the King disapproved of the Carlton House system, the Queen was 'won over to the Prince's wishes by his attention and presents in jewels, &c.', as well as by the bewitching Lady Jersey; as Lord Colchester related, 'a few nights ago, Lady Jersey was invited with the Prince's party to the Queen's house, and put to a card table with the Princess Augusta and Lady Holdernesse', not at all what one would expect to be afforded to a woman of doubtful reputation.[12] On another occasion when the Countess was at the Queen's House, the Prince repeatedly went over to Lady Jersey's table to squeeze her hand in a public display of affection, as well as insult to his wife.[13]

Whilst the Queen openly patronised Lady Jersey, favouring her before her daughter-in-law, the Prince and Princess of Wales had 'an open difference' on the topic of the Countess which was to foreshadow a battle of wills between them over the summer of 1796. This prompted a retort from the Prince of Wales that Caroline should be pleased his attachment was 'an inclination of ancient date rather than to a young and beautiful woman' ('*une inclination date qu'a une jeune et belle femme*').[14] One can scarcely imagine her fury, had the Countess known of this comment.

There was never any real suggestion that Lady Jersey sought to benefit financially from her connections with the Prince, whose finances in any event continued to be in a parlous state. Lord Colchester noted a single allegation of financial corruption on her part, as distinct from the exercise wisely or otherwise of her influence, in his diary on 24 February, although there is another curious comment some years after the Countess's fall from favour. Colchester's comment recounted: 'Lady Jersey is said to have put the Privy Seal to a grant of timber in Cornwall, which has been cut down, and the money paid to her. And about six months ago Macewan [*sic*] and another of the pages, supposed to have been privy to it, were sent to live in Scotland' – presumably so as to avoid interrogation on the topic.[15]

No more is heard of this story, and given the enormous unpopularity of the Countess, that fact alone should be suffice to prove that the rumour was false. To do her justice, there is no evidence that she ever sought to exploit her position for financial gain. Power, status and patronage, not money, were what mattered to her. Even so, her reputation was becoming blackened. The same year her daughter, Caroline (now Lady Paget), gave birth to a daughter; the baby's paternal grandfather, the Earl of Uxbridge, refused to allow his wife to attend the child's christening 'if Lady Jersey comes to it'.[16]

Lady Jersey's reputation suffered further, as she was increasingly seen as the architect of the Carlton House system under which the ever more popular Princess continued to suffer. So far as the Prince was concerned, it was said 'Lady Jersey rules his mind'.[17] The papers, too, were beginning to pick up the story as Farington noted in his diary on 25 May: 'the Princess of Wales' situation is strongly hinted at in the papers: and Lady Jersey pointed at as the cause of the breach between the Prince & Princess.'[18]

Frances Jersey was also the likely cause of another, and subtler, slight to the Princess. The King had commissioned from Gainsborough Dupont (the famous Gainsborough's nephew) a portrait of the Princess in her Wedding

Robes of State, but the portrait was rejected for the 1796 Summer Exhibition at the Royal Academy on the somewhat specious grounds that the artist, in telling the Hanging Committee that the frame was not quite ready, did not show the council sufficient respect, and then 'that they were full'. Given who had commissioned the portrait, its subject, the popularity of the Princess and the fact that paintings commonly arrived for the exhibition at the last moment, as well as 'the extraordinary public interest' in the picture, it seems much more likely that pressure was brought to bear on the Royal Academy not to include it in their exhibition by those inimical to the Princess. Of course, the Prince of Wales and his mistress were the first amongst those. It is, too, just the sort of gratuitous and malicious taunting of a rival that appealed to Lady Jersey.[19]

Perhaps her malice went even further this time in conjunction with her ally the Queen, as *The True Briton* of 9 September asked:

> How comes it that the Portrait of the Princess of Wales is not to be seen at the *Queen's House*, amongst other portraits of the Royal Family? The Duchess of York's has been there some time; and without the Princess the illustrious group is strangely incomplete.

As the activities of Frances Jersey became more widely known, so her stock fell ever further with the public at large as well as those closer to events – as the Irish beauty and kinswoman of Wellington, Frances Calvert, found out to her cost, as she described:

> Lady Jersey became very unpopular with the mob, and one evening, as I was going through Covent Garden in my chariot ... I was taken for her (I have always been considered very like her), and my carriage and servants were well pelted with mud before we got clear of them.[20]

She was also the topic of numerous satirical prints, which as noted were the fashion of the age, and a widely circulated and a popular means of social comment. In the manner of the time, no punches were pulled in their crudeness or obscenity.

So in 1796 Cruickshank published a print entitled *Future Prospects, or symptoms of Love in High Life* in which, as the Prince and Princess of Wales argue, Lord Jersey, with cuckold's horns, peers around the door to announce that his wife awaits the Prince in the next room, where you see the Countess bare breasted and legs apart on the sofa. In another, called *The Grand-Signior Retiring,* he depicted the complicit Lord Jersey escorting the Prince to Lady Jersey's bed.[21]

James Gillray was not to be outdone and his *Fashionable Jockeyship* of the same year has Lord Jersey carrying the Prince piggy-back to Lady Jersey's bed, with the Countess portrayed as an old crone, whilst his *The Jersey Smuggler Detected;– or – good cause for Separation: Marriage Vows are False as Dicers Oaths* shows Princess Caroline finding the Prince of Wales in bed with Lady Jersey.[22]

The principal players in the drama inevitably would know these prints, and the messages they were sending far and wide.

In April 1796, Princess Caroline started in earnest to fight back against Frances Jersey's all-pervading role in her life, which was eventually to result in the Countess's resignation and the royal couple's separation. It did not start well – only in part because of the Princess's clumsy style. In a letter to the Prince, after saying she had to write because she never saw the Prince by himself, she complained she was constantly forced to dine alone with Lady Jersey, *'une personne que je ne peut aimé n'y estimé* et *qui est voter* [sic] *maitresse'*, and that she had to spend all day long shut up with her. She went on to ask that the Prince no longer compel her to dine with Frances Jersey. This prompted an angry, and self-serving, reply from the Prince the same day. After denying that he compelled her to dine with Frances Jersey, he went on:

> I am more immediately call'd to notice the indelicate expression you have used towards me in the allusion you make to Lady Jersey. Beleive [*sic*] me, Madam, that the persons who endeavour to poison your mind with the vile calumnies which have been propagated in the world respecting Lady Jersey are no less seriously your enemies than mine. They hope to further their malignant views by fomenting discord between you and me … I declared to you on your arrival [that Lady Jersey was not] my *mistress, as you* indecorously term her, but a friend to whom I am attached by strong ties of habitude, esteem and respect … But let me remind you that the intimacy of my friendship with Lady Jersey, under all the false colour which slander has given to it was perfectly known to you before you accepted my hand [when, prompted by Caroline's asking about the anonymous letters received in Brunswick, I, said the Prince] then took the opportunity of explaining to you that Lady Jersey was one of the oldest acquaintances I had in this country & that the confidence resulting from so long a friendship had enabled her to offer advice which contributed not a little to decide me to marriage.[23]

Having failed in this request to rid herself of the Countess, Caroline tried a different tack. A month later she wrote again asking, this time, that Lady Jersey be removed entirely as a Lady of the Bedchamber. To this to the Prince answered that he had intended that there would be no further discussion on the topic of Lady Jersey but that in view of the Princess' letter he was compelled to reply. After noting that Princess Caroline had never accused Lady Jersey of a single instance of inattention or disrespect (although there were certainly many), he once more refused Princess Caroline's request saying that, in any event, were he to dismiss Frances Jersey, 'her removal would confirm every slander which has been so industriously propagated relative to her conduct towards you as well as to the nature of her intimacy with me' – and that would clearly be wrong![24]

So, once more, the Princess had lost and the Countess won, retaining her position and her control not only of Caroline but also of the Prince. This control was all the more remarkable because even during these months the Prince of Wales was seeking to lure Mrs Fitzherbert back: 'He wanted her back as his wedded, waiting wife to go home to every evening',[25] perhaps in reaction to Lady Jersey's domineering style, and in May he despatched his brother Prince Ernest to Maria Fitzherbert with a letter seeking a reconciliation, which resulted in the following report from Prince Ernest:

> I have seen Mrs Fitz., shewn her the letter; she is frightened to death, knows not what to say, as is natural to be assumed as you have come upon her *so* unexpectedly. She owns a very sincere regard for you, but I cannot get anything else out of her *as yet*. She has promised to meet me at Payne's tomorrow at *4 o'clock*. I hope to be luckier. She always owns this, that *if* she did make it up you would not agree a fortnight; *cela reste a voir*. Tomorrow evening I shall *be able* to say what has passed at Payne's.[26]

In fact, all this came to nothing. Frances Jersey's position as the Prince's mistress remained unchallenged. Nor was there to be a reconciliation with Mrs Fitzherbert until 1799, when the Countess had already left the Prince's stage. What this episode does show, though, beyond the Prince's extraordinary inability to know his own mind, was that the Countess truly deserved her nickname of 'the Enchantress' in her control over him, as the *Gazetteer*, recalling Maria Cosway's portrait, noted on 28 May.

In this she was probably helped by the support of the Queen, who was also earning great unpopularity for her alliance with the Countess and implicit endorsement of her treatment of the Princess. As *The Morning Chronicle* reported on 30 May: 'Lady Jersey is honoured with the confidential patronage of the Queen. Her Ladyship is daily at Buckingham House; and in all her proceedings is countenanced by the Queen.'

The *Morning Herald* of the following day put it another way: 'We are sorry to add, that the influence of the Circe [that is Lady Jersey] is still increasing, and that it meets with countenance in *another quarter,* altogether surprising as it is unnatural.'[27]

The '[an]other quarter' was, of course the Queen, and *The Sun* the same week explained, tongue-in-cheek, that all this came about through the services of the Countess's great friend Lady Harcourt, who was also an intimate of Queen Charlotte.[28] This, though, was not true. The captivating Countess had no need for help in leading the Queen to give full rein to her predispositions, which certainly entertained no fondness for her daughter-in-law.

However, over the coming weeks and months of 1796 there was a step-change both in the public's and the press's attitude to the Prince and his mistress, becoming ever more explicitly critical of them both, and in the increasingly vocal support of the Prince's much mistreated wife.

On 2 June *The True Briton* published a vicious article on the Prince, calling him a Jacobin and describing him as incorrigible and having a total disregard for the opinions of the world. Lady Jersey did not escape lightly either, being accused of total disregard for the duties of conjugal life,[29] causing the self-deluding Prince when forwarding the article to his father to refer 'to the most villainous aspersions thrown upon the most perfect of characters', meaning of course the Countess.[30] *The True Briton* also offered the advice that: 'The *fashionable cant term* now, for the contempt which misconduct ought to excite, is being sent to *Jersey*.'[31]

The same day, the *Whitehall Evening Post* was just one of the papers to publish a paragraph on the Countess not calculated to amuse her:

> Lady Jersey, who now cuts so *conspicuous* a figure in the Morning Papers, has been married upwards of *thirty years* and has seven *grandchildren*. Her married daughters are Lady Ann Lambton, Lady William Russell and Lady Paget ... She has several younger children, one of whom is only three months old. Her Ladyship is far advanced in her *forty-eighth* year.[32]

It was *The Times* of 10 June which published the most damning commentary on the pair, saying:

> When high personages ... discard all the respect they owe to themselves; when they stoop to the most disgraceful connexions, and above all when their vices, disorders and impudences raise just apprehension for the welfare of the State, it is then that the liberty of the Press ought to resume its dignity and denounce and point out to the public opinion him whom public justice cannot attaint.[33]

In short, Lady Jersey's influence was now bringing the royal family itself into disrepute.

As Lady Jersey became ever more unpopular, and increasingly and correctly seen as the root cause of both the Princess's ill-treatment and her separation from the Prince, and as public anger with the Prince grew, Princess Caroline's popularity grew commensurately, as did the pressure on the Countess to resign as a Lady of the Bedchamber.

At the Epsom races in May 1796, 'many persons thronged after the Prince's coracle ... and the eager concourse did not fail to express their disappointment. They expected to see the Princess; but it was Lady Jersey who accompanied his Royal Highness.'[34]

The *Morning Herald* of 26 May added: 'The speed with which the Prince and Lady Jersey rode over the course at Epsom ... is spoken of with astonishment by the beholders of the sight' as they rushed away to avoid any unpleasantness.

For the first time, too, Society – as distinct from the press – began to show its views on Frances Jersey. When the Countess arrived at the Duchess of

Gordon's assembly, she was comprehensively cut as 'the ladies made a lane for her and let her pass unspoken to'.[35]

By contrast, the public's treatment of the Princess was becoming positively adulatory. The Duke of Leeds described her arrival at the opera on two occasions, the first on 28 May: 'I was in my box when the Princess of Wales arrived. The Pitt [*sic*] and some of the Boxes began to applaud, the whole House almost instantly rose and joined the Applause.'[36] In the words of *The Times* of 1 June, 'the house seemed as if electrified by her presence'.

The Prince was out of London that day and the strength of feeling displayed at the opera clearly disconcerted Lady Jersey.

Of the Princess's second appearance at the opera, three days later, the Duke of Leeds wrote: 'The Princess this evening came in during the first Ballet, which was instantly stopped, and the acclamations began, God save the King, &c &c.' On this occasion the Princess had some conversation with the Duke, telling him she did not attribute the Prince's cruel treatment of her to the Prince himself but rather to Lady Jersey, and when the Duke of Leeds expressed his wonder at the Countess not having 'common sense enough to resign on pretext of ill-health, rather than venture actual danger from the mob, she said it was otherwise ordered, and the P would not hear of her resignation'.

The Duke clearly thought that Frances Jersey was now in some physical danger. The Countess seems to have thought so too since, as the Princess went on (accurately) to tell the Duke, that

> Lady J had left her house in Pall Mall and was gone to her Daughters in Berkeley Square [this was Lady Anne Lambton]. The Princess understood she went on Saturday night [28 May]; and on my asking whether in consequence of what passed that night at the opera, she said she believed it was.[37]

Although, as we shall see, the Countess had additional reasons to go and stay with Lady Anne, she does seem to have thought that there was a real threat. *The Times* of 6 June reported:

> On the evening of the Prince of Wales leaving … for his seat in Hampshire, Lady Jersey left her house in Pall Mall *incog.*, not choosing to remain there. She has retired, though not unobserved, to the house of her daughter in Berkeley Square.[38]

The Prince also thought that events were taking an alarming turn. Writing from Hampshire to Lord Moira, after saying that Lady Jersey stood 'in need of much consolation', he expressed alarm 'at the report that the populace meant to attack [the Jersey's house] in Pall Mall. I hope that is not true, but what I dread most is their finding out that she is [gone?] to Berkeley Square, & following her there.'[39]

In the event, no physical attack took place, but behind these displays of public anger a private farce and a private tragedy were at the same time being played out.*

The farce was that, in May, Lord Jersey had written to the King seeking to do the impossible by defending the honour of both his wife and himself, and requesting a private audience with the King to do so at greater length. In his florid and near impenetrable letter the Earl said that no amount of the prevailing 'invidious malice' to the Jerseys, and particularly the Countess, would induce them to resign their posts in the Prince's household, going on, 'I owe it to my own & Lady Jersey's credit & honor, & not less conspicuously to that spirit of generosity & honor, which the whole conduct of his Royal Highness [the Prince of Wales] to Lady Jersey & myself has breathed in every instance, & which would be totally sacrificed by such a step.'[40]

In short, that the actions of both the Prince and the Countess were beyond reproach and that they were the victims of a witch-hunt. When *The True Briton* heard of the letter it summed it up neatly: 'Lord Jersey is said to have asked an audience of the King, to assure His Majesty that Lady Jersey was the most pure and virtuous woman living!!!'[41]

It is just possible that the Earl believed what he wrote. He was soon once more to publicly defend his wife against the indefensible; but how he could do so credibly is impossible to imagine. If he did believe what he said it was self-delusion of the greatest kind. Possibly, though, he did not and was merely doing what his domineering wife demanded of him to try and keep her post. More important was that the King clearly did not believe it either; when the audience did take place, the King listened to Lord Jersey 'with great complacency' before 'opening the door himself, [giving] him a bow; on which his Lordship retired, as may be supposed, not a little embarrassed'.[42]

The private tragedy was more in touch with reality. On 9 June *The True Briton* reported:

> Lady Jersey's last child is so ill, that it is thought impossible for [him] to recover, if indeed [he] is still alive. Lady Jersey has been extremely ill, in consequence of her maternal anxieties on this occasion.

This 'last child' was of course the little boy born the previous October, whose name history does not record and who was widely believed to be the Prince's son. Lord Jersey confirmed this report when writing to Lady Spencer later that month: 'We have been for eight or ten weeks in extreme anxiety for the little boy, who I may say was in imminent danger almost the whole of the time ... He is now now in a fair way of doing well.'[43]

---

* Nevertheless, the Prince's concerns were justified. As *The London Packet* reported in its 8–10 June edition: 'On Monday night [6 June] a number of persons assembled before the house of the Hon. Mr Lambton, in Berkeley-square, who married one of Lady Jersey's daughters, on a supposition that her Ladyship was in the house, but being assured they were mistaken, they departed in a very peaceful manner'.

Sadly the Earl's optimism was misplaced, and the boy had a relapse and died on 28 May – the same day as the first demonstration of the Princess's popularity at the opera and the day the Countess fled her house to stay with Lady Anne Lambton, making it a double blow for Frances Jersey. It was, of course, also the reason the Prince told Lord Moira of Frances Jersey's great need for consolation. The press picked up the little boy's death, and on 7 June *The Times* commented in the context of the Prince's absence from court on the King's birthday three days earlier, reflecting the widespread assumption as to the child's parentage:

> The loss of the infant son of Lady Jersey ... is given amongst other reasons as the cause of the absence of a high Personage from Court on Saturday last. As there can be no good reason assigned, the above may do as well as any other.

The Morning Post of 14 June also took the opportunity to attack the Countess, commenting of the Birthday that 'some wicked insinuations are made ... respecting the non-appearance of certain Royal Jewels [on the person of Princess Caroline] on the birth-day. It is not true, as surmised, they were sent to Jersey'.[44]

The Countess now seemed to be in real danger. Accordingly after her retreat from Pall Mall Frances Jersey sought to keep a low profile. So *The Morning Post* reported that 'Lady Jersey's *light blue Coach* has not been visible for several days – [instead the Prince took to visiting her, so that] the Prince's Livery Servants may be seen Every Day at her Ladyship's door';[45] and then, as the *St James's Chronicle* wrote on 7 June, the Jerseys discreetly left London and its threats: 'On Saturday Morning [4 June] Lord Jersey called at Lady Ann Lambton's house in Berkeley Square in a hackney post-chaise, and only one servant on horse back, for Lady Jersey, and both set out for the country; but whither they are gone is not known'. This departure from London of a person – who in the words of *The True Briton* 'had given so much disgust to the Public' – was, it said, 'prudent'.[46]

Horace Walpole had foreseen the necessity of the Jerseys leaving Town, for not only was it prudent but worse, as he said, '[Lady Jersey's] present position is not tenable'. She was, however, not alone in leaving. Walpole added that Lady Harcourt, who was a Lady of the Bedchamber to the Queen, 'is gone to Nuneham for a long season, on pretence of [being ill with] St Antony's fire'. The real reason for her departure being, one imagines, that Lady Harcourt, herself not entirely free of criticism in the press in relation to Princess Caroline, wanted to avoid an increasingly difficult situation at court.[47]

This had been triggered by Princess Caroline renewing her fightback against the Countess, with her writing once more to the Prince on 30 May. In this letter, after reminding him how Frances Jersey had treated her at Brighton – where the Countess had been very impertinent to her[48] – she demanded the Countess's immediate dismissal.[49] The effect over the ensuing weeks was confusion, bitterness and anger in relation to Frances Jersey's position, such was the public antipathy to her, as well as real worry about the threat the public's response posed.

On 3 June Georgiana Devonshire told her mother that 'it is said [Lady Jersey] has ask'd for her dismissal but the P. has refused', but five days later she was telling her mother:

> The obscurity that reigns about the Prince's family continues. The Queen, I hear, is still against her [the Princess], I hear from authority that Ly J is going to publish an *éclaircissement*, that, she says will alter public opinion. What it can be I guess not, for however she may incriminate the Pss, that can not justify herself. She is returned to her house in Pall Mall which is more bold than wise.[50]

The Countess was showing her steel in the face of danger, but others too were worried and not only for her safety. Public opinion concerning the Countess and the treatment of the Princess was increasingly one of anger. The royal family was being dragged into the ferment and itself seemed under threat as a result of its associations with Frances Jersey. Thus Princess Elizabeth wrote to her brother the Prince on 3 June: 'Friends & foes are all of the opinion that a *resignation must* take place for the sake of the country & the whole Royal Family, for if you *fall* all must fall,'[51] whilst a day later 'a frighten'd letter'[52] from Thomas Tyrrwhitt to the Prince sought to warn him of what Lord Moira described to the Prince as 'this extraordinary ferment. Things are indeed, very bad. It would be treachery to your Royal Highness not to discover to you how violently the tide of prejudice runs.'[53]

The Bishop of Waterford summed the situation up when he wrote to Lord Charlemont on 7 June:

> I am much pained to find the rage against the prince of W[ales] is increased. The princess, on account of the supposed ill-treatment which she receives from the prince, is become the greatest favourite with people of all ranks, the great vulgar and the small. When she enters the opera-house she is received with bursts of applause. The prince is gone to the country, to avoid insult, and yesterday remained there, and would not venture to attend the birthday. Lady Jersey is the cause of all this bustle, – she ought to resign office, and will not; The Prince ought to dismiss her; he will not. The court at the Queen's house ought privately to order Lady Jersey to resign, and remove from London; no such thing is done. The Prince has no good advisers [the Countess having removed them]; if he has, he does not attend to them. Why can he not show respect and attention, and appear to have affection, though he has none. In his situation hypocrisy would be a sort of virtue. It would make him popular, the princess happy, and save his favourite from much shame and great danger.[54]

The public outrage though had its effect, and the Prince was changing his position on Lady Jersey's remaining as a Lady of the Bedchamber. He was now prepared to countenance her retirement, although not on the terms the Princess demanded. Whilst the Princess had originally required her immediate dismissal, Lord Moira, who was acting as the Prince's intermediary, had succeeded in moderating the demand; as the Duke of York said to Moira on 9 June, 'I am rejoiced to hear that you have persuaded the Princess not to press the measure of the immediate dismissal of Lady Jersey, it would only irritate the Prince and in reality cannot be, at least in my opinion, of any consequence to her,' because, in a display of the Duke's perception of the extraordinary extent of Lady Jersey's unpopularity, 'it is totally impossible for Lady Jersey ever to show herself again in the country.'[55] He was not alone in thinking that Lady Jersey would have to go abroad until the public outcry against her died down.

The Prince had in response proposed that Lady Jersey should resign her post 'when the ferment was over, in perhaps 2 or 3 months' but that she was to be 'received at dinner parties, [and] assemblies as an indifferent [that is normal] person'. He was therefore irritated when Caroline construed this as a firm commitment that the Countess would resign in three months' time, and in the interim that she, the Princess, would not see Frances Jersey and 'never would suffer Lady J. to set her foot in any house in which she was, as long as she lived, & that if she came to dinner she would get up from the table & go & dine in her own room'.[56]

Somehow things got even more confused. As a friend of Lady Stafford wrote:

> The Prince requested that Ly Jersey should not be dismissed abruptly, lest it be said he *sacrificed* her to the Princess. Her RH agreed to it provided she never saw her again, that he might take his time in effecting her resignation ... Lord M[oira] has written a letter ... saying that she had consented (*provided* Ly J resigned) to receive her at dinner at Carlton House whenever the Prince chose to invite her ...'

But Lord Moira's story got to Lady Jersey who peremptorily

> sent for Ld Cholmondley [one of Caroline's supporters] at 12 o'clock last night to tell him this, [when] he assured her she was misinformed & advised her to go abroad ... Ld Cholmondley has written to the Prince ... that Lord Moyra has misunderstood the Princess as it is her firm resolution never to receive Ly J on any terms, at the same time the resignation may be accomplished with as much delicacy as they choose, as she has no wish to have it made publick that she requires it.[57]

It was doubtless at this meeting that Lady Jersey told Lord Cholmondeley, according to Mrs Fitzroy, a lady in waiting to Caroline and the future Lady Southampton, 'that she was ready to quit the Pss's service and should resign in the course of a fortnight'; though this seems to have been linked to the proposition 'that she should dine at C. H. as usual whenever the P asked her, as she found there was no objection made to that', which was, of course, rejected. No more is heard of a possible rapid resignation.[58]

It soon became clear that the Princess and the Prince were at cross-purposes. Princess Caroline thought that until she resigned Lady Jersey was barred from London, rather than merely being banned from approaching her. It also took a great deal of difficulty before the Princess accepted that Lady Jersey was to be admitted at formal occasions. The tension was further increased by the Princess believing that Lady Jersey had publicly abused her baby daughter, Princess Charlotte. When he heard of this charge, the Prince responded that the allegations by the Princess were 'as false as hell, for … Lady J. is incapable of ever having said anything with respect to my daughter', going on to conclude that there was 'a decided resolution in the Princess to persecute and eventually destroy if she can Lady Jersey, which I would rather suffer death than admit'.[59]

And so confusion and bitterness multiplied. Princess Elizabeth wrote again to her brother in June urging a resolution of the matter and saying that she feared '*the putting off the resignation* is a bad plan',[60] whilst, at least according to the Marchioness of Stafford, 'Lady Jersey now writes daily to the Prince desiring him to remain firm for her dismissal not to take place for three months etc. etc. and by that time all will blow over.'[61] For his part, the Prince thought he could not exclude Lady Jersey from his house since by doing so 'he must thereby confess to the public that there has been ground for the various charges so licentiously laid against him'.[62] So far as Princess Caroline was concerned, as the future Lady Southampton said, 'the Pss says there is no end of this business, & as Ly J persists in not resigning she wants to know if she may not dismiss her: will settle it at once.'[63]

There is indeed a draft and caustic letter amongst the Granville manuscripts, apparently in the hand of Lord Thurlow who was advising the Princess, evidently doing just that. It reads:

> After what has passed, attending the Princess must wound Lady Jersey's Delicacy and be intolerably irksome to her. Therefore as she wishes not to give Lady Jersey any Pain, The Princess disposes of her Attendance.[64]

No such letter of dismissal was however sent by the Princess.

The press was watching events closely and reported variously that Lady Jersey was resigning and that Lady Jersey was not resigning. Accurately or not, *The True Briton* reported that an independent MP

> has avowed his determination to rise in his place, on the meeting of Parliament, and move an Address to His Majesty, beseeching him to dismiss a certain *Earl* and *Countess* from the Household of a Great Personage; in case they should be so indecent as to brave the Public by retaining their positions till that time.[65]

Georgiana Devonshire summed up the position when writing to her mother on 10 June:

> I have only time tell you that there is not the least danger about Ly J., and nobody knows where she is, or anything about her. I hear she is obstinate as to resigning and I wish you cd advise him [Lord Jersey] to resign and make her, to let the storm blow over … The D of B assures me that both the Duke of Grafton and Lord Paget justify Lord Jersey, that is, think him deceived.[66]

Edward Jerningham's sister-in-law observed at this time that the Countess 'has sadly lost sight of her usual prudence in managing her affairs'.[67]

So all believed that the Countess had lost her normal sense under the avalanche of disapproval. However, the idea that the Duke of Grafton and Lord Paget thought Lord Jersey was 'deceived' is extraordinary. That such men, men of real judgement and standing, one a former First Minister (albeit a close friend of the Earl) and the other a son-in-law who was to become an illustrious soldier, thought Lord Jersey ignorant of what was really happening despite all the noise and all the publicity is incredible; his *naivité* must have been extreme, once more, under the thrall of his enchantress of a wife. This is all the more so the case since, according to Lady Spencer, Lady Jersey whilst duly avoiding Carlton House was at this time continuing to see the Prince every day in the Jerseys' country house in Hammersmith,[68] where their children were staying, presumably to keep them out of danger from the London mob.[69]

Hammersmith, a village a few miles west of London, was in an area much frequented by the beau monde of the eighteenth century. Daniel Defoe, in his *Tour*, referred to the 'many noble seats … in Istleworth, Twittenham, Hammersmith, Fulham, Puttney, Chelsea, Battersea, and the like [*sic*]'. At the end of the century these included Brandenburg, Chiswick, Syon, Osterley and Strawberry Hill, all of which save the first survive to this day.[70]

Hammersmith itself was then the market garden of London, so that 'three quarters of the fruit sold in Covent Garden towards the end of the century came from a seven-mile stretch of road, lined with orchards, running through Hammersmith, Chiswick and Brentford to Isleworth and Twickenham'.[71]

Presumably the house the children were staying at in Hammersmith, a 'cottage' with five bedchambers, was the same as the house that some years later *The Morning Post* described on its sale, somewhat unusually claiming the identity of its previous owner as a selling point. It described it as a 'desirable residence, with gardens and paddock, altogether about two acres, nearly inclosed [*sic*] with brick wall, and planted with fruit trees [which] was formerly in the occupation of Lady Jersey'.[72]

Early in June 1796 Countess Spencer wrote to her daughter asking for news, given the storm of events:

> What is to be the denouement about the Jerseys pray let me have a line … if you hear anything … I think her attempting to brave a storm like that

> which is risen against her is madness – surely the best way ... would be for them both to resign instantly & get abroad for a year or two ... I must pity Lord Jersey though nobody else will.[73]

Life for the younger Jersey children too must have been very uncomfortable in these years and worthy of pity. Not only was their mother the subject of very public, and very vociferous, vilification but also there was fear for their, as well as her, physical safety. This was not confined to the events of May and June 1796. As we will see, events were to take a nasty turn when the children were in Brighton, without their parents, a few months later and, in the following year, they were to suffer humiliation as a result of the public ostracism of their mother. Further, poor Lady Sarah certainly suffered much discomfiture in coming out into Society at a time when her mother was ignored at public events and tolerated only out of pity for the young daughter whom she, presumably deliberately, brought with her in part at least as a human shield.

Indeed, not for the first time in these turbulent years, the normally clever and astute Countess failed to entertain reality or the sensible course – on this occasion the impossibility of continuing as a Lady of the Bedchamber – and appears to have sacrificed self-interest and the interests of her children in favour of some wider objective, whether malice, obstinacy or pride. It is as if her status, power and patronage had gone to her head, making her self-deluding to the exclusion of all common sense.

Still, only two days after Georgiana Devonshire's letter, the deadlock over the Countess's position was broken and resolution came very rapidly. On 12 June the Princess had written to the King to say that there could be no reconciliation with the Prince without '*la retraite absolue de Lady Jersey de mon service et de ma société privée*'.[74] Shortly thereafter it seems, according to Mrs Fitzroy's understanding at least, the Duke of York told Princess Caroline, 'His Majesty pledges himself that Lady J shall be dismissed.'[75] Then on about 18 June, the Prince of Wales wrote a declaration for delivery to the King 'in which HM will observe that everything that the Princess deemed to wish has been complied with as far as will not degrade the Prince'.[76] Whilst clearly some debate continued about precisely when Lady Jersey could be admitted to Carlton House and when she could not (without degrading the Prince), on 23 July the King wrote to the Prince saying that, with the Prince's consent, he had told Caroline that Lady Jersey was to retire forthwith and thereafter was not to be admitted to the Princess's private society whether at Carlton House or any where else – though this should not prevent her attending the Prince's Drawing Rooms or public assemblies.[77]

The King's aim in all of this was to achieve a reconciliation between the Prince and his wife and avoid the scandal of a separation, formal or otherwise. He thought that harmony would prevail once Lady Jersey had retired from the Princess's service, and was supported in this view by the Princess herself. In this, of course, he was to be disappointed. Any prospect of marital harmony had long since been lost – and whilst Lady Jersey was about to lose her position in the Princess's household she was not about to lose her hold over the Prince.

So on 29 June Frances Jersey resigned under pressure from all sides. In doing so she did not fail to take the opportunity to display her malevolence and her scorn of the Princess. When her letter of resignation to Caroline became public, *The Times* wrote of it:

> Lady Jersey has written a letter to the Princess of Wales on her resignation which is one of the most disrespectful we ever recollect to have read. Her Ladyship begins by stating that her wish was to have resigned long since, but that his Royal Highness would not suffer it on the ground that it would only tend to justify the calumnies reported of her. She then insinuates who the person is who has propagated all the scandal against her, and concludes by assuring the Princess she shall to the last moment of her life *be proud to serve the Prince of Wales*. Throughout the letter there is not one word of respect towards her Royal Highness.[79]

Indeed the malice, scorn and clear desire to insult, as well as the total hypocrisy, shine out from that letter:

> I seize the earliest opportunity in my power to have the honour of informing your Royal Highness that I have this day obtained the permission of H.R.H. the Prince of Wales to resign into *his* hands the situation of Lady of the Bedchamber in yr R. H.'s Family, a situation which I had the honour of being appointed to by *him* at the same time with the rest of those who compose yr Royal Highness's Household.
>
> The same duty & attachment which I shall ever be proud to profess for H.R.H. & which induced me to accept of that appointment, urged me to obey his commands in retaining it long after the infamous & unjustifiable paragraphs in the public papers rendered it impossible for a person of the rank & situation which I hold in this country (indeed for anyone possessing the honest pride & spirit of an Englishwoman) to submit to hold a situation which was to make her the object of deep & designing calumny.
>
> The Prince of Wales represented to me upon my mentioning my earnest request to H.R.H. for my instant resignation that such a step would not only be regarded as confirmation of every absurd & abominable falsehood that had been so industriously fabricated for the *present purpose*, but that it would be farther promoting the views of those who had been so wickedly labouring to injure H.R.H. in the public mind & through him to degrade the rest of the Royal Family. But the moment is now come when I can with propriety withdraw myself from such persecution & injustice, with the conscious satisfaction of *knowing* that I have *by my silence* & forbearance on my part given the strongest proofs of my duty to the Royal Family, & of that respectful

> attachment & gratitude to H.R.H. the Prince of Wales which never can end but with my life.[80]

A document in the Royal Archives refers to a draft of this letter of resignation in which, mysteriously, Lady Jersey concludes by saying that she was resigning 'on account of Mrs Fitzherbert'. What she had in mind in writing that is unclear, and in any event the reference did not survive into the final letter.[81]

Lady Jersey did not of course fail to get such further revenge following her resignation as was available to her. It can be no coincidence that, within ten days of her resignation, Jack Payne, now the Keeper of the Privy Seal to the Prince of Wales but also a stout supporter of Princess Caroline, was dismissed from his post in the Prince's household.[82]

That apart, the life of the Prince and his mistress was to continue after her resignation very much as before. Indeed, following the resignation the Prince saw more of the Countess than ever. He spent as much time as he could at the Grange and later at his new country estate in Dorset, Crichell House, where he could see her, and in the late summer he went down to spend some time with her in Bognor. The Prince also spent time with Lady Jersey at the Pavilion where the Countess 'has her bed in the Prince's dressing room'.[83] He was also to install her at last in the house in Warwick Street adjoining Carlton House, formerly Field Marshall Conway's.[84] How this future was to take shape was foreshadowed when Lady Stafford, another ally of the Princess, wrote of a dinner she attended with the Prince and the Princess. The Prince, she said, behaved as if trying to show he never wanted to see the Princess again, and as soon as dinner was over he left to visit Lady Jersey. 'He protests' said Lady Stafford, 'he will never go to the Opera with the Princess and is entirely directed by Lady Jersey. This is call'd a Reconciliation.' She added that: 'Her Ladyship [i.e. Lady Jersey] yesterday modestly rode through the courts of Carlton House, and out of the Gate, attended by a servant in the Prince's livery.'[85]

Indeed, the conduct of the Countess caused wider comment although not without some grudging admiration. Hare, noting that Lady Jersey had been insulted in public, observed that her appearances in public were 'more to the credit of personal courage than to the delicacy of her feelings'.[86] Whilst Lady Spencer thought that public disapproval of Lady Jersey was such that it would be best if both the Jerseys should go abroad 'for a year or two', since that 'would quiet the world, and I think nothing else will' and would also be 'I will not say the most honourable, but the least dishonourable thing they can do'. She did, though, have a few kind words for her old friend, the Earl, whom she pitied but who had 'erred grievously, I am confident [she said] it has been from tenderness to her and affection for his children, in short from a thousand better motives than will ever be believed'.[87]

The whole business had been conducted very much in the public arena with the press, society and public looking on, almost universally disapproving and vocally so. Lady Jersey was rapidly becoming a figure of such disrepute that there was public speculation whether she would have the effrontery to attend the Queen's Drawing-Room on 1 July. The *Gazetteer* wrote the previous day:

> That there are more extraordinary circumstances in this world than our philosophy can ever dream of, is a fact we must irresistibly admit; yet we may contend ... that the Countess of Jersey will not ... attend ... the drawing-room. The laws of good breeding, humanity, indispensible propriety, and common decency must bear us out.

They did not. Frances Jersey was not one to be put off by such considerations or by public opinion. As Lady Stafford told Lord Granville Leveson Gower: 'They say her Ladyship is to be at the Drawing-Room this Day. I hope the Mob will attack her ...'[88]

14

Vilification: The Apogee of Disrepute

The manner of the times was violent, and not just physical. There was 'a cacophony of violence: newspapers, cartoons and street ballads blasted their targets with scabrous insults and Billingsgate scurrility'.[1]

Lady Jersey was now its target.

The following months of 1796 were no less uncomfortable, and at times no less frightening, for the Countess than the previous year. She faced, first, a barrage of abuse in the press in respect of events dating back almost a year, and then a vivid manifestation of the hatred she inspired and the physical threat that hatred presented to both her and her family.

The first signs of Lady Jersey's new difficulties started to appear in the press at the end of May 1796. On 24 May *The Times* wrote: 'A letter superscribed to Brunswick has been sent by way of Jersey, where it lay concealed for some days, and was there opened by a person to whom it was not addressed.'[2]

Other newspapers soon picked up the story. *The Observer* wrote on 29 May: 'Lady —— is said to be one of the most adroit hands in England at *opening a letter* that is *not* directed to herself.'

The identity of 'Lady ——' and the story that lay behind these reports was widely known and was 'the topic of conversation in every company'. It amounted to this. Somehow letters from Princess Caroline to her parents in Brunswick in which she was critical of both the Queen and Lady Jersey had been intercepted and opened by Lady Jersey, who not only read 'such a description of [herself] as she merits' in them but also 'relayed their contents to the Prince and the Queen'.[3]

Public opinion was outraged on the part of the Princess, although it was not alone:

> The Queen is enraged because in her [i.e. Caroline's] letter to the D. of Brunswick – she said the Queen countenanced Lady Jersey.–The King is almost distracted – all the world are raving against the Prince.– and could a Mob get but once, Lady Jersey into their Clutches – they would pull her heart out.[4]

However, whilst Lady Jersey's guilt was widely assumed it was not yet proven. Over coming days the facts behind the story began to emerge. In the summer of the previous year the Princess of Wales, then in Brighton, had entrusted the delivery of some letters she had written to her parents to the Rev Dr Randolph, formerly her English teacher in Brunswick, who was going to Brunswick for his own purposes. Unfortunately on his coming from Brighton to London, Dr Randolph had news that his wife was unwell and so postponed his journey. Wanting, therefore, to return her letters to the Princess, when back in London he sought instructions as to what to do with them. Lady Jersey told him, on behalf of the Princess, to send the letters, addressed to her, Lady Jersey, at the Pavilion in Brighton where she was in residence. Since the normal practice was that letters forwarded from Carlton House to Brighton were sent by the Brighton Post Coach leaving the Golden Cross at Charing Cross, this is how Dr Randolph was told to send the packet and this is accordingly what he did. However, although the Coach operator's records show that they received the packet from Dr Randolph at the Golden Cross, the Princess never received her letters in Brighton, and despite diligent searches both in London and Brighton the packet was never found.

Curiously, when some time later Dr Randolph volunteered to come back to London to help the search for the packet there he was told by Lady Jersey: 'Your coming to town will be of no use, and their Royal Highnesses wish you not to do it; they lament you did not leave the packet at Carleton House, directed for the Princess, as the porter there would have conveyed it safely.'[5]

This is all the more odd because Dr Randolph had been told specifically at Carlton House to use the Post Coach, and Lady Jersey herself told Randolph to address the packet to her.

At the same time, the press became ever more specific in their accusations and increasingly mocking of Lady Jersey. So *The Morning Post* wrote on 18 July 1796:

> Those letters are reported to have spoken in very severe terms of certain Great Personages, and it was said Lady Jersey intercepted them, and shewed them to the Great Personages complained of ... The scurrilous passages against Lady Jersey ... have too probably prejudiced the Public against her ... It will be found she has been grossly libeled, and that much cunning, misrepresentation, and industry have been employed to influence the Public against her ... The Princess long made her a bosom friend but a female German companion, jealous of Lady Jersey's influence, wished to see it destroyed ... There is as much intrigue carried on by certain persons as ever was practised at the Court of Versailles and there is too much reason to believe, that the Princess is duped, and Lady Jersey sacrificed by it ... The truth, however, will now speedily be before the Public, and they must judge for themselves.

The public did just that and had little doubt as to what had happened and who was to blame. Although the letters had disappeared and were never found, somehow their contents were universally known, and the public's finger of guilt clearly pointed at the Countess. Unfortunately for her husband it was, therefore, once more left to Lord Jersey to try and achieve for his wife the 'justice Lady Jersey's character claims' and rescue his wife from 'the calumny, which the false representations of the business have so shamefully and unjustly drawn upon Lady J'.[6]

He sought to do this, somewhat clumsily, by publishing all the correspondence which had passed between him and his wife and Dr Randolph as they sought to establish all the facts, although the *London Chronicle* commented doubtfully 'how far it is likely to produce the desired effect, the Public to whom the appeal is made [of his wife's innocence] –, are left to decide'.[7]

In fact, when he did publish the correspondence, it made things worse. *The Times* commented that its publication 'has darkened, instead of elucidating this very mysterious transaction', going on to say 'the simple question now is who received the parcel from the office in Brighton'.[8] Others judged that 'Lord Jersey has completely failed in proving his point; for in fact he has proved nothing'.[9] Even more tellingly, as a friend of Mrs Thrale observed:

> The mysterious story of the packet [is] not rendered less mysterious by Lord Jersey's curious pamphlet [and] remains unexplained. His Lordship has proved an excellent advocate for his wife for he has told the public what they did not know before that such a package was *really* addressed her and that unless by some very strange chance which is by no means accounted for it *must* have gone through her hands.[10]

Typically trenchant, *The True Briton* on 22 July asked why Lady Jersey, instead of 'beating around the bush' did not 'come forward with a *positive declaration* that she *never received* the parcel', because the Earl's pamphlet proved nothing in her favour. It then picked up on another point: 'It [is] not unreasonably deemed very strange that Lady Jersey should endeavour to prevent Dr Randolph from coming to London, to make enquiries after the parcel', and in so doing used the names of the Prince and Princess of Wales, 'she best knows with what authority'. The consensus was clearly that she was indeed guilty as accused. As Joseph Farington confirmed in his diary for 24 July: 'Lady Jersey had been the subject of conversation [at Strawberry Hill] & Lord Orford [as Horace Walpole had now become] seemed fully convinced of her having intercepted the letter.'

What was more incredible, as Farington went on to say, was that 'Lord Jersey has been with the King to complain of the Princess of Wales having endeavoured to take away Lady Jersey's character' – presumably in the contents of the intercepted private letters. On this occasion the King was even less sympathetic to the Earl and, in response to Lord Jersey's complaints, humiliatingly for the Earl 'made no reply but bowed him out of the room'.[11]

And then, all of a sudden, the furore died. On 29 August, Mrs Fitzroy wrote saying 'the whole business has [been] dropped; Higher powers began to be alarmed, for I am convinced another Lady was an accomplice.'[12]

The other 'Lady' she referred to was of course the Queen, another steadfast enemy of Princess Caroline and, so it was thought by some, implicated in the theft of Caroline's letters.

So it seems the royal family, frightened by the possible consequences of the raging scandal and the part played in it by the Queen, applied pressure to stem it. If that is indeed correct, it only supports what seems to be the truth of the matter. Everybody, including the Jerseys, acknowledged that the Princess's letters were opened and shown or described to the Queen and went on to become public knowledge. All acknowledged, too, that the letters were sent to the Pavilion addressed to Lady Jersey. There she had every opportunity to open them and to describe their contents to the Queen, her particular friend. To do so would not only be totally in character for Lady Jersey but also completely consistent with her dealings with the Princess and her desire to torment, diminish and control her. Once the (presumably sealed) letters had been opened there was no way they could be returned to the Princess so they, and their evidence against the Countess, were doubtless destroyed. In all it seems more than likely that, despite her brazen, and her husband's naïve, protestations, Lady Jersey was indeed guilty of the charge brought against her in the court of public opinion of having intercepted, opened and read the Princess's private correspondence – and used their contents against her.

Of even greater significance was that the public believed her guilty, and the cumulative effect of this further scandal, following rapidly on the drama and outrage leading to her resignation as a Lady of the Bedchamber, was shortly to be demonstrated.

In the normal way both the Prince and his wife were expected in Brighton in July, with rooms being fitted up in readiness for the infant Princess Charlotte.[13] In the meantime, Lord and Lady Jersey 'engaged a house opposite to the Pavilion, the same which Mrs Fitzherbert occupied when she was last at that place' for the summer,[14] causing *The True Briton* of 16 July to comment: 'The landlord of Lady Jersey's house at Brighton is stated to be a brass-founder. The tenant too deals in brass'; a few days later *The Telegraph* added: 'In the house which Lord Jersey was to occupy in Brighton, there is a communication with the Pavilion. This, we must conclude, was intended to accommodate Lady Jersey, whenever she had occasion to pay her respects to the Princess.'[15]

Towards the end of July the (in)famous Countess's arrival in Brighton was expected daily and, in the words of *The Sun*, her 'visit engrosse[d] the whole conversation of the Fashionables' in Brighton.[16] Nevertheless, whilst her arrival was duly, and incorrectly, reported at the end of the month,[17] and although her housekeeper and children had arrived earlier in the month, her visit was not to take place.[18]

On 26 July Mrs Fitzroy described to Lady Stafford what had happened:

> The lady has not yet left town. – Her carriage was even loaded for that purpose on Saturday evening; but she rec'd an express from Brighton, to advise her not to go there immediately as printed handbills were distributed & posted up against all the houses to say she was coming & to invite a mob to meet her. – I am sorry she was stopped. – Her insolent letter [of resignation as Lady of the Bedchamber] was in the Papers yesterday. She is very much mistaken if she imagines it meets with the Publick approbation. Thank God that [letter] in addition to her Book has completely finished her Character & what is more lucky, she has only to thank herself for her folly. The disgust both publications have caused is no small comfort.[19]

The reference to 'her Book' is probably to a pamphlet published that year by a venal journalist John Matthews, under the pseudonym of Anthony Pasquin, which amounted to an apologia for the Countess. Entitled *The New Brighton Guide; involving a complete, authentic and honourable solution of the recent mysteries of Carlton House*, it was probably commissioned by the Countess or the Prince, as they were to do on another occasion some years later. As its title indicates, its purpose was to give some 'independent' explanation and justification of Frances Jersey's actions.

It completely failed in its objective. The public remained convinced of the Countess's guilt.

Meanwhile the *Whitehall Evening Post* of 28 July described in detail what had happened in Brighton in 'a most extraordinary circumstance. Lady Jersey's children having arrived on Monday last, the populace showed great indignation at it, and assembled tumultuously before the house, declaring that Lady Jersey should not take up her residence at it. Some gentlemen intervened, promising to represent what had passed to her Ladyship, to whom an express was sent off; and we understand she has *prudently* determined *not* to make her appearance at Brighton.'

It must have been terrifying for the children, and very worrying on that account for their mother. It shows the degree of hatred the Countess inspired.

The Times the following day was crueller still, careless of the childrens' welfare and mocking of their various parentages. After describing these events it went on:

> Surely nothing can be more infamous than this! Admitting all the falsehood told of Lady Jersey to be true, it is not the less wicked to attempt to raise a Mob to tear her Children to pieces, several of whom are connected with the most respectable Families in the Kingdom, and are themselves as respectable as the Families with whom they are connected.

There was more to follow, as Lady Spencer wrote to Georgiana Devonshire from Brighton the day after:

> The Prince of Wales arrived here last night and heard what really happened that a stuffed mawkin with a feather had been carried round about two days before with Lady J— written full-length upon it, and was afterwards burnt. He is outrageous, it is likewise said that she was here but went away very early this morning.[20]

Mrs Howe was probably more accurate when she wrote to Lady Stafford:

> Lady J having been persuaded by Mr Villiers not to go to Brighton, she has sent her children back & it is imagined the Prince will come away when the races are over. The Princess has been informed she is not to be there; a few days ago the mob there dressed up a figure as a fine lady in feathers &c, & fastened a label on the back inscribed the *W of Babylon* & carried it around from house to house begging money for buying burning materials, & got some.[21]

Lady Jersey was no more popular in London where she stayed than she was in Brighton, as Mrs Thrale wrote:

> The Town does nothing but rave [i.e. rage] about the Prince of Wales & Lady Jersey & how She ridicules the Princess ... Our honest King and his honest Populace join to support the Foreign suffering Wife, but there are those who abet the Countess and her Royal Paramour – many say the Queen encourages Lady Jersey – what Times! what Wonders! what Horrors![22]

This topic of disapproving conversation was exacerbated by news from Carlton House. At the end of July Princess Caroline told the Duke of Leeds that

> she understood Lady Jersey was [now indeed] to have the house, formerly Marshall Conways, lately inhabited by [the now dismissed] Jack Payne, and which the Prince bought a few years since, adjoining to Carlton House Gardens; that a wall was to be built as a sort of screen on the side of Carlton House, and that this and other works necessary would probably be done in her absence' in the country.[23]

On this the Princess's understanding was correct, and obvious to all was that the building works were to allow the lovers to meet unobserved.

For his part, it was said that the burning of Lady Jersey in effigy by the townspeople of Brighton had determined the Prince never to go there again, and a story circulated that the Pavilion was to be let.[24] Indeed, the Prince only spent a short period in Brighton that year. His cutting short of his visit was, wrote *The Times,* 'considered as a retaliation for the conduct of the people of [Brighton] with respect to a certain Lady'.[25] This prompted a humble public address by 'the principal inhabitants of the town of Brighthelmstone', in which, after assuring the Prince of their regret and their attachment to his person, they expressed the hope that he would honour the town with 'a continuation of your royal Residence and protection', as a result of which, wrote *The Telegraph* of 10 August, the Prince 'with characteristic condescension and benevolence has been soothed into an oblivion of injury'.[26]

Nevertheless, the Countess, who was now driving around in a plain coach without arms so as to avoid identification, would not go to Brighton that year.[27] As *The Telegraph* wrote caustically on 7 August: 'Lady Jersey is determined not to go to Brighton, as she declares nothing shall induce her to visit any place where she is not likely to meet with respect. She has not, however, yet decided upon any abode that will suit her.'

The press continued to snipe at the Countess with great regularity and much scorn. Typical of their barbs was *The True Briton's* observation a few days later, that 'the Government of [the British dependency, the Channel Island of] *Jersey* [whose ownership was fought over with France] has lately passed through several hands – It is not the only thing of the name that has done the same'.[28]

Clearly the Countess' life was very uncomfortable, even for one with such steely strength of character. This is evident, too, from a letter she wrote from London, where she remained for the time being, to Edward Jerningham:

> I am ashamed of having been so long silent, or rather I am sorry that I have not written; because you may think me ungrateful, when I am merely unhappy. My life at present, is, as you know, intolerable to endure and more than insipid to describe. The P. stayed in town till Friday noon, and returned on Saturday. The time has been passed either in seeing Charlotte's nursery, which brings afresh to my mind my angel Augustus, or in cheating myself into fancied amusement by going to the shops for things I do not want, and cannot afford to buy... So much for my days! My nights are sleepless and weary, my appetite as you saw it, and in short my whole existence such as but for hope could not last many weeks. Every day has produced fresh proofs of treachery from all quarters. Your account of Lady Harcourt does not surprise me ... The conduct of the Primate, as usual, is perfect. The Brighton people have made every sort of apology, but in vain; and I conclude their recantation will deter others from running into the same error. Critchil, I hope, will do, and that we shall pass many Christmases there *en dépit des envieux* ... You shall hear again the moment my date is fixed for going out of this accursed house: it cannot be above a week longer that I am condemned to such purgatory. I think I may begin and sin as if I had been born but yesterday; this sejour must have expiated all and more than I could have committed in my long life. Vale![29]

A few days later the Countess was writing again to Jerningham, this time in a much more cheerful frame of mind:

> Though I wrote to you the other day I must say one word to you again: it is to tell you that the Primate has outdone himself in kindness and good nature, and arrangements are so made that the remainder of the summer and autumn will be delicious. We go on Wednesday to Bognor ... And I think now it is time for you to turn your eyes towards the South. My mother has had letters from Ireland with an account of Lord Moira's having done much good in my defence. The tide is certainly turning here, and at Bath. The Brighton people have addressed the P. to stay, and they would have mentioned me in the address if it had not been declined. Adieu! Pray, write soon and often. I shall want amusement and kindness for the next fortnight. God bless Father Edward.[30]

If the first of these letters was self-deluding, the second was certainly wishful thinking, notwithstanding the content of her next letter to Father Edward; the tide was most certainly not turning and in fact the Countess's life was to become even more difficult over the coming months. Nevertheless, the Countess clearly enjoyed her visit to Bognor, or pretended she did, as she described in a letter to Jerningham from there dated 16 August:

> Thank you very much, Father Edward for your long and comfortable letter ... I do not know what day [the Prince] will come though; but I think in the next week, and I shall certainly see him. This place is delightful, in itself quiet, cheerful, clean. The air is delicious, and the country around it beautiful. But it wants some of God's creatures. My house is delightful, much better than any lodging at Brighton; my eating– and drawing–room just the size and shape of my rooms at the Pavilion. Sir R. Hotham, the King of the place, has taken me under his protection, sends me fruit, has put up a tent for me and the children under my windows, and appears to like me excessively. He is a clean old man, with white hair, white eyes, and white hands; was a great merchant; and has laid out above £100,000 in making this place. He will die contented if any of the Royal Family inhabit one of his houses. *Vous sentez bien qu'il est au pieds de Francisca*!
>
> Mrs. Damer is here with Miss Burny [*sic*]. She called upon me last week and was fort aimable. We have met since riding, and greet each other most cordially. But nothing more will happen; for I am not capable of forcing myself upon her, and I do not conceive that my family party would suit her or her friends. I have got books, work, drawing, music, in short every sort of comfort, which gives me no sort of amusement. The state of my poor mind requires dissipation and hurry; and I was never so well as the day I travelled from London. As I cannot afford to spend much money in post-houses, I must wait until Mahomet comes to the mountain, and not finish the saying.

1. Frances, Countess of Jersey, by Thomas Beach (*c.* 1795). Private collection; image courtesy of Sotheby's.

2. Frances, Countess of Jersey, mezzotint by Thomas Watson, after Daniel Gardner, (1774). © National Portrait Gallery, London.

3. George Bussy, 4th Earl of Jersey, by Nathaniel Dance (1770). From the collection at Althorp.

4. Charlotte, Lady William Russell, by John Hoppner. Private collection; photo © Philip Mould Ltd, London/Bridgeman Images.

5. Maria Anne, Mrs Fitzherbert, by Sir Joshua Reynolds. By consent of the owners; on loan to the National Portrait Gallery, London; photograph © National Portrait Gallery, London.

6. 'A trip to Cock's Heath', by William Humphrey, after John Hamilton Mortimer (1778). © The Trustees of the British Museum.

7. 'Future prospects or symptoms of love in high life', published by S. W. Fores (1796). © The Trustees of the British Museum.

8. Lady Caroline Villiers, Lady Paget, and her son Henry, by John Hoppner. © National Trust Images/John Hammond.

9. Lady Sarah Bayley [Bayly], by Mrs Joseph Mee. Royal Collection Trust/ © Her Majesty Queen Elizabeth II 2016.

10. Lady Anne Villiers, Lady Lambton and her children, print of a portrait by John Hoppner (1797). © National Trust/Christopher Warleigh-Lack.

11. George IV as Prince of Wales, by John Hoppner. By kind permission of the Trustees of the Wallace Collection.

12. 'Fashionable-jockeyship', by James Gillray (1796). © National Portrait Gallery, London.

13. Sarah Sophia, Countess of Jersey, by Sir George Hayter. © National Portrait Gallery, London.

14. John Ponsonby, 1st Viscount Ponsonby, by Henry Bone, possibly after Sir Thomas Lawrence (1812). © National Portrait Gallery, London.

15. Georgiana Poyntz, Countess Spencer, by Thomas Gainsborough (*c.* 1780–1781). © Devonshire Collection, Chatsworth. Reproduced by permission of Chatsworth Settlement Trustees.

16. Georgiana, Duchess of Devonshire, by Thomas Gainsborough. © Devonshire Collection, Chatsworth. Reproduced by permission of Chatsworth Settlement Trustees.

Feby. the 19.

CASTLE HOWARD
J14/1/622A

My Dr. Ld. Carlisle

having just received a letter from Mr. Hamilton who tells me you have spoke to him about Mr. Bortes, I cannot help thanking you for remembering him. I should have wrote to you long ago, but I took a panick at the thoughts of any body seeing my letters, for I could write nonsense with great comfort to you which I should not like to have read by others, & if you will promise me upon your honor never to show my

17. Letter (first page) from Frances, Countess of Jersey, to Frederick, 5th Earl of Carlisle, dated 19 February ?1784. From the Castle Howard Archive, reference J14/1/622A. Reproduced by kind permission of the Howard family.

letters you shall hear from me often enough. I bid Mr. J. ask this question for me a great while ago, but he has been so busy, or so idle that he has not wrote to you — pray write to me soon & tell me a great deal about yourself — Ever Yrs. sincerely

F. J.

18. Letter (second page) from Frances, Countess of Jersey, to Frederick, 5th Earl of Carlisle, dated 19 February ?1784. From the Castle Howard Archive, reference J14/1/622A. Reproduced by kind permission of the Howard family.

19. Frederick, 5th Earl of Carlisle, by Sir Joshua Reynolds (1769). From the Castle Howard Collection. Reproduced by kind permission of the Howard family.

20. Princess Caroline of Brunswick, by Sir Thomas Lawrence. © National Portrait Gallery, London.

> Pray write to me instantly, and tell me the day that you will arrive. We cannot lodge you; but we will feed you, and procure a room close to us ... Lord J is gone to see Howards [?] at the Grange, returns today. The Prince has taken Critchil, and it will do well in every respect. Adieu! Still continue to pray for F.[31]

It is easy to imagine the elderly Sir Richard Hotham as putty in the hands of the fascinating and beautiful Countess. It is intriguing, too, to see her awareness of, and pride in, the power of her charms, as well as the recognition of having little in common with the bluestockings Mrs Damer and Miss Burney. Most interesting of all, though, is her recognition of her own character's need for 'dissipation and hurry' before she could be properly amused.

Lady Jersey may have thought, as she said to Jerningham, that the tide of her unpopularity was turning, but in this she was wrong. The press continued to publish biting commentaries on her and, typically, it was *The True Briton* that pushed these to the limit when it wrote on 31 August: 'The Prince of Wales was last week expected at *Bognor*, where we are informed some of His Royal Highness's stud had arrived.'

Nevertheless, some sort of attempt was made on the Countess's part to prevent the press publishing at least some of the worst items. On 1 August Col McMahon wrote to tell the Prince that he, with James Christie (the auctioneer and a founding Proprietor of *The Morning Post*), had managed to stop *The True Briton* publishing 'a most false & infamous paragraph against Lady Jersey'.[32] Again, McMahon was writing to the Prince a fortnight later to say that instructions had been given to his representatives 'to use every precaution towards hindering any insinuations from appearing [in the press] against her Ladyship', going on to report that 'some fresh paragraphs to Lady —— on the subject of Coventry, having been sent to the evening papers' had been successfully suppressed.[33]

Inevitably, though, these attempts to control the press and their attacks on the Countess were, Canute like, doomed to fail. Only a day after the latter of these interventions, *The True Briton* was reporting mockingly that 'Lady Jersey is now at *Bognor-Rock*. The few persons who were there have precipitately left it, amongst whom is Sir Richard Hotham himself.'[34]

Mrs Fitzroy joyfully embellished this story when writing to Lady Stafford at the end of August, saying that Lady Jersey had been forced to leave Bognor 'as the company all went to Sir Richard Hotham (the Proprietor of the place) to say that if he allowed Lady J to remain there, they were resolved to quit it: upon which He sent to inform her she could have her house no longer. She removed the next day to Worthing where I believe she is at present. It is quite a happiness to reflect on the mortifications that woman has met with lately.'[35]

Sadly for Mrs Fitzroy's pleasure, both stories were incorrect, as she had to acknowledge only a few days later:

> I was sorry [she wrote to Lady Stafford] to find the account I sent your Ladyship in my last from Bognor Rocks was erroneous. Lady Jersey is

> settled there & so is the Prince of Wales. He has taken a large house and sent for His cooks, Maitre d'Hotel &c. &c. – Myself I think it is with a view to giving dinners and asking Ladies to dine with him, in order to meet Lady Jersey for at present nobody but Mrs Damer takes notice of her.[36]

Whilst the last may well have been true, what Mrs Fitzroy could not quite bring herself to acknowledge was that, not only had the Countess not been forced to flee Bognor, but also that, in the words of Horace Walpole, whilst 'the beautiful fugitive from Brighthelmston' was there the town 'was thronged with the most fashionable company',[37] including the Countess's long-suffering husband.[38]

Even if, to a greater or lesser extent, the company at Bognor snubbed the Countess, she seemed to enjoy herself – or at least convince herself that she was doing so – whilst the Prince was there. On 2 September she wrote to Edward Jerningham: 'The Primate arrived last night. And when I have got over the agitation of seeing him again after three weeks absence, I shall be more comfortable than I have been for some months. At present I feel giddy with something I suppose is joy.' She went on, after telling Jerningham that he was very disagreeable in not visiting her, to say that the Prince was 'in great beauty, spirits, and *pour aimable il est toujours* like himself'.[39]

This was followed, only a few days later, by another letter to Jerningham in which, after berating him once more for not visiting her, she commented 'do not think I am out of humour because I scold. I am very well, very happy, and very gay. Our future plans you shall know when we meet. At present I can only tell you that the Primate is delighted with the quiet life and with the place, and seems not to have any desire to change it.'[40]

Then, in her third letter to Jerningham within a week, she told him, 'I am very comfortable here at present', before going on to talk about her plans for Christmas with the Prince and, abandoning hope of seeing Jerningham in Bognor, suggesting that he 'make some arrangements for being of the Christmas party [at Crichell House] in Dorsetshire. This is now a secret; so pray do not say a word of my motions.'[41]

The Prince left Bognor on 10 September, leaving the Countess behind. He went away, she told Edward Jerningham:

> Very sorry indeed to go, having passed his time quite to his liking. He is going to fly round Dorsetshire, make a nest for me and my young ones, and perch in London this day se'enight when we shall meet him and take possession of our new house [in Warwick Street], into which they begin moving our furniture the moment what belongs to [Field Marshal Conway] is taken away. I am not sure how long we shall stay in town; but I conclude not many days. You must come to see us on Friday the 30th. The Dorsetshire part of my project [that is Christmas at Crichell] you must keep to yourself; but the house may be talked of, and the delay about the

furniture mentioned, that people may not say we use his. Adieu! ... believe me ever very sincerely and affectionately

Yours,
F.

Pray write to me by return of the post. A letter from you is always acceptable; but *here* and *now* invaluable.[42]

So despite the public's scandalised reaction – of which we shall see more – to the Prince giving the Countess and her husband the house in Warwick Street, Lady Jersey's only concerns were that she might be accused of using the late Field Marshal's furniture – and that, in the absence of the Prince from Bognor, she needed the companionship of letters from Jerningham.

There is one more surviving letter from the Countess sent whilst she was in Bognor. This is located in the Jersey archives and can be dated to this time. Merely addressed 'Dear Sir' and dated 'Bognor Sept 24', its terms clearly refer to the recipient as having spent much time with the Countess at Bognor and having recently left there on a journey. Its style is obviously flirtatious. Given these facts, and the fact that Lady Jersey did not refer in any of her letters to any other companion in Bognor, it is probable that this letter was to the Prince of Wales. If that is the case, it is remarkably a, and indeed the sole, surviving letter from the Countess to the Prince during the period of their affair.

It runs as follows:

I have this morning received your kind letter with the Books by the Coach. Had you written by the Post I should sooner have had the pleasure of knowing you are safe at your Journey's end & that you have followed my advice in calling upon [illegible]. I am sure you will not repent any [illegible] you showed to that person ... Pray never think of saying anything civil to us about your sejour here, we ought to thank you eternally for the many pleasant hours you made us pass & I can sincerely assure you that we miss & and regret you every day – the weather is as much changed as the Society and the only event that has happened is [my?] being wet through on horseback – The face of Bognor is dismal indeed, something like your Duke's I fancy. Why did you not tell me how he received you. Tomorrow we give dinner to Sr Richard &c and on Thursday we shall proceed to London ... Your little friends have found some golden [illegible] which they intend to give to you. They are almost wild with joy at the idea of moving, & getting into a large house. Perhaps I should make an apology for talking so much about them, but this is a subject upon which I have no modesty.[43]

With the Prince gone, the Countess's stay in Bognor however was not easy, and her need for the comfort of Jerningham's letters ever more important. As Mrs Howe wrote: 'I hear not a soul visits Lady Jersey at Bognor not even the Sheridan's who inhabit the next house. When the Prince was there he drove her about in an open carriage, Mr Lambton refused her being at any of his houses, on which she has quarreled with him, & would not allow Lady Sarah going abroad with Lady Ann Lambton.'[44]

It is remarkable indeed that Lady Jersey's reputation was so bad that even her son-in-law refused her admittance – prompting retribution by way of Sarah being banned from consorting with her sister.

Nor was Society's disapproval of the Countess confined to Bognor. When she went to court once back in London in October, Mrs Matthew Montagu, wife of Elizabeth Montagu's nephew, recorded that 'no lady at the Drawing-Room spoke to her but manifested by their behaviour the greatest disapprobation of her conduct'.[45] Further, there was open speculation that the Countess would either by choice or by necessity, in order to achieve some form of acceptance, bring the debutante Lady Sarah out into Society 'on the supposition she will be asked into company out of compassion for the young lady'.[46] That she did so is not entirely to the Countess's credit.

Against this unhappy background, the Jerseys duly left Bognor for their new house in London at the end of September. Once there they found that yet another storm was brewing.

The house in Warwick Street was not only a topic much discussed in (and much disapproved of by) Society but was also the subject of considerable comment in the press, one of whose readers was Queen Charlotte. Alarmed by what she read, and fearing that Frances Jersey was about to bring yet more trouble in her wake, the Queen wrote to the Prince on 23 September that 'on Wednesday evening when alone I took up a newspaper & read an article which mentions that Field Marshall Conway's house was fitted up and given to Lord Jersey by his Royal Highness the Prince of Wales'. The Queen went on that, although she did not believe everything she read in the papers, if the story were true '[after] all the uneasiness you & all of us had gone through this last year, & the many unpleasant scenes which have passed on account of that family [the Jerseys] in many different places ... the world in general would make it a new instrument against you', adding, 'I dread the consequences for yourself, Charlton House [*sic*], and the inhabitants of the next [that is the Jerseys], & the effects of such a public insult makes me shudder', and pleaded with her son to exercise caution in the matter.[47]

The Queen's plea was forlorn. The Prince replied at length, in his usual self-serving manner, saying that the arrangement was merely to enable Lord Jersey the better and more economically to perform his duties as his Master of the Horse, and that any fair-minded person would understand it as such. What is more, he could not conceive how it could be construed as an insult to the Princess.[48] In this, of course, he was wrong. The Jerseys moved into their new house and the arrangement was, said Mrs Fitzroy, 'universally reprobated';[49] Mrs Fitzroy was no friend of Frances Jersey but others used similar descriptions to describe it. Farington confided to his diary after a dinner party: 'The conduct of the Prince of Wales was spoken of and reprobated. – He has given the house, late Genl. Conways, in Warwick St. to Lord Jersey; and he can go to it by a private way.'[50]

The only surprise is that Farington did not couple the Countess's name with that of the Prince, because that is surely what everyone thought. *The Times* summed up the whole business when it wrote on 29 September:

> We cannot believe the report that a certain Countess of *New Coventry* has taken up her abode at the late Field Marshall Conway's house adjoining to Carlton House. After having been dismissed from the Household of the Princess of Wales, the public would not think it decorous that she should be again placed so near HRH.

So close in fact that, as Princess Caroline complained, the Countess's windows looked directly into those of her apartment.[52]

The Times was right about the public's opinion, but both the Prince and Frances Jersey were unmoved.

Lord Glenbervie provides an insight into the perception of Lady Jersey at this time amongst those not in the Princess's camp by comparing the Countess with two of the mistresses of Louis XIV of France. She, he said, 'is certainly much handsomer, at least as clever, less prudish, but fully as good as [the sober and intelligent] Madame de Maintenon and that Lady Jersey was not a [dramatizing, demanding and very beautiful] Madame de Montespan that with the Prince she has the advantage of being older' – which drew the response from Lady Margaret Fordyce that 'Lady Jersey's reign will not last for ever, for that nobody could think of a mistress of half a century'.[53]

Entertainingly, Glenbervie also observed that there was 'a remarkable coincidence in several of the circumstances of a late subject of public discussion and public scandal [meaning of course the Prince and his mistress] with those which produced with very similar effects about the time of Charles II's marriage with the Infanta of Portugal', in that before his marriage Charles too had a mistress called Villiers, whose husband received promotion to procure his acquiescence to the affair and whom, on her arrival, the Queen was determined should be excluded from her presence.[54]

In the following months Society rallied ever more against the Countess. A constant topic of gossip was the treatment Frances Jersey received both from her peers and at court as a result of these serial scandals and the very public and bitter disapproval she had provoked. The reports of how she was treated vary according to whether the reporter was of the Princess's party or not, although even those who were of the Princess's camp found themselves admiring the Countess both for her beauty and for her courage. Initially there was speculation whether, given her extreme unpopularity, she would even dare go to the Drawing Room on 20 October when she was due to present Lady Sarah to the King and Queen. Of course, the steely Countess did dare go with her daughter – who must have found it very difficult – and famously this became the occasion when the discomfiture of Fawkener and a family likeness told the world of Lady Sarah's true paternity.[55]

It cannot have been a pleasant occasion for the Countess. It must have been an awful one for Lady Sarah, both in anticipation and at the time. It seems that the King avoided the Countess although the Queen was relatively gracious to her (and the more criticised as a result), and Lady Jersey succeeded in presenting Lady Sarah to her. Others at the Drawing Room showed their profound disapproval of Lady Jersey. The Countess of Sutherland, an ally of Caroline's, described what happened:

> The drawing room yesterday was full, Ly Jersey & her Daughter arrived late, Ly J looking very beautiful, Ly Worcester can tell you what effect it had on the King as she was close by – as for the Queen she seemed at first to avoid her but spoke to her after some little turning & returning in a very gracious manner as did the Princesses and many of the observers for they were numerous & observing thought her Majesty do more than was necessary in the very obliging manner in which she spoke to her, & paid her Compliments on her Family &c. In short people did not seem to think it alright, & to tell the truth in my opinion the best excuse for the Queen is the idea of *la sacrifice au Diable pour l'apaiser*, as after all Ly J's malicious conduct to her daughter-in-law, & after the fuss she made formerly about distinctions of character it is a strange thing to show such a preference as she does to her. However nobody followed her example for everyone kept out of Ly Jersey's way & ran off on her approach.[56]

As to the King's treatment of the Countess, another ally of the Princess, Mrs Caroline Howe told Lady Stafford:

> I am afraid the King shirked speaking to Lady Jersey three or four times on Thursday whilst she tryed to get at him having Lady Sarah to present. She introduced her to Ly Holderness, & to Lady Grandison & Lady Gertrude, & I think it has been clever of her to bring out Ly Sarah this year tho' they say she is but 16, as it will certainly be a help to notice of herself, and already I hear people say, how hard will be for the girl who is only to be pitied that she should be shunned &c &c'.[57]

Glenbervie's report of her reception was a little bit more positive in that he noted that the Queen had spoken to Lady Jersey 'at least as much as to most other ladies', though he also went on to record that this 'was not in general liked by the persons present'.[58] *The Morning Post*, however, claiming first hand authority, merely maintained that the Countess was 'graciously received'.[59]

Without doubt the Countess was cut by many of those at the Drawing-Room, but typically, in her own eyes at least, she did achieve something, if only self-esteem, from facing down the wall of hostility confronting her. As the Countess of Sutherland told Lady Stafford:

> You will find Lady Jersey in high *feather* when you come, I hear the Royal family are determined to support her ... She certainly was *cut* by everybody else at the drawing room, I think of course one ought to avoid her *there* in order *not* to toad eat the Queen – It is a great triumph to all the ladies formerly neglected by her Majesty for they say that it cannot now be a mark of *purity* to be spoken to by her, all this diverts me very much.[60]

Lady Harcourt, formerly a close friend but now (for reasons we can guess) an angry enemy, was even more forthright when writing to the Countess Spencer:

> I suppose you will hear the Queen abused, because Lady —— returned to Court ... I know from good authority that the reception at St James's was *not* such as any other person, the lady in question excepted, would have been proud of, and yet I hear from authority equally good then she pretends to look upon it as a sort of triumph – the line was upon the present King's accession drawn between such persons as were and were not to be received at Court.[61]

So it was that the Countess faced almost universal vilification and, through her relationship, brought Queen Charlotte into almost as much disrepute as herself. Not only was the Queen's behaviour to her daughter-in-law regarded as 'infamous' but also, in the words of Mrs Fitzroy, 'her M has rendered herself amazingly *un*popular by the reception she gave Lady Jersey at the D. R. – I only wish people would have spirit enough not to go to her Birthday ...'[62]

Lady Jersey's unpopularity, and the public disapproval of her, continued to snowball. Mrs Fitzroy gleefully and scornfully recorded in December: 'Lady Jersey is constant in her attendance at all the Tripos, but even then has no one to speak to but the respective Ladies of the House and her newly acquired friend Lady Rancliffe! A capital protection for her.'*

Mrs Fitzroy went on, rejoicing in the Countess's misfortunes:

> I think it must be mortification to [the Prince] & the Queen, that notwithstanding all their protection, Ly Jersey is not countenanced. I suppose you heard that the Mayor of Bath came up to Town on purposes to tell the Prince that unless Ly J left Bath before H R Hss got their [*sic*], he could not answer for the reception he would meet with – all ranks are outrageous at the idea of his coming at the time she was. The hint was taken & Lady Jersey came off at a moments notice. This is really fact.[63]

---

* *Tripos* comes from the French 'tripot', meaning a gambling den of ill-repute and by extension a place where disreputable people come together. Accordingly here it means female members of society whose reputations were less than fragrant and that, without the Prince, Lady Jersey and the unfortunate Lady Sarah were largely confined to entertainments hosted by them.

There appears to be some basis for this tale. Certainly Col McMahon had been instructed by the Prince the same month as Mrs Fitroy's report to wait on the Countess when he gave her 'all the particulars regarding Bath … which … had the best effects', so possibly it was really fact.[64]

Meanwhile the Countess found yet another reason to upset public opinion. As *The Observer* reported on 6 November, the Prince 'has purchased a lease of a house near his new seat at Crickell, as is stated, for Lord and Lady Jersey'. More trenchantly *The True Briton*, reflecting public opinion, proclaimed three days later: 'We hope it is not true that the P— has taken a house in Dorsetshire, *close to his own*, for Lord and Lady Jersey, because we hope it is not true that any Persons can suppose that, on account of high rank, *they may brave* the Public Opinion.'

All of which, with a relentless barrage of abuse, combined to ensure that life continued to be very difficult for the Countess, and very unpleasant for Lady Sarah, even at court. Mrs Fitzroy reported on an evening at court in January 1797:

> Lady Jersey was there in the morning I am happy to say looking quite hideous as she was loaded with *white paint*. She Cd not persuade her poor daughter to dance so they did not come in the evening. Lady Sarah is pretty – but that is all – but looks frightened to death. I don't think Lady Jersey was very graciously recd … The applause the Princess met with on Tuesday at the Opera was delightful.[65]

The Telegraph on 24 January was even more scathing, mocking too the inappropriateness of the Prince's devices to Lady Jersey, when reporting on a splendid masquerade the previous night: 'There was a *Syren*, rather stricken in years, (supposed to be the Lady Jersey) who wore two devices from the Royal Armorial bearings, vis *Ich Dien*, and *Honi soit, qui mal y pense*.'

Then, when Lady Jersey was entertaining at home, *The True Briton's* version of events, commenting on the rather doubtful company at the Countess's, went as follows:

> Lady Jersey gave a Concert last Monday at her house adjoining and forming part of Carleton-House; the company consisted of many amiable personages – His Royal Highness the Prince of Wales, Lady Elizabeth Luttrell, Mrs Sturt, Mrs Musters, Mrs Campbell, Lady Jane Aston, the Dowager Lady Buckingham … and some of her Ladyship's particular friends.[66]

Adding, by way of clarification of the reputations of the ladies present, a couple of days later: 'In the concert given by Lady Jersey last week, the horns [of cuckolded husbands] were particularly present.'[67]

Although the Duchess of Gordon did invite the Countess along with the Prince to her assembly in January (according to *The Sun* Lady Jersey wore 'a coal black wig'), the Duchess, said Mrs Fiztroy, was ashamed of her being there and sent her excuses to Lady Jersey when in return she was invited to the Countess's concert. Again, at Mrs Walpole's assembly the same month, she reported that nobody would go into the room where Lady Jersey was even to make their curtsy to their hostess, as she was sitting next to Lady Jersey.[68]

In short, 'Lady Jersey is invited nowhere but to the Tripods – & there she carries her poor daughter – every night to each, though there are not a dozen people in town.'[69]

At the same time the Countess was also losing some of her closest allies. So in a letter commonly attributed to the autumn of 1798 but properly attributable to the summer of 1796 Lady Stafford tells of the Jerseys' old friend Lord Harcourt having 'lay'd his commands upon his wife to give up all intercourse with Lady Jersey, who is, as he says, the vilest, most artful of Women, and who by her deceit and pretended Goodness has deceived him for many, many Months'.[70]

Quite what Lady Jersey had done to offend Lord Harcourt is unclear. His disapproval was presumably the result of her treatment of him rather than on account of her sexual mores and treatment of her husband. This because, as Glenbervie wrote of Lord Harcourt's wife, the royal family cordially hated her, and:

> The King particularly does, and with his intimates amuses himself extremely with the scandal about Lady Harcourt and her two bastard children by a Parson H., a handsome young clergyman who lived several years in the house [at Nuneham].[71]

The Queen, too, was beginning to distance herself from Frances Jersey, recognising the unpopularity the connection was causing her, writing to the King in January 1797:

> Since the unpleasant affairs of the Prince & Princess of Wales ... & as your Majesty at the time could not clear my character when things were at the worst in London, *from being privately connected with Lady Jersey*, I then determined never to appear in [public] but where duty called me.[72]

Indeed, it seems to be the beginning of a process that ultimately, and extraordinarily, led to the Queen encouraging her son to resume his affair with Mrs Fitzherbert. As a start in May the Queen, admittedly provoked by the Prince's political posturing, vowed she would never speak to Lady Jersey again at Court. Lady Southampton clearly enjoyed adding her comment: 'Had the Queen never done so, she would have raised herself much in the esteem of the world ...' She also provided the following piece of gossip that shows there were limits even to the Countess's influence: 'The Prince of Wirtemberg has been to [the Prince's house at] Critchell, and he was received with the utmost propriety. Lady J was sent away which occasioned a scene, as she chose to be very angry, but the Prince was stout.'[73]

Lady J was, though, respectable enough to attend the Drawing-Room following the marriage of the Prince of Wirtemberg with the Princess Royal on 18 May and, together with Lady Sarah, kissed hands with the Prince and new Princess.[74] According to the *Observer* she wore 'an elegant dress in white and silver, festooned with china asters and green painted leaves; body and train of the white striped gauze, with silver spangled Circassian tops ornamented with diamonds'.[75]

Whilst the sources are unclear as to whether she attended the marriage ceremony itself in the Chapel Royal, it seems unlikely that she did. This is arguably the case, as it seems clear that she did not attend the formal ball and supper that followed at Windsor Castle on the following Monday night. This, so *The Morning Post* wrote on 24 May 1797,

> was given on the most magnificent, grand, and extensive scale imaginable. The Royal Family and Nobility assembled in St George's Hall at eight o'clock, and at nine the dancing commenced ... [It] continued till twelve, when the company began supper. During the time the Band in the Orchestra kept playing. After supper the company went down one dance, "The Prince of Wales' Fancy", and at four o'clock their Majesties, and the Princesses left the Castle for the Queen's Lodge, and the Nobility retired to their respective lodgings.[76]

The Morning Post lists Lord Jersey as one of those present at the ball and supper but there is no mention of the Countess also being there. It seems she was not. Lady Southampton wrote to Lady Stafford a week later, doubtless with some pleasure, saying just that. She was doubtless too controversial a figure to be invited, whilst her husband was probably only invited in his capacity as Master of the Horse in the Prince's household.

Lady Southampton went on to describe in the same letter how the Prince was handling the constant barrage of criticism, abuse and even hatred directed at him and his mistress. The answer was not well. In her words: 'I hear from everybody the Prince looks the picture of misery. I don't wonder at his being unhappy in these dreadful times.'[77]

Perhaps, then, he looked for comfort in less difficult arms. The Prince was notoriously fickle in his relationships and Mrs Fitzherbert had suffered from him having a series of affairs with other women. Up until then, though, there had been no (serious) reports of infidelities on his part during his affair with Lady Jersey. Possibly this now changed because on 2 February Cruickshank published a new cartoon entitled *A New Scotch Reel Altered from the Brunswick Minuet and the Old Jersey Jig*. In it is depicted a drunken Prince of Wales being lured away from Lady Jersey and her bedroom (with a coronet with the monogram 'J' above the bed) by the Duchess of Manchester to hers. Lady Jersey, looking on in her nightclothes, threatens, 'I'll discover the correspondence in revenge,' whilst her husband, from under her bed, complains 'Upon my Honor I don't think he uses us well after giving me all this trouble for nothing.'[78]

Of course, it is quite possible that Cruickshank was wrong. Certainly there is no other mention of the Prince having an infidelity with the Duchess of Manchester. Nevertheless, it would be in keeping with his character and there is no doubt that in the coming months the Prince's eye, at least, did indeed rove elsewhere. Perhaps this was the first sign of the Countess's hold on him weakening, but that had been predicted confidently – albeit incorrectly – many times before. Whatever the truth, the Countess maintained her position in the Prince's favour so that when *The Morning Chronicle* reported on a 'grand route' [*sic*] given the following month for foreign ambassadors and their ladies, it also recorded that Lady Jersey was of the Prince's party.[79]

His misery, or perhaps just the level of sustained abuse, may also have prompted another of his attempts at self-justification. April 1797 saw the publication of a further pamphlet by the shabby journalist John Williams (also known as Anthony Pasquin). This latest, entitled *A Looking Glass for the Royal Family,* was presumably again composed at his behest by Colonel McMahon with a view to justifying the Prince of Wales – and his lover.[80] Taking the form of a letter to Lord Cholmondley, its stated objectives were the 'unmasking of the false adherents to the Princess of Wales; the refutation of the slanders administered ... towards her august husband; and the present general condition of the women of fashion in this country', meaning of course the Countess of Jersey. Effectively it was an attack on Princess Caroline, in the course of which it managed also to support and even eulogise Lady Jersey over its thirty-six pages and condemn the 'libellers wounding the honour and character of the Countess of Jersey' along with *The Times* and *The True Briton* for their attacks on her.[81]

Once again Williams' pamphlet failed in all its objectives, as the Jerseys discovered when they went to Brighton in July, if not before. As Lady Newdigate wrote from there at the end of that month:

> Many great arrivals yesterday. Amongst ye rest Ld and Ldy Jersey and family: they have a house upon ye Steyne just opposite to the Pavilion, the owner of wch is expected tonight. They will gain their Ends by impudent perseverance, for nobody seems to think that there will be any Bustle made this Year. *We* shall receive them civilly ...'[82]

The Newdigates may have received the Jerseys civilly, but virtually nobody else did, as she wrote a few days later:

> P of W was [at the racecourse] on horseback & always by Lady J's coach when ye horses were not running. She has never appeared except in her Carriage & nobody visits her or seems to make any fuss about her. Our Ladys Maids hear that she and her Daughters walk upon ye Steyne when

> nobody else does & that yesterday ye Mob hissed her as she stood at her window, which faces the Pavillion.[83]

And then, humiliatingly for the Countess:

> I am told that Lady Jersey was with all her beautiful children at ye fireworks ye other night, not amongst ye Great but seated on a bench amongst the vulgar, who made 2 attempts to Hiss her, but were not joined by Townspeople & Company as last year. They will undoubtedly let her stay but she lives for ye P alone, for nobody, a few young Men excepted, go to her house or are seen with her.[84]

How terrifying this must have been for her poor children.

Indeed the ostracism of the Countess was almost total. As *The Times* reported on 8 August, after the Prince had left Brighton, 'Lady Jersey lives quite a recluse life at Brighton. She seldom appears abroad, and her only amusement is having evening card-parties,' causing another newspaper to add the caustic rider: 'The Company there [in Brighton] do not think themselves *good enough* for her.'[85]

One of her few visitors after the Prince had departed was Samuel Rogers. The Countess's treatment in Brighton explains why his description of his flirtation with her ran, 'I dined alone with her, rode alone with her, spent an evening alone with her, the last she spent in Brighton; and how I was domesticated with her daughters ... such daughters'. The thirty-four-year-old poet went on, 'I hope the Prince is jealous of me, for I am most furiously so of him'; he continued to visit the Countess in later years. On one such occasion he expressed regret to her that he had never married, saying 'if I had a wife ... I should have somebody to care about me'. To which Lady Jersey's spine-chilling, and very telling, response was: 'How could you be sure that your wife would not care more about somebody else than about you?'[86]

Such was the woman.

One has to ask why Frances Jersey stayed in Brighton once the Prince had left the town in the summer of 1797. Probably in part it was because she had no choice as London was empty for the summer. She doubtless, too, enjoyed her 'young Men' visitors – young men were as susceptible to her charms as she was to theirs – but the main reason was almost certainly that her inner steel would not allow an admission of defeat by leaving.

She was now without doubt the most unpopular woman in the kingdom.

She did not improve her reputation either when, attending the opera on her return to London in the autumn, she provoked comment in *The True Briton*:

> Lady Jersey might be expected to have more policy, to say nothing of virtue, delicacy, and higher motives, than to appear in the Prince of Wales' box, after all that has been said in the *Scandalous Chronicle*.

> The Public would doubtless feel a high gratification in seeing an illustrious Female, who has proper title to the box, appear in it; and they must suffer a painful emotion every time they behold the place occupied as it has *lately been*.[87]

The Countess rose above such criticism, and in the New Year *The True Briton* was once more complaining:

> Lady Jersey is almost every night in one or other of the Theatres, in a certain *private box*, where she ought never to appear, considering what has been said. – It is a pity that some of her friends to not advise her to pay more deference to Public Opinion.[88]

Perhaps on this occasion they did, because on 27 February 1798, the *Morning Herald* reported that at a production of the ballet *Joan of Arc* at Covent Garden:

> Lady Jersey, last night took her seat in the Duke of Bedford's box at Covent Garden [he was of course her son-in-law's brother and Lady William Russell, a strong character, had a habit of commandeering the box to the irritation of his family]; her Ladyship has not occupied a place in the Prince's box for some weeks passed![89]

Possibly this was also another sign of her hold on the Prince weakening, although there is an alternative explanation. In the New Year, as the Countess of Sutherland had told Lady Stafford, there had been a row between Lady Jersey and the Prince of Wales: 'Have you heard that the P of W has made a liberal donation to a celebrated lady (Mrs Eliot) & that Ly J *comme du raison* takes this very ill, and talks of going abroad.'[90]

She did not go abroad, but Grace Elliott, known as Dally the Tall, was a celebrated, if not infamous, courtesan who in 1781 had had a brief affair with the Prince of Wales; from 1786 she had lived in Paris as the mistress of the Duke of Orleans. Quite why the Prince felt the need to make a donation to her is unclear but, with the Duke having been guillotined and Elliott having been imprisoned during the Terror in revolutionary France, it may be that she was in need of funds.[91] Come what may, the Prince's contribution to one of his former lovers did not go down well with the Countess, so that perhaps a tantrum was the explanation for her absence from the royal box.

In the meantime, sad news arrived from Italy. The Countess's son-in-law, William Lambton, who had long been ailing and travelling in Italy with his wife, Lady Anne, for the benefit of his health, had died of consumption in Pisa on 30 November 1797. The immediate result was twofold. First, his brother Robert Lambton together with Lord Villiers set off to Italy to bring Lady Anne home.[93] The second was to prompt a short exchange of correspondence between Lord Jersey and Countess Spencer full of pathos and recognition of the destruction by Frances Jersey of the very long and very intimate relationship between the two of them.

It started with the Earl writing to Lady Spencer to thank her for her condolences on Mr Lambton's death but went on: 'It is now almost two years since any intercourse has been between us,' and then, after complaining that enquiries after Lady Spencer's health had routinely been ignored by her, continued 'that whatever *unjustifiable & injurious* treatment myself and family have met with from *indifferent* persons has made no lasting impression on my mind,' but when an attachment of forty years has 'given way to Newspaper, and party, [that] has, I confess, excited my utmost astonishment.'[94]

In short, that Lady Spencer had allowed her mind to be poisoned against her old friend by the press and by feuds.

Another letter from Lord Jersey to Lady Spencer followed a few days later. After complaining of 'the extraordinary change in Behaviour in other parts of your family to me' which led him to think himself 'totally abandoned by you', he professed the same friendship, esteem and regard for Lady Spencer as before – although, as he said, the behaviour he complained of had accounted for his ceasing to write to her.[95]

The old friendship was therefore now at an end.

Whilst there is a draft note written by Lady Spencer assuring the Earl that her friendship for him was 'the same it ever was', there was no mention in it of his wife – and further it is unclear whether it was ever sent. Whilst invitations to visit were still issued, the reality was clearly different.[96] After many hundreds of intimate, charming and sometimes wistful letters over forty years the correspondence between them had now withered away to only a handful each year. Of course, all relationships change but this one had been very close and had lasted a very long time.

As the Earl had feared many years before, it could not survive Lady Spencer's dislike of, and distaste for, the Countess of Jersey, both in her public actions and particularly in those relating to Lady Spencer's daughters Georgiana Devonshire and Harriet Bessborough and the fact that, as he must, Lady Spencer's oldest friend stood by his wife despite everything.

Robert Lambton and Lord Villiers' journey across wartime Europe to rescue Lady Anne in Italy was not easy, and with the need for various passports took several months. It was not until early May 1798 that the *Whitehall Evening Post* was able to report:

> Lady Lambton is now on her way to London from Florence with her family, accompanied by Lord Villiers and Ralph Lambton, Esq. the brother of her late husband, who are all expected to arrive in the course of a week ... Mr Lambton died exceedingly rich, and has left Lady Ann in possession of every comfort which pecuniary assistance can afford to console her for the loss of a valuable husband.

Specifically, it wrote that in his will he had left the sumptuous amount of £2,000 per annum to Lady Anne in pin money; £18,000 to each of his four younger children; all his landed property, including the coal mines, to his eldest son; and provided that the building of the new and very grand Lambton Hall was to continue. Finally, Lady Anne was to retain the same retinue as he had for himself, the horse and hounds excepted.[97]

Eventually the *London Chronicle* of 8 May 1798 reported Lady Anne's return to Yarmouth with her brother and family on the Prince of Wales' packet, and on 11 May Lord Jersey wrote one of his (now few) letters to Lady Spencer telling her of his daughter's arrival back home:

> Yesterday Lord Villiers & Anne, with her Children got safe to town; she seems to have suffered every degree of misery & affliction, with great fatigue both of Body & Mind, & the first return to her Family renewed every sensation of distress, & produced a most affecting scene: but time I trust and the attentions of us all, will restore her spirits to a proper tone & strength.[98]

It was indeed to take time, and her husband's unexpected death and the lonely months that followed before her brother's arrival in Italy had clearly shaken her deeply – even though as we shall see she was like her mother a woman of strong character.[99] A few days later, Lord Jersey wrote again to report that, even then, 'Anne's spirits are too low, to allow subjects likely to bring her mind back to former scenes of anxiety, to be too often entered upon.'[100]

A poignant postscript to these events was the report in *The True Briton* of the Royal Academy's Summer Exhibition for 1798, where exhibit number 210 was a *Portrait of Lady Anne Lambton and children* by J. Hoppner, RA. It was, said the newspaper, 'one of the finest ornaments of the Exhibition. There is a beautiful expression of maternal tenderness in the face of Lady Lambton … blended with *"a sadden'd tint,"* such as might be supposed to mark the features of an *affectionate widow,*' though how the artist could achieve this given that Lady Anne was still not returned from Italy must remain a mystery![101]

The summer of 1798 also proved to be the beginning of the end for Lady Jersey's affair with the Prince of Wales. However, even whilst rumours of her downfall swirled, the Countess's position seemed secure. The renowned actress Sarah Siddons was in Brighton 'playing Mrs Beverley for the amusement of the Prince of Wales – Lady Jersey, Lady Deerhurst and Lady Lade'.[102] The Prince accompanied by Lady Jersey, said Sarah Siddons, frequented the theatre with great attention and decorum.[103]

With some trepidation, Mrs Siddons accepted an invitation to dine with the Prince in late July. She told a friend that she did not like the prospect of meeting Lady Jersey at supper, but 'realising that a refusal would displease the individual whom … Farington wrote of with a capital letter – 'Him' and 'His'– she swallowed her scruples.'[104]

In the event, the Countess was her charming and beautiful self and in Sarah Siddons' words:

> The evening went off much more easily and agreeably than I had imagined ... Lady Jersey is really wonderful in her appearance. Her hair was about an inch long all over her head, and she had ty'd round her head one single row of white beads; this I thought was ill judg'd. She certainly wou'd look handsome if she wou'd not affect at forty-eight to be eighteen.[105]

Even now, however, the beautiful Countess's position was under threat and, despite appearances, she probably knew it. It was common knowledge in 1798 that the Prince was infatuated with Lady Horatia Seymour, wife of one of the Countess's earlier victims, and who that year briefly became his mistress. Unusually for the Prince, Lady Horatia was his own age, a mere thirty-two. There is much speculation that her daughter Minny, born the same year, was also the Prince's.[106]

In the circumstances, it is likely Frances Jersey was aware of the competition.

15

The End of the Affair

In August 1798 Lady Stafford wrote to Granville Leveson Gower of yet more competition facing the Countess:

> We are told the Prince has discarded Lady Jersey in consequence of HRH being enamour'd of a Miss Fox, who lived with Lord Egremont, and who has several children. Some say she is youngish and pretty, others that she is oldish, fat and looks like a good House-Keeper. Elderly Dames seem to be his taste.[1]

Rumours of Lady Jersey's dismissal had been circulating for some time. Early that month one newspaper had commented in terms which would have been clear to its readers that 'the change of Society and manners which has taken place at the Pavilion, gives the most heartfelt satisfaction to every lover of his country; it is now, everyway worthy of the heir apparent of the British Empire'.[2]

The rumours had also reached Mrs Howe by the time she wrote to Lady Stafford on 7 August: 'the Prince of Wales after the races ... [at Brighton] are over, leaves for the Summer, & it is said refused a certain lady going down there, and declared he should be rid of her for the summer'.[3]

Mrs Howe's report is probably true but, as we know, the Countess did indeed go to Brighton where she accompanied the Prince to the theatre and at dinner with Sarah Siddons, so demonstrating once more the extraordinary hold she had over him, as with others of her lovers, even against his own desires.

Nevertheless, although the downfall of Frances Jersey had been wrongly predicted – though devoutly wished for – on many occasions in the past, this time there was truth in the reports. The Countess of Jersey's fall from royal favour was however to prove nearly as protracted as her ascent into the royal bed.

In a sign of things to come, Col McMahon was at Cheltenham in August when, doubtless not by chance, he saw Maria Fitzherbert, later reporting to the Prince that she had heard gossip about the Prince's intrigues with an actress.[4] This, of course, was the same Miss Fox of whom *The True Briton* wrote a little later: 'The *Fox* which was said to have annoyed the *purlieu's* of Jersey, remains very quietly in the neighbour of Knightsbridge. She has three *Cubs*, but they are very well provided for.'[5]

The reality, though, was that all those close to the Prince knew the Countess was doomed and expected a rapprochement between him and Maria, even if it was to be a considerable time in coming. Lord Moira wrote to Col McMahon on 30 August in that expectation:

> The new arrangement [i.e. the rapprochement] will be the more for the comfort of the person we love than in any former stile; and it would have been regarded as indulgently by the public had there been an affectation to conceal it. That which most offends great bodies of people is any appearance of braving their opinion. I am apprehensive there has not been skill in the management of this business.[6]

At the same time, the Prince was receiving encouragement from his family to go back to Maria Fitzherbert, obviously also in the knowledge that the Countess's time was over. In the autumn, his sister Princess Augusta wrote to him chiding him for his 'dejected appearance' and urging a reconciliation with Mrs Fitzherbert which, she said, 'would surely make both of you happy'.[7]

Such encouragement was not confined to the Prince's siblings. Even Lady Jersey's former intimate Queen Charlotte was to do the same in February of the following year. Writing in his diary years later Lord Glenbervie recorded that:

> Mrs Fitzherbert showed Lady Anne Barnard a letter to her [Mrs Fitzherbert] in the Queen's own handwriting pressing her to be reconciled to the Prince and written at the time of his rupture with Lady Jersey and when he affected to be or was very ill, and told his sisters that he was quite sure he would die if the reconciliation did not take place between Mrs Fitzherbert and him. This was a strong step for so moral a Queen to take. The ostensible motive was concern for her son's health. But a different and less amiable motive may suggest itself.

That less amiable motive, Glenbervie suggested, was to spite Princess Caroline at a time when her principal rival, the Countess, was being rejected. The Queen, he added, is 'believed never to have forgiven her daughter-in-law' for her disparaging comments in the intercepted letters to her parents.[8]

The Prince needed little encouragement. He was already in contact with Maria Fitzherbert, as another sister, Princess Mary, wrote to him in October:

> As for your amiable *left-hand* (as you call her) [i.e. Maria Fitzherbert] I have firstly to inform you she *has been* very ill but is recovered, and I understand from *some* who have *seen* her is in *greater beauty than ever*.

> In the 2nd place, I am to inform you since I have been in Weymouth I have received two letters from her & *have* given *your* message in one I wrote to her this morning.[9]

Whatever was happening to the Prince's relationship with Lady Jersey, for the time being no one was prepared to strike the fatal blow, and Lady Jersey clung on. Observers were confused. In the late autumn of 1798 Edward Jerningham, who was to be one of the Prince's emissaries to the Countess conveying her dismissal, explained to his sister-in-law:

> To ascend to a higher order of Amourship, I think Lady Jersey is now in the Transit of Venus – it was very evident her reign was drawing to its Period. I believe I have mentioned this circumstance before, but the singularity attending the progression of this affair is that the lady will not acknowledge any Difference or Diminution of Regard on his side. This embarrasses the Prince exceedingly, for he wishes to let her down gently and separate amicably, which he thinks cannot be done if he should Dismiss her in town and unequivocally: I have given her intimations and broad suggestions which she will not understand or at least does not seem to understand.[10]

Those who thought they understood what was going on were happy indeed. So the Countess's old friend and new enemy, Lord Harcourt, wrote to Jerningham at about this time: 'Every person engaged in the tragical interlude exhibited to the public at the old theatre in Warrick Street [*sic*] will feel, himself and herself, happier than when they were the objects of public attention. At least most sincerely do I wish that any prediction may prove true.'[11]

Whatever observers thought, and even though she was not prepared to acknowledge it, perhaps the ever astute Frances Jersey did recognise reality. There is an undated letter to Edward Jerningham in which she mentions a prospective visit to her mother in Bath when, said the Countess:

> I shall tell her all is over, all is well, and that now we have only to divert ourselves, - and laugh at past dangers and storms. I conclude you will be cautious of the enclosed and dispose of it immediately. Remember to see the Primate, and to send me an account of your visit. – I shall keep your letter and read it over when ever the devil of suspicion lays hold of me.[12]

Even so, those who looked on would continue to be confused, doubtless in part deceived by the Prince's gentle approach, though whether this was really because of his kindness rather than fear of a tempestuous response from the Countess may be doubted. As a result, at the end of October Lady Stafford was writing:

> Ld Jersey was at the drawing-room with either the Prince or the Princess I did not hear which; I do not believe his lady has loosned [*sic*] her hold, all what I know is she left Brighthelmstone the very same day the Prince did, and there was no appearance of any alteration of sentiments.[13]

The Russian Ambassador's coruscating and caustic wife, Princess Lieven, was more perceptive, at least in retrospect. She was to refer to the Countess of Jersey as 'the little leech' because of the way she hung onto her lover long after he had moved on and the public had seen that he had moved on.[14]

By the late autumn of 1798, the Prince had had enough and decided that a more direct means of effecting Lady Jersey's dismissal was required. On 24 November Col McMahon wrote to Edward Jerningham asking him '*without fail* to meet the Prince ... at 1 o'clock tomorrow on special business'.[15]

This meeting with the Prince may well have been the one that Jerningham refers to in the letter to his sister-in-law just quoted. That letter had gone on to say that a week earlier the Prince, who was confined with a sprain, had summoned Jerningham to talk to him about Lady Jersey. The Prince told him that he, the Prince, would the next day hobble over to Lady Jersey and try to bring her 'to a conference and would promise never to withdraw from her and her family his protection. But [Jerningham interpolated, the Countess] had art enough to evade the conference,' so that despite the Prince's efforts things remained 'in the same uncertain and undecided situation'.

After commenting that 'the Delicacy, the Reluctance, or call it what ever name you please' shown by the Prince to Lady Jersey was 'very extraordinary', Jerningham went on that he had, presumably at the Prince's request, written to the Countess saying that he had been at Carlton House, and that the Prince had spoken in the highest terms of her and 'that it was in her power to secure his Friendship and that the P had desired me to say something to that effect'.

This approach, though, was too oblique.

Frances Jersey responded to it by telling Jerningham never to mention the Prince's name again, telling him he was mistaken and saying that he was 'an honest Iago'.

At this, Jerningham confessed that he was now at a loss how to act. The Prince for his part sent him a message through McMahon instructing him 'to continue [his] visits to her, but not to enter upon the subject of separation unless she begins, and then I am to keep their same language'.[16]

Even so, despite the pussyfooting, perhaps the message was getting through. At the end of November, the royal family were at Covent Garden in the Prince's private box together with the Countess of Harrington and her family. Lady Jersey was not in the box and, instead, was 'in that of the Duke of Bedford ... [with] a party of her female friends'.[17]

It seems that Jerningham, as one of Lady Jersey's best friends, now became the Prince's chosen instrument in an attempt to get the Lady Jersey to acknowledge her dismissal. He was summoned to meet the Prince by increasingly peremptory letters on at least three occasions in January and February 1799.[18] On one of the occasions in which he sought to deliver the message to the Countess on the Prince's instructions her abrupt response to her old playwrite friend was: 'Damn you I wish you well in your new trade'[19]

Acknowledgement of the message was finally, and eventually, achieved. Whether this was Jerningham's work or someone else's is unclear. One source suggests an additional channel of communication although there is no further evidence of this. According to this, the Prince of Wales 'one day said to Col Willis "I am determined to break off my intimacy with Lady Jersey; and you must deliver the letter which announces to her my determination". When Willis put it into Lady Jersey's hand, she said, before opening it, "you have brought me a gilded dagger."'[20]

Whoever the messenger, the deed was now done – and was known to the world. On 25 January, Mrs Howe wrote to Lady Stafford: 'it is now said & in a degree believed that the Prince has at last broken his attachment and connection with Lady Jersey.'[21] Then on 12 February 1799 the Prince of Wales felt able to write to the Duchess of Rutland, in a letter to which we will return, that after an affair of five years 'everything is *finally at an end*' between him and Frances Jersey.[22]

That the Countess did not take her dismissal well, as we shall see, will come as no surprise.

What was it that brought the Prince's relationship with Frances Jersey to an end? First there was the man himself, a self-indulgent, fickle and inconstant man incapable of long-term relationships. Second there was the Countess; despite her multifaceted brilliance, she must have been an exhausting woman to live with, constant in her demands, vociferous in her wishes and certain of her rights. Doubtless this was not helped either by the trouble she brought in her wake, in particular the barrage of abuse and vitriol both in the press, in Society and in the country at large. The biggest reason, though, was another woman: the Prince's 'one true love', Maria Fitzherbert.

It is clear that the Prince never really reconciled himself to his parting from Mrs Fitzherbert. We have already seen that for some time the Prince had been anxious that Mrs Fitzherbert should rejoin him, although even in February 1799 she was still rejecting his overtures.[23] The Prince sought help in winning a rapprochement with her from both the Duchess of Rutland and the Duchess of Devonshire and in his letter to the former on 12 February, in pursuit of his aims, he authorised the Duchess to 'hint at, even assert if you please, that everything *is finally at end* IN ANOTHER QUARTER' to Maria.[24] Early in February he was also thanking the Duchess of Devonshire for her help in persuading Mrs Fitzherbert to come back to him, commenting 'there *never was an instant in which I did not feel for her*, as I am afraid she never felt for me'; she was, he said, the only person who can '*ever* give me a *taste again for life*'.[25]

Mrs Fitzherbert took her time. She had learned lessons from the past. In June, the Prince was still pleading to her to come back to him, threatening that if she did not do so he would make their marriage public, claim her as his wife and face whatever the consequences might be. He went on to describe his life with Frances Jersey: '*The wretched experiences of the last five years* have made life only desirable in one shape to me, and that is you.'[26]

By July *The Times* was reporting, albeit prematurely, that the Prince and Maria Fitzherbert were once more inseparable, and before long they were – for a few more years at least.[27] So it was that, in the words of Lord Wentworth, the Jersey reign was quite over.[28]

Even so, the Countess still deluded herself on two scores.

First, there is in the Royal Archives a copy of an extraordinary letter dated 8 June 1799 from Lady Jersey, then in Bath, to Lady Lavington, the Polish-born intimate of Queen Charlotte. She wrote:

> So I find the Prince has *forgiven* all your past offences as he has mine ... he has been here incog. having heard the Bath waters did not agree with me, he came with a determination to take me away, but thinks me looking so divinely, that he is determined I shall stay a week longer ... He has promised me to dine at Kew to meet Pitt on Sunday next ... He is doting still about a certain lady ...'[29]

Which, of course, was Maria Fitzherbert.

The terms of the letter, assuming it to be genuine, defy belief. The Prince may have been in Bath but it was surely impossible (as well as out of character) for him to have been there incognito. As to the actions and words ascribed to him, it is inconceivable given all that we know that he did or said what the Countess described. Perhaps the explanation for this delusional letter was that the Countess was massaging her injured pride.

The second delusion consisted in the Countess's thinking there was a conspiracy against her that had so led to her downfall and, in this, Georgiana Devonshire was the principal conspirator. There is an undated letter from the Duchess to Lady Melbourne that from internal references can be dated to August or September of 1799, in which Georgiana writes of Frances Jersey:

> Peste I hear is furious with me &c. & and thinks we were all in a league against her – it would be easy enough to undeceive her – but perhaps it is better to let time do that. I have written to her on her daughter's marriage and propose calling – but my Mother & her friends are all in a fever now least my thinking her unhappy should give her an opening to regain her sway over me – I believe she is too proud to attempt it – & indeed it is long since she has had any power over me except of tormenting; however on G's account I mean to be very cautious for once in my life – for should Peste reproach me & accuse me, I should be distrest [*sic*] not to show some kindness & she would be a bad person for my girls in any way ... I have said not a word of this to anybody but you know how Peste has ever us'd me & yet what I must [feel about ?] a person who I had [loved ?] so long thinking me capable of trying to undermine them. It was all that visit ... in the Spring in which I again refused going to her in that house – & she then told me it was ... settled for her quitting it – & she now says it was in that visit I persuaded him to turn her out – I think she ought to know how little one persuaded him to any thing.[30]

So the Countess thought that not only had the Duchess engineered her downfall but also had achieved her removal from the house in Warwick Street, which did indeed shortly take place. Presumably in doing so Frances Jersey attributed motives to Georgiana which would come naturally to the

Countess herself, that is seeking retribution for her having engineered the breakdown in the close relations which had formerly existed between the Prince and Georgiana.

On both charges the final sentence of Georgiana's letter says it all: 'I think she ought to know how little one persuaded him to any thing.'

Of course, the Prince did indeed want the Jerseys out of the Warwick Street house for very obvious reasons, and as early as April he was talking of making it available to others.

His goal was delayed as a result, in the Prince's words, of 'the indisposition of Lady Elizabeth Villiers, who has been on the point of death in consequence of having broken a blood vessel some few days back'.[31]

Accordingly it was not until 2 July that *The Times* was able to report the next indignity the Countess was to suffer: 'Lady Jersey has removed from the house adjoining Carlton House to that which was Lord Talbot's, in Stratford Place.'[32]

There is some suggestion that the Prince gave the Countess a financial settlement on his ending their affair, just as there had been rumours that he had bought her at its start. The Prince despite his desperate financial situation had somehow managed to borrow £40,000 from the Landgrave of Hesse-Cassel. This, no less a person than Lord Minto said, 'has probably enabled him to settle with Lady Jersey, who is going abroad'.[33] There is no further mention of this, as regards the Countess, and any settlement with her, like stories of her going abroad, are probably incorrect – particularly given not only the Prince's precarious financial position but also the Countess's later applications to the Prince for a pension, coupled with the grievous financial position of the Earl at the time.*

During her years of power, Lady Jersey had alienated many of her former friends, including Lady Spencer and her two daughters, the Duchess of Devonshire and the Countess of Bessborough. Her former close friends Lord and Lady Harcourt were others. This was the result of the haughty, opinionated and manipulative behaviour that she adopted whilst in royal favour. An undated letter from Harcourt to Jerningham sometime after the Prince's dismissal of her vividly illustrates the intensity of the widespread hatred. Talking of the Prince of Wales, Harcourt says fawningly (and not a little hypocritically):

> I feel the warmest gratitude towards him for his goodness to me, a sentiment that is still heightened by the circumstance of his having formerly shown the most marked dislike to me; thanks to the malicious insinuations and base misrepresentations of some of those most despicable, as well as most hateful, of all creatures, *true courtiers*.[35]

He referred, of course, to the Countess of Jersey. One would love to know what for certain she had done to deserve such a charge, though doubtless

* It does seem that the Prince commissioned Richard Cosway to paint a miniature of the Prince for the Countess sometime in 1799, perhaps as a parting gift – since any other explanation for his doing so at that time would be bizarre.[34]

it was merited. What is clear, though, is that Harcourt was not alone in suffering extreme unhappiness at the behaviour of the Countess of Jersey whilst she had the Prince's favour.

Now that she did not, her injured pride famously drove her to seek to embarrass the Prince whenever she could. One well-known story told by Samuel Rogers of about this time tells of the Countess manufacturing the opportunity to be offensive to the Prince at a party at Henry Hope's in Cavendish Square. Lady Jersey took Rogers aside, so she said, to tell him something of importance. There they met the Prince of Wales who stopped, looked at Lady Jersey, drew himself up and passed on. Lady Jersey returned the stare and turned to Rogers with a smile and boasted 'Didn't I do it well?' 'The particular communication seems, then, not to have needed to have been made.'[36]

Vengeful and bitter the Countess may have been after parting from the Prince. This, however, was largely a matter of detail regardless of how it affected the Prince. Her real legacy was much larger and was to last a lifetime. The Prince's relations with a wife he detested, both in the years already passed and those to come, were to poison his reputation in the eyes of the nation until his death. They reflected, too, no credit on the institution of monarchy itself in the estimation of the public, which consequently needed the redemption offered it under the Prince's successors. It was Frances Jersey who had orchestrated that ill-fated marriage for her own unscrupulous and personal objectives and, to the extent that help was needed, assisted in reducing it to bitterness and acrimony.

With her parting from the Prince now definitive, it was perhaps fortunate for the Countess that her own family affairs were becoming more dominant.

Lady William Russell's penchant for requisitioning the Duke of Bedford's box at the opera has already been mentioned. Clearly a strong-minded woman like her mother, it seems that she was more than a match for her eccentric husband in other respects, over and above her continuing affair with the Marquess of Lorne. As a harbinger of things to come Lady John Russell wrote to her husband at about this time that Lady William 'abuses Ld William more and more – I find he swears to his Income as you have done I am told they have give up Streatham', the house which had been given to them by his brother the Duke. Lord William was apparently financially incompetent and, as we shall see, before too long it was not just Streatham that Lord William would need to give up as he headed towards ignominy and bankruptcy, despite the challenges of his wife.[37]

At the same time, Lady Elizabeth Villiers was also still causing concern. As we know, in April she had been close to death; even in August her father was writing to Lady Spencer of his having been in for 'so long a state of anxiety of mind for the once desperate situation of Elizabeth's health; & afterwards very hazardous & still precarious'. Added to all of which, the Countess herself had 'an alarming accident' in her curricle.[38]

Fortunately, Lady Sarah, the Countess's fourth and, yet again, beautiful daughter, who had perhaps been the principal victim of the Countess's ostracism in recent years, was now giving rise to more congenial gossip. In late 1799 Georgiana Devonshire wrote to her daughter: 'I have not been out this long time. I hear assemblies are [illegible] from the competition concerning Lady Sarah.'[39]

One of those competitors for Lady Sarah Villiers' hand – and the successful one – was Charles Nathaniel Bayly, a West Indian sugar baron. In the closing years of the eighteenth century such men with their sugar estates and slaves in the West Indies, most notably William Beckford, were prodigiously wealthy, and Bayly himself was the owner of four estates and almost 850 slaves in Jamaica.[40] As the Earl of Jersey proudly wrote to Lady Spencer in August: 'my daughter Sarah is to be married to Mr Bayly a young man whose Character promises every expectation of happiness; and wth a fortune of about £20,000 pr Ann.'[41]

This was indeed a princely sum.

The wedding took place on 12 September 1799, as reported the *Whitehall Evening Post*.[42]

There was to be a melancholy postcript to this, at least for Bayly and his wife. Not only was Bayly, in the manner of the time, to be unfaithful to his wife, but also, after beginning married life in the richest style, the abolition of the slave trade, followed by the emancipation of slaves and then the admittance of cheap foreign slave-grown sugar into the British market, was to have a devastating effect on Bayly's wealth. In years to come he was to lose virtually all his money, be forced to sell his picture collection and to end his days in a grace and favour apartment at Hampton Court Palace. In the will he made in 1850 he bemoaned that his marriage settlement was now little better than a dead letter, and the jointure of £4,000 a year for his wife and the £20,000 portion for his children on his death were assuredly academic. So great, he said, had been the losses on his estate that he was now reduced to £300 a year.[43] *

At the time Sarah was getting married, her brother, the eighteen-year-old William Augustus Villiers, was going off to war. In March 1798 he had purchased a Cornetcy in the 7th Regiment of Light Dragoon Guards.[44] It is probably no coincidence that the Regiment's then Colonel was William's brother-in-law, Lord Paget, so enabling Lord Jersey to write to Lady Spencer: 'in consequence he is not left to the wide world entirely at first starting.'[45]

As part of the French Revolutionary Wars that had been raging on the Continent for years, in June 1799 Britain signed an alliance with Russia for the joint invasion of Holland, then under French occupation, with a view to the restoration of the Prince of Orange, an operation known as the Helder Expedition. Under this directive the first troops set sail for Holland from Britain on 13 August and, whilst the 7th Light Dragoon Guards were not part of the original expeditionary force, they were soon to follow.[46]

* I am indebted to Alice Munro–Faure for this information on Charles Nathaniel Bayly and on his will.

They embarked for Holland from Ramsgate early in September. Cornet Villiers was amongst those who went under the command of Lord Paget.[47] On arriving in Holland the whole regiment disembarked, save for a handful of officers and men together with some horses, who were on a small brig called *The Union* that immediately returned to Ramsgate to repair damage which it had suffered on the first night of the voyage.[48] Cornet Villiers was amongst this delegation of officers. *The Unio*n, however, never got back to England – it and its occupants were captured by the French and carried into Calais as prisoners of war.[49]

Fortunately for him, William Augustus's captivity was short lived. The Helder Expedition was a dismal failure, and on 18 October the invading forces agreed to a capitulation; the British were to evacuate Holland by 30 November. Accordingly Villiers' colleagues in the 7th Light Dragoon Guards embarked for home on 23 October.[50] *The Union* and her occupants arrived back in Ramsgate about a week after the rest of the Regiment had left Helder, presumably having been released by the French as part of the terms of the British capitulation.[51]

There was, therefore, a happy end to this story. Clearly the Countess will have known that her younger son was off to war. Whether she knew of his capture before he was released is less clear. It was certainly some time before the newspapers caught up with the story. Only on 14 November did the *Whitehall Evening Post* report: 'We are concerned to learn, a detachment of the 7th regiment of Light Dragoons, consisting of Lt Pryke, the Hon Cornet Villiers, and 18 privates and horses, were captured on board a transport returning from Holland, by a French privateer, and carried to Calais.'

By then, of course, the cornet was long since back home with his regiment. Over the next few years they, and he, were quartered in various parts of the country: in 1803 and 1804 they were in East Anglia to guard against the feared invasion by Napoleon's forces. However, it was not until in embarking for Corunna in Spain in 1808 in the course of the Peninsular War that they were again to see active service. By then William Augustus had left the regiment having retired from it in 1806 with the rank of Major.[52]

Even as the tale of William's capture unfolded, the Countess seems to have been enjoying unusual, and untypical, calm away from the limelight. In late September she was with her husband in 'East Bourne' as a result of 'the necessity of ... sea-bathing, to remove the disagreeable effects of her accident in the Curricle' – perhaps once again caused by her recklessness.[53] Some time later that year she wrote to Edward Jerningham from Middleton in positively pastoral terms:

> I am quite alone; for my husband has gone to the Duke of Grafton's to hunt. My girls are very pleasant. I read to them, and they draw all day and all night. When they leave me I work very hard on the harp. I enjoy all the delights of good health, good spirits and good humour; it is a perfect calm,

> but a calm that inspires neither melancholy nor regret. *Ma retraite est Mon Louvre, et j'y commande en Reine*, &c. &c. All my brats are well; the two old ones desire their compliments.[54]

Whatever the Countess pretended, though, she was not a lover of a quiet life and over the coming years she was to devote herself energetically to the promotion of her family, as well as to a new affair – even though she was now approaching fifty. She was also to face some sadder events.

16

Satan's Representative on Earth

Frances Jersey's reputation was now beyond redemption. Nevertheless, whilst not enthusiastically welcoming her back following her rupture with the Prince, Society once more opened its doors to her as acceptable. For the most part the social ostracism ceased and, once more, her name appeared in many of the newspaper reports of the balls, assemblies and masquerades of the new century.

Accordingly she was present at the Queen's Birthday on 20 January 1800 (the Prince of Wales was not; he was then seriously ill), where *The Morning Chronicle* reported only on the splendour of her dress and in complimentary terms:

> The Countess of Jersey – Appeared in the most singular dress at Court. Her Ladyship wore a robe of poppy velvet, and petticoat of the same, embroidered in gold stripes; the sleeves of the robe were trimmed with poppy velvet; and in her head-dress she wore a bandeau and a plume of large poppy feathers.[1]

Instead of prompting the abuse of recent years, her presence at court also provoked *The Morning Post* of 20 January 1800 to write politely of the Countess: 'The general appearance of Lady Jersey occasioned much admiration at the Drawing room on Saturday.'

Even the normally vituperative *The True Briton* restrained itself, publishing in March a verse in praise of a ball just given by the Marquess of Abercorn which included a line on Lady Jersey and another lady guest that ran 'and Jersey and Talbot the crowd did approve'.[2]

The cost of being allowed back into Society was, of course, the loss of office in the Prince's household and the consequent loss of income, which the Jerseys could ill afford. In January 1800 the Earl was dismissed from his position as Master of the Horse to the Prince and, indeed, the office itself was thenceforth abolished.[3]

Typically, the Prince did not at the same time reimburse Lord Jersey the considerable sums of money due him in relation to his fees as Master of the Horse – or, indeed, those that the Earl had (very foolishly) spent out of his own funds on behalf of the Prince.[4] This was to cause the Earl much embarrassment over the next few years.

The Earl nevertheless received his dismissal with typical style, as the *London Packet* reported:

> The Earl of Jersey is said to have received his note of dismission from the Prince of Wales as he was going to Court on the Birth-day. The noble Earl immediately alighted from his carriage, sent his servants home to take off the Royal Liveries and returned to his residence in a hackney coach.[5]

Miss Lloyd succinctly described the Jerseys' return to the real world in a letter to Countess Spencer in February: 'What a kettle of fish the Jerseys have made at last, nobody pities them.'[6]

Society was also disapproving of, or perhaps simply confused by, the roles now played by the principal characters in the dramas of recent years. So Lady Jerningham wrote in March to her daughter:

> The affair of Mrs Fitzherbert and the Prince, becomes very incomprehensible, it is a fact that he meets her whenever he Can and a conversation ensues that takes them both out of the Company. On Saturday, Lady Kenmare tells me, that Mrs Fitzherbert, Mrs Butler, and the Prince were in a high Box all Night in conversation. The Princess at the opera and also Lady Jersey. I comprehend it no longer, for I had thought Mrs Fitzherbert a woman of principle.[7]

Lady Jerningham, and doubtless others, did not know the social machinations which lay behind the scenes. As a condition of their rapprochement, Mrs Fitzherbert insisted that all relations between the Prince and Lady Jersey should be completely broken off.[8] For her part the Princess was satisfied as she had got rid of the loathed Lady Jersey, and she 'and the Fitz having had some sort of common cause for some years have carried on tacit courtesys to each other in a variety of ways'.[9] Thus, Lady Jersey having been excluded, the remaining members of the triangle were content that it should continue.

The Countess took advantage of her new acceptance to glitter once more in Society alongside her daughters. In the spring of 1800 her participation in the daily see and be seen promenade in Hyde Park was described by *The Morning Post*: 'Yesterday all the splendour of Spring embellished this delightful *promenade*. – The throng consisted of one variegated column of beauty and fashion, from Piccadilly to Kensington Gardens.' Amongst those who ornamented the scene were Lady Jersey and Lady Anne Lambton, who was now clearly being promoted once more in the marriage market by her mother.[10]

Lady Anne glittered in her own right too. Her appearance at the Drawing-Room in May provoked the description of her as 'superbly dressed, with a bouquet of diamonds in her bosom of amazing grandeur and brilliancy'.[11] The widowed Lady Anne was thought a considerable catch not only on account of her beauty but also with an income of £10,000 a year. In June the papers were soon reporting that she was to be married to Tom Sheridan, R. B. Sheridan's son. The engagement might have happened but no marriage followed.[12]

Lady Anne's diamonds were in the fashion of the day. By the mid-eighteenth century diamonds had replaced rubies and emeralds as the favoured stone for jewellery in England. The development of sophisticated cutting techniques enabled diamonds to be brilliantly cut and this, with the new practice of setting the stones in claw feet proud of their settings, made them the ideal ornament for candlelit Georgian society, with light glittering through all their facets.[13]

It is difficult in our time to imagine this candlelit society, but in the eighteenth century 'the ability to offset the darkness of the season's winter night with effective and expensive lighting ... was essential to life within the beau monde'. That ability was conferred by candles, in great quantity. The beau monde, of course, favoured expensive wax candles over cheaper tallow ones made from animal fat, and many flickering candles were needed to light their houses for the balls, dinners and entertainments laid on by the *ton*. On one occasion Sir Robert Walpole had no less than 130 candles shimmering in his dining room.[14] One can see the diamonds sparkling.

By now all seemed to be going very well for the Jerseys except, perhaps, for the Earl's financial difficulties – possibly compounded by Anne's grand and brilliant diamonds, although the borrowing of friends' jewels was commonplace at the time.[15] And yet, another problem was fast looming. Despite Lady William Russell's challenges to her husband, it looks as if his financial affairs were also growing very difficult. In March, they had moved out of their house in Streatham, presumably for financial reasons. They moved into old Bedford House, a house built in the reign of Charles II on the north side of what is now Bloomsbury Square, and described by Hesther Piozzi as 'neither splendid nor commodious, neither Ancient nor Modern, can do nothing better – than be pulled down'.[16]

The move seems to have depressed Lady William. As Lady John Russell wrote to her husband at the time: 'The D of B— writes me word that Ly W is at B. H. very low & that he has persuaded her to go with him to Woburn that she is to have some days in her room & then appear in company.'[17]

When she wrote to Lord Jersey a few days later, Lady John was less sympathetic and seemed now to regard Lady William as something of a prima donna, saying: 'You must go to her room as she means to be there on the footing of a disconsolate princess & to receive visits in her room – I suppose the great personage will ride down on some of his miraculous courses and I beg you to remain to see the farce & send me your orders.'[18]

There may have been other explanations. In the view of Lord Melbourne, 'Lady William was very odd, and dreamy and stupefied with opium, large and red' when he knew her; this may well have also contributed to her early death a few years later.[19]

The summer of 1800 finally saw the effective reconciliation between the Prince and Mrs Fitzherbert and its proclamation to the world. The pair made a public appearance at a subsequent breakfast, given by the Duchess of Devonshire at Chiswick House, where Lady Jersey was also present and, once more, took the opportunity of tormenting the Prince. As Lady Jerningham described the scene:

> The Prince ... stood almost the whole time by his Band, with Dr Burney, ordering different pieces of Musick. Lady Jersey was Coasting around the spot where he stood, with her daughters, Lady Ann Lambton and Lady Elizabeth Villiers [who had not yet been presented and appears to be quite a girl]. The Prince was quite annoyed with her and eyed her askance; but she is resolved to plague Him; she professes it to be her Resolution.[20]

A flavour of life led by Society in these years, which now included the more or less rehabilitated Countess of Jersey, is given in the description of a fête held in July 1800 by Lady Cholmondley at Charlton, when typically there would be three or four hundred guests. It was, said *The True Briton*:

> In the first style of simplicity and elegance. The Gardens were tastefully decorated and very brilliantly illuminated ... The Supper was elegant ... and the Company throughout the evening were in high spirits. The Dancing was kept up to a very late hour, and when day broke was adjourned to the lawn.[21]

The Morning Post echoed the 'great brilliancy' of the party, adding that the company, which included Lord and Lady Jersey, 'danced by day-light on the lawn, after the sun rose in the morning'.[22]

The Countess's rehabilitation, though, was still qualified, even if the ever naïve Lord Jersey felt entitled to complain to Countess Spencer of 'the unjustifiable conduct of *numbers* towards me, & mine, grounded on malice & political schemes & arts, I despise most truly and have shown that I do'.[23]

In fact, whatever the Earl thought, his wife would never be able to escape her past.

Regardless, this did not seem to spoil her enjoyment of Brighton, where the Jerseys arrived in the first week of August. As *Jackson's Oxford Journal* reported: 'Lady Jersey arrived at Brighton on Friday last, attended by a most sumptuous entourage. She has for the present taken up residence in the house of her daughter, Lady Anne Lambton, on the South Parade, nearly opposite the Pavilion.'[24]

The proximity of the Countess's residence to the Pavilion may have been more to do with her daughter than with the Countess. As *The Morning Post* said, the Pavilion was crowded and its inmates included not only Lord Villiers but also a Mr Charles Wyndham, who was shortly to play a cameo role in the life of the Jersey family.[25]

Philip Francis described the scene at Brighton:

> This sweet place is not at all like Balls, though it produced a very fine one last night, and a beautiful supper at which I assisted with a pretty Davidson on each side of me ... I shall make you stare with the account I can give of persons. In the meantime be satisfied with a List of their Names [which included the Marchioness of Wolsely, the Countess of Lucan, Lady Impey, the Countess of Berkeley, Lady Anne Lambton, Lady Sarah Bailey {*sic*}, Mrs Wilmot, the Duchess of Marlborough, the Marchioness of Donegal, Lady Jersey] 'and Lord knows how many more, all as good as those I have reckoned.[26]

Despite Lady Jersey's sumptuous entourage, storm clouds were looming over the Jerseys' financial affairs. The Earl had serious problems. Never rich, his unpaid fees and expenses as Master of the Horse had pushed him to the verge of bankruptcy – in those days a matter of complete disgrace, as Lord William Russell was to discover. In Lord Jersey's words when he wrote to the Prince of Wales on 28 October, in part prompted by a message from the Prince, himself ever short of money,[27] to render a statement of account of the debts due to him:

> The Difficulties which have arisen to me from so large a Deficiency have encreased [*sic*] into Embarrassments so severe & so pressing upon myself & my family, both in the present & the future, that it is become an indispensable Duty to lay the same with all submission at your Royal Highness's feet.[28]

In response a few days later McMahon wrote, more than evasively, on behalf of the Prince to the Earl. He said that certain arrangements which the Prince had long since made had unexpectedly not yet met their completion but that every consideration was being given to Lord Jersey's claims, and positive directions signified with all convenient dispatch to discharge them – adding that the Prince of Wales had given orders that Lord Jersey's claim should bear the very earliest attention to the entire amount thereof, but that hopefully in the not distant period the Prince will have the means to pay a part of the sums outstanding.[29]

And so on and on from an impoverished Prince – none of which will have given the Earl any confidence let alone substantive support.

Somehow the Earl, encouraged by the Prince to ward off his creditors, muddled through for another year, but in January 1802 things came to a head as the Earl was faced at last with the debtors' prison. Lord Jersey wrote to McMahon with more than a hint of desperation on 27 January:

> These means are come to their expiration; that delay ceases to prevail, & I am daily and hourly threatened with actions & legal proceedings against me, which I have not the power or ability to withstand & stop ... I feel

> myself bound to endeavour, if possible, to rescue my family, & myself from the indignities heaped upon me from all Quarters, & to save them in fact from the disgrace & Ruin actually hanging over their heads ... It is to His Royal Highness I must look ... With all humility ... I am confident I need say no more.[30]

No more is heard and no more correspondence on the topic is to be found. There is, however, a receipt in the Royal Archives dated 21 June 1802, signed by the Earl of Jersey for the sum of £5,000 received from the Prince of Wales.[31] Ultimately it seems the Earl was rescued from his immediate financial embarrassments by the Prince paying his debts, although in future years the Countess was once more to turn, with typical brazenness, to the Prince for financial help.

At the time these desperate events were evolving, two intriguing vignettes of the Countess of Jersey emerge, one regarding her financial integrity and the other casting light on the sexual mores of a highly sexed woman.

The first arises from a letter written in January 1801 from Thomas Tyrwhitt to Lady Jersey about arrears of the revenue of the Duchy of Cornwall, which of course was part of the Prince of Wales' estates. Why, at a time when the Countess no longer played any part in the Prince's life, should this be of any concern to her? Was it that the Countess had indeed sought financial gain from her position during her time as the Prince's mistress or had in fact the Prince, as Lord Minto had thought, made some financial settlement to her on their parting? Unfortunately there is nothing more to cast light on the matter.[32]

The second is more salacious. Just before Christmas 1800 the Earl of Carlisle's son and heir, Lord Morpeth, proposed to and was accepted by Georgiana Devonshire's elder daughter Georgiana or 'Little G'. Although only twenty-seven at the time, Morpeth had enjoyed a fast life and 'had been linked with several women, including Lady Jersey'.[33] Georgiana, though, believed that his 'former follies' were now a thing of the past and told her mother that 'I really believe he has renounc'd play'.[34] Nevertheless it seems that, prior to this development, the Countess of Jersey had enjoyed her own connection with Lord Morpeth. When she wrote to Georgiana Devonshire to congratulate her on her daughter's engagement, the Duchess was indignant, saying to her mother:

> I have had a most extraordinary performance from Ly Jersey. Not naming G more than wishing us joy & then a most [violent?] encomium on *Morpeth* as she calls him ... I wrote very coolly to say that I was happy as I could be for the prospect of losing her from [illegible] their happiness – & [yet?] I thought so highly of him, I did not know anyone more deserving *of her*. I was pleased with Lord M's indignation at her not mentioning G especially as where she founds her affection for him upon [that is Frances Jersey's brief affair with Morpeth], long acquaintance cannot be full of very favourable recollections to him.[35]

So Frances Jersey had also had, and was known to have had, an affair (where it must be certain that, with her age, experience and character, she was once more the seducer not the seduced) with a young man who, when she was nearly fifty, was not only twenty or more years her junior but also the son of another of her lovers and half-brother to at least one of her daughters.

What an extraordinary woman. What charms the bewitching and beautiful Countess of Jersey must have had, even to men so much younger than her. And what appetites!

Then, suddenly and without warning, in February 1801 Lady Anne Lambton remarried. *The Morning Post* of 13 August the previous year had speculated about the attentions being paid to Lady Anne in Brighton by the supremely eligible young Duke of Bedford. Yet he was not her new husband. Instead it was the Hon Charles Wyndham, the younger brother of the prodigiously wealthy Earl of Egremont.[36] He was, however, disreputable in the extreme – fast, a roué and the worst kind of intimate of the Prince of Wales.

Wyndham's past affairs were numerous. In 1786 he had planned to elope with Harriet Duncannon, Georgiana Devonshire's younger and married sister, but as we know this had been nipped in the bud. In the 1780s he had also embarked on an affair with the celebrated courtesan Grace Elliott, 'Dally the Tall', and some thought that he was the father of her daughter (although the competitors for that claim included both Lord Cholmondeley and the Prince of Wales).[37] In the 1790s he had a 'connexion' with a Mrs Sophia Hodges of 'the left hand variety', which resulted in two children.[38] Finally it was he who drew Lady Worsley, who was later to be at the centre of one of the great sex scandals of the time, 'off the path of virtue' and who was her first 'truly passionate love'.[39]

In addition to his serial affairs, such were Wyndham's financial extravagances that his brother, when the 3rd Earl, had to pay the vast sum of £200,000 to £300,000 to settle his debts.[40]

The King himself summed up the public's view of Charles Wyndham, and his association with the Prince, crushingly with the words: 'The conduct that makes all good men despise a St Leger and a Windham is more criminal in the Heir Apparemt of the Crown.'[41]

This was the man that Lady Anne Lambton chose to marry and to do so in haste, without even her father knowing beforehand, as Georgiana Devonshire's journal tells us:

> Lady Anne Lambton's sudden marriage with Charles Wyndham; that he had proposed one-day & been married the next – that they went to [illegible] where Lord Jersey by chance passing and seeing a [illegible, servant?] of his daughter enquired for her and was told she was in bed with Mr Wyndham. Lord Jersey never having heard the report.[42]

Why Lady Anne married Wyndham, and why in such a rush, is not known. She was certainly one both attracted by and attractive to fast company, including the Prince of Wales. On his side, besides her beauty, Wyndham presumably had money as one of his motives, though in this he was to be disappointed. In any event the marriage was a disaster and a short lived one. Within days Lady Anne had left him and never returned. Quite what provoked this turn of events is equally unknown. Wyndham's past life might provide some clue, as might Farington's entry in his diary later that year, observing that, following Mr Lambton's death, Lady Anne 'has conducted herself most imprudently & is now involved in debt, & is married to Charles Wyndham, but they separated in a few days. – She now resides at Lambton upon a very moderate scale of expence, her servants being at Board Wages and she does not keep a carriage.'[43] So money may have been a factor in the break up of the marriage as well as its formation.

Whatever the reasons, Charles Wyndham soon felt the need to leave the country, implying the whiff of some scandal. As *The Morning Post* wrote on 23 May 1801: 'The Hon Charles Wyndham, to the great regret of the *sporting world*, and an extensive circle of friends, is arrived at Yarmouth on his way to the Continent, where he intends to reside for some time.'

Lady Anne and her parents would not be amongst those who regretted his departure.

The news of Lady Anne's disastrous marriage was rapidly followed by even sadder news for the Countess. One of the constants in Frances Jersey's life was her widowed mother, Frances Johnston, who had retired to live in Bath. Of her, Frances Jersey had written, with apparently beguiling honesty, to Louisa Ponsonby, ironically both the mother of a future lover and a future mother-in-law of one of her daughters, 'I hope to see my mother ... you who know how amiable she is, & how much I love her will guess with what impatience I long for that time ... Fanny.'[44] It seems that Frances Johnston was, outside her children, the focus of one of the few unqualified loyalties in the Countess's life, though it is disappointing that nothing survives recording Mrs Johnston's views on her daughter's adventures. Sadly for the Countess, as the papers reported on 4 March:

> Died ...
>
> At Bath, aged 74, Mrs Johnstone, widow of Gen. Johnstone, and mother of the present Countess of Jersey.[45]

Frances Jersey had now lost one of her principal supporters.

Nevertheless her children moved on.

Despite the debacle of Lady Anne's marriage, she was soon to make her way at the highest levels of Society with particular panache, frequently in the company of the Prince. In the meantime, there were two more marriage campaigns within the Jersey family. Both were to end in failure, in the short term at least. The first was that of Lord Villiers, the second of his sister, Lady Elizabeth, yet another Villiers beauty.

Lord Villiers too was not wanting in good looks. He was 'outstandingly good looking',[46] and in the words of Lady Shelley: 'When we were standing near the window overlooking Piccadilly, Georgiana called me to look at three *elegants* of the day, who happened to be passing: Lord Anglesey [as Lord Paget was to become], Lord Villiers, and John Shelley, then in his great beauty.'[47] Villiers was also, taking after both his parents, an outstanding sportsman, described by Nimrod 'as the hardest, boldest, most judicious, and perhaps the most elegant rider to hounds whom the world ever saw'.[48]

On this occasion the object of Lord Villiers' pursuit was Lady Sarah Fane.

Sarah Fane was the raven haired, and very handsome, daughter of the Earl of Westmorland. She was also prodigiously rich. Her mother was the daughter of the banker Robert Child and had eloped to Gretna Green with the Earl. In retribution, Robert Child's will entailed his fortune so that no future Earl of Westmorland would benefit from it.[49] The consequence of this action was that, when she was just twenty-one, Lady Sarah Fane would inherit the vast bulk of her grandfather's wealth.[50] The newspapers had estimated at that time that her fortune would 'not be less than 40,000l per annum';[51] Horace Walpole had been told that on her coming of age she would be worth over £1,000,000.[52]

The papers were also reporting in December 1801 that Lady Sarah is 'said to destine her hand to Lord Villiers'.[53]

It did, however, take Lord Villiers some time before he played his hand. He had perhaps been distracted by a death in the family. On 2 March, the 5th Duke of Bedford, Lord William Russell's eldest brother, had died unexpectedly after being hit by a ball whilst playing tennis in the great court at Woburn. The Russell family was devastated, particularly the Duke's two brothers, and it fell to Villiers to try and provide some solace to them. In this role, Richard Fitzpatrick wrote of him: 'I find Ld Villiers an admirable assistant, full of both good sense & affectionate feeling in endeavouring to interrupt the effects of too frequent solitary reflections in the minds of the unhappy brothers.'[54]

The Duke's death also sent out one more signal of the financial storm clouds looming over his youngest brother Lord William Russell, who beside being rather eccentric was either incompetent or a spendthrift, despite his wife Lady Charlotte's challenges. In the long run it only delayed disaster, but in the Duke's will he directed that all Lord William's debts should be paid and, in addition to that, left a further amount of £35,000 to him.[55]

It was only in July 1802 that Lord Villiers wrote to Lord Westmorland asking for Sarah's hand. He was refused, Lord Westmorland writing back to him on 4 July:

> My Lord
>
> I was honoured with your letter of 3 July, delivered to me by Lord Paget. From a very particular situation & circumstances in which my daughter Lady Sarah is placed it is in my judgement as well as that of Mr Childs executors most essential to her that she shd not only enter into any engagement or marriage. Having the concurrence of Lady Sarah in this opinion I must express to you the determination both in her name & mine

> of declining the Honor of your Lordship's proposal allow me at ye same time to add my concern at communicating what is not consistent to your wishes & to assure you of the respect with which
>
> I am
> Your … Servant
> Westmorland.[56]

If true, the seventeen-year-old Lady Sarah was indeed wise in avoiding premature decisions when so much money was at stake. Perhaps at heart Villiers recognised the point, as he responded graciously to Lord Westmorland a few days later:

> Deeply as I feel regret & disappointment at the determination … My sentiments towards Lady Sarah bind me to an implicit obedience to you & her will without remonstrance, however difficult the task it may be for me, feeling as I do, to agree with the motives which have operated on your Lordship's & her mind.
>
> Notwithstanding the surprise your Lordship expressed to Lord Paget, I trust you will believe that not even the very sincere attachment I bear to Lady Sarah [wld?] have induced me to take the step I did, without the hope that my sentiments had made such an impression on her mind as to want only the sanction of your Lordship's approbation.[57]

Villiers' aspirations to Lady Sarah were genuine indeed and he was not to give up. In fact, his rejection was the starting point of a campaign for Lady Sarah's hand on his part lasting nearly two years. In the meantime, though, he was understandably downhearted and, perhaps, concerned about competing suitors for Lady Sarah. In August, Lady Bessborough wrote to Granville Leveson Gower saying that she had seen Lord Jersey and Lord Villiers, adding 'Ld. V. looking in great beauty, but very grave, and I thought not so cordial as he used to be to me'.

Lady Bessborough, who was of course Georgiana Devonshire's younger sister Harriet, went on in her letter to speculate that there might be some jealousy on the part of Lord Villiers in relation to Granville Leveson Gower who, variously described for his looks as an Adonis and an Apollo, was indeed another competitor for Lady Sarah Fane's hand and mentioned that Harriet Bessborough was tainted by association with him.[58]

The unlikely reason for this was that Lady Bessborough and Leveson Gower, later the 1st Earl Granville, were lovers. As we shall see, Leveson Gower's pursuit of Lady Sarah was perhaps not as committed as it might have been for this very reason. Thirteen years younger than the Countess, he had been her lover since the mid-1790s and she was to have two children by him, one of whom was to become the Duchess of Leeds. Their affair was to continue until 1809 when, extraordinarily, Leveson Gower, with the Countess's blessing, married Harriet Cavendish, daughter of the Duchess of Devonshire and so the Countess's niece.[59]

Inevitably, given what was involved, other suitors too were rumoured and were to emerge over the course of time. One of these others was Lord Craven, of whom Mrs Howe wrote with some sympathy for the young lady: 'I heard the other day the Lord Craven has a mind for Lady Sarah Fane. I have a wish for her if she would ask my advice, they say she is a charming girl every way, I have never seen her since she was a child, but I pity her present situation.'[60]

Granville Leveson Gower for his part was not satisfied in merely pursuing Lady Sarah Fane at the same time as having an affair with Lady Bessborough. Earlier in the year the Countess, then at Chatsworth with her sister, was caused considerable anxiety by reports of his flirtation with 'Lady Sarah Villiers', presumably meaning Lady Sarah Bayly (as she now was), the sister of his rival.[61] Whether those anxieties were increased as a result of Lady Sarah's mother's reputation is an intriguing question. The stories of the flirtation appear to be true, as some months later Lady Bessborough was still referring to Lady Sarah when writing to Leveson Gower as 'your love'.[62]

Lady Sarah Bayly was presented at court on the Queen's Birthday that year. On the occasion, *The Morning Post* described her wearing:

> A petticoat and drapery of the most beautiful embroidered white crape in silver; the robe was also of white crape, and trimmed with a very elegant Vandyke silver fringe to correspond with the petticoat; the whole forming a dress perfectly simple, though truly elegant. The head-dress was a plume of feathers with diamonds and pearls. Her Lady Ship was extremely well-dressed, and looked with divinely.[63]

She did not, though, accompany her mother to Margate that August. That was left to her three unmarried sisters, Fanny, Elizabeth and Harriet. Georgiana Devonshire's daughter Harriet Cavendish, or Harryo as she was known, who was about to go and stay in neighbouring Ramsgate, told her sister what she thought of her prospective visit: 'I hear it is as full as possible. The Jerseys are there, Lady Southampton and Mrs. Fitzroy, Alas!'[64]

Those two seaside towns were to witness a series of dramas that summer. Prime among these was Frances Jersey's latest, and possibly last, affair. Her new conquest was John Ponsonby, 'a very young man, who subsequently married her daughter'.[65]

All of which is true save that Ponsonby was not that young. At thirty he was indeed eight years younger than the Prince and certainly was very young to have a mistress of forty-seven.

John Ponsonby was the elder son of the 1st Baron Ponsonby. In 1800 he was working as an MP as a prelude to embarking on a diplomatic career. 'He was a handsome man, dissipated, and without political prospects.'[66] That probably understates things on every score. He was the love of the life of one of the most celebrated courtesans of the age, Harriette Wilson, who regarded him as 'the handsomest man in England', describing his beauty as legendary.[67] There is, too, a story that, when in revolutionary Paris as he was about to be strung up from a lamp post as a suspected agent of Pitt, some passing ladies interceded on account of his beauty and persuaded his captors to set him free. This may just be a myth. What is assuredly not is that he shared the Prince of Wales' taste in women; not only did he have an affair with Lady Jersey but also in the early 1800s was engaged to Lady Conyngham who, too, was to become a mistress of the Prince, although Ponsonby jilted her a few days before the wedding.[68]

The Countess of Bessborough described what happened when writing to Leveson Gower, saying that Frances Jersey was at Margate

> where she has made a new conquest and a most violent one – John Ponsonby, who strange as it may seem has his head completely turn'd by her. And as Ly. Jersey's system always is having no happiness without a rival to trouble and torment, she has the pleasure of knowing that poor Ly. Coningham is expecting John every day at Spa.

Of the last sentence, Lady Bessborough commented that it was very ill-natured, and the words were Mrs Wilmot's, not hers; but she admitted they were true 'for it was what gave me a worse opinion of her [that is Lady Jersey] even at the time I knew more off her that all her lovers'.[69]

Harryo Cavendish described what she saw of this business to her sister in mid-September:

> I saw Lady Fanny Villiers yesterday, and think her very beautiful but not much prettier than Lady Elizabeth, who is the greatest beauty, or Lady Harriet, who, although as black as ink, is uncommonly pretty. I am very angry with John Ponsonby, who is desperately in love with odious Lady Jersey and never leaves her side.[70]

Fanny had actually been extremely ill earlier in the year, as Lord Jersey told Lady Spencer when he joined his family in Margate, saying that over the spring and the beginning of the summer he had been

> in a scene of trouble & most severe illness in my Family, nearly very nearly indeed having lost my daughter Fanny; and had it not been for the most [illegible] attentions & watchfulness of Lady Jersey, with a fatigue that I did not think any person scarcely could go thro', added to the skillful & efficient attendance of the Physicians she could not have been saved; thank God she is now recovered.[71]

But then Lady Jersey's latest affair took an extraordinary turn. She put a stop to it. As Harriet Bessborough wrote:

> I must make amende honourable to Lady Jersey, to whom I (in common with everyone here) have been very unjust. John Ponsonby says he was in love with her, which occasion'd his acquaintance with the family, but so far from treating him with coquetry, as people said, she behaved perfectly well, put an entire stop to it, and his passion has taken a more natural course.[72]

That perhaps was erring too much in the Countess of Jersey's favour. She did stop the affair, but an affair it was.

The new and more natural course for Ponsonby's passion was even more extraordinary than Frances Jersey's terminating of the affair. John Ponsonby had proposed to the Countess's daughter Lady Fanny Villiers and had been accepted.

The historian of the Ponsonby family describes Lady Fanny as 'the most beautiful debutante of her day' and says that her romance with John Ponsonby was a case of love at first sight.[73] Certainly her portrait by Opie shows a very striking lady. Harryo Cavendish described her as 'beautiful beyond description ... an engaging, affectionate gentle person' (albeit one who was treated by Ponsonby 'with affected contempt and brutality').[74] Lord Byron described her 'as beautiful as Thought'.[75]

The courtesan Harriette Wilson – who had no cause to love Lady Fanny, who in later years had put a stop to Ponsonby's affair with her – was more critical. Whilst acknowledging her beauty, Harriette described Fanny as not at all clever and very deaf following a violent attack of scarlet fever 'during which her life was despaired of'. Presumably this was the illness she had suffered earlier in the year, but that Fanny was very deaf is much to be doubted.[76] Indeed Farington described Fanny, when Opie was painting her portrait in 1803, as being only 'a little deaf'.[77] Even more doubtful is the story that Harriette Wilson also put about that Lady Fanny 'spent her days playing with a mouse who lived in the wainscot' which she trained to eat from her hand.[78]

News of Lady Fanny's betrothal was greeted in varying ways. Her father, typically, wrote to Lady Spencer to tell her the news, saying, 'I write ... to communicate her Marriage with Mr Ponsonby. You know him well, & lucky as I know him to be in his Choice for there does not exist one to be preferred to Fanny, we are confident she has not the smallest risk of happiness [*sic*].'[79]

Georgiana Devonshire's reaction was more measured:

> John Ponsonby is going to be married to Ly Fanny Villiers. She is beautiful but rather young for him being only 17 next April. He has had many kind letters from his Mother & Sister but his Father was from home and he has not yet heard from him ... The D of D will not however asked them to dinner [presumably until Ponsonby's father gave his approval] ... I am sorry because I think Lady Jersey a terrible person to belong to – I do not [illegible] on the score of character but she is *méchante et très tracassière*.

The Duchess, clearly now completely disenchanted with Frances Jersey, went on to mention the first sign of similar concerns elsewhere which would soon be causing the Bessborough family great anxiety: 'The alarm is also about here. Duncannon is inclined to admire & flirt with Lady Elizabeth Villiers and Lady Jersey encourages it to the greatest degree.'[80]

Duncannon was Harriet Bessborough's eldest son.

The Ponsonby family, too, were not happy with matters, presumably for just these reasons. As Georgiana Devonshire wrote to her mother in

October: 'I believe the Ponsonby's are unhappy with it but as neither he nor Ly Jersey hint at this & as I only know it confidentially I take care it shall not be traced to me as Ly Jersey is willing enough to have or pretend to have cause of dislike to me & would say I set it about.'[81]

James Hare, in contrast, looked at it from a different perspective, recognising Ponsonby's character: 'John Ponsonby will not make a comfortable husband, I am afraid.'[82]

That was also true. Despite all of which, the wedding was to go ahead. Lady Jersey was probably only in part acting when she wrote to Ponsonby's mother, a long-standing friend of hers, in December: 'It almost breaks my heart to part with Fanny.'[83]

The wedding took place on 13 January 1803.

As the Countess wrote the next month, she remained down-spirited at the loss of Fanny and, at the wedding, had taken five drops of laudanum to calm herself. Fanny on the other hand was very composed and, said Lady Jersey, her 'adoration of him [Ponsonby] is excessive'.[84]

'After the ceremony was performed', recounted *The Morning Post*, 'the new married couple, and some friends, set off in two coaches and four for the Countess of Jersey's beautiful villa in Kew-lane.'[85]

Even as Ponsonby proposed to Lady Fanny at Margate, the next drama, already signalled, was unfolding at nearby Ramsgate. When Georgiana Devonshire wrote to her mother from there in September 1802 she confined herself to saying, doubtless with relief, 'The Jerseys are at Margate we do not see them very often – Lady Fanny is recovered & remarkably handsome. Lord Jersey is I believe expected very soon.'[86]

She probably wanted to keep it that way; even if, it seems, she did visit the Countess on one occasion, saying, perhaps sardonically, in a letter to her sister: 'I am going to the play at Margate to meet Ly Jersey – [these?] graciousnesses.'[87]

However, before long that was to change. The first harbinger of this and the trouble which was to ensue came in the form of Lord Duncannon's flirtation with Lady Elizabeth Villiers, along with Lady Jersey's encouragement of it, as the Duchess of Devonshire had earlier noted.

This was the beginning of a two-year saga in which Duncannon's affections wavered between his cousin Harryo Cavendish and Lady Elizabeth Villiers. Originally he seemed to have fallen for Harryo but then, once in Ramsgate, he deserted her for Elizabeth. Harryo Cavendish good-naturedly described the goings-on in a letter to her sister, now Lady Morpeth, on 19 September: 'Duncannon, when he is at Margate is desperately smitten with Lady Elizabeth Villiers, but sticks to me [in Ramsgate] with an astonishing good grace.'[88]

Lady Jersey liked what she saw as much as Lady Elizabeth did. As the Countess of Bessborough observed: 'She has set her mind on marrying Duncannon to Lady Elizabeth and John [that is Duncannon] seems extremely struck with her ... For Ly. E is very pretty and a good deal of a flirt.'

Lady Bessborough went on to say that Lady Jersey had expressed the hope that she did not disapprove of the potential match. Of course she did, said

Lady Bessborough to Leveson Gower, 'I should extremely, for I should not like the connection ... And I think John too young and too Boyish for his age to marry.'[89] Indeed, she went further and declared it would kill her to have Lady Jersey as her son's mother-in-law.[90] In these strong sentiments her daughter Caroline (the future Lady Caroline Lamb, the ostracised lover of Lord Byron) joined her in describing Lady Jersey as 'odious' and as 'Satan's representative on earth' whilst expressing the hope that 'Duncannon will escape from the clutches of that rattlesnake'.[91]

None of which had any effect on Duncannon. Indeed Lady Melbourne's rather wild children – including a future Prime Minister – were hotly urging him to ignore his mother's dread of the connexion and marry Lady Elizabeth.[92] Further, he was flattered by Lady Jersey's attentions.

The whole business generated considerable alarm as, later in September, Harryo Cavendish described to her sister:

> The *families* are rather in alarm at a violent flirtation of [Duncannon] with Lady E. Villiers, as the connexion would not be desirable. He will not speak even to Miss Fitzroy (though she is in the greatest beauty and I really think seriously in love with him) and never leaves the other, who seems, though not so pretty as Miss F much more amiable.[93]

Lady Bessborough described that alarm to Leveson Gower:

> You cannot think of what trouble I have been in about Duncannon and Ly Elizabeth Villiers. She is so very pretty and her manner so pleasing that Lady Jersey need not take half the pains she does to make poor John in love with her ...

Before going on to say that John admired the flirtatious Lady Elizabeth and was flattered by all the fuss they made of him, adding:

> But I am sure [he] has not thought further than liking to talk to a very pretty girl who marks a strong preference for him, and fear of Lady Jersey laughing at him and telling him he is in the leading strings if he refuses any supper or party she asked him to.

Lady Bessborough then tells the story of Lady Jersey seeing Duncannon at the theatre and calling him over to ask him whether his mother had appointed the Manners family [the Devonshire House governess] in Miss Trimmer's place to take care of him.

All of which prompted the Countess's final comment on Lady Jersey:

> She has, besides, a talent at ridicule (the most powerful one with a very young man) greater than anyone I ever knew ... What I dread for John is all this going on till he is really seriously in Love with the Girl or till ... he has made his attentions so particular, that Ly. J will have a right to complain if it goes no further.

Which perhaps, as we will see, it did.[94]

The Bessboroughs' anxieties were not helped by their brother-in-law the Duke of Devonshire. As Harryo Cavendish wrote to Miss Trimmer, a little wickedly:

> It is quite entertaining to hear [her Uncle, Lord Bessborough], though I really pity him, as papa insists upon asking the Jerseys to dinner tomorrow and my Uncle says he will certainly *dine in his own room*. I think it is wrong to have them, but papa is really so very gay it is in vain to hope for anything like quiet, and if we do go out, it is difficult to avoid them.[95]

So, in October, Lady Bessborough felt she had to intervene – and she did so with some success, as she wrote to her lover: 'I must tell you how much reason I have to be pleas'd with Duncannon. Having to combat all Ly Jersey's wit and Lady E. V.'s beauty was trying my influence high.'

She said that she had warned Duncannon of the impropriety of his attentions if he meant nothing by them, and of the danger of mistaking 'a fantaisie' for real affection. He replied abruptly, 'Use a better argument, and say you do not like it and wish me to avoid it,' which is promptly what she then did and explained her reasons. Duncannon said nothing in reply but, she said, looked very grave for a day or two, and then said he would return to London from Ramsgate. He was to go and stay with friends until the family, going along with him, were to leave for Paris which, as a result of (a short lived) peace with France, much of Society was taking the opportunity of visiting a little later in the year.[96]

And that is what he did. For the time being the Countess of Jersey's campaign was thwarted. As one would expect, though, she did not regard this as a defeat and, in due course, was to return to the charge.

It was left to the jilted Harryo Cavendish to sum up for her sister Lady Morpeth the events of the autumn. Describing Duncannon, she said, 'I do think him trifling, inconstant and inconsequent to the greatest, most dreadful and even unparalleled degree.'[97]

Whilst Frances Jersey's plans for Lady Elizabeth's marriage were stalled with the Bessboroughs abroad in Paris, her eldest son resumed his once-rebutted pursuit of Lady Sarah Fane with, in Byron's words, 'her beautiful cream-coloured complexion and raven hair'.[98] Unlike in his sister Elizabeth's campaign for Duncannon's hand, there is no sign of Lady Jersey aiding Villiers in his suit, although there is no doubt she supported it to the utmost.

Lady Sarah, though, was to lead all her suitors, including Lord Villiers, in a pretty quadrille.

In the New Year of 1803 it seemed that Lord Granville Leveson Gower was Lady Sarah's favoured suitor, or at least so it seemed to his mother Lady Stafford, even if his attentions were distracted by his affair with Harriet Bessborough. As Lady Stafford wrote to him: 'Spectators fancy you the favour'd lover, and take Occasion to report how much Lord Villiers is to be pitied, for that he is really and truly in Love with her, and scruples not to own himself miserable, but since you are attach'd elsewhere and follow her for her Fortune.'[99]

Indeed as Lady Morpeth said to her mother around this time:

> I saw Lord Villiers a little while at the Opera, looking thin & ill – Lady Sarah and [her sister] Lady Augusta were there with Lady Westmorland but he was almost all the time in the opposite box with Mrs Bouverie & Mrs Villiers … I met Lady Jersey in the passage, She was very gracious in her enquiries after you & after me – she has not been here ought I to allow her?[100]

Certainly Granville's star seemed to many to be in the ascendant. In Harryo Cavendish's words: 'I never saw anything so coquettish as Lady S. F.'s manner to Ld G on Wednesday night; she never took her eyes off him, and I'm sure saw nothing that was going on. He seemed either angry or sorrowful, I do not know …' to which Lady Bessborough added to Lord Granville the commentary that 'if she thinks at all about you she cannot be much in love with Lord Villiers'.[101]

Harryo Cavendish, writing to her sister Lady Morpeth on 20 January, seemed to echo this and Granville's hopes:

> Lord Granville's arrival in town *s'explique*. He is gone to The Priory [Lord Abercorn's house at Stanmore] today where he will find Lady Sarah and he is in such tearing spirits and seems to be pleased with himself, that I think he must have great hopes of success.[102]

A few days later she was writing of that visit to the Abercorns:

> Lady W[estmorland] is really as mad as it is possible to be … Lady Sarah had only three *adorateurs* on her hands: Tom Sheridan, who acted despair … Lord Craven who seemed to think it the best joke that ever was … and Lord Granville, seeming to have made a vow that he would take everything for the best, smiling with self congratulation when she turned her back.[103]

Granville's visit to The Priory was not, it seems, a success, and conversely Villiers was possibly now in the ascendant. Accordingly Harryo Cavendish, writing on 30 January, described events in a different tone:

> Lord Villiers and him [Granville Leveson Gower] met in our box last night, and each looked like the favoured, and the least successful [perceived to be Granville Leveson Gower] was certainly the most triumphant in manner at least … Lord Granville is in great spirits about his *proceedings*, though nobody can very tell why, as he has not seen Lady Sarah since the Priory, which I am sure was not a very encouraging meeting.[104]

Perhaps Lord Villiers' heroics in Hyde Park that winter helped his cause. As the papers reported in February:

> Hyde Park has not contained so great a crowd since the Review of the Volunteers, as assembled on Sunday to see the skaiters. At half-past three about 4,000 were on the ice, and more than double that number on the banks of the Serpentine River, almost all of them well-dressed persons ... The North side of the Serpentine was lined with gentlemen's carriages three deep, and the string of them reached back to the Piccadilly gate, and forward nearly round the ring. Such a bustle of velvet and silk pelisses, of muffs, and of tippeys, has seldom been seen in Hyde Park promenade. The skaters were numerous; but the chosen band *took their ice* facing the carriages ... Here a party of eight or nine young men of fashion display the ornamental flourishes of the art to the amusement of the numerous circle, many of them persons of the first rank. Amongst these skaters was the Marquess of Lorne, Lord Villiers, Sir J Shelley, Captains Caulfield and Upton. The ice in this part, protected from the north winds by the trees, was not so strong as further east ... A crowded circle was formed round these superior skaiters ... the ice gave way in part of the circle, and two ladies, a gentlemen, and a girl about 14, sunk. Fortunately it was that part of the circle next the shore, and the water was not more than 3 feet deep. The ladies and gentlemen were soon got out, leaving their muffs, tippets and hats floating behind with no other injury than a good ducking, and a great fright; but the girl was so overcome with the fright, that she was falling down, sinking, and would soon have disappeared under the ice, had not Lord Villiers dived in and saved her.[105]

By this time the real competitors for Lady Sarah's hand had been narrowed down to Lord Granville and Lord Villiers; there was much speculation as to who would win. Nevertheless, there was no doubt that Villiers was being helped by the fact that 'Granville was but a laggard lover despite the constant spurrings of both his mother and Lady Bessborough'.[106]

Perhaps unsurprisingly, Lady Sarah was not the first objective of Lord Villiers' matrimonial ambitions. In a manner typical of the times, according to Lady Shelley, a source to be trusted in the case of Lord Villiers, he had earlier wanted to marry Lady Tarleton, as she was to become, the illegitimate daughter of the celebrated Perdita Robinson, actress and former mistress of the Prince of Wales, 'but poverty, and perhaps family pride, made this impossible. At that time Villiers had no income whatsoever,' and his father was 'utterly ruined.'[107]

Villiers' objective had shifted to Lady Sarah, and the press and Society watched the pursuit with fascination, only in part as a result of Lady Sarah's extreme wealth.

As the *Bury & Norwich Post* had it, not without some exaggeration:

> Lady Sarah Fane's *debut* at Court on Thursday, attracted thither all the young beaux of family and fashion. Amongst others were Lords Villiers and Craven, the Marquesses of Lorne and Douglas. Her ladyship is heiress to 45,000l. per annum, and consequently is a *dear Child*'.

Nevertheless it seemed that Lady Sarah was 'persistent in her determination of making no choice between Lord Villiers and Lord G and no engagement till she is of age but she has so generous a motive that one must admire her for it'.[109] As Mrs Ponsonby wrote to Lady Holland in May 1803: 'Lady S Fane has not yet deigned to cast a benizon eye on any of her admirers Ld Granville, Ld Villars ... and many others, she talks and dances with them all but will certainly not marry any of them.'[110]

Even Lady Bessborough was beginning to believe this when she wrote to Lord Granville in September, quoting a letter from Lady Sarah's mother:

> I suppose you heard of our company at Worthing. I wonder what could possess Ld G. L. to come, and I wonder still more what could tempt him to return. I suppose jealousy of Ld Villiers [who was also at Worthing] must have been the motive, but they are all losing their time and their trouble, and *neither* has the least cause either for hope or jealousy. Ly Sarah is perfectly indifferent to both, and both she and I feel extremely offended at Mr Brummell's impertinence, who chuses [*sic*] to set it about that there is an attachment subsisting between Lord V and Ly. S., which is perfectly groundless.[111]

In fact Beau Brummell was right – and the Countess of Westmorland could not have been more wrong. Unbeknown even to her mother, when in Worthing that year Lady Sarah, as she later confessed to the Countess of Bessborough, 'enjoy'd the seeing Villiers in secret there and making all the arrangements for their Marriage'.[112]

Eventually that came to pass. It was, though, only in the spring of 1804 that it happened, as Georgiana Devonshire described:

> It is I believe a secret, but I have reason to think, that Ly Sarah has decided in favour of Ld Villiers. Poor Ld Granville (whom she has certainly [illegible: treated?] ill) is gone out of town very low. Do not ... mention my having said this to you.[113]

A delighted Lord Jersey wrote to Lady Spencer ten days later, on 23 April 1804, confirming the news: 'Lord Villiers's marriage with Lady Sarah Fane, it is decided ... [the decision] being made only on Saturday.'[114]

Indeed his son's marriage was to make the Earl very happy. But there was also a sadness about this letter to Lady Spencer. It was to be his last to her. With it ended a correspondence of many hundreds of letters from him to Countess Spencer spanning thirty-five years, often on a daily basis, although falling away somewhat over the last decade and very considerably so in the final few years. The correspondence displays both Lord Jersey's intense love for his family and an extraordinary and close relationship with Lady Spencer, although not without the occasional squall more often than not caused by his wife. Indeed it was she who, towards the end, effectively destroyed that relationship.

Villiers' marriage with Sarah (or Sally) Fane took place on 23 May 1804 in Lord Westmorland's house in Berkeley Square. The ceremony was performed by the Bishop of Cloyne in the presence of the parents of both the bride and groom, along with Lady Sarah's sisters, Lord Villiers' younger brother, William Augustus, and Lady Sarah's guardian, Mr Dent.[115] After the ceremony, the newlyweds went for their honeymoon to Osterley Park, Robert Child's house west of London, which Lady Sarah was to inherit on her coming of age.[116]

There are persistent stories that the young couple eloped and were married in Gretna Green. These are wrong and without any foundation. They doubtless arise from confusing Lady Sarah with her mother, who did indeed elope to marry Lord Westmorland to Robert Child's fury. If any further proof were needed, there is Lady Sarah's thirty-page marriage settlement, dated the day of their marriage, in the Jersey family papers.[117]

Unlike the Bessboroughs, and indeed the Ponsonbys, the Westmorlands do not seem to have had any objection to Lady Jersey becoming their daughter's mother-in-law. In these years the Countess once more participated fully in Society's events despite her existing reputation. About the only place she did not frequent were Maria Fitzherbert's entertainments.[118] In Georgiana Devonshire's words: 'The Assemblies in London are chiefly taken up with the amusement of watching Ly Jersey & Mrs Fitz run their heads against each other. For Ly J is everywhere & much handsomer from [*sic*] ever from wearing less [illegible, paint?].'[119]

Even if the Prince of Wales was to be a guest at an entertainment that was no bar to the Countess also being invited. So in February 1803, when the Marchioness of Abercorn had a large party at her house with cards and supper, the guests included both the Prince and the Countess.[120]

She was present, too, at the formal occasions like the Queen's Birthday that year, where 'amongst the Ladies most noticed for the brilliancy, neatness and striking harmony of the dresses, as well as for the elegance of their persons were ... Countess .... of Jersey'.[121]

On this occasion, as ever indulging in her love of clothes, she wore a

> petticoat of purple crape, tufted with frosted silver; the sash of purple crape, crossed with embroidery of silver, and foil stone on black velvet, tufted in silver, variegated to correspond with the petticoat; the whole fastened up with elegant silver rouleaus and tassels. The train was a black velvet, richly embroidered in foil–stone and silver; the tops of the sleeves of silver tufted crape, tastefully fastened up with silver cords and tassels.[122]

When she could, however, she continued to contrive to annoy the Prince. In the summer of 1803, as she told the artist Hoppner, she met the Prince of Wales on the stairs of the Royal Opera House and had to make room for him to pass – in her words 'not instantly noticing him she did not do as he wished', and accordingly apologising to the Prince.

One can visualise her performance. There can be no doubt that this was a deliberate slight and the Prince thought so too. The next day Col McMahon called on her to tell her that it 'was the desire of the Prince that she would not speak to him'. A nerve was clearly touched because the Countess responded bitterly, said McMahon, that 'there is a popish combination against her.

[And that h]er acquaintance with Ned Jerningham has ceased and she speaks of him with great contempt'.[123]

It seems the Countess had wantonly discarded her most loyal friend, presumably as a consequence of his being the Prince's emissary in the ending of their affair.

With the Bessboroughs now back from France, that autumn of 1803 also saw the renewal of Frances Jersey's campaign to win Duncannon's hand for Lady Elizabeth. Over the next few tortuous months Duncannon was to vacillate, swinging like a weather vane, between favouring Lady Elizabeth and favouring his cousin Harryo Cavendish, with whom some say there was an understanding from their childhoods that they would eventually marry.[124]

Duncannon was certainly an immature twenty-two year old and really did not know his own mind. In all of this, Harryo Cavendish acted with great dignity, if sometimes with great impatience. Lady Elizabeth, with her manifest charms, did so with perhaps a little less dignity.

So in September 1803 Harryo wrote to her sister, Lady Morpeth: 'The Jerseys are just arrived in Town. I am more afraid of them than of Buonaparte, and expect a most desperate attack on Mary Le Bone,' meaning the Bessboroughs and their house in Cavendish Square.[125]

To which Georgiana Morpeth responded by asking 'how Duncannon continues', provoking the answer from Harryo that she had not a clue:

> You could not ask me a question that would puzzle me more ... for there never yet was created so inexplicable and *unaccountable* a person. We dislike Lady E from thinking that she has been very artful and making great advances to him. In short, if he escapes them, I shall think a little of his good sense and a great deal of his good luck.[126]

Clearly frustrated, she amplified this sentiment two days later:

> Duncannon has been seeing a good deal of the Villiers lately, but I cannot make out what his plans or intentions are, and most likely if it were possible, the *découverte* would not repay me for the pains, as he seems boyish and uncertain to the most worrying degree, and, I am convinced, changes his mind and inclinations in the day as often as the clock strikes. You may think by this guess that we have not interchanged one syllable for the last 4 days and I am so tired of his folly that I do not look forward to a speedy reconciliation.[127]

In the meantime, the Bessboroughs, now staying with Georgiana at Devonshire House in Piccadilly, were doing what they could to avoid entertaining Lady Elizabeth. Early in November, Georgiana Devonshire invited Madame Zamoiska to dinner there to meet Lady Jersey, as Harryo explained:

> Duncannon has gone to [the Abercorn's at] the Priory, and the opportunity was seized to ask [Lady Jersey, who despite all was clearly still, to some

extent, persona grata] though even under that circumstance Lady Elizabeth is left out. I pity *her* very much, also as I think his passion, which was never very deep, is certainly overcome. However, in this weathercock cousin of mine's disposition, it may soon be revived again, and one cannot trust to the continuation of any one thing about him for about five minutes.

When Lady Jersey did arrive she did not impress either Harryo or Madame Zamoiska, as Harryo continued:

> Lady Jersey came all rolled up in schawls [*sic*], gesticulating and squeaking in the most ludicrous manner. "Lady Harriet, you must have thought me a beast when I wrote you that note." "My dear Madam, if you could know how utterly impossible it was I could ever think you a greater one than I do now" was really *au bout de mes lèvres*. I did not think Madame Zamoiska very gracious to her.[128]

And on and on went Duncannon's vacillations. When Lady Elizabeth came back to London only a few days later, Harryo Cavendish summarised the effect of Lady Elizabeth's charms in another letter to her sister:

> Duncannon's love is just returned to Town, to what purpose and with what effect I do not know. He seems to forget her entirely when she is absent, but there is no security if one considers the art of attack and I am afraid, the weakness of the defence.[129]

The continuing confusion as to where the participants in this love triangle stood in relation to one another is summed up in a letter from Harryo to Lady Morpeth written from Bath in mid-November. Here, in the space of very few paragraphs, she described the events of recent weeks.

First that she and Duncannon had made up after a quarrel so as to become 'friends with a vengeance' but, that on reflection, she was unhappy with his attachment to Lady Elizabeth, although, when he did see Lady Elizabeth, he did not seem the least bit altered.

Then Duncannon acknowledged he was undecided and unhappy, dropping hints that he was 'entangled in this affair with the Jerseys, and wished extremely to get off from it'.

For her part, Harryo was lectured furiously by Mrs Trimmer that her 'coquetry was dreadful and that, without caring for my cousin, I had made him in love with me, merely to enjoy the triumph of having supplanted Lady E'.

Harryo and Duncannon promptly quarreled once more and for at least ten days would not speak, and then suddenly Duncannon 'went off to the Jerseys, saw *her* twice every day and, even when we made up, was very cold to me. During this time I once or twice met him walking in the path and he joined us. He did not seem in the least in love with her, but tearing about in the most buoyant spirits and extremely flattered, evidently with her manner to him, which though she has more excuses than most people, was certainly a very wrong one.'

At this stage Lady Bessborough once more intervened to discourage his attentions to Lady Elizabeth. To this Duncannon 'answered as if he was dying for her – Lady E – but agreeing to leave off seeing her. Instead of depressing his spirits this seemed to take a load off his mind and, though before my aunt *il jouait le Désespoir*, with us he was gayer than usual.'

Duncannon soon changed his mind and confessed to Harryo that he had broken his promise to his mother not to see Elizabeth and 'meant to marry Lady E., *immediately*'. Harryo, though, saw this as a ruse to test her sentiments toward him, to which she reacted angrily and told him that she thought him very weak and foolish and that she never wished to speak to him again. The result was that for six weeks more they did not speak, with the consequence that Duncannon 'really was miserable the whole time ... it touched me ... and it was the only time I have ever felt the slightest *penchant* for him'.[130]

So by the middle of November Harryo was writing:

> With regard to my cousin – I believe that at present he is, or fancies himself, in love with me ... but you know my opinion of his boyishness inconstancy and, alas, fickleness, and it would scarcely create in me surprise to hear of his making desperate love to Lady E tomorrow.[131]

This time it was Lady Jersey's turn to intervene in an attempt to achieve just that:

> We heard today [wrote Harryo Cavendish] that the Jerseys have taken the box next to ours at Covent Garden – this coup de main will not, of course, remain unknown – and that Lady E V looked in to our box, all over it and then was for the rest of the evening in a deep melancholy. This is not affected; by all accounts '*ce petite conte est joué trop au naturel*'.[132]

Around this time Harryo had commented that she was sure that Duncannon 'does not think of Lady E. at present'.[133] Within days, though, she was writing from Bath, contradicting herself, 'Do not be surprised if you see in the papers that he is married to Lady E. I hear *they* [the Jerseys] are making greater preparations than Buonaparte.'[134]

Neither Harriet Bessborough nor Georgiana Devonshire were happy with the state of affairs. What was worse, the impressionable and inconstant Duncannon had now become infatuated with the charismatic Lady Jersey herself, and there were concerns that if she ordered him to marry Lady Elizabeth that is what he would do. As for Georgiana, she wrote 'I feel anxious about Harriet and Duncannon ... It must not go on – something must be decided,'[135]

And then, all of a sudden, it was all over. For whatever reason, Duncannon abandoned both Lady Elizabeth and Harryo Cavendish and the following year married Lady Maria Fane, Sally's sister. Harryo Cavendish, who felt sorry for Lady Elizabeth (if not her mother) at the outcome of her pursuit, was to marry Duncannon's mother's lover, Granville Leveson Gower. Sadly for her, and for the Countess of Jersey's ambitions, Lady Elizabeth Villiers despite all her beauty and her charms was to die unmarried and young.

It is not clear what happened to cause this break but, on 30 December 1803, Harryo wrote to Lady Morpeth about Duncannon: 'Do not talk of his ever being a *nearer relation*. You do not know me if you ever for a moment think it possible. I told you some time ago that it would not surprise me if he returned to Lady E., but after what passed the last time he was here [in Bath], I own it does.'

It seems Duncannon avoided coming to Bath at this time lest Lady Elizabeth worry about his relationship with Harryo. Harryo for her part now seemed to think that all was over with Lady Elizabeth, too. Given what she went on to say in that letter and the reference to something having happened on an earlier occasion in Bath, it looks as if Duncannon had jilted Lady Elizabeth in favour of Harryo only to find that Harryo had had enough and now rejected him. This is consistent with Harryo's letter also saying:

> No Bath gales will could blow him into my good graces. And I shall feel my conscience acquitted towards Lady E., as she is (excepting a little too much giving in to her dear Mama's plans) a great favourite of mine and too amiable and pretty to be discomposed by the jerks of a weathercock … Send me word if Lady E. is in beauty and admired and above all attribute the question merely to curiosity [and not to jealousy].[136]

It seems, too, that Duncannon's withdrawal from the young ladies affected both of them differently, which would also be consistent with this hypothesis. Harryo was able to continue serenely after the withdrawal, by her dismissal, of her cousin's attentions. Lady Elizabeth on the other hand, and reflecting her being rejected following a very public campaign, was less happily placed. This is all consistent with the scruples Harryo described to her mother in September 1804:

> I believe I am wrong about Lady E. and yet I think you will do me the justice to own it is natural I should have a thousand scruples about her, that I even would not forgive myself if I had not. Her situation (whatever may have been the blameable or excusable in her conduct) is a most particularly delicate one, and whatever may in future may be decided upon to try and prevent it being either mortifying or injurious to her, I not only consider a duty to the really one of the first wishes of my heart.[137]

A few weeks later she was again writing to her mother on the subject of Lady Elizabeth:

> I have heard much praise of the girl since I have been here, and I believe whatever we may have heard to the contrary has been dictated by prejudice

> or policy. Do you know what part *dear* Jo[hn] Ponsonby takes? If he now protects Lady E I shall think everybody else ought, for he was not inclined to do so, and I think would not, unless he had strong reasons for it.
>
> Does my aunt blame me? I think she *ought not*, but conclude she *will*, but from the most amiable if not the most just motives ...
>
> Though I am perfectly decided as to my own sentiments, whatever happens I neither wish them to be known or hope for his marrying Lady Elizabeth.
>
> I think he might make someone happy, but not Lady E. after all that has passed and not Lady H [i.e. Harryo herself] whatever may pass.[138]

With her marriage prospects to Duncannon now evaporated and her position compromised by his very public rejection of her, Lady Elizabeth needed to find redemption in an alternative suitor. Accordingly, Lady Jersey once more took her comprehensively under her wing, and at the rash of routs, masquerades, balls and other entertainments over the coming months, which formed much of the marriage market for the beau monde, Lady Elizabeth was the Countess's constant companion – their beauty and dresses frequently admired in the press.

One such occasion, the Queen's Birthday in 1804, stands out for its description of the Countess's dress. There Lady Jersey, now aged over fifty, appeared in a white satin dress of the kind that would challenge many who were years her junior. We do not know for sure, but can be confident that Frances Jersey, with her style, fully rose to that challenge. As *The Morning Post* said, Lady Jersey:

> Was very elegantly dressed in the most rich and beautiful white satin, superbly embroidered in patent pearl ... Her Ladyship's dress, which we understood was one of a number produced by Mrs Sowerby, certainly attracted general admiration by its neatness, elegance, and novelty. Head-dress profusion of diamonds and rich ostrich feathers.[139]

Another occasion, this time a masquerade, stands out for the Countess's choice of fancy dress, not least for her nubile daughter. This was the masked ball given by Lady Louisa Manners in Pall Mall in July 1805. As the *Bury & Norwich Post* reported, the ball 'was attended by 450 personages of the first distinction, in character or fancy dresses ... The Prince of Wales entered in a domino, with Mrs Fitzherbert ... in a beautiful Swiss dress ... The Countess of Jersey and Lady E Villiers, as Greek Slaves'.[140]

Despite these splendours, other difficulties ensued for the Jersey family. The same month saw Lord and Lady Villiers have a nasty accident. Riding in their curricle at Osterley, the horses took fright and, the curricle colliding with a post, they were both thrown out. *The Morning Post* described what happened:

> They lay for some time senseless on the ground, till by the assistance of Sir H Featherstonhaugh, who was riding near them, they were put into

> a carriage and conveyed home. Surgical aid was immediately procured, both were blooded, and we are happy to announce they were yesterday considerably recovered.[141]

Lady Villiers' head was badly cut, and when Lord Morpeth dined with them a few days later her head remained bound up and he thought she still looked ill.[142]

Nevertheless they were sufficiently recovered to go to Tunbridge Wells towards the end of the month, taking a house there for the summer.[143] There they cut fine figures. Lord Villiers sported one of the most elegant equipages in town and was said to drive a four-in-hand in good style.[144] Lady Villiers, it was reported, 'promenades daily on the Parade, elegantly dressed *a la Parisienne*. Her Ladyship's beautiful raven tresses sport on her shoulders, confined by three knots of brown ribbon.'[145]

They were joined there by the Earl of Jersey but not, apparently, the Countess. It was there on 22 August 1805 that the Earl suddenly died. As *The Times* reported:

> He was on a visit to Viscount and Viscountess Villiers, at their house, Prospect Lodge, and had accompanied them that morning to the Wells. Upon his return from the walks to Prospect Lodge, after drinking the waters, he fell down in a fit and instantly expired. The body of his Lordship was taken to lodging house in Vale Royal, where it at present remains.[146]

Harriet Bessborough filled in some of the details when writing to Lord Granville. The Earl had, apparently, been walking with Lord Villiers who, 'finding him silent all at once, turned round and saw him extended on the ground quite dead. It was a spasm of the heart.' She added that 'Sally [as Sarah Villiers was known] was with him at the time – how shocking for her! She is behaving with the greatest kindness to Ly J., and shewing her every possible attention.'[147]

The Earl's unexpected death had a surprisingly profound effect on Frances Jersey, as the Countess of Bessborough also described:

> This morning [she wrote] I receiv'd a note from Ly. Jersey entreating me to come and see her, and reminding me that poor Ld. J. had been the earliest friend my Father [Lord Spencer] ever had. I went and found her really very ill and very much affected; I expected it, tho' everybody laughed at me for saying so, for she certainly us'd to treat him very ill. I do not mean only in infidelities (Heaven knows bad enough!), but she made him unhappy – teaz'd and turn'd him into ridicule in every possible manner; yet I was quite certain the moment I heard of his death that she would be miserable.
>
> But die, and she'll adore you – then the bust, the Temples rise, &c., &c. *Sally* met me on the stairs and kiss'd me. I found Ly. J. very low and looking very ill. She threw her arms round me, and told me she had very often tried to hate me, but could not – that she had lov'd me when I was an

> infant, and should continue doing so as long as we both liv'd. Afterwards she told me I could form no Idea what it was to be separated for ever in one moment from a person who had been one's constant companion for five and thirty years, and who, when all the world deserted her, continued to show her undiminish'd and unremitting kindness. Sally is kindness itself to her – never leaves her.[148]

The Earl's death also called caused others to reflect on his life, his wife and his marriage. One of his oldest (former) friends, Lady Spencer, wrote to another, Lord Harcourt:

> Almost every occurrence in the former part of our lives, my dear Lord Harcourt, has united you & Lord Jersey so closely together in my memory, that the shock I felt when I first heard of his death, was immediately followed by the reflection that you would feel it as I did.
>
> Many unhappy circumstances tended to disunite him, for some years, from us both, but I have ever retained a sincere regard for him, who, with yourself, was so highly valued by Lord Spencer. I am happy to find his children have ever shown him the tenderest duty & affection, & are greatly & justly afflicted with the loss of so indulgent a father. Lady Jersey too is deeply affected; can she be otherwise?[149]

Queen Charlotte herself wrote on 29 August to Lady Harcourt, fearing for Lord Harcourt's nerves following the death of Lord Jersey:

> I know that of latter years their intimacy could not be kept up in the manner it used to be; but ... Connections formed in the early part of our life are most Commonly lasting. The poor deceased was never bad in himself, but weak & indulging to a little bewitching Wife, which made him appear to some wanting in Sense, and to others unfeeling, for Himself & to many others, I grant it would have been better had he shown more Spirit, at least it appears so; but in Domestic affairs, none but those who belong to them can form a true Judgement ...
>
> His children seem to be attached to him & I hear are very much hurt & as to the Widow, she is reported to be in Constant Fits since the News reached Her. This is scrutinized enough; but I own I believe it: for Common humanity would feel for such an event happening in any Family, without having any connection with it; & therefore I think that having lived so many years together, she will feel the Shock more Severely, & I do not think Her void of Feeling.[150]

Some thought that, even so, some good might come out of the Earl's death. Lady Hawkesworth wrote to her sister:

> 'Poor Lord Jersey's death, though there are no edifying details, may also have its use, for I hear it has shocked his wife excessively, & it *may* make her reflect poor creature whilst she has time.'[151]

And perhaps it did, for both she and the family were very hard hit by the Earl's death. As Georgiana Devonshire described to her mother after visiting them all at Osterley early in September:

> I was in Osterley yesterday & gave your letter but not at first for they were in the greatest distress. Lord Villiers is very ill has been blooded several times & keeps his bed. They say now it is not dangerous but an [affliction] of the head from agitation. He has not been quite well since his father was buried ... I could not say much to Ly Jersey, but I did to Ly Villiers who pressed my hand and said tell Lady Spencer it came from *us all* ... Lady Jersey seems ... ill & has I think a good chance of happiness. She has given up all her old ways. She looks beautiful but wears spectacles to read with & is become quite an old woman. Mrs [illegible] thinks she means to make it an [epocher?] in her life and she is all gentleness.[152]

Whether Lord Villiers' illness was caused by grief or, as some thought, was a consequence of his accident earlier in the summer is unclear.[153] He was the focus of Lord Harcourt's reply to a letter from Lady Spencer, reflecting on 'the sudden death of so old friend':

> It is a great consolation, to think that from the time of his son's marriage, he enjoyed as large a portion of happiness as he had experienced of misery, during many years preceding that event – as for Lady Jersey, supposing her not to possess an adamantine heart, she must be, at this moment, one of the most unhappy beings on this earth – as such I feel the utmost compassion for her, and am resolved (as far as I am *myself* concerned) to show her every kindness and attention in my power.[154]

The Earl's death left his wife not only emotionally shattered but also in a precarious financial position. He was, said Lady Shelley, utterly ruined and 'it became necessary for Lord Villiers, when he ... inherited the family estates, to discharge his father's debts at a tremendous personal sacrifice'.[155] Under his will, the Earl left his widow a mere £600 together with a life interest in various jewels, watches, rings and ornaments, as well as the carriages she personally used; he also left her with the balance of his personal estate after all other legacies. The bulk of his landed estates went, of course, to his heir, with some going to his unmarried daughters, Ladies Elizabeth and Harriet.[156]

As we will see, the now Dowager Countess was to turn both to the Prince of Wales and to her eldest son to resolve her financial difficulties over the coming years.

In the immediate aftermath of her husband's death Frances Jersey went, in October, to stay with her elder son and his wife in Worthing, where the Earl, as he now was, remained very ill. The Countess of Bessborough described visiting them there:

> His Mother is with them, and I see intends to renew all her former intimacy with us. The Prince of Wales put himself in a passion when I came back,

> saying my Sister [Georgiana Devonshire] and I had always had been and always would be her dupes. I said she had behav'd very well praising Ly Maria [that is Maria Fane who had married Duncannon] extremely and speaking well of Duncannon, which, considering all the past, I thought good-natured of her. He [the Prince] answered (and I'm afraid it is true; he knows her very well) that he would have sworn she would do so – that her aim was renewing with us. She did all she could to make D. marry her daughter in spite of us, and when that fail'd, after abusing us all like Pick pockets, she at once turns about and seems as much pleas'd at D.'s marrying into Sally's family because it is still a connection.[157]

This is interesting for several reasons. First it confirms that there was at least sensitivity, if not guilty feelings, about the part Duncannon had played in relation to Lady Elizabeth; second that, for once, the Prince of Wales read the Countess of Jersey like a book; and finally it emphasises a perhaps insecure Countess's desire to stay in with Georgiana Devonshire and her sister despite everything.

There is one more vignette to be related about the Earl's death, as told by Harryo Cavendish to her sister early in November:

> The Jersey family are all in town, furious that Mr Wyndham's riding about in the lightest and gayest colours he can find. They seem to think that Lady Ann has become the model of a patient resigned wife and when I think of that injured excellence in her blue Landau, I'm tempted to send him a pink coat with orange buttons.[158]

In other words, that in the family's eyes the Earl's son-in-law was failing in the respect due to the late Earl, even as they failed to recognise that his daughter now moved in a very fast set, details of which she hid from her family. As her sister Caroline said, 'Anne keeps her Affairs very secret, for she never tells me one word for the dinners and suppers or who she ever sees.'[159]

17

The Years of Scandals

Following her husband's death, the Dowager Countess of Jersey retreated into a period of mourning and, for a time, was rarely seen in Society.

At the same time her mantle of leadership in Society would progressively pass to her son and his attractive, vivacious and charismatic wife, Sally (or Sarah), the new Countess of Jersey. It was Sarah who would become the centre of attention and was to then rule Society for many years to come. Known universally as 'Silence' because of her loquacity, she is said by some to have been acutely sensitive of her mother-in-law's reputation. For all that, she was no saint – as we shall see.

Nevertheless, the Dowager Countess had by no means left the stage. What is more, the years to come were to present her and her family with some great challenges and some great scandals.

Nor had she lost her charms and attraction to young men or her strength of will. Following her husband's death, she had moved out of the house in Berkeley Square into one in the neighbouring Charles Street.[1] Harryo Cavendish told of her activities there at the end of December 1805: 'Little Delmé in high feather and full of the Dow. Lady Jersey, who in the solitude of London in December, cultivates him and Frederick Byng and has them always with her.'[2]

Frederick Byng was Viscount Torrington's son who, in 1805, was a mere twenty-one years old. Delmé was the son of Peter Delmé, known as Peter the Czar because of his great wealth, which he and his wife, the sister of Frances Jersey's former lover the Earl of Carlisle, much reduced at the gaming tables before he shot himself in April 1789. 'Little Delmé' was not much older than Byng.[3]

As to the Countess's willpower, Harriet Bessborough tells of the summons she received just an hour after Duncannon had left for Roehampton following his marriage to Lady Maria Fane in November:

> The Dowr. Ly. Jersey insisted on my going there the moment the marriage was over; she made such a point of it I was oblig'd to comply. I drew

> my shawl close to hide my favour, but she pull'd it open, on which Ly. A Windham chose to go into hysterics; *je ne savois quel contenance tenir*.[4]

The 'favour' was presumably some token for Duncannon's marriage to Lady Maria, and one imagines Lady Anne's hysterics were prompted by this on account of the travails that Lady Elizabeth had endured following Duncannon's jilting of her.

But there seems more than willpower involved here. It very much looks as if Lady Jersey wanted to see the favour and to provoke a drama. She had earlier abused the Bessboroughs about Duncannon's actions. Was this another attempt to discomfort them? It looks to be a very deliberate attempt to make a point, before moving on.

For the main, though, the Countess was invisible in 1806. Apart from a single attendance at the Queen's Drawing-Room on 15 May there is no mention of her at any entertainments. Nor even is there any record of her response to the death of her one-time bosom friend, Georgiana Devonshire, on 30 March.[5]

All this changed in 1807 when, once more, she began to appear regularly in Society. This was not welcomed by everybody. Countess Spencer, who was contemplating going to Tunbridge Wells for the summer, wrote to Harriet Bessborough in May: 'There are not many people I wish to avoid, but there are a few, the Prince is one, & the Dowr Lady Jersey another. Let me know if they are likely to be there the end of June or beginning of July.'[6]

Later that year, in a more philosophical frame of mind, Lady Spencer discussed the failings of Society in its treatment – that is, acceptance – of some of its more notorious members and the possibility that Society should have excluded them, with much personal benefit. The company in which Lady Spencer places Frances Jersey is telling indeed:

> Had the exclusion been confined to Dev[onshire] H[ouse] alone, my dear Harriet I should have been sorry, but when one considers that the too frequent admission of the Dowr Ly Jersey, Ly Holland, Ly Hamilton, Mrs Fox, your poor cousin, Mrs Bouvery, Mr Fawkener & others into all companys, we must acknowledge there is great merit in the uniform steadiness that has been able to enclude [presumably she means 'exclude'] them all, & to set an example much wanted & which if it was followed might perhaps produce a greater change in the manners of the times than any other single circumstance could do, I am the more ready to acknowledge the propriety of this behaviour as my conscience is most cruelly sore upon this subject. who knows, if I had had more firmness, how much it might have operated upon your dear sister's conduct & your own, & what bitter regrets it may have saved us all.[7]

Given the sexual indiscretions of both her daughters, this was a bit rich on the part of the Countess. In addition to various rumoured affairs, Georgiana

Devonshire had a brief affair with the Duke of Dorset, and her long and acknowledged affair with Earl Grey resulted both in a temporary banishment abroad and in a daughter. Harriet Bessborough's peccadilloes, in addition to her affairs with Charles Wyndham and, over the long term, with Lord Granville, included being caught in flagrante delicto in 1789 with Richard Brinsley Sheridan.[8] It was not even as if the sisters were discreet in the conduct of their affairs. As Lady Mary Coke said at the time of Harriet's affair with Sheridan, 'I am sorry to say that Lady Duncannon is now as much talked of for Mr Sheridan as she ever was for Charles Wyndham.'[9]

Even so, Frances Jersey would have derided Countess Spencer's sanctimony had she known about it. She would have been much more wounded by other views of her in Society, as Lady Lyttleton, writing from Brighton, described:

> [Lady Jersey] is here undergoing that most painful operation, the loss of all the admiration, attention and flattery which used to surround her. Indeed she has undergone it, being sixty years old – but she's still very beautiful, very full of affectation and coquetterie, and nothing can persuade her that she is more than thirty, which is rather ridiculous.[10]

Following his father's death William Augustus was also losing former advantages. In this case paternal guidance and authority, whose loss was compounded by an indulgent and adoring mother, and his career was falling into disarray and ultimately disrepute.

Having enlisted into the 7th Regiment of Light Dragoons in 1797 as a cornet, he had gradually risen through promotion to be, by 1806, a major in that regiment serving under his brother-in-law, Major-General Henry, Lord Paget.[11] Thereafter, things seem to have fallen apart.

In January 1806, William Augustus (who with the King's consent had in 1802 changed his name to 'Mansel, pursuant to the last will and testament of Louisa Barbara, late Baroness Vernon, deceased'[12]) resigned from the 7th Light Dragoons.[13] Quite why he did this is unclear although there may be some connection with the fact that 'early in 1806 [the regiment] embarked for Ireland', a troubled province where they were to remain for more than four years.[14]

Things then took a bizarre turn. In the summer of 1806 *The London Gazette* reported that he had purchased a cornetcy, the lowest rank of officer and a very considerable demotion from major, in the 25th Regiment of Light Dragoon Guards.[15]

Some amends were made a few months later when he transferred, also by purchase, to be a lieutenant in the 21st Regiment of Light Dragoon Guards.[16] If that was not enough, *The London Gazette* records in May 1807 that 'Lt Honourable W Villiers Mansell, [transferred] from the 21st Light Dragoon Guards, to the 9th Regiment of Light Dragoon guards, to be Lieutenant.'[17]

What lay behind these manoeuvrings is unclear. Such evidence as exists suggests that William Augustus was getting into bad habits and bad company, as well as not wanting to serve abroad. His move to the 9th Light Dragoon

Guards was, however, the end of his career in the Army. In August 1808 he 'became non-effective' by reason of resignation from the 9th Light Dragoons and was never again to appear in the Army List.[18]

The explanation, beyond the absence of paternal authority, may lie in some correspondence from Georgiana Devonshire to her daughter 'Little G' some time in 1805. In the first of these letters she wrote:

> The Jerseys are in great trouble about young Mansel – with some noble qualities such as having given his 2 unmarried sisters 5,000 each, after Lord Vernon's death He seems in some things (now that by his Father's death he has no control) to be like [illegible] – he drinks drams in the morning has quitted the army – gone into the navy at 25. He went in a sailors jacket quite drunk to the play & made a great riot.[19]

In a subsequent letter Georgiana Devonshire wrote:

> I saw Ly Jersey yesterday – she is very much out of spirits and so is Ld Villiers in a coup de tete of young Mansell. he is grown tired of the Army & has got into bad naval connections at Ipswich. He is therefor going to sell out and at 25 to commence midshipman.[20]

The idea in those times, when midshipmen were typically in their early teens, of a twenty-five-year-old midshipman was beyond belief. William Augustus was clearly becoming a wastrel, albeit a generous one, and an individual trapped in a sad situation.

Thereafter there is virtually nothing more to be heard of him until, in 1813, he came into his very substantial inheritance of the Briton Ferry estate. It seems that before that time he had been banished, probably to Canada, in disgrace.[21] It was there, in Pictou, Nova Scotia, that very soon after coming into his inheritance he died, unmarried, on 3 January 1814.[22]

What the Countess made of this is only to be imagined. References to William Augustus in the family correspondence are rare, but such as there are suggest a particularly deep affection was felt by the Countess for her younger son, perhaps brought on by his sickly youth, whom she referred to in a letter to Edward Jerninghan as 'my angel Augustus'.[23] One suspects she indulged him and was greatly saddened by his banishment.

It seems that Frances Jersey also had difficulties in these years with the new Countess of Jersey. Sally Jersey was a forceful and domineering character who was used to getting her own way.[24] It was therefore inevitable that there should be a falling out between her and her mother-in-law. The difficulties between the two headstrong women seem to have gone much wider and to extend to real friction between her and her husband's sisters as well. In a touching letter that Sally wrote to her husband in July 1807, when pregnant and against the eventuality of dying in childbirth, she wrote: 'Tell your Mother & Sisters how I loved them how I wish [to be their friend?] & how much their [treating?] me as a stranger hurt me & offended me.'[25]

Similarly, when meeting Lady Anne the following year, Sally wrote: 'I dined with Ly Anne ... who was *very triste* I was quite hurt.'[26]

Clearly the worst offender was the Dowager Countess, of whom Sally complained crushingly at the same time: 'Yr Mother I do not speak of, she is past remarks'[27] – and indeed she must have been a dreadful mother-in-law, autocratic and interfering, but Sally's complaints were not limited to her or even to her and Lady Anne. In another letter to her husband at about this time, she wrote: 'the persecution the cruelty your Mother & Sister have pursued towards me. I forgive them all the little [horrors?] they have occasioned me but let not my Children suffer from their selfishness & indifference as I have done.'[28]

The result seems to have been a real anger between the Earl and another of his sisters, Caroline Paget. However, in August 1808 Caroline and her brother resolved their differences, as Caroline described to her brother in law Sir Arthur Paget:

> I must tell you that Villiers and I are reconciled. He said so he could not bear to see me so altered to him &c &c &c & a thousand things that were kind & as he used to be & and at the same time denied all the things which Ly J had ever said, & expected me to believe him which I could not but promised [*sic*] for his sake I would forget it all that he & I might live on good terms ... I would not instantly change my opinion about her but that I can never do for I know her too well.

So it seems that Frances Jersey had been making mischief by telling tales of her son, and possibly her daughter-in-law, to Caroline, so increasing the animosity between them perhaps as part of a spiteful campaign against Sally Jersey. However amongst the good news of reconciliation there was also bad news, as Lady Caroline went on: 'I am sorry to say Charlotte continues very ill ...'

Lady William Russell, the eldest of the Countess's children, was in Worthing, where as Caroline described:

> She is scarcely able to sit up when her bed is made, the Dr has been here for 2 days, but she did not see him. I do not feel happy about her, I found her so much worse when I came back [from a Ball at the Pavilion in Brighton, where she had also seen her brother], and she is weaker every day'.[29]

It was probably of Lady William that Samuel Rogers was writing in a letter, which is clearly misdated to October of that year: 'I have dined twice with Lady Jersey, whose daughter is still lingering, very cheerful, but with no chance of recovery. Every evening she flatters herself that her feverish fit will not come on, and then it comes. She does not leave her room.'[30]

Lady William's health was degenerating fast. On 27 August her brother left Osterley to visit her in Worthing where she was reported to be dangerously ill.[31] She died there on 31 August 1808 aged thirty-seven.[32]

Perhaps Sally Jersey's relations with her mother-in-law had not been helped by her clearly having difficulty in providing her husband with an heir. In the autumn of 1805, Harryo Cavendish had written to her sister: 'I hear Lady Boringdon [Sally Jersey's sister Augusta] is with child. Lady V[illiers] burst into tears when she heard it and coloured like fire when mama asked about it.'[33]

A few days later Harryo Cavendish described Sally as looking

> so very ill that it was quite melancholy to see her. She is quite a skeleton, pale as death and seems dreadfully out of sorts. Lady Harriet [Villiers] was with her with the Jersey complexion and arrived *comme une bombe*, looking beautiful. She is very amiable. Lady Aberdeen sat by Lady Jersey at the table where I was. They seemed great friends but she talked very little and seemed so very melancholy, it made me quite unhappy. I think it must be sorrow not to be with child, and I do pity her from my heart.[34]

Eventually, marking one of the happier events amidst some difficult years for the Jersey family, on 4 April 1808 a son and heir to the 5th Earl of Jersey and his Countess was born: George Augustus Frederic.[35]

With an irony that will become apparent later, in May 1808 that same Lady Boringdon deserted her husband and ran off with Sir Arthur Paget, whom following her divorce she was later to marry.[36] As a sign of things to come, Caroline Paget made a very obvious statement by visiting the now socially outcast Augusta Boringdon in September of that year in the company of her dead sister's lover. As Lady Caroline Lamb described: 'Lady [Caroline] Paget's fate I fear is not a happy prospect; she has been always well spoken of hitherto I believe, but was certainly injudicious in her husband's absence in going from her sister's death bed with the Duke of A[rgyll] to Lady Boringdon.'[37]

As it happened, fate was to deal Lady Paget a greater blow, and put her in a better light, than being tainted by association with Augusta Boringdon. The company she chose when visiting Augusta was to prove, too, a sign of that future.

For a time it seemed that the happier events surrounding the family would also include the marriage of the jilted Lady Elizabeth. In November 1806 Harryo Cavendish had written to her sister that she had been told by Kitty Monck that 'Lady Elizabeth Villiers [is going to be married] to Mr Irby "by the force of passion driven". If this is so, and Kitty declares her authority is excellent, the capability of those Lady Villiers have in falling in love is extraordinary, considering the objects.'[38]

Harriet Bessborough had heard the same story.[39] Sadly it proved unfounded, and it was another year before Lady Elizabeth and marriage were once more spoken of in the same breath. Then in December 1807 her suitor was the same Little Delmé who two years earlier had been paying court to her mother. As Harryo Cavendish told her sister: 'Mr Delmé is going in a week to Mr Bailey's [presumably the husband of Lady Sarah Bayly], where he will find his last flame, Lady Elizabeth Villiers, and from thence to Bath.'[40]

A little later, Harryo updated her sister with the news of Delmé's rejection and the umbrage he was taking:

> Little Delmé I find proposed to Lady E. Villiers before he left town, but unlike his patient adherence to Caro [Caroline St Jules, the natural daughter of the Duke of Devonshire and Lady Elizabeth Foster] after her refusal, he resents this last with all his little might and will not go near her or her mother.[41]

One marriage which did come to pass despite these ambivalences was that of Frances Jersey's youngest daughter, Lady Harriet, to Richard Bagot in December 1806.

Richard Bagot, known as 'Dandy Dick', was the youngest son of the 1st Lord Bagot.[42] Destined for the church, he was described by Glenbervie a few years earlier as a cockscomb 'in dress and manner to a degree of affectation, bringing to one's mind those characters in the age before our time who used to have the term beau affixed to their names'.[43] He was despite that to prove a good husband to Lady Harriet and to be the father of twelve children as well as an eminent churchman becoming, in due course, Bishop of Oxford and later Bishop of Bath and Wells.[44]

The Morning Chronicle described Lady Harriet's wedding dress and the excitement it caused on the morning of her marriage on Sunday, 21 December 1806. The dress, it wrote:

> was a most superlative elegant wedding suit ... composed of the finest India muslin that can possibly be procured, trimmed with the richest lace, and so tastefully ornamented, that it may be considered as a perfect model for the fashionable world ... [It was being taken on Sunday morning at 1.30 by a Mrs Fitzgerald to Lady Jersey's house from a dressmaker favoured by Lady Jersey, Mrs Sowerby's in New Bond Street] when she was stopped in Berkeley-square by two ruffians with intent to rob her ... She refused to surrender her valuable charge, and ... continued to struggle with the villains until some persons were heard coming up ... The robbers then ran off.[45]

The dress was, of course, only part of Harriet's trousseau. There is a bundle of receipts and bills found at Osterley in 1925 that provide a fascinating insight into the manners of the time. There is a large bill for £381–15–11½ (that is 381 pounds, 15 shillings and 11½ pence), annotated 'Mrs Sowerby's Bill for Harriet', which bears another note saying 'This bill is correct F Jersey March 6, 1807'.

The receipt for payment of the bill does not mention the halfpenny!

Other bills include a perfumer's bill of £14-6–0 for a pot of almond paste and bottles of essence of rose and of jasmine, another for £4-18-0 for four ivory hair brushes and bills for two tortoiseshell combs and five ivory ones. The bill for three hats, a 'fine white cap', a 'diamond straw hat' and a 'Dunstable Cottage Bont', is for £4–14–4, whilst that for 'two long stays' was

£3–12–0 and the one for 'making & marking 36 fine pocket handkerchiefs' was £1–4–0. The bill for no less than 25 pairs of shoes was £13.

In total the milliner's bill alone amounted to £234–4–9½.[46]

The Morning Chronicle reported on the wedding the following day:

> Her Ladyship was, at half after two yesterday, married to the Honourable and Rev R Bagot, in the presence of her mother, brother, and some other friends, at her mother's house in Charles-street, Berkeley–square. The marriage ceremony was performed by the Right Reverend Bishop of Exeter. After it was over the happy couple set off to spend the honey–moon at Osterley Park, the seat of Earl of Jersey, brother to the lovely bride.[47]

The difficult years for the Jerseys then continued, and in 1809 they faced two scandals. The first it seems was never picked up by the press. The second dominated it for months.

The first concerned Lord William Russell. The financial difficulties which for years he had struggled with came to a head. He was bankrupt. The first sign of this was a letter Caroline Paget (known to her friends as Car) wrote to Sir Arthur Paget, to whom she was very close, on 31 March 1809. In this she said she needed to see him to seek his advice on 'a subject I can scarcely [illegible] to write ... & hope that I can be sure you will not mention this letter to *anybody*'.[48] A week later she wrote again to Sir Arthur: 'I have a letter ... From Ld Wm confessing all that he hinted to me the other day which I believe I told you & from the state of which he is obliged to leave his children.'[49]

Bankruptcy in the early nineteenth century was a serious matter and a serious disgrace; the choice was between others bailing you out, flight, and the debtors' prison. The widowed Lord William, or rather his brother the Duke of Bedford, chose flight, with the result that his children needed to be entrusted to the care of other members of the family. As Car Paget related some time later:

> Ld William came yesterday ... and leaves this evening; he's going to Scotland immediately, and he says *for ever* which is to him in some respects worse than death ... I cannot forgive his brother consenting to his banishment. It is decided [in relation to Lord William's children] that Gertrude and Frances should live with the Duchess [of Bedford], William with Lady Jersey [that is Sally] and Eliza with me. She is now at Woburn and I am to have her when I like. My excuse to Mama by no means satisfied her, for, unless I *particularly wish to be alone* with Ld Wm, she had not the least objection to meet him, she tells me, and that I must fix a day, which I shall not do till I hear from you ...
>
> Car.
>
> You are very good about Mama; she is certainly pleasanter with company, but it is hardly fair on you.[50]

So it seems that Frances Jersey wanted to visit Car Paget. Her daughter – even though as we will soon see she had problems of her own – did not welcome that, and was using Lord William's disgrace as an excuse not to see her. Sir Arthur, on the other hand, was happy to come at the same time as the Countess, who it seems was less demanding and less over-bearing when there was company than when she was alone with her daughter. We shall see that Caroline was not alone amongst the Countess's children in seeking to avoid their mother's company in the years to come.

Nor were any of Lord William's children, who following his flight needed to be farmed out amongst the family, entrusted to the care of their maternal grandmother – although her age, as much as her reputation, could account for that.

Lord William's flight to Scotland was presumably because Holyrood Palace was then a sanctuary against debts. He was to remain in Scotland for some time, and it was probably from there he wrote a rather poignant letter, from 'Wood-end Cottage', to Lady Holland later in the year:

> I have myself received letters from my Boys of the same date, but still it has been a further gratification to me to hear from you of their being so well spoken of – they seem highly pleased with their situation – Captain Stuart is very good to them and they talk with much delight of the kindness they experience from Lord and Lady Amherst.[51]

On which note, Lord William Russell leaves this story. In due course, he was to return to England. An increasingly sad and eccentric figure, he spent much of his remaining years abroad; ultimately he was to die in his bed, his throat cut by his valet.[52]

The second, and much larger, scandal involved Car Paget herself. Hers was not an easy marriage. In January 1808 her brother-in-law, Charles Paget, was describing her as 'poor dear excellent Car, with as much or more reason to complain than ever'.[53] Even so, when in early 1809 her husband was serving in Spain under Sir John Moore, fighting Napoleon's forces in the Peninsular War – the news not good – she wrote to Sir Arthur in January 1809:

> I wrote to P[aget] soon after I arrived here [at Beau Desert, the Earl of Uxbridge's seat] with the Children's letters. I feel very anxious for the next accounts from Spain, indeed all my thoughts are *horrid*.[54]

She need not have worried, for Paget's well-being at least, since he returned to England safely on 20 January 1809.[55] What she could not foresee were the dramatic events that would shortly follow. At the beginning of March, Paget abruptly left her and eloped with Lady Charlotte Wellesley, the wife of the future Duke of Wellington's youngest brother, Henry. The news caused uproar in the press and in Society. As Harryo Cavendish wrote to her brother Lord Hartington on 8 March:

> London is full of impenetrable fog and horror at Lord Paget's elopement – he went off the day before yesterday with Lady Charlotte Wellesley. It is

> in every way shocking and unaccountable. He has left his beautiful wife and 8 or 9 children and she a husband she married about 5 years ago, for love, and is quite a Héro de Romance in person and manner, with 4 poor little children. He left a letter for [his father] Lord Uxbridge saying he had great esteem and affection for Lady Paget but could not resist taking the step he has done ... I believe Lady Paget is a very great fool though do not imagine that I mean that or anything as an excuse for him – I think him inexcusable and detestable.
>
> How the White Hart will ring with my aunt Spencer's comments on this event and how dearest Douaire Zara and Sarah will mourn over the world and its enormities.[56]

Paget had, so Harryo wrote in a letter to her brother the following day, been 'long irresistibly attached to Lady Charlotte' and could not resist doing what he had done, when 'Henry Wellesley made some discoveries the day before she went off – very high words passed between them and he told her that either she or him must leave the house. The next morning, before anybody was up, she walked out ... and drove to Lord Paget's home,' from whence they eloped.[57]

London rang with the news and rumours abounded. One rumour, untrue, reported in *The Times* claimed that the fugitives were pursued by Sir Arthur Wellesley (as Wellington then was) himself and captured near Uxbridge. This was followed, so the story went, by a duel between Sir Arthur and Lord Paget which resulted in the latter being fatally wounded.[58]

Nevertheless, even before he eloped Lord Paget had doubts in his mind about his wife. He had gone so far as 'to speak to Car most distinctly upon the subject of *her* future' and questioned her as to whether there was an attachment between her and the Marquess of Lorne (or the Duke of Argyll as he now was) with whom she had visited Augusta Boringdon. In her turn, she solemnly vowed to his brother Charles Paget that there was 'nothing to create the slightest fear in our minds as to any understanding between herself and Lorne. She owned the greatest friendship and regard for him (two dangerous feelings to cherish) but no more.' Nevertheless the relationship had not only been noticed by Paget but also had 'already begun to gain some observation in the world', where Car's name was already linked with the Marquess of Lorne's.[59]

In short, Society saw an affair between the pair.

In the days immediately following Paget's elopement there were various attempts at reconciliation and to persuade Lady Charlotte Wellesley, for the sake of the children, to return to her husband and break off all correspondence with Lord Paget. These all failed.[60]

There were reports, too, that Paget had resigned all his regimental and staff appointments. This went down well with public opinion which, despite all, saw a 'feeling of respect for public decorum' entitling him to lenient consideration.[61]

So that she could get away from all the drama, in mid-March Car went to stay in a cottage outside London belonging to Lord Kinnaird.[62]

Summarising public opinion at the time, Lady Williams Wynn wrote:

> What a misfortune to his family that he [Paget] did not find in Spain the Tomb of honour which they say he so eagerly sought. For his companion in disgrace we must in charity remember the heavy degree of insanity which prevails throughout her family, but it is indeed horrible & alarming to see how these instances of depravity multiply upon us.[63]

With perhaps more sympathy, Harryo Cavendish wrote to Hartington on 16 March:

> Lady Paget is in great distress but I fancy his conduct to her has for a long time been inexcusable. He has written to Lord Uxbridge to say that hers has always been irreproachable and that her encouragement of Sir Arthur and Lady Boringdon, for which she has been so much blamed, was in obedience to his express command. You should hear Miss Berry upon the subject – "oh that is a pretty story, a very pretty story. Lady Charlotte leaves 4 children, the youngest 4 months old and just weaned, oh, but it is a pretty story. Lord Paget devotes himself to ruin and disgrace and for what a strapping lass I would hardly hire for my kitchen maid."'[64]

Meanwhile, despite her travails, Caroline Paget was writing to her brother-in-law Sir Arthur on 17 March to congratulate him on the birth of a daughter by his wife, the former Lady Boringdon:

> From my heart … warmest congratulations on dear Augusta's being now safer … I know what you have suffered … I shall ever regret not having been able to be a comfort to you [by being with you].

The letter bears a postscript signed by 'A Wyndham' sending her best wishes to Lady Augusta.[65]

A day later Car was again writing to Sir Arthur and, after saying she could not go to him to support him and Lady Augusta because she could not leave her children since 'all my 4 little children are dependent on me alone', she commented, 'I must wait patiently to submit my fate, I think it hard one – & confess I find … miserable.'[66]

Car was not alone in writing to Sir Arthur. On 20 March Frances Jersey wrote also to him, as ever putting sentiment before convention:

> My Dr Arthur
>
> I know you are plagued with letters yet I must tell you how happy I am that Augusta is well & that you have a little girl. If it is not the most beautiful arrival in the world it is much to blame – pray give a thousand loves to Ly Augusta Paget, and Miss Paget, and believe me ever affec yours.
>
> F J.[67]

Writing towards the end of the month, the *Hampshire Telegraph* reported the state of affairs:

> Lord Paget has made his appearance in town, in good health ... His Lordship, in his letters, expresses the most poignant sorrow and sincere contrition from his offence. Lady Paget kept her bed for two days after his Lordship's elopement, and has not left her house in Upper Brook-street since the event. The Countess of Uxbridge sleeps at home, in old Burlington Street, but spends the rest of her time with her Ladyship.[68]

Soon after, for the time being at least, other scandals took over the public's attention. As Sarah Spencer, Lady Lyttleton wrote: 'Everybody was scandalized as they ought to be with the dreadful *esclandre* of Lord Paget and Lady Charlotte Wellesley; but everybody has almost forgotten it, as it happened a good ten days ago.' The attention, as she understood from reports from London, of everyone was now on a new scandal, one involving the Duke of York, a younger brother of the Prince of Wales, and his mistress Mrs Clarke.[69]

On 21 March, the Duke of Argyll paid a visit on Car Paget, doubtless for not entirely altruistic reasons. He reported to Arthur Paget: 'I have today seen poor Ly P she is better than I have [illegible] hoped ... I wrote a note to P[aget] offering to be of any use ... and received a kind one in return for ... What insanity.'[70]

Indeed, and what hypocrisy on his part.

The support which Car had provided to Sir Arthur following his elopement was reciprocated, and in her troubles Sir Arthur Paget was a friend indeed. Car wrote to him on 2 April thanking him and saying, '[I] hate myself for not having thanked you as I ought for the kindness you have [shown?] to me ... I can never forget it & however it may end my gratitude to you will be eternal.'[71]

With that everything went quiet. Lady Charlotte and Lord Paget apparently retired for the time being to Devon and for two months nothing more was heard of the affair.[72]

Then, in May, there was talk of reconciliation between Lord and Lady Paget – not without some angry misunderstanding. On 12 May, Paget was writing to Sir Arthur that:

> You must be too well aware of the wavering & unsteady conduct of Lady Paget previous to this last communication ... imagine that I could be in the least surprised at what is now occurred. But what seems totally to have escaped your memory is, the conversation that took place between us, when you announced her acquiescence in my terms namely that I shd return home without any stipulation whatsoever – Let me remind you of it. I said 'Arthur, Lady Paget [illegible]'. You answered (and it was not my ears alone that heard it) *'Paget, you do her injustice, she will be too happy to see you again'*.

> It would indeed have required courage ... to accede to the terms now after I have been infamously treated & my feelings trifled with ...
>
> Here I drop the subject.[73]

The end result was recorded by Farington in his diary on 26 May:

> It was stated [at a dinner party he had gone to] that Lord Paget has returned to His Wife & family, but [said] he would not do it on any compromise. His motive, He said, for returning was on acct of His Children, but he would visit Lady Charlotte Wellesley whenever he pleased. She is at Brompton. She had been remarked for great levity of manner before she was married.[74]

And so it seemed that Paget 'had been persuaded by his brothers to agree to an arrangement whereby he became, at any rate in the eyes of the world, reconciled to Car ... [and] on 17 May Paget returned to his wife and children in Brook Street and the next day set off with them for Beaudesert'.[75]

In the meantime, there had been other developments. Henry Wellesley had sued Lord Paget for criminal conversation. As *The Times* reported on 13 May, the previous day judgment was given in the Sheriff's Court, in an undefended action, against Lord Paget and had awarded Wellesley £20,000 in damages.[76] Then, on 16 May, *The Morning Chronicle* published an exchange of letters between Lord Paget and Lady Charlotte's brother, Col Cadogan, in which the colonel had challenged Lord Paget to a duel in justification of his sister's honour. Lord Paget's response, however, was to refuse to fight, saying: 'It distresses me beyond all description to refuse you that satisfaction which I am most ready to admit you have a right to demand; but, upon the most mature reflection, I have determined upon the propriety of this line of conduct.'

In doing so he also acknowledged that there was no justification for his conduct, but explained that, because by his actions he had ruined Lady Charlotte, his life was hers and not his own. In this, Lord Paget was without doubt acting with honour.[77]

This all was to change whilst he was in Devon with Lady Charlotte. He there received a further challenge from Col Cadogan which, this time, he accepted. The meeting took place at 7.00 a.m. on 30 May on Wimbledon Common. The following day's *The Morning Chronicle* described what happened:

> The ground having been taken at 12 paces distance, they were directed to fire together ... Cadogan fired, Lord Paget's flashed – this having been decided to go for a fire, a question arose, whether Lord Paget had taken aim as intending to hit his antagonist. Both the seconds being clearly of opinion that this was not his intention.

As a result the seconds would not allow proceedings to continue, to which Lord Paget responded: 'As such is your determination, I have no hesitation in saying that nothing could ever have induced me to add to the Injuries I have already done the family, by firing at the brother of Lady Charlotte Wellesley.' The parties then left the ground.[78]

Paget was now desperate to get abroad again in some military capacity. On 18 July he was successful and left London, embarking the next day on HMS *The Revenge*, commanded by another of his brothers, to take part in the Walcheren campaign in the Low Countries. This expedition was to fail most miserably but at least it meant that Paget was out of the country until the first week of September.[79] For the four months following his return he lived, or so it seemed at least, under the same roof as Car, spending much of his time at Beaudesert in Staffordshire and in London.[80]

After this the charade of reconciliation with his wife rapidly fell apart and collusion took over. In early 1810 Henry Wellesley finally divorced his wife, and in April Car commenced proceedings to divorce Paget. At the time, although a husband could obtain a divorce on the ground of his wife's adultery, it was not possible under English law for a wife to divorce her husband for the same reason. It was, however, possible to do so under Scottish law even if the adultery did not take place in Scotland, but to do that the parties had to reside in Scotland for forty days. To comply with this requirement and enable Car to get a Scottish divorce, Paget and Lady Charlotte took a house in Perthshire around April 1810; Car's proceedings in Scotland for divorce were begun in October.

There were two additional problems. Both parties to the divorce had to swear that there was no connivance, which there clearly was. This problem was overcome by something akin to perjury, for everybody now knew that Car was in effect engaged to the Duke of Argyll. The second difficulty presented was that the law did not permit the guilty divorced husband to marry the woman with whom he had committed adultery, which clearly Paget wanted to do. As a result it was necessary to manufacture circumstances where Paget was detected in bed with someone other than Lady Charlotte. This was done by persuading chambermaids and others to swear that they did not know the identity of the woman they saw in bed with Paget.

Despite, or perhaps because of, all of this the Scottish courts granted Car a divorce from Paget in October 1810 and on 29 November she married the Duke of Argyll, her dead sister's long-term lover. Before the end of the year Paget had married Lady Charlotte.[81]

Car may have declared before her wedding that her good fortune was so great 'that till the business was absolutely over, she should not be able to believe it', but in Scotland, and indeed elsewhere, the whole proceedings were looked at in a rather different light.[82]

Of them, Glenbervie wrote in his diary:

> The scandalous plan which is said to have been concerted between [Lord Paget and Lady Charlotte Wellesley] and Lady Paget and the Duke of Argyll ... Lady C has been divorced from Mr Wellesley by Act for crim con with Lord Paget but he is still married so can't wed. Lady P to get a divorce from him in Scotland so as to marry Argyll but under Scots law two guilty

> parties can't marry so ... the concert therefore between the four is that Lord Paget shall, by connivance, be detected by Lady Paget or witnesses appointed for that purpose in bed with someone hired for the occasion which will then enable all of them to get married when proof of any new act of adultery on Lady Paget's part would not answer the case.[83]

Indeed, the whole arrangement was very doubtful – so doubtful that there were concerns not only as to its legality but also whether the Duke's title would be able validly to pass to any son under the marriage. Perhaps fortunately in the circumstances the marriage never produced a son so that the issue never had to be tested.

Certainly the divorces and the remarriages provoked varying responses, from the droll, through the disbelieving, to the downright disapproving.

Lord Holland fell in the first category, writing to Richard Fitzpatrick in September about the various suits in Scotland, which 'it is confidently reported are to end in Ld Paget marrying Ldy Charlotte & D of Argyle Ldy Paget – it will be comical enough if a trip to Scotland so often resorted to for the purpose of making a marriage [at Gretna Green] should be found equally efficacious for undoing it.'[84]

Lady Bessborough's version of events claimed that Lord Paget had fled to Scotland under an assumed name with an unnamed lady who wore a black veil at all times, even in bed. His wife tracked him down and served a writ on him and sued for a divorce, then promptly marrying the Duke of Argyll with Lord Paget marrying Lady Charlotte Cadogan.[85]

Writing in November, Lady Jerningham had it that:

> You will perhaps have heard that Lady Paget is positively to be married to the Duke of Argyle. She was to set off yesterday for Scotland with Lady Charlotte Campbell, and the Duke will receive them. It is a very odd affair and Lord Paget will not admire meeting his quondam wife with a higher Rank of Duchess and an obsequious Husband. For He has always treated her with the most shameful Contempt, and now He must be a little more Careful in his expressions. At the same time it is in fact a most irregular proceeding.[86]

Whilst Lord Auckland wrote: 'They write from Scotland (I suppose not seriously) that the Duke and Duchess of Argyll have invited Lord and Lady Paget to pass the honeymoon altogether at Inverary,' the Duke's seat in Scotland.[87]

The disapproval, too, was fierce. Mrs Grant, a clearly dour Edinburgh lady, wrote in October:

> You can not think how fiercely the popular indignation burns against Lord and Lady —— for contaminating our Highland glens – the seat of pure unviolated conjugal faith – with their residence of six weeks in order to obtain a divorce.[88]

Dr Hall, the Dean of Christ Church, writing to Mrs Piozzi a few days later was equally blistering in his commentary: 'After living almost *openly* as even you know with Lady William Russell for many years, [the Duke of Argyll] will marry no one but *her sister* – the deserted Lady Paget whose husband is wild to wed his *own favourite* …' going on to describe the entire proceedings as an 'Enormity'.[89]

For all these reasons Mrs Piozzi summarised the marriage of Car to the Duke as 'Incest, Perjury and Sacrilege'[90] – which on two scores it certainly was and, on the third, came very close. But then, as we shall see, the Duke – and he was not alone in this amongst the Countess of Jersey's sons-in-law – had a penchant for sisters.

Lady Jersey, though, was much more positive and welcomed the outcome. Presumably knowing the plans being put in place for Car to marry the Duke of Argyll, she had written to Sir Arthur Paget earlier in the year to say:

> I must write to you, I am so happy about Car, I must vent myself, I know no one that feels just as I do upon the subject but yourself, & you must be the victim. Surely there is every reason to rejoice & I am not too sanguine when I think she will be more comfortable than ever. I am out of patience with those who croak & had more pleasure in pitying her than they have been seeing her happy & well … Eliz is certainly better has less Fever & more strength … I am teazed to death with what I think the absurdity of that world which always interests itself in an odious way about what does not concern it.[91]

She was fierce, too, in the defence of her daughter after the event, even in the face of disapproval from her elder son and his wife – again putting sentiment before convention. As Lord Paget wrote to Sir Arthur in May 1811:

> I saw Dwr Ly Jersey who was pretty good. Such a *tirade* upon her son & Daughter in Law. The latter in discussing the late marriages &c – after saying everything that was coarse added I am sure the Dss will *not* be received. Upon being told she actually was well received, She said – But I am certain she will not be admitted at Court, which opinion being also [corrected?] –She added – Well I am positive she cannot *walk at a Coronation*!!! That is worth something.[92]

There was one more complainant to be heard. Like his brother-in-law, John Ponsonby, the Duke of Argyll had some years earlier had an affair with the courtesan Harriette Wilson. When that came to an end, he had transferred his affections to Harriette's younger sister, Amy (also a courtesan), and she, according to Harriette Wilson's (rather unreliable) memoirs:

> Had long been led to believe, according to her own account that she was to become the legitimate wife [and her, as yet unborn, child the heir] of the Duke of Argyll. At last, when Amy was very near her confinement, Argyle … opened to her, with the utmost delicacy he was master of, the appalling fact

> that he was about to marry Lady [Paget] ... Amy had a hysterical fit, or was afflicted with sore eyes, I forget which; but I know that she was very bad.[93]

It was, of course, inevitable that Amy would be disappointed. So eventually was Car. The Argylls were fully received into Society but eventually, despite all they had gone through, they separated.

Lord Melbourne, Queen Victoria's first Prime Minister, had a take on this. As he explained to the Queen in 1838:

> The Duchess of Argyll was a fine woman ... but silly ... all the Pagets [her children by Lord Paget], the women, were excessively fond of their Mother, the Duchess of Argyll, and of the Duke too ... which was very odd ... as he couldn't bear her; I believe [said Lord Melbourne] he liked her when he married her; but he soon got tired of her and lived away from her.[94]

As a result, the Duke, needing a mistress for his house, sent for his natural daughter Catherine to fulfill that role. Catherine, who had been born in 1806, said of herself 'that her mother was the Countess of M., and this association is so far corroborated by the fact that there was a great deal of scandal about that Lady's connection with Lord Lorne (as he then was)'.[95]

For the time being, Frances Jersey was happy for her daughter's sake. And yet, whilst all this was playing out, she had also suffered another personal tragedy – just briefly hinted at. Within the space of eighteen months she was to lose a second daughter. Lady Elizabeth Villiers had clearly not been well, and although in her letter of early 1810 the Countess had said that Elizabeth was better, it was a short lived improvement in her health. On 28 March 1810, as *The Morning Chronicle* announced the following day:

> DIED
>
> Yesterday at her Mother's house, in Piccadilly, Lady Elizabeth Villiers.[96]

So at twenty-seven, and despite all her and her mother's efforts, the beautiful and flirtatious Lady Elizabeth Villiers died unmarried.

Fortunately other members of the family fared better.

Lady Sarah was enjoying the life of the wife of a sugar baron, as *The Morning Post* reported from Weymouth:

> The town has to boast more company than has been known for several seasons past; the arrivals of last week have nearly filled it, and Russell's Royal Hotel, notwithstanding the many improvements and additions it has undergone, Mr Bayly and Lady S Bayly occupy the best suit of apartments, and are living there with a degree of splendour equal to their fortune and rank – their equipage and retinue is in the first style of fashion.[97]

Whilst Lady Fanny, often reported to be mistreated by her husband Ponsonby, was standing up to him, with her mother's typical force of character, over the matter of the affair he was having with the same Harriette Wilson. This, according to Harriette, had started in 1806 and was terminated in 1809. There is conflicting evidence as to the precise dates – but not as to the reason for its coming to an end. That, according to Harriette, was because 'Mrs Fanny would have it so'.[98]

Writing of the letter of dismissal she received from Ponsonby, Harriette said:

> I remember little of the style or nature of the letter. Something I read about a discovery made by Lady Ponsonby, and a solemn engagement or promise extorted from him to see me only once more in which interview, he had intended to have explained and arranged everything; but could not.

According to her own testimony, Harriette refused Ponsonby's offer of a pension of £200 a year.[99]

Writing some years later to Byron, Harriette described how she felt about the ending of the affair, saying:

> Lord if you could only suffer for one single day the agony of mind I endured for more than two years after Ponsonby left me, because *Mrs Fanny* would have so, you would bless your stars and your good fortune, *blind*, *deaf* and *lame* at eighty-two.[100]

This may be true. Harriette always maintained that Ponsonby was the love of her life. Still, chagrin and jealousy are also possible reasons for her feelings, because soon afterwards Ponsonby began an involvement with Harriette's youngest sister, Sophia, a mere fourteen and just launched in her career as a courtesan. One of Harriette's biographers suggests that humiliation was the reason that no mention of this liaison appears anywhere in Harriette's memoirs.[101]

So Ponsonby's tastes extended not only to mother and daughter but also, like the Duke of Argyll's, to sisters.

18
The Final Mischiefs

Around 1810 the Dowager Countess of Jersey retired to the spa town of Cheltenham. This did not mean that she also retired from Society or that, in retrospect at least, she ceased to provoke comment and controversy. Indeed, history records that, borne out of a desire for revenge, over the next few years she deliberately and maliciously caused repeated trouble and embarrassment to the Prince of Wales and his family.

History has been unkind to Frances Jersey on this score. As we shall see, the mischiefs she is accused of were committed not by her but by her daughter-in-law Sally Jersey; history has failed to distinguish between the two Countesses of Jersey. It assumed that the lady with the reputation was the guilty one.

The younger Countess, Sally, was an extraordinary and forceful lady. Creevey, writing from Middleton, described her:

> Shall I tell you what Lady Jersey is like? She is like one of her numerous gold and silver dicky birds that are in all the shew rooms of this house. She begins to sing at eleven o'clock, and, with the interval of the hour she retires to rest, she sings till 12 at night without a moment's interruption. She changes her feathers for dinner, and her plumage both morng. and eveng. is the happiest and most beautiful I ever saw.[1]

With her black hair and perfect complexion she was indeed a handsome woman. Even in the 1830s, Balzac, who saw her at the opera in Paris, described her as the perfect type of English aristocratic beauty.[2]

With her wealth, beauty and force of character she was a queen of Society – as one of its Lady Patronesses, ruling the exclusive Almack's with a rod of iron, she famously once refused the Duke of Wellington admission. For some years she cordially disliked the Prince of Wales, and for all that was far from being a saint. She had numerous affairs over the years including, almost certainly, one with Palmerston, with her husband consistently refusing to fight in defence of her honour, saying that if he was to start doing so he would have to fight every gentleman in town.[3] As one of Palmerston's biographers has it:

> In view of the moral tone of society in Regency days, and the reputation of Palmerston and of the Lady Patronesses [of Almack's] there can be very little doubt as to the nature of [Palmerston's] relationship with Lady Jersey ... Although the popular tradition of the period represented English women as being virtuous, proud and unattainable ... this did not apply to Lady Jersey, Lady Cowper and Princess Lieven.[4]

Contemporary evidence supports this, with Creevey writing at the time that 'it was very current that, when Lady Cowper went abroad, Palmerston transferred his allegiance to Lady Jersey'.[5]

The newspapers also certainly credited Sally Jersey's infidelities. There is amongst the Jersey family manuscripts – one cannot help wondering why – an undated press cutting, annotated '1837', which reads as follows:

Things of Sport.

Most *sporting* things in couples go,
E'en those the head adorns;
As VANE and Jersey truly know –
From Partridges to *horns*. [6] *

For his part her loving husband reciprocated with at least one affair, this with Princess Borghese, Napoleon's sister.[7]

The entertainments of Cheltenham were, to Frances Jersey, doubtless less glamorous than those in London, even if the company was relatively smart. The *dejeuné a l'ambigu* given by Baron Pfeilitzer in Cheltenham in September 1810 does sound a little bit dull in comparison, even with its 'elegant cold collation, consisting of every rarity of the season, with the choicest wines' and the table being laid in the grounds for 120 guests.[8]

So Frances Jersey was regularly reported to be at entertainments in town, whether Lady Ossulton's 'elegant assemblage of Fashionables',[9] the Duchess of Devonshire's 'Music Party' with the concert beginning at 10 o'clock and supper at 2 a.m.,[10] or the Duchess of Montrose's ball 'of the most splendid description'.[11] About the only entertainment in London that the Countess was not invited to was the Prince of Wales' fête at Carlton House in honour of the King's birthday on 19 June 1811, to which, according to a censorious Farington, 'the number of invitations issued amounted to 3,000, and was indiscriminate, including persons of all descriptions as to Politics & manners ... [including] the Duke & Duchess of Argyle ... Thus are morals and principles disregarded.'[12]

But even if the 3,000 indiscriminate invitations included the disapproved-of Argylls, they did not apparently include the Dowager Countess of Jersey.

---

* That is the horns of a cuckolded husband.

Her son and daughter-in-law were there but Frances Jersey's name is not amongst the eighty-five other countesses and dowager countesses whom *The Morning Post* reported as being present.[13]

They did, on the other hand, include her daughter, Lady Anne Wyndham, who was now frequently to be seen as a guest of the Prince of Wales both in London and in Brighton. *The Morning Post* described Lady Anne's dress at the Prince's fête in the following terms:

> Rich white satin dress, lustered with small spangles, and bordered with silver net, sleeves of Honiton Brussels, looped up with diamonds, a long drapery of silver tissue, spangled over, and edged with silver fringes, fastened on the left shoulder with silver brilliants. Head–dress a superb plume of feathers with diamonds.[14]

It seems that the Prince made a habit of not inviting Frances Jersey to his fêtes in honour of the King's birthday, however many other people were invited. With that said, the Countess took her exclusion with a sense of humour if not a typical degree of hauteur. As John Cam Hobhouse (Lord Broughton) wrote of a similar occasion in 1814:

> Went in the evening to Lady Jersey's, where was a small party attended by those not invited to the Prince's fête – about twenty. Lord and Lady Holland, Duchess of Somerset, Mr and Mrs Rawdon, Lady Rancliffe, Mr and Mrs Tierney, Mr D Rouse and lastly [Beau] Brummel, who was received with a smile for repetition of *fades pleasanteries* on the occasion of their exclusion.[15]

The Countess, nevertheless, continued to perform her loyal duties in the light of George III's periodic attacks of insanity, and was recorded on two occasions late in 1810 as being, amongst many others, 'an inquirer at St James's Palace as to the state of the King's health'.[16]

She was too, along with a raft of high society, to be one of the subscribers to a letter in *The Morning Chronicle* early in January 1811 complaining about the increased cost of boxes at the opera. They clearly objected to the high-handed behaviour of the proprietors, writing:

> The undersigned Subscribers to the Opera considering the circular letter of Mr Taylor dated November 22, 1810, to be highly offensive and improper, and not believing the augmentation of the price of subscription to be necessary, have determined to resist such augmentation, and withdraw their patronage from Mr Taylor, unless he shall agree that all their Boxes shall be continued at the former Prices.[17]

We do not know if he did, although it is quite possible that he was forced to. Given the popularity of the theatre, the price of theatre tickets was a flashpoint for violence, with audiences hating any increases whatever the reason. Two years earlier, John Kemble, the manager of Covent Garden, came under vicious attack for raising prices following the rebuilding of the theatre after it was destroyed by fire. After more than two months of rioting, Kemble was forced to give in and restore his prices to their former level.[18]

At the end of the Season, the Countess returned to Cheltenham.[19] As *The Morning Post* of 6 May reported: 'That delightful and highly favoured spot, Cheltenham is resuming its wanted gaity; [the Countess of Jersey is amongst] a long list of Fashionables [who] grace the walks of a morning.'[20] And it was not just the walks that the Countess was gracing. It was the custom that productions at the theatre should be under the patronage of individual members of the beau monde. So on 23 May 1811 the *Cheltenham Chronicle* was reporting that the theatre had opened two days earlier under the auspices of the Countess of Buckinghamshire and that it was looking forward to the next performance which it understood was to be 'under the patronage of Lady Jersey, in whose walk through the circle of fashion we doubt not but she will select for the promotion of the drama, as great an assemblage of female loveliness as graced the boxes when the influence of the Countesss of Buckinghamshire was so successfully exercised'.[21] And indeed it was, as the same newspaper reported:

By Desire and under the Patronage of
The Right Honourable Countess of Jersey

Theatre Royal, Cheltenham
This Present Thursday, the 23 May
Will be performed Colman's comedy of
The Heir at Law
To which will be added the Farce of
Plot and Counterplot on the Portrait of Cervantes
to begin exactly at Seven o'clock
Places to be taken at the Box-office only,
Cambray Colonnade, and Tickets to
be had from 10 till 4 every day.[22]

None of which had prevented the Dowager going back to London, a few days earlier, to enjoy Mrs Calvert's 'very magnificent ball and supper ... in Mansfield-street ... [where] to complete this unrivalled entertainment, a dejeune of tea, coffee, chocolate, & c was provided'.[23]

There was, however, no mention of the Dowager being present at her daughter-in-law's Rout in Berkeley Square early in July. Doubtless Sally preferred, given her mother-in-law's character and the history of their relationship, to avoid inviting Frances Jersey to her parties although, to give her credit, the guest list on this occasion was only some 200 names.[24] Nevertheless, over the coming years, it was rare indeed for the Dowager's name to be amongst the reported guests at her daughter-in-law's numerous entertainments.

And then arrived the first intimations of mortality amongst her friends. On 2 August 1811 *The Morning Post* recorded the death of William Fawkener:

> Mr Fawkener's death was so sudden, that his servant had no knowledge of his indisposition when he went up at his usual time to dress him, and found that he had just expired.[25]

The following Tuesday, 6 August, it added:

> On Thursday the remains of the late William Fawkener, Esq were removed with great solemnity from his house, in the Circus, Bath, and interred on Saturday last in a vault prepared by himself in Kingsbury Church–yard. The Procession was joined, on Wilsdon Green, by the Earl of Orford [his relative Horace Walpole] and the intimate friends of the late Mr Fawkener.[26]

It is unlikely that Frances Jersey was one of those intimate friends in attendance since on Tuesday 6 August she was at Lady Anne's house in Curzon Street, London attending the marriage of her granddaughter, 'Miss Lambton, to the Hon. Mr. F. Howard, third son of the Earl of Carlisle', another of her former lovers.[27]

After the ceremony, 'the Lady's brother, Mr. Lambton, gave a most elegant and sumptuous dinner of turtle, venison and every delicacy the season could afford, with wines of the choicest quality'.[28]

Sadly, the marriage was to be short-lived, for less than four years later Frederick Howard was to die at Waterloo.[29]

The same grandson of the Countess, Mr Lambton, was very soon thereafter involved in a rather less conventional form of matrimony. At the end of 1811 he eloped to Gretna Green with Henrietta Cholmondeley, the illegitimate daughter of Lord Cholmondeley and a French actress, Mme St Alban, where they were married on 1 January 1812. In fact the Cholmondeleys approved of the match and the couple were soon more conventionally remarried in the Cholmondeley's parish church with their blessing.[30] The explanation for the elopement doubtless lies rather in Henrietta's parentage, even though her mother had left her £20,000, and the fact that, in the words of the *Bury & Norwich Post*, 'Mr L. is not yet of age, and his estates, with the accumulation of his long minority are now estimated at 60,000 l. a year. The C. family are no ways adverse to the match.'[31] Indeed: and it was much more likely that his mother, Lady Anne, would have been. In fact, parental refusal to approve the match had prompted the elopement.

Succession planning was also taking place elsewhere in the family. William Augustus was to succeed to the Briton Ferry Estate in the Vale of Glamorgan under Lady Vernon's will on the death of Lord Vernon on 18 June 1813 and had already, as her will required and with the King's permission, changed his name to Mansel in 1802.[32] Even before Lord Vernon's death, planning was in hand. The 4th Earl's cousin, Louisa Barbara, Lady Vernon, was concerned that her husband was a wastrel and, accordingly, had left him only a life interest in the estate that she had inherited from her father. Even so, it seems that Lord Vernon, in the quarter of a century following his wife's death, sought to milk the estate as much as he could, and one of the means of his doing so was by granting leases of various parts of it.

In 1812, perhaps in the expectation that Lord Vernon's death could not be long delayed, the Jerseys started to take pre-emptive action. Of course, it was William Augustus who was due to inherit the Briton Ferry estate but, perhaps in view of his wayward character or his exile to North America, it seems that his brother the 5th Earl was to take the leading role in proceedings. Accordingly, in January 1812 William Augustus sold to his brother and two of his agents a year's interest in one of the properties in the estate, known as Tal y Coba Uchaf, which was leased to a Mr Smith, presumably to enable them to push forward a test case.[33]

The air was thick with conspiracy but it seems that Lord Jersey and his agent, Alex Murray, thought that in Lord Vernon's granting of leases there was a '*fatal* deviation from the power of leasing' under which he held the estate for his life.[34] They therefore planned to challenge the validity of the leases granted by Lord Vernon and so restore the capital value of the estate. They recognised that there were many 'difficulties we shall have to encounter, but I hope, properly overcome, and settle, when the *explosion* takes place for which the Mine is now laid, and remains secret to every person here, except Mr Thomas Junr who by his silence to his own family has shown himself worthy the confidence I reposed in him'.[35]

Following which Mr Smith was promptly ousted from the property that Lord Vernon had leased to him.

All did not go according to plan. The validity of the leases was to become the subject of a long-running action in the courts. Initially the Earl lost his argument in the Court of King's Bench. This decision was then reversed in the Earl's favour in the Exchequer Court.[36] The case then went to the highest Court in the land, the House of Lords, which eventually ruled in 1821 against the Earl that the lease, and therefore in all probability all the other leases granted by Lord Vernon, was validly granted. By this time, William Augustus was long dead, the Earl had inherited the entire estate from him and the Countess herself was not long to live.[37]

In these years there was yet more trouble in the family – and Sally Jersey was once more the cause. By common consent, her sister-in-law Lady Harriet Bagot was 'perfectly beautiful and very pleasing and amiable'.[38] She was, though, clearly very fond of her elder brother and was not sympathetic to his treatment at the hands of his wife. As Harryo Cavendish, now Harriet, Lady Granville, wrote to her sister in 1812:

> Lady Harriet [Bagot] seems to be compassionate her brother [*sic*] and to think him, in spite of good fortune, or as Newhouse would say 'plenty of money', much to be pitied, and worn to the greatest degree with voluble *tracasseries*.

The result was, as Harriet Granville went on, 'I do not think Lady Jersey *en bonne odeur* with the Dicks'.[39] Whether this amounted to a family feud, as Harryo suggested some months earlier, is unclear. Nevertheless her comments on the voluble Sally Jersey at that time are clearly disapproving, stating: 'I have a horror of family feuds, and you may depend upon my keeping all knowledge of them to myself and not going on, as somebody said of Lady Jersey, "like a watch after the main spring is broken."'[40]

Harriet Granville gave news, too, of other members of the family. A letter she wrote in December 1812 suggests either that Harriette Wilson got the dates of her affair with John Ponsonby wrong in her memoirs or that, for some years after its ending, Ponsonby continued to have an affair with her younger sister Amy (which too was put to an end by Fanny). Harryo wrote:

> Lady Ponsonby is beautiful beyond all description, and seems an engaging, affectionate gentle person with an understanding crushed by his [Lord Ponsonby's] affected contempt and brutality, for I am convinced he is in fact desperately in love with her all the time. They have, I hear, what is called come to an understanding. He is to give up Miss Wilson and all that sort of thing, as Lady Stafford would say, and she is to renounce all her little manoeuvres round the Ring in the opera. He is not to laugh at her with the Duchess of Bedford and she is not to complain of him to Lord Tyrconnel.

On Harriet Bagot her views were:

> Lady Harriet is a little miracle of goodness. She is the quietest, best and happiest person I ever met with; Dick is a good sort of man and a very good husband.

Whilst she thought:

> Lord Ponsonby was very affected and agreeable, his affectation is not offensive it is not skin deep, like that of many people, and therefore, as far as society goes, there is no cause for complaint.[41]

Another Villiers sister, this time Lady Sarah Bayly, was also complimented, on this occasion by comparison to her mother. Of Lady Sarah, Maria Edgeworth wrote in 1813: 'We are going to dine at Lady Levinge's this day to meet Lady S: Bailey a daughter of Lady Jerseys – like her mother in person and as unlike her in mind I understand as her friends could wish.'[42]

As to that mother, and despite the mischiefs attributed to her in later years which we shall now come to, she was now beginning to withdraw from Society. Whilst in April 1813 *The Morning Post* reported her presence at 'the Misses Prichard [who] on Thursday evening opened their splendid mansion, in Green-street, Park–lane, with a Ball and Supper. A temporary room was erected in the garden for dancing,'[43] from this time forward the Dowager's presence was rarely to be noted at the entertainments of the beau monde.

This in itself is also relevant to the mischiefs attributed to Frances Jersey. It is said they were manufactured by the Countess to embarrass the Prince, motivated by a spurned woman's desire for revenge. Like a lot of stories about the Countess, much of this is myth. To understand what really happened and whether the Dowager was in fact the cause of these mischiefs, you need to understand the background to her relations with the Prince of Wales (or the Prince Regent as he now was) and Princess Caroline in these years. Those relationships are best demonstrated by the Countess's continuing financial difficulties and the assistance she sought from the Prince to alleviate them.

In short, she needed the Prince's help and so was unlikely to annoy him out of sheer gratuity. Indeed, as we shall see, not only did the Prince, to the extent of a pension at least, seem favourably inclined to her, but when she was the subject of untrue stories she approached him to deny them vigorously.

So in January 1813 Lady Jersey wrote to the Prince's Secretary, Col McMahon, on the possibility of the Prince giving her a pension:

> I have received your letter of yesterday, & in justice to myself I must remind you of your calling upon me on the 12th of August 1811 & asking me 'why I would not have a pension?' I answered I cannot ask for one. You then said that the Prince felt hurt that I was in an uncomfortable situation & that the moment the restrictions were taken off it would be the first thing he would do, to grant me one & we entered as much further into the subject as to agree that such a thing could be done without its being made public. All that passed in this conversation, as well as your answer to a letter which I wrote to you upon the subject (in which you told me I must address myself to the Prince & *ask* for a pension) I understood to be indirect messages from him, nothing but what I looked upon as an absolute promise from him would have induced me to do so. I thought my letter to him a mere matter of form & now I find that I have put myself in the disgraceful shape of a beggar! I do entreat that you will relate these facts to him in order that I have if I have been mistaken, if I have misunderstood his intentions & your assurances, that I may no longer feel in the humiliating state in which I must remain whilst my way of thinking upon the subject remains unexplained. Many of my friends have at different times advised me to apply for a pension, have urged that as the widow of a faithful servant of His R. H. left without a sufficient income to support my rank, I might hope that I had some claim to one but I felt that it was quite impossible to *ask*, and no power but a command from him could have forced me to take a step so repugnant to my feelings of respect to His R. H. or of delicacy to myself. Should you dislike to show this letter to the Prince, or to state to him all that has passed, I have no objection to writing to him when I shall *most fully* explain that no blame can attach to the part you have acted, that all the distress which I now enjoy is owing to my having miscomprehended you when I saw you here.[44]

So, needing money and believing that she was being invited to apply for a pension, the Countess had done so only to find her understanding was wrong. As a consequence the proud Countess felt humiliated. Whether she also really felt the respect for the Prince which she mentioned is another matter.

What is particularly surprising, not only in the context of the past but also in the light of future events, is the Prince's apparent sympathy for the Countess. This lies badly with the stories we shall come to of his being irritated by her.

In any event, seemingly McMahon did just what she asked of him. There is in the Royal Archives at Windsor Castle an undated letter from the Countess to Col McMahon which does not appear in Professor Aspinall's edition of the correspondence of the Prince of Wales. This letter fits perfectly with Lady Jersey's letter just quoted. In it, she thanks McMahon for his letter and his promise to show hers to the Prince and says that, in so doing, he had removed the mortification of her being thought to have acted in a way so different from what she thought she was doing. She went on, somewhat gushingly, to describe McMahon's reply to her as handsome and just what she expected from him, and assuring him of the high opinion 'I have invariably had of your integrity & goodness of heart'. She closed with the comment 'you will make me very happy by telling me how my letter was received'.[45]

So the issue of the Prince giving a pension to the Countess was clearly on the table even if there were misunderstandings about it; as we shall see, the issue continued to be a live one for some months. Obviously, therefore, Frances Jersey would have continued to be anxious not to anger the Prince Regent. It was for just this reason that she wrote to him again on 6 April 1813 in the following almost submissive terms:

> At the risk of your displeasure of your thinking me presuming, I must entreat that your Royal Highness will read this letter. I have been three weeks in Staffordshire, at my return I hear from various quarters, it has been asserted that I have been in Her Royal Highness the Princess of Wales confidence, & one of her *advisers* in the late transaction; that I was in the habit of meeting her at Lady Oxford's and that I went out of town the moment I did in order not to appear to be one of her counsellors. I entreat that your Royal Highness will believe that I do not intend by this letter to force myself into your Royal Highness's presence any longer than whilst I justify myself – but Sir I have long smarted under the effects of the malice of my enemies without knowing of what I have been accused, and now that I am possessed of a specific charge against myself, I will not end my life under so vile an aspersion. Permit me then to assure you by everything most sacred that I have never directly or indirectly had any communication with the Princess since I sent to her my letter of resignation, & that I have never been at Lady Oxford's house since last summer when I was there at a Ball. If your Royal Highness recollects my character, you will remember that to *advise* was never my taste, & if *truth* respecting me has reached your Royal Highnesses ears you will know that I have ever expressed myself with that dutyful respect, & attachment to your Royal Highnesses interests

> which I ought to feel. If your Royal Highness could imagine what I have suffered from this accusation you would pardon my venturing to enter into an explanation.
>
> Should you be graciously pleased to make it known to me that you are not offended at the liberty I have taken and that you believe what I have asserted you will relieve me from great unhappiness.[46]

So there were evidently rumours, which the Countess strenuously denied, that she was now aligning herself with the Princess of Wales whom, of course, the Prince detested. Given past history, such a story lacks any credibility whatsoever. Given, too, as we shall see, the Princess of Wales's reaction to such stories they are clearly entirely untrue. The very submissiveness of the Dowager gives the lie to the allegations that she deliberately sought to annoy the Prince or frustrate his wishes.

What is true, though, is first that the Countess did not want the Prince to believe the stories and, second and most important in connection with the 'mischiefs', that the Dowager's daughter-in-law, Sally Jersey, was at this time indeed allying herself both with Princess Caroline and with Princess Charlotte – who was much closer in age to Sally Jersey in any event.

The stories circulating at the time, which have continued down the years, simply confused the two Lady Jerseys.

The Prince probably knew this anyway. Only a few months earlier he had been angered when, as he was making a speech to the House of Lords with the two Princesses also there, Princess Charlotte had nodded a greeting to Lord Jersey in recognition, in the Prince's eyes, of some form of alliance vicariously with the Prince's hated wife.[47]

The Dowager Lady Jersey clearly felt acquitted of the charges as, in August 1813, she once more raised the issue of a pension with Col McMahon, writing in a tenor quite incompatible with a mischief maker:

> I have written, since you think I am not forbidden, & am sure it is most respectful to do so. I send my letter to you for I think it better not to let my ser[van]t go to C. H. am I not right? ... Now my good friend I must thank you for all the trouble which you have taken ... I did not venture to say, what I will in confidence to you, how *much* I am distressed that what you sent came from a very different fund than I intended. Do you understand me?[48]

So not only was the Countess writing to the Prince but it also seems that she had already received some money from him, although what she meant by it coming from a 'different fund' is entirely unclear.

Whatever she received, it was not enough and, still needing his help, she was to write another, and the last surviving, letter on the topic to the Prince on 12 December 1813. In it she said:

> It is with the greatest reluctance that I again obtrude myself upon your Royal Highness but my situation is such that I am in a manner compelled

> to do so. I have only 700 per an which considering my former situation will scarce afford me the necessaries of life May I not hope that as a Peeress, and the widow of a faithful servant who had the honour of holding a high situation in your Royal Highness's family, I may have some claim upon your Royal bounty for a pension ... I am convinced that upon reading [this letter] your Royal Highness will feel I have suffered much before I could bring myself to write it.[49]

Whether Frances Jersey received anything further from the Prince is unclear. Whether she would much longer need to is less so. As we will see, her rich elder son was to give her considerable financial help. Not only that but, on the death of her younger son, William Augustus, she was also to receive significant sums of money from his estate.

This episode shows one thing beyond the brazenness of Lady Jersey in applying for a pension to a former lover whom she had consistently sought to irritate in the past. It was not in her best interests to be, nor was her assumed tone that of, the source of the various bigger mischiefs against the Prince hence attributed to her.

Further, the fact that she was not in reality the authoress of these mischiefs is reinforced by other happenings over the months in point.

Cornelia Knight, Princess Charlotte's Lady Companion, wrote in early February 1813 of the Prince taking her aside at Carlton House, when he 'warned me against Lady Jersey, whom he had observed talking to Princess Charlotte the night before at the ball, and said he did not choose [she, Lady Jersey] should be too intimate at Warwick House [which was now Charlotte's home], but does not give any particular reasons for it'.

When Cornelia Knight related this to Princess Caroline, the latter's response was:

> As to Lady Jersey, she said she knew not what the Prince had against her. He had been the first to urge her visiting his daughter, and Lady Jersey declared she would come unless she heard from his own lips a positive revocation of the order.[50]

The Lady Jersey so described by Princess Caroline cannot conceivably have been Frances Jersey.

Again a month later Princess Charlotte was writing to her friend, companion and adviser Miss Mercer Elphinstone about rumours that the Dowager Countess was seeing a lot of Princess Caroline, to which Charlotte's dismissive reaction was:

> Conceive what a lie they have told everywhere, that the Pss *saw the Dow. Ly Jersey* constantly at her house – a person she hates more than anything in the world, & whom she has never seen for 17 years. As soon as I heard of it I wrote her word, & I rcvd. an answer, as I supposed, saying there was not a word of truth in it.[51]

It is clear that the Lady Jersey now getting close to the Royal Princesses was in truth Sally Jersey, and that the Prince Regent did not welcome it because he never liked his friends or acquaintances, let alone former favourites like Sally Jersey, to associate with those who (like the Dowager) he had rejected.

This was the background to all the mischiefs.

The first concerned a portrait of Princess Charlotte. In the summer of 1813, Princess Charlotte was having her portrait painted by the miniaturist George Sanders, who had also painted Fanny Ponsonby, as a gift to her father. In the words of Cornelia Knight:

> We used to go very often to his study for these sittings. Sanders is a very particular man, very correct, very religious. So far from taking the liberty of admitting anybody when her Royal Highness was there, it was with great difficulty we could prevail on him to let in Miss Mercer, Lady Tavistock, Lady Jersey, or the Miss Fitzroy's, when the Regent particularly desired it.[52]

It is commonly said that this Lady Jersey was Frances Jersey and that her purpose in attending the sittings was to annoy the Prince.[53]

It was not. It was clearly Sally Jersey for all the reasons just explained. She was there as a friend of Charlotte's – though she was increasingly becoming an object of suspicion and distrust to the Prince Regent as a result – through her friendship with Princess Caroline. By early August Princess Charlotte was writing to Mercer Elphinstone, saying that 'Ly Jersey's visits at Sanders' was one of the stumbling blocks' to a pleasant life at Windsor Castle. Indeed by now the Prince both disliked and constrained the intimacy between Sally Jersey and Charlotte.[54] Ultimately he decreed that all future sittings would take place at Warwick House rather than at Sanders' studio so he could control the sittings' attendees. Sadly the result was that the portrait was never completed because the particular Sanders was unhappy with the light at Warwick House.[55]

If any doubt remains as to which Lady Jersey it was who was becoming the friend and ally of Princess Caroline and her daughter, the events of future years were conclusive. Apart from Sally's visits to and very loud support of Caroline during and after the trial of Caroline (which Frances did not emulate), the happenings of 1814 are compelling.

After the Battle of Leipzig in 1813 and the invasion of France by the Allies the defeated Napoleon was sent into exile on Elba and, once more, France was open to British visitors. In July 1814 the Earl and Countess of Jersey left London for Paris.[56] There is no evidence, or even the possibility, that the Dowager did likewise, either with them or independently. Accordingly, when Queen Charlotte wrote of 'Lady Jersey' to the Prince Regent on 20 September 1814 after the Jerseys' return from Paris, there can be no doubt either that the Lady Jersey she was referring to was Sally.

This is because in that letter she stated that Lady Jersey had been to Paris, where she had made some purchases for Charlotte, and that Lady Jersey wanted to know where she should send them. Charlotte, the Queen went on, had been told that no parcel should be sent to her without the Prince's approval and that 'Lady Jersey's conduct to you [the Prince] justifyed you in disapproving of her as a friend for yr daughter'. Accordingly, the Queen asked the Prince for his instructions.

Queen Charlotte also warned of the friendship of Lady Jersey with Miss Mercer – 'you know much better than I do of the friendship between Ldy Jersey & Miss Mercer' – and that, in turn, there was no control over the correspondence between Miss Mercer and Princess Charlotte so that it would be very easy to smuggle a letter to Charlotte through her. Nevertheless, the Queen left it to the Prince as to what should be done about the whole business.[57]

In context, clearly the Lady Jersey she was referring to was Sally Jersey. Equally clearly there was very real dislike and mistrust of Sally Jersey. This distrust and dislike, in combination with her being disapproved of as a friend for Princess Charlotte, was caused by Sally Jersey's befriending of Princess Charlotte and, in particular, Princess Caroline. Both the Prince and the Queen disliked and distrusted Caroline, the Prince with considerable venom, so that Sally was guilty by association.

This accords with Byron's experience. A frequent visitor to the Earl and Countess of Jersey in these years, Lord Byron saw Sally, a former favourite of the Prince, fall out of favour with the Prince shortly after he met her.[58]

One example of this falling out related to a miniature portrait of Sally. The miniaturist, Mrs Mee, had painted a gallery of beauties, including Sally Jersey, for the Prince Regent, but when he received them in the spring of 1814 he sent back the one of Sally Jersey. This prompted Byron, an intimate of the Countess, to write to Lady Jersey on 29 May: 'Dear Lady Jersey – Don't be very angry with me – I send you something of which – if ill done – the shame can only be mine.'

They were in fact verses entitled *Condolatary Address to Sarah Countess of Jersey on the Prince Regent's returning her picture to Mrs Mee*. They were not very polite about the Prince. Accordingly, when the *Champion* of 31 July that year published them without Byron's consent, furthermore naming him as the author, he was 'discomfited' as they included lines which in his words were of 'impudent lèse majesté'.[59]

Indeed the Prince's continuing distrust and mistreatment of Sally was to provoke her husband to defend his wife against the Prince's behaviour towards her and his impugning her reputation. On 27 May 1816 *The Morning Chronicle* reported that the Earl 'had an audience of the Prince Regent, on Friday last, at Carlton House'.[60]

Lord Jersey made and signed a note of his conversation with the Prince on the day of the audience. He noted that he had defended his wife, her reputation, character and proper relations with Princess Charlotte – in particular by not encouraging her against her father. In response the Prince acknowledged that all of what the Earl said was true but, even so, the Prince's prohibition on Sally Jersey visiting Princess Charlotte was to continue.[61]

A final piece of evidence as to the real identity of the visitor lies in Queen Victoria's journals. There, the Queen records Lord Melbourne telling her:

> When the Regent wanted to prevent Lady Jersey going so often to see Princess Charlotte, Lord Jersy [*sic*] asked for a Private audience, and the Regent said to him ... if you come to speak about your wife, I cannot speak to you.[62]

Accordingly, even though the index to Professor Aspinall's collected correspondence of the Prince attributes these last events to the elder Lady Jersey, it is wrong to say it was Frances whose presence at Sanders' sittings so annoyed the Prince. History has got it wrong. Here, as in years to come, it was Sally Jersey rather than her mother-in-law who was the mischief maker, albeit probably not a malicious one.

History blamed trouble on the Lady Jersey with a reputation.

The next 'mischief' involved the Emperor of Russia. Following the Battle of Leipzig and Napoleon's exile, in 1814 the Emperor with the King of Prussia and other European dignitaries visited England as part of the celebrations of the overthrow of Napoleon. Whilst in England, it is commonly said that the Prince Regent was angered by the Emperor waltzing with the Prince's one-time lover, Frances Jersey.[63]

Certainly the Emperor and the Prince did not get on and, indeed, the Emperor seems to have done as much as he could when in England to avoid the Prince's entertainments, for reasons which Lady Holland explained:

> The Emperor and the Regent are as great enemies as possible, each party sneering and even abusing the other. The *ton* at C House is to ridicule all the Emp. and his sister [the Grand Duchess of Oldenburg] do. The Emp. shrugs up his shoulders at the sight of Ly Hertford and at the length of the dinners. *'Qel Goût! les grosses femmes et les grosses bouteilles.'* He objects to the practice in England of sitting so long a dinner. He says, beside the *ennui* it is a sad waste of life, time and pleasure; three quarters of an hour he reckons quite sufficient for any of the duties of the table.

The Emperor compounded his unpopularity with the Prince by writing to the Princess of Wales before leaving London, styling her his '*chère cousine*' and lamenting that particular circumstances prevented him from visiting her – this despite the Prince Regent having previously written to the Emperor imploring him not to visit the Princess.[64]

What is not true, as is commonly said, is that it was Frances Jersey who was waltzing with the Emperor. Once again history has confused the two Countesses of Jersey, as we shall see.

One of the first entertainments given for the Emperor on his visit was the Countess of Cholmondeley's ball on 13 June 1814, attended not only by the Emperor but also by the King of Prussia, the Prince Regent and twelve foreign Princes. As *The Morning Post* reported two days later: 'The Emperor of Russia opened the ball with the Countess of Jersey.'[65]

Creevey described the Prince's reactions the following day:

> He already abuses the Emperor lustily, and his (the Emperor's) waltzing with Lady Jersey last night at Lady Cholmondeley's would not mend his temper, and in truth he only stayed five minutes and went off sulky as a bear.[66]

Indeed it seems to have been worse than this. As Lord Broughton recalled in his autobiography:

> I heard that at Lady Cholmondeley's ball the Countess of Jersey was walking with the Emperor Alexander, when she happened to be so near the Prince of Wales that she dropped him a curtsey. The Prince turned on his heel; the Emperor whispered to Lady Jersey – '*Pas fort gallant* ça'. Lady Jersey told this to me.[67]

The Lady Jersey referred to in all these quotations can only have been Sally Jersey, the queen of Society, and not the sixty-one year-old Dowager who had increasingly retired from high society. Indeed the indexes to both published collections of Creevey's papers also reflect that fact. The anger and irritation of the Prince reflects not his dislike of a rejected mistress but rather his normal anger at anyone who allied themselves with his discarded wife, compounded by that person dancing with a guest he disliked.

Other evidence supports this view.

The Morning Chronicle of 14 June 1814 reported that 'the Earl and Countess of Jersey will entertain her Imperial Highness the Duchess of Oldenburg and a large party, to dinner, on Monday next, at their house in Berkeley-square,'[68] whilst two days later the newspapers were reporting that 'the Emperor of Russia ... went to the Countess of Jersey's ball where he remained till 6 o'clock'.[69]

So it was in Sally Jersey's house in Berkeley Square that the parties were held; the entertainments were being given by the Earl and Countess of Jersey.

The Dowager Countess on the other hand was at no time in these years reported as hosting any entertainments, let alone in London – and probably did not at this time have the money to do so.

Letters from Lady Holland add to the colour. She tells of the Prussian General Blücher dining at Holland House, when the Jerseys – plural – were amongst the party. Then she tells of him dancing a polonaise with Lady Jersey at the Countess's party. Finally she tells the story of the Emperor's promise to go to Lady Jersey's ball on his return from a visit to Oxford. When at 2:30 a.m. he had not arrived back in London, the company were beginning to despair and to disperse. However:

> The Russians who were present said they knew their *cher Empereur* so well, that, as he had promised, he might not perhaps come in time for the *Ball* but he certainly would not go to bed in London before he had made her a visit. Accordingly at half past three he arrived, without guards or even an aide-de-camp or any companion. On entering the room he endeavoured to dispel all form, put his hat into a corner, and began waltzing. He stayed 12 minutes at supper, and then returned to dancing with different ladies. He remained till 6 o'clock, and appeared very happy. He desired Lady Jersey not to let people be full dress.[70]

The Emperor's waltzing was not quite over. On 20 June, as *The Morning Post* reported, White's had given a grand fête at Burlington House where the Tsar was also present: 'The company began to dance at twelve o'clock, led off with waltzes by the Emperor of Russia and the beautiful Countess of Jersey.' Doubtless the Prince Regent, who was there too, was unhappy at that as well.[71]

Amongst all of this there is not one piece of evidence suggesting that Frances Jersey was the Countess who danced with the Emperor to the annoyance of the Prince, beautiful as she still was at the age of sixty-one. On the contrary, everything points in the direction of the Countess concerned being Sally Jersey before she and her husband left for Paris.

It is from Paris that we find the final piece of evidence, in the letters of Harriet Granville. In the summer of 1817, Harriet was there with her husband. At the time Sally Jersey was also in France, arriving in Paris from Lyon in the middle of June. Harriet Granville, who always refers to Sally Jersey as 'Lady Jersey', wrote to her sister that month: 'Granville drank Russian tea last night with Mme [actually, Princess] Bagration and a *dame d'honneur*. She talked to him ... of the Emperor's admiration of Lady Jersey.'

The reference in its context is clearly to Sally, and the admiration was the result of waltzes and entertainments in 1814.[72]

The third occasion on which Frances Jersey is said deliberately to have caused mischief to the royal family was in relation to the proposed marriage of Princess Charlotte. The Prince Regent proposed, in the summer of 1813, that she should marry the Hereditary Prince William of Orange. Princess Charlotte was initially reluctant, but by the end of the year had come round to accept the idea and was, thereafter, effectively betrothed to him. Over the coming months she had second thoughts and, in the middle of June 1814, she wrote to him impetuously calling off the engagement.

It is said that Lady Jersey was the architect, or at least a force, behind this change of mind. The source for this is probably Lord Holland's *Further Memoirs of the Whig Party 1807–1821* in which he claimed that 'Lady Jersey had a hand in the Whig intrigue against the Orange match in June 1814'.[73]

Credence has apparently also been placed in some correspondence at this time between the Prince Regent and his mother in relation to Princess Charlotte, when he wrote:

> I am well acquainted with the wickedness, perseverance, & trick, of that infernal Jezabel Lady Jersey, and & of all her Jacobin[ic]al set of connexions, & that there is no one base, or infernal scheme, plot, or plan that they will stick at, to accomplish their views. Therefore we cannot be too much upon our guard, or too much on the alert.[74]

In both cases it has been generally assumed that the Lady Jersey referred to is Frances Jersey and that her motive for causing trouble was malice and the desire of a spurned woman for revenge. Thus Professor Webster, in the introduction to Professor Aspinall's edition of the correspondence of George IV, writes: 'Lady Jersey ... tried to pay off old scores by making mischief in the Orange marriage but it does not seem that her influence on Princess Charlotte was considerable.'[75]

Other writers have been less restrained. One, for example, writes that it was well known in the royal family that Lady Jersey had abetted the Whigs to break off the Orange match, and that from the time of her impudent request for a pension from the Prince of Wales she had worked steadily against him.[76]

These accusations do not hold water. The truth is that, once again, there is confusion between the two Countesses of Jersey. Put aside the history of Frances Jersey's relations with Princess Charlotte's mother, which makes any connivance on her part with Charlotte inconceivable: it is clear that such mischief as was made was made by Sally Jersey. Holland's reference was neutral, only to 'Lady Jersey', which could have been either of them and, indeed, more accurately Sally as Frances was properly styled 'Dowager Lady Jersey'. Then, tellingly, the Prince's comments about the Jezabel to his mother were not only contained in a letter to the Queen responding to her request, in her letter dated 20 September 1814 quoted above, for instructions about Sally Jersey's parcel from Paris and the Queen's warning about Sally Jersey, but also were in the context of those two topics. In both letters the Lady Jersey referred to is clearly Sally. The Jezabel is therefore Sally Jersey and not the Dowager.

Since it seems the Prince did give Frances Jersey some financial aid it is bizarre, too, to suggest that her actions were prompted by his rejection of her request for a pension.

Finally there is the memorandum, at the National Archives, which the Earl of Malmesbury wrote in June and July 1814, with an addendum written in 1817, setting out his considered views of the reasons for Princess Charlotte's rejection of the Prince of Orange. This contemporary record, seemingly unread by other historical authorities, is the best evidence we have.

In it Lord Malmesbury recognised that there were stories that the Duke of Sussex and 'Lady Jersey' had been interfering in the marriage proposals although there was not any evidence that that was in fact the case. From what

Malmesbury wrote, it is clear that the Lady Jersey he was referring to was Sally Jersey. Admittedly he goes on to say that Sally was ambivalent about Prince William seemingly playing a double part, both undermining him and grieving at his departure. Nevertheless, recognising that Princess Charlotte may have been influenced by 'mischievous and artful advisers ... Russian intrigue is suspected' to prevent the union of British and Russian fleets, he concludes that, ultimately, the rejection of Prince William was due to Charlotte's temper and impetuosity coupled with youthful lack of judgement. She had been frustrated in her desires to go to some of the parties held in London during the visits of the Emperor of Russia; the King of Prussia and the Prince of Orange declined to support her; and then she had been unhappy at the news that, once married, she would have to spend six months each year in Holland and acted impetuously.[77]

Whether or not Sally Jersey had any role in this is not clear. On the other hand it is clear beyond all doubt that Frances Jersey had none. So, once more, Frances Jersey is innocent of the charges laid against her. Again it is a case of mistaken identity with, no doubt, an element of wishful thinking attributing mischief to the one with a reputation. If anyone was guilty of the charge, and the case is at best unproven, it was Sally Jersey and not her mother-in-law. She, certainly, was close to Princess Charlotte and it was doubtless her who gave Lord Holland a copy of Princess Charlotte's letter dismissing Prince William, so giving rise to the story in the first place.[78]

So history has demonised Frances Jersey. There is no doubt that the Prince was repeatedly angered by the actions of a Countess of Jersey; but they were Sally Jersey's actions. And they were not inspired by malice on her part. She, along with many parts of Society, sympathised profoundly with Princess Caroline and abhorred her treatment by her husband. It was Sally's befriending of Caroline and her daughter that provoked the Prince's wrath. Frances Jersey is acquitted on all scores.

There was, however, a much bigger and continuing mischief for which the Countess was to blame. That was the very fact of the marriage of the Prince to Caroline. Conceived for the Countess's own purposes, it remained a source of trouble long after the Prince and Caroline had separated. The Prince could never resist the opportunity of tormenting his wife, a wife he detested. Only two years earlier than the events just described, for example, he had done so by severely limited Caroline's contact with their daughter. Whilst the government supported him, the public, incited by Caroline's ally Lord Brougham, were outraged, and the Regent's reputation amongst his subjects suffered once more from the consequences of that unfortunate marriage.[79]

This was the final, and enduring, mischief of Frances, Countess of Jersey.

19

The Fading Beauty

All the Dowager's daughters were now married, and the only family member who was not was William Augustus, now in exile in Canada. Now over sixty, Frances Jersey was not often seen in Society. Nor was she seen much within her family. She made the occasional visit from Cheltenham to London and once was reported as visiting Lady Harriet Bagot in Lichfield.[1] One recalls Car Paget seeking to put off her mother's visit some years earlier, so perhaps all her daughters apart from the kindly Harriet now did the same. Lady Sarah in particular may have felt ill-used by her mother.

Certainly the Dowager was noticeably absent from Sally Jersey's parties. Sally, as one of the leaders of the beau monde, had regular, indeed numerous, dinners, concerts, balls, routs and other entertainments in London over the years. She also had a stream of visitors to Middleton. Both in London and in Oxfordshire members of the family were commonly amongst the guests, whether Lady Anne, the Bagots, the Argylls or the Baylys. Over the coming years there is not a single mention of her mother-in-law being one of Sally's guests or visitors in either place.[2]

One of the ironies is that Mrs Fitzherbert did number amongst them, and the invitations were reciprocated. Indeed, Sally Jersey seems to have struck up a friendship with Maria Fitzherbert. When the Jerseys were in Brighton in October 1815, Mrs Fitzherbert was also there although 'indisposed'. According to *The Morning Post*, 'The Countess of Jersey paid her a visit of some length.'[3]

It may be it was this occasion which prompted an undated letter from Maria Fitzherbert to Sally Jersey thanking her

> a thousand times for your kind letter and enquiries after me. I have had a very serious attack of illness for the last two months & tho' I am getting better I have not as yet been able to leave my room ... Pray remember me kindly to Lord Jersey ... Brighton Wednesday Morng.[4]

One does not need to speculate long as to the reasons for the Dowager's absence from Sally's entertainments. Nevertheless there is a second note written in these years by Sally Jersey to her husband against the eventuality of her dying in childbirth, which tells us much about both her views on propriety and her views on her mother-in-law:

> Let neither my sons or girl [*sic*] see much of the Dss of Argyle – she is without sense or principle & sometimes her manners are [unprepossessing?] ... Her conduct ... I forgive – but I cannot pass her over without warning ... of her ... You know my feelings about everyone – I feel no resentment, no not even against the D Css [that is the Dowager Countess]. I have had too much happiness.[5]

For her part, the Dowager had her share of happiness and of sadness. In June 1815 a rumour circulated about her granddaughter, another Car Paget. As Lady Caroline Capel said: 'Is it true that Car Paget is to marry Lord March?'[6]

That indeed would be a match to be proud of as Lord March was heir to the Duke of Richmond.

The rumour was true, although the marriage did not take place for another two years, on 10 April 1817. Those present at the wedding included the bride's mother, the Duchess of Argyll, and two of her aunts, Lady Anne Wyndham and Lady Sarah Bayly. The Dowager Countess was not reported as being present, but then neither were the current Earl and Countess nor the bride's father, now the Marquess of Anglesey.[7]

Then there was an alarm about Lady Harriet Bagot. On 23 August 1816 *The Morning Chronicle* reported her death at Lord Bagot's seat in Wales, going on:

> Five young children are suddenly bereft of an amiable and accomplished mother. Her Ladyship died on Tuesday last, of the typhus fever six weeks after her accouchement ... Her Ladyship was the youngest daughter of the late Earl of Jersey, and married, in December 1806, the Hon and Rev Richard Bagot, the brother of Lord Bagot.[8]

One does not know if Frances Jersey read this report and if so what her reaction to it was. Fortunately *The Morning Chronicle* had been misled. The same day's *The Morning Post* had seen the mistake and reported accurately that it was the wife of Lord Bagot and not that of Dick Bagot who had died.[9]

There were, though, other real sadnesses. We have already mentioned the death of twenty-year-old Fanny Lambton's husband, Frederick Howard, at Waterloo in June 1815, in the same month that the rumour about young Car Paget and Lord March was circulating. Frederick Howard's death was commemorated by Lord Byron (Frederick's father, the 5th Earl of Carlisle, was a relative of and had been the guardian of Byron) in the 29th stanza of

Canto III of Byron's *Childe Harold's Pilgrimage*, where Byron also apologised for abusing Lord Carlisle some years earlier:

> Their praise is hymn'd by loftier harps than mine;
> Yet one I would select from that proud throng,
> Partly because they blend me with his line
> And partly that I did his sire some wrong,
> And partly that bright names will hallow song;
> And he was of the bravest, and when shower'd
> The death–bolts deadliest the thinn'd files along,
> Even where the thickest of war's tempest lower'd,
> They reach'd no nobler breast than thine, young gallant Howard![10]

The blow which the Dowager felt most keenly was certainly that reported on 2 March 1814:

> Died ...
>
> In America, the Hon Wm V Mansel, 2d son of the late Lord Jersey.[11]

So Frances Jersey's 'angel' Augustus had died, unmarried and in exile in Pictou, Nova Scotia, on 3 January 1814, aged thirty-three. There is no record of how this afflicted the Countess but she was clearly very attached to Augustus. He was buried in the Laurel Hill Cemetery, Wellington Street, Pictou and it is said that 'he spent the last years of his life carousing in the taverns of Creighton Street', Pictou, where he was known as 'the Prince of Pictou'.[12]

Another anecdote has it that, in 1845 when Augustus's tomb was in disrepair, one John Paterson wrote from Pictou to England seeking money for its repair and, in a nice touch, Sally Jersey sent £30 to have it restored.[13]

As a consequence of the unmarried Augustus's death, 'The Earl of Jersey succeed[ed] to his immense fortune' of Briton Ferry.[14]

Although, if Lady Charlotte Bury is to believed, Augustus did not forget his mother in his will. This perhaps was the end of her financial problems. As Lady Charlotte wrote in her journal: 'I heard that Lord J—— has got all Mr M——'s fortune, and that he has left his mother £3,000 a year, and Lady —— £1,000'[15]

Perhaps, though, she had got it wrong, as Creevey wrote at the time of the Dowager's death that it was Lord Jersey who had come to the Countess's financial rescue, saying:

> Let me add to the honour of Jersey, and indeed of his wife (for it was her money, not his), that he had raised his mother's jointure from £1,100 per ann. to £3,500, and that he has paid at different times £6,000 and £2,000 in discharge of her debts.[16]

That certainly would have ended any serious financial embarrassment for Frances Jersey.

These years, too, saw the swansong of the Countess's life in society. She would commonly come to London for a few weeks in the summer to attend a small number of entertainments whilst staying at the Pulteney Hotel in Piccadilly.[17] During her visit in 1816, when she attended Lady Heathcote's ball in Grosvenor Square, thus perhaps reflecting the lessening of mutual animosity, at supper 'the principal table was laid with seventy covers ... the Regent and his amiable brother [were] at the table ... Amongst the leading personages at this table may be named ...[the] Dowager of Jersey.'[18]

This rather suggests that Frances Jersey, even if not popular with the Prince, was not regarded at the time as the avowed gadfly or Jezabel to him which history asserts. Entertainingly, Mrs Fitzherbert and Lady Hertford, another intimate if not lover of the Prince, were both also there. Despite all of which, 'His Royal Highness was in excellent spirits, and did not retire until four o'clock in the morning.'[19]

Later that year, the Dowager Countess was sufficiently sprightly to visit both Brighton and Leamington Spa.[20] She was, though, beginning to be aware of her years. Farington wrote in his diary in December 1816 of:

> A remarkable anecdote of the Dowager Lady Jersey expressive of her mortification at becoming Old with its consequences. – She was heard to say whilst supposing herself to be alone and whilst she was looking at herself in a glass – 'it will better to go to H-ll at once than live to be old & ugly'.[21]

The proud Countess was certainly old after years of acting thirty years younger than her age. Ugly, though, she was not:

> We are told that 'her beauty in the autumn of life (she had been known as "the beautiful Miss Twysden") was rather changed in style than diminished in degree; her graces, natural and acquired, of mind and manner, which equalled if they did not exceed, her personal charms, were perfected in the school of the great world and the Court'.[22]

Nor should we imagine, even though now needing spectacles to read, a wizened old lady with stereotypically blackened teeth. Even in the eighteenth century white teeth were admired, and to have scales or scuff on one's teeth was frowned upon. Toothbrushes were imported from France and Turkey and toothpaste was used consisting of a ground abrasive, like cuttlefish, coral or alabaster, combined with sweetening agents such as rose- or orange- flower water in order to keep teeth clean and white.[23]

Even so, knowing the power that her beauty had brought her, the Countess might be forgiven for lamenting its turning.

The following year the Countess was in London for Mrs Sloane's ball and, indeed, on the same night the Marchioness of Hertford's assembly. At the first, 'above 300 persons of fashion' were present, with dancing beginning at midnight, supper at two in the morning and departure at five o'clock. At the second, 'At midnight upwards of 1,000 people had arrived ... All the leading avenues were completely blocked up' as the guests made their way to Hertford House.[24]

Nor was the Countess yet finished with the season for 1817. She was at Mrs Dupré's assembly three days later and,[25] at the end of June, is reported to have attended the Queen's Drawing-Room, where she wore

> a superb suit of blond silk laceries, tastefully arranged over a petticoat of the richest white satin, pocket holes ornamented with blond lace, and finished with rich blond lace trimmings, &c.; body and train of white satin, with a profusion of point lace. Head dress, a beautiful plume of ostrich feathers and diamonds.[26]

Elegant to the end.

Before retiring to Cheltenham for the year, the Countess attended a ball at Almack's 'attended by a brilliant circle', with dancing from half-past midnight until four o'clock;[27] along with the Regent, she also attended Lady Heathcote's assembly.[28]

That, however, was the turning point, and the Countess from now on attended few parties as age took its toll. In 1818 the only entertainment which she is reported as attending in London was another of Lady Heathcote's assemblies where, once more, both the Prince and Mrs Fitzherbert were also present.[29]

She was back in London for the final time in the summer of 1819. On this occasion she went to a 'Grand Fancy Ball at Almack's'. Sally Jersey went as an 'Indian Queen', and both the Prince and Mrs Fitzherbert were there too. Sadly there is no report of what the Dowager wore, though one imagines that now she was past dressing up, even as a nun.[30]

Nevertheless, she proved that her brain and her tongue remained as sharp as ever and her views on the Regent unchanged, even if more rarely expressed, as Lady Jerningham wrote that July: 'It is reported that the Dowr Lady Jersey, on hearing that the Regent personated both King and Queen, in the Drawing-Room, said He was a sequence: King, Queen and Knave!'[31]

The same month, along with the Duke and Duchess of Argyll, Frances Jersey was at the King's Theatre to see a performance of Rossini's *Barber of Seville* in which, as *The Morning Post* gushingly reported, 'the singing of GARCIA and BELLOCHI was inimitable, nor did AMBROGETTI, ANGRISANI and PLACCI fall short of their wonted excellence'.[32]

And then on Tuesday 3 August 1819, nearly fifty years after her entry into Society, the Countess made her last recorded appearance on its stage. Fittingly this was, as *The Morning Post* reported, at her daughter, the Duchess of Argyll's ball:

> A magnificent Fete was given yesterday evening, at her Grace's residence in Upper Brook–street ... a temporary ball-room was erected forming a chain with the *suite* apartments on the drawing–room floor ... Dancing commenced at eleven ... at two the company retired to the supper rooms.[33]

And then the Countess withdrew for the final time.

Even as the Countess was withdrawing from Society, there was another reminder of her legacy. In May 1816 Princess Charlotte had married, for love, Prince Leopold of Saxe-Coburg. In November 1817 she had given birth to a stillborn son and, although she was initially said to be doing extremely well following the birth, a few hours later she suffered a haemorrhage and died. The news came as a profound shock both to her family and to the nation.[34]

Returning to England from abroad a few days later, Lord and Lady Holland witnessed the universal grief:

> Everyone they met on the road from Dover to London, including post boys and turnpike men, was wearing some kind of mourning. But the outburst of grief, thought Holland was more an indication of the unpopularity of the Prince Regent and his brothers 'than the childish affection for Royalty, which the people of England so frequently display'[35]

Frances Jersey was a material cause of that unpopularity.

A subscription fund was rapidly set up for the erection of a public monument to the late Princess, under which subscribers were to give one guinea each towards its cost. The list of subscribers was published in *The Times* on 30 December 1817. Not surprisingly those listed included both the Earl and Countess of Jersey, whose closeness to the late Princess Charlotte is vividly demonstrated by a letter from Prince Leopold inviting them, sometime thereafter, to Claremont, the house near Esher where he and his wife had lived and she had died. In it the Prince asked them:

> To do me the honour of dining and sleeping at Claremont Sunday next the 23rd ... Amusements I have none to offer you but you will feel interested in seeing poor Claremont again connected as it now is with the memory of one so dear to you.[36]

Equally unsurprisingly, the list of subscribers for Princess Charlotte's monument did not include the Dowager Countess of Jersey.

The outpouring of emotion caused by the death of Princess Charlotte was to be eclipsed a few years later by the death of George III on 29 January 1820. Rejecting an offer of an annuity of £50,000 in return for foregoing her rights as Queen, Princess Caroline arrived in England on 5 June that year to claim them. She was rapturously greeted in the streets of London by cheering crowds but her arrival forced the new King's hand. He insisted on initiating proceedings for divorce and the disqualification of Caroline from becoming Queen. In August the House of Lords gathered to hear the evidence of immorality against the Queen and to decide on the government's Bill of Pains and Penalties which, if passed into law, would result in Caroline's divorce and disqualification. These proceedings came to be known as the 'Trial of Queen Caroline'.[37]

All of which galvanized the nation into two camps and into a general uproar. Sally Jersey was just one, albeit one of the most vociferous, of those espousing Princess Caroline's cause. Some say that this was, in part at least, to annoy her mother-in-law who, of course, had been the enemy of Caroline for many years.[38] Yet there is no evidence of this. On the contrary, as we have seen, Sally Jersey had long been a friend of Caroline and, in particular, her daughter, and in recent years had been regarded by the Prince as an enemy as a consequence. Further she felt, now at least, no resentment of her mother-in-law. Put simply, she, like half the nation, detested the Prince's treatment of his wife both in the past and in the present. Indeed, 'the outcry against him was terrific. The Press ... outdid itself in scurrility.'[39]

The 'Trial of the Queen' dominated the news, gossip and conversation. The King was portrayed as 'a monster of depravity and a wicked and cowardly schemer against his injured wife'. Some speculated whether his coronation would ever take place, and the future Prime Minister Robert Peel was not alone in asking whether the monarchy could survive. Revolution seemed a possibility. Even though the evidence of Caroline's indiscretions seemed overwhelming, she was still regarded by many as a wronged and much persecuted victim.[40]

The Bill of Pains and Penalties was, despite all this, eventually passed in the House of Lords in November 1820, albeit by a narrow margin, with Lord Jersey voting against it. However, Lord Liverpool, the Prime Minister, promptly announced that the Bill would be withdrawn rather than face the threat of violent popular disorder as a result of the government trying to force it through the House of Commons so as to become law.[41] Accordingly Caroline remained Queen, even though never crowned.

Harriet Granville wrote to Lady Morpeth on 13 November to describe the public's reaction:

> I have the following effusion from Silence to Granville: 'You never saw anything like the universal joy of the country. All the way we came people of every rank cheering, and in the towns and most respectable persons came to shake hands with Lord Jersey and thank him for his vote. The Queen was in everyone's mouth, in everyone's hat, upon every cart and in every house. They drew us through the towns, and there was not one person drunk!'[42]

These turbulent events too were part of the Dowager Countess's legacy. Once again the Prince's actions in relation to a disastrous marriage a quarter of a century earlier and a hated wife resulted in his being pilloried, his unpopularity soaring and the monarchy itself falling seemingly under threat. The architect of that marriage was Frances Jersey.

Within months, though, the public lost interest in the fate of Princess Caroline. Instead it became 'coronation mad'. The ceremony, which was to take place on 19 July 1821, was an exercise of extraordinary pageantry, with a budget more than three times the cost of George III's coronation. It was, in the words of Sir Walter Scott, to provide a 'degree of splendor which [foreign visitors] averred they had never seen paralleled in Europe'. There had not been a coronation for sixty years and the nation was entranced as the plans for it unfolded.[43]

In the months running up to the ceremony, with Sally Jersey's encouragement Princess Caroline had sought to create her own court by replicating a royal Drawing-Room at Brandenburgh House and by giving concerts which were attended by, amongst others, Sally Jersey.[44] Nevertheless by the time of the coronation, as Lady Cowper wrote, 'Even Ly Jersey ha[d] left her'.[45]

Instead, and somewhat remarkably, the younger Jerseys were reconciled with the King. As early as 9 June 1821 Lady Cowper was writing to her brother:

> Ld & Ly Jersey have announced now that they stay for the Coronation – *comme c'est ridicule* – but I must bridle my tongue for I am going today to dine alone with her & to explain why I don't seem so fond of her as I used to be.[46]

Then, three days before the coronation, 'the Countess of Jersey gave a grand rout ... in Berkeley Square ... It was attended by upwards of 200 distinguished fashionables, including most of the Foreigners who are arrived to attend the Coronation'.[47]

The ultimate proof of reconciliation was that Sally Jersey's sons were two of the six royal pages at the ceremony, an appointment which Lady Jersey refused until the King himself asked her in writing.[48] So complete was the reconciliation that at the coronation the Jersey boys were 'almost the only boys [the King] took any notice of'.[49]

There were two other ladies, however, with whom there was no reconciliation. The first was Princess Caroline, who famously found the doors of Westminster Abbey closed against her at the coronation. The second was her hated rival Frances Jersey, who was probably not invited either but certainly did not attend, remaining instead at Cheltenham.

And then, suddenly, death intervened.

On 23 July 1821, four days after her former lover's coronation, the Dowager Countess was taken ill at Cheltenham. She died there two days later on 25 July.[50] Her funeral took place on 1 August when, as *The Morning Post* of the following day reported:

> The Remains of the Countess Dowager of Jersey were interred yesterday morning in the family vault at Middleton Park, Oxfordshire.[51]

The Dowager Countess was approaching seventy when she died. Nevertheless it seems that her death was unexpected, as the Duke of Wellington wrote to Sally Jersey two days later: 'It must have shocked you as well as Lord Jersey but I hope that you will not become nervous again.'[52]

The reactions to Frances Jersey's death were varied, but she had long ceased to be the figure she once was and for some was even to be pitied. In a real sense she was now just history.

Jerningham put it in its context, writing on 3 August:

> Poor Lady Jersey died at Cheltenham about a week ago; the news came to London on the day of the Duc de Grammont's fête at Almacks where the King was, with Lady Cunningham [Lady Conyngham, his current mistress].[53]

Or as he put it, rather more starkly and more pityingly, some days later: 'The Poor Dowr Lady Jersey is dead.'[54]

The Gentleman's Magazine whilst recording the bare facts of her death and burial added the understated comment: 'She was very unpopular at the period of the unhappy marriage of our present Sovereign.'[55]

Lord Clarendon was even more practical. As Creevey wrote that August:

> The other day Lord Jersey received a letter from Lord Clarendon begging him to come to him, which he did. He [Lord Clarendon] then told him that he was going as executor to open his [Lord Jersey's] mother's papers. The seal was then taken off, and letters from the Monarch to his former sweetheart caught Jersey's eye in great abundance. Lord Clarendon then proceeded to put them all in the fire, saying he had merely wished Lord Jersey to be present at their destruction, and as a witness that they had never been seen by anyone. Very genteel, this, on Lord Clarendon's part to the living Monarch and memory of his mistress, but dammed provoking to think that such capital materials for the instruction and improvement of men and womankind should be eternally lost![56]

For the time being some other papers survived. On the death of the King's former Private Secretary, Col McMahon, his executor Sir William Knighton found some 'very delicate' papers relating to the private affairs of the King, particularly in relation to Princess Caroline and Lady Jersey. These he instantly took to Carlton House in order to put them, as was said, in the hands of their rightful owner who, presumably, then had them destroyed.[57]

It was not long, however, before the demonisation of Frances Jersey in print began, sealing her reputation in history and turning many a myth into fact. Robert Huish's largely apocryphal *Memoirs of George IV* was to be published in 1831 and put many untrue stories about the Countess into the public consciousness. Before then, though, other publications appeared. Amongst these, two stand out.

The first was an anonymous pamphlet, published in 1806, entitled the *Delicate Investigation* (a formal investigation was being carried out at the behest of the Prince into the possibility of Princess Caroline being guilty of adultery). The pamphlet was subtitled a *Plain Letter to his Royal Highness upon his Plain Duties*. Even though it was written ten years after the events it (fairly accurately) describes, it drips with venom directed at Lady Jersey.

It records that, scarcely had the wedding of the Prince and Caroline taken place,

> when the bride is told, through officiousness or malevolence, that amongst the suite who had the honour to attend Her Royal Highness, there was at least one old lady, the wife of a contemptible degraded Peer who was equally a dishonour to her rank, a disgrace to her sex, and an insult to her Royal Highness.[58]

It goes on to say, bitingly, that the affair between the Prince and Lady Jersey

> must be discovered, and her Royal Highness be informed, that this courtgoing-lady, the wife of an Earl, the mother and grandmother of children, chosen of course for her superior virtue and reputation to attend the Royal Highness did immediately before, if not when upon the journey to meet Her Royal Highness, sleep shamefully and adulterously with the intended husband of Her Royal Highness, to the eternal infamy of the lady, at least.
>
> Could the Princess just married to such a Prince, with such a woman still about her person, aye and about her husband's person too, feel any emotions but those of scorn and abhorrence! She could not'[59]

The second was a short book, again anonymous, published the year after the Countess's death under the title of the *Death-bed Confessions of the Late Countess of Guernsey* – by which, of course, it meant the late Countess of Jersey.

In this Princess Caroline was presented as the innocent she largely was, whilst the late Countess was depicted as the 'viper that has been secretly wounding [her] ... for the last five-and-twenty years' with the aim of alienating Princess Caroline from her husband and his family. As proof of this, the Countess confesses to various offences which have varying degrees of semblance to the truth.

First she acknowledges that, in order to get closer to the Prince of Wales, she persuaded the Queen that she should be made lady-in-waiting to Princess Caroline, 'to secure her husband for myself'.

Then she admits writing to the Queen 'detracting' Princess Caroline and telling Caroline herself about the Prince's relations with Mrs Fitzherbert.

She confesses, too, to spiking Caroline's cider with brandy so that the Princess is drunk at her own wedding.

And, as a final example, the Countess allows that she told the Prince that Caroline had said to her that 'she had *known* several [men] more elegant in form than his R– H– [and] ... took care to lay such emphasis on the word *known*', so as to create the worst impression possible.[60]

Founded on fact as some of these 'confessions' were, all were exaggerated and some completely untrue. But all, wrapped in the venom that she inspired, ultimately entered the pantheon of mythology that is the story of the Countess of Jersey.

20

The Verdict of History

Frances Jersey left thirty-six grandchildren and a reputation so bad that is has not been challenged in the 200 years since her death.

Writing in 1924, Margaret, Countess of Jersey, tells the story of the death of one of Frances Jersey's grandchildren, Lady Clementina Villiers, nearly forty years after Frances's death:

> As for [Sally Jersey's] beautiful daughter Lady Clementina, she was locally regarded as an angel, and I have heard that when she died the villagers resented her having been buried next to her grandmother, Frances Lady Jersey, as they thought her much too good to lie next to the lady who had won the fleeting affections of George IV.[1]

That was in the little Parish Church of Middleton Stoney, the Church of All Saints. The church, surrounded by a low wall, sits within the park at Middleton itself. On one side of the church is a memorial chapel to the Jersey family, built in 1805. In it can be found separate plaques in memory of various members of the family. There is a plaque for the 4th Earl as well one for each of his father and his son, the 5th Earl. There is one, too, in memory of Augustus, who is recorded as being buried in 'Picton', Nova Scotia, and also one for Sally Jersey.

There is none for Frances Jersey.

Such was her reputation.

The Countess was, though, an extraordinary woman who led an extraordinary life. She was a glittering leader of Society in a glittering age. She was one of the great beauties of her time with enormous style and great wit. Her charm, when she chose to use it, was legendary, even bewitching. She had enormous force of will and could, like an enchantress, bend people to her will – even against their better judgement. Well into middle age she had huge sex appeal and an attractiveness which infatuated even those a generation younger than her. She was the epitome of a woman of the beau monde.

She was very spirited and devoted to pleasure and to parties. Physically, as her exploits on the hunting field show, she was brave to the point of rashness. She had great moral courage, unshakeable self-belief and a backbone of steel. How otherwise could she have deliberately faced up to the very public vilification she was confronted with and, in her own view at least, faced it down?

She was devoted to her friends and to children, and not just her own. For her children she campaigned indefatigably and was capable of great kindness to others and to those in trouble. She would eagerly throw herself into helping her friends in all manner of ways. In Countess Spencer's words, 'she has a better heart than she appears to have'.

Unlike many of those friends, though, politics barely interested her and she avoided the bane of the age, gambling.

Instead, Frances Jersey's primary interest was herself and in the pursuit of pleasure and the pleasures of Society. In that she was a veritable chameleon.

Capable of great affection, warmth and solicitude to her friends, she was also self-centred, vain and selfish – and dismissive of former friends. Normally sensible, even shrewd, she was capable of serious misjudgements of what was wise, acceptable or even right. She was often self-deluding and was increasingly regarded as fast, unreliable and unprincipled. She could be manipulative, malicious and cruel. She had a habit of losing friends. When it did not suit her to treat others well, she was capable of treating them very badly. In particular she took delight in tormenting her rivals when she was in a position of strength and they were not.

In her pomp as the royal mistress she exploited her position in personal ways although notably not in financial ones. She saw the opportunity and advantages of becoming the Prince's lover and seized them. Having succeeded in that, she was supercilious, domineering and often malevolent. To maximise her influence, she treated all – of both sexes – who had previously been close to the Prince badly and was divisive and dismissive so as to separate them from him.

She treated her adoring but naïve husband with extraordinary arrogance and cruelty, making him very unhappy over the years. She mocked the Earl both to his face and behind his back, in both words and actions. She drove him, who was in some ways indeed in trepidation of her, to do her sometimes absurd bidding. She was a serial adulteress, although in her time this was scarcely remarkable; nevertheless, the Countess was having one affair or another almost continually over some thirty years and humiliated her husband by flaunting the fact. Her children had at least four different fathers, possibly more.

Frances Jersey was highly sexed and generally it was her who took the initiative in her affairs. She had no scruples in embracing as her lovers both a father and his son, thirty years her junior and a half- brother to her children, or even a future son-in-law. Even so, by the standards of the time, this too was hardly exceptional.

Even adding all of this together does not justify the odium which history has attached to the name of the Countess of Jersey. Many, both in her time and in other times, are guilty of similar sins without having achieved the same degree of ill repute. Nor do many of the stories about the Countess which over the years have acquired the veneer of truth as a result of history, in the nature of a self-fulfilling prophesy, coming to believe the worst of one who already had a bad reputation.

So we have seen that the story of the Countess forcing Princess Caroline on her arrival at Greenwich to change into an unflattering dress and rouging her cheeks in order to create a bad impression on the Prince is not true. This canard, though, at least has the merit of reflecting some elements of reality. Other stories, like encouraging the Princess to eat onions because the Prince liked the smell, putting Epsom salts in the Princess's food and spiking her drinks with brandy to make her drunk, do not even have that merit. Nor do they reflect any likelihood and do not need to detain us for a moment.

We have seen, too, that the mischiefs commonly attributed to Frances Jersey's desire for revenge following her dismissal are simply not the acts of the Countess. She was indeed piqued, and acted accordingly, in the years that followed. However it was not her who, to the irritation of the Prince, attended Princess Charlotte's sittings for her portrait. Nor was it her who waltzed with the Emperor of Russia to the annoyance of the Prince Regent. It was not her, either, who was the infernal Jezabel who meddled – if indeed anyone did meddle – with the Prince's planned marriage of his daughter to the Hereditary Prince of Orange.

The real mischiefs of Frances Jersey, and the real legacy of this extraordinary woman, lie elsewhere. That is in the unhappy marriage of the Prince of Wales and Princess Caroline. This disastrous marriage, sponsored by the Countess for her own purposes and to bolster her own ambitions, was her first sin. It in its turn was to generate two further and enduring sins.

The first was that through the malevolent and cruel treatment of Princess Caroline during the early years of the marriage, encouraged by Lady Jersey, the Prince blackened both their reputations beyond redemption. The actions of the 'viper', the Prince's flaunting of his mistress, the Carlton House system, the ever present hated Lady of the Bedchamber, the arrogance of the Countess, the theft of Caroline's letters, and the scorn and disdain heaped upon the Princess by the Countess and a husband who hated her provoked immense public anger against them both and much sympathy for the Princess.

The second was to flow from this and become an open sore for years to come. So much did the Prince hate, and perhaps resent, his gauche wife that he could not resist the temptation of injuring Princess Caroline whenever he had the opportunity to do so, even long after he had ceased to have the encouragement of the Countess. Whenever he did so, whether it was the 'Intimate Enquiry', restricting Caroline's access to her daughter, the 'Trial of the Queen' or Caroline's exclusion from his coronation, the result was the same. In all cases, until Caroline turned her back on the doors of Westminster Abbey, there was public outcry against the Prince and public sympathy for the wronged Princess against her cruel and dissolute husband. The effect was that a disliked Prince and King, although there were also other reasons for his unpopularity, simply reminded his subjects of that fact and turned unpopularity into widespread derision.

Indeed, twice on account of this marriage and the treatment of Princess Caroline by the Prince and Frances Jersey the Monarchy itself had seemed under threat and its survival uncertain, so violent was the public reaction to their deeds.

Even on the death of George IV in June 1830 the mood was hardly grieving as the country recalled his dissolute character and his misdeeds.

In short, 'the general mood was hardly one of mourning at his passing'.[2]

In the words of Charles Greville on the King's death:

> Nobody thinks any more of the late King than if he had been dead fifty years, unless it be to abuse him and to rake up all his vices and misdeeds ... nobody ever was less regretted ... and the breath was hardly out of his body before the press burst forth in full cry against him, and raked up all his vices, follies, and misdeeds, which were numerous and glaring enough.

To which Mme de Lieven added that the King was

> completely forgotten, and if remembered, it is only to criticise his morals. It is in the middle and lower classes especially that this side of his character has left a very unfavourable impression – an impression which overshadows much that was striking and brilliant in his reign. His glory is forgotten, and his vices exaggerated; so true is it that what a nation most appreciates in its sovereign is domestic virtue.[3]

Even his funeral, though 'a fine sight', evoked little sadness. Lord Ellenborough wrote of it in his diary:

> King George IV is gone to his grave with all the pomp of royalty, and splendid the pageant was; but it was considered a mere pageant even by his household, who had lived so intimately with him for years. There was no regret. A coronation could hardly be gayer.[4]

It was left to *The Times*, admittedly no friend of the late King, to add the brutal epitaphs, and in so doing remind the world of the role of the Countess of Jersey.

First, as a supporter of the Princess of Wales, it thundered in the King's obituary on 28 June:

> The Princess of Wales would not, it is probable, under any circumstances have made her husband a fit member of the marriage state.
>
> To supply that absent grace to his character she must have reclaimed him; and the wife who would reclaim a libertine must begin by awakening his affections. But the affections of the Prince of Wales! where were they? of what nature? by what engaged, or by whom? His passions, alas! were

> known to be far otherwise excited. His pity might have been touched but if Caroline of Brunswick herself could feel that sentiment, she disdained to sue for it.
>
> Her reception in her husband's house was a stain to manhood. A fashionable strumpet usurped the apartments of the Princess – her rights – the honours due to her, – and everything but the name she bore, and the bonds which galled and disgraced her. The Master of the mansion felt not his own dignity insulted, when the half-drunken menials made their Royal mistress the subject of gross ribaldry or spiteful abuse! She complained to her parent; her letters were intercepted, and the seals violated; the offence of her misery was unmercifully punished ... Unsated malice, vengeance, perjury and persecution followed her.

It went on:

> The late King had many generations of intimates with whom he led a course of life, the character of which rose little higher than that of animal indulgence.[5]

Then, famously, on the day following the King's funeral it wrote of him:

> An inveterate voluptuary, especially if he be an artificial person, is of all known beings the most selfish. Selfishness is the true repellant of human sympathy. Selfishness feels no attachment, and it invites none; it is the charnel-house of the affections ...
>
> The truth is, however, – and it speaks volumes about the man, – that there never was an individual less regretted by his fellow-creatures than this deceased King.[6]

So King George IV went to his grave disgraced by, and to be remembered in the light of, his many misdeeds, not least his marriage to and treatment of Princess Caroline. And in that Frances Jersey played no mean part.

That is her legacy and for that and what flowed from it she must take the blame. In the space of a handful of years Frances Jersey destroyed an already doubtful reputation and helped blacken that of a future King. That apart, her conduct was neither exceptional for her time nor unconscionable in any other. For 200 years she has been treated as the personification of malevolence, often on the back of falsehoods. She was a remarkable woman. She was not all bad let alone that bad.

History has been harsh to Frances, Countess of Jersey.

21
Afterword

And what remains now of these glittering times and these dramatic events? Some injustice, indeed. And some reputations – pungent, fragrant or otherwise: Georgiana Devonshire, no saint, remains a name familiar to many to this day, even if that of her husband does not. Harriet Bessborough's name too features large in the biography sections of libraries (even in her time she was known as a serial adulteress), though her mother's does not. Lady Jersey's obviously lives on as well but more in the nature of a disreputable footnote to history, her husband forgotten. Lady Melbourne's name is mostly remembered through her son, Queen Victoria's first prime minister, even though he (like most of his siblings) was not, despite his name, Lord Melbourne's child. As a future king, the Prince of Wales, another multiple sinner, is clearly well remembered – and indeed the current Prince of Wales doubtless had him in mind when he told his then wife that all Princes of Wales have affairs.

Some titles survive too, some with greater resonance than others: Jersey, Devonshire, Carlisle, Spencer and, under a different name, Hanover all still exist. Others, Melbourne for one, do not.

A surprising number of the places where this story unfolded also survive. Middleton Park does not. It was demolished in the 1930s by the 9th Earl of Jersey and replaced with a Lutyens mansion. The Earl of Jersey sold the new house in 1946 (it is now apartments) to go and live, serendipitously, in Jersey. Sadly, many of the family's paintings were destroyed in a warehouse fire in Jersey shortly thereafter. The little church in the grounds of Middleton, and its plaques or the absence of a plaque, remains. The house itself served as a military hospital during the Second World War so part of the church's graveyard is now a Commonwealth War Graves Commission cemetery.

Osterley, with its Adam interiors, brought to the Jerseys by the 5th Earl's marriage to Sally Fane, survives and is now owned by the National Trust.

Miraculously, Chatsworth, in its full glory, remains in private hands as does Blenheim Palace. So too does that jewel of the north, Castle Howard. Despite the unbridled malice of Manny Shinwell, Minister of Fuel & Power in Clement Attlee's post-war Labour Government, Wentworth Woodhouse has also survived, just.

Roe, the Bessborough's house in Roehampton, survives in part. Its Grade 1 listed portico, with huge unimpeded views over Richmond Park and foxes strolling on the lawns, is now an appendage to the concrete and plate-glass of Roehampton University. Wimbledon Park House, the Spencers' country house outside London, has gone. Its gardens in part now a public park, Wimbledon Park, next to the home of the All England Tennis Club, hosts of the Wimbledon Lawn Tennis Championship, the Spencers' ornamental lake now a boating lake. Devonshire house in Piccadilly, too, has long since been demolished as has Almack's in King Street, St James's although remembered in the name of a modern office block on its site.

Two other jewels, though, have survived. Owing to the generosity and commitment of Lord Rothschild, the Spencers' townhouse in St James's, Spencer House, has been restored to its former glory, whilst in west London Chiswick House, now owned by the London Borough of Hounslow, retains much of its former glory and all of its former beauty.

On the other hand, whilst the Prince's Pavilion at Brighton has also survived, Carlton House, despite the enormous sums he spent on it, was demolished in 1825.

So much of what surrounded the Countess lives on that it is still possible to walk in the footsteps of Frances Jersey – and even, if you choose, where her husband fell – in many of the places she frequented in her pomp. There, one can imagine her presence and her world and see, surviving to this day, the glory and elegance of an aristocratic century, a century in which the beautiful and bewitching Enchantress glittered.

List of Illustrations

15. Georgiana Poyntz, Countess Spencer, by Thomas Gainsborough (*c.* 1780–1781). © Devonshire Collection, Chatsworth. Reproduced by permission of Chatsworth Settlement Trustees.
16. Georgiana, Duchess of Devonshire, by Thomas Gainsborough. © Devonshire Collection, Chatsworth. Reproduced by permission of Chatsworth Settlement Trustees.
17. Letter (first page) from Frances, Countess of Jersey, to Frederick, 5th Earl of Carlisle, dated 19 February ?1784. From the Castle Howard Archive, reference J14/1/622A. Reproduced by kind permission of the Howard family.
18. Letter (second page) from Frances, Countess of Jersey, to Frederick, 5th Earl of Carlisle, dated 19 February ?1784. From the Castle Howard Archive, reference J14/1/622A. Reproduced by kind permission of the Howard family.
19. Frederick, 5th Earl of Carlisle, by Sir Joshua Reynolds (1769). From the Castle Howard Collection. Reproduced by kind permission of the Howard family.
20. Princess Caroline of Brunswick, by Sir Thomas Lawrence. © National Portrait Gallery, London.

Notes

Foreword

1. *8th Report of The Historical Manuscripts Commission (HMC) and Appendix* Parts 1–3, London, HMSO, 1881. pp. 92b–101b.
2. *Creevey, Selected and Reedited by John Gore*, London, John Murray, 1948, ('Creevey'), p. 216.
3. Aspinall, A. ed., *The Correspondence of George, Prince of Wales 1770–1812*, 8 Vols, London, Cassell, 1953–1971, ('Aspinall PoW'), Vol. 2, p. 446, note 9 to letter 852.
4. Ibid.
5. Aspinall PoW, Vol. 1, pp. v-vi.
6. Aspinall, A. ed., *The Letters of King George IV 1812–1830*, 3 Vols, Cambridge, Cambridge University Press, 1938, ('Aspinall Giv'), Vol. 1, p. lxxii.
7. Creevey, p. 216.

1 – The Beautiful Miss Twysden

1. *The Times*, 29 June 1830.
2. White, Jerry, *London in the 18th Century, A Great and Monstrous Thing*, London, Vintage, 2013, ('White London'), p. 395.
3. Halstead, Edward, *The History and Topographical Survey of the County of Kent*, Vol. 5, 1798, pp. 91–106.
4. British Library Additional MSS ('Add MSS'), 34177, f. 49.
5. Twisden, Sir John Ramskill, Bt, *The Family of Twysden or Twisden. Their History and archives*, London, John Murray, 1939 ('Twysden Family'), p. 301.
6. Twysden Family, p. 301.
7. *Dictionary of Irish Biography*, Cambridge University Press, 2010.
8. Delaney, Mrs Mary, *The Autobiography and Correspondence of Mary Granville, Mrs. Delaney*, London, Richard Bentley, 1862, Vol. 3, p. 173, 14 November 1752.

9. Jersey, Margaret Countess of, *Records of the Family of Villiers, Earls of Jersey*, London, Morton, Burt & Sons, 1924 ('Jersey Records'), p. 23.
10. Twysden Family, p. 304.
11. Berkeley, the Hon Grantley, *My Life and Recollections*, London, Hurst and Blackett, 1865, Vol. 1, p. 213.
12. Twysden Family, pp. 304–305.
13. Twysden Family, pp. 303–304.
14. *London Evening Post*, 27 February 1753.
15. Twysden Family, p. 306.
16. Jersey Records, p. 23.
17. Coxe, Howard, *The Stranger in the House*, London, Chatto & Windus, 1939, pp. 28–29.

2 – The Prince of Macaronies

1. Keynes, John Maynard, *The Collected Writings, Vol. X, Essays in Biography*, London, Macmillan, 1972, pp. 62–63.
2. Walpole, Horace, *Correspondence, Yale Edition*, ed. W. S. Lewis, 48 Vols, London, Oxford University Press, 1937–1983 ('Walpole Correspondence'), Vol. 32/I, p. 247, 3 August 1775.
3. Kelly, Linda, *A History of London's Most Celebrated Salon, Holland House*, London, J B Tauris & Co Ltd, 2013 ('Kelly Holland House'), p. 209.
4. Chatham, Hester Pitt, Lady, *So Dearly Loved, So Much Admired: Letters 1774–1801*, ed. Vere Birdwood, London, HMSO, 1994, p. 84, 24 July 1750.
5. Kelly Holland House, p. 163.
6. *Whitehall Evening Post*, 4 June 1754.
7. Walpole Correspondence, Vol. 35, pp. 71–72.
8. London Metropolitan Archives, City of London, Jersey Collection ('LMA Jersey MSS') LMA/ACC/1128/216, nd ?1841–1842.
9. LMA Jersey MSS LMA/ACC/1128/238, nd ?1755.
10. Jersey Records, p. 36.
11. Climenson, Emily J. ed., *Passages from the Diary of Mrs. Philip Lybbe Powys, AD 1756 to 1808*, London, Longmans Green, 1899, pp. 197–198, 1778.
12. Norton, E. J. ed., *Gibbon, Edward – The Letters of Edward Gibbon*, 3 Vols, London, Cassell and Company, 1956, no. 10, Vol. 1, p. 36, *c.* 15 November 1756.
13. History of Parliament online, *The History of Parliament: the House of Commons 1754–1790,* ed. L. Namier, J. Brooke, 1964.
14. Anson, Sir William R., *Autobiography and Political Correspondence of Augustus Henry, 3rd Duke of Grafton*, London, John Murray, 1898 ('Grafton Biography'), pp. 75–81.
15. Friedman, Joseph, *Spencer House: The Chronicle of a Great London Mansion*, London, Zwemmer, 1993, pp. 132–133.
16. Cunnington, C. Willett & Phyllis, *Handbook of English Costume in the Eighteenth Century*, Boston, Plays, Inc, 1972, ('Cunnington Costume'), p. 23.

17. Doran, John, *Lady of the Last Century*, London, Richard Bentley, 1873, p. 205.
18. Dewes, Simon, *Mrs. Delaney*, London, Rich & Cowan Ltd, 1940, p. 246.
19. Harcourt, William ed., *The Harcourt Papers*. 14 Vols, Privately Printed, 1880–1885 ('Harcourt Papers'), Vol. 7, p. 242, 11 September 1763.
20. Harcourt Papers, Vol. 7, p. 240, 2 August 1763.
21. Lennox, Lady Sarah, *The Life and Letters of Lady Sarah Lennox, ed. The Countess of Ilchester and Lord Stavordale*, London, John Murray, 1901, Vol. 1, p. 135, 16 October 1763.
22. Coke, Lady Mary, *The Letters and Journals of Lady Mary Coke*, Bath, Kingsmead Reprints, 1970, ('Coke Journals'), Vol. 1, p. 12, 31 May 1767.

3 – Courtship and Marriage

1. Beckett, J. V., *The Aristocracy in England 1660–1914*, Oxford, Basil Blackwell, 1986, p. 487.
2. Cannon, John, *Aristocratic Century, The peerage of eighteenth century England*, Cambridge, Cambridge University Press, 1984, p. 85.
3. Add MSS 75672, nd, ?September 1769.
4. Add MSS 75672, 10 October 1769.
5. Add MSS 75672, 26 November 1769.
6. Add MSS 75672, 4 December 1769.
7. Add MSS 75672, 18 December 1769.
8. Add MSS 75672, 29 January 1770.
9. Add MSS 75672, 1 February 1770.
10. Add MSS 75672, 9 February and 25 March 1770.
11. Add MSS 75672, 9 February 1770.
12. Add MSS 75672, 6 February and 9 February 1770.
13. Add MSS 75672, 22 February 1770.
14. LMA Jersey MSS LMA/ACC/1128/376, ?26 March 1770.
15. LMA Jersey MSS LMA/ACC/1128/238, 27 March 1770.
16. Add MSS 75673, ?27 March 1770.
17. National Archives PRO 30/29 ('Granville MSS'), PRO 30/29/4/2/33, 2 April 1770.
18. Coke Journals, Vol. 3, p. 231, 3 April 1770.

4 – Respectability

1. Jersey Records, p. 23.
2. Wheatley, Henry B. ed., *The Historical and Posthumous Memoirs of Sir Nathaniel Wraxall 1772–1784*, London, Black & Son, 1884. Vol. 5, p. 36.
3. Cokayne G. E., *The Complete Peerage*, London, St Catherine's Press, 1929, Vol. VII, pp. 90–91.
4. Queen Victoria's Journals website ('Queen Victoria's Journals'), RA VIC/MAIN/QVJ (W) 17 November 1838 (Lord Esher's typescripts). Retrieved 10 September 2015.

5. Stokes, Hugh, *The Devonshire House Circle*, The London and Norwich Press, 1917, p. 137.
6. Foreman, Amanda, *Georgiana, Duchess of Devonshire*, London, HarperCollins Publishers, 1998 ('Foreman Georgiana'), p. 77.
7. King, Dean, *Patrick O'Brian, A Life Revealed*, New York, Henry Holt and Company, 2000, pp. 106–107.
8. Add MSS 75673, 14 October 1770.
9. Cunnington Costume, p. 349.
10. Hibbert, Christopher, *George IV: Prince of Wales 1762–1811*, London, Longman, 1972 ('Hibbert Prince'), p. 131.
11. Harcourt Papers, Vol. 7, p. 287, 25 June 1770.
12. Add MSS 75673, nd.
13. Harcourt Papers, Vol. 7, p. 289, 30 June 1770.
14. Add MSS 75673, 9 July 1770.
15. Add MSS 75673, 17 July 1770.
16. Add MSS 75673, 25 July 1770.
17. Add MSS 75673, 30 July 1770.
18. Add MSS 75673, 8 August 1770.
19. *Memoirs of the Life and Correspondence of Hannah More, ed. William Roberts*, London, R B Seeley and W Burnside, 1834, Vol. 3, p. 26.
20. Add MSS 75673, 16 August 1770.
21. Harcourt Papers, Vol. 7, p. 290, 23 August 1770.
22. Add MSS 75673, 17 ?September 1770.
23. Add MSS 75673, 14 October 1770.
24. Add MSS 75673, ?October 1770.
25. Add MSS 75673, 28 October 1770.
26. MSS 75673, nd 1771.
27. Add MSS 75673, postmark 2 May 1771.
28. Add MSS 75673, nd ?1771.
29. Add MSS 75673, nd ?1771.
30. Add MSS 75673, nd ?1771.
31. Add MSS 75673, nd ?1771.
32. Add MSS 75673, 27 June 1771.
33. Add MSS 75673, 14 July 1771.
34. Add MSS 75673, 21 July 1771.
35. Add MSS 75673, 11 August 1771.
36. Add MSS 75673, nd 1772?.
37. Harcourt Papers, Vol. 3, p. 113, 1772.
38. Harcourt Papers, Vol. 7, p. 298, June 1772.
39. Paston, George, *Social Caricature in the Eighteenth Century*, New York, Benjamin Blom, 1968, p. 17.
40. Add MSS 75673, July 1772.
41. Harcourt Papers, Vol. 7, p. 297, 11 July 1772.
42. Add MSS 75673, 19 July 1772.
43. Add MSS 75673, 17 August 1772.
44. Add MSS 75673, 31 August 1772.

45. Add MSS 75673, 23 September 1772.
46. Add MSS 75673, 27 October 1772.
47. Add MSS 75673, 8 November 1772.
48. Add MSS 75673, 27 November 1772.
49. Add MSS 75673, 20 December 1772.
50. Add MSS 75673, 24 December 1772.
51. White London, p. 307.
52. White London, p. 307.
53. White London, p. 308.
54. Add MSS 75673, 12 January 1773.
55. Add MSS 75673, 3 March 1773.
56. Add MSS 75673, 20 May 1773.
57. Add MSS 75673, 28 May 1773.
58. Add MSS 75673, 24 May 1773.
59. Add MSS 75673, 31 May 1773.
60. Add MSS 75673, 15 June 1773.
61. Add MSS 75673, 18 June 1773.
62. Add MSS 75673, 27 June 1773.
63. Add MSS 75674, 5 July 1773.
64. Add MSS 75674, 28 July 1773.
65. Add MSS 75674, 9 August 1773.
66. Add MSS 75674, 19 August 1773.
67. Harcourt Papers, Vol. 7, p. 300, 19 August 1773.
68. Add MSS 75674, 23 August 1773.
69. Add MSS 75674, 30 August 1773.
70. Add MSS 75674, 5 September 1773.
71. Add MSS 75683, 26 September 1773.

5 – Les Liaisons Dangereuses

1. Stone, Lawrence, *The Family, Sex and Marriage in England 1500–1800*, London, Weidenfeld and Nicolson, 1977 ('Stone, Sex and Marriage'), pp. 530–533.
2. Harvey, A. D., *Sex in Georgian England*, London, Gerald Duckworth & Co Ltd, 1994, pp. 57–58.
3. Gattrell, Vic, *City of Laughter – Sex and Satire in 18th Century London*, London, Atlantic, 2006, p. 358.
4. Stone, Sex and Marriage, pp. 530–533.
5. Boucé, J-P., *Sexuality in eighteenth-century Britain*, Manchester, Manchester University Press, 1982, p. 18 and Oxford Dictionary of National Biography ('DNB').
6. Piggott, Charles, *The Female Jockey Club*, London, D. I. Eaton, 1794, p. 179.
7. Chatsworth MSS, 5th Duke's Group ('Chatsworth MSS'), 442, 16 October 1782.
8. Perry, Norma, *Sir Everard Fawkener, friend and correspondent of Voltaire*, Banbury, Voltaire Foundation, 1975 ('Everard Fawkener'), p. 147.

9. Walpole, Horace, *The Last Journals, 2 Vols*, London, John Lane The Bodley Head, 1910 ('Walpole Last Journals'), Vol. 1, p.37, footnote.
10. Selwyn, George, *George Selwyn, His Life and Letters*, ed. E. S. Roscoe, London, T Fisher Unwin, 1899, p. 138, note.
11. HMC, *The Manuscripts of the Earl of Carlisle preserved at Castle Howard, HMC 15th Report Appendix Part VI*, London, HMSO, 1897 ('HMC Carlisle'), pp. 521–522.
12. Blackmantle, Bernard (Westmacott, Charles), *The English Spy, 2 Vols*, London, Methuen & Co, 1825, Vol. 1, p. 71.
13. Steele, Mrs Elizabeth, *The Memoirs of Mrs. Sophia Baddeley, 3 Vols*, Dublin, privately printed, 1787 ('Sophia Baddeley'), p. 164.
14. Deffand, Marqise du, *Lettres de la Marquise du Deffand à Horace Walpole (1766–1780), ed. Mrs. Paget Toynbee, 3 Vols*, Londres, Methuen & Cie, 1912, Vol. 2, p. 562, 21 December 1773.
15. DNB.
16. Add MSS 47582, ?December 1773.
17. Add MSS 47582, 15 December 1773.
18. Add MSS 47582, 22 February 1774.
19. *The Diaries of Sylvester Douglas, Lord Glenbervie, 2 Vols*, ed. Francis Bickley, London, Constable, 1928 ('Glenbervie Diaries'), Vol. 2, p. 15.
20. Sophia Baddeley, Vol. 1, p. 88.
21. Harcourt Papers, Vol. 7, p. 305, 18 January 1774.
22. White London, p. 39.
23. White London, p. 39 and p. 235.
24. Porter, Roy, *English Society in the 18th Century*, Revised Edition, London, Penguin Books, 1991 ('Porter 18th Century'), p. 39.
25. White London, p. 63.
26. White London, p. 66.
27. White London, p. 189.
28. Harcourt Papers, Vol. 8, p. 62, 20 January 1774.
29. Williamson, G. W., *Daniel Gardner, painter*, London, John Lane, 1921, p. 136.
30. Harcourt Papers, Vol. 7, p. 308, 23 February 1774.
31. Harcourt Papers, Vol. 7, p. 309, 26 March 1774.
32. Add MSS 75674, 24 February 1774.
33. Add MSS 75674, nd 1774.
34. Add MSS 75674, 4 March 1774.
35. Add MSS 75674, 7 March 1774.
36. Chatsworth MSS, 33, 17 October 1774.
37. Harcourt Papers, Vol. 7, p. 309, 26 March 1774.
38. Add MSS 75576, 4 April 1774.
39. Add MSS 75674, 9 April 1774.
40. Harcourt Papers, Vol. 7, p. 309, 26 March 1774.
41. White London, p. 115.
42. Harcourt Papers, Vol. 7, p. 310, 23 April 1774.
43. Add MSS 75674, 25 April 1774.
44. White London, pp. 321–322.

45. Add MSS 75674, 25 April 1774.
46. Add MSS 75674, 25 April 1774.
47. Add MSS 75674, 29 April 1774.
48. Add MSS 75576, 29 April and 1 May 1774.
49. Add MSS 75674, 12 May 1774.
50. Add MSS 75674, 30 April 1774.
51. Add MSS 75674, 23 June 1774.
52. Add MSS 75674, 29 June 1774.
53. Harcourt Papers, Vol. 7, p. 312, 1 July 1774.
54. Add MSS 75674, 6 July 1774.
55. Add MSS 75674, 20 July 1774.
56. Add MSS 47582, 20 July 1774.
57. Add MSS 47582, 3 August 1774.

6 – The Social Whirl

1. Moore, Thomas, *The Journal of Thomas Moore, ed. Wilfred S. Dowden, 6 Vols*, London, Associated University Press, 1983, Vol. 1, p. 95.
2. Add MSS 75674, 31 July 1774.
3. Harcourt Papers, Vol. 7, p. 313, 31 July 1774.
4. Harcourt Papers, Vol. 7, p. 313, 31 July 1774.
5. Add MSS 75674, 3 August 1774.
6. Add MSS 75674, 14 August 1774.
7. Add MSS 75674, 19 August 1774.
8. Add MSS 75674, 11 September 1774.
9. Add MSS 75674, 21 September 1774.
10. Chatsworth MSS, 50, 24 November 1774.
11. Add MSS 75692, 13 October 1774.
12. Add MSS 75674, 29 November and 10 December 1774.
13. Minto, Countess of, *Memoir of Hugh Elliott*, Edinburgh, Edmonson and Douglas, 1868, pp. 76–77.
14. Add MSS 75674, 12 May 1775.
15. Walpole Correspondence, Vol. 35, p. 471, 28 May 1775.
16. Harcourt Papers, Vol. 7, p. 321.
17. Add MSS 75674, 11 July 1775.
18. Walpole Correspondence, Vol. 32/I, p. 247, 3 August 1775.
19. Harcourt Papers, Vol. 7, p. 322, 17 July 1775.
20. Add MSS 75674, 27 August 1775.
21. Harcourt Papers, Vol. 7, p. 324, 10 September 1775.
22. Add MSS 75674, 14 September 1775.
23. Add MSS 75683, 14 September 1775.
24. Add MSS 75675, 11 October 1775.
25. Add MSS 75675, 31 October 1775.
26. Stokes, Hugh, *The Devonshire House Circle*, The London and Norwich Press, 1917, p. 150, December 1775.

27. Add MSS 75692, 22 January 1776.
28. Foreman Georgiana, pp. 45–49.
29. Delany, Mrs Mary, *The Autobiography and Correspondence of Mary Granville, Mrs. Delany, ed. Rt Hon Lady Llanover*, 6 Vols, London, Richard Bentley, 1862, Vol. 5, p. 204, 2 April 1776.
30. Add MSS 75675, 15 July 1776.
31. Debrett, *Correct Peerage of England, Scotland and Ireland*, London, 1802.
32. Chatsworth MSS, 112.1, *c.* 25 December 1775.
33. Add MSS 75675, 28 July, 14 August and 4, 11 and 19 September 1776.
34. Chatsworth MSS, 126, 1 August 1776.
35. Chatsworth MSS, 128.1, 3? August 1776.
36. Add MSS 75675, 29 September 1776.
37. Chatsworth MSS, 139, 25 August 1776.
38. Add MSS 75675, 2 October 1776.
39. Chatsworth MSS, 154, 10 October 1776.
40. Chatsworth MSS, 44, 9 November, 1774.
41. Add MSS 75674, 7 December 1774.
42. Add MSS 75675, 2 November 1775.
43. Chatsworth MSS, 160, 18 October 1776.
44. Chatsworth MSS, 136, 2 August 1776.
45. Chatsworth MSS, 136, 10 August 1776.
46. Foreman Georgiana, p. 55.
47. *Anglo-Saxon Review*, June 1899, p. 237, 1 November 1776.
48. Add MSS 75675, 12, 18 and 26 June 1776.
49. Harcourt Papers, Vol. 7, p. 319, 16 December 1774.
50. Add MSS 75674, 17 December 1774.
51. Add MSS 75674, 19 December 1774.
52. Add MSS 75674, 21 December 1774.
53. Add MSS 75674, 24 December 1774.
54. Add MSS 75674, 3 January 1775.
55. Add MSS 75674, 7 January 1775.
56. Nethercote, H. O., *The Pytchley Hunt: Past and Present*, London, Sampson, Low, Mardston, Searle & Rivington, Limited, 1888, p. 6.
57. Paget, Guy, *The History of the Althorp and Pytchley Hunt 1634–1920*, London, Collins, 1937 ('Paget Pytchley'), p. 71.
58. Paget Pytchley, p. 77.
59. Paget Pytchley, pp. 47–48.
60. Add MSS 75576, 7 January 1775.
61. Paget Pytchley, p. 45.
62. Walpole, Horace, *The Last Journals of Horace Walpole During the Reign of George III from 1771–1783*, 2 Vols, London, John Lane The Bodley Head, 1910, Vol. 1, p. 485, October 1775.
63. HMC Carlisle, p. 301, 7 November 1775.
64. Add MSS 47582, 9 September 1774.
65. Bleackley, Horace, *The Beautiful Duchess, Being an Account of the Life and Times of Elizabeth Gunning Duchess of Hamilton and Argyll*, London, John Lane The Bodley Head, 1927 ('Bleackley Duchess of Hamilton'), p. 198.

66. White London, pp. 293 and 321.
67. Birkenhead, Sheila, *Peace in Piccadilly, The Story of Albany*, London, Hamish Hamilton, 1958, p. 16.
68. White London, pp. 340–343.
69. Foreman Georgiana, p. 50.
70. Borthwick Institute for Archives, University of York, Archives of the Earls of Halifax ('Halifax MSS') /A1.2.7.4, nd.
71. Castle Howard Archive, 5th Earl of Carlisle's MSS ('Castle Howard MSS'), J/18/20/96, nd.
72. Croft, Sir Herbert, *The abbey of Kilkhampton; or monumental records for the year 1980* [sic], London, 1780, pp. 4–5.
73. Castle Howard MSS, J/18/20, nd.
74. Castle Howard MSS, J/18/32/37 and 38, nd.
75. Add MSS 47582, 20 April and 24 June 1777.

7 – Tunbridge Wells and Coxheath Camp

1. Add MSS 75675, 18 July 1777.
2. Add MSS 47582, 28 July 1777.
3. White London, pp. 253 and 256.
4. Sophia Baddeley, Vol. 1, p. 82.
5. Chatsworth MSS, 182, 21 August 1777.
6. Chatsworth MSS, 188, 10 to 16 September 1777.
7. Chatsworth MSS, 189, 17 to 23 September 1777.
8. Chatsworth MSS, 190, 23 September to 2 October 1777.
9. Chatsworth MSS, 189, 23 September 1777.
10. Add MSS 75675, 14, 26 and 27 August and 3, 15, 21 and 28 September 1777.
11. Add MSS 75675, 27 August 1777.
12. Jersey Records, p. 27.
13. Add MSS 75683, August? 1777.
14. Harcourt Papers, Vol. 7, p. 329, 20 August 1777.
15. Add MSS 75675, 24 August 1777.
16. Add MSS 75675, 28 September 1777.
17. Harcourt Papers, Vol. 7, p. 48, 6 October 1777.
18. Walpole Last Journals, Vol. 2, p. 84.
19. Garrick, David, *The Letters of David Garrick, ed. David M. Little and George M. Kahrl*, 3 Vols, London, Oxford University Press, 1963 ('Garrick Little'), Vol. 3, p. 1207, 21 December 1777.
20. Garrick Little, p. 1205, 15 December 1777.
21. Add MSS 75694, 19 December 1777.
22. Add MSS 75675, 16 January 1778.
23. Doran, John, *Lady of the Last Century*, London, Richard Bentley, 1873, p. 205.
24. Add MSS 75675, 1 March 1778.
25. Harcourt Papers, Vol. 3, p. 291, nd.
26. Add MSS 45923, 11 October 1775.

27. Herbert, Charles, 'Coxheath Camp 1778–1779', *Journal of the Society for Army Historical Research*, Vol. 45, 1967 ('Herbert Coxheath'), p. 129.
28. Archenholz, J. W. von, *A Picture of England: containing a description of the laws, customs and manners of England*, 2 Vols, London, printed for Edward Jeffery, 1789, pp. 209–210, June 1778.
29. Rubenhold, Hallie, *Lady Worsley's Whim, An Eighteenth Century Tale of Sex, Scandal and Divorce*, London, Chatto & Windus, 2008 ('Rubenhold Worsley'), p. 47.
30. Foreman Georgiana, pp. 62–64.
31. Herbert Coxheath, p. 134.
32. Harcourt Papers, Vol. 7, pp. 334–335, 12 July 1778.
33. Herbert Coxheath, p. 146.
34. Rubenhold Worsley, p. 49.
35. Anon, *Coxheath Camp: a novel. In a series of Letters by a Lady*, Dublin, Messrs Price, Whitestone etc, 1779, p. 164.
36. Rubenhold Worsley, p. 49.
37. Foreman Georgiana, p. 65.
38. Foreman Georgiana, p. 66.
39. Add MSS 75675, 21 June 1778.
40. Harcourt Papers, Vol. 7, p. 334, 1 July 1778.
41. Add MSS 75675, 16 July 1778.
42. Halifax MSS /A1.2.7.1, 8 August 1778.
43. Add MSS 75675, 8 September 1778.
44. Add MSS 75675, 27 September 1778.
45. Foreman Georgiana, p. 67.
46. Add MSS 75577, 29 October 1778.
47. Foreman Georgiana, p. 67.
48. Foreman Georgiana, p. 129.
49. Foreman Georgiana, pp. 59–61.
50. Devonshire, Georgiana Duchess of, *The Sylph: a Novel*, York, Henry Parker, 2001, originally published 1778 ('The Sylph'), p. 78.
51. The Sylph, p. 100.
52. The Sylph, p. 81.
53. Foreman Georgiana, p. 68.
54. Halifax MSS /A1.2.7.5, December 1778.
55. Chatsworth MSS, 237, 5 December 1778.
56. Douglas-Home family, Earls of Home MSS: NRAS 859 ('Douglas-Home MSS'), Vol. 488, 20 December 1778.
57. Anon, *Sketches from Nature, in High Preservation, by the Most Honourable Masters; containing upwards of eighty Portraits, or Characters of the Principal Personages in the Kingdom*. London, printed for G Kearsley, 1779, p. 34.

8 – The Fawkener Years

1. Chatsworth MSS, 204, 16 April 1778.

2. Chatsworth MSS, 209, 22 April 1778.
3. Chatsworth MSS, 218, 30 July 1778.
4. Chatsworth MSS, 226, 18 October 1778.
5. Chatsworth MSS, 225, 15 to 17 October 1778.
6. Add MSS 75683, 4 January 1779.
7. Douglas-Home MSS, Vol. 488, 29 December 1788.
8. Selwyn, George, *The Correspondence of George Selwyn and his Contemporaries, ed. John Heneage Jesse*, 4 Vols, London, Bickers & Son, 1882 ('Jesse Selwyn'), Vol. 4, pp. 103–104, April 1779.
9. Harcourt Papers, Vol. 7, p. 336, June 1779.
10. Halifax MSS /A1.2.7.6, 10 June 1779.
11. Add MSS 75694, 19 July 1779.
12. Add MSS 75676, 23 September 1779.
13. Douglas-Home MSS, Vol. 489, ?1 October 1779.
14. Add MSS 75676, 28 September 1779.
15. Harcourt Papers, Vol. 7, p. 340, 30 September 1779.
16. Jesse Selwyn, Vol. 4, p. 268, October 1779.
17. Foreman Georgiana, p. 67.
18. Add MSS 75676, 22 October 1779.
19. Halifax MSS /A1.2.7.8, 30 November 1779.
20. Harcourt Papers, Vol. 8, pp. 63-64.
21. *Lloyds Evening Post*, 21 October 1796.
22. Glenbervie Diaries, Vol. 1, p. 89.
23. Jersey Records, p. 27.
24. Add MSS 75578, 25 March 1780.
25. Add MSS 75578, 8 and 10 April 1780.
26. Add MSS 75676, 15 April 1780.
27. Add MSS 75676, 24 April 1780.
28. Add MSS 75676, 3 May 1780.
29. Add MSS 75692, 12 May 1780.
30. Add MSS 75692, 19 May 1780.
31. Add MSS 75676, 22 May 1780.
32. Add MSS 75676, 13 May 1780.
33. Add MSS 75677, 5 June 1780.
34. Marshall, Dorothy, *Eighteenth Century England*, London, Longmans, Green and Co Ltd, 1962 ('Marshall Eighteenth Century'), pp. 477–479.
35. White London, pp. 540–541.
36. White London, pp. 541–542.
37. Add MSS 75677, 8 June 1780.
38. Harcourt Papers, Vol. 7, p. 342, 9th June 1780.
39. Add MSS 75677, 10 June 1780.
40. Add MSS 75677, 11 June 1780.
41. Add MSS 75677, 13 June 1780.
42. Add MSS 75677, 21 June 1780.
43. Harcourt Papers, Vol. 7, pp. 345–346, 28 June 1780.
44. Walpole Correspondence, Vol. 29 /II, p. 72, 8 August 1780.

45. Add MSS 75677, 30 August 1780.
46. Add MSS 75677, 6 October 1780.
47. Bettany, Lewis ed., *Edward Jerningham and His Friends*, New York, Brentano's, 1919 ('Jerningham Bettany'), p. 59.
48. Holland, Henry Fox, Lord, *To Lady Sarah Bunbury in imitation of Lydia*, ? London, ?1770.
49. Walpole Last Journals, Vol. 2, p. 122.
50. HMC Carlisle, p. 468, 2 March 1781.
51. Anon (William Pearce), *The Bevy of Beauties: A Collection of Sonnets*, London, R Baldwin, J Faulder, 1781.
52. Taylor, John, *Records of My Life*, 2 Vols, London, Edward Bull, 1832, Vol. 2, p. 406.
53. Harcourt Papers, Vol. 7, p. 348, 30 July 1781.
54. Add MSS 75677, 14 August 1781.
55. Add MSS 75606, 2 October 1781.
56. Chatsworth MSS, 370, 4 October 1781.
57. Chatsworth MSS, 472, 8 December 1782.
58. HMC Carlisle, pp. 521-522, 14 October 1781.
59. Add MSS 75677, 8 November 1781.
60. Hawkins, Laetitia, *Memoirs, anecdots* (sic), *facts and opinions collected and preserved by LMH*, 2 Vols, London, 1824 ('Hawkins Memoirs'), pp. 28–30.
61. Granville MSS PRO 30/29/4/7/63, nd ?1782.
62. HMC Carlisle, p. 573, 8th February 1782.
63. Hawkins Memoirs, pp. 28–30.
64. White London, p. 280.
65. White London, p. 283.
66. White London, pp. 288-289.
67. HMC Carlisle, p. 575, 11 February 1782.
68. Halifax MSS /A1.2.7.9, February 1782.
69. Anon, *Ways and Means: or, a sale of the L***s S*******l and T****** by R****l P.********n*, London, printed for G Kearsley, 1782.
70. HMC Carlisle, p. 597, 18 March 1782.
71. Halifax MSS /A1.2.7.9, February 1782.
72. Add MSS 75677, 1 June 1782.
73. Add MSS 75692, August 1782.
74. HMC Carlisle, pp. 610–611, 29 March 1782.
75. Harcourt Papers, Vol. 7, p. 360, 18 September 1782.
76. Add MSS 75677, 7 October 1782.
77. Add MSS 75694, 17 October 1782.
78. Chatsworth MSS, 444, 26 October 1782.
79. Add MSS 75677, 14 November 1782.
80. Add MSS 75677, 18 November 1782.
81. Add MSS 75694, 23 November 1782.
82. Add MSS 75677, 22 November 1782.
83. Harcourt Papers Vol. 8, pp. 69–70, nd.

84. Add MSS 75677, 28 November 1782.
85. Add MSS 75677, 30 December 1782.
86. Add MSS 75677, 13 January 1783.
87. George III, *The Correspondence of King George III from 1760 to December 1783*, ed. Sir John Fortescue, 6 Vols, London, Macmillan and Co. Limited, 1928. ('Fortescue George III'), Vol. 6, 4350, 12 May 1783.
88. Fortescue George III, Vol. 6, 4349, 11 May 1783.
89. Add MSS 75579, 10 May 1783.
90. Add MSS 75579, 17 May 1783.
91. Douglas-Home MSS, Vol. 492, 1 December 1782.
92. Douglas-Home MSS, Vol. 493, 12 June 1793.
93. Walpole Correspondence, Vol. 29, pp. 305–306, 31 May 1783.
94. Walpole Correspondence, Vol. 29, p. 306 n.
95. Add MSS 75677, 20 May 1783.
96. Add MSS 75579, 22 and 23 May 1783.
97. Add MSS 75677, 27 May 1773.
98. Foreman Georgiana, p. 117.
99. Douglas-Home MSS, Vol. 493, 28 May 1783.
100. Douglas-Home MSS, Vol. 493, 31 May 1783.
101. Walpole Correspondence, Vol. 25, p. 411, 29 May 1783.
102. Add MSS 75579, 27 May 1783.
103. Add MSS 75912, 31 May 1783.
104. Add MSS 75678, 3 June 1783.
105. Add MSS 75678, 8 June 1783.
106. Add MSS 75579, 4 July 1783.
107. HMC, The *Manuscripts of the Duke of Rutland Preserved at Belvoir Castle*, HMC 14th Report Appendix Part I, Volume III, London HMSO, 1896 ('HMC Rutland'), p. 70, 3 August 1793.
108. Add MSS 75579, 7 June 1783.
109. Bleackley Duchess of Hamilton, p. 236.
110. Harcourt Papers, Vol. 7, p. 363, 19 August 1783.
111. Add MSS 75678, 22 August and 3 September 1783.
112. Add MSS 75678, 22 September 1783.
113. Add MSS 75606, 29 September 1783.
114. Add MSS 75678, 9 October 1783.
115. DNB.
116. HMC Carlisle, p. 639, 15 October 1783.
117. Add MSS 75678, 21 October 1783.
118. Chatsworth MSS, 654, 13 to 23 October 1783.
119. Douglas-Home MSS, Vol. 493, 18 August 1783.
120. Douglas-Home MSS, Vol. 493, 25 October 1783.
121. Add MSS 75694, 22 November 1783.
122. Add MSS 75678, November 1783.
123. Add MSS 75912, 27 November 1783.

124. Extracts from the *Correspondence of Georgiana, Duchess of Devonshire*, ed. The Earl of Bessborough, London, John Murray, 1955 ('Bessborough Georgiana'), p. 71, January 1784.
125. Glenbervie, Sylvester Douglas, Lord, *The Glenbervie Journals*, ed. Walter Sichel, London, Constable, 1928 ('Glenbervie Journals'), p. 196, 23 September 1813.
126. Everard Fawkener, p. 141.
127. Foreman Georgiana, pp. 179–180.
128. Glenbervie Diaries, Vol. 2, p. 15, February 1807.

9 – The Westminster Election and a New Lover

1. Castle Howard MSS, J14/1/622A, 19 February nd.
2. Porter 18th Century, p. 260.
3. *The Historical and Posthumous Memoirs of Sir Nathaniel William Wraxall 1772–1784*, ed. Henry B. Wheatley, 5 Vols, London, Black & Son, 1884 ('Wraxall Posthumous Memoirs'), Vol. 5, p. 37, 1784.
4. Add MSS 75684, 8 January 1784.
5. Add MSS 75684, 29-31 January 1784.
6. Add MSS 75684, 19 April 1784.
7. Walpole Correspondence, Vol. 29 /II, p. 329, 2 February 1784.
8. Add MSS 75684, 3 and 7 February 1784.
9. Add MSS 75684, 21-22 February 1784.
10. Foreman Georgiana, p. 135.
11. Chatsworth MSS, 598, 8 February 1784.
12. Foreman Georgiana, p. 48.
13. Add MSS 75684, 23-25 February 1784.
14. Add MSS 75607, 15 March 1784.
15. Chatsworth MSS, 608, 17 March 1784.
16. *The Anglo Saxon Review: A Quarterly Miscellany*, ed. Lady Randolph Churchill, September 1899, p. 73, 17 March 1784.
17. Add MSS 45911, f 8, nd.
18. Add MSS 75678, 29, 30 and 31 March and 5 and 7 April 1784.
19. Marshall Eighteenth Century, pp. 516–518.
20. Lewis, Judith S , Sacred *to Female Patriotism: Gender, Class and Politics in Late Georgian Britain*, New York/London, Routledge, 2003 ('Lewis Patriotism'), pp. 46–47.
21. Lewis Patriotism, p. 128.
22. Wraxall Posthumous Memoirs, Vol. 3, p. 346.
23. Hanger, George, Baron Coleraine, *The life, adventures and opinions of Col G H written by himself*, 2 Vols, London, 1801, Vol. 2, p. 452.
24. White London, pp. 545–546.
25. Papendiek, Mrs. Charlotte Louisa Henrietta, *Court and Private Life in the Time of Queen Charlotte – being the Journals of Mrs. Papendiek*, ed. Mrs. V. D. Broughton, 2 Vols, London, Bentley & Son, 1887, Vol. 1, p. 210.
26. Lewis Patriotism, p. 132.

27. 'Mary Hamilton afterwards Mrs. John Dickenson at Court and at Home', from *Letters and Diaries 1756 to 1816,* ed. Elizabeth and Florence Anson, London, John Murray, 1925, p. 178, 23 and 27 April 1784.
28. E.g. Foreman Georgiana, p. 142 and Gleeson, Janet, *An Aristocratic Affair, The Life of Georgiana's Sister, Harriet Spencer, Countess of Bessborough*, London, Bantam Press, 2006, p. 67.
29. Anon, *History of the Westminster Election containing every material occurrence from its commecement* (sic) *on the first of April to the final close of the poll, London, 1784* ('Westminster Election'), p. 224.
30. Add MSS 75678, 10 April 1784.
31. Add MSS 75678, 30 April 1784.
32. Add MSS 75678, 15 May 1784.
33. Add MSS 75678, 17 May 1784.
34. Kelly Holland House, p. 3.
35. Westminster Election, p. 377.
36. Add MSS 75678, 25 and 28 May 1784.
37. Add MSS 75679, 22 June 1784.
38. Add MSS 75679, 25 July 1784.
39. Add MSS 75679, 8 August 1784.
40. Add MSS 75679, 4 September 1784.
41. Add MSS 75679, 12 September 1784.
42. Chatsworth MSS, 648, 11 September 1784.
43. Leveson Gower, Iris, *The Face Without a Frown, Georgiana Duchess of Devonshire*, London, Frederick Muller, 1944, p. 123.
44. Chatsworth MSS, 650, 23 September 1784.
45. Add MSS 75679, 19 September 1784.
46. Porter 18th Century, pp. 191–192.
47. Chatsworth MSS, 649, 23 September 1784.
48. Add MSS 75679, 26 September 1784.
49. Add MSS 75679, 28 September 1784.
50. Add MSS 75679, 9 October 1784.
51. Add MSS 75679, 22 October 1784.
52. Add MSS 75679, 15 October 1784.
53. Add MSS 75679, 7 November 1784.
54. Add MSS 75679, 25 October and 25 December 1784.
55. Douglas-Home MSS, Vol. 495, 27 January 1785.
56. Add MSS 75679, 12 and 16 February 1785.
57. Add MSS 75679, 19 February 1785.
58. Add MSS 75679, 23 February 1785.
59. Add MSS 75679, 9 January 1785.
60. Add MSS 75581, 8 March 1785.
61. Add MSS 75679, 26 April 1785.
62. Add MSS 75913, 14 May 1785.
63. Add MSS 75679, 13 and 23 June 1785.
64. Add MSS 75679, 30 June 1785.
65. Add MSS 75679, 11 July 1785.

66. Add MSS 51723, 4 October, 1802 (f 154).
67. Add MSS 75679, 8 September 1785.
68. Porter 18th Century, p. 25.

10 – A Growing Family and Growing Ill-repute

1. Queen Victoria's Journals RA VIC/MAIN/QVJ (W) 13 February 1839 (Lord Esher's typescripts). Retrieved 2 April 2015.
2. Queen Victoria's Journals RA VIC/MAIN/QVJ (W) 13 February 1839 and 20 August 1838 (Lord Esher's typescripts). Both retrieved 2 April 2015.
3. Add MSS 75679, 1 September 1785.
4. Add MSS 75679, 9 January 1786.
5. Chatsworth MSS, 706, 25 January 1786.
6. Chatsworth MSS, 886, 18 July 1788.
7. Bligh, Richard, *Reports of cases heard in the House of Lords: on appeals and writs*, 1827, Vol. 2, p. 304.
8. Childs, Jeff, 'Landownership changes in a Glamorgan parish, 1750-1850; The case of Llangyfelach', *Morgannwg: transactions of the Glamorgan Local History Society*, Vol. 38 – 1994.
9. Add MSS 75679, 20 February 1786.
10. Add MSS 75913, 20 February 1786.
11. Add MSS 75680, 1 April 1786.
12. Add MSS 75680, nd, 3 April 1786?.
13. Add MSS 75680, 6 and 8 April 1786.
14. Add MSS 75680, 15 April 1786.
15. Add MSS 75680, 22 April and 9 May 1786.
16. Add MSS 75680, 2 June 1786.
17. Add MSS 75684, 23 June 1786.
18. Add MSS 75680, 20 June 1786.
19. Harcourt Papers, Vol. 6, pp. 174–175, September 1785.
20. Add MSS 75680, 9 May 1786.
21. Foreman Georgiana, p. 180.
22. Add MSS 75680, 6 November 1786.
23. Jersey Records, pp. 37–38.
24. HMC, *Reports on the Manuscripts of the Duke of Somerset etc*, 15th Report, Appendix, Part VII, London, HMSO, 1898, p. 279, 27 April 1787.
25. LMA Jersey MSS LMA/ACC/1128/238, 3 May 1787.
26. Whitley, William T., *Artists and Their Friends in England 1770–1799*, 2 Vols, London, The Medici Society, 1928, p. 82.
27. *Whitehall Evening Post*, 20 January 1787.
28. *World & Fashionable Advertiser*, 4 May 1787.
29. *World & Fashionable Advertiser*, 22 June 1787.
30. Add MSS 75680, 11 May 1787.
31. Add MSS 75680, 11 June 1787.
32. Add MSS 75680, 18 July 1787.

33. Granville MSS PRO/29/4/7/65, 6 September 1787.
34. DNB.
35. Jerningham Bettany, p. 236, 7 September 1786.
36. Jerningham Bettany, p. 236, 5 October 1787.
37. Douglas-Home MSS, Vol. 496, 29 November 1796.
38. *The Morning Chronicle*, 8 January 1788.
39. Bleackley Duchess of Hamilton, pp. 236–237.
40. Clayden, P. W, *The Early Life of Samuel Rogers*, London, Elder & Co, 1887, p. 335.
41. Chatsworth MSS, 283, 28 April 1788.
42. Add MSS 75680, 1 May 1788.
43. Add MSS 75680, 7 May 1788.
44. Add MSS 75681, 6 June 1788.
45. Add MSS 75695, 14 September 1788.
46. Douglas-Home MSS, Vol. 498, 20 July 1788.
47. Add MSS 75681, 22 November 1788.
48. Add MSS 75681, 13 December 1788.
49. Jesse, Captain, *The Life of George Brummell, Esq*., 2 Vols, London, John C Nimmo, 1886, Vol. 1, p. 152.
50. Add MSS 75681, 27 March 1789.
51. Add MSS 75681, 31 March 1789.
52. Add MSS 75681, 9 April 1789.
53. Add MSS 75681, 10 and 22 April 1789.
54. Add MSS 75681, 23 May 1789.
55. Add MSS 75585, 25 May1789.
56. Add MSS 75681, 30 May 1789.
57. Sheridan, Betsy, *Betsy Sheridan's Journal*, ed. William LeFanu, London, Eyre & Spottiswoode, 1960, pp. 167–168, 14–15 June 1789.
58. Add MSS 75681, 15 June 1789.
59. Minto, Sir Gilbert Elliot, First Earl of, *Life and Letter of Sir Gilbert Elliot, First Earl of Minto*, ed. The Countess of Minto, 3 Vols, London, Longmans Green & Co, 1874, Vol. 1, p. 332, 17 June 1789.
60. Wilson, Frances, *The Courtesan's Revenge*, London, Faber and Faber, 2003, pp. 61–66.
61. Douglas-Home MSS, Vol. 499, 13 June 1789.
62. *General Evening Post*, 23 June 1789.
63. Add MSS 75681, 23 June 1789.
64. *Bath Chronicle*, 16 July 1789.
65. Add MSS 75681, 11 July 1789.
66. *The World*, 14 July 1789.
67. Add MSS 75681, 28 July 1789.
68. Add MSS 75681, 7 October 1789.
69. Add MSS 75681, 17 November 1789.
70. Add MSS 75695, 13 November 1789.
71. Add MSS 75681, 25 November 1789.
72. Chatsworh MSS, 1025, 15 December 1789.

73. Add MSS 75681, 2 December 1789.
74. Chatsworth MSS, 1037, 12 February 1790.
75. Chatsworth MSS, 1132.1, 3 September 1792.
76. Add MSS 75681, 2 December 1789.
77. *General Evening Post*, 30 January 1790.
78. Add MSS 75681, 14 June 1790.
79. Add MSS 75681, 5 July 1790.
80. Add MSS 75681, 27 July 1790.
81. Add MSS 75681, 15 September 1790.
82. *The World*, 2 October 1790.
83. Add MSS 75681, 4 October 1790.
84. Add MSS 75681, 13 November 1790.
85. Add MSS 75682, 22 September 1791.
86. *The Diary of Lady Frances Shelley*, ed. Richard Edgcumbe, 2 Vols, London, John Murray, 1912, Vol. 1, p. 21, 1805.
87. *Morning Herald*, 14 February 1792.
88. Add MSS 75693, 26 January 1791.
89. Add MSS 75682, 15 August 1791.
90. Granville MSS PRO/30/29/4/8/51, 25 September 1791.
91. Granville MSS PRO/30/29/4/8/53, 14 November 1791.
92. Granville MSS PRO/30/29/4/8/54, 21 November 1791.
93. Add MSS 75682, 25 November 1791.
94. The Gazetteer, 26 November 1791.
95. Add MSS 75586, 27 November 1791.
96. Add MSS 75682, ?2 January 1792.
97. Add MSS 75682, 3 February 1792.
98. Add MSS 75682, 10 March 1793.
99. Colville, Sir John, *Those Lambtons, A Most Unusual Family*, London, Hodder & Stoughton, 1988, p. 27.
100. Add MSS 75681, 6 June 1791.
101. *The Jerningham Letters*, ed. Egerton Castle, 2 Vols, London, Richard Bentley and Son, 1896 ('Jerningham Castle'), Vol. 1, p. 49, 21 June 1791.
102. Add MSS 75681, 15 June 1791.
103. Elwin, Malcolm, *The Noels and the Milbankes, Their Letters for Twenty-Five Years 1767–1792, Presented as a Narrative,* London, Macdonald, 1967, p. 407, 1 January 1792.
104. Reid, Stuart J, *Life and Letters of the First Earl of Durham 1792–1840*, 2 Vols, London, Longmans, Green, and Co, 1906, Vol. 1, p. 38.
105. Add MSS 75682, 30 April 1792.
106. Add MSS 75695, 21-27 February 1792.
107. *The Gazetteer*, 1 March 1792.
109. Add MSS 75682, 29 May 1792.
109. Graham, E. Maxton, *The Beautiful Mrs. Graham and the Cathcart Circle*, London, Nisbet & Co Ltd, 1927, pp. 280–281, 1 June 1792.
110. DNB.
111. Add MSS 75695, 13-19 March 1792.

112. Granville MSS PRO 30/29/4/8/57, 21 July 1792.
113. Aspinall, A. ed., *The Later Correspondence of George III*, 5 Vols, Cambridge, University Press, 1962-1970 ('Aspinall George III'), Vol. 1, Letter 811, 27 November 1792.
114. Porter 18th Century, p. 114.
115. Jerningham Bettany, pp. 236-237, 5 August 1791.
116. Jerningham Bettany, pp. 248-249, 30 September, nd.
117. Jerningham Bettany, p. 237, 2 September 1792.
118. Jerningham Bettany, p. 237, 23 October 1792.
119. Jerningham Bettany, p. 238, 15 November 1792.
120. Jerningham Bettany, pp. 241-243, 4 and 9 November 1795.
121. Foreman Georgiana, p. 273.
122. Add MSS 75682, 29 March 1792.
123. Add MSS 75682, 6 February 1793.
124. Add MSS 75682, 27 June 1793.
125. Bessborough, Earl of and Aspinall, A. ed., *Lady Bessborough and her Family Circle*, London, John Murray, 1940, p. 67, 29 January 1792.

11 – Mrs Fitzherbert's Overturn

1. Glenbervie Diaries, Vol. 2, p. 27, 21 November 1807.
2. Aspinall PoW, Vol. 2, p. 38, n 1 and p. 286, n 1.
3. Glenbervie Diaries, Vol. 2, pp. 15, 27 and 28, 18 February and 21 November 1807.
4. Hibbert Prince, pp. 129–131.
5. Wardroper, John, *Kings, Lords and Wicked Libellers – Satire and Protest 1760–1837*, London, John Murray, 1973, p. 167.
6. Broadley, A. M. & Melville, Lewis ed., *The Original Memoirs of Lady Elizabeth Craven (Later Margravine of Anspach and Princess Berkeley of the Holy Roman Empire) 1750–1828*, 2 Vols, London, John Lane The Bodley Head, 1914, Vol. 1, pp. lxxxxix and xc, 20 April 1793.
7. Add MSS 75682, 20 May 1793.
8. Add MSS 75682, 25 July 1793.
9. *The World*, 16 August 1793.
10. *The Gazetteer*, 17 August 1793.
11. Blake, Mrs Warrenne ed., *An Irish Beauty of the Regency – The Unpublished Journals of the Hon Mrs. Calvert*, London, John Lane The Bodley Head, 1911, p. 8.
12. Granville MSS PRO 39/29/5/4/48, ?1793.
13. Harcourt, Elizabeth Countess of, *Mrs. Harcourt's Diary of the Court of King George III (1789–1791)*, London, Miscellanies of the Philobiblon Society, Vol. XIII, 1871-1872, p. 41, 21 November 1790.
14. Jerningham Bettany, p. 239, ? October 1793.
15. White London, pp. 356 and 361.
16. Jerningham Bettany, p. 240, 1 November 1793.

17. Turquan, Joseph and Ellis, Lucy ed., *La Belle Pamela (Lady Edward Fitzgerald) 1773–1831: D'après des correspondence et memoires inedits, des traditions et documents de famille*, 2 Vols, Paris, Émile-Paul frères, 1923-24, Vol. 2, p. 174, n 1.
18. Munson, James, *Maria Fitzherbert: The Secret Wife of George IV*, London, Constable, 2001 ('Munson Fitzherbert'), p. 261.
19. Munson Fitzherbert, p. 262.
20. Munson Fitzherbert, p. 263.
21. Add MSS 75682, 10 December 1793.
22. Granville MSS PRO/30/29/5/4/51, ? October ?1793.
23. Hibbert Prince, p. 131.
24. Leslie, Anita, *Mrs Fitzherbert*, London, Hutchinson, 1960, p. 89.
25. Add MSS 75682, 27 January 1794.
26. *Whitehall Evening Post*, 1 February 1794.
27. *The Morning Chronicle*, 5 June 1794.
28. Jupp., Peter ed., *The Letter Journal of George Canning, 1793–1795*, London, Royal Historical Society, 1991, p. 66, 12 February 1794.
29. Aspinall PoW, Vol. 2, p. 443, n 1, 24 June 1794.
30. Aspinall PoW, Vol. 2, 848, ?7 July 1794.
31. Aspinall Pow, Vol. 2, 848, 8 July 1794.
32. Munson Fitzherbert, p. 265.
33. Munson Fitzherbert, pp. 266-267.
34. Leveson Gower, The Hon F. ed., *The Letters of Harriet, Countess Granville*, London, Longmans, Green, and Co, 1894 ('Granville (Harriet) Letters'), Vol. 1, p. 93, 18 July 1794.
35. *The Sun*, 25th July 1794.
36. Aspinall PoW, Vol. 2, 854, 26 July 1794.
37. Munson Fitzherbert, p. 267.
38. Munson Fitzherbert, p. 268.
39. Munson Fitzherbert, p. 269.
40. Granville MSS PRO 30/29/4/9/68, 20 August 1794.
41. Bloom, Edward A. and Bloom, Lillian, *The Piozzi Letters, The Correspondence of Hester Lynch Piozzi 1784–1821*, 6 Vols, Newark, University Press, London and Toronto Associated University Press, 1991 ('Piozzi Letters'), Vol. 2, pp. 193–194, 22 August 1794.
42. Leslie, Anita, *Mrs. Fitzherbert*, London, Hutchinson, 1960, p. 95.
43. Aspinall PoW, Vol. 2, 852, 24 July 1794.
44. Aspinall PoW, Vol. 2, 852, 24 July 1794.
45. *The Oracle*, 26 July 1794.
46. Argyll, Duke of ed., *Intimate Society Letters of the Eighteenth Century*, London, Stanley Paul & Co, 1910 ('Argyll Letters'), p. 658, nd.
47. Aspinall PoW, Vol. 2, 941, 22 August ?1794.
48. Huish, Robert, *Memoirs of George the Fourth*, 2 Vols, Thomas Kelly, 1831 ('Huish George IV'), Vol. 1, p. 263.
49. Munson Fitzherbert, p. 268.
50. Munson Fitzherbert, p. 276.

51. Ashton, John, *Florizel's Folly*, London, Chatto & Windus, 1899, p. 174.
52. Balderstone, Katherine C. ed., *Thraliana, The Diary of Mrs. Hester Lynch Thrale (later Mrs. Piozzi) 1776–1809*, 2 Vols, Oxford, Clarendon Press, 1942, Vol. 2, p. 917, 17 March 1795.
53. Huish George IV, Vol. 1, p. 334.
54. Foreman Georgiana, p. 290 n.
55. Garlick K. and Macintyre A./Cave K., *The Diary of Joseph Farington RA*, 16 Vols, Yale University Press, 1978 ('Farington Diaries, Yale'), Vol. 1, p. 232, 8 September 1794.
56. LMA Jersey MSS LMA ACC/1128/185/51, 4 September 1794.
57. Hibbert Prince, p. 135.
58. Holland, Henry Edward, Lord ed., *Holland, Henry Richard, Lord – Memoirs of the Whig Party in my Time*, 2 Vols, London, Longman, Brown, Green and Longmans, 1852 and 1854 ('Holland Memoirs'), Vol. 2, p. 144.
59. Holland Memoirs, Vol. 2, pp. 145–146, quoted in Hibbert Prince, p. 135.
60. Jerrningham Bettany, p. 219, 20 September 1794.
61. Walpole Correspondence, Vol. 12, p. 120, 1 October 1794.
62. Aspinall PoW, Vol. 2, 871, 8 October 1794.
63. Holland Memoirs, Vol. 2, p. 147.
64. Glenbervie Diaries, Vol. 2, p. 88, 30 October 1810.
65. Add MSS 75682, 30 October 1794.
66. Jerningham Bettany, pp. 240–241, 10 September 1794.
67. Jerningham Bettany p. 241, 30 September 1794.
68. Aspinall PoW, Vol. 2, 877, 25 October 1794.
69. Aspinall PoW, Vol. 2, p. 472 n 2, 1 November 1794.
70. Aspinall PoW, Vol. 2, 877, 25 October 1794.
71. Melville, Lewis, *Regency Ladies*, London, Hutchinson & Co, 1926, p. 82.

12 – The Arrival of Princess Caroline

1. Granville MSS PRO 30/29/4/9/73, 11 November 1794.
2. Aspinall PoW, Vol. 2, 894, 19 November 1794.
3. Add MSS 75682, 27 November 1794.
4. *The Morning Chronicle*, 12 December 1794.
5. Malmesbury, 3rd Earl ed., *The Diaries and Correspondence of James Harris, First Earl of Malmesbury*, 4 Vols, London, Richard Bentley, 1844 ('Malmesbury Diaries'), Vol. 3, p. 167, 9 December 1794.
6. *The Sun*, 5 December 1794.
7. Add MSS 75682, 15 December, 1794.
8. Aspinall PoW, Vol. 2, p. 516, n 1.
9. Aspinall PoW, Vol. 2, 920, ?22 December 1794.
10. Aspinall PoW, Vol. 2, 921, 22 December 1794.
11. LMA Jersey MSS LMA ACC/1275/001, 002 and 003, nd.
12. Aspinall PoW, Vol. 2, 923, 23 December 1794.

13. Aspinall PoW, Vol. 2, 917, 19 December 1794.
14. Malmesbury Diaries, Vol. 3, p. 188, 28 December 1794.
15. *The Morning Chronicle*, 30 December 1794.
16. Add MSS 34453, 2 January 1795.
17. Add MSS 75682, 9 January 1795.
18. *Norfolk Chronicle*, 10 January 1795.
19. *The Morning Chronicle,* 12 January 1795.
20. Hamilton, Lady Anne, *Secret History of the Court of England from the Accession of George the Third to the Death of George the Fourth*, 2 Vols, London, Eveleigh Nash, 1903, Vol. 1, p. 100.
21. Aspinall PoW, Vol. 2, 919, 21 December 1794.
22. Aspinall PoW, Vol. 2, 935, 31 December 1794.
23. Aspinall PoW, Vol. 3, 948, 14 January 1795.
24. Aspinall PoW, Vol. 3, 948, 16 January 1795.
25. Aspinall PoW, Vol. 3, 951, 19 January 1795.
26. Aspinall PoW, Vol. 3, 959, 6, 7 and 8 February 1795.
27. Biddulph, Violet, The *Three Ladies Waldegrave (and their Mother)*, London, Peter Davies, 1938, p. 220.
28. Aspinall PoW, Vol. 3, p. 27 n, 7 February 1795.
29. Aspinall PoW, Vol. 3, 961, ?12 February 1795.
30. Foreman Georgiana, p. 297.
31. *Lloyds Evening Post*, 9 March 1795.
32. Hill, Draper, *Fashionable Contrasts : Caricatures by James Gillray*, London, Phaidon Press Ltd, 1966, plate 61, notes pp. 164–165.
33. *The Oracle*, 7 February 1795.
34. Connell, Brian, *Portrait of a Whig Peer, Compiled from the Papers of the Second Viscount Palmerston 1739–1802,* London, Andre Deutsch, 1957 ('Connell Palmerston'), p. 315.
35. Add MSS 75682, 13 March 1795.
36. Munson Fitzherbert, p. 277.
37. Huish George IV, Vol. 1, p. 328.
38. Robins, Jane, *Rebel Queen – The Trial of Caroline*, London, Simon & Schuster, 2006, pp. 10–11.
39. *The Sun*, 6 April 1795.
40. Malmesbury Diaries, Vol. 3, p. 217, 5 April 1795.
41. Nightingale J, *Memoirs of the Public and Private Life of Caroline, Queen of Great Britain*, London, 2 Vols, J Robins & Co, 1820, pp. 46–47.
42. Aspinall PoW, Vol. 2, 918, 20 ?December 1795.
43. Hare, Augustus J. C., *Story of My Life*, 6 Vols, London, George Allen, 1900 ('Hare Life'), Vol. 6, p. 369.
44. Malmesbury Diaries, Vol. 3, p. 217, 5 April 1795.
45. Walpole Correspondence, Vol. 12, p. 138, 7 April 1795.
46. Somerset, Anne, *Ladies in Waiting: From the Tudors to the Present Day*, London, Weidenfeld and Nicholson, 1984, p. 250.
47. Anon, *Plain Letter to His Royal Highness Upon His Plain Duties*, London, 18—, p. 4.

48. Bury, Lady Charlotte, *The Court of England Under George IV*, 2 Vols, London, John Macqueen, 1896 ('Bury George IV'), Vol. 1, pp. 142–143.
49. Mundy, Harriot Georgina ed., *The Journal of Mary Frampton*, London, Sampson Low, Marston, Searle & Rivington, 1886, p. 84, April 1795.
50. *The Sun*, 6 April 1795.
51. Bury George IV, Vol. 1, p. 13.
52. Malmesbury Diaries, Vol. 3, p. 217, 5 April 1795.
53. Huish George IV, Vol. 1, p. 329.
54. Aspinall PoW, Vol. 3, 1094, 21 April 1796.
55. Munson Fitzherbert, p. 277.
56. Munson Fitzherbert, p. 277.
57. Munson Fitzherbert, p. 281.
58. Fraser, Flora, *The Unruly Queen: The Life of Queen Caroline*, London, Macmillan, 1996, p. 64 citing Royal Archives 'Geo IV Box 12/39'.
59. Hone, William, *Hone's Political Tracts*, London, William Hone, 1822.
60. *Whitehall Evening Post*, 9 April 1795.
61. Russell, C. C. E., *Three Generations of Fascinating Women and other sketches from family history*, London, Longmans & Co, 1904, pp. 65–66.
62. Browning, Oscar ed., *The Political Memoranda of Francis Fifth Duke of Leeds*, London, Camden Society, 1884 ('Leeds Memoranda'), p. 220, 8 April 1795.
63. Munson Fitzherbert, p. 278.
64. Hibbert Prince, p. 147.
65. Leeds Memoranda, p. 220, 8 April 1795.
66. Leeds Memoranda, p. 220, 8 April 1795.
67. Musgrave, Clifford, *Life in Brighton from the earliest times to the present*, London, Faber and Faber, 1970, p. 120.
68. Minto, Countess of ed., *Life and Letters of Sir Gilbert Elliot, First Earl of Minto*, 3 Vols, London, Longmans Green & Co, 1874, Vol. 3, pp. 13–14, 14 July 1798.
69. Hare Life, Vol. 4, p. 308, ?May 1795.
70. Holme, Thea, *Prinny's Daughter: A Life of Princess Charlotte of Wales*, London, Hamish Hamilton, 1976, p. 33.
71. Chatsworth MSS, 1285, 12 April 1795.
72. *The Morning Chronicle*, 21 April 1795.
73. White London, p. 215.
74. *The Morning Chronicle*, 17 April 1795.
75. Bury George IV, Vol. 1, p. 22.
76. Bessborough Georgiana, p. 213, 20 April 1795.
77. Balderstone, Katherine C. ed., *Thraliana, The Diary of Mrs. Hester Lynch Thrale (later Mrs. Piozzi) 1776–1809*, 2 Vols, Oxford, Clarendon Press, 1942 ('Balderstone Thraliana'), Vol. 2, p. 921, 17 April 1795.
78. Bloom, Edward A. and Bloom, Lillian, *The Piozzi Letters, Correspondence of Hester Lynch Piozzi*, 6 Vols, Newark, University of Delaware Press, London and Toronto, Associated University Press, 1991, Vol. 2, p. 258, 5 May 1795.
79. White London, p. 223.
80. Connell Palmerston, p. 318.
81. Connell Palmerston, p. 319.

82. Balderstone Thraliana, Vol. 2, p. 928, 12 May 1795.
83. Wraxall Posthumous Memoirs, Vol. 5, p. 384.
84. Add MSS 75682, 8 June 1795.
85. Paget, G. C. H. V., 7th Marquess of Anglesey, One *Leg, The Life and Letters of Henry William Paget First Marquess of Anglesey KG 1768–1854*, London, Jonathan Cape, 1961 ('Paget One Leg'), p. 53.
86. *The The True Briton*, 22 June 1795.
87. Walpole Correspondence, Vol. 12, p. 142, 19 August 1795.
88. *The Morning Post*, 14 August 1795.
89. Aspinall PoW, Vol. 3, p. 100, n, 30 June 1795.
90. *St James's Chronicle*, 7 July 1795.
91. Fraser, Flora, *The Unruly Queen, The Life of Queen Caroline*, London, Macmillan, 1996 ('Fraser Unruly Queen'), p. 71.
92. Dasent, Arthur Irwin, *A History of Grosvenor Square*, London, Macmillan & Co., Limited, 1935, pp. 217–218.
93. Granville MSS PRO 30/29/4/9/75, 22 August 1795.
94. Granville MSS PRO 30/29/4/6/55, nd 1795.
95. Walpole Correspondence, Vol. 12, p. 150, 26 August 1795.
96. Walpole Correspondence, Vol. 12, pp. 149-150, 26 August 1795.
97. Walpole Correspondence, Vol. 12, p. 15, 1 September 1795.
98. Aspinall PoW, Vol. 3, 1031, 28 August 1795.
99. Aspinall PoW, Vol. 2, p. 482, n 1, 4 September 1795.
100. *The Oracle*, 14 September 1795.
101. *The Oracle*, 6 October 1795.
102. LMA Jersey MSS LMA/ACC/1128/238, nd.
103. Jerningham Bettany, p. 241, 16 October 1795.
104. *The Oracle*, 23 October 1795.
105. Granville MSS, PRO 30/29/4/9/78, 24 October 1795.
106. Ashton, John, *Old Times: A Picture of Social Life at the end of the Eighteenth Century*, London, John C Nimmo, 1885, p. 320.
107. Blunt, Reginald ed., '*Mrs. Montagu 'Queen of the Blues', Her Letters and Friendships from 1762 to 1800*, 2 Vols, London, Constable and Company Limited, 1923, Vol. 2, p. 317, 13 September 1795.
108. Fraser Unruly Queen, p. 71.
109. Hibbert Prince, pp. 149–150, citing Vehse, Höfed, 'Hauses Braunnschweig', quoted by Greenwood in *Lives of the Hanoverian Queens of England*, Vol. 2, p. 1911.

13 – Love in High Life

1. *The Morning Chronicle*, 13 February 1796.
2. *The Sun*, 18 February 1796.
3. Villiers, Marjorie, *The Grand Whiggery*, London, John Murray, 1939, p. 130.
4. Chatsworth MSS, 1324, 8 January 1796.
5. Aspinall PoW, Vol. 3, 1067, 10 January 1796.
6. Fraser Unruly Queen, p. 77.

7. Glenbervie Diaries, Vol. 1, p. 60, 18 January 1796.
8. Aspinall PoW, Vol. 3, 1408, Monday evening [?1796]
9. *The True Briton*, 27 January 1796.
10. Munson Fitzherbert, p. 288.
11. *The Sun*, 9 February 1796.
12. Colchester, Charles Lord ed., *The Diary and Correspondence of Charles Abbott, Lord Colchester*, London, John Murray, 1861 ('Colchester Diary'), Vol. 1, p. 37, 25th February 1796.
13. Munson Fitzherbert, p. 286.
14. Fraser Unruly Queen, p. 79 and Aspinall PoW, Vol. 3, 1094, 24 April 1796.
15. Colchester Diary, Vol. 1, p. 36, 24 February 1796.
16. Hylton, Lord ed., *The Paget Brothers, 1790–1840: Selections from the Family Correspondence of Sir Arthur Paget*, London, John Murray, 1918 ('Paget Brothers'), p. 113 n.
17. Farington Diaries, Yale, Vol. 2, pp. 548-549 and 553, 15 and 21 May 1796.
18. Farington Diaries, Yale, Vol. 2, p. 557, 25 May 1796.
19. Whitley, William T, *Artists and Their Friends in England 1700–1799*, 2 Vols, London, The Medici Society, 1928, Vol. 2, pp. 205–206.
20. Blake, Mrs Warrenne, ed., *An Irish Beauty of the Regency – The Unpublished Journals of the Hon Mrs. Calvert*, London, John Lane The Bodley Head, 1911, p. 10, nd.
21. Gattrell, Vic, *City of Laughter – Sex and Satire in the 18th Century*, London, Atlantic, 2006 ('Gattrell Satire'), p. 325.
22. Gattrell Satire, pp. 326 and 644.
23. Aspinall PoW, Vol. 3, 1094, 21 April 1796.
24. Aspinall PoW, Vol. 3, 1113, 26 and 27 May 1796.
25. Leslie, Anita, *Mrs. Fitzherbert, London, Hutchinson*, 1960, p. 111.
26. Aspinall PoW, Vol. 3, 1111, 17 May 1796.
27. Anon, *A Review, with suitable remarks and reflections, of the misrepresentations and contradictions which have been circulated in all the Daily Papers relative to a late domestic fracas in a family of the first rank etc* ('Domestic Fracas'), London, 1796, p. 25.
28. Walpole Correspondence, Vol. 12, p. 189, n, 1 June 1796.
29. David, Saul, Prince *of Pleasure, The Prince of Wales and the Making of the Regency*, London, Little, Brown and Company, 1998, p. 262.
30. Aspinall PoW, Vol. 3, 1119, 2 June 1796.
31. Aspinall PoW, Vol. 3, 1186 n 2, 16 August 1796.
32. *Whitehall Evening Post*, 2 June 1796.
33. Aspinall PoW, Vol. 3, 1113 n 1, 26 May 1796.
34. *The Gazetteer*, 23 May 1796.
35. Hibbert Prince, p. 155, citing Farington Diaries, Yale, Vol. 1, pp. 199-200.
36. Leeds Memoranda, p. 221, 28 May 1796.
37. Leeds Memoranda, p. 222, 31 May 1796.
38. Aspinall PoW, Vol. 3, 1125, 4 June 1796, n 1, citing The Times of 6 June 1796.
39. Aspinall PoW, Vol. 3, 1125, 4 June 1796.

40. Aspinall PoW, Vol. 3, 1109, 13 May 1796, Royal Archives ('RA') GEO/MAIN/39184, 13th May 1796.
41. *The True Briton*, 2 June 1796.
42. *Morning Herald*, 14 June 1796 as cited in Domestic Fracas, p. 33.
43. Add MSS 75684, 18 May 1796.
44. *The Morning Post*, 14 June 1796 as cited in Domestic Fracas, p. 16.
45. *The Morning Post*, 3 June 1796.
46. *The True Briton,* 2 June 1796.
47. Walpole Correspondence, Vol. 12, pp. 188–189 and notes, 2 June 1796.
48. Granville MSS PRO 30/29/4/11/6 (Mrs L. Fitzroy to Lady Stafford), 12 June 1796.
49. Aspinall PoW, Vol. 3, 1115, 30 May 1796.
50. Bessborough Georgiana, p. 217, 3 June 1796.
51. Aspinall PoW, Vol. 3, 1121, 3 June 1796.
52, Aspinall PoW, Vol. 3, 1125 and 1126, 4 June 1796.
53. Aspinall PoW, Vol. 3, 1132, 6 June 1796.
54. HMC, *The Manuscripts and Correspondence of James, First Earl of Charlemont*, Vol. 2 – 1784–1799, Thirteenth Report, Appendix, Part VIII, London, HMSO, 1894, p. 273, 7 June 1796.
55. HMC, *Report on The Manuscripts of Reginald Rawdon Hastings of the Manor House, Ashby de la Zouche*, 78 Vol. 3, London, HMSO, 1934, pp. 211–212, 9 June 1796.
56. Aspinall PoW, Vol. 3, 1137, 10 June 1796.
57. Granville MSS PRO 30/29/4/11/2, nd, 'Clarges St, Wednesday 6 o'clock'.
58. Granville MSS PRO 30/29/4/11/1, nd.
59. Aspinall PoW, Vol. 3, 1139, 10 June 1796.
60. Aspinall PoW, Vol. 3, 1144, ?12 or 13 June 1796.
61. Granville MSS PRO 30/29/4/11/11, ?June 1796.
62. Aspinall PoW, Vol. 3, 1145, 13 June 1796.
63. Granville MSS PRO 30/29/4/11/6, 12 June 1796.
64. Granville MSS PRO 30/29/4/11/13, ?June 1796.
65. *The True Briton*, 10 June 1796.
66. Bessborough Georgiana, p. 217, 10 June 1796.
67. Jerningham Bettany, p. 111, 21 June 1796.
68. Bessborough Georgiana, p. 218, June 1796.
69. Jerningham Bettany, p. 111, 21 June 1796.
70. Rudé, George, *Hanoverian London 1714–1808*, London, Secker & Warburg, 1971, p. 47.
71. Rudé, George, *Hanoverian London 1714–1808*, London, Secker & Warburg, 1971, p. 22.
72. *The Morning Post*, 18 November 1811.
73. Chatsworth MSS, 1347, 9 June 1796.
74. Aspinall PoW, Vol. 3, 1143, 12 June 1796.
75. Granville MSS PRO 30/29/4/11/8, ?June 1796.
76. Aspinall PoW, Vol. 3, 1150, ?18 June 1796.
77. Aspinall PoW, Vol. 3, 1160, 23 June 1796.
78. Hibbert Prince, p. 158.

79. *The Times*, 25 July 1796 cited in Aspinall PoW, Vol. 3, 1167 n 1, 29 June 1796.
80. Aspinall PoW, Vol. 3, 1167 n 1, 29th June 1796.
81. RA GEO/ADD/21/87, nd.
82. Aspinall PoW, Vol. 3, 1172, 10 July 1796.
83. Aspinall PoW, Vol. 3, p. 123.
84. Hibbert Prince, p. 159.
85. Granville, Castalia, Countess ed., *The Private Correspondence of Lord Granville Leveson Gower*, London, John Murray, 1916 ('GLG Correspondence'), Vol. 1, p. 123, 29 June 1796.
86. Stuart, Dorothy Margaret, *Dearest Bess, The Life and Times of Lady Elizabeth Foster afterwards Duchess of Devonshire from Her Unpublished Journals and Correspondence*, London, Methuen & Co Ltd, 1955, p. 74.
87. Bessborough Georgiana, p. 219, 9 July 1796.
88. GLG Correspondence, Vol. 1, p. 124, 1 July 1796.

14 – Vilification: The Apogee of Disrepute

1. Porter 18th Century, p. 100.
2. Domestic Fracas, p. 19, citing *The Times* of 24 May 1796.
3. Farington Diaries, Yale, Vol. 2, p. 559, 26 May 1796.
4. Piozzi Letters, Vol. 2, p. 350, 30 May 1796.
5. *The Times*, 20 July 1796.
6. *The Times*, 20 July 1796.
7. *London Chronicle*, 19 July 1796.
8. *The Times*, 22 July 1796.
9. *The True Briton*, 20 July 1796.
10. Piozzi Letters, Vol. 2, p. 380, 2-10 October 1796.
11. Farington Diaries, Yale, Vol. 2, p. 615, 24 July 1796.
12. Granville MSS PRO 30/29/4/11/25, 29 August 1796.
13. Bessborough Georgiana, p. 209, 14 July 1796.
14. Cited in Roberts, Henry D, A *History of the Royal Pavilion Brighton*, London, Country Life Limited, 1939, p. 41.
15. *The Telegraph*, 30 July 1796.
16. *The Sun*, 21 July 1796.
17. *The Telegraph*, 26 July 1796.
18. Walpole Correspondence, Vol. 12, p. 200 n, 17 July 1796.
19. Granville MSS, PRO 30/29/4/11/22, 26 July 1796.
20. Bessborough Georgiana, p. 219, 30 July 1796.
21. Granville MSS PRO 30/29/4/9/86, 1 August 1796.
22. Balderstone, Katharine C. ed., *Thraliana, The Diary of Mrs. Hester Lynch Thrale (later Mrs Piozzi) 1776–1809*, 2 Vols, Oxford at the Clarendon Press, 1942, Vol. 2, p. 963, 30 July 1796.
23. Leeds Memoranda, p. 233, 30 July 1796.
24. Granville MSS PRO 30/29/4/11/23, 5 August 1796.
25. Walpole Correspondence, Vol. 12, p. 200 n, 9 August 1796.

26. *The Telegraph*, 10 August 1796.
27. Walpole Correspondence, Vol. 12, p. 200, 9 August 1796.
28. *The True Briton*, 8 August 1796.
29. Jerningham Bettany, p. 247, ?August 1796.
30. Jerningham Bettany, pp. 243-244, nd.
31. Jerningham Bettany, p. 246, 16 ?August 1796.
32. Aspinall PoW, Vol. 3, 1181, 1 August 1976.
33. Aspinall PoW, Vol. 3, 1185, 16 August 1796.
34. *The True Briton*, 17 August 1796.
35. Granville MSS PRO 30/29/4/11/25, 29 August 1796.
36. Granville MSS PRO 30/29/4/11/26, 12 September 1796.
37. Walpole Correspondence, Vol. 12, p. 204, 16 August 1796.
38. Granville MSS PRO 30/29/4/9/89, 26 August 1796.
39. Jerningham Bettany, p. 244, 2 September 1796.
40. Jerningham Bettany, p. 244, 5 September 1796.
41. Jerningham Bettany, p. 245, 14 September 1796.
42. Jerningham Bettany, p. 245, 14 September 1796.
43. LMA Jersey MSS LMA/ACC/1275/004, 24 September ?1796.
44. Granville MSS PRO 30/29/4/9/93, 29 September 1796.
45. Blunt, Reginald ed., *Mrs. Montagu 'Queen of the Blues', Her Letters and Friendships from 1762 to 1800,* 2 Vols, London, Constable and Company Limited, 1923, Vol. 2, p. 324, 17 October 1796.
46. Granville MSS PRO 30/29/4/9/94, 8 October 1796.
47. Aspinall PoW, Vol. 3, 1194, 23 September 1796.
48. Aspinall PoW, Vol. 3, 1194, 26 September 1796.
49. Granville MSS PRO 30/29/4/11/27, 2 October 1796.
50. Farington Diaries, Yale, Vol. 3, p. 696, 17 November 1796.
51. Quoted in Aspinall PoW, Vol. 3, p. 272, 29 September 1796.52. Leeds Memoranda, p. 23, 22 September 1796.
53. Glenbervie Diaries, Vol. 1, p. 74, 7 October 1796.
54. Glenbervie Diaries, Vol. 1, p. 88, 16 October 1796.
55. Glenbervie Diaries, Vol. 1, p. 88, 20 October 1796.
56. Granville MSS PRO 30/29/5/4/68, nd, probably 21 October 1796.
57. Granville MSS PRO 30/29/4/9/95, 22 October 1796.
58. Glenbervie Diaries, Vol. 1, p. 90, 26 October 1796.
59. *The Morning Post*, 26 October 1796.
60. Granville MSS PRO 30/29/5/4/70, nd, *c.* 21 October 1796.
61. Add MSS 75684, nd, annotated 30 October 1796.
62. Granville MSS PRO 30/29/4/11/32, 17 November 1796.
63. Granville MSS PRO 30/29/4/11/33, 12th December 1796.
64. Aspinall PoW, Vol. 3, 1218, 1 December 1796.
65. Granville MSS PRO 30/29/4/11/36, 19 January 1797.
66. *The True Briton*, 30 January 1797.
67. *The True Briton*, 1 February 1797.
68. Granville MSS PRO/30/29/4/11/37, 29 January 1797.
69. Granville MSS PRO 30/29/4/11/34, 10 January 1797.
70. GLG Correspondence, Vol. 1, p. 221, ?August/September 1796.

71. Glenbervie Diaries, Vol. 1, p. 214, 7 April 1799.
72. Aspinall George III, Vol. 2, 1495, 22 January 1797.
73. Granville MSS PRO 30/29/4/11/43, 7 May 1797.
74. *The Morning Post*, 19 May 1797.
75. *Observer*, 21 May 1797.
76. *The Morning Post*, 24 May 1797.
77. Granville MSS PRO 30/29/4/11/44, 31 May 1797.
78. Baker, Kenneth, *George IV, A Life in Caricature*, London, Thames & Hudson, 2005, p. 45
79. *The Morning Chronicle*, 1 April 1797.
80. Wardroper, John, *Kings, Lords and Wicked Libellers – Satire and Protest 1760–1837*, London, John Murray, 1973, pp. 179-180.
81. Williams, John, *A Looking Glass for the Royal Family*, London, H D Symonds, T Bellamy, 1797.
82. Newdigate-Newdegate, Lady ed., The *Cheverels of Cheverel Manor*, London, Longmans, Green, and Co, 1898 ('Newdigate'), p. 192, 23 July 1797.
83. Newdigate, p. 195, 26 July 1797.
84. Newdigate, p. 198, 28 July 1797.
85. LMA Jersey MSS LMA ACC/1128/238, nd, unspecified newspaper.
86. Clayden, P. W, *The Early Life of Samuel Rogers*, London, Smith, Elder & Co, 1887, pp. 335–337, 14 November 1797.
87. *The True Briton*, 23 November 1797.
88. *The True Briton*, 20 January 1798.
89. *Morning Herald*, 27 February 1798.
90. Granville MSS PRO 30/29/5/4/79, 1 January 1798.
91. DNB.
92. Reid, Stuart J, *Life and Letters of the First Earl of Durham, 1792–1840*, 2 Vols, London, Longmans, Green and Co, 1906, Vol. 1, p. 36, 30 November 1797.
93. GLG Correspondence, Vol. 1, p. 190, 27 December 1797.
94. Add MSS 75682, 16 January 1798.
95. Add MSS 75682, 22 January 1798.
96. Add MSS 75682, nd, ? January 1798.
97. *Whitehall Evening Post*, 5 May 1798.
98. Add MSS 75682, 11 May 1798.
99. Add MSS 75682, 24 January 1798.
100. Add MSS 75682, 15 May 1798.
101. *The True Briton*, 3 May 1798.
102. Piozzi Letters, Vol. 2, p. 525, 14 September 1798.
103. Manvell, Roger, *Sarah Siddons, Portrait of an Actress,* London, Heinemann, 1970 ('Manvell Siddons'), p. 223, 1 August 1798.
104. Parsons, Mrs Clement, *The Incomparable Siddons*, London, Methuen & Co, 1909, p. 250
105. Manvell Siddons, p. 204.
106. Smith, E. A., *George IV*, New Haven and London, Yale University Press, 1999 ('Smith George IV'), p. 290.

15 – The End of the Affair

1. GLG Correspondence, Vol. 1, p. 220, 26 August 1798.
2. Ashton, John, *Florizel's Folly*, London, Chatto & Wimdus, 1899, p. 199.
3. Granville MSS PRO/30/29/4/9/117, 7 August 1798.
4. Munson Fitzherbert, pp. 288–289.
5. *The True Briton*, 4 October 1798.
6. Aspinall PoW, Vol. 3, 1376, 30 August 1798.
7. Aspinall PoW, Vol. 3, 1415, nd.
8. Glenbervie Diaries, Vol. 2, p. 13, 1 February 1807.
9. Aspinall PoW, Vol. 3, 1392, 7 October 1798.
10. Jerningham Castle, Vol. 1, p. 137, ?November 1798.
11. Jerningham Bettany, p. 103, nd.
12. Jerningham Bettany, p. 249, nd.
13. Granville MSS PRO 30/29/4/9/119, 29 October 1798.
14. Murray, Venetia, *High Society, A Social History of the Regency Period 1778–1830*, London, Viking, 1998, p. 56.
15. Jerningham Bettany, p. 255, 24 November 1798.
16. Jerningham Castle, p. 137, ?November 1798.
17. *The Star*, 29 November 1798.
18. Jerningham Bettanny, pp. 255, 11 and 30 January 1799.
19. Hibbert Prince, p. 170.
20. Bishop, Morchand ed., *Recollections of the Table Talk of Samuel Rogers*, London, Richards Press, 1952, p. 266 n.
21. Granville MSS PRO 30/29/4/9/121, 25 January 1799.
22. Aspinall PoW, Vol. 4, 1422, 12 February 1799.
23. Aspinall PoW, Vol. 4, p. 12, n 1.
24. Aspinall PoW, Vol. 4, 1422, 12 February 1799.
25. Munson Fitzherbert, p. 289.
26. Aspinall PoW, Vol. 4, 1454, 11-12 June 1799.
27. Munson Fitzherbert, p. 291.
28. Munson Fitzherbert, p. 290.
29. RA GEO/ADD/MSS/21/21, 8 June 1799.
30. Add MSS 45548, f 33, ?August/September 1799.
31. Aspinall PoW, Vol. 4, 1450, 30 April 1799.
32. Aspinall PoW, Vol. 4, p. 62, n 2, 2 July 1799.
33. Aspinall PoW, Vol. 4, p. 91 n, 15 December 1799.
34. Barnett, Gerald, *Richard and Maria Cosway – A Biography*, Westcountry Books, The Lutterworth Press, 1995, p. 186.
35. Jerningham Bettany, p. 104, nd.
36. Clayden, P. W., *Rogers and his Contemporaries*, 2 Vols, London, Smith Elder & Co, 1887, Vol. 1, p. 144, nd.
37. Russell, Lady John, *Letters of Lady John Russell to Her Husband 1798–1801*, London, Chiswick Press, 1933 ('Russell Letters'), p. [ ], ?October 1798.
38. Add MSS 75682, 19 August 1799.

39. Castle Howard MSS J/18/20, nd.
40. Draper, Nicholas, 'The Price of Emancipation: Slave-Ownership, Compensation and British Society at the End of Slavery', *Cambridge Studies in Economic History*, 2013 ('Draper Emancipation')..
41. Add MSS 75682, 19 August 1799.
42. *Whitehall Evening Post*, 19 September 1799.
43. Draper Emancipation.
44. *London Chronicle*, 13 March 1798.
45. Add MSS 75682, 31 March 1798.
46. Barrett, C. R. B., *The 7th Queen's Own Hussars*, London, Royal United Services Institution ('Barrett 7th LDG'), p. 240.
47. Cannon, Richard, *Historical Record of the Seventh, or, Queen's Own Regiment of Hussars: containing an account of the formation of the regiment in 1690 and its subsequent services to 1842*, London, J W Parker, 1841 ('Cannon 7th Hussars'), p. 64.
48. Barrett 7th LDG, p. 247.
49. Barrett 7th LDG, p. 245.
50. Fortescue, Sir John, *A History of the British Army*, 14 Vols, London, Macmillan, 1899–1930, Vol. 4 Part 11, p. 700.
51. Barrett 7th LDG, p. 271.
52. Cannon 7th Hussars, p. 67.
53. Add MSS 75682, 29 September 1799.
54. Jerningham Bettany, p. 230, nd.

16 – Satan's Representative on Earth

1. *The Morning Chronicle*, 20 January 1800.
2. *The True Briton*, 21 March 1800.
3. *The Morning Post*, 21 January 1800.
4. Hibbert Prince, p. 174.
5. *London Packet*, 24 January 1800.
6. Add MSS 75695, 3 February 1800.
7. Jerningham Castle, Vol. 1, p. 160, 17 March 1800.
8. Wilkins, W. H., *Mrs Fitzherbert and George IV*, 2 Vols, London, Longmans, Green, and Co, 1905, Vol. 2, p. 15.
9. Munson Fitzherbert, p. 293.
10. *The Morning Post*, 7 April 1800.
11. *Caledonian Mercury*, 26 May 1800.
12. Price, Cecil ed., The *Letters of Richard Brinsley Sheridan*, 3 Vols, Oxford, Clarendon Press, 1966, Vol. 2, p. 131, June 1800.
13. Greig, Hannah, *The Beau Monde, Fashionable Society in Georgian London*, Oxford University Press, 2013 ('Greig Beau Monde'), p. 49.
14. Greig Beau Monde, p. 42.
15. Greig Beau Monde, p. 59.
16. Piozzi Letters, Vol. 3, pp. 175–176, 29th March 1800.
17. Russell Letters, p. 71, nd.

18. Russell Letters, p. 72, nd.
19. Queen Victoria's Journals RA VIC/MAIN/QVJ (W) 8 November 1838 (Lord Esher's typescripts). Retrieved 2 April 2015.
20. Jerningham Castle, Vol. 1, p. 193, 7 July 1800.
21. *The True Briton*, 21 July 1800.
22. *The Morning Post*, 22 July 1800.
23. Add MSS 75682, 4 August 1800.
24. Jackson's Oxford Journal, 9 August 1800.
25. *The Morning Post*, 14 August 1800.
26. Francis, Beata ed., *The Francis Letters – Letters of Sir Philip Francis and other members of the family*, 2 Vols, London, Hutchison & Co, 1901, Vol. 2, pp. 461–462, 19 August 1800.
27. Aspinall PoW, Vol. 4, 1566, 28 October 1800.
28. RA GEO/MAIN/39699-700, 28 October 1800.
29. RA GEO/MAIN/39701, 3 November 1800.
30. RA GEO/MAIN/39774, 27 January 1802.
31. RA GEO/MAIN/31512, 21 June 1802.
32. Aspinall PoW, Vol. 4, 1588, 28 January 1801.
33. Foreman Georgiana, p. 333.
34. Chatsworth MSS, 1543, 18 December 1800.
35. Chatsworth MSS, 1564, 14 January 1801.
36. *The Morning Chronicle*, 6 February 1801.
37. Glenbervie Diaries, Vol. 2, p. 284, 3 January 1818.
38. Wyndham, H. A., *A Family History, 1688–1837. The Wyndhams of Somerset, Sussex and Wiltshire*, London, Oxford University Press, 1950, p. 226 and Genealogy.
39. Rubenhold Worsley, p. 130.
40. Maxwell, The Rt Hon Sir Herbert Bt, *The Creevey Papers – A Selection of the Correspondence and Diaries of the late Thomas Creevey MP*, London, John Murray, 1905 ('Creevey Maxwell'), p. 164.
41. Aspinall PoW, Vol. 1, 44, p. 61, 6 May 1781.
42. Chatsworth MSS, 1611C, 7 February 1801.
43. Farington Diaries, Yale, Vol. 5, p. 1619, 14 September 1801.
44. Halifax MSS, /A1.2.7.3, 22 September nd.
45. Bury & Norwich Post, 4 March 1801.
46. Askwith, Betty, *Piety and Wit: A Biography of Harriet Countess Granville 1785–1862*, London, Collins, 1982, p. 37.
47. Edgcumbe, Richard ed., *The Diary of Lady Frances Shelley*, 2 Vols, London, John Murray, 1912, Vol. 1, p. 44.
48. Lobel, Mary D. ed., *The Victoria History of the Counties of England – A History of the County of Oxford*, Vol. 6, Ploughley Hundred, London, Oxford University Press, 1959, p. 246.
49. Howell-Thomas, Dorothy, *Duncannon, Reformer and Reconciler 1781–1847*, Norwich, Michael Russell, 1992, p. 72.
50. LMA Jersey MSS LMA/1128/011 and 012, will of 16 July 1782 and codicil.
51. Jackson's Oxford Journal, 5 December 1801.

52. Walpole Correspondence, Vol. 12, p. 73, 23 November 1793.
53. Jackson's Oxford Journal, 5 December 1801.
54. Add MSS 51799, 5 March 1802.
55. Buckingham and Chandos, Duke of, *Memoirs of the Court and Cabinets of George III*, 3 Vols, London, Hurst and Blackett, 1853, Vol. 3, p. 196.
56. LMA Jersey MSS LMA/ACC/1128/185/54, 4 July 1802.
57. LMA Jersey MSS LMA/ACC/0510/274, ?9 July 1802.
58. GLG Correspondence, Vol. 1, p. 345,13 August 1802.
59. Foreman Georgiana, p. 293 and p. 397.
60. Granville MSS PRO 30/29/4/9/132, 18 August 1802.
61. Villiers, Marjorie, *The Grand Whiggery*, London, John Murray, 1939 ('Villiers Grand Whiggery'), p. 163.
62. GLG Correspondence, Vol. 1, p. 334, 26 March 1802.
63. *The Morning Post*, 5th June 1802.
64. Leveson Gower, Sir George ed., *Hary-O, The Letters of Lady Harriet Cavendish, 1796–1809*, London, John Murray ('Hary-O Letters'), p. 26, 15 August 1802.
65. Leslie, Doris, *The Great Corinthian: A Portrait of the Prince Regent*, London, Eyre & Spottiswoode, 1952, p. 131.
66. DNB.
67. Wilson, Frances, *The Courtesan's Revenge*, London, Faber and Faber, 2003, ('Wilson Courtesan's Revenge'), pp. 81–82.
68. Wilson, Harriette, *Harriette Wilson's Memoirs*, London, Peter Davies, 1929 ('Harriette Wilson'), p. 72.
69. GLG Correspondence, Vol. 1, p. 359, 21 September 1802.
70. Hary-O Letters, p. 34, 19 September 1802.
71. Add MSS 75682, 1 October 1802.
72. GLG Correspondence, Vol. 1, p. 359, September 1803.
73. Ponsonby, Major General Sir John KCB, *The Ponsonby Family*, London, Medici Society, 1929, p. 79.
74. Wilson Courtesan's Revenge, p. 84, citing Hon F. Leveson Gower ed., *The Letters of Harriet, Countess Granville*, London, Longmans, Green, and Co, 1894, Vol. 1, p. 43.
75. Marchand, Leslie A. ed., *Byron's Letters and Journals*, 12 Vols, London, John Murray, 1973–1982 ('Marchand Byron'), Vol. 5, p. 216.
76. Harriette Wilson, pp. 101–102 and p. 99.
77. Farington Diaries, Yale, Vol. 6, p. 2196, 19 December 1803.
78. Harriette Wilson, pp. 98-99.
79. Add MSS 75682, 1 October 1802.
80. Castle Howard MSS J/18/20 f 69, nd.
81. Chatsworth MSS, 1651, 15 October? 1802.
82. Chatsworth MSS, 1662, 8 November 1802.
83. Halifax MSS /A1.2.7.10, 28 December 1802.
84. Halifax MSS /A1.2.7.11, 14 February 1803.
85. *The Morning Post*, 4 February 1803.
86. Chatsworth MSS, 1647, 24 September 1802.

87. Castle Howard MSS J/18/20, 'Friday', nd
88. Hary-O Letters, p. 34, 19 September 1802.
89. GLG Correspondence, Vol. 1, p. 359, nd September 1802.
90. Foreman Georgiana, p. 357.
91. Masters, Brian, *Georgiana Duchess of Devonshire*, London, Hamish Hamilton, 1981, pp. 251–252.
92. Villiers Grand Whiggery, p. 166, nd September 1802.
93. Hary-O Letters, p. 36, 22 September 1802.
94. GLG Correspondence, Vol. 1, pp. 363-364, 4 October 1802.
95. Hary-O Letters, p. 38, 12 October 1802.
96. GLG Correspondence, Vol. 1, p. 365, nd October 1802.
97. Hary-O Letters, pp. 86-87, 29 November 1802.
98. Jersey Records, p. 55.
99. GLG Correspondence, Vol. 1, p. 417, nd.
100. Castle Howard MSS J/18/21 f 90, nd.
101. GLG Correspondence, Vol. 1, p. 417, nd.
102. Hary-O Letters, p. 45, 20 January 1803.
103. Hary-O Letters, p. 47, 25 January 1803.
104. Hary-O Letters, p. 49, 30 January 1803.
105. *The Bury and Norwich Post*, 2 February 1803.
106. Hary-O Letters, p. 41, ?January/February 1803.
107. Edgcumbe, Richard ed., *The Diary of Lady Frances Shelley*, 2 Vols, London, John Murray, 1912 ('Shelley Diary'), Vol. 1, p. 42.
108. Bury & Norwich Post, 16 February 1803.
109. GLG Correspondence, Vol. 1, p. 454, nd.
110. Add MSS 51724, 8 May 1803.
111. GLG Correspondence, Vol. 1, p. 433, September 1803.
112. GLG Correspondence, Vol. 2, p. 109, 28 August 1805.
113. Chatsworth MSS, 1766, 13 April 1804.
114. Add MSS 75682, 23 April 1804.
115. *The Morning Post*, 24 May 1804.
116. Knox, Tim and Palmer, Anthea ed., *Aspects of Osterley: Nineteenth Century Chatelaines*, Rogers, Kevin, High Wycombe, National Trust, *c.* 2000, pp. 50–52.
117. LMA Jersey MSS LMA/1128/015, 23 May 1804.
118. *The Morning Post*, 2 April 1803.
119. Castle Howard MSS J/18/20, 17 February 1803.
120. *The Times*, 11 February 1803.
121. *Observer*, 23 January 1803.
122. *The Times*, 19 January 1803.
123. Farington Diaries, Yale, Vol. 6, p. 2075, 5 July 1803.
124. Hary-O Letters, p. 55.
125. Hary-O Letters, p. 57, 10 September 1803.
126. Hary-O Letters, p. 59, ?4 October 1803.
127. Hary-O Letters, p. 60, 6 October 1803.
128. Hary-O Letters, p. 64, 2 November 1803.
129. Hary-O Letters, p. 65, 4 November 1803.

130. Hary-O Letters, p. 76, 17/18 November 1803.
131. Hary-O Letters, p. 79, 19 November 1803.
132. Hary-O Letters, p. 81, 22 November 1803.
133. Hary-O Letters, p. 81, 22 November 1803.
134. Hary-O Letters, p. 87, 29 November 1803.
135. Foreman Georgiana, p. 375.
136. Hary-O Letters, p. 91, 30 December 1803.
137. Hary-O Letters, p. 103, 29 September 1804.
138. Hary-O Letters, p. 110, ?November 1804.
139. *The Morning Post,* 19 January 1804.
140. *Bury & Norfolk Post*, 24 July 1805.
141. *The Morning Post*, 4 July 1805.
142. GLG Correspondence, Vol. 2, p. 91, 10 July 1805.
143. *The Morning Post*, 27 July 1805.
144. *The Morning Post*, 2 August 1805.
145. *The Morning Post*, 9 August 1805.
146. *The Times,* 24 August 1805.
147. GLG Correspondence, Vol. 2, pp. 107 and 108, 25 and 28 August 1805.
148. GLG Correspondence, Vol. 2, p. 109, 28 August 1805.
149. Harcourt Papers, Vol. 8, pp. 88–89, 29 August 1805.
150. Harcourt Papers, Vol. 6, pp. 80–81, 29 August 1805.
151. Grosvenor, Caroline and Beilby, Charles (Lord Stuart of Wortley), *The First Lady Wharncliffe and her Family 1779–1856*, 2 Vols, London, William Heinemann, 1927, Vol. 1, p. 110, nd.
152. Chatsworth MSS, 1817, 9 September 1805.
153. Add MSS 75594, 10 September 1805.
154. Add MSS 75684, 4 September 1805.
155. Shelley Diary, Vol. 1, p. 42.
156. LMA Jersey MSS LMA/ACC/1401/177, Earl of Jersey's Will dated 16 April 1791.
157. GLG Correspondence, Vol. 2, p. 120, 10 October 1805.
158. Hary-O Letters, p. 128, 6 November 1805.
159. Paget Brothers, pp. 16-17, nd 1803.

17 – The Years of Scandals

1. *The Morning Post*, 22 December 1806.
2. Hary-O letters, p. 142, late December 1805.
3. Roscoe, E. S. and Clergue, Helen ed., *George Selwyn, His Letters and Life*, London, T Fisher Unwin, 1899, p. 99 n.
4. GLG Correspondence, Vol. 2, p. 135, 16 November 1805.
5. *The Times*, 16 May 1806.
6. Bessborough, Earl of in collaboration with Aspinall, A. ed., *Lady Bessborough and her Family Circle*, London, John Murray, 1940 ('Bessborough Family Circle'), p. 159, 15 May 1807.

7. Bessborough Family Circle, pp. 160–161, 8 July 1807.
8. Price, Cecil, ed., *The Letters of Richard Brinsley Sheridan*, 3 Vols, Oxford, Clarendon Press, 1966, Vol. 1, p. 208.
9. Douglas-Home MSS, Vol. 499, 25 August 1789.
10. Wyndham, The Hon Mrs Hugh ed., *Correspondence of Sarah Spencer, Lady Lyttleton 1787–1870*, London, John Murray, 1912 ('Lyttleton Correspondence') p. 36, 19 October 1808.
11. War Office, Lists of all the Officers of the Army and Royal Marines, London, War Office ('Army List'), 1798–1806.
12. *The London Gazette*, 6 June 1802.
13. *The London Gazette*, 25 January 1806.
14. Cannon, Richard, *Historical Records of the Seventh, or Princess Royal's, Regiment of Dragoon Guards*, London, Longman, Orme, Clowes, 1839, p. 61.
15. *The London Gazette*, 1 July 1806.
16. Army List 1806.
17. *The London Gazette*, 26 May 1807.
18. Shepp.ard, Major E. W., The *Ninth Queen's Royal Lancers, 1715–1936*, Aldershot, Gale & Polden, Ltd, 1939, p. 347.
19. Castle Howard MSS J/18/20 f 92, nd.
20. Castle Howard MSS J/18/20 f 93, nd.
21. Jersey Records and RootsWeb: NOVA-SCOTIA-L Archives.
22. Phillips, D. Rhys, *The History of the Vale of Neath, Swansea*, 1925, p. 390 citing the *Cambrian* of 14 February 1814.
23. Jerningham Bettany, p. 248, nd ?1796.
24. Shelley Diary, Vol. 1, p. 37.
25. LMA Jersey MSS LMA/ACC/0510/275, 29 July 1807.
26. LMA Jersey MSS LMA/ACC/0510/281, 1 November 1808.
27. LMA Jersey MSS LMA/ACC/0510/280, 31 October 1808.
28. LMA Jersey MSS LMA/ACC/0510/282, ?November 1808.
29. Add MSS 48404B, f 29, 17 August 1808.
30. Clayden, P. W., *Rogers and his Contemporaries*, 2 Vols, London, Smith, Elder & Co, 1889, Vol. 1, pp. 52–53.
31. *The Morning Post*, 29 August 1808.
32. Debretts, *Peerage of the United Kingdom of Great Btitain and Ireland*, 17th Edition, Vol. 1, London, 1828 ('Debrett').
33. Hary-O Letters, pp. 127–128, 6 November 1805.
34. Hary-O Letters, p. 141, 29 December 1805.
35. Debrett.
36. Greig, James ed., The *Farington Diary*, 6 Vols, London, Hutchinson & Co, 1922. ('Farington Greig'), Vol. 5, p. 65, 18 May 1808.
37. Bessborough Family Circle, p. 172, 17 September 1808.
38. Hary-O Letters, p. 170, 22 November 1806.
39. GLG Correspondence, Vol. 2, p. 230, post marked 4 December 1806.
40. Hary-O Letters, p. 268, 8 December 1807.
41. Hary-O Letters, p. 273, nd December 1807.
42. Jersey Records, p. 37.

43. Glenbervie Diaries, Vol. 1, p. 350, 16 October 1802.
44. DNB.
45. *The Morning Chronicle*, 22 December 1806.
46. LMA Jersey MSS LMA/ACC/1128/103, December 1806.
47. *The Morning Chronicle*, 22 December 1806.
48. Add MSS 48404B f 79, 31 March 1809.
49. Add MSS 48404B f 83, ?7 April 1809.
50. Add MSS 48404B f 89, May/June 1809.
51. Add MSS 51681, 20 October 1809.
52. Blakiston, Georgiana, *Woburn and the Russells*, London, Constable, 1980, p. 188.
53. Paget One Leg, p. 90.
54. Paget Brothers, p. 107.
55. Paget One Leg, p. 89.
56. Hary-O Letters, pp. 307–308, 8 March 1809.
57. Hary-O Letters, pp. 309–310, 9 March 1809.
58. *The Times*, 11 March 1809.
59. Paget One Leg, pp. 91–92, 3 March 1809.
60. Paget One Leg, p. 96.
61. *The Morning Chronicle*, 13 March 1809.
62. Paget One Leg, p. 100.
63. Leighton, Rachel ed., *The Correspondence of Charlotte Grenville, Lady Williams Wynn and her three sons, Sir Watkin Williams Wynn Bart, Rt Hon Charles Williams Wynn, and Sir Henry Williams Wynn 1795–1832*, London, John Murray, 1920, pp. 144–145, 14 March 1809.
64. Hary-O Letters, p. 311, 16 March 1809.
65. Add MSS 48404B, f 71, 17 March 1809.
66. Add MSS 48404B, f 73, ?18 March 1809.
67. Add MSS 48415, f 191, 20 March 1809.
68. *Hampshire Telegraph*, 20 March 1809.
69. Lyttleton Correspondence, p. 63, 20 March 1809.
70. Add MSS 48404, f 127, 21 March 1809.
71. Add MSS 48404B, f 81, 2 April 1809.
72. Paget One Leg, p. 102.
73. Add MSS 48404A, 12 May 1809.
74. Farington Diaries, Yale, Vol. 9, p. 3470, 26 May 1809.
75. Paget One Leg, p. 103.
76. *The Times*, 13 May 1809.
77. *The Morning Chronicle*, 16 May 1809.
78. *The Morning Chronicle*, 31 May 1809.
79. Paget One Leg, pp. 105 and 109.
80. Paget One Leg, p. 109.
81. Paget One Leg, p. 109.
82. Paget One Leg, pp. 109–110.
83. Glenbervie Diaries, Vol. 2, pp. 73-74, 7 October 1810.
84. Add MSS 51799, 23 September 1810.
85. GLG Correspondence, Vol. 2, p. 365, 9 September 1810.

86. Jerningham Castle, Vol. 1, p. 379, 13 November 1810.
87. HMC, *The Manuscripts of J B Fortescue Preserved at Dropmore*, 30th Report, Vol. X, London, HMSO, 1927, p. 83, 10 December 1810.
88. Grant, J. P. ed., *Memoirs and Correspondence of Mrs Grant*, 3 Vols, London, 1844, Vol. 1, p. 274, 24 October 1810.
89. Piozzi Letters, Vol. 4, p. 310, 27 October 1810.
90. Piozzi Letters, Vol. 4, p. 321, 21 December 1810.
91. Add MSS 48415, ?before 22 February 1810.
92. Add MSS 48404A, 12 May 1811.
93. Harriette Wilson, p. 215.
94. Quenn Victoria's Journals RA VIC/MAIN/QVJ (W) 8 November 1838 (Lord Esher's typescripts). Retrieved 2 April 2015.
95. Russell, C. C. E., *Three Generations of Fascinating Women and other sketches from family history*, London, Longmans & Co, 1904, pp. 199–200.
96. *The Morning Chronicle,* 29 March 1810.
97. *The Morning Post*, 9 August 1809.
98. Wilson Courtesan's Revenge, pp. 84 and 89.
99. Harriette Wilson, p. 146.
100. Paston, George and Quennell, Peter, *To Lord Byron: Feminine Profiles based on unpublished letters 1807–1824*, London, John Murray, 1939, pp. 160–161.
101. Wilson Courtesan's Revenge, p. 89.

18 – The Final Mischiefs

1. Creevey Maxwell, Vol. 2, p. 296, 23 January 1820.
2. Ridley, Jasper, *Lord Palmerston*, London, Constable & Co, 1970 ('Ridley Palmerston'), p. 167.
3. Ridley Palmerston, pp. 42–44.
4. Ridley Palmerston, p. 71.
5. Creevey Maxwell, Vol. 2, p. 268, 24 November 1833.
6. LMA Jersey MSS LMA/ACC/1128/238, nd, annotated '1837'.
7. Granville (Harriet) Letters, Vol. 1, p. 110, 18 June 1817.
8. *Cheltenham Chronicle*, 27 September 1810.
9. *The Morning Post*, 18 April 1809.
10. *The Morning Post*, 30 January 1811.
11. *The Morning Post*, 1 March 1811.
12. Farington Greig, Vol. 7, p. 3, 15 June 1811.
13. *The Morning Post*, 21st June 1811.
14. *The Morning Post*, 21st June 1811.
15. Dorchester, Lady ed., *Lord Broughton – Recollections of a Long Life*, 6 Vols, London, John Murray, 1910, Vol. 1, p. 159, 21 July 1814.
16. *The Morning Post*, 24 November and 15 December 1810.
17. *The Morning Chronicle*, 17 January 1811.

18. Goff, Moira, Goldfinch, John, Limper-Herrz, Karen and Peden, Helen, *Georgians Revealed: Life, Style and the Making of Modern Britain*, London, The British Library, 2013, p. 88.
19. *Cheltenham Chronicle*, 2 May 1811.
20. *The Morning Post*, 6 May 1811.
21. *Cheltenham Chronicle*, 23 May 1811.
22. *Cheltenham Chronicle*, 23 May 1811.
23. *The Morning Post*, 13 May 1811.
24. *The Morning Post*, 5 July 1811.
25. *The Morning Post*, 2 August 1811.
26. *The Morning Post*, 6 August 1811.
27. *The Morning Chronicle*, 10 August 1811.
28. *The Morning Post*, 10 August 1811.
29. Jerningham Bettany, p. 59, 18 June 1815.
30. Colville, Sir John, *Those Lambtons, A Most Unusual Family*, London, Hodder & Stoughton, 1988, p. 29.
31. *Bury & Norwich Post*, 5 February 1812.
32. Phillips, D. Rhys, *The History of the Vale of Neath, with illustrations*, Swansea, 1925, p. 390.
33. Reports of cases argued and determined in the courts of Common Pleas, Court of Exchequer Chamber, Volume 10, John Bayly Moore, 1820 ('Common Pleas Reports'), p. 352.
34. LMA Jersey MSS LMA/4195/009, 24 September 1813.
35. LMA Jersey MSS LMA/4195/009, 30 September 1813.
36. Common Pleas Reports, p. 352.
37. Reports of cases heard in the House of Lords: on appeals and writs, Volume 2, Richard Bligh, 1827, p. 305.
38. Granville (Harriet) Letters, Vol. 1, p. 29, 13 November 1811.
39. Granville (Harriet) Letters, Vol. 1, p. 40, 11 September 1812.
40. Granville (Harriet) Letters, Vol. 1, p. 29, 13 November 1811.
41. Granville (Harriet) Letters, Vol. 1, p. 43, 30 December 1812.
42. Colvin, Christina ed., *Maria Edgeworth – Letters from England 1813–1844*, Oxford, Clarendon Press, 1971, p. 56, 16 May 1813.
43. *The The Morning Post*, 24 April 1813.
44. Aspinall Giv, Vol. 1, 232, 27 January 1813.
45. RA GEO/MAIN/20394, nd.
46. Aspinall Giv, Vol. 1, 263, 6 April 1813.
47. Bury George IV, Vol. 1, p. 89, 2 December 1812.
48. Aspinall Giv, Vol. 1, 307, 12 August 1813.
49. Aspinall Giv, Vol. 1, 359, 12 December 1813.
50. Knight, Miss Cornelia, Autobiography *of Miss Cornelia Knight, Lady Companion to Princess Charlotte of Wales*, 2 Vols, London, W H Allen & Co, 1861 ('Knight Autobiography'), Vol. 1, pp. 212–213.
51. Aspinall, A. ed., *Letters of Princess Charlotte*, London, Home and Van Thal, 1949 ('Charlotte Letters'), p. 60, 7 March 1813.
52. Knight Autobiography, Vol. 1, p. 240, ? June 1813.

53. E.g. Holme, Thea, *Prinny's Daughter, A Life of Princess Charlotte of Wales*, London, Hamish Hamilton, 1976, p. 114 and Stuart, Dorothy Margaret, *Daughter of England, A New Study of Princess Charlotte and her Family*, London, Macmillan & Co, 1951 ('Stuart Daughter of England'), p. 117.
54. Charlotte Letters, p. 62, 2 August 1813.
55. Stuart Daughter of England, p. 117.
56. *The Morning Chronicle*, 28 July 1814.
57. Aspinall Giv, Vol. 1, 486, 20 September 1814.
58. Marchand Byron, Vol. 3, pp. 271-272.
59. Marchand Byron, Vol. 4, p. 120, 29 May 1814 and LMA Jersey MSS LMA ACC/1128/193, Sally Jersey's Commonplace Book, 29 May 1814.
60. *The Morning Chronicle*, 27 May 1816.
61. LMA Jersey MSS LMA/4195/017, 24 May 1816.
62. Queen Victoria's Journals RA VIC/MAIN/QVJ (W) 20 May 1838 (Lord Esher's typescripts). Retrieved 10 September 2015.
63. E.g. Stuart Daughter of England, p. 175 and Smith George IV, p. 149.
64. Ilchester, Earl of, *The Home of the Hollands 1605–1820*, London, John Murray, 1937 ('Ilchester Hollands'), p. 293.
65. *The Morning Post*, 15 June 1814.
66. Creevey, p. 117, 14 June 1814.
67. Dorchester, Lady ed., *Lord Broughton – Recollections of a Long Life*, 6 Vols, London, John Murray, 1910, Vol. 1, pp. 149–150, 16 June 1814.
68. *The Morning Chronicle*, 14 June 1814.
69. *Ipswich Journal*, 18 June 1814.
70. Ilchester Hollands, pp. 292–293.
71. *The Morning Post*, 22 June 1814.
72. Granville (Harriet) Letters, Vol. 1, p. 100, 14 June 1817.
73. Stavordale, Lord ed., *Lord Holland – Further Memoirs of the Whig Party 1807–1821*, John Murray, 1905 ('Holland Further Memoirs'), p. 200.
74. Aspinall Giv, Vol. 1, 504, 24 November 1814.
75. Aspinall Giv, Vol. 1, p. lxxii.
76. Daughter of England, p. 228.
77. National Archives: Cole MSS 30/43/25/10, June and July 1814.
78. Holland Further Memoirs, p. 199.
79. Kelly Holland House, p. 81.

19 – The Fading Beauty

1. *The Morning Post*, 15 February 1815.
2. E.g. *The Morning Post*, 29 April 1814 and 8 March 1815.
3. *The Morning Post*, 26 October 1815.
4. LMA Jersey MSS LMA/ACC/0510/368, nd.
5. LMA Jersey MSS LMA/ACC/0510/285, 1819, nd.
6. Anglesey, Marquess of ed., *The Capel Letters 1814–1817*, London, Jonathan Cape, 1955, p. 161.

7. *The Times*, 11 April 1817.
8. *The Morning Chronicle*, 23 August 1816.
9. *The Morning Post*, 23 August 1816.
10. Jerningham Bettany, p. 59, nd.
11. *Bury & Norwich Post*, 2 March 1814.
12. The Pictou Historical Society.
13 Website of rootsweb.ancestry.com.
14. Jackson's Oxford Journal, 26 February 1814.
15. Bury George IV, Vol. 2, p. 56, 3 December 1815.
16. Creevey, p. 216, 18 August 1821.
17. *The Morning Post*, 25 July 1816.
18. *The Morning Post,* 22 July 1816.
19. *Examiner*, 28 July 1816.
20. *The Morning Post*, 9 November and 9 December 1816.
21. Farington Diaries, Yale, Vol. 14, p. 4912, 24 December 1816.
22. Chancellor, E. Beresford, *The Lives of the Rakes*, 6 Vols, London, Philip Alan & Co., 1924–1925, Vol. VI, Regency Rakes, p. 119.
23. Inglis, Lucy, *Georgian London*, Oxford, Oxford University Press, 2013, p. 169.
24. *The Morning Post*, 11 June 1817.
25. *The Morning Post*, 14 June 1817.
26. *The Morning Post*, 28 June 1817.
27. *The Morning Post*, 4 July 1817.
28. *The Morning Post*, 14 July 1817.
29. *The Morning Post*, 16 July 1818.
30. *The Morning Post*, 25 June 1819.
31. Jerningham Castle, Vol. 2, p. 140, 9 July 1819.
32. *The Morning Post*, 12 July 1819.
33. *The Morning Post*, 4 August 1819.
34. Smith George IV, pp. 164–165.
35. Kelly Holland House, p. 103.
36. LMA Jersey MSS LMA/ACC/0510/364, nd.
37. Smith George IV, p. 181.
38. Airlie, Mabell Countess of, *Lady Palmerston and her Times*, 2 Vols, London, Hodder and Stoughton Ltd, 1922, Vol. 1, p. 51.
39. Kelly Holland House, pp. 113–114.
40. Smith George IV, p. 181.
41. Smith George IV, p. 181.
42. Granville (Harriet) Letters, Vol. 1, p. 193, 13 November 1820.
43. Smith George IV, pp. 186–187.
44. Colchester Diary, Vol. 3, pp. 218–219, 17 April 1821, *The Times*, 15 June 1821 and *The Examiner*, 17 June 1821.45. Lever, Tresham ed., *The Letters of Lady Palmerston*, London, John Murray, 1957, p. 87, 20 July 1821.
46. Add MSS 45550, 9 July 1821.
47. *The Morning Chronicle*, 18 July 1821.
48. Bamford, Francis and Wellington, Duke of ed., *The Journal of Mrs Arbuthnot*, 2 Vols, London, Macmillan & Co Ltd, 1950, Vol. 1, p. 109, 19 July 1821.

49. Grosvenor, Caroline and Beilby, Charles ed., *The First Lady Wharncliffe and her Family (1779–1856)*, 2 Vols, London, William Heinemann, 1927, Vol. 1, p. 298, 19 July 1821.
50. Cokayne, G. E., *The Complete Peerage*, Vol. VII, London, St Catherine's Press, 1929.
51. *The Morning Post*, 2 August 1821.
52. LMA Jersey MSS LMA/ACC/0510/393, 27 July 1821.
53. Jerningham Castle, Vol. 2, pp. 201-202, 3 August 1821.
54. Jerningham Castle, Vol. 2, p. 203, 7 August 1821.
55. *Gentleman's Magazine*, Vol. 91, p. 180.
56. Creevey Maxwell, p. 367, 18 August 1821.
57. Stoddard, R. H. ed., *Personal Reminiscences of Ellis Cornelia Knight and Thomas Raikes, Bric a Brac Series*, 1874, pp. 304–305, 4 November 1836.
58. Anon, *Plain Letter to His Royal Highness Upon His Plain Duties*, London, 18—, 1806 ('Plain Letter'), pp. 24–25.
59. Plain Letter, p. 25.
60. Anon, *Death-bed Confessions of the Late Countess of Guernsey*, London, Jones & Co, 1822, pp. 9–10, 12-14 and 17.

20 – The Verdict of History

1. Jersey, Dowager Countess (Margaret), *Fifty-One Years of Victorian Life*, London, John Murray, 1923, p. 67.
2. Smith George IV, p. 273.
3. Smith George IV, p. 273.
4. Smith George IV, p. 274.
5. *The Times*, 28 June 1830.
6. *The Times*, 16 July 1830.

Bibliography

Manuscript Sources

Bodleian Library, Oxford

Duncan, A. I. M., A *Study of the Life and Public Career of Frederick Howard, Fifth Earl of Carlisle* (Oxford D. Phil. 1981)

Borthwick Institute for Archives, University of York

Hickleton MSS (Archives of the Wood family, Earls of Halifax): A1.2.7. Twelve letters from Frances, Countess of Jersey to Louisa, Lady Ponsonby, mother of John (later, Lord) Ponsonby, with family and social news, 1778–1803

British Library, London

Althorp MSS: Add MSS 75576, 75577, 75578, 75579, 75580, 75581, 75582, 75583, 75584, 75585, 75586, 75587, 75588, 75594 and 75595. Many hundreds of letters to Margaret Georgiana, Countess Spencer from her son, George John, 2nd Earl Spencer, and a few from his wife, Lavinia, Countess Spencer, 1764-1814

Add MSS 75606, 75607 and 75608. Correspondence of Lady Spencer with her daughter, Henrietta, wife of Frederick Ponsonby, Viscount Duncannon, 3rd Earl of Bessborough and a few to her daughter Georgiana, wife of William Cavendish, 5th Duke of Devonshire, 1768?–1814

Add MSS 75669, 75670, 75671, 75672, 75673, 75674, 75675, 75676, 75677, 75678, 75679, 75680, 75681 and 75682. Many hundreds of letters to Georgiana, Countess Spencer from George Bussy Villiers, 4th Earl of Jersey, drafts of some letters from Lady Spencer to Lord Jersey and a few letters to Lady Spencer from Frances Villiers, Countess of Jersey, *née* Twysden, and from her son, George, Viscount Villiers, 1759–1804

Add MSS 75683 and 75684. Letters to Lady Spencer from George Simon Harcourt, Viscount Nuneham, 2nd Earl Harcourt, including a few letters to Lady Spencer from his wife Elizabeth and some letters to Lord Nuneham from his father, 1st Earl Harcourt, 1756–1814

Add MSS 75692 and 75693. Letters to Lady Spencer from Frances, wife of William Henry Fortescue, Earl of Clermont, including a few from Lord Clermont, 1770–1801

Add MSS 75694 and 75695. Letters to Lady Spencer from Miss Rachel Lloyd, Housekeeper at Kensington Palace, 1773–1803

Add MSS 75911, 75912, 75913, 75914, 75915 and 75920. Letters to George, 2nd Earl Spencer from his mother, Lady Spencer, 1769–1813

Add MSS 75923 and 75924. Letters to 2nd Earl Spencer from his sister Georgiana, Duchess of Devonshire, 1777–1806

Add MSS 75925. Letters to 2nd Earl Spencer from his sister Henrietta, wife of Frederick, 3rd Earl of Bessborough, 1777–1820

Auckland MSS: Add MSS 34453. Correspondence and papers, political and private, of William Eden, 1st Baron Auckland, Vol. xlii, August 1794–May 1796

Fox MSS: Add MSS 47582. Letters to Hon Richard Fitzpatrick from William Augustus Fawkener, 1773–1777

Holland House MSS: Add MSS 51681. Letters to Lord Holland from Lord William Russell, husband of Charlotte Anne, Lady William Russell, née Villiers, 1802–1834

Add MSS 51723. Letters to Lady Holland from Georgiana, Duchess of Devonshire and Henrietta, Countess of Bessborough, 1797–1832

Add MSS 51724. Letters to Lord Holland and to Lady Holland from Mrs F. Ponsonby, George, 2nd Earl Spencer and others, 1795–1831

Add MSS 51729. Letters to Lord Holland and Lady Holland from 5th Earl of Jersey and Sarah, Countess of Jersey, 1812–1840

Add MSS 51799. Correspondence between Lord Holland, Hon Richard Fitzpatrick, Georgiana, Duchess of Devonshire and others, 1792–1830

Lamb MSS: Add MSS 45548. Letters to Elizabeth Lamb, Lady Melbourne from Georgiana, Duchess of Devonshire, *c.* 1780 – *c.* 1805 (ff. 1–35). Letters to Lady Melbourne from Henrietta Ponsonby, Countess of Bessborough, 1791–1814 (ff. 36–78b). Letters to Lady Melbourne from Lady Elizabeth Foster, afterwards Cavendish, Duchess of Devonshire, 1789–1816 (ff. 79–97b)

Add MSS 45549. Letters to Lady Melbourne from her daughter Lady Cowper (afterwards Lady Palmerston), 1805–1817, some letters from Lady Melbourne to Lady Cowper and some letters to Lady Melbourne from her son-in-law, Lord Cowper, 1802–1805

Add MSS 45550. Correspondence of Lady Cowper with her brother Frederick, 3rd Viscount Melbourne, *c.* 1802–1825

Add MSS 45911. Letters to Lady Melbourne from Georgiana Cavendish, Duchess of Devonshire, 1780–1802 (ff. 1–53). Letters to Lady Melbourne from Lady Bessborough, 1791– *c.* 1812 (ff. 15, 28–35b and 58). Letters to Lady Melbourne from Lady Elizabeth Foster, afterwards Cavendish, Duchess of Devonshire, 1789 – *c.* 1812 (ff. 11, 13, 22, 46 and 60–65)

Leeds MSS: Add MSS 27915. Letter from Frances, Countess of Jersey to Caroline, Princess of Wales, 29 June, 1796, copy (f. 26)

Paget MSS: Add MSS 48404 A. Letters from Henry William, Lord Paget, 1st Marquess of Anglesey, to his brother Sir Arthur Paget, PC, GCB, 1798–1835

Add MSS 48404 B. Letters to Sir Arthur Paget from Caroline Elizabeth, Lady Paget, *née* Villiers, first wife of Henry William, Lord Paget, later 1st Marquess of Anglesey, and a few letters to Sir Arthur Paget from Lord Paget, 1804–1817 (ff. 1–111). Letters to Sir Arthur Paget from George William Campbell, 6th Duke of Argyll, second husband of Lady Paget, 1808–1811 (ff. 95 and 111–137b)

Add MSS 48406. Letters to Sir Arthur Paget from George Villiers, afterwards Child-Villiers, 5th Earl of Jersey and his wife Sarah Sophia, *née* Fane, 1807–1830 [ff. 103–150b]

Add MSS 48415. Two letters to Sir Arthur Paget from Frances Villiers, Dowager Countess of Jersey, 1809 and 1810 (ff. 191 and 203)

Streatfeild MSS: Add MSS 33919. Miscellaneous genealogical, biographical and other memoranda consisting of short descents or pedigrees of Kentish and other families, including the Twysden family, (f. 318b)

Twysden MSS: Add MSS 34173. Letters to and from various members of the Twysden family and others, relating to family matters, from the seventeenth to the nineteenth centuries

Add MSS 34177. Miscellaneous papers relating to the Twysden family, including genealogical notes, from the sixteenth to the eighteenth centuries

Wilde MSS: Add MSS 43727. Correspondence between Caroline, Princess of Wales and the Prince of Wales and other members of the Royal circle relating to her matrimonial affairs, 1796–1820, copies, (ff. 16–42)

Castle Howard, Yorkshire

Carlisle MSS: J/14/1, J/18/20, J/18/21 and J/18/32. Personal correspondence of the 5th Earl of Carlisle with Frances, Countess of Jersey and of Georgiana, Lady Morpeth, Lord Morpeth and Georgiana, Duchess of Devonshire.

Chatsworth, Derbyshire

Chatsworth MSS, 5th Duke's Group: Correspondence of Frances, Countess of Jersey, W. A. H. Fawkener, Richard Fitzpatrick, the 5th Earl of Carlisle, the Countess of Bessborough, Viscountess Melbourne, James Hare, Georgiana, Duchess of Devonshire, Countess Spencer, Lady Elizabeth Foster and the 5th Duke of Devonshire

London Metropolitan Archives, London

Jersey MSS: ACC 0510/256 to 601 (with limited exceptions). Correspondence of Sarah Sophia, Countess of Jersey, her husband George, 5th Earl of Jersey, and in one case George, 4th Earl of Jersey, 1790–1821

ACC 1128/011, 012, 015, 103, 138, 169, 184, 185, 188 to 193, 216, 234, 238, 239, 267, 268, 283, 313 and 369. Correspondence, journals, common-place books, scrapbooks, pedigrees, legal documents and other papers of the Villiers family, 1358–1829

ACC 1275/001 to 005. Correspondence of Frances, Countess of Jersey, *c.* 1796

ACC 1401/117. Letters of Administration and Will of George, 4th Earl of Jersey, 1791–1821

ACC 4195/009, 010, 012, 013, 015 and 017 to 019. Jersey family papers re South Wales property, family pedigrees, family papers and family correspondence

Middlesex Sessions, County Administration Section: MA/D/A/01/052. Attested copy of the Marriage Settlement dated 23 May 1804 between, George, Viscount Villiers, Lady Sarah Fane, John, Duke of Bedford and others

National Archives, London

Granville MSS: PRO 30/29. Papers and correspondence of the Leveson Gower family, in particular letters from the 5th Earl of Carlisle, the Duke of Rutland, the Duke of Dorset, Lady Mary Coke, the Countess of Bessborough, the Marchioness of Stafford, Mrs Fitzroy (Lady Southampton), Lord Thurlow, Lady Harriet Bagot (*née* Villiers), George Canning, Lord Holland, Georgiana, Lady Morpeth (*née* Cavendish), Lady Augusta Murray, Miss Rachel Lloyd, Hon Mrs. Caroline Howe, Viscountess Irwin, Lady Sackville, William A. H. Fawkener, Countess Waldegrave, the Countess of Sutherland, the Marchioness of Abercorn, the

Duchess of Beaufort, Lady Louisa Macdonald and Harriet, Countess Granville (née Cavendish) 1769–1827

Cole MSS: PRO 30/43. Papers and correspondence of Sir Galbraith Lowry Cole, his wife Lady Frances Cole and her parents James Harris, 1st Earl of Malmesbury and his wife Harriet Mary, Countess of Malmesbury, 1752–1843

National Register of Archives (Scotland), Edinburgh

Douglas-Home Family, Earls of Home MSS: NRAS 859/Volumes 485 to 501. Letters from Lady Mary Coke 1775–1791 to her sister, Anne, Countess of Stafford, and after the Countess's death in 1785 to her husband, in the form of a weekly journal

Royal Archives, Windsor Castle

Georgian Papers: RA GEO/MAIN/20394, 29674, 39728–9 and 42102–6, RA GEO/ADD21/21 and 87 and RA GEO/MAIN/7066, 31512, 39184–6, 39699–39701, 39711 and 39774. Correspondence of Frances, Countess of Jersey and of George, 4th Earl of Jersey

Queen Victoria's Journals website: RA VIC/MAIN/QVJ (W) 20 May 1838, 20 August 1838, 8 November 1838, 17 November 1838 and 13 February 1839. Lord Esher's typescripts. Conversations of Queen Victoria with her Prime Minister, William Lamb, 2nd Viscount Melbourne

Primary Printed Sources

Adair, Rt Hon Sir Robert, *Sketch of the Character of the late Duke of Devonshire* (London: W Bulmer & Co, 1811)

Airlie, Mabell Countess of, *In Whig Society 1775–1818* (London: Hodder and Stoughton, 1921)

Almon, John, *Biographical, literary and political anecdotes of several of the most eminent persons of the current age*, 3 Vols (London: T N Longman and L B Seely, 1797)

Andrews, John, *Remarks on the French and English Ladies in a Series of Letters;—interspersed with anecdotes* (London: T Longman & G Robinson, 1783)

Angelo, Henry Charles William, *Angelo's Pic Nic; or, Table Talk including numerous recollections of public characters* (London: John Ebers, 1834)

Annual Register for the Year 1821, Vol. 63 (London: Baldwin, Cradock, and Joy, 1822)

Anon, *Coxheath Camp: a novel. In a series of Letters by a Lady* (Dublin: Messrs Price, Whitestone etc, 1779)

Anon, *A Review, with suitable remarks and reflections, of the misrepresentations and contradictions which have been circulated in all the Daily Papers relative to a late domestic fracas in a family of the first rank etc* (London: 1796)

Anon, *An Asylum for Fugitive Pieces in Prose and Verse, Vol. III* (London: printed for J. Debrett, 1795)

Anon, *Plain Letter to His Royal Highness Upon His Plain Duties* (London: 18—)

Anon, *Sketches from Nature, in High Preservation, by the Most Honourable Masters; containing upwards of eighty Portraits, or Characters, of the Principal Personages in the Kingdom* (London: printed for G Kearsley, 1779)

Anon, *The Bevy of Beauties: A Collection of Sonnets* (London: R Baldwin, J Faulder, 1781)

Anon, *Ways and Means: or, a sale of the L***s S*******l and T******l, by R***l P.********n* (London: printed for G Kearsley, 1782)

Arbuthnot, Charles, *The Correspondence of Charles Arbuthnot*, ed. for The Royal Historical Society by A. Aspinall, Camden Third Series Vol. LXV (London: Royal Historical Society, 1941)

Arbuthnot, Mrs, *The Journal of Mrs Arbuthnot*, ed. Francis Bamford and the Duke of Wellington, 2 Vols (London,: Macmillan & Co Ltd, 1950)

Archenholz, J. W. von, *A Picture of England: containing a description of the laws, customs and manners of England*, 2 Vols (London: printed for Edward Jeffery, 1789)

Argyll, Duke of ed., *Intimate Society Letters of the Eighteenth Century*, 2 Vols (London: Stanley Paul & Co, 1910)

Aspinall, A. and Smith, E. Anthony eds, *English Historical Documents, Vol. 11, 1783–1832* (London: Eyre & Spottiswoode, 1959)

Auckland, William Lord, *The Journal and Correspondence of William, Lord Auckland*, ed. The Bishop of Bath and Wells, 4 Vols (London: Richard Bentley, 1861)

Barfoot, Peter & Wilkes, John, *The Universal British Directory of Trade and Commerce, Vol. 1* (London: Champante & Whitrow, 1793)

Barfoot, Peter and Wilkes, John, *Directory to The Nobility, Gentry, and Families of Distinction, in London* (London: J Wilkes, Champante & Whitrow, 1793)

Barlow, Frederick, *The Complete English Peerage or a Genealogical and historical account of the peers and peeresses of this realm, to the year 1775*, 2 Vols (London: Printed for the Author, 1775)

Berkeley, Eliza, 'Singular Tale of Love in High Life', *Gentleman's Magazine 66* (August 1796)

Berkeley, The Hon Grantley F., *My Life and Recollections*, 2 Vols (London: Hurst and Blackett, 1865)

Berry, Mary and Agnes, *The Berry Papers being the Correspondence hitherto Unpublished of Mary and Agnes Berry*, ed. Lewis Melville (London: John Lane, The Bodley Head, 1914)

Berry, Miss, *Extracts from the Journals and Correspondence of Miss Berry from the Year 1783 to 1852*, ed. Lady Theresa Lewis, 3 Vols (London: Longmans, Green, and Co, 1866)

Bessborough, Lady, *Lady Bessborough and her Family Circle*, ed. The Earl of Bessborough in collaboration with A. Aspinall (London: John Murray, 1940)

Binns, John, *Recollections of the Life of John Binns* (Philadelphia, published by the author, 1854)

Blackmantle, Bernard (Westmacott, Charles M.), *The English Spy*, 2 Vols (London: Methuen & Co, 1825)

Broughton, Lord (John Cam Hobhouse), *Recollections of a Long Life*, ed. Lady Dorchester, 6 Vols (London: John Murray, 1910)

Buckingham and Chandos, Duke of, *Memoirs of the Court and Cabinets of George the Third*, 3 Vols (London: Hurst and Blackett, 1853)

Burghersh, Lord, *Correspondence of Lord Burghersh, afterwards 11th Earl of Westmorland, 1808–1840*, ed. Rachel Weigall (London: John Murray, 1912)

Burke, Edmund, *The Correspondence of Edmund Burke* ed. T W Copeland, 10 Vols (Cambridge: Cambridge University Press, 1958–1978)

Burke, John B., *Genealogical & Heraldic Dictionary of the Peerage and Baronetage, 11th Edition* (London: Henry Colburn, 1849)

Burke, John B., *General & Heraldic Dictionary of the Peerage and Baronetage of the British Empire* (London: Henry Colburn, 1828)

Burke, Sir John B., *Burke's Peerage and Baronetage, 106th Edition* (London: 1999)

Bury, Lady Charlotte, *The Court of England Under George IV*, 2 Vols (London, John Macqueen, 1896)

Bury, Lady Charlotte, *The Diary of a Lady in Waiting* (London: John Lane the Bodley Head, 1908)

Butler, Lady Eleanor, *The Hamwood Papers of the Ladies of Llangollen and Caroline, Hamilton*, ed. Mrs G. H. Bell (London: Macmillan and Co., Limited, 1930)

Byron, Lord, Byron's Letters and Journals, ed. Leslie A. Marchand, 12 Vols (London: John Murray, 1973–1982)

Byron, Lord, *Lady Blessington's Conversations of Lord Byron*, ed. Ernest J. Lovell (Princeton: Princeton University Press, 1969)

Byron, Lord, *Lord Byron's Correspondence*, ed. John Murray, 2 Vols (London: John Murray, 1922)

Calvert, The Hon Mrs, *An Irish Beauty of the Regency – The unpublished Journals of The Hon Mrs Calvert,* ed. Mrs Warrenne Blake (London: John Lane The Bodley Head, 1911)

Campan, Madame, *Memoirs of the Private Life of Marie Antoinette*, 2 Vols (London: Henry Colburn and Co and M Bossange and Co, 1823)

Campbell, Thomas, *Dr Campbell's Diary of a Visit to England in 1775*, ed. James L. Clifford (Cambridge: University Press, 1947)

Canning, George, *The Letter Journal of George Canning, 1793–1795*, ed. Peter Jupp. (London: Royal Historical Society, 1991)

Capel, Lady Caroline, *The Capel Letters 1814–1817,* ed. The Marquess of Anglesey, FSA (London: Jonathan Cape, 1955)

Carey, George Saville, *The Balnea; or an impartial description of the watering places in England,* Third Edition (London: West & Hughes, 1801)

Cavendish, Lady Harriet, *Hary-O, The Letters of Lady Harriet Cavendish 1796–1809*, ed. Sir George Leveson Gower and Iris Palmer (London: John Murray, 1940)

Charlotte, Princess, *Letters of the Princess Charlotte*, ed. A. Aspinall (London: Home and Van Thal, 1949)

Chatham, Hester Pitt, Lady, *So Dearly Loved, So Much Admired: Letters to Hester Pitt, Lady Chatham from her relations and friends 1774–1801*, ed. Vere Birdwood (London: HMSO, 1994)

Cokayne, G. E., *The Complete Peerage, Vol. VII* (London: St Catherine's Press, 1929)

Cokayne, G E., *The Complete Peerage, Vol. VIII* (London: St Catherine's Press, 1932)

Coke, Lady Mary, *The Letters and Journals of Lady Mary Coke*, ed. J. A. Home, Facsimile Edition, 4 Vols (Bath: Kingsmead Reprints, 1970). (Originally printed 1889–96)

Colchester, Charles Abbot, Lord, *The Diary and Correspondence of Charles Abbot, Lord Colchester,* ed. Charles, Lord Colchester (London: John Murray, 1861)

Combe, William, *The Royal Dream; or the P._____ in a Panic; an eclogue with annotations* (London: 1785)

Craven, Lady Elizabeth (Later Margravine of Anspach and Princess Berkeley of the Holy Roman Empire), *The Beautiful Lady Craven, The Original Memoirs of etc (1750–1828)*, eds A. M. Broadley & Lewis Melville, 2 Vols (London: John Lane The Bodley Head, 1914)

Creevey, Selected and Reedited by John Gore (London: John Murray, 1948)

Creevey, *The Creevey Papers – A Selection from the Correspondence and Diaries of the late Thomas Creevey MP,* ed. The Rt Hon Sir Herbert Maxwell Bt (London: John Murray, 1905)

Croft, Sir Herbert, *The abbey of Kilkhampton; or monumental records for the year 1980* [sic] (London: 1780)

Curwen, Samuel, *Journal and Letters of Samuel Curwen, an American Refugee in England, from 1775 to 1784* (London: Wiley and Putnam, 1842)

Debrett, *Debrett's Peerage of the United Kingdom of Great Britain and Ireland, 17th Edition, Vol. 1* (London: 1828)

Debrett, J., *Correct Peerage of England, Scotland and Ireland* (London: J. Debrett, 1802)

Debrett, J., *Debrett's Correct Peerage of England, Scotland and Ireland, Vol. 1* (London: J. Debrett, 1803)

Debrett's Genealogical Peerage of Great Britain and Ireland (London: Pickering, 1849)

Delany, Mrs Mary, *The Autobiography and Correspondence of Mary Granville, Mrs Delany*, ed. The Rt Hon Lady Llanover, 6 Vols (London: Richard Bentley, 1862)

Devonshire, Georgiana, *Extracts from the Correspondence of Georgiana, Duchess of Devonshire*, ed. The Earl of Bessborough PC GCMG (London: John Murray, 1955)

Devonshire, Georgiana Duchess of, *The Sylph: a Novel* (York: Henry Parker, 2001). (Originally published 1779)

Dodington, George Bubb, *Diary 1749–1761* (Salisbury: E Easton, 1784)

du Deffand, Marquise du, *Lettres de la Marquise du Deffand à Horace Walpole (1776–1780)*, ed. Mrs Paget Toynbee, 3 Vols (Londres, Methuen & Cie, 1912)

Dudley, Earl of, *Letters to Ivy from the First Earl of Dudley*, ed. S. H. Romilly (London: Longmans, Green, and Co, 1905)

Dunvan, Paul, *Ancient and Modern History of Lewes and Brighthelmstone* (Lewes: W. Lee, 1795)

Eden, Miss, *Miss Eden's Letters*, ed. Violet Dickinson (London: Macmillan and Co, 1919)

Edgeworth, Maria, *Letters from England 1813–1844*, ed. Christina Colvin (Oxford: Clarendon Press, 1971)

Erskine, Beatrice, *Lady Diana Beauclerk. Her Life and Work (letters to her daughter Mary, Countess of Walworth from 1797 to 1807)* (London: T. Fisher Unwin, 1903)

Farington, Joseph, *The Diary of Joseph Farington RA*, eds K. Garlick and A. Macintyre/K. Cave, 17 Vols (Yale: University Press, 1978)

Farington, Joseph, RA, *The Farington Diary*, ed. James Greig, 6 Vols (London: Hutchinson & Co, 1922)

Ffrench, Yvonne, *News from the Past 1805–1887, the autobiography of the nineteenth century* (London: Victor Gollancz, 1934)

Fitzgerald, Lady Edward, *La Belle Pamela (Lady Edward Fitzgerald) 1773–1831: d'après des correspondence et mémoires inedits, des traditions et documents de famille*, eds Joseph Turquan et Lucy Ellis, 2 Vols (Paris, Émile-Paul frères, 1923–24)

Ford, Ann, *A Letter from Miss F__d (Ann Ford), addressed to a person of distinction* (i.e. William Villiers, 3rd Earl of Jersey) (London: 1761)

Foster, Vere, *The Two Duchesses, Georgiana Duchess of Devonshire and Elizabeth Duchess of Devonshire – Family Correspondence 1777–1859* (London: Blackie & Son Limited, 1898)

Fox, Charles James, *Memorials and Correspondence of Charles James Fox*, ed. Lord John Russell, 4 Vols (London: Richard Bentley, 1853)

Frampton, Mary, *The Journal of Mary Frampton*, ed. Harriot Georgina Mundy (London: Sampson Low, Marston, Searle & Rivington, 1886)

Francis, Philip Sir, *Memoirs of Sir Philip Francis KCB with correspondence and journals,* ed. E J Parkes, 2 Vols (London: 1867)

Francis, Sir Philip and other members of the family, *The Francis Letters*, ed. Beata Francis, 2 Vols (London: Hutchinson & Co, 1901)

Garrick, David, *The Letters of David Garrick*, eds David M. Little and George M. Kahrl, 3 Vols (London: Oxford University Press, 1963)

Garrick, David, *The Private Correspondence of David Garrick*, ed. H. Colburn, 2 Vols (London: Henry Colburn and Richard Bentley, 1831)

George III, *The Later Correspondence of George III*, ed. A. Aspinall, 5 Vols (Cambridge, University Press, 1963–1967)

George IV, *The Letters of King George IV 1812–1830*, ed. A. Aspinall, 3 Vols (Cambridge University Press, 1938)

George the Third, King, *The Correspondence of King George the Third from 1760 to December 1783*, ed. The Hon Sir John Fortescue, 6 Vols (London: Macmillan and Co., Limited, 1928)

George, Prince of Wales, *The Correspondence of George, Prince of Wales 1770–1812*, ed. A. Aspinall, 7 Vols (London: Cassell, 1953–1971)

Gibbon, Edward, *The Letters of Edward Gibbon*, ed. J. E. Norton, 3 Vols (London: Cassell and Company, 1956)

Glenbervie, Lord, *The Diaries of Sylvester Douglas, Lord Glenbervie*, ed. Francis Bickley, 2 Vols (London: Constable, 1928)

Glenbervie, Sylvester Douglas Lord, *The Glenbervie Journals*, ed. Walter Sichel (London: Constable & Company Ltd, 1910)

Grafton, Augustus Henry 3rd Duke of, *Autobiography and Political Correspondence of Augustus Henry 3rd Duke of Grafton*, ed. Sir William R Anson (London: John Murray, 1898)

Grant, Anne McVicar, *Memoir and Correspondence of Mrs Grant*, ed., J. P. Grant, 3 Vols (London: 1844)

Granville, Harriet Countess, *A Second Self: The Letters of Harriet Granville 1810–1845*, ed. Virginia Surtees (Salisbury: Michael Russell, 1990)

Granville, Harriet Countess, *Letters of Harriet Countess Granville 1810-1845*, ed. The Hon F. Leveson Gower, 2 Vols (London, Longmans, Green, and Co, 1895)

Granville, Harriet Countess, *The Letters of Harriet, Countess Granville*, ed. The Hon F. Leveson Gower (London: Longmans, Green, and Co, 1894)

Grenville, Richard Earl Temple KG and Grenville, George The Rt Hon, *The Grenville Papers*, ed. W. J. Smith, 4 Vols (London: John Murray, 1853)

Greville, Charles C. F., *The Greville Memoirs*, ed. Henry Reeve, 3 Vols (London: Longmans, Green, and Co, 1874)

Greville, Charles C. F., *The Greville Memoirs*, ed. Henry Reeve, A New Edition, 8 Vols (London: Longmans, Green, and Co, 1896)

Greville, Charles C. F., *The Greville Memoirs,* ed. Roger Fulford, (London: B T Batsford Ltd, 1963)

Greville, Robert Fulke, *The Diaries of Colonel the Hon Robert Fulke Greville,* ed. F. McKno Bladon (London: John Lane The Bodley Head Limited, 1930)

Gronow, R. H., *Reminiscences* (London: Smith, Elder and Co., 1865)

Grossley, P. J., *A tour of London, or new observations on England and its inhabitants* (London: 1772)

Guernsey, Countess of (pseudonym*), Death-bed Confessions of the Late Countess of Guernsey* (London: Jones & Co, 1822)

Hamilton, Lady Anne, *The Epics of the Ton, or Glories of the Great World* (London:1807)

Hamilton, Mary, *Mary Hamilton afterwards Mrs John Dickenson at Court and at Home. From Letters and Diaries 1756 to 1816*, eds Elizabeth and Florence Anson (London: John Murray, 1925)

Hanger, George Baron Coleraine, *The life, adventures and opinions of Col G H written by himself*, 2 Vols (London: 1801)

Harcourt, *The Harcourt Papers*, ed. William Harcourt, 14 Vols, (Privately Printed: 1880–85)

Harcourt, Elizabeth Countess of, *Mrs Harcourt's Diary of the Court of King George III (1789–1791)* (London: Miscellanies of the Philobiblon Society Vol. XIII, 1871–1872)

Hare, Augustus J. C., *Story of My Life,* 6 Vols (London: George Allen, 1900)

Hartley J. ed, *History of the Westminster Election containing every material occurrence from its commecement* [sic] *on the first of April to the final close of the poll* (London: 1784)

Hawkins, Laetitia Matilda, *Anecdotes, Biographical Sketches and Memoirs* (London, Windsor (printed), 1822)

Hawkins, Laetitia Matilda, *Memoirs, anecdots (sic), facts and opinions collected and preserved by LMH*, 2 Vols (London: 1824)

Headlam, Cuthbert, *The Letters of Lady Harriot Eliot 1766-1786* (Edinburgh: T and A Constable, 1914)

Heathcote, Ralph, *Letters of a Young Diplomatist and Soldier During the Time of Napoleon,* ed. Countess Gunther Groben (London: John Lane the Bodley Head, 1907)

Historical Manuscripts Commission, *8th Report and Appendix Parts 1-3* (London: HMSO, 1881)

Historical Manuscripts Commission, *Report on the Manuscripts of the Earl of Denbigh (Part V)* (London: HMSO, 1911)

Historical Manuscripts Commission, *The Manuscripts of J B Fortescue Preserved at Dropmore, 30th Report Vol. X* (London: HMSO, 1927)

Historical Manuscripts Commission, *Report on the Manuscripts of Reginald Rawdon Hastings of The Manor House, Ashby de la Zouch, 78 Vol. III* (London: HMSO, 1934)

Historical Manuscripts Commission, *Report on the Manuscripts of Earl Bathurst* (London: HMSO, 1923)

Historical Manuscripts Commission, *Reports on the Manuscripts of The Earl of Eglinton etc, 19th Report, Appendix I* (London: HMSO, 1885)

Historical Manuscripts Commission, *Reports on the Manuscripts of the Duke of Somerset etc, 15th Report, Appendix, Part VII* (London: HMSO, 1898)

Historical Manuscripts Commission, *The Manuscripts and Correspondence of James, First Earl of Charlemont, Vol. II – 1784-1799, Thirteenth Report, Appendix, Part VIII* (London: HMSO, 1894)

Historical Manuscripts Commission, *The Manuscripts of J B Fortescue Preserved at Dropmore, Vol. III* (London: HMSO, 1934)

Historical Manuscripts Commission, *The Manuscripts of Lord Kenyon, Historical Manuscripts Commission, 14th Report, App.endix, Part IV* (London: HMSO, 1894)

Historical Manuscripts Commission, *The Manuscripts of the Duke of Rutland Preserved at Belvoir Castle, Historical Manuscripts Commission 14th Report Appendix Part I, Volume III* (London: HMSO, 1896).

Historical Manuscripts Commission, *The Manuscripts of the Earl of Carlisle Preserved at Castle Howard, Historical Manuscripts Commission 15th Report App.endix Part VI* (London: HMSO, 1897)

Holland, Henry Fox, Baron, *To Lady Sarah Bunburu* [sic] *(ie Bunbury), in imitation of Lydia (his sister in law on her affair with Frederick Howard, the 5th Earl of Carlisle)* (? London: ? 1770)

Holland, Henry Richard Vassall, Lord, *Further Memoirs of the Whig Party 1807–1821*, ed. Lord Stavordale (London: John Murray, 1905)

Holland, Henry Richard, Lord, *Memoirs of the Whig Party in my Time*, ed. Henry Edward, Lord Holland, 2 Vols (London, Longman, Brown, Green, and Longmans, 1852 and 1854)

Hone, William, *Hone's Political Tracts* (London: William Hone, 1822)

Horn D. B. and Ransome M. ed., *English Historical Documents, Vol. 10, 1714–1783* (London, Eyre & Spottiswoode, 1957)

Huish, Robert, *Memoirs of George the Fourth*, 2 Vols (Thomas Kelly, 1831)

Jefferys, Nathaniel, *A Review of the Conduct of HRH the Prince of Wales in his Various Transactions with Mr Jefferys* (London:1801)

Jerningham, Edward, *Edward Jerningham and His Friends*, ed. Lewis Bettany (New York: Brentano's, 1919)

Jerningham, Edward, *The Jerningham Letters* ed. Egerton Castle, 2 Vols (London, Richard Bentley and Son, 1896)

Jersey, Dowager Countess of (M. E.), *Fifty-One Years of Victorian Life* (London, John Murray, 1923)

Jersey, George Bussy, Earl of, *The Correspondence between the Earl and Countess of Jersey, and…Dr Randolph upon the subject of some letters belonging to HRH the Princess of Wales (ed by GBV)* (London: 1796)

Jersey, Margaret Elizabeth Villiers, Countess of, *Records of the Family of Villiers, Earls of Jersey* (London: Morton, Burt & Sons, 1924)

Jersey, William Villiers 3rd Earl of, *A Letter to Miss F___d* (London: 1761)
Jones, Sir William, *Letters of Sir William Jones*, ed. G. Cannon, 2 Vols (Oxford: Clarendon Press, 1970)
Junius, *The Letters of Junius*, ed. John Cannon (Oxford: The Clarendon Press, 1978)
Knight, Ellis Cornelia and Raikes, Thomas, *Personal Reminiscences*, ed. R. H. Stoddard (Bric a Brac Series, 1874)
Knight, Henrietta, Baroness Luxborough, *Letters written by the late ... Lady Luxborough to William Shenstone Esq.*, ed. John Hodgetts (Dublin: Caleb Jenkin, 1776)
Knight, Miss Cornelia, *Autobiography of Miss Cornelia Knight, Lady Companion to Princess Charlotte of Wales*, 2 Vols (London: W H Allen & Co, 1861)
Knox, Family of (Jane), *Memoirs of a Vanished Generation 1813–1855*, ed. Mrs Warrenne Blake (London: John Lane, 1909)
Kynynmound, Emma Eleanor Elizabeth Elliot Murray, Countess of Minto, *Notes from Minto Manuscripts* (Edinburgh: privately printed, 1862)
La Roche, Sophie v, *Sophie in London 1786, being the Diary of Sophie v la Roche* (London: Jonathan Cape, 1933)
Langdale, The Hon Charles, *Memoirs of Mrs Fitzherbert* (London: Richard Bentley, 1856)
Lascelles, Lady Caroline, Dover, Lady and Gower, Countess, *Three Howard Sisters, Selections from the Writings of Lady Caroline Lascelles, Lady Dover and Countess Gower 1825 to 1833*, ed. Maud, Lady Leconfield, revised and completed by John Gore (London: John Murray, 1955)
Leeds, Francis Fifth Duke of, *The Political Memoranda of Francis Fifth Duke of Leeds*, ed. Oscar Browning (London: Camden Society, 1884)
Leighton, Rachel ed., *The Correspondence of Charlotte Grenville Lady Williams Wynn and her three sons, Sir Watkin Williams Wynn Bart, Rt Hon Charles Williams Wynn, and Sir Henry Williams Wynn 1795–1832* (London: John Muurray, 1920)
Lennox, Lady Sarah, *The Life and Letters of Lady Sarah Lennox 1745–1826*, ed. The Countess of Ilchester and Lord Stavordale, 2 Vols (London: John Murray, 1901)
Leslie, Shane, *The Letters of Mrs Fitzherbert* (London: Burns Oates, 1940)
Leveson Gower, Lord Granville, *The Private Correspondence of Lord Granville Leveson Gower*, ed. Castalia, Countess Granville, 2 Vols (London: John Murray, 1916)
Lichtenberg, G., *Lichtenberg's Visit to England as described in his letters and diaries* (Oxford: Clarendon Press, 1938)
Lieven, Princess, *Letters of Dorothea, Princess Lieven, during her Residence in London, 1812–1834*, ed. Lionel G Robinson (London: Longmas, Green, and Co., 1902)
Lieven, Princess, *The Private Letters of Princess Lieven to Prince Metternich 1820–1826*, ed. Peter Quennell (London: John Murray, 1937)
Lobb, R., ed., *Ambulator, or a pocket companion in a Tour round London* (London: 1793)
Lyttleton, George Lord, *Memoirs and Correspondence of George, Lord Lyttleton: from 1734 to 1773*, compiled and edited by Robert Phillimore, 2 Vols (London: James Ridgway, 1845)
Lyttleton, Sarah Spencer Lady, *Correspondence of Sarah Spencer, Lady Lyttleton 1787–1870*, ed. The Hon Mrs Hugh Wyndham (London: John Murray, 1912)
Macdonald, John, *Memoirs of an Eighteenth-Century Footman* (London: Century, 1985). (Originally published 1790)
Malcolm, James Peller, *Anecdotes of the Manners and Customs of London during the Eighteenth Century* (London: Longman, Hurst, Rees and Orme, 1808)
Malmesbury, James Harris, First Earl of, *The Diaries and Correspondence of James Harris, First Earl of Malmesbury*, ed. the Third Earl of Malmesbury, 4 Vols (London: Richard Bentley, 1844)

Matthews, William, *British Diaries: An Annotated Bibliography of British Diaries Written between 1442 and 1942* (London: Cambridge University Press, 1950)

Matthias, Thomas James, *An epistle in verse to the Rev Dr Randolph occasioned by the publication of the Correspondence of the Earl and Countess of Jersey and the Doctor upon the subject of some letters belonging to the Princess of Wales* (London: 1796)

Matthias, Thomas James, *An Equestrian Epistle in Verse to the Rt Hon The Earl of Jersey occasioned by the publication of the correspondence between the Earl and Countess of Jersey and the Rev Dr Randolph upon the subject of some letters belonging to the Princess of Wales* (London: 1796)

Matthias, Thomas James, *The grove. A satire. By the author of the pursuits of literature with notes, including various anecdotes of the King etc (Including Lord Jersey and Lady Jersey)* (London: printed for the author, 1798?)

Melbourne, Elizabeth M. L., Countess, *Byron's 'Courbeau Blanc': The Life and Letters of Lady Melbourne*, ed. Jonathan Gross (Houston, Texas: Rice University Press, 1997)

Minto, Sir Gilbert Elliot, First Earl of, *Life and Letters of Sir Gilbert Elliot, First Earl of Minto*, ed. The Countess of Minto, 3 Vols (London: Longmans Green & Co, 1874)

Montagu, Mrs Elizabeth, *Mrs Montagu 'Queen of the Blues': Her Letters and Friendships from 1762 to 1800*, ed. Reginald Blunt, 2 Vols (London: Constable and Company Limited, 1923)

Moore, Thomas, *The Journal of Thomas Moore*, ed. Wilfred S Dowden, 6 Vols (London: Associated University Press, 1983)

Moore, Thomas, *The Letters of Thomas Moore*, ed. Wilfred S Dowden, 2 Vols (Oxford: Clarendon Press, 1964)

More, Mrs Hannah, *Memoirs of the Life and Correspondence of Mrs Hannah More*, ed. William Roberts, 4 Vols (London: R B Seeley and W Burnside, 1834)

Morgan, Lady Sydney, *Lady Morgan's Memoirs 1783–1859: Autobiography, Diaries and Correspondence*, ed. W. H. Dixon, 2 Vols (London: 1863)

Morgan, Lady Sydney, *Passages from My Autobiography* (New York: D Appleton and Company, 1859)

Morgan, Lady Sydney, *The Book of the Boudoir*, 2 Vols (Paris: A and W Galignani, 1829)

Moritz, Carl Philip, *Journeys of a German in England in 1782*, ed. R. Nettel (London: Jonathan Cape, 1965)

Morris, Gouveneur, *A Diary of the French Revolution*, ed. Beatrice Cary Davenport, 2 Vols (London: G G Harrap & Co, 1939)

Namier, L. B., *Additions and Corrections to Sir John Fortescue's Edition of The Correspondence of King George The Third* (Manchester: Manchester University Press, 1937)

Newdigate, Family of, *The Cheverels of Cheverel Manor*, ed. Lady Newdigate-Newdegate (London: Longmans, Green, and Co., 1898)

Nightingale, J., *Memoirs of the Public and Private Life of Caroline, Queen of Great Britain*, 2 Vols (London: J Robins & Co, 1820)

Nimrod, *Nimrod's Hunting Reminiscences, Comprising … Notices of the Crack Riders … of England* (London: John Lane The Bodley Head Limited, Reprint 1926). (Originally printed 1843)

Osborne, Lady Sarah Byng, *Political and Social Letters: Letters of Lady Sarah Byng Osborne 1721–1773* (Palo Alto: Stanford University Press, 1930)

Paget, Sir Arthur, *Diplomatic and other Correspondence of Sir Arthur Paget 1794–1807*, ed. Sir A. B. Paget, 2 Vols (London: W Heinemann, 1896)

Paget, Sir Arthur, *The Paget Brothers, 1790–1840: Selections from the Family Correspondence of Sir Arthur Paget,* ed. Lord Hylton (London: John Murray, 1918)

Palmerston, Lady, *The Letters of Lady Palmerston*, ed. Tresham Lever (London: John Murray, 1957)

Palmerston, Viscount and others, *The New Whig Guide* (London: 1819)

Papendiek, Charlotte Louisa Henrietta Mrs, *Court and Private Life in the Time of Queen Charlotte: being the Journals of Mrs Papendiek*, ed. Mrs V. D. Broughton, 2 Vols (London: Bentley & Son, 1887)

Pasquin, Anthony (pseudonym for Williams, John), *The New Brighton Guide; involving a complete, authentic, and honourable solution of the recent mysteries of Carlton House* (London: printed for H D Symonds ... and T Bellamy, 1796)

Pasquin, Thomas (i.e. Williams, John), *The Pin Basket. To the Children of Thespis: a satire (Dedicated to the Countess of Jersey)* (London: 1796)

Paston, George and Quennell, Peter, *To Lord Byron: Feminine Profiles based on unpublished letters 1807–1824* (London; John Murray, 1939)

Pepys, William Weller, Sir, Bart, *A Later Pepys: the correspondence of Sir W W Pepys Bart, Master in Chancery, 1758–1825*, ed. Alice C. C. Gaussen, 2 Vols (London: John Lane, 1904)

Pickering, A. M. W., *Memoirs of Anna Maria Wilhelmina Pickering*, ed. Spencer Pickering (London: Hodder & Stoughton, 1903)

Piggott, Charles, *The Female Jockey Club or a Sketch of the Manners of the Age* (London: D I Eaton, 1794)

Piozzi, Hester, *The Intimate Letters of Hester Piozzi and Penelope Pennington 1788–1821*, ed. Oswald G Knapp (London: John Lane, The Bodley Head, 1914)

Piozzi, Hester Lynch, *The Piozzi Letters: Correspondence of Hester Lynch Piozzi 1784–1821*, eds Edward A. Bloom and Lillian Bloom, 6 Vols (Newark: University of Delaware Press, London and Toronto: Associated University Press, 1991)

Powys, Caroline, *Passages from the diaries of Mrs Philip Lybbe Powys of Hardwick House, Oxon: AD 1756 to 1808*, ed. Emily J. Climenson (London: Longmans, Green, 1899)

Pukler Muskau, Hermann, Prince, *A Regency Visitor: The English Tour of Prince Pukler Mulkau described in his letters 1826–28* (London: Collins, 1957)

Reid, Stuart J., *Life and Letters of the First Earl of Durham 1792–1840*, 2 Vols (London: Longmans, Green, and Co, 1906)

Reports of cases argued and determined in courts of Common Pleas, Court of Exchequer Chamber, Volume 10 (John Bayly Moore, 1820)

Reports of cases heard in the House of Lords: on app.eals and writs, Volume 2 (Richard Bligh, 1827)

Rogers, Samuel, *Recollections by Samuel Rogers (with a biographical notice by W Sharpe)* (London: 1859)

Rogers, Samuel, *Recollections of the Table Talk of Samuel Rogers*, ed. Morchand Bishop (London: Richards Press, 1952)

Rose, George, *The Diaries and Correspondence of The Rt Hon George Rose*, ed. Leveson Vernon Harcourt, 2 Vols (London: Richard Bentley, 1860)

Russell, G. W. E., *Collections & Recollections* (London: Smith Elder & Co, 1898)

Russell, Lord G. William, *Letters to Lord G William Russell from various writers, 1815–1847*, 3 Vols (London: printed for private circulation, Chiswick Press, 1915)

Russell, Lady John, *Letters of Lady John Russell to her Husband 1798–1801* (London: Chiswick Press, 1933)

Sandwich, John Montagu 4th Earl of Sandwich, *The Private Papers of John Earl of Sandwich, First Lord of the Admiralty 1771–82*, 4 Vols (London: Publications of the Naval Record Society Vols 69, 71, 75 and 78, 1932–8)

Selwyn, George, *George Selwyn: His Letters and Life*, eds E. S. Roscoe and Helen Clergue (London: T Fisher Unwin, 1899)

Selwyn, George, *Correspondence of George Selwyn and his Contemporaries, With Memoirs and Notes by John Heanage Jesse*, 4 Vols (London: Bickers & Son, 1882)

Seward, Anna, *Letters of Anna Seward: Written Between the Years 1784 and 1807*, 6 Vols (Edinburgh: Archibald Constable and Company and others, 1811)

Seward, Anna, *The Swan of Lichfield, being a Selection from the Correspondence of Anna Seward*, ed. Hesketh Pearson (London: Hamish Hamilton, 1936)
Shelley, Frances, Lady, *The Diary of Lady Frances Shelley*, ed. Richard Edgcumbe, 2 Vols (London: John Murray, 1912)
Sheridan, Betsy, *Betsy Sheridan's Journal*, ed. William LeFanu (London: Eyre & Spottiswoode, 1960)
Sheridan, R. B., *Sheridan's plays: now printed as he wrote them: and his mother's unpublished comedy A journey to Bath*, W. Fraser Rae (London, David Nutt, 1902)
Sheridan, Richard Brinsley, *The Dramatic Works of Richard Brinsley Sheridan*, ed. Cecil Price, 2 Vols (Oxford, Clarendon Press, 1973)
Sheridan, Richard Brinsley, *The Letters of Richard Brinsley Sheridan*, ed. Cecil Price, 3 Vols (Oxford: Clarendon Press, 1966)
Simond, Louis, *An American in Regency England: The Journal of a Tour in 1810–1811*, ed. Christopher Hibbert (London: The History Book Club, 1968)
Stanhope, Lady Elizabeth Spencer, *The Letter Bag of Lady Elizabeth Spencer Stanhope*, ed. Anna Maria Diana Pickering (afterwards Stirling), 2 Vols (London: John Lane, 1913)
Steele, Mrs Elizabeth, *The Memoirs of Mrs Sophia Baddeley*, 3 Vols (Dublin: privately printed for the author, 1787)
Sterne, Laurence, *The Life and Opinions of Tristram Shandy, Gentleman*, 2 Vols (London: Macmillan and Co. Limited, 1900)
Stuart, Dorothy Margaret, *Dearest Bess: The Life and Times of Lady Elizabeth Foster afterwards Duchess of Devonshire from Her Unpublished Journals and Correspondence* (London: Methuen & Co Ltd, 1955)
Stuart, Lady Louisa, *Gleanings from an Old Portfolio: Correspondence between Lady Louisa Stuart and her Sister Caroline, Countess of Portarlington*, ed. Mrs Godfrey Clark, 3 Vols (Edinburgh: privately printed, 1895)
Sutherland, George Granville Second Duke of, *Stafford House Letters*, ed. Lord Ronald Gower (London: Kegan Paul, Trench, Trubner & Co., Ltd, 1891)
Talbot, Thomas Mansel, *The Penrice Letters 1768–1795*, ed. Joanna Martin (Swansea: West Glamorgan Archive Service, 1993)
Taylor, Eliza, *The Letters of Eliza Pierce (Eliza Taylor) 1751–1775* (London: F Etchells & H Macdonald, 1927)
Taylor, John, *Records of My Life*, 2 Vols (London: Edward Bull, 1832)
Taylor, Miss Elizabeth, *Authentic Memoirs of Mrs Clarke* (London: Thomas Tegg, 1809)
Thoms, William, *The Book of the Court* (London: Henry G Bohn, 1844)
Thrale, Hester Lynch, *Thraliana, The Diary of Mrs Hester Lynch Thrale (Later Mrs Piozzi) 1776–1809*, ed. Katharine C. Balderstone, 2 Vols (Oxford: Clarendon Press, 1942)
Ticknor, George, *Life, Letters, and Journals of George Ticknor*, 2 Vols (Boston: James R Osgood and Company, 1876)
Twitcher, Jemmy, *The Life, Adventures, Intrigues and Amours of the celebrated Jemmy Twitcher* (i.e.John Montagu, Earl of Sandwich) (London: Jonathan Brough, 1770)
Waldegrave, James 2nd Earl, *The Memoirs and Speeches of James, 2nd Earl Waldegrave 1742–1763*, ed J. C. D. Clark (Cambridge: Cambridge University Press, 1988)
Waldegrave, James Earl of, *Memoirs from 1754 to 1758* (London: John Murray, 1821)
Walpole, Horace, *Horace Walpole's Correspondence, the Yale Edition*, ed. W. S. Lewis, 48 Vols (Oxford: Oxford University Press, 1937–1983).
Walpole, Horace, *Memoirs of Horace Walpole and his Contemporaries*, ed. Eliot Warburton, 2 Vols (London: Henry Colburn, 1851)
Walpole, Horace, *Memoirs of the Reign of George the Third*, re-ed. G. F. Russell Baker, 4 Vols, (London: Lawrence and Bullen, 1894)

Walpole, Horace, *Reminiscences written in 1788 (notes of conversations with Lady Suffolk)* (Oxford: Clarendon Press, 1924)
Walpole, Horace, *Reminiscences written in MDCCLXXXVIII for the amusement of Miss Mary and Miss Agnes Berry* (London: R Taylor & Co, 1805)
Walpole, Horace, *The Last Journals of Horace Walpole During the Reign of George III from 1771–1783*, 2 Vols (London: John Lane The Bodley Head, 1910)
War Office – Lists of all the Officers of the Army and Royal Marines (London: War Office, for each of the years 1772 to 1774, 1777, 1779 and 1797 to 1814)
Whately, T., *Remarks on some of the Characters of Shakespeare By the Author of Observations on modern Gardening* (London: T Payne & Son, 1785)
Wildman, Joseph, *The Force of Prejudice: A Moral Tale*, 2 Vols (London: 1799)
Williams, John, A *Looking Glass for the Royal Family* (London: H D Symonds, T Bellamy, 1797)
Wilson, Harriette, *Harriette Wilson's Memoirs* (London: Peter Davies, 1929)
Wilson, Harriette, *The Game of Hearts: Harriette Wilson and her memoirs* (London: Gryphon Books, 1957)
Windham, Rt Hon William, *The Diary of Rt Hon William Windham 1784 to 1810*, ed. Mrs Henry Baring (London: Longmans, Green, and Co, 1866)
Windham, William, *The Crewe Papers: Section I Windham Letters* (London: Philobiblon Society, Vol. 9, 1854 etc, 1865–66)
Wraxall, Sir N. W. Bt, *Historical Memoirs of His Own Time*, 4 Vols (London: Richard Bentley, 1836)
Wraxall, Sir Nathaniel William, *The Historical and Posthumous Memoirs of Sir Nathaniel William Wraxall 1772–1784*, ed. Henry B. Wheatley, 5 Vols (London, Black & Son, 1884)
Wynn, Charlotte Williams, *The Correspondence of Charlotte Grenville, Lady Williams Wynn, and her three sons*, ed. Rachel Leighton (London: John Murray, 1920)
Wynne, Elizabeth, *The Wynne Diaries, 1789–1820*, ed. Anne Fremantle, 3 Vols (London: Oxford University Press, 1935)
Yorke, Philip Chesney, *Life and Correspondence of Philip Yorke, Earl of Hardwicke Lord High Chancellor of Great Britain*, 3 Vols (Cambridge: University Press, 1913)

Secondary Printed Sources

Abbott, Elizabeth, *A History of Mistresses* (London: Duckworth Overlook, 2010)
Adburgham, Alison, *Silver Fork Society: Fashionable Life and Literature from 1814 to 1840* (London: Constable, 1983)
Airlie, Mabell Countess of, *Lady Palmerston and her Times*, 2 Vols (London: Hodder and Stoughton Ltd, 1922)
Andrew, Donna T., *Adultery a la Mode: Privilege, the Law and Attitudes to Adultery 1770–1809 (*History: Vol. 82, Issue 265, 1997, pp. 5–23)
Archaeologia Cantiana, Vol. 58, (1945)
Ashton, John, *Old Times: A Picture of Social Life at the end of the Eighteenth Century* (London: John C Nimmo, 1885)
Ashton, John, *Florizel's Folly* (London: Chatto & Windus, 1899)
Askwith, Betty, *Piety and Wit: A Biography of Harriet Countess Granville 1785–1862* (London: Collins, 1982)
Aspinall, A., *Politics and the Press c. 1780-1850* (London: Home & Van Thal Ltd, 1949)
Bagot, William, Baron, *Memorials of the Bagot Family; compiled in 1823* (Blithfield: Wm Hodgetts, 1824)
Baily, F. E., *The Love Story of Lady Palmerston* (London: Hutchinson & Co, 1938)
Baker, Kenneth, *George III: A Life in Caricature* (London: Thames & Hudson, 2007)
Baker, Kenneth, *George IV: A Life in Caricature* (London: Thames & Hudson, 2005)

Barker, Hannah and Chalus, Elaine ed., *Gender in Eighteenth-Century England, Roles, Representations and Responsibilities* (London and New York: Longman, 1997)

Barnett, Gerald, *Richard and Maria Cosway: A Biography* (Westcountry Books: The Lutterworth Press, 1995)

Barrett, C. R. B., *The 7th, Queen's Own, Hussars*, 2 Vols (London: Royal United Service Institution, 1914)

Bateman, J. V., *The Great Landowners of Great Britain and Ireland* (Leicester: Leicester University Press, 1971). (Reprint of 4th Ed, London, Harrison, 1883)

Battiscombe, Georgina, *The Spencers of Althorp* (London: Constable, 1984)

Beckett, J. V., *The Aristocracy in England 1660–1914* (Oxford: Basil Blackwell, 1986)

Besant, Sir Walter, *London in the Eighteenth Century* (London: Black, 1902)

Biddulph, Violet, *The Three Ladies Waldegrave (and their Mother)* (London: Peter Davies, 1938)

Birkenhead, Sheila, *Peace in Piccadilly: The Story of Albany* (London: Hamish Hamilton, 1958)

Black, Jeremy, *The English Press in the Eighteenth Century* (London: Croom Helm, 1987)

Blakiston, Georgiana, *Lord William Russell and his Wife 1815–1846* (London: John Murray, 1972)

Blakiston, Georgiana, *Woburn and the Russells* (London: Constable, 1980)

Bleackley, Horace, *Ladies Fair and Frail: sketches of the demi-monde during the eighteenth century* (London: The Bodley Head, 1919)

Bleackley, Horace, *The Beautiful Duchess: Being an Account of the Life and Times of Elizabeth Gunning Duchess of Hamilton and Argyll* (London: John Lane The Bodley Head Ltd, 1927)

Borer, Mary Cathcart, *Mayfair, The Years of Grandeur* (London: W H Allen, 1975)

Bouce, Paul-Gabriel ed., *Sexuality in eighteenth-century Britain* (Manchester: University Press, 1982)

Bovill, E. W., *English Country Life 1780–1830* (London: Oxford University Press, 1962)

Brenan, Gerald and Statham, Edward Philips, *The House of Howard*, 2 Vols (London: Hutchinson & Co, 1907)

Brereton, J. M., *The 7th Queen's Own Hussars* (London: Cooper, 1975)

Brereton, J. M., *A History of the 4th/7th Royal Dragoon Guards and their predecessors 1685–1980* (Catterick: Published by the Regiment, 1982)

Bridges, Yseult, *Two Studies in Crime* (London: Hutchinson & Co, 1910)

Broughton, Lord (John Cam Hobhouse), *Recollections of a Long Life*, ed. Lady Dorchester, 6 Vols (London: John Murray, 1909)

Brown, A. G., *Persons, animals, ships and cannon in the Aubrey-Maturin sea novels of Patrick O'Brian* (London: McFarland, *c.* 1999)

Burton, A. E., *The Georgians at Home 1714–1830* (London: Longmans, 1967)

Calder, Timothy, *The Encyclopaedia of Brighton* (Lewes: East Sussex County Libraries, 1990)

Campbell, Cynthia, *The Most Polished Gentleman: George IV and the Women in his Life* (London: Kudos Books Limited, 1995)

Cannon, John, *Aristocratic Century: The peerage of eighteenth-century England* (Cambridge: University Press, 1984)

Cannon, Richard, *Historical Record of the Seventh, or, Princess Royal's Regiment of Dragoon Guards* (London: Longman, Orme, Clowes, 1839)

Cannon, Richard, *Historical Record of the Seventh, or, Queen's Own Regiment of Hussars: containing an account of the formation of the regiment in 1690 and its subsequent services to 1842* (London: J W Parker, 1841)

Cannon, Richard, *Historical Record of the Ninth, or, The Queen's Royal Regiment of Light Dragoons, Lancers: containing an account of the formation of the regiment in 1715 and its subsequent services to 1841* (London: J W Parker, 1841)

Chancellor, E. Beresford, *Memorials of St James's Street* (London: Grant Richards Ltd, 1922)

Chancellor, E. Beresford, *The Lives of the Rakes*, 6 Vols (London: Philip Alan & Co., 1924–1925)

Chancellor, E. Beresford, *The XVIIIth Century in London* (London: B T Batsford Ltd, 1921)

Chapman, Caroline, *Elizabeth and Georgiana: The Duke of Devonshire and his two Duchesses* (London: John Murray, 2002)

Childs, Jeff, *Morgannwg: transactions of the Glamorgan Local History Society, Vol. 38 – 1994, Landownership changes in a Glamorgan parish, 1750–1850: The case of Llangyfelach*

Clayden, P. W., *Rogers and His Contemporaries*, 2 Vols (London: Smith, Elder & Co, 1889)

Clayden, P. W., *The Early life of Samuel Rogers* (London: Smith, Elder & Co, 1887)

Coke, David & Borg, Alan, *Vauxhall Gardens, A History* (New Haven & London: Yale University Press, 2011)

Cole, Hubert, *Beau Brummell* (London: Hart-Davis, MacGibbon, 1977)

Colville, Sir John, *Those Lambtons, A Most Unusual Family* (London: Hodder & Stoughton, 1988)

Connell, Brian, *Portrait of a Whig Peer: Compiled from the Papers of the Second Viscount Palmerston 1739–1802* (London: Andre Deutsch, 1957)

Cooper, Leonard, *British Regular Cavalry 1644–1914* (London: Chapman & Hall, 1965)

Coxe, Howard, *The Stranger in the House: A Life of Caroline of Brunswick* (London: Chatto & Windus, 1939)

Cunnington, C. Willett & Phyllis, *Handbook of English Costume in the Eighteenth Century* (Boston: Plays, Inc, 1972)

Dasent, Arthur Irwin, *A History of Grosvenor Square* (London: Macmillan and Co., Limited, 1935)

Dasent, Arthur Irwin, *Piccadilly In Three Centuries* (London: Macmillan and Co., Limited, 1920)

David, Saul, *Prince of Pleasure, The Prince of Wales and the Making of Regency* (London: Little, Brown and Company, 1998)

Davidoff, Leonore, *The Best Circles: Society Etiquette and the Season* (London: Croom Helm, 1973)

Davis, I. M., *The Harlot and the Statesman* (Bourne End: The Kensal Press, 1986)

Derry, John W., *The Regency Crisis and the Whigs* (Cambridge: University Press, 1963)

Dewes, Simon, *Mrs Delany* (London: Rich & Cowan Ltd, 1940)

Dictionary of Irish Biography (Cambridge: University Press, 2009)

Doran, John, *Lady of the Last Century (Mrs Elizabeth Montagu)* (London: Richard Bentley, 1873)

Draper, Nicholas, *The Price of Emancipation: Slave-Ownership, Compensation and British Society at the End of Slavery* (Cambridge: Cambridge Studies in Economic History, 2013)

Duffy, Michael, *The English Satirical Print 1600–1832: The Englishman and the Foreigner* (Cambridge: Chadwyck-Healey, 1986)

Elwin, Malcolm, *The Noels and the Milbankes: Their Letters for Twenty-Five Years 1767–1792, Presented as a Narrative* (London: Macdonald, 1967)

Fairweather, Maria, *Madame de Stael* (London: Constable, 2005)

Farr, Evelyn, *Before the Deluge: Parisian Society in the Reign of Louis XVI* (London: Owen, 1994)

Fletcher, Ian, *Galloping at Everything: The British Cavalry in the Peninsular War and at Waterloo, 1800–15* (Staplehurst: Spellmount, 1999)

Foreman, Amanda, *Georgiana, Duchess of Devonshire* (London: Harper Collins, 1998)

Fortescue, Sir John, *A History of the British Army*, 14 Vols (London: Macmillan, 1899–1930)

Foster, Elizabeth, *Children of the Mist* (London: Hutchinson of London, 1960)
Fraser, Flora, *The Unruly Queen: The Life of Queen Caroline* (London: Macmillan, 1996)
Friedman, Joseph, *Spencer House: The Chronicle of a Great London Mansion* (London: Zwemmer, 1993)
Garratt, G. T., *Lord Brougham* (London: Macmillan and Co., Limited, 1935)
Gattrell, Vic, *City of Laughter: Sex and Satire in 18th Century London* (London: Atlantic, 2006)
George, E., *'Fox's Martyrs; The General Election of 1784'*, *Transactions of the Royal Historical Society*, 21 (1939)
Girouard, Mark, *Life in the English Country House* (New Haven and London: Yale University Press, 1978)
Gleeson, Janet, *An Aristocratic Affair, The Life of Georgiana's Sister, Harriet Spencer, Countess of Bessborough* (London: Bantam Press, 2006)
Goff, Moira, Goldfinch, John, Limper-Herz, Karen and Peden, Helen, *Georgians Revealed: Life, Style and the Making of Modern Britain* (London: The British Library, 2013)
Gosse, Philip, *Dr Viper, The Querulous Life of Philip Thicknesse* (London: Cassell & Company Ltd, 1952)
Great Britain Cavalry Regiments. Seventh Queen's Own Hussars – The Queen's Own Hussars (London: Malcolm Page, 1968)
Greig, Hannah, *The Beau Monde: Fashionable Society in Georgian London* (Oxford: Oxford University Press, 2013)
Grenby, M. O., *The Anti-Jacobin Novel: British Conservatism and the French Revolution* (Cambridge: Cambridge University Press, 2001)
Grosvenor, Caroline and Beilby, Charles (Lord Stuart of Wortley), *The First Lady Wharncliffe and her Family (1779–1856)*, 2 Vols (London: William Heinemann, 1927)
Gun, W. T. J., *Studies in Hereditary Ability* (London: Allen & Unwin, 1928)
Guttsman, W. L., ed, *The English Ruling Class* (London: Weidenfeld and Nicolson, 1969)
Halsted, Edward, *The History and Topographical Survey of the County of Kent* (Vol. 2, 1797, Vol. 5, 1798)
Hamilton, Anne Lady, *Secret History of the Court of England from the Accession of George the Third to the Death of George the Fourth*, 2 Vols (London: Eveleigh Nash, 1903)
Harvey, A. D., *Sex in Georgian England, Attitudes and Prejudices from the 1720s to the 1820s* (London: Gerald Duckworth & Co Ltd, 1994)
Hedley, Olwen, *Queen Charlotte* (London: John Murray, 1975)
Herbert, Charles, 'Coxheath Camp 1778–1779', *Journal of the Society for Army Historical Research*, Vol. 45 (1967), 129–148
Hibbert, Christopher, *George III: A Personal History* (London: Viking, 1998)
Hibbert, Christopher, *George IV: Prince of Wales 1762–1811* (London: Longman, 1972)
Hibbert, Christopher, *George IV: Regent and King 1811–1830* (London: Longman, 1973)
Hicks, Carola, *Improper Pursuits: The Scandalous Life of Lady Di Beauclerk* (London: Macmillan, 2001)
Higman, B. W., *Jamaica Surveyed, Plantation Maps and Plans of the Eighteenth and Nineteenth Centuries* (Barbados, Jamaica and Trinidad and Tobago: University of the West Indies Press, 2001)
Hill, Bridget. *Eighteenth Century Women: An Anthology* (London: George Allen & Unwin, 1984)
Hill, Bridget, *Women, Work, and Sexual Politics in Eighteenth Century England* (Oxford: Basil Blackwell, 1989)

Hill, Draper, *Fashionable Contrasts: Caricatures by James Gillray* (London: Phaidon Press Ltd, 1966)
Hilton, Boyd, *A Mad, Bad, and Dangerous People? England 1783–1846* (Oxford: Clarendon Press, 2006)
Holme, Thea, *Caroline: A Biography of Caroline of Brunswick* (London: Hamish Hamilton, 1979)
Holme, Thea, *Prinny's Daughter: A Life of Princess Charlotte of Wales* (London: Hamish Hamilton, 1976)
Howell-Thomas, Dorothy, *Duncannon: Reformer and Reconciler 1781-1847* (Norwich: Michael Russell, 1992)
Hudson, Roger, ed., *The Grand Tour 1592–1796* (London: The Folio Society, 1993)
Ilchester, Earl of, *The Home of the Hollands 1605–1820* (London: John Murray, 1937)
Inglis, Lucy, *Georgian London: into the streets* (London: Viking, 2013)
Jenkins, Elizabeth, *Ten Fascinating Women* (London: Odhams Press Limited, 1955)
Jenkins, Philip, *The making of a ruling class: The Glamorgan gentry 1640–1790* (Cambridge: Cambridge University Press, 1983)
Jesse, Captain, *The Life of George Brummell, Esq.*, 2 Vols (London: John C Nimmo, 1886)
Jones, Louis C., *The Clubs of the Georgian Rakes* (New York: Columbia University Press, 1942)
Kelly, Ian, *Beau Brummell* (London: Hodder & Stoughton, 2005)
Kelly, Linda, *Holland House* (London: I B Tauris & Co Ltd, 2013)
Keynes, John Maynard, *The Collected Writings of John Maynard Keynes, Vol. X, Essays in Biography* (London: Macmillan, 1972)
King, Dean, *A Sea of Words: lexicon and companion for Patrick O'Brian's seafaring tales* (New York: Henry Holt, *c.* 1995)
King, Dean, *Patrick O'Brian, A Life Revealed* (New York: Henry Holt and Company, 2000)
Knight, Derrick, *Gentlemen of Fortune: the men who made their fortunes in Britain's slave colonies* (London: Muller, 1978)
Knox, Tim and Palmer, Anthea ed., *Aspects of Osterley: Nineteenth Century Chatelaines* (Rogers, Kevin, High Wycombe: National Trust, *c.* 2000)
Lamington, Lord, *In the Days of the Dandies* (Eveleigh Nash, 1906)
Laver, James, *The Age of Illusion: Manners and Morals 1750–1848* (London: Weidenfeld and Nicolson, 1972)
Leslie, Anita, *Mrs Fitzherbert* (London: Hutchinson, 1960)
Leslie, Doris, *The Great Corinthian: A Portrait of the Prince Regent* (London: Eyre & Spottiswoode, 1952)
Leslie, Shane, *Mrs Fitzherbert: A Life, chiefly from unpublished sources* (London: Burns Oates, 1939)
Leveson-Gower, Iris, *The Face Without a Frown, Georgiana Duchess of Devonshire* (London: Frederick Muller Ltd, 1944)
Levy, M. J., *The Mistresses of George IV* (London: Peter Owen, 1996)
Lewis, W. S., *Three Tours through London in the years 1748, 1776, 1799* (New Haven: Yale University Press, 1941)
Lewis, Judith S., *Sacred to Female Patriotism: Gender, Class and Politics in Late Georgian Britain* (New York/London: Routledge, 2003)
Locke, Amy Audrey, *The Seymour Family: History and Romance* (London: Constable & Co, 1911)
Loftis, John, *Sheridan and the drama of Georgian England* (Oxford: Blackwell, *c.* 1976)
London Topographical Society, *The A to Z of Georgian London, Introductory Notes by Ralph Hyde, London* (London; London Topographical Society Publication No 126, 1982)
Manvell, Roger, *Sarah Siddons: Portrait of an Actress* (London: Heinemann, 1970)

Marshall, Dorothy, *Eighteenth Century England* (London: Longmans, Green and Co Ltd, 1962)

Martelli, George, *Jemmy Twitcher: A Life of the Fourth Earl of Sandwich, 1718–1792* (London: Jonathan Cape, 1962)

Masters, Brian, *Georgiana Duchess of Devonshire* (London: Hamish Hamilton, 1981)

Mayne, Ethel Colburn, *A Regency Chapter: Lady Bessborough and her friendships* (London: Macmillan & Co Ltd, 1939)

McCord, James, 'Taming the Female Politician in the Early 19th Century', *Journal of Women's History,* Vol. 13, Part 4, (2002)

Melville, Lewis, *Brighton: Its History, Its Follies, and Its Fashions* (London: Chapman & Hall, Ltd, 1909)

Melville, Lewis, *Regency Ladies* (London: Hutchinson & Co, 1926)

Mingay, G. E., *English Landed Society in the Eighteenth Century* (London: Routledge and Kegan Paul, 1963)

Minto, Countess of, *A Memoir of the Right Honourable Hugh Elliott* (Edinburgh: Edmonston and Douglas, 1868)

Mitchell, Austin, *The Whigs in Opp.osition 1815–1830* (Oxford: The Clarendon Press, 1967)

Mitchell, Leslie, *Holland House* (London: Duckworth, 1980)

Mitchell, Leslie, *The Whig World 1760–1837* (London: Hambledon and London, 2005)

Moore, Thomas, *Memoirs of the Life of The Rt Hon Richard Brinsley Sheridan,* 2 Vols (London: Longman, Hurst, Rees, Orme, Brown, and Green, 1825)

Morgan, Cliff, *Briton Ferry (Llansawel)* (Briton Ferry: the Author, 1977)

Munson, James, *Maria Fitzherbert: The Secret Wife of George IV* (London: Constable, 2001)

Murray, Venetia, *High Society: A Social History of the Regency Period 1778–1830* (London: Viking, 1998)

Musgrave, Clifford, *Life in Brighton from the earliest times to the present* (London: Faber and Faber, 1970)

Myer, Valerie Grosvenor, *Harriette Wilson, Lady of Pleasure* (Ely: Fern House, 1999)

Nethercote, H. O., *The Pytchley Hunt: Past and Present* (London: Sampson Low, Mardston, Searle, & Rivington, Limited, 1888)

New, Chester, *Lord Durham: a Biography of John George Lambton 1st Earl of Durham* (Oxford: Clarendon Press, 1929)

Newdigate-Newdegate, Lady Anne, *The Cheverels of Cheverel Manor* (London: Longmans Green, 1898)

Oliphant (afterwards Graham), Margaret and Cathcart Family, *The Beautiful Mrs Graham and the Cathcart Circle* (London: Nisbet & Co., 1927)

Oxford Dictionary of National Biography.

Paget, G. C. H. V., 7th Marquess of Anglesey, *One-Leg, The Life and Letters of Henry William Paget First Marquess of Anglesey KG 1768–1854* (London: Jonathan Cape, 1961)

Paget, Guy, *The History of the Althorp and Pytchley Hunt 1634–1920* (London: Collins, 1937)

Parker, Matthew, *The Sugar Barons: Family, Corruption, Empire and War* (London: Hutchinson, 2011)

Parreaux, Andre, *Daily Life in England in the Reign of George III* (London: George Allen & Unwin Ltd, 1969)

Parry, Sir Edward, *Queen Caroline* (London: Ernest Benn Ltd, 1930)

Parsons, Mrs Clement, *The Incomparable Siddons* (London: Methuen & Co, 1909)

Paston, George, *Side-Lights on the Georgian Period* (London: Methuen & Co, 1902)

Paston, George, *Social Caricature in the Eighteenth Century* (New York: Benjamin Blom, 1968). (First published London 1905)

Pearson, John, *Stags and Serpents: The Story of the House of Cavendish and the Dukes of Devonshire* (London: Macmillan, 1983)
Perry, Norma, *Sir Everard Fawkener, friend and correspondent of Voltaire* (Banbury: Voltaire Foundation, 1975)
Phillips, D. Rhys, *The History of the Vale of Neath, with Illustrations* (Swansea: 1925)
Plowden, Alison, *Caroline and Charlotte: regency scandals 1795–1821* (Sutton: Stroud, 2005)
Plowden, Alison, *Caroline & Charlotte: the Regent's wife and daughter 1795–1821* (London: Sidgwick & Jackson, 1989)
Plumb, J. H., *The First Four Georges,* (London: B T Batsford Ltd, 1957)
Ponsonby, Major-General Sir John KCB, *The Ponsonby Family* (London: Medici Society, 1929)
Porter, Roy, *English Society in the 18th Century*, Revised edition (London: Penguin Books, 1991)
Powell, Violet, *Margaret, Countess of Jersey* (London: Heinemann, 1978)
Powis, Jonathan, *Aristocracy* (Oxford: Basil Blackwell, 1984)
Renny, Robert, *An History of Jamaica* (London: J Cawthorn, 1807)
Reynard, Frank H., *The Ninth (Queen's Royal) Lancers, 1715–1903* (Edinburgh: William Blackwood and Sons, 1904)
Ribeiro, Aileen, *Dress and Morality* (London: B T Batsford, 1986)
Ribeiro, Aileen, *Dress Worn at Masquerades in England, 1730–1790* (London: Garland, 1984)
Ribeiro, Aileen, *The Art of Dress, Fashion in England and France 1750 to 1820* (New Haven: Yale University Press, 1995)
Ridley, Jasper, *Lord Palmerston* (London: Constable & Co, 1970)
Rizzo, Betty, *Companions Without Vows: Relationships Amongst Eighteenth Century Women* (Athens and London: The University of Georgia Press, 1994)
Roberts, Henry D., *A History of the Royal Pavilion Brighton* (London: Country Life Limited, 1939)
Roberts, R. Ellis, *Samuel Rogers and his Circle* (London: Methuen & Co Ltd, 1910)
Robins, Jane, *Rebel Queen: The Trial of Caroline* (London: Simon & Schuster, 2006)
Rowley, Trevor, *Excavations at Middleton Stoney, Oxfordshire including a brief history of the parish of Middleton Stoney* (Oxford: Oxford University Department for External Studies, 1977)
Royal Bank of Scotland – Heritage Archives (heritagearchives.rbs.com/wiki/Nathaniel_Bayly) (2011)
Rubenhold, Hallie, *Lady Worsley's Whim: An Eighteenth-Century Tale of Sex, Scandal and Divorce* (London: Chatto & Windus, 2008)
Rude, George, *Hanoverian London 1714–1808* (London: Secker & Warburg, 1971)
Russell, C. C. E., *Three Generations of Fascinating Women and other sketches from family history* (London: Longmans & Co, 1904)
Sadleir, Michael, *Blessington-D'Orsay: A Masquerade* (London: Constable & Co Ltd, 1933)
Saul, David, *Prince of Pleasure: The Prince of Wales and the Making of the Regency* (London: Little Brown and Company, 1998)
Scott, Hon Caroline Lucy, Lady, *A marriage in high life by Lady Charlotte Bury* (Paris: Baudry's European Library, 1836)
Shepp.ard, Major E. W., *The Ninth Queen's Royal Lancers, 1715–1936* (Aldershot: Gale & Polden Ltd, 1939)
Sichel, Walter, *Sheridan, Including a Manuscript Diary by Georgiana Duchess of Devonshire*, 2 Vols (London: Constable & Company Ltd, 1909)
Smith, E. A., *George IV* (New Haven and London: Yale University Press, 1999)
Somerset, Anne, *Ladies in Waiting: From the Tudors to the Present Day* (London: Weidenfeld and Nicolson, 1984)
Steinmetz, Andrew, *The Gaming Table: its votaries and victims*, 2 Vols (London: 1870)

Stokes, Hugh, *The Devonshire House Circle* (London: The London and Norwich Press, 1917)
Stone, Lawrence, *The Family, Sex and Marriage in England 1500–1800* (London: Weidenfeld and Nicolson, 1977)
Stone, Lawrence and Stone, Jeanne C. Fawtier – *An Open Elite? England 1540–1880* (Oxford: Clarendon Press, 1984)
Stuart, Dorothy Margaret, *Daughter of England: A New Study of Princess Charlotte and her Family* (London: Macmillan & Co Ltd, 1951)
Sykes, Christopher S., *Private Palaces: Life in the Great London Houses* (London: Chatto & Windus Ltd, 1985)
The Royal Commission on Historical Manuscripts, *Principal Family and Estate Collections*, 2 Vols (London: HMSO, 1996)
Thirkell, A. M., *The Fortunes of Harriet* [sic]*: the surprising career of Harriette Wilson* (London: Hamish Hamilton, 1936)
Thompson, Col C. W., *Seventh (Princess Royal's) Dragoon Guards: The Story of the Regiment (1688–1882)* (Liverpool: Daily Post, 1913)
Tillyard, Stella, *Aristocrats, Caroline, Emily, Louisa and Sarah Lennox 1740–1832* (London: Chatto & Windus, 1994)
Tisdall, E. E. P., *The Wanton Queen, The Story of Britain's Strangest Queen* (London: Stanley Paul & Co Ltd, 1939)
Tolstoy, Nikolai, *Patrick O'Brian, The Making of the Novelist* (London: Century, 2004)
Trethewey, Rachel, *Mistress of the Arts: The Passionate Life of Georgina Duchess of Bedford* (London: Headline Book Publishing, 2002)
Twisden, Sir John Ramskill, Bt, *The Family of Twysden or Twisden: Their history and archives. From an original by Sir J R Twisden. Completed by C H Dudley Ward* (London: John Murray, 1939)
Victoria History of the Counties of England, The, *A History of the County of Oxford, Volume VI, Ploughley Hundred,* ed. Mary D. Lobel (London: Oxford University Press, 1959)
Victoria History of the County of Northamptonshire, FSA, Vol. 3, ed. William Page (History Online, 1930)
Villiers, Marjorie, *The Grand Whiggery* (London: John Murray, 1939)
Wardroper, John, *Kings, Lords and Wicked Libellers: Satire and Protest 1760–1837* (London: John Murray, 1973)
Wharton, Grace, *The Queens of Society* (London: Jarvis & Son, 1890)
Wheately, Henry B., *London Past and Present: its history, associations and traditions*, 3 Vols (London: John Murray, 1891)
White, A. S., *A Bibliography of Regimental Histories of the British Army* (London: The London Stamp Exchange, 1988)
White, Jerry, *London in the 18th Century: A Great and Monstrous Thing* (London: The Bodley Head, 2012)
White, R. J., *Life in Regency England* (London: B T Batsford, 1963)
Whitley, William T., *Artists and Their Friends in England 1700–1799*, 2 Vols (London: The Medici Society, 1928)
Wilkins, W. H., *Mrs Fitzherbert and George IV*, 2 Vols (London: Longmans, Green, and Co, 1905)
Williamson, George Charles, *Daniel Gardner, painter* (London: John Lane, 1921)
Wilson, Frances, *The Courtesan's Revenge* (London: Faber and Faber, 2003)
Woodham-Smith, Cecil, *Queen Victoria, Her Life and Times, Volume One: 1819–1861* (London: Hamish Hamilton, 1972)
Wyndham, H. A., *A Family History, 1688–1837. The Wyndhams of Somerset, Sussex and Wiltshire,* (Oxford: Oxford University Press, 1950)

Periodicals

Colburn's United Service Magazine:1876, Part 2, p. 341, Notes on the History and Services of the Twenty-First Regiment of Dragoons, London, Hurst and Blackett, 1876

Country Life: Vol. LX (July-Dec, 1926)
Vol. C (July-Dec, 1946)

Eighteenth Century Life: Vol. 17, Number 3, 1993, p. 60, Stott, A., 'Female Patriotism: Georgiana, Duchess of Devonshire and the Westminster Election of 1784'.
Vol. 26, Part 1, 2002, p. 46, Lana, R., 'Women and Foxite Strategy in the Westminster Election of 1784'.

Gentleman's Magazine: 1752, 1770, 1805, 1806, 1807, 1808, 1810, 1814, 1815, 1817, 1821.

Studies on Voltaire and the Eighteenth Century: Vol. 49, 1967, 'Voltaire's British Visitors, ed Sir Gavin de Beer and André-Michel Rousseau'

The Anglo-Saxon Review: A Quarterly Miscellany, ed. Lady Randolph Churchill, Vols 1 and 2, June and September, 1899 – 'Correspondence of Georgiana, Duchess of Devonshire'

History Today: Vol. 6, 1956, p. 655, Cargill, Morris – Jamaica and Britain
Vol. 26, 1976, p. 241, Turner, Stephen – Almack's and Society
Vol. 28, 1978, p. 463, Ribeiro, Aileen – The Macaronis
Vol. 28, 1978, p. 113, Cowie, L W – Carlton House

The Army Quarterly:Vol. XLIX, 1939/40, p. 103, Burne, Lt Col Alfred H. – An Amphibious Campaign – North Holland, 1799

The Macaroni and Theatrical Magazine, or, Register of the fashions and diversions of the times: London, Oct 1773 to Oct 1774

The Rambler's Magazine: 1783 (April and June).

The Town & Country Magazine: 1775.

Newspapers

Bath Chronicle: 1784–1796
Gazetteer and New Daily Advertiser: 1787–1796
General Evening Post: 1735–1800
Hampshire Telegraph & Portsmouth Gazette: 1802–1806
Hampshire Telegraph and Sussex Chronicle: 1802–1806
Jackson's Oxford Journal: 1762–69, 1800–1821
Lloyds Evening Post: 1775–1795
London Chronicle: 1757–1800
London Evening Post: 1750–1780
Morning Herald: 1780–1799
The Morning Post: 1773–1821
Public Advertiser: 1755–1794
St James's Chronicle: 1762–1799
Staffordshire Advertiser: 1795–1800
Telegraph: 1795–1797
The Alfred, Westminster Evening Gazette: 1810
The Bury and Norwich Post: 1801–1821
The Cheltenham Chronicle, and Glocestershire [sic] *General Advertiser*: 1809–1821
The Examiner: 1808–1821
The Ipswich Journal: 1802–1821
The Lancaster Gazetteer: 1801
The London Gazette: 1795–1813
The London Packet: 1795–1800
The The Morning Chronicle: 1772–1821

Observer: 1791–1821
The Oracle: 1789–1799
The Star: 1791–1797, 1778–1779
The Sun: 1793–1800
The Times: 1785–1821
The World (formerly The World and Fashionable Advertiser): 1787–1794
The True Briton: 1793–1800
Whitehall Evening Post: 1750–1799

Index